PREACHING THROUGH THE BIBLE

BY
JOSEPH PARKER

VOL. 3

LEVITICUS — NUMBERS XXVI

BAKER BOOK HOUSE
Grand Rapids, Michigan

Standard Book Number: 8010-6875-4

Library of Congress Catalog Card Number: 59-10860

Reprinted 1971 by
Baker Book House Company

Originally printed
under the title,
The People's Bible

Printed in the United States of America

CONTENTS.

NUMBERS I.—XXVI.—

CONTENTS.

"The **Bible** is the flaming book which men fear will be destroyed; but sooner will you pluck the stars out of heaven, than one star out of this divine book. . . . All theories respecting the history and structure of the Bible may be mooted and disputed; but there it is, a book whose fruits rise higher, smell sweeter, taste more flavoursome, inspire more health, than any or all others that have been produced upon the plane of human life."—HENRY WARD BEECHER

THE THIRD BOOK OF MOSES

CONSIDERED as embracing the history of one month only, this may claim to be the most remarkable book in the Old Testament. Containing twenty-seven chapters; ranging its contents under sixteen different categories; and requiring to be actively represented within the space of say eight-and-twenty days, it may, in its own degree, claim an energy not inferior to the book of Genesis. The same fearlessness of treatment is distinctive of both books. The reverent audacity which represented creation as the work of six days—whatever the measure of a day may be—did not shrink from focalising into one month the whole discipline of life. Moses loses nothing by diffuseness. Even in days that were made long by intolerable monotony—in which men lived centuries because of weariness—Moses did not shrink from a condensation unparalleled in human literature. His words could hardly have been fewer if he had lived in our time of feverish haste and tumult. To put up the heavens and the earth in one chapter was a miracle in authorship, yet, well pondered, it was the only thing to be done,—any poet could have built them in endless stanzas, and any philosopher could have begun the infinite story in a book too large for the world to hold : Moses chose the more excellent way, creating creation with a swiftness that has dazed a literal criticism ever since ;— literal criticism that has but one season in its dreary year, a year that knows nothing of snow-blossom, or wedded light and song. But this very haste was part of the man. The Moses of poetry required fifty-one days for the revolution of his Iliad ; the Moses of revelation only took a week for the settlement of the heavens and the earth, and in that week he found one whole day of rest for the Creator. This action was entirely characteristic of Moses, for he was the most wrathful man as well as the meekest,—killing, smiting, destroying, and burning with anger, as well as praying like the father-priest of his people. In a sense obvious enough he was the protoplastic Christ,—for was not he who described himself as " meek and lowly in heart," the scourger of trespassers, and did he not burn the religious actors of his day ? Moses and Christ both did things with startling rapidity ; in their very soul they were akin ; they were " straitened " until their work was " accomplished,"—the Pentateuch and the Gospels have action enough in them to fill innumerable volumes, yet there is an infinite calm in both, the haste being in the temporary framework, the calm being in the eternal purpose.

Think of these seven-and-twenty chapters constituting the discipline of one month. The reflections started by this circumstance culminate in a sense of pain, for who can bear this grievous toil or endure this sting of accusation ? There is no respite. Egyptian burdens were for the body, but those wilderness exactions tormented the soul, and by so much made Egyptian memories bright. The trial of muscle is nothing to the trial of patience. Men may sleep after labour, but an unquiet conscience keeps the eyes wide open. This discipline afflicted both the body and the soul, and thus drained the entire strength of the people. This conscious toil must have been accompanied by an unconscious inspiration, a reciprocal action impossible in theory but well understood in spiritual experience. We resume our burdens in the very act of dreading them. We pray the next prayer in the very process of waiting for answers to a thousand prayers to which God has paid no known heed. Yesterday's sacrifice has nothing to do with this day's sin, except to remind us, that to-day must provide its own sacrifice. This was so with the Jews ; this is precisely so with ourselves, yet we boast our liberty, and suppose that in leaping one inch from the earth we have broken the tether of gravitation. As put before us in this manual called Leviticus the discipline of the month seems to be more than we could endure, and this we say in ignorance of the fact that our own manual imposes a severer discipline. Our pity for the Jews arises out of the apparently ineradicable sophism that spiritual service is easier than bodily exercise. A most deadly sophism is this, and prevalent yet, notwithstanding the rebuke and condemnation of universal history. It was not in dressing and keeping the garden that Adam failed, but in obedience, in spiritual trust, in child-like simplicity. Not a word is said about indolence ;—garden-keeping is an easy virtue; but to obey, to trust, to love, to be truly true in all the heart's loyalty and hope, who is sufficient ? Not Eve, not Adam,—not woman, not man. It was a bold thing on the part of any fabulist to fix the point of failure in the heart ; an inspired fabulist may-be,—an allegorist under the very touch of God. Yet disobedient man must always be brought back by bodily subjugation, simply because the body responds quickly to the chastisement of justice. The flesh aches, and burns, and begs like a coward that the smiter will drop his lash. Spiritual reproach, affectionate entreaty, argument made strong by a thousand unanswerable pleas, go for nothing ; but one stroke of the cutting thong brings the criminal to beg for mercy. It is easier to get at the bone than to get at the conscience. That is the difference between a martyr and a criminal,—a man all spirit and a man all body. The Christian manual has but little to say to the body, except through the medium of the spirit, but through that medium it has much to say. Not until the spirit is right can the body be right ; but the spirit being right the body becomes a holy temple and a living sacrifice The Jews kept up a magnificent tragedy of symbolism, but Christians must represent an infinitely more magnificent tragedy of reality. It was easy to kill a bullock at the door of the tabernacle, or to slay a sheep on the northward side of the altar, or to pluck away the crop of the turtle-dove or young pigeon, and cast it beside the altar on the east part by the place of the ashes ; but who can slay a will, or burn a purpose, or give up every pulse of the heart's love ; who can nail his vanity to the cross, or shut out the charming world, or slay the pleading senses one by one, or crucify the passion set on fire of hell ?

In no spiritual sense, then, is Leviticus an obsolete book. Moses is not dead. The inventors of the alphabet have some rights even in Paradise Lost, and quite a large property in Euclid. It is not grateful on our part to forget the primers through which we passed to the encyclopædias, though their authors were but our intellectual nurses. In no mere dream was Moses present when Christ communed with him concerning the Exodus that was to be accomplished at Jerusalem, and in no dramatic sense did Elijah watch the consummation of prophecy. Marvellous fables, lies grand enough to be true, ventures heroic enough to be divine, and all massed into coherence without trace of joint or seam ;—verily it is easier to believe than to disbelieve, to pray than to sneer ! The wonder is that Christians should be so willing to regard the Pentateuch as obsolete. This is practically a foregone conclusion, to such an extent certainly that the Pentateuch is tolerated rather than studied for edification by the rank and file of Christians. Without the Pentateuch Christ as revealed in the Gospels would have been impossible, and without Christ the Pentateuch would have been impossible. I venture upon this proposition because I find no great event in the Pentateuch that is not for some purpose of argument or illustration used by Christ himself or by his disciples and apostles in the interests of what is known as evangelical truth. It lies within easy proof that Christ is the text of the Old

Testament and that the Old Testament is the text of Christ. What use is made in the New Testament of the creation of the universe, the faith of Abraham, the rain of manna, the lifting up of the serpent, and the tabernacle of witness; the sublime apology of Stephen epitomises the Old Testament, and the epistle to the Hebrews could not have been written but for the ritual of Exodus and Leviticus. In its purely moral tone the Old Testament is of kindred quality with the New. Take an instance from Leviticus. Three forms of evil are recognised in one of its most ardent chapters, namely Violence, Deceit, and Perjury, a succession amounting to a development, and unwittingly, it may or may not be, confirming that law of evolution which is as happily illustrated in morals as in physics. Men begin with acts of violence, then go on to silent deceit and calculation, and then close with a profanation of the holiest terms,— the early sinners robbed gardens and killed brothers; the later sinners "agreed together" to "lie unto God." It is something, therefore, to find in so ancient a book as Leviticus the recognition of an order which is true to philosophy and to history. But the proof that Moses and Christ are identical in moral tone is to be found in the process which offenders were commanded to adopt. By no sacerdotal jugglery was the foul blot to be removed; by no sigh of selfishness could the inward corruption be permitted to evaporate; by no investment of cheap tears could thieves compound for felony. First, there must be restoration; then there must be an addition of a fifth part of the whole; then the priest must be faced as the very representative of God and a trespass-offering be laid upon the altar, and after atonement Forgiveness would come, a white angel from heaven, and dwell in the reclaimed and sanctified heart,—all the past driven away as a black cloud, and all the present filled with a light above the brightness of the sun. What is this but an outline or forecast of what Christ himself said when he drove the hostile and vindictive man from the altar, bidding him first be reconciled with his brother and at peace with society? Christianity is not a substitute for morality; it is morality inspired, glorified and crowned.

Say that the ritual was sanitary rather than doctrinal or theological. What then? All divine things are first sanitary, but not necessarily bounded by that term. By admitting that the ritual was sanitary we begin an *à fortiori* argument of infinite cogency, instead of abandoning the definitely theological position. If the body requires so much care, what of the spirit? If the laws of bodily health were revealed, has no message been delivered to the soul? Is cleanliness vital, and purity quite unimportant? Is leprosy deadly, and internal cancer most harmless? No degradation of the Deity is more obvious than the thought which bounds his revelation and his discipline by the wants of a body which must die, or by an occasion which is as mechanical as it is transient. It would, too, be a circumstance wholly unprecedented if God had suddenly changed the level of his movement, by coming down from the purpose to crush the serpent's head and reinstate his own image, to the direction of ablutions, donations, and ordinances, without metaphysical meaning or religious intent. The irony would involve profanity. In the estimate of such a book as Leviticus something is due to the argument founded upon harmony. Something, too, is due to the history and genius of names. To call a stone upon which flesh is burned for sanitary purposes an *altar* is to mock the very spirit of every honest paganism ; and to call a health-officer, or inspector of nuisances, a *priest* is to be frivolous at the expense of decency. The larger interpretation is generally the right one, right by virtue of its nobleness, and right by virtue of the effects which must follow its practical application. It is along this line that one of the most powerful arguments for the inspiration of the Bible reveals itself. Take, for example, this very book of Leviticus : do not, in the first instance, vex the mind by the mere detail, but inquire into the central thought and purpose of the writer, and let the detail adjust itself. Grant that the innermost thought of the book is the idea which may be represented by the word *cleanness.* That term fixes the point of inspiration, and not only its point but its measure and quality. Anything else may be simply incidental and illustrative ; it is enough to seize the inspired term and magnify it by natural evolution into its whole meaning, so that every point of the area may be covered. It will be found that the practice of genuine cleanness, chemical as well as mechanical, will be followed by a philosophy, and that the morality of cleanness will be followed by a theology. Accustom a man to look out for bullocks and rams and lambs " without blemish," and he will find that he cannot stop at that point ; he has begun an education which can only culminate in the prayer—" Create in me a clean heart, O God, and renew a right spirit within me," though no word of that holy thought was named in the original instructions. This view of inspiration need not create any alarm, for it has been invariably adopted in the interpretation of the parables of Jesus Christ, and by its adoption the central purpose of each parable has been relieved of every complication arising from the use of merely pictorial and symbolical terms. Of necessity it is only the *thought* that can be divinely inspired, because the words are part of the common speech of the world and are tainted by misuse, or burdened with grievous responsibilities. Thus God is put to disadvantage by having to employ terms which have been disennobled by mutilation and false setting. But this difficulty is wholly got rid of by looking for the inspired thought, the one idea, the sacred purpose, the spirituality that cannot be polluted or defaced. If, therefore, the idea of Leviticus is cleanness it is useless to deny its inspiration ; it is useless, too, to imagine that cleanness is a commonplace, for all history proves the contrary, and useless to attempt to put partial cleanness in the place of absolute cleanness, for then by parity of reasoning partial honesty would be sufficient, and partial sanity would be the same thing as a sound mind.

That this view is not fanciful may be tested by applying its doctrine to any and every part of the Bible. It dissolves every difficulty, and invests the record with complete and immutable authority. Take one or two perplexing instances for the purpose of illustrating its philosophy. For example, the command to offer Isaac : the frivolous objections to the account as it stands in the English version cannot but be well remembered ; grammar has attempted to rearrange some of the words; the customs of heathen nations are supposed to have suggested the mechanism of the offering ; and so, by external processes, men have tried to bring the narrative within the lines of probability. But why this elision of the word " burnt " and the heathenising of the term "knife" when the central thought of the incident is so evidently noble,—that central thought being that all we have is God's, and that nothing, how dear soever and tender, is to stand between the heart and absolute obedience to the divine will ? The frivolity which quibbles about the fire and the knife, quibbles about Dives and Lazarus, because of Abraham's bosom and the realism of the rich man's body suffering at the very moment when his flesh was buried in the earth. Thus the spirit is sacrificed to the letter, and inspiration is either impoverished or debased. Look for a moment, in further illustration, at such a book as the Song of Solomon. Again and again it has been pointed out that a Song so luscious in its love is surely not an inspired poem ; it is unworthy of a place in so sublime a book as the Bible ; it is infatuated sentimentalism ; it is the very disease of love. I venture to deny the charge, and to claim inspiration for the Song. What is the central thought of the poem ? It is the supreme love of the soul for Christ. *That* is the inspired thought ; as for " the kisses of his mouth," the " cheeks comely with rows of jewels," the house of cedar, and the chariot of the wood of Lebanon, these are but struggles to express the inexpressible ; and therefore to quibble about the head being as most fine gold, the neck being like the tower of David, and the eyes being as the eyes of doves by the rivers of water, is to sacrifice that which is substantial to that which is incidental, and to displace inspiration in favour of the formalities of mechanism.

Leviticus is the gospel of the Pentateuch, glistening with purity, turning law into music, and spreading a banquet in the wilderness. But its ritual is dead. This is hard to believe ; hard because religious vanity is fond of ritualism, and ritualism makes no demand upon the deepest conscience: yet ritualism had a divinely-appointed function in the education of the awakening mind, and was the only influence which could hold the attention of a people to whom freedom was a new experience. Specta-cular religion is alphabetic religion, and therefore to revert to it is to ignore every characteristic and impulse of manhood and progress. But they who say so, must be prepared to complete the philosophy which that conten-tion initiates. It is not enough to dismiss ritualism on the ground that it has been displaced by spiritual worship ; admit that such is the case, and other and broader admis-sions are involved in the plea, and can only be shirked at the expense of consistency. It is generally admitted, for example, that the Old Testament law has been dis-placed by a New Testament principle. So Ritualism and Law, in their ancient forms, have passed away. But let us be careful. When we say Ritualism and Law, we mean in reality the *letter,* and it is evident that if any one letter can be displaced every other letter may be outlived and completed. And what is " the letter " but the symbol of flesh, visibleness, objectivity, historic fact and bulk ? The Apostle Paul went so far as to say that even Christ was no longer known " after the flesh "—yea, though he had been known after the flesh, that kind of knowledge was for ever done away, and another knowledge had permanently taken its place. The Church has never adopted the whole meaning of that teaching. Willing enough to consign Leviticus to the shades, the Church still clings to some sort of bodily Christ, the figure of a man, a bulk to be at least imaginatively touched. This is easily accounted for without suggesting superstition, and yet it might be done away with without imperilling faith. We are held in bondage by a mistaken conception of personality. When we think of that term we think of ourselves. But even admitting the necessity of this, we may by a correct definition of personality acquire a higher conception of our own being. Instead of saying that personality is this or that, after the manner of a geometrical figure, binding it to four points and otherwise limiting it, say that personality is the unit of being, and instantly every conception is enlarged and illuminated, the meaning being that personality is the starting point of conscious existence, not the fulness but the outline, not the *maximum* but the *minimum*, the very smallest conception which the mind can lay hold of,—the Euclidic " point " to be carried on into ratios and dimensions which originate a new vocabulary. We do not, then, define " God " when we describe him as a " Person," we merely *begin* to define him ; in other words, we say, God cannot be *less* than a Person, what more he is we must gradually and adoringly discover. So far as Christ is concerned there is one enlargement of his personality which no school of thinkers will dispute, rhetorically expressed by M. Renan, when he says of Jesus—" A thousand times more living, a thousand times more loved since thy death than during the days of thy pilgrimage here below, thou wilt become to such a degree the Corner Stone of humanity, that to tear thy name from this world would be to shake it to its foundations." If ritualism has been displaced by spirituality, and if law has been suspended by a principle—in other words, if the local has made way for the universal—why shrink from the admission that limited personality has been exchanged for unlimited Influence ? If along that line of thought

any sincere and reverent mind can go out in adoration
and thankfulness, why embarrass its noble and ennobling
rapture by unprofitable, because indeterminable, discus-
sions upon the metaphysics of personality? I have no
difficulty whatever in realising the personality of Christ,
and in that recognition I find the strength and joy peculiarly needed by one order or quality of mind, so much so
that without it life would be de-centralised and prayer
would fail of its destiny, but where other minds can find
rest and inspiration it is better that they should live
high up in sunshine than that they pine in the prison of
darkness. In the one case profit is possible ; in the other
death is certain.

Contemporary judgment and charity may be assisted,
in view of the ever-enlarging future, by imagining the
writer of Leviticus face to face with the Church of the
present time. Note the extreme singularity of the circumstances. We say (some hardly knowing what they
mean) that the book is inspired, yet no ordinance of it
is perpetuated ; we say that the book is canonical, yet no
ritual obligation is binding ; on no account could we
permit the elision of the book, yet no one observance
would we reproduce. We claim, too, that our religion
has in some way absorbed, fulfilled, completed, and
abolished the book by consummation, in other words it
is claimed that Christianity is Judaism interpreted and
glorified. From our standpoint, particularly if we are
clerically minded—this construction may be satisfactory,
but the immediate question is, How would *Moses* regard
nineteenth century worship, say of a Low Church and
Evangelical type, as the true evolution of Leviticus?
Where is the resemblance? The eye that can see the
similitude is surely looking through an adapted medium.
Yet the mystery would be dissolved if the book of
Leviticus were not open to reference. The man is the
completion of the child, but the child is no longer in
existence : the fruit is the fulfilment of the blossom, but
the blossom is no longer available for comparison or

contrast. Christianity is the consummation of Leviticus,
but Leviticus remains, unlike the child and the blossom,
and offers a series of dissonances or dissimilarities, of the
most positive quality. Yet if Moses were living now he
would be unchurched if he refused to identify the meaning of Leviticus in the service of the Christian sanctuary
—the Papist nearest in gorgeousness, the Protestant
claiming to be nearest in doctrine, and the Nonconformist
Moses would, in the absence of inspiration, be, in this
matter, the arch-heretic of the century.

LEVITICUS.

***

Leviticus i. 1.

"And the Lord called unto Moses, and spake unto him out of the tabernacle of the congregation."

THE ANCIENT RITUAL.

WHEN the Ten Commandments were given the Lord called unto Moses from the top of mount Sinai. Now he calls from "the tent of meeting." He is about to speak more minutely, and to enter upon statements which were better made in the quietness of a holy place, than delivered in a theatre of lightning and thunder and earthquake. The one was a great declaration of morals, a solemn code of behaviour or action ; the other related to sacrifice, worship, divine communion and the whole life of the heart. The lightning and the thunder have passed, and the earth throbs and heaves no longer, but is quieted to hear the peaceful law. Moses enters the sanctuary. It is a church made with hands, and it stands at the foot of " the mount which burned with fire." Sometimes our worship seems to require ALL SPACE, so much are our souls exalted, and so loud is our cry of distress or our psalm of adoration. The mountain is not high enough, the sea is wanting in width, and the horizon is too near to constitute a church, because our souls are lifted up with great emotions and our love glows with an infinite fire. In those high moods we tell the mountains to rejoice ; we bid Lebanon clap its hands ; and call upon the sea to help our offering of praise. Afterwards we fall into another and calmer mood ; a mood subdued almost into timidity ; then we would curtain ourselves in and draw our former publicity within

the bounds of comparative secrecy. The sky is too vast; we
are afraid of its very immensity; so under roof and lamp of
our own making we render our worship, giving God praise,
and whispering the prayer which is almost spoiled by speech.
This verse gives us the picture of God and man meeting in a holy
place; say in close quarters; say as if space were annihilated
and the infinite had taken up the finite into itself. Man needs
instruction in the art or act of worship. The worship itself may
be what is sometimes called instinctive. Hence man has been
called a religious being; hence we are told that worship or the
spirit of worship is in man; and hence too we have been mis-
takenly told that every man may worship God as he pleases.
That is a sophism which needs exposure. The will of man has
no place whatever in worship, except to receive the direction
or command of God as to its expression. There are emotions
of the heart, inarticulate sometimes, fierce sometimes, tender
emotions of every force and tone that run through the whole
gamut of human feeling; but we are not to say which part shall
be uttered and which shall be silent; we are like little children to
be taught how to worship our Father God.

"Speak unto the children of Israel, and say unto them, If any man of you
bring an offering unto the Lord, ye shall bring your offering of the cattle,
even of the herd, and of the flock.

If his offering be a burnt sacrifice of the herd, let him offer a male without
blemish: he shall offer it of his own voluntary will at the door of the
tabernacle of the congregation before the Lord.

And he shall put his hand upon the head of the burnt offering; and it
shall be accepted for him to make atonement for him.

And he shall kill the bullock before the Lord: and the priests, Aaron's
sons, shall bring the blood, and sprinkle the blood round about upon the
altar that is by the door of the tabernacle of the congregation.

And he shall flay the burnt offering, and cut it into his pieces.

And the sons of Aaron the priest shall put fire upon the altar, and lay
the wood in order upon the fire:

And the priests, Aaron's sons, shall lay the parts, the head, and the fat,
in order upon the wood that is on the fire which is upon the altar:

But his inwards and his legs shall he wash in water: and the priest shall
burn all on the altar, to be a burnt sacrifice, an offering made by fire, of a
sweet savour unto the Lord " (i. 2-9).

Here is a singular conjunction of the legal and the voluntary.
Jehovah fixes the particulars; but the man himself decides on
the act of sacrificial worship. Observe how the Lord works

from the opposite point from which the first of the Ten Commandments was given.   There God called for the worship : here
he leaves the man to offer the worship and proceeds to tell
him how.   The first was general, the second was particular.
The offering was to be of the cattle ; it was to be a male without
blemish ; it was to be offered at the door of the tabernacle ; the
priests were to do part and the man himself was to do part.
So we see again that man needs instruction in the act of worship.
The question must ever arise, How shall we come before God ?
The disciples of Jesus Christ came to him, and said, " Lord, teach
us how to pray."   We all pray ; we cannot help praying.   Some
times in our secularistic pride we only use such common words
as " I wish," " I long for," " I hope," " I desire,"—these are feeble
ways of putting what is in every human heart, namely, the desire
which means prayer.   Jesus Christ taught his disciples how to
pray, that is, he gave them instruction as to the meaning and
mode of worship.   So then, we have a manner or science of
worship even in the Christian sanctuary, dictated and authorised
by Jesus Christ himself.   The preparation of the heart and
the answer of the tongue are from God.   No man was at liberty
in the ancient Church to determine his own terms of approach
to God.   The throne must be approached in the appointed way.
We are not living in an era of religious licentiousness.   There is
a genius of worship, there is a method of coming before God.
God does not ask us to conceive or suggest methods of worship.
He himself meets us with his time-bill and his terms of
spiritual commerce.   God is in heaven and we are upon the
earth ; therefore should our words be few.   The law of approach
to the divine throne is unchanged.   The very first condition
of worship is obedience.   Obedience is better than sacrifice, and
is so because it is the end of sacrifice.   But see, how under
the Levitical ritual, the worshipper was trained to obedience.
Mark the exasperating minuteness of the law.   Nothing was
left to haphazard.   The bullock was to be offered at the door
of the tabernacle ; the sheep was to be killed on the northward
side of the altar ; the blood of the fowl was to be wrung out
at the side of the altar ; the crop was to be plucked away with
the feathers and was to be cast on the east side of the altar
by the place of the ashes ; fine flour and oil were to be the

ingredients of the meat offering, whether it was burnt upon
the altar or baken in the oven, or in the frying-pan, and loaves
and honey were not to enter into the sacrifice by fire. So the
law runs on until it chafes the obstinate mind. But man was
to yield. He had no choice. His iron will was to be broken
in two and his soul was to wait patiently upon God. When,
however, we are in the spirit of filial obedience the very
minuteness of the law becomes a delight. God does not speak
to us in the gross; every motion is watched, every action is
determined, every breathing is regulated; man is always to
yield; he is not a co-partner in this high thinking. So our inventive genius of a religious kind often stands rebuked before
God. We like to make ceremonies; methods of worship seem
to tempt one side of our fertile genius, and we stultify ourselves
by regarding our inventiveness as an element of our devotion.
We like to draw up programmes and orders and schemes of
service and sacrifice. What we should do is to keep as nearly
as we can to the Biblical line, and bring all our arrangements
into harmony with the law of heaven. The law can never give
way. Fire never surrenders; it is the fuel that must go down.

The worship was to be offered through mediation. In every
sacrifice the priests, Aaron or the sons of Aaron, were present.
The priestly element pervades the universe; it is the mystery of
life and service. The sinner did not come immediately before God
and transact his business with the Infinite face to face. Is there
then any priestly element in Christianity? It is the very consummation of priestliness. Our sacrifices are acceptable to God
by Jesus Christ. Our great High Priest is passed into the
heavens. There is one Mediator between God and man, the Man
Christ Jesus. Jesus is the Mediator of the new covenant. The
difficulty with us is that we think we can all be official priests.
We forget that now there is only one Man who continueth for
ever, because he hath an unchangeable priesthood. Jesus is the
Intercessor, he pleads his blood; his cross is in heaven; it
rests against the throne. "I saw in the midst of the throne a
Lamb slain from the foundation of the world." All things are
coloured with his blood. It is a great mystery and not to be
understood by reason in its cold moods; only when we are
burning with unutterable love to God, do we catch any hint of

the meaning of these sovereign mysteries. We have no need of priestly help from any human point of view. Brethren pray for us. Ministers will pray for their people, but not as their substitutes; their prayers are eloquent with the cry of human necessity and the psalm of human adoration. Not in any priestly but in a profoundly sympathetic sense, we are all priests in Christ—a holy priesthood.

The service was voluntary. Notice the expression, " He shall offer it of his own voluntary will." The voluntariness gives the value to the worship. We can only pray with the *heart.* Prayers we can say with the mouth, but to say prayers may not be to pray. To pay a tax is to keep a law, but to give bread to the hungry is to draw out the heart and to put a gift in the very hand of God. So in Christian worship, the voluntary and the legal are combined. There is in this great ritual a wonderful mixing of free will and divine ordination; the voluntary and the unchangeable; the human action and the divine decree. We cannot understand it; if we are able to understand it then it is no larger than our understanding: so God becomes a measurable god, merely the shadow of human wit, a god that cannot be worshipped. It is where our understanding fails or rises into a new wealth of faith, that we find the only altar at which we can bow, with all our powers, where we can utter with enthusiasm all our hopes and desires. So we come with our sacrifice and offering, whatever it may be, and having laid it on the altar, we can follow it no further—free as the air up to a given point, but after that bounded and fixed and watched and regulated—a mystery that can never be solved, and that can never be chased out of a universe in which the Infinite and finite confer.

The worship of the ancient Church was no mere expression of sentiment. It was a most practical worship; not a sentimental exercise; it was a confession and an expiation,—in a word an atonement. This fact explains all. Take the word "atonement" out of Christian theology, and Christian theology has no centre, no circumference, no life, no meaning, no virtue. See the man bringing his bullock—what is he going to do? To make God a present? He is going to confess sin; he is about to say, "My sin deserves death, but it hath pleased thee, mighty King, to accept a type of my death, therefore do I shed the blood of this beast before thee." He is about to say, "Sin means suffering; suffering must accompany sin;" to express it therefore did he put the knife into that dedicated bullock. We have lost many of the spiritual ideas, I fear, suggested by this symbolism, from the range of our Christian worship. Who remembers that sin is a debt? Who brings before his mind in all its pathos and humiliating effect the great fact that sin must be confessed, admitted, specifically owned,—that each man must say "*My* sin"? Who is there that really feels that he is not master of his own sin, having power to put an end to it as if he had never committed it? The devil says, "You have sinned; that may be perfectly true, but what you have got to do is to repent of your sin, and all will be well." He knows that our repentances, unless springing from the right source and regulated by the right influence, do but harden the heart and give the tempter a wider sweep and advantage over us. The enemy says to the withered branch perishing by the roadside, "It is quite true that you are withered, but repent, and all will be well." Never. There must come a hand that can lift the branch up and put it back in the tree, so that it may draw the life-juice from the root and connect itself with the all-blessing sun. A vital work must be done. You cannot wash yourself clean. The sea will not wash you. The cleansing is an act Divine.

The ancient worship was marked by every variety of offering. What a wonderful list do we find in the first three chapters of Leviticus! A bullock, a sheep, a turtle-dove, a young pigeon, fine flour, first-fruits, a goat. The great law seems to say to us, "What have you to offer?" The law is not hard and fast. The rich man and the poor man each has his opportunity. They could not all bring alike; it was not every man who had a bullock to offer, or a turtle-dove, or a young pigeon, or a handful of flour,— the meaning was the same; the meaning was not to be measured by the gift; the gift itself was the meaning when measured by the heart. Has this time of oblation passed? It cannot pass; only our offering is no longer an atonement, it is now a grateful expression for an atonement already offered. So the Lord says to each of us, "What have you?" One man has time, and gives it willingly unto the Lord; another has social influence, and is true to his Saviour in the exercise of all the power that comes out of his station in society; another has sympathy,—power of advising, entering into other people's feelings and encouraging them, in all good and holy ways. The Lord takes what we have. He blesses the giver and the gift.

If we could read this book of Leviticus through at one sitting, the result might be expressed in some such words as these,—" Thank God we have got rid of this infinite labour ; thank God this is not in the Christian service ; thank God we are Christians and not Jews." Let not our rejoicing be the expression of selfishness or folly. It is true we have escaped the bondage of the letter, but only to enter into the larger and sweeter bondage of the spirit. It makes the heart sore to think that so many persons are under the impression that Christianity is a do-nothing religion, and that by becoming Christians we enter into the liberty of idleness. When we think of the bullock, and the sheep, and the goat, and the turtle-dove, and the young pigeon, and the fine flour, the heave-offering, and the wave-offering, and the trespass-offering— offerings all the year round, never ending, or ending only to begin again ; the smoke always ascending, the fire always alight, we say, "Thank God we are Christians." What do we mean ? Had the Jew more to do than we have to do ? No; or only so in a very limited and mechanical sense. The Jew gave his bullock or his goat, his turtle-dove or his young pigeon ; but now each man has to give *himself.* We now buy ourselves off with gold. Well may the apostle exhort us, saying, " I beseech you, therefore, brethren, by the mercies of God, that ye present your bodies a living sacrifice, holy, acceptable unto God, which is your reasonable service." Wonderful is the law which lays its claim upon the ransomed soul,—none of us liveth to himself, and no man dieth to himself; whether we live, we live unto the Lord ; whether we die, we die unto the Lord ; living or dying we are the Lord's. We have escaped measurable taxation, but we have come under the bond of immeasurable love. We have escaped the letter, we have been brought under the dominion of the spirit. Let us be careful, therefore, how we congratulate ourselves on having escaped the goat-offering and heifer-offering, and turtle-dove and young pigeon sacrifices; how we have been brought away from the technicality and poverty of the letter into the still further deeper poverty of selfishness. As Christians, we have nothing that is our own; not a moment of time is ours; not a pulse that throbs in us, not a hair of our head, not a coin in the coffer belongs to us. This is the severe demand of love. Who can rise to the pitch of that self-sacrifice? None. The Jew gives his tenth, and another tenth, and another tenth, and another tenth, even unto five-tenths, or one-half, and we say, " All that is done for ever; it has passed away with the obsolete ritual, and now we are under the law of love," as if God had brought us into something less rather than into something more. The Jew had a night in which he might rest from his labour, but in Christianity, as to the spiritual exactions of its service it may be truly said there is no night; if we cease from the more active labour during the night it is that we may be prepared to resume it with increased energy with the first light of dawn.

NOTE.

Five animals are named in the Law as suitable for sacrifice; the ox, the sheep, the goat, the dove, and the pigeon. It is worthy of notice that these were all offered by Abraham in the great sacrifice of the Covenant (see Gen. xv. 9). These animals are all clean, according to the division into clean and unclean animals, which was adopted in the Law. They were the most important of those which are used for food, and are of the greatest utility to man. The three kinds of quadrupeds were domesticated in flocks and herds, and were recognised as property, making up in fact a great part of the wealth of the Hebrews before they settled in Palestine. It would thus appear that three conditions met in the sacrificial quadrupeds: (1) they were clean according to the Law; (2) they were commonly used as food; and being domesticated (3) they formed part of the home-wealth of the sacrificers.—*Abridged from the Speaker's Commentary.*

Leviticus i.

THE CHANGEABLE AND THE UNCHANGEABLE.

IN addition to what we have already said, there are some things in this first chapter which will justify varied repetition. What an important part the word "if" plays in the opening chapters of Leviticus! At first we did not seem to see it, but by frequent repetition it urges itself upon our notice as a term of vital importance in the argument of the subject, whatever that subject may be. We cannot enter into the subject except through the gate *if*. It is God's word. The meaning must be profound; the meaning must be in excess of the visible insignificance of the word. It is but a film of a word after all. Is there a less word in all the language? Yet it is no film in its moral significance and in its moral effect; it is a granite wall thicker than the earth and high as the sky. Even God condescends to make terms with us. One of the greatest of English writers has been perplexed by the suggestion that God is almighty. He says—No; either His almightiness must be surrendered, or His all-goodness. If He were almighty, He never could permit the evil which is now afflicting mankind. The argument is inconclusive, hiding, from my point of view, a most obvious sophism. Yet this is a ground upon which the almightiness of God must be surrendered. He is no mightier than we in one direction. Viewed in the light of that direction we would seem to be almighty. We can withhold our consent or we can give it. A great *if* must be crossed before even God can continue his purposes of wisdom and love in our education and redemption. We are almighty in obstinacy. The word is not unfamiliar; we hear it in the expression, "To-day if ye will hear his voice, harden not your hearts." God has fixed the time, made the proposition, offered the whole hospitality of his heart and heaven, and then waits for our treatment of his necessary *if*. We hear it in the statement latest in all the sacred books, "If any man will open the door." What! Cannot God break through any door that ever was framed and fashioned? No! To break through is not his object. Destruction is but the very poorest aspect of the working of almightiness. God's aim is persuasion, the winning of consent, the bringing over of the whole force of the will : and then almightiness must stand still and wait a beggar's answer. Nowhere is the greatness of man so broadly and vividly confessed as in the Bible. They do injustice to Holy Scripture who suppose that it is continually contemning, abusing, and degrading human nature. The whole scheme of education and redemption revealed in the Bible awaits the consent of the creature. God is ready, and we keep him waiting at the door; the King is in the chariot, and the horses are prancing, eager to be gone on some celestial journey, and we keep them all waiting. It is a daring assumption. No book that is not conscious of infinite resources and vindications could base itself upon such a theory of human nature.

Through the gate *if* we enter into the temple of obedience. Having crossed the threshold, then law begins to operate. After the *if* comes the discipline—the sweet, but often painful necessity. Observe the balance of operation : Man must reply; having replied, either in one form or the other, necessary consequences follow. It is so in all life. There is no exception in what is known as the religious consciousness and activity. The great sea says in its wild waves, "If ye will walk on me and become citizens of this wilderness of water, then you must submit to the law of the country; you must fall into the rhythm of the universe; you must build your wooden houses or your iron habitations according to laws old as God; you need not come upon my waters; I do not ask you to come; when you come I will obliterate your footprints so that no man may ever know that you have crossed me; but if you come you must obey." The earth says, "If ye will build upon me, please yourselves: I do not ask you to build upon me; I shall swing around the sun if no stone be laid upon the top of another, and be as glad in my path of light as though I carried temples and towers and cities; but if ye will build, you must obey the law; I cast down everything that is out of plomb; I will not carry any structure with any guarantee of permanence that is not built by the geometry of the sun; I do not ask you to build, but if you build you then come under the dominion of laws which cannot be set aside permanently. For a time they may be evaded or trifled with, or apparently suspended; but they will assert their permanence and vindicate their justice." We have therefore no liberty after a certain time. That is quite right; it is the law of all life. But we never give up our liberty in response to the laws of the universe without our surrender being compensated after God's measure. We are accustomed to speak of the law: we quote sharp and imperative terms from the Pentateuch, saying, "These words are very emphatic, and are all-inclusive, and often touch the point of severity; they do not tamper with us, or compromise with us, or leave us any liberty." That is an unjust criticism, if it be all we have to say. There was a time when God was suppliant; there was an hour in which he prayed; there was a time when God was on his knees asking a beggar to allow him heart-room. Let us therefore take in the whole case, and state it in all its lines and elements, and we shall find a marvellous harmony of forces—a union and reconciliation constituting a coherent and sublime ministry.

We call this the law, but it is the law with a golden fringe of mercy. The law gave great choice of offering. It said, "If you bring a burnt offering, bring it of the herd if you have one. If you have not a herd of cattle, bring it of the flocks; bring it of the flock of the sheep; but if you are too poor to have a flock of sheep, bring a goat from the flock of the goats; only in all cases this condition must be permanent: whatever you offer must be without blemish. But if you have no cattle, no sheep, no goats, then bring it of the fowls : bring turtle-doves or young pigeons; the air is full of them, and the poorest man can take them." Is that not mercy twice blessed? We are not all masters of cattle that browse upon the green hills; nor are we all flockmasters, and amongst flockmasters there are rich and poor. God says, "Let your offering be according to your circumstances, only without blemish, and it shall be accepted."

What was the object of the offerings? Atonement. What is the meaning of the word "atone"? To cover. How then does the word *atone* refer to sin? By covering it, hiding it, concealing it and so destroying it. The object of the offerings was to atone,

to cover, to hide. "Blessed is the man whose sin is covered"—
and sin can only be covered or hidden in one way. No cloth of
human weaving can ever conceal it; it will rise and show its
figure before the vision of the world through all the silk and
purple ever thrown upon it. There is an appointed covering;
have we accepted it? Observe, this is the law of all life. To
atone in the sense of covering is not a religious idea only; it is
the thing which is being done every day by every man. Where,
then, is the awful dogmatism of the Scriptures, and the appalling
arbitrariness of the divine decrees and requirements? God
looks down from heaven and sees us engaged in the continual
endeavour to cover our sin, and he says, "It cannot be done;
you have undertaken the impossible; that miracle does not lie
within the compass of human invention or mortal strength; you
are right in endeavouring to cover it; you are working according
to a law, the full operation of which you do not understand; I
will provide the covering." One reason for attending to the
proposition is that all our coverings have failed. We have
heaped rocks upon the sin, and the tremendous vitality of the
wrong has heaved off the rock; we have bribed the sin to be
quiet, and it has devoured our investments and balances and
prosperities, and has then looked at us with a look of insatiable
hunger. Knowing this, we are prepared to listen to the new
proposal. God undertakes what we ourselves have been undertaking and failing in. It may be the Lord will succeed where
we have been baffled by mocking perplexities.

What was the method of the offerings? The hands were to
be laid upon the head of the victim. Whether the priest laid his
hands upon it or the man himself, the act was symbolic and
representative—a most beautiful and pathetic symbol. The
hands were laid upon the head, and the meaning of the imposition was that the sin was communicated by being recognised,
acknowledged, confessed with a contrite heart. These are
symbols we must not take out of human history until we are
prepared to remove from the history of our race one of the most
pathetic signs which has blessed it with religious accentuation.
"My faith would lay her hands on that dear head of thine."

We say that all this is changed. Is it? What is changed?

I am not aware that the change has taken place in any sense that would justify contempt for the ancient history. Changes have taken place, but they have only transpired in the sense of completion and fulfilment. What is confirmed? God has chosen the offering now. We are no longer called upon to say,—Shall it be a burnt sacrifice of the herd? or shall the offering be of the flocks, whether of the sheep or of the goats? or shall the burnt sacrifice be of fowls, whether turtle-doves or young pigeons? But we are called upon to accept God's choice: "Behold the Lamb of God, which taketh away the sin of the world"—the Son of man for the sons of men, Emmanuel: God with us—always explaining itself to the consciousness and the necessity and the love, but never condescending to exchange the mystery for words which men can change into pointless controversy. What is changed?— The mere mechanism, the personal expense, the humiliation— undoubtedly, but not the Atonement. Really next to nothing has been changed. The accidentals or accessories have all been changed, but the central truth—the Atonement—remains for ever. There is no short and easy method with sin. It never has been one of the easy problems of human history. It has pained all men. It has distressed the supreme intellect of the world, and brought that intellect into the darkness and silence of despair. It has driven men away to find in beauty some solace for a conscious hideousness within; and men have found it to be cold and monotonous work, to be worshipping unresponsive sculpture, painting, and art of every name and kind. Men have sought by excess of the very thing itself to destroy sin, and if they could have gone forward from indulgence to indulgence, from insanity to insanity, they might have escaped the remorse of this world; but God has so constituted the universe that men have moments of sobriety, times of mental and moral reaction, periods in which they see themselves and their destiny with an appalling vividness, and in those hours it is found that the sin which began the mischief is still there. There is no way out of it but God's way. We have tried most of the ways ourselves, and it is but just to acknowledge that all our trials have ended only in the embitterment of our lot. "If we say that we have no sin, we deceive ourselves, and the truth is not in us. If we confess our sins, he is faithful and just to forgive us our sins, and to cleanse us from all unrighteousness." Seeing therefore that I must grapple with this problem of sin : that in proportion as I grow in wisdom I am conscious of the presence of the sin—something that marks the fairest sheet upon which I would write my history, something that plagues the heart in its innermost delights, something that twists and perverts everything I do that is of the quality of goodness—I will look into God's proposal. It is a proposal amounting to a miracle. He says, " Your sin is red like crimson, I will make it white as snow ; it is a scarlet thing, I will make it like speckless wool : come now, let us reason together." It is for me to accept the invitation. This will I do : I will arise and go to my Father, and say unto him, " I have sinned, and the spot marks the guilt I can never erase." What is changed ? Not the priestly idea, though the priestly person is changed. There is one Mediator, or Priest, between God and man, the Man Christ Jesus. We have a High Priest that abideth for ever. All we do in relation to the heavens we do through the medium of Jesus Christ, the Son of God, and the Priest of the universe. He is able to save unto the uttermost all that come unto God by him, seeing he ever liveth to make intercession for us.

So then, now I examine the change, I find it is practically no change at all. In things accidental, accessory, contributory, in mere externals, the change is very great, but a very great change within a very small compass. What is left is this : God, sin, atonement, priestliness. Now I understand what Jesus said : " Think not that I am come to destroy the law, or the prophets : I am not come to destroy, but to fulfil." What remains ? The different offerings, they remain. We can never offer the same thing to God. Every man offers according to his quality and resources. What is prayer to one man is no prayer to another. God is judge. If I bring a turtle-dove or a young pigeon, when I might have brought the head of the herd, the poor bird will not be accepted ; it will fly downwards. If I bring out of the flocks the best of the sheep, it will not be accepted if I could have brought my sacrifice of the herd, a male without blemish. We bring what we have. We do not all contribute in the same kind. The greatest contributors may be those who seem to contribute nothing. Even in the matter of giving of our wealth, Jesus Christ has a law of measurement. He said, concerning one

who gave two mites, which make one farthing, " She **hath given**
more than they all." Some contribute thought, inspiration,
personal magnetism ; some communicate the contagion of enthusiasm ; some give new ideas concerning the old truths, or set old
truths in new lights and aspects ; some give of the herd, some
of the flock, and some of the aviary ; some but two mites. What
is it gives the value to the offering ? The spirit. The primest
bullock that ever browsed is a worthless offering, if it be given
with begrudgement or reluctance ; and the poorest effort in
speech, in service, in prayer, in oblation, is a miracle, if done
with the passion of the heart.

NOTE.

If a man were rich and could afford it, he would bring his burnt sacrifice, with which he designed to honour God, out of his herd of larger cattle.
He who considers what God is will resolve to give him the best he has ;
else he gives him not the glory due unto his name. . . Those of the middle
rank, who could not well afford to offer a bullock, would bring a sheep or a
goat, and those who were not able to do that would be accepted of God if
they brought a turtle-dove or a pigeon. It is observable that those creatures
were chosen for sacrifice which were most mild and gentle, harmless and
inoffensive ; to typify the innocence and meekness that were in Christ, and
to teach the innocence and meekness that should be in Christians.

*   *   *   *   *   *

The Jews say this sacrifice of birds was one of the most difficult services
the priests had to do. The priest would need to take as much care in offering this sacrifice as in any of the others ; to teach those that minister in holy
things to be as solicitous for the salvation of the souls of the poor as of the
rich ; their services are as acceptable to God, if they come from an upright
heart, as the services of the rich ; for he expects according to what a man
hath, and not according to what he hath not (2 Cor. viii. 12). The poor
man's turtle-doves or young pigeons are here said to be an offering of a sweet
savour, as much as those of an ox or a bullock, that hath horns and hoofs.
Yet, to love God with all our heart, and to love our neighbours as ourselves,
is better than all burnt-offerings and sacrifices (Mark xii. 33).—*Commentary,*
HENRY AND SCOTT.

Leviticus 1. (continued).

THE ORDER OF THE ANCIENT OFFERINGS.

THERE is something very remarkable in the order in which the offerings, patriarchal and Jewish, were presented unto the Lord. I do not advise young readers to make themselves learnedly familiar with patriarchal and Jewish usage or ritual, but I do recommend them to look sufficiently into the old histories to make themselves acquainted with the elements that are permanent, and which throw light upon a development which was consummated in the cross and in the whole priesthood of Jesus Christ. The order of offering itself is a revelation. I do not go beyond that order to find proof that the book which sets it forth in historical sequence is a book inspired. The order in which the offerings were presented enables me to address every man as religious. It is a large sanctuary that throws out its sacred screen until it includes the man who is supposed not to be in church at all. God builds no little houses. He is not given to making small, dwarfed sanctuaries that can hold but a few. He means his Church to be typified by the blue sky when there is no cloud or fog in it, when it is at its very best in all the infinitude of its summer glory. It is then the blue dome best emblematises the Church and Kingdom of him who is all heart when he loves and all light when he guides.

I would that I could sufficiently prepare your minds, if they have not already undergone adequate preparation, for the statement of the order in which the offerings occurred. I could announce them at once. I do not want to throw the announcement away. I want to dally with you until I get you into the true tone and temper of mind for a revelation so brilliant and startling. I want to lead you away from commerce and anxiety, to excite you to a pitch of expectation, so that you may realise the infinite grandeur of the development.

The first offering that was presented in patriarchal ages was the burnt-offering. It was an appeal to fire. It did not mean destruction. The meaning of the burnt-offering was that which ascends. Think of it; that man first directed his attention to fire as a medium of worship. The flesh was not regarded as destroyed by burning, but as being sent up to God as a sweet-smelling savour. It was a typical offering of the hope of the whole life of the man who offered the sacrifice. Being put into modern language it meant, " I am God's creature; my life is his; I give it to him; on the wings of fire my life ascends to his holy place, and daily I rise to the source of my being." All religious acts mean more than they seem to mean. No religious act is measurable by words. It is not to be brought within a parenthesis, and yarded off into so many inches or ells; therefore it is more than probable that those who offered the burnt-offering had some deep conceptions of a moral kind. But these do not appear in the act; they are latent; they are hidden and stowed away in the consciousness of the worshipper who is dumb because of the vastness of the work he has undertaken. But the elementary meaning is ascending, returning as fire to the sun, for your fire in your little grate is a child of the sun, and when it flickers and spurts and crackles and blazes, what is it doing but seeking its source? Find Abel and find Noah, and others of patriarchal times, lighting their fire and offering their burnt-offering, and you find the very first principle of natural religion. That burnt-offering might represent the operation of an instinct. Man is spoken of as a religious being. He goes out after the unknown God, and you cannot keep him back. He will make a God rather than not have one. He aspires, he ascends; earth is too little for him, time chokes him. He is almost God, even as fire in its blaze and glow and heaven-seeking flame is almost a human spirit at times. It burns for God, it seeks him fervently.

The patriarchal burnt-offering represented the indestructible God-seeking element in human nature. In that sense the fire upon the altar never goes out. There are men amongst us to-day who are not in the Church, and who have no hymn-book and no pastor, and no *locus standi* in ecclesiastical courts, who are presenting the burnt-offering. They stand with Abel, they worship with Noah; they are in the twilight far back, but they are still within God's great day of worship and grace and hope. The burnt-offering is the expression of an instinct. Now these men have dropped the word *God*. Perhaps they do not like it; perhaps the associations which have gathered round it have somewhat discouraged, or even distressed, them; perhaps they have been troubled by sectarian definitions of that infinite term, and by endeavours to house the Eternal within bricks of a merely denominational boundary, but they offer the burnt sacrifice to the Secret, the Force, the Totality of Being, the Something beyond, the *plus*, whatever it is. When they lift their necks and sigh because they have no speech, they are offering the burnt sacrifice; they are going up in pure flame to the Unmeasured and the Unnamed. Do I drive such men away as heathen, pagan, and alien? God forbid. I would they could offer at another altar which I shall presently name; meanwhile, if they sigh, they will be saved; if they want to know, they shall know; if they are offering the fire of an earnest and fervent wish, that fire will be accepted in its fullest meaning. Yet I would speak these words cautiously, and with distinct reservation, because, as a Christian teacher, I have to enforce Christian truth. I am speaking of men now who are sincere, real-hearted, simple-minded, without disingenuousness or complexity of thought, but who have come up to a point unknown, a secret unnameable, an uncontrollable force, and who worship by lifting silent eyes, or sighing out their wondering hearts, after that which they have not yet understood. The Lord accept their fire, and make their hearts warm with ever-growing desire after himself.

What was the next offering presented in patriarchal times and under the Jewish ritual? It was the peace-offering. The peace-offering had a double aspect. It was heaved, the action being the uplifted hand, ejaculated, thrown up, to the enthroned God, and there was a secondary action, lateral, waving, having great human meanings, pathetic outgoings towards human moods, human obligations, social trespasses and sins. Certain portions of the victim were offered upon the altar in burning, and the remainder of the flesh was eaten by the man who offered the sacrifice, and those who were associated with him. In heathen sacrifices the portion that was not burnt was saved to furnish materials for a feast.

There are some persons who do not understand eating and
drinking. They are merely animal exercises to them. They do
not like toasts; they disapprove them; and they are perfectly
right under their narrow definitions. But· to eat should be a
religious exercise; the lifting of a hand over a table of feast
should mean, " God be with us, every one ; God forgive our sins
and bind us in tenderer love." Let us learn from the old heathen
nations, when they had burnt part of the offering to the gods,
they kept the other for a social feast, that eating and drinking·
are sacramental acts when performed by religious souls—they
may be acts that can be done in stable or stye, they may be made
sacraments unto God.

The peace-offering had therefore a divine uplifting and a
human outlook and application. At times the innate brotherhood
of the race declares itself in bursts of benevolence. We have
to be at peace with one another. What is the meaning of
apologising, pardon-seeking, mutual explanation, agreeing with
the adversary quickly whilst he is in the way with us ? What
is the meaning of going to one another, and saying, " Brother,
I have sinned against you ; I have done you wrong " ? That
is the permanent element in the old patriarchal, Jewish, and
pagan peace-offering. So, then, up to this point we are under
the operation of what I may term religious instinct. Heathen
nations have found out the things I have now been speaking
about—fire seeking, tremblingly, a source, with a modesty that
makes it quiver, with an energy that cannot be turned aside ;
and a peace-offering, meaning, " I have injured you, we have
injured one another, we have done to one another the things we
ought not to have done ; we apologise, we repent, we express
contrition ; we have a wave-offering; let us all accept it, and
be at peace among ourselves."

The burnt-offering, the peace-offering—what next ? The SIN-
offering ! It is a beautiful development. The sin-offering comes
under law and is full of mystery. Unlike the burnt-offering
and the peace-offering, it is not wholly measurable by an instinct.
It roots itself in an instinct, but goes beyond it. The sin-offering
is a revelation : not in patriarchal annals but in Mosaic records
we read how the blood shed in sacrifice was to be treated.
Now we come to *blood.* Where do you first read of the blood,

in this relation? You should make yourselves, younger readers, familiar with the beginnings of great rivers; you should explore these Niles of thought. We read of blood in this relation for the first time in the twelfth chapter of Exodus, which treats of the sprinkling of the blood of the lamb on the door-posts of the houses of the Israelites. It was to save them from destruction. The next mention of blood is in the twenty-fourth chapter of Exodus. This should be specially noticed. Blood was now to be used in common with burnt-offerings and peace-offerings of the covenant of Sinai. Thus all that was instinctive was taken up into the region of revelation, and was baptized with blood. The burnt-offering and the peace-offering were no longer instinctive ceremonies, they were baptized with the red blood and made holy unto the Lord as offerings that expressed his revealed will.

When the sin-offering was presented, a portion of blood was offered to the Lord by being put on the horns of the altar, and the rest, except on certain occasions, was poured away at the base of the altar. The blood was the life: to offer the blood was typically to die: in emblem the sinner slew himself. Now look at the development—the burnt-offering, consecration; the peace-offering, the humanity of religion; the sin-offering, atonement, sacrifice, propitiation—words not to be caught within a theory, and to be seen only once in a lifetime. Distrust those who have theories of the atonement. You can only see the atonement for a moment. Christ could only suffer his agony once. Such agonies are not to be repeated. You do not see the atonement with a cold reason: you cannot analyse it and then synthesise and play theologico-metaphysical tricks and games with the heart of God. Once your eyes will be opened you will see it—see the Cross, see the bursting heart, and you will be saved. God's Christianity is a religion of fire. Only under the excitement of the soul, which amounts to a divine inspiration, an opening of the eyes by God himself, can we see the Cross. I once saw it: it abides within me as the sun abides: after you have seen it for a moment with the open eye, close the eye and the sun is still there. It is in you. As to reasoning about it, and logically persuading a man that God died for him—logic and God are never brought together in this connection; it is an unholy union; see the Sin and you will see the Mercy!

Through some such process must we all come. You are offering the burnt sacrifice; I thank God, I hail you as a brother. You are offering peace sacrifices, you want good will amongst men, peace on earth, happy family relationships—you want to diffuse the spirit of brotherhood. Thank God; you are not far from the kingdom. Only get a man out of himself to think about anybody else in the world, and he is on the road to God. Now that is not enough: the sin-offering takes up the preliminary sacrifices, gives them their true meaning, their highest application, and extracts from them all that is permanent and valuable in their purpose. We have not come to the mount that might be touched, to Mount Sinai; we have not come to the Jewish shambles, red with blood, reeking with outpoured life—we have come to Calvary, to the slain Man, to the Lamb of God—a great mystery, but I wanted it to round off my thinking, I wanted it as a sky to my earth—I had made a little mud floor which I called earth, I wanted that higher floor to set above it like a sky, rich with one sun, wealthy with innumerable stars.

Where are you? Still following your instinct? I call you to obey a revelation. Still occupying yourself with human relationships? I call upon you to see the divine meaning and purpose. Where are you—at the Cross? Stay there. With Jesus? Never leave him. With the blood that speaketh better things than the blood of Abel? Long for no higher eloquence. Then is my life to be spent in sighing at the Cross? No. How? On the Cross. We are to be crucified with Christ, we are to know the fellowship of his sufferings, we are to be living sacrifices. The Lord drive back those baptized in grace who are making a luxury of Christianity, a pillow of down of Christian revelation—the Lord send them back to the burnt-offering and the peace-offering, for they have mistaken the genius of the last revelation. If our Christian religion is not a passion, it is a lie. The old doctors of the Church said that if Christ was not God, he was not good. "*Non Deus, non bonus.*" If we are not alive with fire we are twice dead—we shall be plucked up by the roots.

And as for thee, earnest man, all flame, know the spirit of judgment is to be united with the spirit of burning, that zeal is to be balanced by knowledge, that the true logic is love, not reason, directed by all the highest powers of the mind. Thou shalt love with all thy *mind*. Intellect itself is to be a flame, cold understanding is to be warmed up into a burning affection. These are great mysteries, but the elect of God will understand them.

PRAYER.

ALMIGHTY GOD, all things do change, but thou changest not: thou art the same, and thy years do not fail. The heavens grow old, and the earth, and all things made by thine almightiness; but thou remainest upon the throne from age to age, ruling, governing, redeeming, and blessing the sons of men. Thou wilt reign evermore: the Lord reigneth, let the earth rejoice. Jesus Christ thy Son shall reign till all enemies are put under his feet. The last enemy that shall be destroyed is death: death shall be swallowed up in victory; then shall there be a shouting of great gladness in thine house, because there shall be no more death. Thou art taking away one and another, still thy Church abides; speech after speech ends and is forgotten, but the word of the Lord abideth for ever. We bless thee for that which is permanent amidst that which is always passing away. Thou thyself art the Living One: the generations come and go, but the Creator sits upon the throne time without end. May we be found worshippers of God through our Lord Jesus Christ, adoring the Father, loving and serving the Son, and receiving constantly the sanctifying ministry of the Holy Ghost, until we become temples of the triune God, and body, soul, and spirit—all, is without flaw, without spot or wrinkle or any such thing,—glorious with the splendour and beautiful with the comeliness of Christ. The Lord light a fire in the midst of us that shall not consume; the Lord address a gospel to every heart that shall call it to its noblest hopes and consecrate it to divinest service. Reordain all thy ministers every day; baptize thy people with a double portion of thy Spirit morning by morning; regard the lambs of the flock with shepherdly tenderness; may all workers work with both hands, and may all sufferers magnify the patience of Christ. Amen.

Leviticus ii. 12-16.

12. As for the oblation of the firstfruits, ye shall offer them unto the Lord; but they shall not be burnt on the altar for a sweet savour.

13. And every oblation of thy meat-offering shalt thou season with salt; neither shalt thou suffer the salt of the covenant of thy God to be lacking from thy meat-offering : with all thine offerings thou shalt offer salt.

14. And if thou offer a meat-offering of thy firstfruits unto the Lord, thou shalt offer for the meat-offering of thy firstfruits green ears of corn dried by the fire, even corn beaten out of full ears.

15. And thou shalt put oil upon it, and lay frankincense thereon: it is a meat-offering.

16. And the priest shall burn the memorial of it, part of the beaten corn thereof, and part of the oil thereof, with all the frankincense thereof: it is an offering made by fire unto the Lord.

THE MEAT-OFFERING.

WE have been accustomed to the terms "burnt-offering," "offering of the flocks," "offering of the fowls," "the burnt sacrifice," "an offering made by fire of sweet savour unto the Lord,"—now we read of a "meat-offering." Is there, then, already in these ancient writings some hint of appropriation, participation in a sacred feast ? The other offerings stand outside of us ; we do not know all the meaning of the mysterious flame ; it is something done by us under the inspiration and direction of God. But is the "meat-offering" a hint of something that is done within us for our spiritual nourishment, for the daily culture of the soul in all its best qualities and moods ? Is it a solitary feast ? or, being solitary at a given historical point, is it suggestive of communion, fellowship, participation with others—yea, with the Master himself in festal blessing ? We have become weary with the burnt-offerings, with slaughters and blood-shedding; but the "meat-offering" seems to hint at eucharistic hospitality,— the appropriation of the body and the blood of Christ in a great symbolic act whose majesty is shaded by its tenderness. We are not yielding to fancy in any wanton or lawless sense in thus finding the germs and beginnings of things. Even the Church has its Genesis; even the Bible has its first book—its seed-house; and blessed are they, as men who are very wealthy in spiritual possessions, who can wisely, and rationally, and truly seize the very plasm out of which all the Church-universe has been developed and consolidated.

The " meat-offering " was to be seasoned with salt. It is wonderful to mark how God in his providence attaches his kingdom to old customs or prevalent practices, or to usages that had great meanings to the common people, so that through them as through parabolical images he might communicate his own highest purposes and meanings. This is what Christianity always does. In going into the nations it studies the customs of the people; it aims very quickly to preach in the native tongue. It does not stand up in its ancient pride and classical elegance and say to other nations, even to peoples who have no grammar or formal speech, " You must learn my tongue." It says, " What is your speech ? How do you hold commerce with one another ? Show me your methods of communicating with one another as to spiritual impression, or purpose, or action that has a meaning and a design, and I will adopt your plans, methods, customs and usages, for through them, better than through any other medium, I can communicate my purpose to you." Christianity is the condescending religion ; Christianity is the religion that can afford to stoop ; there is majesty in its every attitude. Its Founder made himself of no reputation, but took upon himself the form of a slave that he might raise and save the world. There was an ancient Eastern custom as to the use of salt and the meaning of salt as used upon various occasions. There have been countries in which the eating of salt with a man meant eternal friendship. Said one, " I cannot fight with him "—naming a supposed enemy—" because we have eaten salt together." A custom among the Arabs was, in the forming of any serious covenant, to sprinkle salt upon a sword, and for the two covenanting parties to partake of the salt so sprinkled, and the understanding was that nothing should ever be allowed to violate that covenant. It was a covenant seasoned with salt, sealed by the most solemn formalities. Arabs, who can trifle with language, who have a subtlety of mind that can make distinctions where other intelligences fail to perceive any differences, would hold themselves bound by a common participation of salt sprinkled upon a sword never to violate the awful covenant. The Lord adopts our customs wherein they are to us most significant. He begins with the human mind where he can. Instead of formulating some new method unheard of and open to all the perils of controversial interpretation, he says, in effect,—" What are your most solemn usages ? " Finding them to be in themselves innocent, involving no corruptness or malice, he adopts such usages as points of beginning—just as he would invent a parable whereby to express a kingdom. There is a great law here which we ought to study more carefully and apply more fearlessly. Christianity consents to be, in a sense, nationalised—accentuated by the peculiarities of the people who receive it. It cannot be otherwise. It is so amongst ourselves. Every man seasons his sacrifice according to his individuality,— in other words, marks his labour by his own image and super- scription, so that it is *his* labour expressively and exclusively ; it bears upon it the touch of his own soul. When India receives the Christian revelation we shall have Indian preaching, Indian books : the old truths, which never can be changed in substance, expressed in new eloquence, startling allegory, wondrous philo- sophy : words will be turned to new uses and miracles will be wrought in the speech of men. So with every other nation. Each will have its own form of Christianity, its own method of representing the Gospel, its own condiment with which to season its most religious actions. Let us be more fearless herein. Let us recognise the diversity of human qualities, capacities, and general gifts. We must not mechanise the divine kingdom or the eternal book. Where can each man attach himself to this redeeming thought ? should be the supreme question of the Church. The true Church includes all churches. They may not all stand upon one level, but they are all shone upon by the same impartial Sun, all grouped in the same infinite constellation which constitutes the crown of Christ. Can you seize the Christian thought best at the hu- manity of Christ ? then seize it there and despise the theological odium that may be heaped upon you by theological bigots. Can you, on the other hand, at once, as if by some spiritual kinship, enter into the very highest mysteries of the Divine Nature ? Then begin even there—away among the upper places radiant with celestial splendour—and heed not the imputations of fanaticism which may be accorded to you by theological utilitarians. Do you need some other point of attachment ? and have you found one of your own ? Have you found it ?—keep it, it is yours by right of spiritual revelation, or mental conquest, wrought in you as a miracle by God the Holy Ghost. The one thing to be observed is this : that the central truth may be the same—must be the same ; Christ cannot change, his priesthood cannot be altered ; but recognise the sublime possibility that by a thousand different ways of merely particular thinking and seizure of principles we may all at last come into a common light and hail one another in a communion to which we have passed through all the tumult of sometimes angry controversy.

Here is the element of discipline even in worship. We have not been accustomed to associate worship and discipline, but the two cannot be properly or justly — that is, in harmony with the genius of the divine purpose—dissociated. Worship is discipline ; discipline in its highest sense is worship. Is God careless about the way in which he is worshipped, or approached, or sought unto ? Already in these ancient writings we find that it is God himself who marks the road, keeps the gate, gives the password, indicates times, seasons, gifts, quantities methods. There is no human invention in all this poetry of worship, nor is there laxity. No man is left to himself to invent his own religion, to build his own little altar, and to have everything according to his own way of thinking. This is the marvellous apparent contradiction of the divine testimony—individuality, but under divine inspiration ; divine inspiration accommodating itself to national circumstances and to individual capacities, but all the time preserving a central and unchangeable substance. This cannot always be explained in words. We must live some expositions. We must pray ourselves, and through much suffering introduce ourselves, into some of the many provinces of the heavenly kingdom. Even where God adopts a national habit, or an individual capacity and accent, he adopts whatever he takes in hand so as to bring it under continual and most holy discipline. Pray in your own time, but pray at the appointed altar ; bring your offering willingly, but having brought it willingly offer it according to the standard and law of the sanctuary. We must not be lax in our worship. Voluntariness, consent and assent of the mind must not be understood as permitting new ventures, out-of-the-way customs, the very establishment of which conceals a tribute to our own vanity. In the kingdom of Christ there is the largest liberty for individual thought, capacity, expression, and yet there is a centripetal force that binds all diversities to its own great heart. Unity in diversity,—diversity forming itself into unity,—these are the practical mysteries ; but, blessed be God, these are also the daily revelations of the highest spiritual life and relation. Herein we have been unjust to the gracious spirit of Christianity : we have come to church when we pleased, we have listened to Gospel ministration when we were disposed to do so, we have given the offering in any way that best suited the convenience of the moment, we have entered the house of God when our circumstances suggested we should do so,—we have entered it perfunctorily, we have left it hastily, we have scampered through its exercises as through something that must unhappily be done ;—all this has but whitened the sepulchre, has but aggravated the blasphemy which it seemed to conceal. Let no man think that he can alter God's waiting : or set back the ordinances of Heaven : that he can come into the book just where he pleases, how he pleases, and extract from it the message which God left there only for humble souls and broken hearts. There is a discipline of worship. There is a law that watches the altar—a flaming sword moving every way that keeps the tree of Life. We must not debase the name of liberty by reducing its permissions into the extravagances of licentiousness. Discipline in every part of life must be our law ; in our uprising and our downsitting, in all we think, say, do, the whole life must have. upon it the touch, the superintendence, criticism, and sacred intention of spiritual meaning.

Whatever of frankincense, or leaven, or oil, we may bring with the offering, if it be a meat-offering we must not forget the salt. Leaven and oil represent possible fermentation, corruption and depreciation of quality salt represents that which is antiseptic preservative, vital, permanent. The salt may not be required in some offerings, but it is required in one, and that offering the "meat-offering," the participation-offering, the festival-service. There must be some seal with divine meanings in it. Perhaps we may be left in some sense to adopt our own particular seal; but the seal must be there—the vital signature. Your letter means nothing until you have signed it; it is no letter addressed even to the eye, much less to the heart, until it bears the signature of the hand that wrote it and the man that meant it all. Your blessing upon your food may be very brief, but it is a blessing; before eating your bread you may but look up silently unto heaven, but there is a silence that is an infinite prayer. You must for yourself determine in many instances what the seal is to be—whether salt, or an upward look, or a sigh, the confession of unworthiness, or some gentle family hymn sung by the father and the mother and all the children. Fix your own seal. It may be unknown by any other person or family in the whole Church, but it is yours; and in some things God has been pleased to allow us this gracious liberty, this license of spiritual invention, but without the seal which to you has the greatest meaning what you do may be worthless. The one great seal never can be changed, and that is the name of Christ, the priesthood of the Son of God, the ever-speaking blood,—that admits of no variation, or modification, or re-arrangement; it abides for ever. But there are other seals, tokens and intimations, in the use of which we may have much liberty. Your worship may be right as to its form; but it may be offered in a wrong spirit. A man may pray blasphemously; a man may pray profanely. There are prayers that are profanity in its worst form. When you use the altar as a place of judgment upon others—when you pray so as to inflict pain upon those who are supposed to share your intercession— when under the shelter of talking to God you talk bitterly to men of their offences, and shortcomings, and evil deeds—the worship in its act and in some of its general meanings may be right, but being uttered in a wrong spirit it falls downward. Thank God he has a bottomless pit for our pithless, soulless, Christless prayers! You may give the right gift of time, or money, or influence—be it what it may, but being unsalted with your heart's consent, it is not accepted in the treasury of heaven;

it does not amount to a practical and accepted contribution; a voice says, "Thy money perish with thee: both of you rot together or be eaten up by a common canker." You have the right creed, but if it be unaccompanied by sacrifice it is no faith, it is without the salt of real, genuine trust; it is a form of godliness but without the power thereof. This is the position about which we should be most anxiously jealous. It has become so common to think that a creed merely as such—an enumerated and regulated act of beliefs—can save the world. All these we may need, every one of them may be of great importance; but until our creed becomes our faith, until it is taken into the heart and reproduced in the life by loving sacrifice, daily seasoned with salt, continually ablaze to the heavens, it is a creed only which a parrot might repeat—not an inspiration which an angel might covet. Hence we come to have mechanical orthodoxies, hence we add to the profanity of a lifetime the audacity which can sentence men to the right hand or to the left in proportion as they read our books and adopt our lines and our formal positions. Blessed be God! our Maker is our Judge. He looks at the spirit. "To this man will I look." "To which man, Lord?" "The man who is of a broken and a contrite heart and who trembleth at my word." Where has that man ever been regarded as a Christian? Where is his name set down at the top of any human list? Nowhere; and that confession must be followed by a thanksgiving. You may be on the right side of an argument, but if your position be unsalted by enthusiasm your patronage is a burden. You count one by the register, but you are not counted at all by the God of the battle. A right man, a right side, without a right spirit; on the right nominal list without being inflamed by Heaven's pure fire,—that is falsehood, that is irony, that keeps back the kingdom of heaven from its proper advance to-day. Let the cold man leave the Church; we shall be the warmer for that subtraction of coldness. Do not let the formalist patronise the Cross; he hurts us, he hurts the cause, he hurts the Son of God. Take your patronage over to the other side: you grieve the Spirit of God! The offering is nominally right, the contribution is formally to all appearance as it ought to be; but the soul is wanting,—the fire, the enthusiasm, the love, the passion,—the one thing that gives it significance and value.

Leviticus iii.

MINOR OFFERINGS.

IN addition to the great offerings of the Jewish ritual, there were certain minor offerings for which special provision was made. If we take this chapter and view it in the light of the Christian dispensation we shall see more clearly what has been gained by the Christian covenant. These offerings, in themselves considered, the Gentile mind will never be able fully to appreciate. The oblations were not intended for Gentiles, and therefore can only be understood in some of their broadest suggestions by the contrasts which are afforded by the Christian religion. We cannot but be struck by the fact that the penalties of worship, as expressed by all these offerings, are abolished. That the Jewish worship was a system of penalties is evident upon the face of the arrangements. The gifts were really substantial and costly; whatever there might be about them of mere sentiment and spiritual aspiration it is certain that the gifts themselves necessitated very heavy expenditure, and constituted in fact a species of personal taxation. The meaning of this is that sin wherever it is found necessitates punishment. The punishment of sin is in no wise suspended or abrogated by the Christian dispensation, but the sting of penalty is wholly abstracted from Christian worship by the very spirit of Christ. What is now given, even of a costly character, ceases to affect the mind with a sense of its burdensomeness and becomes rather a delight than an imposition, a response of the heart rather than a heavy toil of the reluctant hand. Throughout the Biblical revelation we are never allowed to lose sight of the fact that sin means suffering, and that in some way or other sin must be paid for—not in equivalents but in punishments, which are continually showing themselves unequal to the disastrous occasion. Payment on account of sin is the law of nature. We must not lose sight of this idea simply because there is no money in the transaction,—ailment, decrepitude, incapacity to enjoy and inability to respond to the claims of life, all manner of restlessness, fear and shame,—these are among the heavy payments which sin exacts at the hands of the sinner. It is difficult, too, to rid the mind of the idea that something like payment is involved in the act of worship; by payment in this sense must be understood the idea of compensation or doing something for the sake of blotting something else out, and thus, as it were, balancing accounts with Heaven. The Christian spirit delivers the soul from all this sense of mechanism and burdensomeness; though the worship is due and though the homage is paid, and thus words are imported into the exercise which savour of a commercial kind, yet what is due is rather an expression of spontaneous love, and what is paid is rather the inspiration of a grateful heart than any action that can be brought under the name of imposition or taxation.

It is impossible to compare this chapter with the law of Christian worship without observing how all narrow conceptions of God and of his requirements of the human soul are utterly abolished. The Jewish system was really a small one in all its conceptions of God. Jehovah was a task-master, a king who had prizes to give away and appointments to make in his celestial kingdom. He was an image of terror and of continual apprehension; his anger was to be appeased by suffering on the part of those who had offended, or by the offering of symbolic sacrifices. The day's account could be settled within the day itself. The service was the labour of a hireling and not the sacred answer of the heart to the claim of divine love. All this is done away in the Christian dispensation. The idea of master, despot, ruler, in the low and base senses of these terms, has no place in Christian thinking. God is Father, pitiful and kind; Lord, as gracious as he is mighty; the Eternal who is continually incarnating himself in the separate moments of time. Worship is no longer confined to definite places as if it would be unacceptable unless offered under localising and narrowing conditions. Not in any mountain, nor in any metropolis exclusively is worship to be offered; the whole earth is now a church and every man is related to the priesthood of the Son of God. With those narrow conceptions all degrading thoughts of God are abolished. God is degraded to human thought when he is conceived of as a tyrant or as one who comes to claim mere suffering at the hands of the sinner. We are led to see that suffering is only intended as a means towards spiritual education, and is only used because through it alone can some parts of our nature be vitally and redeemingly touched. The suffering thus acquires a new character because it is invested with a new purpose. It is not suffering only, or suffering without moral suggestion and comfort; it is suffering as an educator, as a severity edged with mercy, as a mere point in a long and tedious process by which the soul is delivered from evil servitude and brought into sacred and holy liberty. Along with narrow conceptions and degrading thoughts of God all merely bodily exercises are done away. "Bodily exercise profiteth little." Long education was required to expel from the human mind the sophism that bodily exercise is needful to spiritual enlargement. Being in the body we use to a larger extent than is often supposed, the creatures of the flesh. It pleases us to think that we are able to do something or to suffer something which must of necessity have an effect upon the obligation created by our daily guilt. The ministrations which we offer to our vanity are often of the subtlest kind. Even in our Christian worship there is a tendency of the mind towards all that is meant by "bodily exercise": it may be by much speaking, it may be by overstraining the mind in an effort to be mechanically correct, it may be some superstitious idea of what is due to the majesty of God, it may be many things which cannot be named in words; but in the last analysis it will be found that the offering of bodily exercise conceals itself oftentimes within our most sacred spiritual abstractions and services. That Christianity seeks to deliver the soul from all such bondage, is one of its highest titles to the trust and veneration of men. Christianity risks itself upon its absolute spirituality. It is willing to part with all its externals in order that it may establish itself in the simple and unadulterated confidence of the heart. It has gone so far as to be willing to lay aside miracles, and prophecies, and tongues, and all signs and wonders—considering these but as so many bodily exercises —in order that it might set up a kingdom of spiritual truth and establish a service of spiritual consecration. Christianity has even gone so far as to say in the person of its greatest expounder, the Apostle Paul, that henceforth even Christ himself is not known after the flesh. What has become of the body of Christ is now a small question compared with what is the meaning of the rule of the Spirit of Christ in every province of human thought and life. Great lessons follow from this train of reflection. We must put a stop to all those inferior teachers who would enclose the kingdom of heaven within certain questions of simply a fleshly kind, though those questions may never be defined under such broad conditions. We may debase even the question of inspiration into a merely carnal one; that is to say, we may be so anxious about the inspiration of certain particular individuals, as to where that inspiration began and ended and how it operated, as utterly to overlook the true nature and function of the ministry of the Holy Spirit in the human heart. It is possible to be so anxious to prove the actual rising of the body of Christ from the grave as to forget the higher resurrection, the nobler and grander ascension, the direct personal lordship of Christ over all things in heaven and in earth. There is no occasion so to pervert these suggestions as to deduce the mischievous inference that things introductory, accessory and explanatory, have been denied. Nothing of the kind. Our one object is to define the limit of such externals and illustrations, and to show that they all point towards an inner and inexpressible mystery: the kingdom of heaven in the heart—often without defined boundaries, but embracing all inspiration, conviction, service and hope; involving, in fact, the whole being in the very mystery of immortality and heaven. These reflections have a distinct bearing upon persons who would offer sacrifice or homage with the mere letter of Scripture. It cannot be too persistently re-affirmed that it is possible to know the letter and yet not to know anything of the meaning of the spirit; to be learned in chapter and verse and to be completely qualified for cross-examination in the concordance, and yet never to have come within the sacred enclosure of spiritual revelation and ministry. The letter is true; the letter must be vindicated; but the letter itself is dishonoured when it is considered as final;—it is a magnificent portal to a magnificent palace or temple.

Leviticus iv. 3.

" If the priest that is anointed do sin."

POSSIBILITIES OF GUILT.

BUT that is impossible! Yet how graciously the matter
is suggested! What a wondrous providence is revealed
in mitigations,—remote, gracious suggestions and definitions.
What wonderful *ifs* in the speech of God!—as if his great
heart were glad of some word that merely hinted at an impossible possibility, at something which might occur but could
not ; a voice such as was heard in Eden when the suggestion
was made concerning a certain tree. It never could have entered
into the divine thought that any accountable and loving creature
would touch a tree that had been forbidden. But in this case
we read of an officer—a priest—a priest anointed, so that
there can be no mistake about his identity. The descriptive
clause is perfect and complete in simplicity. Yet how wondrous
a thing in all the wondrousness of love is this door that opens
the verse,—this great astounding *If!* How can a priest sin ?
The oil is upon him ; the holy touch has left its holy impress
upon him. Great names should be equal in moral arithmetic
to great characters. Great offices are not empty forms, mere
sounding words, titles to live upon. Great names are great
offices, and great offices imply great character : for character
alone is strength in the sanctuary,—not brilliance, not genius,
not power of amazing other intellects by lights that look like
revelations ; but solid, genuine, noble character,—indiscretions
may lie upon it a thousand thick, but right down in the core
of it there is genuine sincerity, unuttered and unutterable desire
for God. That is what character really is and always ought
to be and must be. No man can do the Church so much harm
as the priest, the professor, the minister, the person who is

inside the Church. We sometimes talk about *unbelievers.*
Where are they ? How seldom we realise the fact that a
man cannot be an *un*believer outside! The unbelievers are
inside. Do you see that ? Do you feel that ? Only he can
*un*believe who has professed to *believe.* There is a merely
etymological sense in which a man who is outside may be
an unbeliever; but in the deep, moral, tragical sense of the
term the unbelievers are in the pulpit and in the pew. The
unbelievers are not the men who to-day are lecturing against
God and Christ and Revelation : the unbelievers are the
anoirted priests who have slipped out of the enthusiasm of
their piety, who are uttering formal sentences without having
a corresponding burning in the heart, who are living upon paper
which is unsupported by the solid bullion. This is the truth
now urging itself upon us every one, because it is so easy
to deceive one's self and talk about unbelievers, as if they
were the persons who never went to church, who took no part
in religious movements, and who rather turned a deaf ear to
all religious appeals. *They* cannot unbelieve,—*we* can ; the
priest that is anointed can ; the Christian that is baptized in
the name of the Father, the Son and the Holy Ghost can.
The man who sings religious hymns and folds his hands and
closes his eyes in religious attitude can unbelieve. Judgment
must begin at the house of God. Do not suppose that we
are Christians because we are theologians, or that we know
anything about divine pity because we are skilled in the controversy of words. Christianity is a state of the heart, a condition of the soul before God, a continual penitence, a continual
faith, a continual service. Change your views, if you please,
about persons who are called unbelievers. There is no greater
unbeliever than the man who preaches a Gospel he does not
feel ; there is no greater unbeliever than the Church which
having a form of godliness denies the power thereof. This
thought would close many a ministry, would shut up many
a mission to the outsiders called unbelievers ; this would burn
us, yet by the grace and mercy of God would make new men
of us. The world will die and mock the efforts of the Church
unless the Church itself shall take up its old faith and live
in its rightful and natural force. Still there is some comfort

in this subjunctive form and way of putting the case. "If
the priest that is anointed do sin,"—if professing men do fall
below their profession; if Christian aspirants fall below the
level of their own prayer,—if venerable men should turn aside
for one moment to dally with the foe,—if—if—; it is God's
if. It is the way of mercy. Search into every command of
God, and you will find mercy at the heart of it.

Read on: "If the whole congregation of Israel sin." Can
a whole congregation sin? Yes. We must not individualise
too much. Humanity is not a set of unrelated individuals:
humanity is a larger term than the one word "individual,"
or "man," or "person." It is easy for a whole congregation
to sin and for each man in that congregation to declare that
he is not responsible for the sin of the whole. But he is.
If that man has not stood up in the middle of the church,
and cried out in a tone of agony against the evil that is being
done, he is guilty of every sin which the Almighty charges
upon the congregation as a whole. Men may be cowards
in congregations who are brave men in their own individuality.
Nothing tries a man's quality much more than making him
a member of a crowd. Men will do things in crowds they
would never dream of doing in their individual capacity and
under their own sign-manual. Responsibility becomes diffused,
the moral sense becomes scattered and distracted; and men,
therefore, will do in committees, on boards, in congregations,
in vestries, in churches what they would not do in their own
simple, measurable personality. Wondrous is the insight into
human nature in such an *if* as we have in the thirteenth verse.
"If the whole congregation sin." There is a corporate life
as well as a personal existence. We live in many relations
towards one another and towards God. We are individuals,—
we are also families, we are also citizens, we are also members
of a congregation. We cannot tell where our relations cease,—
how they shrink into comparatively small dimensions and then
broaden out into imperial magnitudes. Life is a mystery involved in great complexity, and revealing itself very startlingly
to every careful student of its expression and action. We
cannot come together as a congregation without having con-

gregational relations to God. Could we teach this truth as it ought to be taught we should all be new men. When we are sitting at boards of direction, when we are dividing with others the responsibility of corporate decisions we should not play the coward by hiding behind some bigger man than ourselves. The safety of every corporation, congregation, imperial or ecclesiastical body, is in the development of the individual conscience. The nation will never be right until the individual is right. How much mischief has been done by bodies of men ! and yet not one member of the several bodies will accept the responsibility of the action or the issue. But every man in a congregation is responsible for the Church, for the treatment of all the institutions of the Church, for a response to every appeal of the Church. He cannot say " the congregation " has done this or that, except in so far as we fix the responsibility upon the individual members. And this tells on both sides. We hear of congregations doing wonderful things in the way of benevolence ; but coming to analysis we find the whole has been done by some half-dozen men. The congregation has no right to assume in its sum total capacity the virtues and the sacrifices of half-a-dozen heroic souls.

Read again : " If any one of the common people sin." How searching is the criticism of God ! " Common people " may sin as certainly as priests and rulers. We have left the congregation in its corporate capacity for one moment, and we are now dealing with—not the common people, but " *any one* of the common people." God will not have *any man* permitted to sin with impunity. He does not release a priest from the obligations which he imposes upon the common people, nor will he excuse the common people because they are not priests. We are all God's little ones. Every man is of importance to God. " It is not the will of your Father which is in heaven that one of these little ones should perish." The same rule applies to moral criticism or to spiritual investigation of conduct. We must not excuse ourselves on the ground that we belong to the commonalty, and therefore may do what we please. God's judgment, like God's commandment, is " exceeding broad."

Thus we have,—If a priest do sin,—If a ruler sin,—If the whole congregation sin,—If any one of the common people

sin. Is there any loophole in that circle? Perhaps there may
be. You cannot anticipate Omniscience. We read in the very
beginning of this chapter,—"If a soul shall sin." Now there is
no loophole. The very first line of the next chapter reads:
"And if a soul sin." Now how will you escape? You are not
"priest," nor "ruler," nor part of a "congregation," nor "one of
the common people"; but can you disclaim the next title,—
"soul"? "If a soul sin,"—yes, it is the soul that sins. That
is a doctrine full of graciousness, but full of mystery, and requires
to be stated with such delicacy of expression, as perhaps but
really few can follow, in all its solemnity and significance. We
have been unkind to the body, we have been mean to the body;
we knew we had it for only a few years—just a handful of days
—and we have abused it as we would abuse an unvalued dog.
We have charged the body with everything. It is mean, it is
false; it is the soul that sins. The body can never, as the
younger son, go far from the soul. We sin when we sin with
the consent of our whole nature,—when the soul likes the tree,
when the soul loves the golden goblet full of poison, when the
soul says, "Give me more! this is a hunger of immortality."
Poor body! what it has had to bear! The soul is a coward.
There is no divinely-intended schism between the body and the
soul, and we must not be permitted to ride off upon the miserable
excuse that the flesh is weak. God leaves no ground upon which
any man can stand, saying,—"He has not mentioned me; I am
no priest, nor do I belong to the congregation, nor am I one of
the common people; I am something else: I have not been
named; I may sin seven days a week and do as I list." Hear
the word of the Lord: "If a soul shall sin"; and again: "If a
soul sin"; and yet again, in the following chapter: "If a soul
sin." There is no escape. Let us be just to ourselves. God
has been coming to the soul all the time; but He must be so
critical and, as it were, analytical as not to leave any man,
woman or child with the appearance of an excuse.

Look at the whole of these *Ifs* and mark their pathos and overlook not their divine courtesy,—as if by this time, in the world's
history, we had wrought ourselves up so high in moral culture
and solidity of character, as to make it a bare possibility that we
might sin. This is the divine generosity; this is the divine

encouragement. There is a time when you change your tone towards your own child When your son is eighteen years of age you change your tone a little; you begin to assume his dignity, his moral pride and ambition. You would not suggest to him that he could now repeat his childish follies; and you wisely make what statements of a cautionary kind you have to make with moderated expression, with the cunning graduation of tone which only love can inspire and sustain. "By this time," you say, "another tone will be needed," and you adopt that tone, and if the young soul knew the meaning of it, he would see more of your real love in that changed tone than in the first command-ment given with so frank a simplicity, and with so direct an emphasis.

Then after all those hypothetical cases we find God devising ways of escape. The Book of Leviticus is full of doors opening back upon the Father's heart. " If the priest that is anointed do sin" tell him what to do,—how he shall bring his " young bullock without blemish," and how he shall bring it " unto the door of the tabernacle of the congregation before the Lord, and shall lay his hand upon the bullock's head, and kill the bullock before the Lord," and "take of the bullock's blood " and " dip his finger in the blood, and sprinkle the blood seven times before the Lord, before the rail of the sanctuary," and " put some of the blood upon the horns of the altar of sweet incense before the Lord, which is in the tabernacle of the congregation; and shall pour all the blood of the bullock at the bottom of the altar of the burnt offering." Tell him what to do. The record might have gone in the contrary direction : " If a priest that is anointed do sin, report it to me, and all the tabernacles of thunder shall be shaken, and not one bolt of lightning hidden in all the treasury of heavens shall be spared ; the criminal shall be shot through and through with lightning and buried amid the indignation of angels ! " No ; the Book of Leviticus shows the very genius of Deity in finding ways whereby offences may be sponged out and offenders made as if they had not fallen. But there is no trifling with sin. Read all the provisions made after each *if,* and you will find that repentance is always costly ; read the detail of the sacrifices, and you will find how exacting is God. A man cannot sin in an off-handed manner and God say, " Let bygones be bygones, and begin again to-morrow as if life had had no yesterday." It is a fearful thing to fall into the hands of the living God. If the priest has sinned, he is not regarded as a priest, but as a sinner. So with every member of the sinning tribe, repentance is costly, return is marked by exactions of the most minute and critical kind. You cannot get back to God but through the medium of sacrifice, blood, propitiation, atonement.

Now what says the New Testament about priest, ruler, congregation, common people, soul?—"If we confess our sins, he is faithful and just to forgive us our sins, and to cleanse us from all unrighteousness." "The blood of Jesus Christ, God's Son, cleanseth us from all sin." It is still the way of blood. Do not vulgarise that term; do not narrow your conceptions of it and try to make it some vulgar excuse for not accepting the awful term. Blood means life, reality, divine agony, an outpouring of the soul. Sin has not changed its character, nor can the method of sin's redemption be changed as to its highest expression and meaning. "Without shedding of blood is no remission." It is so between ourselves. If we understood the compact aright, all forgiveness expresses blood-shedding, or we may return to our old alienation. So the great Christian Gospel is heard amongst us this day, saying so solemnly, so sweetly, with all the trumpets of heaven, "The blood of Jesus Christ, God's Son, cleanseth us from all sin." Come priest, ruler, congregation, common people, every soul,—come, for there is yet room,—"Behold the Lamb of God, which taketh away the sin of the world."

Leviticus iv.

SINS OF IGNORANCE.

THE expression, "If a soul shall sin through ignorance," opens a very wide region of thought. One would wonder whether it is possible that sin can be committed in ignorance— that is to say, whether the ignorance does not do away with the sinful character of the deed. Is not sin a wilful action? Is not its wilfulness the very essence of its guilt? So we would think; yet again and again in the ritual we find that ignorance is never made into a sufficient excuse for sin. The sense of mystery which we may feel in regard to this matter can only be relieved by looking for analogous instances in the field of nature. This I would lay down as an excellent law of Biblical interpretation. Thus, given instances of mystery which afflict the soul with a sense of burdensomeness, or even of injustice, to find out how far such circumstances are illuminated or explained by actions within the province of observation and reason take, for example, sins of ignorance in a strictly physical department of life. Suppose it to be possible for anyone not to know the nature of fire, and in that state of ignorance to expose himself to its action, would the fire cease to operate because the man is ignorant? would nature suspend her operations in pity, saying, This man does not understand the nature of heat, and therefore he shall not feel the effects of its excessive use or application? Nothing of the kind occurs in nature. Nature is full of healing and kindness and compassion, always seeking to comfort the wounded and to staunch the fountains of blood, and yet nature makes no note of the persons who misunderstand or misapply her laws. Suppose a man should exclude the living air from his habitation, will nature say that the man, not understanding the utility of the atmosphere, must be excused because of his ignorance? Nature, like her Lord, teaches through suffering. There is no law written on all the dominion of nature with a broader and clearer hand than that all sin is followed by penalty. Exclude the air, and you exclude vitality; shut out the light, and you impoverish the life; doom yourself to solitude, and you doom yourself by the same fiat to extinction. It is in vain to plead that we did not know the nature of air, or the utility of light, or the influence of high things upon things that are low; we must be taught the depth of our ignorance and its guilt by the intensity and continuance of our personal suffering. Leaving the region of nature and coming into the region of civilisation, we find that even in legal affairs violations of law are not excused on the ground of ignorance. The judge upon the bench does not hesitate to inform the trespasser that he ought to have known the law of which he pleaded ignorance. Again and again this has been known to be the case. That some modification may be allowed, or some concession, is perfectly possible; but it is distinctly made as a concession, and in no sense as a right. The law has been violated, by neglect, or through ignorance, or wantonly; and whether in the one way or the other, there it stands in an offended attitude, and nothing can cause it to consent to change its posture. It insists upon the amendment of recognition and the compensation of suffering on the part of the offender. Turning from purely legal criticism of this kind, we find the same law in operation in social affairs. A man is not excused from the consequences of ill-behaviour on the ground that he did not know the customs of society or the technicalities of etiquette. He may be pitied, he may be held in a kind of mild contempt, his name may be used to point a moral; but at the root of all this criticism lies the law that the man is a trespasser, and that ignorance cannot be pleaded as a complete excuse. This canon of judgment has a very wide bearing upon human affairs. Were it to be justly and completely applied, it would alter many arrangements and relations of life. There are many things which we ought to know, and which we ought to be; and instead of excusing ourselves by our ignorance, we should be stimulated by its effects to keener inquiry and more diligent culture. That sense of ignorance will possibly show us in what critical conditions our life is being spent. Life is not a broad surface which any eye can read, and which any capacity can comprehend. Life is a mystery, a complication, a series of causes and effects, a most complex organism which requires continual study and vigilance We know not upon what we may be launched by the very shortest journey we can take. He is living the life of a fool who imagines that life is a simple affair lying between four visible and measurable points. There is a superficial existence which can be measured as it were by the foot-rule, and weighed in common scales; but life, as inspired and directed by the Holy Ghost, is a sublime mystery. It admits of distinctions, and of classifications absolutely infinite in number. It is the part of Christianity so to operate upon human life as to show the greatness of that life to itself. As the Bible is a progressive revelation, so life is a progressive Apocalypse. To be told in plain and frank terms that man is made in the image and likeness of God is simply to startle the mind with a bold and possibly incredible proposition. That proposition does lie at the very base of Biblical revelation, but its full explanation is only to be realised as the centuries come and go, and after a breadth of education stretching through the experience of many generations. The first thing that a man was told is the last thing which man can understand. Thus we come to the beginning from the end, and only by doubling life back upon itself do we begin to take in the profoundest meanings of the very first statements which were addressed to the reason and the imagination. It is only in the Apocalypse that we begin to understand the Pentateuch. Yet even in such expressions as " If a soul sin through ignorance " we begin to see the meaning of the mystery of the divine nature of man. What watchfulness is imposed upon us by the fact that it is possible to sin through ignorance ! If sin were a mere act of violence, we could easily become aware of it, and with comparatively little difficulty we might avoid its repetition. But it is more and other than this. It is committed when we little think of its commission; we inflict wounds when we think our hands are free of all weapons and instruments; we dishonour God when we suppose we are merely silent about him. The voice of nature and of experience, as well as of revelation, is— " The place whereon thou standest is holy ground." The sin may be in a look, in a far-off suggestion, in a tempting tone, in attitudes that have no names, and in breathings that are inarticulate. Neglect may be sin as well as violence. There is a negative criminality as well as a positive blasphemy. All this makes life most critical and most profoundly solemn. The commandment of God is exceeding broad. Being a divine commandment it comes of continual and minute exactions covering all life with the spirit and obligation of discipline. Not a moment is our own ; not a single atom of all the stupendous universe comes within our proprietorship ; to-day or to-morrow we may be translated into other spheres of existence ; we cannot make a law of any kind that is not local and temporary—a mere convenience for a moment ; all the great laws were written before the universe was formed, and they will continue to exist through all changes and developments and processes of being ; by their very nature they are eternal, and being eternal they cannot be affected by the conditions which are continually changing the attitude and complexion of our earthly life. Let us be just to the Biblical revelation in all such matters as these sins of ignorance ; let us remind ourselves again that we recognise such sins in nature, in law, in social etiquette, in all the various relations of life, and that when we come upon them in the Bible we ought to approach them with a familiarity which itself amounts to an exposition and a vindication. There is nothing arbitrary in these enactments and demands. The God of Providence is the God of the Bible. Providence is the Bible in action, and the Bible is Providence in exposition and contemplation.

The mercy is shown that a special offering was provided for the sin of ignorance. It was recognised as a specialty, and provided for as such. Our business should never be to find the excuse, but rather to confess the sin. The great and gracious law applies here as elsewhere : " If we confess our sins, God is faithful and just to forgive us our sins, and to cleanse us from all unrighteousness." It is not our place to provide sacrifices. Even the Jews had no sacrifices to provide in the sense of inventing them. The part which the Jew had to act was simply a response to a divine enactment, and in reality that is exactly what we have to do. It is not our business to say how a way can be found out of this sin or that, or what argument can be set up in palliation of the crime which has been committed ; the provision has been made, and that provision we must accept unless we are prepared to fall under a penalty which never fails to follow in the wake of evil-doing. The sin of ignorance never goes alone. Imagine a life so well lived that nothing can be charged upon it but sin due to ignorance! Such a life is an impossibility. It is also impossible for life to be marked only by what are called little or minor sins. There are no such sins, and in proportion as the mind leans to the thought that such sins are possible, is the mind the victim of a most mischievous, and may be fatal, sophism. Life cannot be reduced to a mere negation. We know not what the conditions of life may be in other worlds, but in the region which is described by time, life itself would seem to be steeped in sin, and sin may be regarded, in some sense, as a necessity of life; not a necessity as involving the sovereignty of God, but as revealing the mystery of human nature, under local and probationary conditions, to itself. If one righteous man could have been found upon the earth, the atonement of Christ would have been unnecessary. Atonement does not relate to numbers, or to individuals, or to exceptional instances, as if Christ should have said, " I will die for those who are tainted, for the few or the many who have apostatised "; in that case his death would have been the mere romance of philanthropy, or the fanaticism of perverted divinity; Jesus Christ found no righteous man, and therefore he tasted death for every man; he died for a world lying in the wicked one, and not for certain populations who had been less fortunate than other portions of mankind. Human nature is one. Human sin is one. Divine atonement is one. We disintegrate the universe and turn into trifling the sublime purpose of God when we individualise, and specialise, and make exceptions on behalf of the virtue of this class or that class. The solemn and appalling truth is that there is none righteous, no not one ; and however the sin may be critically described, it is simply for the purpose of showing that the sacrifice provided is equal to the refinement and mystery of any new definition that may startle the imagination by its delicacy or unsuspected operation. Take this view of the sacrifices, and it will be shown that the divine mind has anticipated every possible form of human evil and offence. Happily, therefore, the mind can never be surprised into despair by having forced upon it the conviction that some new sin has been invented, or some new conditions have so surrounded a sin as to take the offence out of the catalogue of the crimes for which divine provision has been made. The specification of sins is not intended to show the keenness and breadth of the divine criticism, but to supply an answer to temptations that might assail the soul and drag it towards the darkness of despair. Let every soul, then, boldly say, as if in solemn monologue, Whatever my sin may be, it is provided for in the great Offering established as the way of access to the Father ; I will invent no excuses; I will seek for no new methods of payment or compensation ; I will bring no price in my hand, no excuse on my tongue, nor will I hide even in the depths of my consciousness any hope that I can vindicate my position before God ; I will simply fall into the hands of the Living One, and look upon the Lamb of God which taketh away the sin of the world. In that spirit I will go forward to judgment, and in that spirit I will encounter the mysteries of destiny.

NOTE.

It was in the sprinkling of the blood, the proper sacrament of sacrifice, that the distinction between the guilt offering and the expiatory offering, in the narrow sense, came most clearly to the front ; and it is easy to understand why it would reveal itself most plainly here. As it was right that the blood of an expiatory offering for public transgressions should be made far more conspicuous to eyes and sense, so it was sprinkled on an elevated place, or even on one which was extraordinarily sacred. The way, too, in which this was done was marked by three stages. If the atonement was made for an ordinary man, or for a prince, the priest sprinkled the blood against the high towering horns of the outer altar, and poured the remainder, as usual, out at its base ; if it was made for the community, or for the high-priest, some of the blood was seven times sprinkled against the veil of the Holy of Holies, then some more against the horns of the inner altar, and only what was then left was poured out, as usual, at the base of the outer altar. The third, and highest stage ot expiation was adopted on the yearly day of atonement. On the other hand, in the case of the guilt offering, no reason existed for adopting any unusual mode of sprinkling the blood. It was sprinkled, just as in other cases, round the sides and foot of the outer altar. As soon as this most sacred ceremony of the sprinkling was completed, then, according to the ancient belief, the impurity and guilt were already shaken off from the object to which they had clung.—EWALD.

Leviticus v.

MORAL CONTAGION.

IN reading this chapter take notice of the expression, "if a soul touch any unclean thing, whether it be a carcase of an unclean beast, or a carcase of unclean cattle, or the carcase of unclean creeping things, and if it be hidden from him; he also shall be unclean, and guilty." Why this continual dread of uncleanness? Call these, if you please, merely sanitary arrangements, yet why this early care about matters connected with human health? Is not the provision totally in excess of the occasion? Is not this an instance of much ado about nothing? Do men require all these instructions and the continual supervision of all this judgment in matters connected with the health and purity of the body? Let that be granted, and nothing whatever is taken from the urgency and solemnity of the spiritual appeal; on the contrary, the very circumstance that so much ado is made about fleshly cleanliness increases the poignancy of the appeal dealing with spiritual health and vigour. Those who suppose that the whole ritual of the Jews related to sanitation must not imagine that even if their position could be proved—which from my point of view is impossible—they have at all impaired the cogency and completeness of any appeal which may be addressed to the moral sense. The fact is, that man could not be made apart from the moral sense to comprehend even such an appeal were it restricted to the body. In other words, we could not be really cleanly in body and soundly in earnest about physical sanitation except through the medium of the conscience as well as through the action of the judgment. The judgment is often but an impotent director of human conduct. We may say with the ancient poet, "We see the right, and yet the wrong pursue." It is really only when the moral sense is thoroughly aroused and inspired that the judgment itself is lifted to its right level and brought into complete action in all practical matters. We will not, therefore, be turned aside from the spiritual appeal which may be founded upon these exhortations by being told that in the first instance the exhortation was related to matters that were purely sanitary. This avoidance of unclean animals and places is not without practical illustration in our own personal experience and action. To-day, for example, we avoid places that are known to be fever-stricken. We are alarmed lest we should bring ourselves within the influence of contagion. The strongest man might fear if he knew that a letter were put into his hand which had come from a house where fever was fatally raging. However heroic he might be in sentiment, and however inclined to boast of the solidity of his nervous system, it is not impossible that even the strongest man might shrink from taking the hand of a fever-stricken friend. All this is natural and all this is justifiable, and, in fact, any defiance of this would be unnatural and unjustifiable. Is there, then, no suggestion in all such rational caution that there may be moral danger from moral contagion ? Can a body emit pestilence and a soul dwell in all evil and riot in all wantonness without giving out an effluvium fatal to moral vigour and to spiritual health ? The suggestion is preposterous. They are the unwise and most reprehensible men who being afraid of a fever have no fear of a moral pestilence ; who running away in moral terror from influences leading towards small-pox, cholera, and other fatal diseases, rush into companionships, and actions, and servitudes which are positively steeped and saturated with moral pollution. That we are more affected by the one than by the other only shows that we are more body than soul. The man who is careful about his body and careless about his soul does not prove the littleness of the soul in itself or in the purpose of God : he simply proves that in his case the flesh is overgrown and has acquired excessive importance. It would be the merest conceit did it not also involve deep moral injury to imagine that human life can be lived without any exposure to moral contagion. This is a mystery which has no words. The temptation does not always come to us in some violent form which can be measured, estimated, and physically or substantially resisted either in action or in argument. The elements which poison the air are of the subtlest kind, and can only be detected by the most advanced chemistry. This is true in the moral atmosphere. What a suggestion may do it is impossible always to foretell. At first it may seem to be of little weight, or it may actually appear to be forgotten, to sink wholly out of memory and consciousness; but it is impossible to tell how long it may lie in the soul latently and under what circumstances it may begin to bear evil fruit in the spirit and the life. Strange, indeed, if such things are possible in nature and impossible in morals! A truly wonderful thing if after all it should be found that physical conditions involve greater mysteries than spiritual possibilities and destinies! This would be an inversion of thought—a turning upside down of all that has been customary in intellectual conception and representation. The Christian whilst protesting against such inversion as irrational and unnatural will accept every mystery that is hidden in nature as indicating a still greater mystery that is to be found in the kingdom of thought and of spiritual activity. It seems to be impossible to escape contagion of a moral kind. All contagion is so wide-sweeping in its influence,—that is to say, it operates at points so far distant from any visible and tangible centre, that we easily dissociate the effect from the cause and imagine harmlessness in the very centres of most active and pestilent mischief. It is of the nature of moral contagion that it operates with equal vigour at every point along the line over which it stretches. It loses nothing by distance; it loses nothing by time. The evil book written a century ago may be bearing fruit to-day, though its author is not only dead but forgotten. Sometimes evil lies a hundred years or more without showing signs of vitality or effectiveness, and then under peculiar conditions is awakened and becomes most active and disastrous. As we grow in moral capacity and in the sensitiveness which accompanies spiritual culture we shall come to acknowledge that stains may be worse than wounds; that one speck upon the honour is infinitely worse than the deepest gash that could be inflicted by the cruellest sword upon the flesh. This is a matter which cannot be taught abstractly or in a moment; it comes after long years of study, thought, experience, and those reciprocal actions which make up the mystery of social life. At first we are affected by a crime; then we are unsettled by the suggestion of an offence; then, still advancing in spiritual culture and sensitiveness, we come to see that though the crime itself may never be done, yet the motive which even for a moment suggested it is a deadlier thing than the crime itself: for the crime is a mere vulgarity which might be partially excused by passion, but the motive is a condition of the heart which indicates the apostasy and utter badness of the soul. A singular thing this, that unclean things may be touched by the soul itself. Literally, the text does not refer in all probability to a purely spiritual action, yet not the less is the suggestion justified by experience that even the soul considered in its most spiritual sense may touch things that are unclean and may be defiled by them. A poor thing indeed that the hand has kept itself away from pollution and defilement if the mind has opened wide all the points of access to the influence of evil. Sin may not only be in the hand, it may be rolled as a sweet morsel under the tongue. There may be a chamber of imagery in the heart. A man may be utterly without offence in any social acceptation of that term—actually a friend of magistrates and judges, and himself a high interpreter of the law of social morality and honour, and yet all the while may be hiding a very perdition in his heart. It is the characteristic mystery of the salvation of Jesus Christ that it does not come to remove stains upon the flesh or spots upon the garments, but to work out an utter and eternal cleansing in the secret places of the soul, so that the heart itself may in the event be without "spot or wrinkle or any such thing,"—pure, holy, radiant, even dazzling with light, fit to be looked upon by the very eye of God.

This is the ideal of Christ: how far we may be from its accomplishment is not the immediate question. It is of the highest consequence to remember what the ultimate purpose of the Son of God is, and then to bring to bear upon that purpose all the instruments and methods, all the ministries and influences which are utilised by the living Spirit. Between the one and the other the happiest harmony will be seen to exist. It is by his own precious blood that Jesus Christ seeks to remove the stain, not of crime but of sin, not of the hand but of the soul. The adoption of such means to such ends involves an inscrutable philosophy No wonder that eternity gone and eternity to come are both charged with this sacred mystery. The Lamb was slain from before the foundation of the world, and the song which celebrates his praise is to be continued long after the earth and all its tragedies have passed away. This mystery is not confined within the bounds of time; those bounds, in fact, do but show one aspect of the mystery; it belongs to eternity on both sides of time, and we shall require eternity for its elucidation, and our comprehension of its gracious meaning. The one thing to be borne in mind at present is that the soul is still exposed to the contagion of uncleanness. We fight against the prince of the power of the air; we fight with ourselves; sometimes we seem to be our own tempters, and to have within us all the mystery of hell. A wonderful thing is this matter of touch. Who can touch pitch and not be defiled? It has not been given to us so to encase ourselves, even so far as the body is concerned, that we shall be impervious to evil influences working in the air. Where, then, is our defence against the evil that is in the world? Jesus Christ does not pray that we may be taken out of the world, but that we may be kept from the evil that is in the world; he will have us here as the light of the world, as the salt of the earth, as a city set upon a hill; he will not operate in any spirit of cowardice and fear, withdrawing us from temporal regions and temporal activities lest the wind should be too cold for us, or the enemy should surprise us into some new lapse, and so spoil our integrity and turn our prayers to confusion. Christ will have us live the heroic life,—a heroism that is often carried to the point of defiance, as if we could not only merely overcome the enemy but actually and absolutely trample him underfoot, in excess of triumph and in redundance of divinely-given strength. We must not altogether take the view of contagion which is full of unhappy and dispiriting suggestions. There is another view, and that we are bound as Christian men to adopt—namely, that good may be as contagious as evil. It is difficult to believe this. Human nature seems to be so constituted that evil outruns good and has altogether an easier task than virtue to accomplish. It is easier to go downhill than to go uphill. It seems to suit human nature better not to do duty than to discharge it, not to submit to discipline than to accept it. This is indeed a practical mystery which can only be accounted for completely and satisfactorily by

the provision which has been made on the divine side to meet it
and overcome it. Still there does remain the sacred and happy
impression that even good has its contagious effect upon society.
Men may be shamed into withholding part of their strength at
least from evil service. Such restraints may not end in a very
high type of virtue; in the meantime the very suspension of
active evil may prepare the way for something better. The force
of example must never be under-estimated. If we once begin to
think that evil is predominant over good, and that the bad man
alone is influential, we may relax in our efforts and underlive the
great purpose of our vocation in Christ. Rather let us hear the
Master's voice saying,—"Let your light so shine before men, that
they may see your good works, and glorify your Father which is in
heaven." The very argument of Christ in the Sermon upon the
Mount is that good men are the light of the world and the salt of
the earth.

In the fourteenth verse of this chapter there is a remarkable
expression, bearing upon a certain type of sin. The law was
that if a soul committed trespass and sinned through ignorance
in the holy things of the Lord, he was to bring for his trespass
unto the Lord a ram without blemish, out of the flocks, and
other offerings,—"and he shall make amends for the harm that
he hath done in the holy thing, and shall add the fifth part
thereto." The ritual was not, therefore, merely sanitary. Those
who would limit it to merely sanitary matters will find it difficult
to reconcile the mere details of sanitation with such arrangements
as were imposed upon the Jewish people or the Israelites with
regard to restitution. What is the law in this case? Whatever
harm was done was, as far as possible, to be undone. That being
the case one would suppose that the property having been
restored, nothing further could be attempted. This is not the
case. Not only was restitution to be completed, but twenty per
cent. was to be added by way of penalty on the one side, and
compensation on the other. It is not enough to prove that a man
who has been injured has been unjustly injured. It is not the
law that a man having been proved not to have committed some
offence charged against him, shall simply accept the acquittal.
Acquittal must be followed by compensation. Where injury has
been done it cannot be met by a mere apology—except, indeed,

by the grace and courtesy of the man upon whom the injury has been inflicted. Society by its very constitution must go further, and demand that the person who has been unjustly accused shall be compensated for the injury which he has sustained in the estimation of his fellow-men, and, indeed, in his own complacency and conscious integrity. Morality of this kind is most acceptable in any book professing to be a revelation of the divine mind. It is at such points especially that we can lay hold of the purposes of the book, and by keeping them steadily in mind, can wait further light and broadening revelation, conscious that a morality so pure and so just must be the beginning of a dispensation that shall vindicate its own spirituality and broader claim. It is peculiarly characteristic of the Bible that it insists upon justice between man and man, that it will not excuse the great man or the small man, but it will have an equal law, and will bring to bear its spirit of discipline upon every soul, whatever may be the conditions and characteristics which give it partiality and preference amongst its fellows. This is a claim of the Bible to human trust and reception. It can never be set aside by criticism, by casuistry, by speculative unbelief; it appeals to the conscience of mankind, and it says to that conscience—Whatever difficulties or mysteries I may yet address to your imagination, hold fast by these plain and substantial truths; if my purpose is absolutely unimpeachable in morality, the very spirit of justice, and honour, and truth; and in proportion as you appreciate the social side of the revelation will every other side be made luminous, and ultimately vindicate itself by its equally practical beneficence.

God will have nothing to do with uncleanness. " Wash you, make you clean; put away the evil of your doings "—is the continual voice of God to the human soul. He will pity weakness; he will not be offended by ungainliness; he understands all the meaning of poverty;—in all these directions we have nothing to fear; but when we hide uncleanness, or endeavour to make excuse for sin, all heaven burns against us with unquenchable anger. This is another aspect of the morality of the Bible. Even when Christ sat down to meat with publicans and sinners, he recognised their character and did not seek to confound their manhood and their merely official position. This must be the clear understanding everywhere : that the Bible will have no immorality, no trifling with righteousness, no compromises with the wicked spirit. The Bible insists upon holiness in the inward parts—a morality that can bear the criticism of the divine righteousness—and how great soever its compassion for weakness, poverty, frailty, and all the various characteristics of fallen humanity that do not involve consent to that which is evil, the Bible can hold no intercourse or parleying whatsoever with any soul that would cling ·to its uncleanness, and yet expect to enjoy the fellowship or complacency of God. This is not only an anomaly, but a miracle which lies beyond the omnipotence of Heaven.

PRAYER.

ALMIGHTY GOD, our altar is already built : we come unto the Cross of Jesus Christ our Saviour, and there offer such prayer as thou mayest inspire in our hearts. Thou hast moved us to pray every day for pardon; if we confess our sins, thou art faithful and just to forgive us our sins. Grant unto us the grace of confession—the power of uttering in thine ear all the tale of sin and wrong, keeping back nothing from the divine eye, but calling attention to everything we have done which is amiss. Thus, by knowing our sin, and naming it in the hearing of God and in the sight of the Cross, may the burden be dissolved, and instead of despair may the joy of conscious pardon and release take possession of our hearts and utter itself in the music of continual praise. We thank thee that thou hast come near to us with gospels of forgiveness. Thou couldest have blinded us with glory, or amazed us with wonders, without associating these disclosures of thy power with tenderness and willingness to redeem and to forgive; but thou hast caused the Cross of Christ to represent the fulness of thy miraculous power ; and we behold in it—not only almightiness, but compassion, not only omnipotence, but the tenderness of the heart of God. Do thou instruct us in all the way of life. Keep quite near to us ; may we never be beyond the reach of thine ear— not only because of our loudness and crying, but when we whisper, may we be so near, thou so near, that we may hold fellowship one with another. Let the sky of our life brighten above our head, let the last cloud be cleansed from the horizon, and let a great brightness of complacency shine upon us from above; then shall we walk in thy light and take counsel of thee, and obey thee with industry and gladness. Write thy word for us every day; accommodate thy light to our vision ; be nearest to us when we most need thee ; and give us triumph in the night-time ; and in despair, in great sorrow, and in floods of tears, may we always be found steadfast in faith, ardent in love, bright in spiritual hope, renewing our confidence continually in God, and purifying the motive by which our whole life's action is determined.

The Lord hear us, and in the hearing give us answers of peace. Amen.

Leviticus vi. 1-7.

1. And the Lord spake unto Moses, saying,

2. If a soul sin, and commit a trespass against the Lord, and lie unto his neighbour in that which was delivered him to keep, or in fellowship, or in a thing taken away by violence, or hath deceived his neighbour;

3. Or have found that which was lost, and lieth concerning it, and sweareth falsely; in any of all these that a man doeth, sinning therein:

4. Then it shall be, because he hath sinned, and is guilty, that he shall restore that which he took violently away, or the thing which he hath deceitfully gotten, or that which was delivered him to keep, or the lost thing which he found,

5. Or all that about which he hath sworn falsely; he shall even restore it in the principal, and shall add the fifth part more thereto, and give it unto him to whom it appertaineth, in the day of his trespass offering.

6. And he shall bring his trespass offering unto the Lord, a ram without blemish out of the flock, with thy estimation, for a trespass offering, unto the priest:

7. And the priest shall make an atonement for him before the Lord: and it shall be forgiven him for any thing of all that he hath done in trespassing therein.

PRACTICAL RELIGION.

A CURIOUS combination of words is this in the second verse— ". . . a trespass against the Lord, and lie unto his neighbour." What have the terms "Lord" and "neighbour" to do with one another? Have we not partitioned off society into special and unrelated departments? Who shall venture to throw down the lines which we have set up and to make one common society of earth and heaven? Already here is a forth-shadowing of the two commandments on which hang all the law and the prophets— namely: "Thou shalt love the Lord thy God . . . and thy neighbour as thyself." There has always been some vital connection between "Lord" and "neighbour";—how is this? Do we not pass too roughly over such conjunctions, taking them as mere matters of course—a jingling of words, hiding no music, modifying no eternity of power and right? We are bungling readers at the best; we do not extract from the word its root, and life, and soul. May not that man sin against his neighbour, and yet say his prayers as if nothing had been done to violate the sanctity of upper and spiritual relations? May not a man kneel upon his overthrown neighbour, and in that attitude of oppression and triumph plead with the complacent heavens? Verily, the Bible is a book which takes part with the "neighbour"; it is a chivalrous revelation. To have come from heaven it comes with wondrous earthly sympathy and sense of right and rule of judgment. From this point of view the book *may* be inspired! When we sin against our neighbour, we sin against God; when we remove the ancient landmark, we violate the altar; when we tell lies to society, we smite heaven with blasphemy. This is the spirit of the book. Such spirit makes us strong, leads out our love in adoration towards the book as towards a living protector, and friend, and guide. Were it full of ghosts—a great theatre of possible spiritual presences, having no relation to our life except to alarm it, we might flee away in terror and leave it to men who have skill in communing with ghostly presences; but it takes care of the flock in the field, it will not allow an ancient hedge to be taken down without a just equivalent being rendered, it will not have a bird's little nest torn to pieces without protest and judgment; it is a domestic book: it looks after the house-fire and the house-table and all things belonging to our little daily life; it has an infinite sky, but, blessed be God, it is also a world about the size of a house —a house watched with the eyes of love. A book that cares so much for "neighbours" is a book which by so much arrests the moral attention and may reward the moral confidence of mankind.

Violence, deceit, false-swearing,—why these are the sins of to-day. There is nothing original in sinning. The old vulgarity, and the old refinement upon it, we find from the beginning. Consider the words, for there is a philosophy in their very order: "violence," "deceit," "perjury." You cannot invert that order without violating the philosophy of true development and evolution. There is an inspiration of order as well as of substance, and that inspiration is written here and proved by the fullest and happiest verification. We all begin with "violence." The first man begins branch-breaking and fruit-stealing. He tells no lie, he has no deep plot against the Eternal: he puts out his hand and wrenches the branch, and the crash of that

wood, hitherto untouched, sends pain through all the garden.
The next man kills his enemy. The world's sin began with
violence; by-and-by violent men see that there is another way
of accomplishing the purpose of the evil heart, so, without
smiting and fire-kindling and rudeness, they begin to conspire
and plot, and attach new meanings to words, and infuse unsuspected colours into the speech of commerce as between man
and man : so language becomes manifold instead of simple : to
the speaker it means one thing, to the hearer it means another
thing, though the terms are the common property of the nation.
After "deceit" comes the profanation of holy terms—the sin
against what may be termed the Holy Ghost of speech. We are,
therefore, no further than this Old Testament text to-day; some
are committing violence, some are plotting deceitful schemes and
conspiracies, and others are standing up and insulting the spirit
of truth—lying not unto men, but unto God. There you have
the range of the devil's power : he oscillates from violence to
perjury, touching the intermediate point of deceit. There is no
genius in such an enemy; he is not fertile in invention; sub-
jected to honest analysis he is to be laid out plainly on the
world's table in three parts,—violence, deceit, perjury ; and all
the sin that can be committed can be brought under these three
categories or one of them. And all this may be done away by
offering to the priest "a ram without blemish out of the flock"!
Bring the "ram" and all will be well! Steal the forbidden fruit,
kill the hated Abel, swear with larger boldness than the audacity
of Ananias and Sapphira, and when you are done, see to it that
you pick out the right "ram," offer it to the pontiff, let him slay
it, and all will be well! That is an easy way out of difficulty!
It is; but it is not the way of the Bible. Many persons who
think they have escaped the Jewish ritual suppose they have
only to see the priest, whisper the tale into his ear, furnish their
"ram," and go home released and sanctified. If they imagine a
delusion so deep and aggravated in its infatuation, then they have
indeed escaped Leviticus and the whole Pentateuch, and every
line of the Gospels and the Epistles—the whole canon of revelation. Mistakes are made about this matter which are of vital
consequence. We have given the enemy occasion to mock us a
good deal in some of these applications ; we have so acted as to
leave upon the enemy the impression that we can obliterate a

whole week's work of violence, deceit and perjury by going to church on Sunday—especially if we are so learned in ancient law as to be quite sure that we have escaped the ancient ritual and now stand in the liberty of wantonness and in the blasphemy of licentiousness. There is to be no Sunday catharism—washing by the priest or washing by the sinner's own hand—until some thing else has been done. What was the ancient law? The offender was to restore that which was taken away by violence, or that about which deceit was practised, or that wherein perjury was committed. That is the first step in the process. The whole thing in controversy must be replaced. Now may the man pray? No. There is no *quid pro quo* in morals. You cannot balance a crime by an apology; and you cannot drive iron into wood and extract it without leaving a wound behind. Extraction is not enough, restoration is not sufficient; after the full quantity has been restored, the man is to add twenty per cent. to it. If he has robbed his employer of one hundred pounds, he must replace the hundred pounds, and he must add twenty pounds to it,—*then* he may go to church! What a blessed thing it would be for some men if they could have escaped Leviticus!— for those men who sneer at the Old Testament as at an obsolete document, made yellow by time, good enough in its day but outworn by the magazines of the hour. You cannot outlive morality, moral judgment, righteousness. There is no back door through what is called natural law by which we can escape the eternal demand and claim of truth. After restoration and the addition of the fifth part thereto, the man was to go and see the pontiff of Israel and arrange about the offering of the ram. The process was not complete until the ram had been offered. We do not sin downward only, we sin upward as well. Every social offence has a religious bearing; every wrong done in the market-place reports itself in heaven. Thus life is solemn : actions have rebounds, and throbs, and issues, often incalculable, often infinite. The criminal has a hard life of it in the Bible. Some men have escaped the Bible; that is the reason they treat one another so violently, or with so fine a deceit, or with so flat a perjury. The moral tone of the Bible begets confidence. The book wants things to be foursquare, real, solid. A book with such a claim cannot be displaced by the most elaborate argument that founds itself upon smoke and rises into the dignity of evaporation. The

Bible will have what is right: therefore, the Bible *may* be inspired! No such morality have I met in any other book accessible to me. Bible morality is critical, minute, detailed,—most critical and exacting. There is no rough and ready method of bringing things to temporary equipoise. Nothing is settled until the root is made right, the fountain is purified, restoration is completed, compensation is effected, and prayer is said over the blood that atones. Mark the process of repentance as well as the process of sin. There is a philosophy in the one as certainly as there is in the other. How was the offender to begin? He was to begin at the moral point. Preachers may be too much afraid of preaching in this tone, because they are afraid of being stigmatised by epithets that have nothing in them but the spite of their own utterers and mean inventors. We must not be afraid of preaching works and laws and rights. We do not honour the Book by such fear; we misinterpret its spirit and misapply its claim. Begin with the moral and work towards the spiritual—restore, compensate, pray. No doubt it would suit some conditions of human nature to begin at the other end, because something might occur in the reverse process to prevent the completion of the whole. Hear not those priests—though their name be Aaron—who tell you to begin in metaphysical regions and work your way downwards, little by little, until you begin to bring back the property you stole. Restore the property before you see the high-priest, and give a fifth part of that which is taken back to the owner of that which was lost. Having done what is possible to humanity, begin the upper movement, and close the process with a look towards God. Let us have no whining, no canting, no sentimentality; let us rebuke the enemy wherein he thinks we are fanatics and can pray ourselves out of duties, bank ruptcies, and moral obligations. Is this preaching morality? I shall be thankful if that impression be made, for it is the one impression I wish to stamp upon the judgment and conscience of all men. This offers opportunities to every one immediately. It is not to be left to the offender first to obtain exactly clear views of the constitution of the Godhead before he begins to repay the man he has robbed. Believe me, we are not thus circumstanced that we have to fix upon a definite theory of the atonement—for even the atonement has been debased into a theory—until we begin to undo that which we have done amiss. We can restore stolen property: we can add to it a fifth part thereof or more,—we may double it; and having done so, we must then ask pardon. Any Iscariot can throw back the thirty pieces of silver; but the only end of such villainy is to be hanged, and to die an unpitied death. We are not at liberty, as Christians, to put down upon a man's threshold the money we stole, or the property we abstracted, and to run away drying our lips and lifting up our eyes to heaven and saying—" All is now well!" We have not lied unto man only, we have lied unto God; we have wounded the Spirit of truth; we have outraged the harmony of heaven. We have a great religious task now to achieve and accomplish. A book insisting upon such regulations will hold its own when all the insects that have gathered upon it to eat it up have fallen away into forgetfulness. All wronged men should revere the Bible; it takes up their case; it insists upon justice being done to them, and upon justice blossoming into restoration, and restoration being crowned with prayer, atonement, and reconciliation. Bad men should dread the Bible; they have not a friend in any one of its pages; not one of its complete proverbs can they quote in vindication of evil spirit or of evil action. Men anxious about social regeneration and harmony should go to the Bible for law, precept and guidance. What is this but Christianity anticipated? Moses and the Lamb are at one here as otherwhere and everywhere. Said Christ—" Think not I am come to destroy. . . . I am not come to destroy, but to fulfil." Did Christ say anything about evil and the method of treating that evil before religious postures were assumed or oblations were attempted? He did. What did he say? He said, in spirit, exactly what Moses said. He saw men coming to the altar about to offer their gifts and to say their prayers, and he stopped them on the road and said to them— " How stands it with you and your neighbour?" "My neighbour?" "Yes. Has thy brother aught against thee? Is there a feeling of hostility in thy heart against thy brother— thy brother-man? If there is, do not go to the altar; you can do nothing there, except dishonour the very stones of which it is built. First go and be reconciled to thy brother—make human and social relations right, begin at the visible point, make an impression upon the parties immediately concerned and through them upon observers,—then go and offer thy gift." Can we part with a book of which this is the moral tone! Here is a lesson for inquirers into the inspiration and authority of Holy Scripture. We cannot all begin at the uppermost points ; many of us cannot seize recondite matters and adjust and determine them by adequate scholarship and information ; but we can all begin our inquiry by asking, What is the moral tone of the book ? What does it want to be at in its actual issue ? It wants to reconcile man with man, to have restoration made where injury has been done ; it would bring every man on his knees to the offended person saying—" I have brought back that which I took away ; I restore fourfold ; pity me, forgive me, stoop over me and lift me up from this proper humiliation." Does the book breathe a spirit of that kind ? If so, no devil wrote it ; no bad man ever inspired it ; no clique of wrong-doers ever got up so complete a conspiracy. It would have father and mother honoured—it would have the old folks at home made young again every day by the action of filial obedience, filial sympathy and filial help ; it would set aside one day for rest every week—sweet holy day : as far as possible, everything should stand still and rest awhile, taking its breath again, and looking the great look that takes in horizons and skies, constellations and thrones and powers ; it would have honesty the law of life ; it would have every loaf of pure flour without any leaven of untruthfulness, sharp practice, or evil skill in outwitting men. Is that the moral tone of the book ? If so, I will not now trouble myself (the young inquirer may say) by questions I cannot now handle and perhaps may never be able to handle, but seeing that the book comes with such assertions of right and such claims, and insists upon them, and will in no sense be eluded, I will begin at that point,— who knows but I may, step by step, go into the interior of the holy temple and see the inner lights and touch the inner mysteries ? That is the right resolve ; the issue of it will be that you will discover that the Sacred Book is one—one as the many-coloured and resplendent sky.

Leviticus vi. 13.

"The fire shall ever be burning upon the altar; it shall never go out."

THE CONTINUAL BURNING.

BUT may not the people cease to sin before morning, and the fire be put out in the night-time? Does it not assume too much about the frailty and sinfulness of man to keep a fire up always? Would it not be better to extinguish it sometimes, just to suggest to the observers that a great hope has sprung up in the divine heart that perhaps this day there will be no more need for sacrifice? If the fire were put out, would not that itself be a gospel? Such are the questions that force themselves upon us when we come face to face with decrees and fiats and laws that have about them the awfulness of eternity. It is the expressions, "for ever," "evermore," "never"—terms which exhaust all time—that the soul cannot peruse without shuddering and inexpressible distress. It would seem as if God had no hope for his people. There is no opportunity for the exercise of feeling on the part of man that God sees a way out of the continual sin which needs the continual sacrifice. There is no touch of grace in this command; it is stern, unrelieved by a tear of pathos, never trembling with the feeling which makes all things sacred. If a man should reason thus concerning this passage, his reasoning would be correct within the points which he has assigned as its scope; but the view is partial, the distances are not properly regulated, the whole idea has not been seized by the observant mind. Suppose the sin should cease, would the fire then be put out? Certainly not. The fire has a double significance; it is not there only to consume the sacrifice, it is there to express the continual aspiration of the soul. The fire still burns. There is an unquenchable fire in heaven. To love is to worship; to love rightly is to worship rightly. The choice of expression is left with us, the choice of posture and method ; but where the spirit is right with God its action is best symbolised by the unquenchable fire, the aspiring flame.

It is instructive and partially distressing to hear many of the congratulations regarding the progress which has been made in the matter of divine worship ; it is most pitiful. Christians congratulate themselves in profane complacency that they have nothing to do with altars and fires and sacrifices of the herd, and of the flocks, and of the fowls, whether of turtle-doves or of young pigeons : they have escaped all that complicated and expensive mechanism—they have escaped more than that, or that fool's boast would not be on their lips. The truly progressive man has escaped nothing ; he is still where the Jew was, with new uses and higher disciplines, with keener penetrations into divine intent and purpose, and with a correspondingly severe and oppressive discipline. But the spirit is found also, not only as expressed in contrasts between Christianity and Judaism, but in contrasts between ancient Christian times and modern Christian usages—the same selfishness of felicitation. Who has not heard modern flippancy, often misappropriating the garb of piety, congratulating itself that it does not live in Puritan times ? Verily, we delight in setting down our escapes from discipline, and burden, and exaction, and training. Modern pietetic flippancy rejoices that it does not listen to the Puritan preacher, who, having preached the hour-glass empty, quietly inverted it in the sight of the people, and preached it empty again. Our felicitations are all of a most pitiful kind. We have escaped all the Jewish ceremony, all the Puritan tediousness—into what liberty have we come ? What is the practical result of all such escapes ? A greater love of brevity, a keener sense of liberty, which really means in such lips licentiousness ; we have nothing to do, nothing to give, nothing to suffer, all to enjoy, and just when we please, and as much as we please, and thus we have sunk into the idolatry of self. To suppose that discipline has ceased is to give up all that is worth living for. Our object should not be to escape discipline, but to make commandments pleasant, to turn statutes into songs in the house of our pilgrimage, to make obedience not a penalty but a delight. Listen to Christian talk to-day, listen to the monologue of your own heart, and the chief delight is found in having escaped all things requiring military discipline, Spartan exaction, obedience that keeps nothing back. When that becomes the law of the family, the family is practically broken up, decentralised, because the altar of discipline is destroyed. When that becomes the law of the Church, there is no Church left; it is a broken-down temple; the owls, and the bitterns, and the satyrs may take possession of the deserted place. What then is there permanent in such commands as the one which is now before us? Let us allow that accidents, accessories, incidental complexions and postures, have all passed away; but the tree has not consummated its purpose when it has shed its blossom. What is the eternal quantity? The altar is the principal feature in the truly consecrated life—an invisible altar, but not the less the place of worship, of meeting with the Divine One, of conference with Heaven,—not a local altar: "neither in this mountain nor yet at Jerusalem," shall men exclusively "worship the Father," but on every mountain and in every city, and in the unstable church of the sea. What then have we lost? A few pieces of stone, a certain construction in rude wilderness masonry; but that was not the altar: it was but the representation of the altar of the soul. The walls and roof we call the church are not the Church; the Church is within those walls and yet infinitely beyond those walls and that localising roof. We should live in a kingdom of symbols, hints, living suggestions— a place awful by the vitality of its inspirations. How can this doctrine be taught to carnal men? It requires a century of millenniums to begin the great spiritual mystery. A misconception of the altar leads to idolatry—to the idolatry of places, and to the idolatry of offices. What we can see is not the altar; the stone altar is a medium through which the soul may get swift glimpses of the altar beyond, where spirits kneel, where souls burn in ardent desire, where angels hover in wonder and in hope. No marvel that we become less and less in mind and affection if we have mistaken any building of stone for God's house. It is the beginning of the house, the outward and visible form of the house, a halting-place where we may unloose the sandal for a time and set up the staff in the corner, and wait awhile, and get breath by praying. We must be up and on, seeking the house not made with hands, of which all good houses and hospitable homes are but dim hints and types.

Aspiration is the highest expression of character. That is the permanent quantity in the text. Fire ascends; it speechlessly says, " This is not my home; I must travel, I must fly, I must return; the sun calls me, and I must obey." A character without aspiration cannot live healthily and exercise a vital and ennobling influence. When religion becomes mere controversy, it has lost veneration; and whatever or whoever loses veneration slips away from the centre of things, and falls evermore into thickening darkness. There is a philosophy in this conception as well as a theology. To aspire is to grow. It is an action full of meaning; it signifies, being expressed in many words, that we are not yet content : there is something in us which seeks completion; there is a spirit weary of solitude that yearns for fellowship, and that cannot be content with any communion of a human and visible kind ; there is a soul in man that holds time and space in solemn contempt, and seeks rest in infinite liberties and harmonies. Without this aspiration man becomes a mere grub; he dwells upon the earth and accommodates himself to his little prison ; no storm of anger rises within because of the poverty of the place; it is good enough to eat and drink in, ample enough to lie down in, and beyond these poor exercises the man so lost has no desire. Here is the place at which the Christian religion directs its most powerful appeal to human attention and confidence. It is a solemn religion, so solemn that many times it cannot argue; it will not criticise; it leaves the region of words and rises to the rapture of silence. Here, too, arises that marvellous pathos which will keep evangelical doctrine from desuetude and contempt. No religion that is not rich in pathos can live long or make itself world-wide in influence. Controversies perish in the air which separates one nation from another ; pathos comes with every wind, shines with every rising day, and glows in every westering sun—" makes the whole world kin."

" Jesus wept "—will be a power in human thought and human need when all critical questions have vexed themselves to death and perished in unholy and unprofitable abortiveness. We are conscious of a perpetual need ; we cannot be satisfied. We mock one another sometimes in language not intended to be mischievous or reproachful when we ask if we cannot *now* rest and be thankful—sit down and enjoy ourselves. We ought to do so with regard to things temporal and measurable, and if things temporal and measurable were all, then the inquiry would take upon itself a very high moral solemnity ; but all this outreaching, striving, discontent—all this aching, poverty, and burning desire for more and more conquest and territory, wealth and influence, has a religious meaning, and that meaning being put into words is that the soul has not room enough in space, duration enough in time, but, by its discontent, expresses the magnificence of its origin and its destiny.

"The fire shall ever be burning upon the altar ; it shall never go out."

Then there are two things in the text—" fire " and " altar." We may have an altar, but no fire. That is the deadly possibility ; that is the fatal reality. The world is not dying for want of a creed, but for want of faith. We are not in need of more prayers, we are in need of more prayerfulness. If the little knowledge we have—how small it is the wisest men know best of all—were turned to right use, fire in its happiest influences would soon begin to be detected by surrounding neighbours and by unknown observers. Of what avail is it that we have filled the grate with fuel if we have not applied the flame ? Does the unlighted fuel warm the chamber ? No more does the unsanctified knowledge help to redeem and save society. We need the fire as well as the altar. Magnificent altars we have built : we have brought stone from afar ; we have hewn it in the field that there might be no noise near the temple ; we have set it up and made ourselves proud in the contemplation of the skilful building. It is nothing ; it is a lie ; it is an imposition ; it is the sign of self-idolatry ; we have mistaken the means for the end, the process for the result. What is needed now is a fire that will burn the altar itself—turn the marble and porphyry and granite and hewn soft-stone all into fuel that shall go up in a common oblation to the waiting heavens.

We may have fire and no altar, as well as have an altar and no fire. This is also a mistake. We ought to have religious places and Christian observances, locality with special meaning, resting-places with heaven's welcome written upon their portals. There is a deadly sophism lurking in the supposition that men

can have the fire without the altar, and are independent of institutions, churches, families, places, Bibles, and all that is known
by Christian arrangement for common worship. We are not
meant to be solitary worshippers. When a man says he can read
the Bible at home, I deny it. He can *partially* read it there, he
can see some of its meaning there ; but society is one, as well as
is the individual, in some degrees and in some relations. There
is a religion of fellowship as well as of solitude. Forsake not
the assembling of yourselves together : there is a touch that helps
life to gather itself up into its full force ; there is a contagion
which makes the heart feel strong in masonry. When a man
says he can pray at home, I deny it—except in the sense that he
can there *partially* pray. He can transact part of the commerce
which ought to be going on continually between heaven and
earth, earth and heaven ; but there is a common prayer—the
family cry, the congregational intercession, the sense that we
are praying for one another in common petition at the throne
of grace. It may be that one voice only is heard, but when
that voice has been touched by the inspiration of Heaven, it
will have priestly tones in it, great expressiveness, touching
every known experience, and speaking in one great language a
thousand otherwise unutterable desires.

It is not enough to kindle a fire : we must renew it. " The
fire shall ever be burning upon the altar ; it shall never go out."
Did not some men burn once who are cold now ? Have not
some men allowed the holy flame to perish ? and is not their life
now like a deserted altar laden with cold, white ashes ? Once
they sang sweetly, prayed with eagerness of expectation, worked
with both hands diligently, were always open to Christian appeal,
localised their lives in one poignant inquiry—Lord, what wilt
thou have me to do ? I know of no drearier spectacle than to
see a man who still bears the Christian name on the altar of
whose heart the fire has gone out. That is a possibility. Lost
enthusiasm means lost faith ; lost passion means lost conviction.
Do not let us delude ourselves with the notion that if we are less
enthusiastic and passionate, vehement and openly heroic, we are
all the stronger and the more truly consolidated men. The devil
there cheats us with long words ; the enemy persuades us with
false reasoning. We easily yield to the logic which bids us be

quiet, be still, refrain. He has the easy task in life who pleads with men to be less and to do less, to think less, read less and act less. He has the heroic part—the great hill to climb—who calls to reluctant travellers, " Excelsior ! " who bids men whose eyelids are heavy with sleep rise and renew the fire, for the midnight hour is near and the temperature is falling fast. That is the position assigned to the Christian teacher, to the Christian apostle, to the father of the family, to Christian Churches, to every man and every institution assuming and employing the name of Christ. We might be better thought of if our appeals were less persistent and tremendous in mortal agony ; but the time of judgment is not yet. Be it ours to escape the fate of people who have lamps but no fire, beliefs but no faith, a bound book but no revelation.

NOTES.

Q. Curtius, giving an account of the march of Darius's army, says : " The fire which they called eternal was carried before them on silver altars ; the Magi came after it, singing hymns, after the Persian manner; and three hundred and sixty-five youths clothed in scarlet followed, according to the number of the days in the year."—BURDER.

The first fire upon the altar came from heaven (chap. ix. 24), so that by keeping that up continually with a constant supply of fuel, all their sacrifices throughout all their generations might be said to be consumed with that fire from heaven, in token of God's acceptance. If, through carelessness, they should ever let it go out, they could not expect to have it so kindled again. Accordingly, the Jews tell us, that the fire never did go out upon the altar, until the captivity in Babylon. This is referred to (Isa. xxxi. 9) where God is said to have " his fire in Zion, and his furnace in Jerusalem." By this law we are taught to keep up in our minds a constant disposition to all acts of piety and devotion, and habitual affection to divine things, so as to be always ready to every good word and work. Though we be not always sacrificing, yet we must keep the fire of holy love always burning ; and thus we mus. pray always.—MATTHEW HENRY.

Leviticus viii. 33; ix. 1-8.

And ye shall not go out of the door of the tabernacle of the congregation in seven days, until the days of your consecration be at an end : for seven days shall he consecrate you.

1. And it came to pass on the eighth day, that Moses called Aaron and his sons, and the elders of Israel ;

2. And he said unto Aaron, Take thee a young calf for a sin offering, and a ram for a burnt offering, without blemish, and offer them before the Lord.

3. And unto the children of Israel thou shalt speak, saying, Take ye a kid of the goats for a sin offering ; and a calf and a lamb, both of the first year without blemish, for a burnt offering ;

4. Also a bullock and a ram for peace offerings, to sacrifice before the Lord ; and a meat offering mingled with oil : for to-day the Lord will appear unto you.

5. And they brought that which Moses commanded before the tabernacle of the congregation : and all the congregation drew near and stood before the Lord.

6. And Moses said, This is the thing which the Lord commanded that ye should do : and the glory of the Lord shall appear unto you.

7. And Moses said unto Aaron, Go unto the altar, and offer thy sin offering, and thy burnt offering, and make an atonement for thyself, and for the people : and offer the offering of the people, and make an atonement for them ; as the Lord commanded.

8. Aaron therefore went unto the altar, and slew the calf of the sin offering, which was for himself.

CONSECRATION AND SERVICE.

IT seems singular and almost frivolous that the priests were commanded not to go out of the door of the tabernacle of the congregation for seven days. This is our own practice. The accident has changed, but this is the philosophy of all calculated and well-set life. We think we have escaped all these mechanisms, whereas we have not escaped one of them. God is one, his method is one, his providence is one. Any variety which may please our little fancy is a very transient delight ; at the root and core of things there is a marvellous, an eternal unity. Men are not permitted to go forth into the priesthood at a step. No priesthood is worth accepting that any fool may step into without notice, without preparation and without thought. The great priesthoods of life are all approached by a seven days' consecration. Men may rush at work, they may "rush in where angels fear to tread"; but looked at comprehensively and weighed wisely, the great philosophy covers all time that he who would accept any priesthood of life— by which is meant any of its highest offices, leaderships and utilities—must approach through a strait gate and go by a narrow way and obey the eternal law of consecration. This is not open to dispute; no theme of controversy is started by this suggestion. The practice of life is described almost literally even in this ancient text. There is no Old Testament in the sense of obsoleteness or exhaustion; there is an Old Testament in the sense of root, origin, first points, germs, authorities. Without the Old Testament we could have had no New Testament, as without eternity time would have been impossible. Does the medical priest run into his priesthood without consecration? is he not hidden for many a day in the tabernacle of wisdom—in the tent in which he meets all the authorities of his science? For a long time he may not prescribe; for a considerable period he has but to inquire and to give proof of capacity and industry. A whole week of time—meaning by that some perfect period — must elapse before he goes forth authoritatively to feel a pulse, or to prescribe a remedy. Why this repetition of Old Testament technicality, of obsolete and most frivolous pedantry? There is no such thing. The Old Testament has a grip of life in all its departments and issues—which is proof enough that it never wrote itself. Does the musical priest rush into his work quite suddenly without notice or preparation, without consecration and endorsement? Allow that in some conspicuous instances which could never be encompassed by mortal law there may have been bushes burning in wildernesses without the enkindling of the fire by human hands; allow for genius, for almost divine fulness of inspiration; still there remains the great common law of education, progress and influence; and seven days' consecration, silence, study, inquiry, qualification must precede a forthcoming priest and the assertion of his power. The same law applies to the preaching of the Gospel. The preacher must be long time hidden, during which no man may suspect that he is a preacher; his silence may be almost provoking; people may be driven to inquire what the purpose of his life is;—he says nothing; he never reveals himself; he looks as if he might be about to speak, but speak he never does; he is full of books and thoughts, and prayer seems to be written upon his transfigured face. What is the meaning of this? He is in the Tent of Meeting; he is in conference with the Trinity; he is undergoing consecration,—in no merely ceremonial sense : in the sense of acquiring deeper knowledge of God, fuller communion with the truth, and entering into closer fellowship with all the mysteries of human life. Even when he seems to be doing things that other men could easily do, it is the other men who are making the mistake. When the medical priest, hoary with long years, touches your pulse, remember that half a century is listening to the ticking of that life-pendulum ; and remember that when any well-qualified critic pronounces an opinion in a moment upon any performance it may be half a century that speaks in the brief and urgent sentence. Our judgments are not to be founded upon the mere flash of the moment; behind what appears to be easy there may be a life-time of study, prayer, and consecration. What is true of all these regions is equally true of every other region in life that is worth occupying—true of every workman, however humble his sphere of industry, true of every head of a business that requires care and thoughtful management, true of every man who attempts wisely to direct public opinion; there must be preparation, consecration, waiting, silence, and then the outcoming of the prepared man to do the work which God means him to execute. Thus life is no little trick, no momentary posture, no empirical venture; but a deep philosophy, a grand tragedy, a tremendous struggle. O! that men were wise, that they understood these things! In all thy ways acknowledge God, and he will direct thy path. Do not run before being sent. Remember that time spent in the wilderness is not time wasted. Never forget that there is a religious silence as well as a religious utterance; and let God **fix the time of consecration and the place of concealment, and** let him begin, continue and terminate the conference. After that all will be easy—not because of any frivolity in itself, but because of the divine store of strength treasured up in the prepared and consecrated heart.

"So Aaron and his sons did all things which the Lord commanded by the hand of Moses" (viii. 36).

Obedience is the best preparation for service. We cannot rule until we can obey. That was the motto of the great Napoleon. It is a philosophy expressed in the briefest terms. Aaron and his sons did not take a primary place; they did not rush upon their destiny; they waited, accepted the law, obeyed it to the letter, stood still like a commanded sun, and would not move until God bade them go forward. It is at this point that many of us lose much. We are impatient : we think we are prepared for action when we are not at all qualified to undertake it. The teacher knows better than the pupil ; the master knows when we have been long enough in the wilderness or undergoing processes of spiritual education and religious chastisement. God is the time-keeper. To obey is to express in the form most suitable to modesty a spirit of genuine greatness. He who obeys, accepts discipline. To obey is to confess the power of others; to obey is to be willing to learn. How often is obedience masked ! It has a look of complete surrender, though it is hooked and seamed through and through with subtle reluctance. In that case it is not obedience. None of the happy issues of obedience are secured by it ; it is but a varied form of vanity, it is but a concealed expression of self-idolatry. The same rule holds good in Christian service. In the words of judgment we read, " Thou hast been faithful . . . I will make thee ruler." The sense is even more clearly and graphically expressed by another word in the same judgment, " Well done, thou good and faithful servant : thou hast been faithful . . . I will make thee ruler." We should have more influence if we were more inspired by the spirit of obedience. Our word would go further if our character justified the assertion of our claim. It has come to a sad state when men undervalue what may be called, or rather miscalled, the negative virtues. We praise open heroism, military adventure, and in doing so we may

within certain bounds be perfectly right ; but we should not
forget patience, obedience, modesty, uncomplaining resignation,
the eyes that are weary with long watching, and the lips that
are sometimes tempted to move to profanation and yet are
recovered suddenly and shaped in prayer. It is no mark of
progress that we undervalue negative virtues, passive qualities,
simple waiting until we are told to go forward. A meek and
a quiet spirit is, in the sight of God, of great price.

The time came when Aaron was to go forward to his work.
" And it came to pass on the eighth day, that Moses called Aaron
and his sons, and the elders of Israel," and gave them their
orders ; and Aaron went forth and took the " young calf for a
sin offering, and a ram for a burnt offering." There is something
very pathetic about a man's first action. We ought to look
lovingly upon the young who try for the first time to realise the
mystery of their vocation. It little becomes us to sneer. We
ourselves, however old and skilled, had to begin. We should
rather remember our own stumblings, and blunderings, and
misadventures, and remembering these, should keep back the
word of stinging criticism and bitter reproach, the utterance of
which on the part of any man is an insult to the Spirit of Christ.
Are any beginning the Christian race ? We who are a mile or
two on must pray that the new runners may run well ; we
remember where we slipped, where we well-nigh fell and should
have fallen quite, but for friendly interposition and gentlest
encouragement given by stronger men. He is not an able man
who shows his ability in cynicism and in sneering. It is the
curse of some families that they are always bitter. They mistake
sneering for ability. It is the sting of a wasp, it is the fang of a
serpent, it is the hoof of an ass,—it is not ability. Ability
sustains, comforts, encourages, builds up with gracious edification
and speaks the word of encouragement when heart and flesh do
fail. We owe everything to encouragement—nothing to bitter
cynicism. Encouragement was given in the case of the early
priests.

" And Moses said, This is the thing which the Lord commanded
that ye should do : and the glory of the Lord shall appear unto
you." Duty and glory—not glory and duty—must be the motto

of life. Read the words,—ponder them : " This is the thing which the Lord commanded that ye should do :—" The sentence is punctuated by a colon ; the thing is supposed to be done, and on the other side of the colon we read—" and the glory of the Lord shall appear unto you " ;—harvest after seed-time, honour after service, heaven after earth, immortality after triumphant death.

Jesus Christ did all that is here ascribed to Aaron and his sons. Christ underwent preparation : for thirty years he was practically silent ; he was being consecrated in a sense we cannot perfectly understand ; he was being set apart, and in the end he brought all the completeness of his strength to bear in redeeming tenderness upon the awful situation of the world. He walked in long silence ; no man dared ask him any question about his reticence. He might have spoken before—so human impatience reasoned ; but he was fulfilling a destiny ; he was representing the most solemn mystery of life. Christ obeyed. In saying so, we are abiding strictly by the Scriptural line ; we are not venturing upon some idle or poetic fancy. He accepted the position : he " became obedient unto death, even the death of the Cross " ; as a Son he served in the Father's house. Study this aspect of the divine character of Jesus ; his Deity suffers no loss by this stoop of his humanity. He is not the less God to the soul, but the more, and the more priestly and the more sympathetic, that he understands all the bending, all the condescension, all the service of life. There is no work of a permitted kind to which the hand can be put which Christ did not do long before he commanded us to attempt its execution. Jesus Christ also had his first work. We read such words as these : " Jesus began to preach." They are tender words ; they touch the heart with a most subtle pathos. Christ, who never himself began—for he was Alpha and Omega, the First and the Last—" began to preach "—heard his own voice in public for the first time. What a beginning it was ! How like a beginning when he began ! He said " Repent !" It was a short discourse,—yes, in words, but a discourse that filled all time with its meaning. Then we read—" This beginning of miracles did Jesus in Cana of Galilee." He who began to preach began to work miracles—did his first wonder. They say that to the true speaker the sentences he utters are greater surprises to himself than to his hearers. Was the miracle greater to Christ than to the observer? Was there any element of surprise in the Redeemer's mind when he saw that the water had blushed into wine? We cannot tell. The human mind must wonder, and put reverent questions, and may do so without profaning sanctities divine. Have we begun? Have we begun to preach? Have we tried to do the first miracle? Have we never begun at all? It is high time to awake out of sleep: the night is far-spent, the day is at hand; redeem the time, buy up the opportunity,—begin now. One man's miracle may be the speaking of a gracious word, or the utterance of a forgiving declaration, or the offering of a hand long withheld, or the serving of the poor and the ignorant and those that are out of the way. Another man's miracle may be begun in opening his lips for the first time in audible prayer. Each man must find out for himself the point at which he must begin his preaching and his miracle. Christ associated duty and glory; he said—" I have finished the work which thou gavest me to do, . . . glorify thou me . . . with the glory which I had with thee before the world was." He, too, would be glorified. Moses finished the work, then the glory of the Lord descended; Aaron did the things that were commanded, then the glory of the Lord appeared; Jesus Christ finished the work which was given him to do, and the glory was not withheld,—a marvellous sentence; it seems to separate the coincident lines and divide them for ever.

" Aaron therefore went unto the altar, and slew the calf of the sin offering, which was for himself " (ix. 8).

There the scene ends. We look for analogies and consummations, but where is the analogous line in this instance? There is a sentence in the New Testament which makes us quail bearing upon this very doctrine. In the Epistle to the Hebrews (vii. 27), that sentence is recorded : " Who needeth not daily, as those high-priests, to offer up sacrifice, first for his own sins, and then for the people's : for this he did once, when he offered up himself." All the meaning of that sentence no man may explain. Does it relate to the latter part of the previous sentence or to the entire declaration? Read again : " Who needeth not daily, as those high-priests, to offer up sacrifice, first for his own sins, and then for the people's: for this—" Which? " . . . first for his own sins, and

then for the people's : for this he did once, when he offered up
himself." He was without sin, and therefore would need no sin-
offering ;—a Lamb without blemish or spot or drawback, he had
no sin to confess ; but when he was baptized he said ". . . thus it
becometh us to fulfil all righteousness " ; and when he was slain,
what know I how much of his pure humanity was itself involved
in the mysterious oblation ? Silence is best. That he had no
sin, he knew no sin, that he was spotless, pure, holy as God in
himself we know ; but representatively, humanly, fleshly, who
can tell—for the exposition must put itself into the form of a
question—the whole meaning of this ineffable mystery ?

Thus stands the sublime appeal : a time of consecration, an act
of obedience, glory crowning duty. To that programme of life
and to no mean policy are we called, every one, by the Spirit of
Christ and the vision of his Cross.

NOTE.

The order of God for the consecration of Aaron is found in Ex. xxix., and
the record of its execution in Lev. viii.; and the delegated character of the
Aaronic priesthood is clearly seen by the fact, that, in this its inauguration,
the priestly office is borne by Moses, as God's truer representative (Heb. vii).

The form of consecration resembled other sacrificial ceremonies in containing, first a sin offering, the form ot cleansing from sin and reconciliation ;
a burnt offering, the symbol of entire devotion to God of the nature so
purified ; and a meat offering, the thankful acknowledgment and sanctifying
of God's natural blessings. It had, however, besides these, the solemn
assumption of the sacred robes (the garb of righteousness), the anointing
(the symbol of God's grace), and the offering of the ram of consecration, the
blood of which was sprinkled on Aaron and his sons, as upon the altar and
vessels of the ministry, in order to sanctify them for the service of God. The
former ceremonies represented the blessings and duties of the man, the latter
the special consecration of the priest.

The solemnity of the office, and its entire dependence for sanctity on the
ordinance of God, were vindicated by the death of Nadab and Abihu, for
" offering strange fire " on the altar, and apparently for doing so in drunken
recklessness. Aaron checking his sorrow, so as at least to refrain from all
outward signs of it, would be a severe trial to an impulsive and weak
character, and a proof of his being lifted above himself by the office which
he held.

From this time the history of Aaron is almost entirely that of the priesthood, and its chief feature is the great rebellion of Korah and the Levites
against his sacerdotal dignity, united with that of Dathan and Abiram and
the Reubenites against the temporal authority of Moses.

The true vindication of the reality of Aaron's priesthood was, not so much
the death of Korah by the fire of the Lord, as the efficacy of his offering of
incense to stay the plague, by which he was seen to be accepted as an
intercessor for the people.—SMITH's *Dictionary of the Bible.*

Leviticus ix. 22; x. 1-7.

And Aaron lifted up his hand toward the people, and blessed them, and came down from offering of the sin offering, and the burnt offering, and peace offerings.

1. And Nadab and Abihu, the sons of Aaron, took either of them his censer [not the appointed censer of the tabernacle], and put fire therein, and put incense thereon, and offered strange [common or ordinary] fire before the Lord [in front of the holy of holies], which he commanded them not [the negative form is often used in Hebrew to express the stronger affirmative].

2. And there went out fire from the Lord, and devoured them, and they died before the Lord [by the same fire. Read 2 Cor. ii. 16, in illustration of alternative uses].

3. Then Moses said unto Aaron, This is it that the Lord spake [an unrecorded law], saying, I will be sanctified in them that come nigh me [I will sanctify myself in them that come near to me], and before all the people I will be glorified [and I will glorify myself before all the people]. And Aaron held his peace [silent assent, not sullenness].

4. And Moses called Mishael and Elzaphan, the sons of Uzziel [the son of Kohath, and father of three sons] the uncle of Aaron, and said unto them, Come near, carry your brethren [kinsmen] from before the sanctuary out of the camp.

5. So they went near, and carried them in their coats [tunics, long, white, sacerdotal garments] out of the camp ; as Moses had said.

6. And Moses said unto Aaron, and unto Eleazar and unto Ithamar [ordinary priests], his sons, Uncover not your heads, neither rend your clothes [give not way to such displays of grief as might reflect upon the providence of God] ; lest ye die, and lest wrath come upon all the people [the connection between the priest and the people was representative and vital] : but let your brethren, the whole house of Israel, bewail the burning which the Lord hath kindled.

7. And ye shall not go out from the door of the tabernacle of the congregation [the entrance of the tent of meeting], lest ye die : for the anointing oil of the Lord is upon you. And they did according to the word of Moses.

BLESSING AND JUDGMENT.

A MOST happy change! We feel as if we could join the thankful and rapturous host of Israel. There has not been much blessing up to this period in our studies. We have come face to face with law, rule, exaction, discipline, and all the

apparatus of profound and life-long education. A tender tone
would have helped us now and again. We have not been without such tone. When we have heard it, we have made the most
of it; we have magnified the tenderness into a great heaven-
filling benediction. We took it as preliminary; we interpreted
it typically; we hailed it as an earnest; we said, " The cloud at
present is only about the size of a man's hand, but quickly the
sky will be charged with rain, and upon the earth it will plash
in gracious benediction." This is the right way to read gentle
providences—all light helps by the way; regard them as earnests,
pledges, hints, and promises in substance. A great human passage is before us. Up to this time we have been dealing with
priests, and ceremonies, and mechanisms; we have been conscious
of the want of what may be represented as the universal; on
every hand we have been bounded, shut up in stern iron, with
a look upward, but no horizon. Now Aaron stretches forth his
hands and blesses the people : stern Moses joins him : they enter
the tent of meeting and return, and they both bless the people.
The ministry is widening; there is a streak of light on the far-
away horizon; the two greatest men have at present seen the
possibility of millenniums of light and rest and comfort; a new
tone is in their voices; feeling begins to enter into the ministry
of law. The people may behave better after this. Who can
rebel immediately after a benediction? Does not a blessing
block us on our rebellious way and make us think a little whether
we may not have been wrong, and whether it is not better to
turn round and go the other—the upward—road? What has
been wanting in our education, personally, domestically, socially,
may be this element of feeling, sympathy, benediction,—this
utterance of infinite hope, this covering up of wounds and
blemishes and shortcomings and life-wanderings by a great and
divine benediction. We seem to have sudden summer coming
upon us in the winter-time of this law and mechanism.

Blessings of this kind do not come alone; other comforts attend
and consummate them. We read in the twenty-fourth verse of
the ninth chapter :

"And there came a fire out from before the Lord, and consumed upon the
altar the burnt offering and the fat : which when all the people saw, they
shouted, and fell on their faces."

It was a rare time in Israel—a time of rapture, of melting tenderness, of that sacred emotion which lifts up the level of the whole life by enlarging and ennobling all the best sentiments of the heart. This is what is now granted to men. All true service is glorified by a consciousness of the Divine presence. Again and again we say, " Did not our heart burn within us ? " We knew hardly why ; we had seen a Stranger : he had conversed with our inmost spirit : he had delivered messages straight to the hearing ear of the soul, every tone of which was heard, every tone of which was new ; and the fire began to burn, and the heart became a new heart—soft, tender, filled with a sense of mystery : love rose above the region of words and shaped itself before the inner vision in apocalypses of symbol and type and wizardry such as might have been inspired by the Holy Spirit : and the air danced with new images, and the sun burned with new light, and all time seemed too short for the expression of the rapture which thrilled the spirit. Then we were charged with fanaticism ; some did not hesitate to say : " These men are drunken ; they have had new wine, and they are under the influence of intoxicants,"—not knowing that we were not drunken with wine wherein is excess, but were filled with the Spirit of God ; and the only word in all the daily language of mortals which touched our experience at all, and gave it articulation, was the word *fire*, because it seems to hold all other words that mean earnestness, purity, elevation, beauty, suggestiveness. The fire in the humblest grate outshines the king's diamonds. The fire, read by open and discerning eyes, is a continual history, battle, unfoldment, revelation.

There have been grand days in the Church—days when the mechanical priest has shaken off his mechanism and blessed the people ; days when great legislators have dropped the bâton of statesmanship, and with free hands stretched out over a wondering people have blessed the common human heart. One may come in the ages who will sit down upon a mountain, and when he opens his mouth he will say, " Blessed, blessed, blessed ! " he will begin his sermon by putting the crown upon all the best history of the heart ; he will begin, where other men close, with congratulation and beatitude.

The history pauses a moment.   It ought here to be punctuated by a whole century.   Some time should elapse before the next sentence is read.   Yet we had better not lengthen the pause, or we may sacrifice reality for poetical completeness.   Our own life to-day is just as hurried, rugged, and contradictory as is this piece of ancient story.   So we may come into the next chapter with an awful familiarity.   Men can go from the altar to forbidden places; men can unclasp their hands from God's grip and put those hands into other keeping.   Poetical justice might have closed the book of Leviticus with the ninth chapter.   It would have been a glorious close,—Aaron moved to feeling: Moses giving way to emotion: the Lord's fire consuming the offering upon the altar: the people singing, shouting, and falling down in adoration.   Why did not the history close there?   That would have been Canaan enough for any nation, paradise enough for any people.   But there *is* another chapter.   The tenth chapter opens with a sketch of character which appears from day to day:

"And Nadab and Abihu, the sons of Aaron, took either of them his censer, and put fire therein, and put incense thereon, and offered strange fire before the Lord, which he commanded them not."

What a set-back in the grand advance!   How often have we been within one step of heaven, and have turned suddenly round and fallen right back to the earth that has every reason to be ashamed of us!   They were priests too; they were the sons of the pontiff.   The evil began in the upper places.   The scepticism is *in* the Church to-day.   It pleases us to organise missions to those who are supposed to be unbelievers; but the unbelief of the day is *in* the Church.   There is (as we have said again and again) no possible *un*belief outside the Church.   There may be ignorance, only partial knowledge, prejudice, perverted judgment; but, as we have again and again averred—and growing time becomes growing conviction,—the enemies of the Church are not outside the Church.   The pulpit may be leprous; the ministry may be filled with scepticism.   They were in the sacerdotal line, who blasphemously took their own censers,— a thing forbidden in the law.   These men were not at liberty to take each his own censer; there was a utensil provided for that action, and for any man to bring his own ironmongery to serve in such a cause was to insult the Spirit of the universe.   This

is how we stand to-day : every man bringing his censer—
his own censer,—which means the prostitution of personality,
the loss of the commonwealth-spirit and of the recognition of
the unity and completeness of the Church. There are men
who spend their time in amending Providence : Nadab and
Abihu represent two such men to-day. There are men who
are always trying to naturalise the supernatural : this is what
Nadab and Abihu did. They said in effect, " This evil fire will
do quite as well ; build your life on reason ; order all the
ministry of your life by coherent and cumulative argument ;
drop the ancient words, and choose and set new words of your
own ; there is no supernatural : let us banish superstition
and inaugurate the reign of reason." Nadab and Abihu had a
kind of church, but a church without the true God,—an unin-
habited shell, a mockery, a base irony—the baser because it was
in a sense religious. There are men who substitute invention
for commandment. This is what Nadab and Abihu did : they
invented a new use of the common censer ; they brought into
new service common fire ; they ventured to put incense thereon
when only the pontiff of Israel was allowed to use such incense ;
they invented new bibles, new laws, new churches, new methods;
they were cursed with the spirit of extra independence and
individuality, with the audacity of self-trust—not with its religious
worship and adoration. This all occurs every day, and it occurs
quite as rudely and violently in the current and flow of our own
history. All this invention and all this deposition of God and of
law comes just as swiftly after our conscious realisations of the
divine presence as this instance came swiftly upon the conscious
benediction of God. " There is but a step between me and
death." It would seem as if a universe might intervene between
true prayer and the spirit of distrust and cursing—yet not a
hair's-breadth intervenes. A man on his knees is next to the
worst self, namely,—a man with clenched fists defying the
heavens. It is possible to lay down the Bible and take up the
unholy book and read the corruptest pages with conscious interest
if not positive sympathy. Thin is the veil which keeps the right
action from the wrong deed. The place of devils is next door to
the sanctuary always. For some men it is never so easy to rebel
as after a great Amen spoken in the ear of Heaven.

Another action of fire is found in this incident:

"And there went out fire from the Lord, and devoured them, and they died before the Lord " (x. 2).

The same fire! Is it not said that the Gospel is a savour of life unto life, or of death unto death ? Fire had just consumed the burnt offering and the fat upon the altar in token of divine complacency and sacred nearness and the acceptance of human worship and that same fire went out from the Lord and devoured the audacious priests—the sacerdotal blasphemers,—ate them up as if they had been common bones! It is an awful flame! "Our God is a consuming fire." Priests, officers, leaders, men of position, men of wealth, play not your little fantastic tricks on God's altar! Your vanity and pomp and fashion and base wealth will be no protection against the anger and righteous judgment of God. The pulpit must obey; the foremost men must obey as the hindmost. The law must have obedience—simple, complete, honest, unquestioning obedience;—ours not to ask the reason, or make objection, or start new difficulty, or invent new methods; but to be found in loving and holy obedience evermore.

This is what has always happened in the history of such men as Nadab and Abihu. History is full of the white ashes of burned heretics. Leave the Lord to handle the infidel—whether he be priest or outside sceptic. The Lord has never been negligent of his own altar. Men have arisen from century to century proposing the use of new censers, granting to every man the use of his own censer—and thus paying a subtle tribute to the vanity of the human heart; in many ages men have arisen to write down the Bible, to tear down the altar, to supersede the sanctuary. For a time they succeeded; but because there was "no deepness of earth" they soon withered away—that is to say, they were not rooted in the Heart of the Universe, which is a living Heart, an eternal Heart; they were planted on the surface of things, and were in very deed quite green and gave promise of blossom and of fruit; but we looked for them; and, lo, they were not; yea, we sought them, but they could not be found. The Lord will burn every Nadab and Abihu, and burn them the more quickly that they were priests. If they had been sound heretics—really out-and-out enemies and assailants—he might have conferred with Moses and Aaron about them as he conferred with an elder man about Sodom and Gomorrah; but he has no parleying when priests do wrong, for the evil is at the altar : there is nothing between the deed and the judgment. It shall be more tolerable for the land of Sodom and Gomorrah in the day of judgment than for preachers, teachers, professors, who have played the fool, and have substituted the traditions of elders for the commandments of God. It is a sad time in the Church when the altar is forgotten. The Lord said " I will be sanctified in them that come nigh me, and before all the people I will be glorified. . . . And Moses called " two of the family " and said . . . Carry out these men and bury them outside the camp "; and Moses would have no mourning by Aaron or Eleazar and Ithamar :

" Uncover not your heads, neither rend your clothes; lest ye die, and lest wrath come upon all the people : but let your brethren, the whole house of Israel, bewail the burning which the Lord hath kindled " (x. 6).

—but there must be no tears on the altar. We must not reflect upon Providence by crying in the church. It was the law that the priest should never leave the altar to go to burials, or interrupt his sacred ministry by shedding tears. He represented God as well as represented the people, and he must abide at his duty whoever died. It was military religion in its mechanical arrangement; it was spiritual obedience in the acceptation of its intention.

" Moses said unto Aaron, and unto Eleazar, and unto Ithamar . . . Ye shall not go out from the door of the tabernacle of the congregation " (the tent of meeting), " lest ye die : for the anointing oil of the Lord is upon you "; if you go out you will reflect upon God's ministry in the world. Aaron must not mourn along the track of the divine judgment; he must remain at the altar; what may occur in his own heart none can tell, for God will not be hard upon him; but he must not be found going after burned men as one might go after those who had died complacently with Heaven and in the discharge of duty.

The reason is given in the words—" For the anointing oil of the Lord is upon you." That oil must separate between you and the appearance of unbelief; that oil is a restraint as well as an inspiration. Is it not so now, varying the terms and the relations of things? If we could enter into the spirit of that restriction, what different men we should be! The name of your country is upon you: dishonour it not. A venerable name, never associated with meanness, cowardice, corruption, or fear of man. Rise to the dignity of the signature which is upon you. When *you* flee, the enemy will say your country has fled; when *you* play the coward, the enemy will say the throne has tottered and the sovereign has succumbed. The holy vow is upon you. You said you would be better and do better. You punctuated the vow with hot tears; your emphasis was quite an unfamiliar tone, so much so that we wondered at the poignancy of your utterance, and felt in very deed that you were speaking the heart's truth. Remember that vow. The vow of the Lord is upon you. If *you* stoop, it will not be condescension, it will be base prostration; if *you* palter with the reality of language, it will not be ability in the use of words, it will be the profanation of the medium which God has established for the conveyance and the interchange of truth. The exalted position is yours. You are the head of a family: if *you* go wrong, the whole family will suffer to the second and third and fourth generations. You are known and trusted in business: if *you* be found mean, untrustworthy, faithless, deceitful, the whole city will feel the anguish of a pang, for you were regarded as a trustee of its honour and its reputation. The anointing oil is upon you in some form or in some way. The name of Christ is upon us all. We cannot get rid of it. In this way or in that we have all to do with Christ, with his name, his honour, his cross, his crown. Tell it not in Gath, publish it not in the streets of Askelon, lest the daughters of Philistia rejoice. Who can tell what savage joy there is when Lucifer, son of the morning, trembles in his orbit—staggers—falls? The anointing oil of the Lord is upon you, and when the Christian professor speaks the base word, does the base deed, bends at the forbidden altar, withholds the sacrifice, forbears to speak the word of faithful testimony and allegiance,—the enemy laughs, and hell says: "Art thou also become as one of us?"

Leviticus x. 12-20.

12. And Moses spake unto Aaron, and unto Eleazar and unto Ithamar, his sons that were left [younger sons should learn lessons from the fate of the elder], Take the meat offering that remaineth [a handful had been burnt on the altar] of the offerings of the Lord made by fire, and eat it without leaven beside the altar [where the altar of burnt offering stood] : for it is most holy :

13. And ye shall eat it in the holy place, because it is thy due, and thy son's due, of the sacrifices of the Lord made by fire: for so I am commanded.

14. And the wave-breast and heave-shoulder shall ye eat in a clean place ; thou, and thy sons, and thy daughters with thee : for they be thy due, and thy sons' due, which are given out of the sacrifices of peace offerings of the children of Israel.

15. The heave-shoulder and the wave-breast shall they bring with the offerings made by fire of the fat, to wave it for a wave offering before the Lord ; and it shall be thine, and thy sons' with thee, by a statute for ever ; as the Lord hath commanded.

16. And Moses diligently sought the goat [the flesh of the goat (ch. ix. 15)] of the sin offering, and, behold, it was burnt: and he was angry with Eleazar and Ithamar, the sons of Aaron which were left alive, saying,

17. Wherefore have ye not eaten the sin offering [ch. vi. 28] in the holy place, seeing it is most holy, and God hath given it you to bear [to remove] the iniquity of the congregation, to make atonement for them before the Lord ?

18. Behold, the blood of it was not brought in within the holy place : ye should indeed have eaten it in the holy place, as I commanded.

19. And Aaron said [he acknowledged his responsibility, though he had not been personally accused] unto Moses, Behold, this day have they offered their [the people's] sin offering and their burnt offering before the Lord ; and such things have befallen me : and if I had eaten the sin offering to-day, should it have been accepted in the sight of the Lord ?

20. And when Moses heard that, he was content.

PRIESTS AND LAWS.

" AND Moses spake unto Aaron,"—the people speaking unto the priest ! That is the eternal law in the true Church. The priest has no existence apart from the people. The people were represented by Moses ; the divine element was represented

by Aaron; but Aaron was *only* a representative—living under
criticism and judgment, and living only—so far as he lived truly—
for the benefit and culture and elevation of the people. The
Bible is the *people's* Bible; it is not the Bible of a class, a priest,
a man-made and man-ruled Church of a mechanical and formal
type, separating itself from the universal instinct, and the universal need of the world. A grand chapter is opened in these
words!—the people speaking unto the priest: the great-heart
speaking to the momentary officer: the instinct of a world
sitting, as it were, in judgment and righteous and generous
criticism upon ceremonies and mediums and momentary arrangements, even though they were divine in their origin and most
beneficent in their purpose. The people are always more than
the priests. The people are always more than the princes.
Kings are nothing but the blossomings of the social tree. Princes
have no existence but for nations. This is a law not to be taught
in one lecture, or to be brought home to the human mind in all
its fulness and generous intent in violent harangue. Knowledge
will secure this end; the spread of wisdom will bring in "the
parliament of man." Meanwhile, no priest must dictate; no
prince must rule despotically. The people are the strength and
the reality, the pith and the whole core of the nations. Moses
must always speak unto Aaron. The pew must always speak
to the pulpit, saying what its need is, telling the man how
far he is speaking to immediate wants and to present necessities,
or how far he is spending eloquent discourse upon people who
are not in existence. Aaron must go down if he pray not
mightily for the people. We cannot have any man continued
amongst us simply because of his office. Office is nothing
except it be associated with noble character, generous impulse,
and divine vocation, and express the eternal thought of God.
But this is an issue not to be hastened. Mechanical operation
can do little or nothing here. Men must grow in grace and in the
knowledge of our Lord Jesus Christ; and not knowing how the
kingdom of the Son of man shall come in—the infinite theocracy
—when no man shall be dragged down but every man shall be
lifted up, and without fire or tempest or high wind rending the
rocks, there shall be heard a still small voice saying, "He is
come whose right it is." Meanwhile, one sign of progress is that

the people shall take an interest in their priests, correcting them, rebuking them, cheering them, responding to them ; when their prayers are offered, all the people shall say, Amen ;—then prayer will be not merely official ; then prayer will be unanimous ; then prayer will mightily prevail.

"And Moses spake unto Aaron. . . . Take the meat offering,"— and he adds,—" for so I am commanded." Moses was not the fountain of authority. There is a spirit in man, and the inspiration of the Almighty giveth him understanding. This was not a clamorous interference with Aaron, an interference merely for the sake of tumult or the assertion of endangered right; it was the representation of a divine purpose and a holy command. This is an instance which shows how the law was looked after. Men make laws and forget them ; they refer to statutes three hundred years old, venerable with the dust of four centuries, and they surprise current opinion by exhumations which show the cleverness and the perseverance of the lawyer. Men are fond of making laws; when they have ignoble leisure, they " improve " it (to use an ironical expression) by adding to the bye-laws, by multiplying mechanical stipulations and regulations, and forgetting the existence of such laws in the very act of their multiplication. God has no dead-letters in his law-book. The law is alive—tingling, throbbing in every letter and at every point. The commandment is exceeding broad; it never slumbers, never passes into obsoleteness, but stands in perpetual claim of right and insistance of decree. It is convenient to forget laws ; but God will not allow any one of his laws to be forgotten. Every inquiry which Moses put to Israel was justified by a statute; he said, "I do but represent the law; there is nothing hypocritical in my examination ; there is nothing super-refined in my judgment ; I am simply asking as the representative of law how obedience is keeping up step with the march of judgment ?" We need such constables to watch the law and to be jealous for its observance and maintenance. Every age needs a grand constabulary force. The time will come when every man will be his own watch, his own critic and judge, and will require no external appeal ; man shall not have occasion to say to man, " Know the Lord,"—for every one shall know him from the least to the greatest ; universality of knowledge shall report itself in unanimity of obedience. God's laws are still alive, we have said; they are alive in nature; even could we sponge them out wherever they are written with ink, we cannot obliterate them as they form part of the very life and economy of creation. Fire still stings; the great sea will drown the vastest navy that ever trespassed on its waves if the laws which govern the ocean be not diligently obeyed—ay, almost to the point of idolatry; men who can use profane language to an invisible God must be up early and sit up late to watch the way of the sea. Thus, at some altar we are always bent: if not at this particular one, then at that. The profanest man is shamed into occasional reverence—bound like a coward at some altar which he would gladly escape. Nature looks after the execution of her own laws; she says to Moses and she says to Aaron and to all the children of men,—I am not mocked; you may mock my Creator, but I am not mocked; you cannot shorten one of my days, you cannot lengthen one of my sunsets, you cannot change the wind from the east to the west, you cannot drive on the procession of the seasons, or substitute one position for another in that serene and glorious march; you may mock my Creator; you may profane your speech by a misuse of his name; you may never look upward in pious wonder, not to say affectionate prayer; but I will not be mocked. So then, this boasted liberty, this magnificent freedom, is itself a caged bird, and the bars of the cage are of no flexible wand but of stiff and stubborn iron. We know we can blaspheme God, and we know that we cannot substitute spring for winter; we will be free and not pray, and we who thus spread paper wings fall down in stupid servitude before laws of ploughing, and sowing, and reaping—as obedient as the oxen that open the furrow. Every inquiry, therefore, which Moses made was founded upon a statute. The commandment of the Lord is everywhere.

"And Moses diligently sought the goat of the sin offering, and, behold, it was burnt: and he was angry with Eleazar and Ithamar, the sons of Aaron which were left alive" (x. 16).

But the flesh ought to have been eaten; a ceremonial law ought to have been observed. The two elder sons of the pontiff had been burnt, and the flesh of the goat of the sin offering had not been eaten, and Moses was angry. He does not name Aaron:

there is a gentle considerateness even in the "meek man's" anger; he will not have the pontiff abased in the sight of the people; he will blame the juniors. But there is an indirect blame that comes back with tremendous recoil upon men nameless who are involved in the responsibility. "And Aaron said unto Moses—" The younger men said nothing; they did not like the fire that burned in the face of Moses, a face soon made radiant either by communion divine, or by indignation because of violated law. So Aaron, recognising his own responsibility, made speech unto Moses. What is the answer to this ceremonial sin? A grand one! A perpetual one! Said Aaron, "Behold, this day have they offered their [the people's] sin offering and their burnt offering before the Lord; and such things have befallen me": and there he sobbed. His two sons had been taken from him by fire: having the anointing oil of the Lord upon him, he was not permitted to go with the dead bodies, to see them buried outside the camp: he remained at his post; but his old heart was sore. We know the experience: still ploughing in the field, whilst a keener plough is ripping up the field of the heart! " . . . and such things have befallen me,"—I will not complain of the judgment: the young men were wrong: God was right: God's holy will be done! But I am a man; we could not eat the flesh to-day, our hearts were sore; if we had eaten the flesh, "should it have been accepted in the sight of the Lord?" The Lord knoweth our frame: he remembereth that we are dust; we know the law, the flesh would under ordinary circumstances have been eaten; but "such things have befallen me," my heart has been torn, my life has been emptied, a great judgment has stretched its black wings over my house-roof, and therefore the law has not been obeyed in the letter. It was a sublime answer; it was a father's explanation; it was a plea of instinct; it was old nature rising against temporary law, a larger law subordinating and for the moment suspending a smaller one. This is God's permission. This is the government under which we live. Instinct has its place in human education as well as ceremonial law, mechanical appointment, and transient stipulations. Aaron here supplies the "one touch of nature" which "makes the whole world kin." His plea holds good to-day. It holds good even in matters purely bodily. The sufferer "ought" to eat;

"But," he says, "such things have befallen me. I ought to partake of food, you are quite right in reminding me of the law; but such things have befallen me : I have just buried my dearest one; I have looked into the grave where my only child lies." Another says, excusing himself, "My child is twice dead · he is gone away, I know not where; I ought to eat and drink and sleep; but such things have befallen me." Thus one law modifies another. The deeper laws assert themselves against the more superficial statutes and ordinances. This plea operates in all social relations. Why was the wedding put off?—"such things have befallen me." Why was the feast postponed?—"such things have befallen me." The hands of the men were upon the bell-ropes, and in a moment more the metal in the belfry would have clashed out in song that would have made the city glad. Why was the belfry dumb?—"such things have befallen me." There are events in life which suspend the feast, which forbid the clash of the joy-bells, hung high in the air, almost eager to swing that they may speak their metallic music to the wondering town. We recall the card of invitation, and substitute it by a card black-edged, eloquent of grief, and in the presence of that dark margin explanation is unnecessary. God is not unpitiful : God is tender; he knows our frame; he says,— "They are but children of the dust; their life is but as a vapour, which cometh for a little time and then vanisheth away; and their days are as a post : they fly quicker than a weaver's shuttle; their breath is in their nostrils." "His mercy endureth for ever." If our very prayer is choked in the throat by ungovernable sorrow, it may in its very off-breaking—in its very interruption—be a mightier prayer than if its eloquence had been rounded in the most resonant periods. We live under a merciful heaven. The sceptre is not of iron, and the hand that holds it is a gentle hand.

There is more in the twentieth verse than the mere letter : "And when Moses heard that, he was content." Some explanations carry their own conviction. We know the voice of honesty when we hear it; there is a frankness about it that can hardly be mistaken. But the meaning lies deeper : there can be no contentment in the presence of violated law. Where a law is violated wantonly, nature can have no rest ; she says,—"I cannot sleep to-night." Thank God she cannot! When she can forget her Maker, the end will have come in darkness, and there will in very deed, in spirit and effect, be no more any God. Law must be satisfied in one of two ways. Law can rest upon the ashes of Sodom and Gomorrah, saying,—"Judgment has been inflicted, righteousness has been vindicated, and the seal of condemnation has been attached to the testimony of evil "; and mighty, imperial, inexorable law sits on the desolated cities— "content." That is not the way in which the Lord would bring about his own contentment; still, there is the law : fall upon this stone and be broken, or the stone will fall upon you and you will be ground to powder. The Gospel is a savour of life unto life, or of death unto death. God would have law obeyed : all his ordinances carried out in simple obedience, every statute turned into conduct, every appointment represented in obedience and praise. Then the universe, faithful to her Creator, the stars never disloyal to their Creator-King,—the whole creation, will say,—CONTENT.

Leviticus xi.

ANIMALS PERMITTED AND FORBIDDEN FOR FOOD.

IT appears from this chapter that laws were not bounded by local circumstances. In that one fact is a divine philosophy, and in that one fact there is a law which, if seized by us and applied to our daily life, will save us from infinite trouble. If the law had been bounded by local circumstances hardly one word of all this elaborate chapter could have been written. The animals that are permitted and that are forbidden had hardly any existence in the wilderness in which the immediate life of Israel was then being spent. The people might have said,— Why permit us to eat animals which are not at hand? Why forbid us to eat food which is not within our reach? Why, in a great desert, lay down rules and regulations about the fish in the sea? Why not confine legislation to immediate environment? That is the rude questioning of human ignorance and impatience. Men of impatient temper will insist upon limiting everything by the exigency of the immediate moment. What wonder if such men have no heaven, no immortality, no future, no sky above their little earth? The philosophy is the same all through and through. Here is the solemn lesson that we are to provide for all life, for all the possibilities of life, for all the yet unknown contingencies of life, as far as they can be forecast and ruled by inspired prudence. Thus in Leviticus we are called to larger life. A very few rules would have done for the local wilderness; the simplicity of the occasion rendered intricate legislation perfectly needless—made it, indeed, quite a burden of superfluity. But life is not all lived in one place; life is not bounded by one little day. It is not enough to look at the immediate point: we must endeavour to bring within our purview all possibilities and argue out the logic of our life upon broad bases, and be sometimes apparently losing our life that we may in the issue the more certainly gain it. Beware of all extemporised law! The very fact of its suddenness deprives it of its dignity. There is no need to make laws under panic. Certain adaptations of law may have to be made suddenly; but the law itself—the abiding and substantial quantity—may be settled an eternity before any direct application becomes necessary. This is the meaning of predestination, foreknowledge, pre-arrangement. The Lamb was slain before Adam fell : sin was provided for before it was committed. The surprise was not in heaven : in heaven eternity rules in all its infinite serenity, its ineffable calm. The very hairs of our head are all numbered. We may easily be thrown into spasm and racked by keen surprise and troubled with many an unexpected tumult; but the Lord liveth in infinite peace ; he knoweth the end from the beginning ; in the wilderness he legislates for the city ; in heaven he legislates for earth ; it was in eternity that he settled the balances in which time's affairs were to be weighed and settled. Better take the long view ; you will be saved from surprise and from the action which may be impaired or perverted by being called upon for instant and unprepared reply. So now in the little world of time men may settle their eternal affairs ; even in this wilderness they can begin their heaven ; close by the grave-side they can sing hymns of immortality. There is no need for haste, or panic, or sore distress of soul, to those who have entered into the divine foresight such as is revealed in this chapter, and who from the beginning have, by the Divine Spirit, settled the issue of all life, and have anticipated and passed not only the bitterness of death, but the solemnity and sternness of judgment.

Suppose we deny the whole of the eleventh chapter of Leviticus, speaking of its pedantry, its frivolity, its unworthiness of a mind infinite and a sovereignty eternal,—suppose we erase the whole chapter—What then ? Here, too, is a grand philosophy : deny the letter, yet there is the chapter as a spirit in the consciousness of every man. To destroy the merely literal chapter is nothing : we leave the fact behind. We *do* elect and we *do* reject. With what, then, do we quarrel ? Simply with the paper and ink and shaped letter—with the law as impressed upon the record by iron. The frivolity, then, is upon our part. If Leviticus were closed, we still turn away from some food with revulsion—from some suggestions with positive disgust; or we yield to other appetences and preferences as if borne towards them by a divine and gentle pressure. Of what avail is it to differ with the letter —to wonder whether the Eternal God would stoop to give directions about this animal and that animal in relation to human consumption—when there is written upon the very surface of life the same law, and we ourselves every day obey an instinct which, indeed, we find it all but impossible to suppress? This reflection would be stripped of most of its value if it related only to the matter of human eating and drinking; but even this suggestion touches the whole circle of human thought and the practical expression of the human will. We deny the super-natural; yet we obey. We all really confess the supernatural: some in solemn testimony well-argued and expressed with great precision of language: others in surprise, in fear, in cowardice for which no preparation had been made, in times of conscience rising to assert itself and making "cowards of us all." It is possible to carry faith in the supernatural clear through the whole line of life; but who ever found it possible to have nothing supernatural through all the undulation and all the uncalculated variety of life? Who has not sometimes been suddenly blanched by what might have been a ghostly presence in the air? Who has not sometimes almost so faltered as to fall upon his knees in attitude of supplication? Who has carried reason, pure and simple, without horizon, without ghostliness, without fear, right through the whole quantity of life? I have never met that man. Though we quibble in argument about the supernatural, we obey; though we discuss in high controversy about faith, yet we live a faith-life, and cannot help it. The atheist walks by faith and not by sight. The very men who are quibbling about the place of faith in the development and education of the human race cease their quibbling that they may obey the necessities of the universe. We suggest objections to the doctrine of the innocent suffering for the guilty, and when we have closed our wordy fray we go out to do the very thing which we had just declared to be impossible: the debater illustrates the fallacy of his own argument. All through life the innocent are as a matter of fact suffering for the guilty: the son of man is dying for the sons of men. The principle of vicaric isness rules the whole economy of human development and progress. Our denials, therefore, are always but in terms : in our own life we re-affirm the doctrine which in our intellectual vanity we had questioned. Thus is God Master : even thus do circumstances make men theologians and force them into truth which they could never accept in merely formal proposition. Hence the axiom— for such it almost is, not only in its terseness but in its truthfulness—that "some men are better than their creed." This is God's interpretation of our life. Were he to be judging by our words, he could convict us of solecism and contradiction amounting to falsehood, and of irony amounting to profanity ; but he looks upon the heart, and about many a man he may be saying, in effect,—" Poor soul ! how he foams in argument, yet how noble he is in suffering ! Poor half-wild creature ! how he vexes himself by the misuse of terms, but how complete he is in patience ! How he troubles himself about the philosophy of prayer—not knowing that the very sigh he heaves after his vexation is itself a noble cry to the Unseen and Infinite." Thus many may come from the east and from the west, from the north and from the south, and be made members of the kingdom of heaven who in mere words have been ranked among the opposition, the sceptical and those who have had no certitude of religious position and hope. Cheer your hearts, then, about your sons and your daughters ! Lift up your heads, for you may not have lost from the Church so many as in your unworthy fear you had supposed. God is the Judge. Behind the denial in words he may find the confirmation in feeling and in action.

Judging by this schedule of regulations as to eating and not eating, it would appear that uses and values are not to be determined along one line only. Some things mentioned here are not to be *eaten;* yet they may be useful. The "not" is a very small limitation : it refers to one direction only. Some animals are to *be* eaten ; yet they are not therefore to be despised. Who can foretell their destiny ? eaten by the poet, they may become poetry ; sanctified by the eater, they may be lifted into new significance. There is no one exclusive standard by which value is to be determined in these matters. This is a very wide law like the others. This man is not a scholar ; but he is a genius ; he has

no information, but he has inspiration. Do not misjudge him.
The other man is not a genius, but he is a scholar; he is useful :
he abounds in knowledge : he can correct a thousand mistakes :
he can direct life upon an upward road. We must, therefore,
—such seems to be the spirit of the law—not confine our judgment
to one direction or to another, but remember that as we are many
members yet one body, so we in our higher relations represent
a great diversity, yet a most solid and gracious unity. Let us be
careful about these matters. This is the infirmity of the critic :
that he can see in one direction only. The glory of the judge is
that he takes in the whole case, balancing, distributing, arranging,
and estimating the entire situation, with the calmness of wisdom
and with the penetration of an upright and unbiassed mind.

A very popular argument is upset by this chapter. There
is an argument which runs in this fashion : Why should we not
eat and drink these things, for they are all good creatures of God ?
The temptation of man is to find a "good creature of God"
wherever he wants to find one. The doctor, yielding to human
infirmity, permits, rather than sanctions or commands, certain
little indulgences, and the receiver of the permission instantly
turns the permission into a statute and commandment and seals
it with the doctorial seal ! We are easily led in the direction of
our preferences. All the animals in this chapter were good
creatures of God, in the sense of having been created by the
Almighty. "And these are they which ye shall have in
abomination among the fowls; they shall not be eaten, they are
an abomination : the eagle, and the ossifrage, and the ospray,
and the vulture, and the kite after his kind ; every raven after
his kind ; and the owl, and the night hawk, and the cuckow, and
the hawk after his kind, and the little owl, and the cormorant,
and the great owl, and the swan, and the pelican, and the gier
eagle, and the stork, the heron after her kind, and the lapwing,
and the bat." Who made these ? God. Then are they not good
creatures of God ? Possibly so ; but they are forbidden in that
particular use. You do not depose the creature from any dignity
to which it is entitled as a creation of God : you do but discern
the right use and purpose of the creature in the intent of God.
This argument must be applied by every man according to his
own circumstances The argument of the chapter does not end

in itself. What does end in itself? There are educational beginnings; there are points to start with. The argument is cumulative and becomes stronger and stronger as the instances are plied in illustration of its meaning. Is God so careful about the body and has he written no schedule of directions about the feeding of the mind? May the body not eat of this, but the soul eat of everything? Are there poisons which take away the life of the body, and no poisons that take away the life of the spirit, the mind, the soul? That is the chapter magnified by spirituality. This is an instance of how things may be made symbols of truth infinitely greater than themselves. It is impossible to believe that God, who takes care of the body, pays no attention to the soul. He who feeds the fowls of the air will feed his children is an argument we do well to reiterate, because we feel at once how true it is and gracious. Why not be consistent with our own reasoning? The very fact that God could take such pains in keeping us back from the use of such animals, begins the infinite argument that his anxiety is to save the soul from poison, corruption, death. "Turn ye, turn ye, why will ye die?" Let your soul delight itself in fatness; Wisdom hath prepared her feast: the viands are heaven-tasted and are all approved: sit down, eat and drink,—yea, eat and drink abundantly; there is no poison in the bread, there is no death in the pot, and the banner over the feast is Love. May a man eat lies,—may a man devour false teaching, and be none the worse for the meal which the soul has eaten ravenously? Has a man to be very critical and dainty about the food which his body consumes, and is he to sit down at every table spread for his intellectual satisfaction and to eat and drink whatever comes without exercising the spirit of criticism and discernment? It is an insult to reason to suggest a vanity so evident and so complete. You are particular about the cleanness of your body, and you are right; but being faithful to that daintiness you must go further and see that the soul is unspotted—pure as heaven's purity. You are most careful not to eat and to drink what will injure and disturb and unsettle you, or subject you to momentary inconvenience: so far you are right; but being right there, do not play the fool in the heedless satisfaction of your mind or in the glutting of your soul beware what is offered for the spirit's consumption—for the Lord has "no pleasure in the death of the wicked." Bread of Life, feed me! Lord, evermore give us this living bread. We would eat of thy flesh and drink of thy blood, and so escape the tyranny and the bitterness of death. We would accept the hospitality of Heaven. We bless thee that thou hast saved us by instinct and by law from eating and drinking that which would injure us : now, Lord, give us the intuition, the inspiration, which will enable us to see in a moment what is false, what is impure, what is unworthy of our soul's inner purpose, and having seen what is so unworthy, may we touch not, taste not, handle not, the unclean thing, but ever keep within our Father's house, where there is bread enough and to spare.

NOTE.

It is noteworthy that the practical effect of the rule laid down is to exclude all the *carnivora* among quadrupeds, and, so far as we can interpret the nomenclature, the *raptores* among birds. This suggests the question whether they were excluded as being not averse to human carcases, and in most Eastern countries acting as the servitors of the battlefield and the gibbet. Even swine have been known so to feed ; and further, by their constant runcation among whatever lies on the ground, suggest impurity, even if they were not generally foul feeders. Amongst fish those which were allowed contain unquestionably the most wholesome varieties, save that they exclude the oyster. Probably, however, sea-fishing was little practised by the Israelites; and the Levitical rules must be understood as referring backwards to their experience of the produce of the Nile, and forwards to their enjoyment of the Jordan and its upper lakes. The exclusion of the camel and the hare from allowable meats is less easy to account for, save that the former never was in common use, and is generally spoken of in reference to the semi-barbarous desert tribes on the eastern or southern borderland, some of whom certainly had no insuperable repugnance to his flesh; although it is so impossible to substitute any other creature for the camel as "the ship of the desert," that to eat him, especially where so many other creatures give meat so much preferable, would be the worst economy possible in an Eastern commissariat—that of destroying the best, or rather the only conveyance, in order to obtain the most indifferent food. The hare was long supposed, even by eminent naturalists, to ruminate, and certainly was eaten by the Egyptians. . . . As regards the animals allowed for food, comparing them with those forbidden, there can be no doubt on which side the balance of wholesomeness lies. Nor would any dietetic economist fail to pronounce in favour of the Levitical dietary code as a whole, as ensuring the maximum of public health and yet of national distinctness, procured, however, by a minimum of the inconvenience arising from restriction.— SMITH'S *Dictionary of the Bible.*

Leviticus xiii., xiv.

THE LAW OF LEPROSY.

THE thirteenth and fourteenth chapters are occupied with the question of leprosy. With that disease we have now, happily, nothing to do in this country; yet those who care to peruse the note at the end of this discourse will find that England was once ravaged by that terrible disease. It would be pleasant to turn over the thirteenth and fourteenth chapters, and to escape to subjects less revolting; but pleasure is not the law of life. It is here that so many men fritter away their days and altogether mistake the divine purpose of education. Men set up their "taste." When a man talks about his "taste," he has no taste to be proud of. Look at this large question in the light of religious history and human progress. What was to be done when leprosy was suspected? "The priest shall look." Would you hasten away from that great saying? Why that is the key of history. You would escape from the richest thought if you escaped from the fact that God has trained the human race from the religious instinct. Where was the doctor? There was no doctor then; he is a later creation. He came in due course and by pressure of necessity, having regard to the widening expanse of civilisation; but the priest was the doctor, —and the priest is the only true doctor in every age. "The priest shall look"? Why not confine himself to his own work? Why not stay within the church and do the priestly rites and ceremonies, and let the leper alone? No work is excluded from the priest. The priest has, indeed, lived downwards and backwards, and given up his heritage and his rights and properties, and has cut down his divine vocation with a ruthless hand; but, rightly interpreted, the minister of God is the doctor of the world, the musician of the world, the father of the fatherless, the leader of the blind, the great schoolmaster, the gentle unwearying shepherd,—he is the son of man. He has allowed himself to be snubbed out of nine-tenths of his work; he has permitted himself to be enclosed in a certain way, and to be shut up within certain boundaries and points; but that is his blame—his apostasy in the Eden which includes the world—and if he has fallen into a little man, it is not because God's vocation was a limited call. The Church is the true lazar-house; the Church is the great hospital; the Church is the dame-school, presided over by gentlest mother, who collects us all around her, and helps us in the spelling and building up and speaking out of words. But we have allowed the fool to prate over us and to tell ministers to confine themselves to their own work, as if they were artisans or specialists, not having right over all flesh, all history, all poetry, all music, all progress. The doctor is but *part* of the minister—a spark flashed out of the greater fire. The true priest—the seer, and interpreter—is the foremost man of the age : beyond him is One only, and that is God. In old history the priests were the doctors; in our own history the priests are the leeches. What is the meaning of this ? The profound philosophy of it is, that it is from the religious point, or instinct, that all history is developed. We are told that of course in the early ages all learning was with the monks. That does not impair the proposition that has been laid down; that circumstance rather increases the evidence of the truthfulness and cogency of that proposition. How did all learning come to be associated with the monk, or religious man ? The same philosophy is here. Life is associated with the religious instinct,— prying into all things, knocking at every door to have it opened, looking over every water and wondering what shores are lying beyond its waves. If religion has allowed itself to be shut up in some church cellar, religion, in its human relations, must blame itself. It was meant to stand on the mountains, to rule the nations, to lead every holy war, and to settle the tumult of the world into the peace of heaven. The largeness of the religious responsibility continues. The Church is responsible for the ignorance of the world. Do not blame the State—a poor little machine, a shed run up in the night-time for protection against the weather. The Church is responsible for every man this day that does not know the name of Christ, the claim of God, the holiness of honour, and the duties of civilisation. The Church is responsible for every child that cannot write its name. But the Church has fallen upon small ideas, little comforts, seventh-day indulgences, half-day hearings, and these marked by extreme reluctance or spoiled by pedantic criticism. The heroic conception—the vocation to seize the world, arrest it, fight its enemies, shut up its hell—has been misinterpreted or forgotten. Read history, and be just to the religious instinct. It is easy to see where civilisation, having entered into elaborate redistribution of offices and positions, may have forgotten its original obligations: it is easy for a man to forget at whose torch he lighted his own ; but search back through the days and nights of history, and you will find that the first torch was kindled by the hand of God. We soon become forgetful ; it is easy to drop into the spirit of ingratitude. We may look at the sky until its very blue becomes commonplace.

All this care, outlined with so complete an elaboration, was not meant for the sake of the individual alone,—it contemplated the protection of the whole body of the people. Why this anxiety about a man who shows signs of the plague ? For his own sake, certainly ; but largely for the sake of the uncontaminated host. The man was to be put outside the camp or to be shut up in a dwelling of his own : for a period he was to be cut off from his people and made to live a solitary life. Did the priest order this punishment with the view of afflicting the poor sufferer himself ? Unquestionably not ; the priest had no wish to add solitude to pain, exile to defilement. The priest represented the spirit of compassion—soft, tender, healing pity ; but it was the large pity that not only looked at the sufferer himself, but regarded the unnumbered hosts who might be affected by the defilement of the leper, were the leper permitted to sustain his customary relations. "No man liveth to himself." The camp was afraid of contagion. Save the untouched by expelling the defiled. Look at the precautions taken by ourselves in case of disease : how we publish the names of affected neighbourhoods ; how we protest against the erection of buildings appropriated to endeavours to cure certain malignant and infectious diseases ; how we blanch under the intelligence that cholera or small-pox has threatened an invasion of the country. What anxiety ! What endeavours to prevent the ravages of the disease! All this is right; but it throws into tremendous and appalling contrast our carelessness about the contagion that poisons the soul. There is a moral contamination; there is a mental defilement. " Evil communications corrupt good manners." " My son, if sinners entice thee, consent thou not." We do not know what evil we are working by the subtle influence of contagion. It is not needful for the infected man to go and deliberately touch the unaffected man, as if by an act of violence : we spoil the air. We drop a word and think no more about it ; but that word is working for evil in the soul of the youth who heard it ; we indulge a jest which hides impurity, and the impurity works when the jest is forgotten ; we throw out a suspicion, and pass away as if we had done no wrong,—better fill the air with poison and kill a thousand men a day than unsettle the soul's faith, trouble the moral confidence, risk the eternal destiny of men. Why are we not consistent with our own logic ? Why do we not complete our own view of cleanness ? Any man who can content himself with external purity is not a pure man ; he is a trickster, a mechanician, a man who attends to externals. Only he is clean in the flesh who is clean in the spirit. You cannot wash a man with an unclean spirit to any effect, even in the flesh ; the evil oozes through the burnished skin ; the iniquity comes through every pore. What we should look after is moral consistency. We are anxious to shut out a disease that would kill the body, and yet open all the doors and all the windows and let in the diseases which infect and poison and damn the soul. Out of thine own mouth will I condemn thee !

It is interesting and instructive to note that the pure man can alone deal effectively and harmlessly with corrupt and pestilent subjects. This lesson can never be taught to some minds. The priest represented purity ; we have seen what pains have been taken to purify him, to sanctify him, and consecrate him ; we have been present in all the process, and now the priest ideally represents purity, divine holiness. We have no instruction to the effect that one leper is to look on another ; the distinct direction is that the priest—the holy, pure man—shall look at the leper—handle him, undertake him. Send the holy to the unholy ; send the Christ of God to the sinners of the earth :

he has " gone to be guest with a man that is a sinner." Religiou⁹
men should take up all bad questions ; but they will not. The
mischief is that such men should take upon themselves the
responsibility of representing the kingdom of God. Why are not
they infidels, if we must have infidels upon the earth for a time ?
I should turn all the imperfect and misinterpreting professors
of Christianity into infidels, for such they are, and they are
such of the very worst type. The Church is burdened with men
who do not understand the genius of the kingdom of heaven.
When our holiest women are found in our unholiest places, know
ye that the kingdom of heaven is at hand : the day is dawning ;
the sweetest wife we have is away seeking the piece that is lost.
But she will be defiled ? Never ! She will be exposed to
danger ? No ! Not when the theologues have balanced their
wordy battles and foolish misunderstandings, but when the holy
lives are sitting down with lives unholy, will the orient whiten
and the day dawn, and Christ " see of the travail of his soul."
It is no sign of piety to turn away from revolting subjects and to
say,—We cannot enter into this because our taste is offended,
and our feelings are shocked. Whoever says so is a knave in
the Church ; he has no right to sit down where Christ sits ; he is
worse than Iscariot ; he is a traitor for whom no death has been
devised sufficiently awful. These people abound on every hand ;
they are the plague of society ! Raise a very evil report about
a man : make it very bad : spare no charge : enlarge the
accusation until it takes in all things revolting, shocking, and
instantly nearly all the pious people you have ever known will
leave the man because the accusations are so shocking. Accuse
him of some trifling violation of etiquette, or propriety, and
twenty men may be willing to share his fate, or abate the force
of the social blow that is aimed at him ; but make the accusation
bad enough : especially introduce into it elements of obscenity,
and you will hear so-called Christian people say that they have
no wish to enter into subjects of that kind. The very people who
ought to say " What are they ? when did they occur ?—let the
witnesses stand up "—will speak of their taste and their sensitiveness, and the delicacy of their bringing-up, and will abandon
the man. *Those* people are the infidels. Do not believe—I
speak to inquirers as to the extent of the divine temple and the

meaning of the divine kingdom—do not believe that wordy
opponents are the infidels; those are the infidels who profess to
know Christ, and yet know nothing of the infinite pity, valour,
nobleness, and deity of his spirit. Let the priest look on the
man accused. The priest must never be afraid. The priest
must enter the house where small-pox is, or leprosy, or cholera;
let others cry fear if they will—the priest resigns his priesthood
when he resigns his courage. Christ was holy, harmless, un-
defiled; yet he was the Guest of sinners, he received sinners,
he ate and drank with sinners, he spake to sinners as never
man spake; to the lost woman he said,—Sister, begin again.

Men turn away from the perusal of such chapters, and look
complacently upon moral leprosy. Men who would walk a mile
to avoid an infected house, will read the very last book that the
devil has published, and allow the devil to cut the pages for
them; men who are so dainty that they could on no account pass
by certain hospitals, have in their libraries books that poison
the soul; men who would be alarmed if they knew that their
children were exposed to companionship with children who have
the *whooping-cough*, will tell lies by the hour;—pitiable men!
shameful men! Men who would not allow any child of theirs to
look upon a drunken man, will allow their children to hear
themselves speaking evil of their neighbour all day long. What
inconsistency! what irony! But this is the difficulty of Christ:
that whatever is objective, tangible, and fleshly, has, by reason
of its substance, an advantage over the moral, spiritual, invisible,
and immortal. The conduct of men is not always against God
only, it is against inward honour, conscience, moral right,
spiritual sensitiveness; the atheism is not a speculation which
challenges the heavens, it is a practice which embitters the
fountains of life.

Read the thirteenth and fourteenth chapters of Leviticus through
without stopping, then read Jesus Christ's cure of leprosy, and
compare the two. The leper said: "Lord, if thou wilt, thou
canst make me clean. . . . I will"—and the man was cleansed.
"Jesus, Master, have mercy on us"; and Jesus said,—"Go show
yourselves unto the priests"; and as they went the burden fell
off, and they stood up in the purity and suppleness of renewed
youth; one soul was so filled with gratitude that he went back

to bless his Benefactor. You can hardly have a more striking instance of the difference between the ancient ritual and the Christian dispensation than by reading the thirteenth and fourteenth chapters of Leviticus, and then reading in immediate connection the history of the cure of leprosy by Jesus Christ. We are all afflicted with leprosy; the disease is within. Jesus Christ is within our cry : we can now make him' hear : let each say with an honest heart, "Lord, if thou wilt, thou canst make me clean; create in me a clean heart, O God, and renew a right spirit within me," and we shall escape all this elaborate ritual, all this exclusion, and separation, and purification, and at a word—the creative, redeeming word—we shall stand up clean men, pure souls. *"Lord, I believe, help thou mine unbelief."*

NOTE.

Many imagine leprosy to be some obscure disease alluded to only in the Bible. Leprosy was also a disease of the Middle Ages, more widely spread and more fearful in its results than any other in ancient or modern times. It is probable that the worst form of leprosy in early Jewish history was that now known as *elephantiasis.* The milder form of Jewish leprosy, called *bohak*, was neither severe nor contagious.

Leprosy in England and Europe arose gradually after the destruction of the Roman Empire, as fast as barbarism spread with its uncleanliness of personal habits, and its resort to animal food and beer as nearly exclusive articles of daily diet. In all ancient towns it was early found necessary to erect hospitals and retreats and churches for those afflicted with leprosy. We have in England, now, hospitals built for lepers, so ancient that theii origin is unknown, such as the St. Bartholomew Hospital at Gloucester, and others. It is known that there were at least 9,000 hospitals in Europe for leprosy alone. Louis VII. of France left legacies to over 2,000 hospitals for lepers in his country. We have extant a touching account of a knight of vast wealth and influence, named Amiloun, expelled from his castle to be a beggar, almost in sight of his vast possessions and stately home; for the Normans in France virtually outlawed, as well as expelled from their homes all lepers, and, as soon as their influence was established in England, they extended their sanitary measures and benevolent enterprise to lepers.

Hugo, or Eudo Dapifer—the steward for William the Conqueror— having received from him vast possessions of land in Essex, built or rebuilt, and endowed a St. Mary Magdalen Hospital for lepers in Colchester. The hospital for lepers, dedicated to the same saint, in the city of Exeter, is of unknown antiquity. Bartholomew, bishop of that city and diocese (1161-1184), finding its usefulness limited for want of funds, and the sufferings ot lepers unlimited, endowed it with considerable wealth. He gave it for ever five marks of silver yearly—the tenth of a certain toll, and the profits arising for ever from the sale of the bark of his wood at Chudleigh. His example stimulated the chapter of St. Peter's, in the same city, to grant a weekly dole of bread for ever. The good bishop Bartholomew wearied the Pope to give a charter to the hospital, making the endowment an everlasting benefaction, as he viewed the curse of leprosy to be as wide-spreading as humanity, and as lasting as the race of man. But he died before his wishes were gratified. However, Pope Celestine III. granted or confirmed a charter in the year 1192, and the charity exists to this day.

Hubert, Archbishop of Canterbury, held a synod at Westminster, in the year 1200, to carry out the decree of the Council of Lateran (1172), to build a number of churches solely for leprous people, for they had long been expelled from all parish churches. They were to have priests, officers, and graveyards exclusively for themselves. They were released at the same time from all claims for tithes for their land or cattle. So careful and determined were our ancestors to remove from sight and smell every leper, that a law was early in existence to enforce their removal out of towns and villages "to a solitary place." The writ is in our ancient law-books, entitled *De Leprose Amovendo*, and it is fully stated by Judge Fitz-Herbert in his *Natura Brevium*. King Edward III., finding that, in spite of the old law, leprous persons were concealed in houses inhabited by other persons, gave commandment to the Lord Mayor and Sheriffs to make proclamation in every ward of the city and its suburbs, "that all *leprous* persons inhabiting there should avoid within fifteen days next," etc., etc.

At the city of Bath, a bath, with physicians and attendants, was endowed —exclusively for lepers—and the endowments are still paid. That the bath was occasionally effiacious, in connection with improved diet, we have sure evidence ; for one leper in late days had fixed to the bath a mural tablet to say that "William Berry, of Garthorpe, near Melton Mowbray, in the county of Leicester, was cured of a dry leprosy by the help of God and the bath, 1737."—GIBSON WARD.

Leviticus xxiii. 44.

"And Moses declared unto the children of Israel the feasts of the Lord."

PLEASANT MINISTRIES.

THE principal Jewish festivals were, the Feast of Passover or unleavened bread; the Feast of Pentecost; the Feast of Weeks or of the harvest, or of the day on which were offered the loaves made of the new wheat; the Feast of Trumpets, called by the Jews *New Year;* and the Day of Atonement, or the Great Sabbath; the Feast of Tabernacles or the Ingathering of the Harvest. Owing to the difficulty of travelling no festival was appointed for winter; there was one in the spring, one in the summer, and four were appointed for the autumn. The feasts of Passover, Pentecost, and Tabernacles were called pilgrimage festivals, and were of a doubly joyful character, commemorative of national events and relating to the blessings of the seasons and the land. Besides the great annual feasts there were more occasional festivals, as, *e.g.,* the weekly Sabbath, the feast of the new moon, the Sabbath year, and the year of Jubilee. With these festivals in their local setting we have nothing to do; our business is with the perpetual truth which glows in the terms, " And Moses declared unto the children of Israel the feasts of the Lord." What a change in his great ministry! Never was man charged with the delivering of so many disciplinary and legal words. It is time that he had something to say with easier music in it, conveying a pleasanter appeal to the imagination and the whole attention of Israel. It was a new mission. The lips of Moses must have grown hard in the delivery of hard speeches. It was his business always to deliver law, to recall to duty, to suppress revolution, to command and overawe the people whose fortunes he humanly led. What wonder if the people dreaded his appearance? That appearance might have been equal to a new Sinai, a new Decalogue,—a harder speech of law and duty and servitude. It was a pleasant thing for Moses, too, this change in the tone of his ministry; he is now speaking of feasts, of festivals,—times of solemn rejoicing,—yea, some of the very feasts which were instituted were designated by names the roots of which signified to dance and be glad with great joy. An awful fate for any man to be merely the legal prophet of his age! A most burdensome mission always to be called upon to rebuke and chastise, to suppress, and to put men down to their proper level, and call them up to their proper obedience! Thus the Lord varies the ministry of his servants. He says, There will be no utterance of new law to-day, but this very day shall be a day of feasting and music and dancing; he will have a home in the wilderness—a glad, warm, happy home all troublesome memories shall be dismissed and one over-mastering joy shall rule this festal day. That is the speech he has been longing to make; but we would not let him. He never wanted to make any other speech; we ourselves forced the hard terms from his reluctant lips. A complete ministry is terrible and gracious. It is terrible by the necessities of the case. Consider the nature with which the ministry of heaven has to deal: "there is none righteous, no not one"; we have turned aside from the right way and are far from the centres of light and rest and peace; sometimes nothing will reach us but fear, terror, awful denunciation of anger, and judgment. Our mother tongue would be deficient of one instrument which alone can touch some men, were we to remove from that sweetest tongue the word "perdition," or the word "hell." We do not want it: we avoid it when we can; we would not set it in our eloquence, or weave it into our music, or use it upon any occasion if we could possibly do without it; it is a word which is used in reply to infinite provocation; he who has pleasure in the use of it knows not its meaning; he who declines its use altogether knows not the mystery of the nature which he has undertaken to reclaim and educate. Paul said, "Knowing therefore the terror of the Lord, we persuade men." The apostle used terror as an instrument of persuasion: not to keep men away from God, but to draw them near to the Father. That is the right use of all solemn terms and fearful judgments, all burning fires, all unutterable and infinite threatenings,—namely, to bring men to consideration, to penitence, to newness of mind. But the ministry is also gentle : there is no gentleness like it. The true ministry of Christ is marked by surpassing and ineffable grace : its eyes are full of tears; its great trumpet-tones are broken down by greater sobs; it pities the weak; it speaks a word of hope to the fallen ; it tells the farthest off that there is time for him to get home before the nightfall, or if he be overtaken with the darkness the light will be in the house he has abandoned; it pleads with men; it beseeches men to be reconciled to God ; it writes its promises in syllables of stars ; it punctuates its speech with fragrant flowers; it breaks down into the omnipotence of weakness by clinging to the sinner when all men have abandoned him in despair. We must establish a whole ministry. The mountain must have two sides : the side where the darkness lingers ; the side where the light plays and dances in many a symbolism. This is human life. The two sides must go together. When the ministry thunders its law, it must be upheld ; when it breaks down in tears over the Jerusalem that has rejected it, it must be regarded as the very heart of God.

Notice the time when the feasts were spoken of. Let us regard the very position of the text as instructive. We have now read up to it ; beginning with the bondage in Egypt, dwelling tearfully and sympathetically upon that pagan servitude,— watching the children of Israel led forth by a mighty hand, we have noted the discipline which afflicted them educationally ; by this time we have become familiar with their hardships,— now it is a welcome relief to the reader to come upon festival, dancing, joy, delight,— one touch of heaven in a very wilderness of desolation. This is the day we have longed for. There was a hope hidden in our hearts that, by-and-by, golden gates would swing back upon happy places and offer us the liberty of heaven. We have come to that Sabbatic time ; now we are in times of jubilee and Sabbath, release, pardon, rapture,—praising God all the time, having found a temple without a roof, a sanctuary without a wall,—an infinite liberty vast as the Being which it adores. This is a picture of life wisely ordered. It is a pity when **any life begins** with the feast.   It is sad to see pampered children.   What can make the wise man's heart sorer than to see children whose every want is anticipated, who have no burdens to carry, no darkness to fear, no enemy to grapple with ? It makes the spirit sad !   The student of history knows what a fate awaits those fair children—those sweet little ones.   Every life must have its battle-field.   The devil never allowed any soul to pass through without having to fight every inch of the way. Blessed are they who had their bondage first—their hard toil in the first years of life, when they went home to a fireless grate, and sat down in the very midst of desolation ; when every wind was a ghostly threat ; when the morning brought but a variety of darkness ; when the night came with new terrors and alarms. Blessed are they who fought early and got the battle over soon ; they had a hard struggle : they were struck on one side of the head and on the other, and thrown down by invisible hands, but they dashed the tears away, or burned them in the fire of new courage, and stood up again like men.   " It is good for a man to bear the yoke in his youth."   A terrible indictment is being written against people who imagine they can invert the purpose of Providence and rule life by new tricks in confectionery and pampering.   Who are the strong men in the city, in the market-place, in any department and sphere of life ?   The men who carry scars and wound-marks—signatures of early battle, medals which testify that they met the foe and flung him in mortal wrestling.   Who are the weak and the frail and the useless—those who are but shells painted in colours that will not stand the wear and tear of life ?   To that inquiry no answer in words need be given.   God's plan is to train us for the feast.   Who enjoys the feast ?   Not the sated appetite, not the cloyed palate ; but the labourer from the field ; the soldier who unbuckles his military robe and throws down his weapons with a soldier's heartiness ; the man who has been out in the long wet night ; the traveller who has just come to the summit of the hill ; the pilgrim who brings with him all the fresh wind, the keen air of night, and the toil of a long ascent. Set down these men, and their very look is a benediction, their very way of eating is itself a religious expression.   This feast has been in the divine view from the very beginning : God has always meant hope, feasting, dancing, joy, liberty. Let us repeat, for our soul's profit, that all things contrary to these have been of our own invention, or have been necessitated by our evil behaviour. " God . . made man upright ; but " men " have sought out many inventions." Let us leave ourselves in the divine hands ; at the last, gathered around the table of God, spread by his hands, every guest shall say, " Thou hast kept the good wine until now."

Notice whose feasts they were, and how joy is ennobled by solemnity. " And Moses declared unto the children of Israel the feasts of the Lord." They were not fools' revels ; they were not inventions even of Moses and Aaron ; they were as certainly divine creations as were the stars that glittered above. The highest joy is always touched with melancholy. It has been said that laughter and tears lie close together ; singular is that, but most true to our own consciousness and experience. We sigh at the wedding. There is so much joy and gracious hilarity, that he is supposed to be criminal to the genius of the occasion who utters one word of gloom ; but the hearing ear has detected, in father or mother or friend, the sigh that meant it all. At the funeral we quote words that should make the face one broad and gracious smile ; we feast at the grave side : the promises never eat so well, with so keen a relish on the part of the eater, as when the soul really feels its need of divine sustenance and inspiration. Did the Lord make feasts ? He may have done so. Is " feasts " not a word too frivolous to associate with the name of the Lord ? No. If we are to judge by analogy,—No. The God of flowers may be the God of feasts. We know the flowers are his ; we know that no Solomon has ever arrayed himself in equal beauty ; he who made those flowers *must* have made a feast somewhere, a feast of reason, a feast for the soul, a luxury for the inner taste, an appeal to the larger appetency. He who made the birds may surely be the God of the soul's music. The birds sing so blithely, without one touch of vanity ; so purely, so independently, without pedantry, without sign or hint of human education ; the God who set their little throats in tune may surely be the God of all pure music,—the mother's broad laugh over her little one, the father's tender voice in the presence of distress and need ; and he who made the birds' throat may have put it into the mind of man to make the trumpet, and the cornet, and the flute, and the harp, and the sackbut, and the psaltery; they *may* be his judging by the happy analogies of nature. He who made summer, may have made heaven! There is but a step between them. When Summer is at her best, what wonder if she should think herself sister of the blue heavens? She is certainly lovely, nothing wanting in the completeness of her beauty : here so lofty and stately, there so pendent and graceful, yonder so fragrant and odorous as if with messages from paradise, and otherwhere so blithe and warm and gentle, climbing up in woodbine to the sick child's little chamber, and uttering messages of hope to the mother's heart, bidding all invalids come out and enjoy the feast. Whoever made that summer *must* have made a heaven; standing in the summer meads, walking through the summer gardens, loitering by summer streams, watching summer heavens, it is easy to sing—

> " There is a and of pure delight,
> Where saints immortal reign ;
> Infinite day excludes the night,
> And pleasures banish pain. "

No other hymn would suit the music of the time!

The gospel is a feast. Jesus Christ makes his kings spread feasts and issue large invitations, and when the mighty and the proud and the grand will not come, he sends men out into the highways and the hedges to bring in the traveller, the beggar, the homeless one. To Christ's feast all are invited; no exception can be made. Yet there are exceptions : the Pharisee, the self-righteous man, the critic of other people, is forbidden; Christ will have no cold souls at his banqueting-board—none there who imagines he is conferring patronage upon God. Man cannot patronise the Church. The Church may have so debased herself as to accept patronage; but therein she has been disloyal to the divine call. Ho, every one that thirsteth,—whosoever will, let him come; the Spirit and the Bride say, Come; let him that heareth say, Come. The great invitation is issued from end to end of the Gospel message, and if we turn to it a deaf ear, the result is hunger, pining, wasting,—death! This feast never cloys. All other feasts bring their own ending; even the glutton says, with a porcine voice, " No more "; the voluptuary and the sensualist withdraw themselves from the feast by which they have been sated; but in the feast of wisdom, in the banquet of grace, there is no satiety. "Doth not wisdom cry? and understanding put forth her voice? She standeth in the top of high places, by the way in the places of the paths. She crieth at the gates, at the entry of the city, at the coming in at the doors. Unto you, O men, I call; and my voice is to the sons of man. O ye simple, understand wisdom: and, ye fools, be ye of an understanding heart. Hear; for I will speak of excellent things; and the opening of my lips shall be right things." "Wisdom hath builded her house, she hath hewn out her seven pillars: she hath killed her beasts; she hath mingled her wine; she hath also furnished her table. She hath sent forth her maidens: she crieth upon the highest places of the city, Whoso is simple, let him turn in hither: as for him that wanteth understanding, she saith to him, Come, eat of my bread, and drink of the wine which I have mingled."

A gracious voice! a glad, grand gospel! If hitherto ye have been living amid the sounding of law, the utterance of decree,—if, up to this moment, ye have been trembling under the sight of the rod and in the presence of gleaming judgment, know ye that now the feast of the Lord is declared, and whoso is shut out is self-excluded!

"HANDFULS OF PURPOSE,"
FOR ALL GLEANERS.

"And the Lord called unto Moses."—
LEVIT. i. I.

The calls of Providence.—Their number and variety.—Every man is conscious of a call to higher life and duty.—Account for it as we may, there is an inward voice alluring us in one of two directions.—The voice of the Lord is not the only voice that addresses human attention.—The devil speaks as well as God.—The two voices can be easily distinguished by any earnest hearer who is determined upon doing the right deed.—There are appeals addressed to self-interest and self-indulgence ; these are the appeals which are never made by God.—There are also appeals addressed to selfish cleverness and ingenuity, showing how prosperity can be secured or how personal interests can be advanced ; such appeals need not be long considered as to their moral value : they bear upon them the stamp of an evil genius.—God's calls are always in the direction of self-sacrifice, beneficence, higher and higher holiness.—God calls through circumstances ; through convictions ; through the spontaneous action of friends of solid character ; we are called upon to beware of every allurement that does not point in a distinctly lofty direction.—God calls to deeper study of the Word.—God calls to beneficent activity on behalf of others.

—It is a deception of the enemy to suppose that we cannot always distinguish the voice of the divine. Whilst that may be true enough as to certain practical details which are so intermixed as not to admit of special moral valuation, it is absolutely false in all matters involving conscience, sacrifice, and loyalty to truth.—The man who wishes to hear the divine voice must cleanse his ears of all worldly noises. These noises often constitute so many prejudices, through which, if the divine word is heard at all, it comes without emphasis and without authority. "He that hath ears to hear, let him hear."— We should hear more divine calls if we listened more attentively.—If God has ceased to speak, therefore, it may be only because we have ceased to listen.—Nature says nothing to the unsympathetic man.—Art delivers no message to eyes that are filled with mean objects.—The speech often depends upon the hearer.—The supreme prayer of life should be : Speak, Lord, for thy servant heareth.

" Without blemish."—LEVIT. iii. I.

This qualification occurs again and again in the designation of sacrifices, and is therefore of supreme importance.—This call for the ideally pure is itself an instrument of discipline.—

Where can we find that which is absolutely without blemish?—Even where we cannot find the ideally perfect we are bound to look for it, for the very act of looking for it trains the attention to true criticism and the conscience to moral exactness.—The sacrifice was not to be almost blameless; or as nearly perfect as possible; it was to be without blemish.—God has always been calling for this description of sacrifice.—Can we find it in ourselves? Experience emphatically says No.—The more we know ourselves the more conscious we are of blemishes, not always visible, indeed, but not the less blemishes that they are invisible to public eyes, and sometimes almost invisible to ourselves. —Let a man examine himself.—All this inquiry for the ideally perfect points to a certain issue.—Not until Jesus Christ himself appeared was it possible to secure a perfectly blameless sacrifice.—He was without sin. He knew no sin. He was the just sacrificed for the unjust.—Sometimes we have to wait long for the explanation of profoundly spiritual terms.— An ideally perfect lamb of the flock or bullock of the herd was simply impossible, if only for the reason that the sentence of death was in every one of them.—The blemished can never give birth to the unblemished. —There is an hereditary taint in all living things; not, of course, a moral taint in all cases, not the less, however, a taint or a fault.—The blemished offered for the blemished is a mere mockery of law and divine claim.—The whole merit of the work of Christ turns upon his absolute pureness, according to Apostolic theology.—There are times when we hardly see the full pith of such a doctrine or feel its necessity; there are other times in the soul's experience when we feel that the purity of Christ was the chief element of his sacrifice.

—We must have a theology that covers all the moods and phases of spiritual experience; that grows with the day; that expands with the summer; and that fills even the winter with light and enriches the night with stars.—We do not want a theology that is adapted to one set of circumstances only. That theology could be easily invented, and could be as easily perverted. We must have a theology so lofty as not to permit of the handiwork of man, and yet so genial and condescending as to elicit the confidence and the love of the poorest and weakest of mankind.—Our judgment is not without blemish; our giving is not without blemish; our affections are not without blemish. Possibly there may be a line of selfish calculation running through all our most religious arrangements.—The object of Christ's priesthood is to make the Church " without spot or wrinkle or any such thing—a glorious Church."— When we would consider what the Church is to be we must fix our attention upon the blamelessness of Christ. —He is the pattern.—He is the consummation.

" . . . the holy things of the Lord."— LEVIT. v. 15.

Are we not told that "the earth is the Lord's, and the fulness thereof"? Do not all things belong to Heaven? Has not God himself said "All souls are mine"? Has he not also said the "silver and the gold are mine," and "the cattle upon a thousand hills?" To these inquiries there can be but one reply. Still, the separation of things into special relations to the Most High is perfectly compatible with the universal proprietorship of God.—It is not always implied that one thing is holy and another sinful.—The term holy often means separated; that is to say, set apart for special and exclusive purposes.—Taken in this sense, the Lord has from the beginning made special claims in his own name.—He has claimed one day in the week for rest and worship.—He has claimed offerings from the flock upon the field in acknowledgment of divine owner-ship.—He has set apart occasions for fast or festival, that the soul might address itself properly to the heavenly mercy.—Self-deception upon all such matters is very easy.—There is a piety which is void by generality.—When men say they give all they have to God, and, therefore, need not set aside particular sums, they confuse things that differ.—The man who lays claim to this entire consecration without having gone through a period of education shows the insidious nature of self-conceit.—Where is the man who has been enabled all at once, without training and without experience, to give all his time and store to the service of God? No such man has yet been discovered in history.—To claim to be such a man is to set up a claim for idolatry. — To regard all things, times, and places as holy is a leap of the imagination which is likely to involve impiety.—It is well for us to begin with one day in seven; one pound in ten; one church in a town, or a district of a town; from these partial appointments and sacrifices we may rise into the higher consecration. —To say that we have found some other way to that consecration than the way which God himself has marked out, is to have anticipated Omniscience and invented a new theory of human nature.—We are called upon to begin at distinct points, and to con-tribute of time, money, and influence, according to a measure; not, indeed, that we may stop there, but that, hav-ing tasted of the goodness of God's dispensation, we may go forward steadily and loyally to perfection and rest.—Even with regard to the body and the mind, as they are known to us, some portions of them may be spoken of as being more peculiarly holy unto the Lord than are others.— Specially should we guard the con-science : the imagination, too, should be bent in worship at the holy altar : the will should be watched as fire is guarded. Errors of judgment may be venial, but when the conscience is bribed or stupefied who can prophesy good of the whole life ?—To have some things marked as holy things of the Lord is to show at least the begin-ning of religious character and aspira-tion.

"*Command Aaron and his sons.*"— LEVIT. vi. 9.

This is a notable instruction.—Aaron and his sons were priests, and might therefore be supposed to be beyond official regulation or personal obedi-ence.—God has no priests or other officers whom he has made indepen-dent of himself.—The commandment of God is exceeding broad, including "the armies of heaven and the children of men."—Theologians are only safe guides in proportion as they can point to the direct commands and institu-tions of Heaven.—A theologian without the Bible is the most enormous of all wicked pretences.—The priest is simply an interpreter, a helper, a stronger brother in the commonwealth of spiri-tual society; when he ventures to speak in his own name the Church should stop its ears or drive him away from the pedestal which he unworthily occupies.—God never gives up the Church, as to its education and pro-gress, to the entire control of men, how great soever in office.—If the priest cannot do without command-ment, how can the people? If priests have to obey God, are the people exempt from obedience to the will of Heaven ? The weaker may learn their duty from the stronger. If Aaron required continual inspiration and command, surely those of us who are of lower grade and smaller capacity cannot be sustained in our spiritual health and force except by the word of God. —There is a strong temptation to invent new commandments—to establish new institutions—to conduct experiments upon human credulity — to modify the arduousness of religious discipline, but whenever a prophet or a priest arises to tempt the soul in these directions he should be instantly called upon to prove his authority by the law and the testimony.—There cannot be two Bibles in the Church : in other words, there cannot be two sources or centres of authority.—Nor is any man at liberty to use private interpretation in the unfolding of the divine word.—Language is a common property ; language has one key of interpretation ; when the discussion becomes one of merely pedantic learning it is of really no interest to the great common heart of the Church ;— the words or laws of God addressed to the general people are so simple and direct that the heart instantly recognises them.—The priest may have the power of reading them so as to invest their very utterance with new nobility, but it is not in priestly elocution or in any artifice of man to change the internal and solid meaning of the divine command.—Any man can get at God's meaning if he is prayerfully determined to acquaint himself with it.

"*. . this is the law.*"—LEVIT. vii. 1.

We are thankful for definiteness.— Again and again this word occurs in the directions given to Moses.—Men are not called upon to make any vital laws for themselves.—They are called upon to a kind of legislation which is either limited by momentary convenience or is expressive of an eternal law underlying the very constitution of life and society.—It would be impossible, for example, to make a. law to steal.— Even if the law were laid down in so many words the heart would instantly detect its wickedness, and the spirit of man, inspired by the Almighty, would rise against it in burning rebellion. Here and there a man might be found base enough to avail himself of such a law ; but the great human heart would disallow and disavow so wicked a pretence.—There will be no difficulty in asserting the law where the mind and the heart are free from prejudice. —God always looks for the honest heart, the pure heart, the contrite heart, the broken heart ; with such a heart God has no difficulty, every word of his addresses itself instantly to that heart's necessity and pain.— We are not at liberty to fix upon isolated lines in the Bible and magnify these into laws ; our duty, where anything is wanting in absolute definiteness, is to compare Scripture with Scripture, and to find out the Biblical and spiritual meaning rather than the narrow letter, which by its very narrowness may fail to express the divine purpose.—The way to understand the divine law is to discover it in the very spirit of the whole Bible.— To find out one line of vital importance it may be necessary to read the whole Scripture through from end to end.— Where does the Bible point to two Christs ? Where does the Bible justify the worship of two Gods ? Where does the Bible encourage the worship of God and Mammon ? The Bible is always calling its readers to definiteness of conviction and preciseness of religious homage.—There is nothing merely dogmatic or narrow-minded in this.—It may be made dogmatic and narrow-minded by those who pervert divine instructions; but definiteness has no necessary connection with arbitrary dogmatism.—The giving of definite instructions saves time; the giving of definite instructions saves the imagination from fruitless wondering and unprofitable speculation.—What doth the Lord thy God require of thee but to do justly, to love mercy, and to walk humbly with thy God? They who turn religion into a difficulty, or spiritual worship into a metaphysical puzzle, have in them an evil heart of unbelief, and are not to be trusted as teachers of the divine law.

". . . that soul shall be cut off from his people."—LEVIT. vii. 27.

There are terrible excisions in life. —Expatriation is one.—Dismissal from the household circle is another.—Expulsion from friendly confidence and association is another.—There is a kinship of souls, and that kinship may be forfeited by evil behaviour.—Excommunication is not a merely priestly invention; it is based upon a divine decree, and is necessary for social health and honour.—Expulsion is threatened to all evil-doers, even by Christ himself. The unprofitable servant is to be cast into outer darkness. —Those who have only known the name of Christ are to be disavowed as utterly unknown to him, and are not to be admitted, however loud may be their too-late knocking at his door. The man without the wedding garment is to be turned away from the feast.— There is something solemnly awful in this notion of excision. The social touch may be lost. He who was once a child at home may be driven away by the scorn of those who have discovered his unworthiness. Had the man never known the warmth of home and the charm of confidence the outer darkness would not be so blank and heavy to him.—It is when he remembers what he has lost that the night settles upon him as a burden which he cannot bear. Cut off! Cut off from his people! Living alone for ever! Or, what may be even worse, living for ever amongst strangers who detest his appearance, who suspect his motive, and who flee from his approach! By such hints as these we may get the beginning of an idea of what is meant by eternal punishment!—We have all been in a sense cut off from our people.—The grand evangelical doctrine is that we may return and be re-established in the household from which we have been ejected.—This is, at all events, an encouraging doctrine, full of tender comfort, and pregnant with a suggestion which may well lift the soul out of the deepest despair.—The word of the Bible is always a word calling upon the sinner to return.—God has no pleasure in the death of the wicked. God is waiting to receive the returning prodigal.—This attitude on his part does not express a mere sentiment. He is the very God who first cut off the soul, that through excision he might magnify the grace of salvation.—The soul knows when it has been cut off from its people.—It has longings and yearnings which tell a bitter tale. It is conscious of necessities which, when allowed freely to express themselves, cry for home and sense of sonship and assurance of security.—Imagine a star cut off from its central sun.—Imagine a branch cut out of the vine and cast away.—Look at a flower plucked up by the roots and disassociated from the processes of the spring.—All these images but dimly suggest the appalling condition of the soul that has been cut off from its natural relations, dispossessed and disennobled by the hand of righteousness.—Out of all these considerations comes a call to caution, circumspection, and religious anxiety. " Let him that thinketh he standeth take heed lest he fall."—Let there be no boasting, as if discipline and watchfulness were no longer necessary.—The prayer of the soul should always be, " Hold thou me up, and I shall be safe."

". . . utterly unclean."—LEVIT. xiii. 44.

This is a ceremonial expression.— People in certain conditions of body were to be pronounced by the priest as " utterly unclean."—The Bible is everywhere careful not to allow the idea of partial goodness or partial uncleanness.—There is a great moral suggestion in all this.—Once let a man consider that he is not so bad as some other man, and instantly false standards of purity are set up.—The Pharisee adopted this method of self-measurement, and separated himself from the publican by certain degrees of supposed righteousness. The consequence was that he went down to his house unjustified.—The idea of partial unrighteousness necessitates the idea of partial self-justification.— A partial righteousness obviates the necessity for a divine atonement.—The Bible proceeds upon the doctrine that "there is none righteous, no, not one "; that " the whole head is sick, and the whole heart faint "; that " the heart is deceitful above all things, and desperately wicked."—" Utterly unclean," is the expression which best defines the condition of the soul as before God.— When we read the words " utterly unclean " in this connection we are to remember that they were only ceremonially used; they in no wise countenance the idea that some persons are morally partially unclean, and others

utterly unclean.—There are degrees of ceremonial purity, but there are no degrees of moral purity or righteousness as before God.—It was to an utterly unclean world that Jesus Christ came. " If we say that we have no sin, we deceive ourselves, and truth is not in us." Every man must feel that he is " the chief of sinners."— This is not a rhetorical expression, nor is it to be judged comparatively as between one man and another ; it is to express the soul's bitter consciousness of its personal unworthiness in view of the purity of heaven.— Every man knows that his own sin is the worst that can be possibly imagined. He knows its aggravations ; he is aware of atmospheric influence and colour, not observable by any other eye, which give deadly heinousness to his whole line of conduct.—We are not called upon to judge ourselves by others : we are simply called upon to put our hand upon our mouth, and to lay our mouth in the dust, and to cry,—Unclean ! unclean !—There is only one method of cleansing revealed in the Bible.—No man cleanses himself.—Without the shedding of blood there is no remission. The blood of Jesus Christ cleanses from all sin.— Jesus Christ, looking upon his Church, says,—" Now ye are clean through the word which I have spoken unto you."—The moral cleanness of the human race is the sublimest miracle of God.

". . . such as he can get."—LEVIT. xiv. 30.

This is an incidental revelation of the considerateness and mercy of God. —All men could not procure the same kind of sacrifices. Some men were rich and others poor, and God determined the nature of the sacrifice by the social condition of the man. God never omitted the sacrifice : however poor was the worshipper, some degree or form of sacrifice he was bound to supply.—This shows that the true sacrifice is in the spirit rather than in the offering which is made by the hand.—God has always acted upon the principle that every man must confess his personal sin.—Now that One Sacrifice has been offered for all, this law of personal offering is still in operation. It no longer refers to the sacrifice on account of sin, for that has been offered once for all by the Son of God ; it now refers to the daily sacrifice of homage, service, profession, and general conduct.—What a variety of offering is even now found upon the Christian altar !—Some men have laid upon that altar the greatest genius ever created by divine inspiration : others have laid upon that altar the humblest mental attributes ; the rich man has piled up his gold, and the widow has dropped in her mites ; but throughout the whole discipline of consecrated life no man is exempted from the operation of this beneficent taxing. We are to give as God has prospered us. The master and the servant must operate in various degrees ; not the master narrowing himself by the circumstances of the servant ; not the servant complaining because of the larger prosperity of the master ; each worshipper is to bring " such as he can get."—This same law applies to work.—All men cannot publicly preach ; all men cannot make public testimony of allegiance to Jesus Christ ; all men cannot give money ; some men have next to no time to give, so heavy are the demands of labour ; but in some way, and in some degree, and at some time everyone can show that he has been redeemed by the blood of Christ, and has in him the new heart which spares nothing within its possession from the altar of the Cross.—How

long will men be in learning the variety of gift, the variety of opportunity, and the variety of responsibility, connected with Christian life ? We are too prone to betake ourselves to ruthless judgments of one another through not distinguishing between differences of capacity, opportunity, and all those circumstances which constitute the situation of life.—This kind of law has an educating influence upon the individual conscience.—It does not reduce the necessity of giving, it multiplies the opportunity of donation. —It is not for any one man to say that some other man should have brought a higher gift or tribute: to his own Master every man standeth or falleth : God will judge righteous judgment herein as in all other things.—Still the general inquiry may be put, leaving every man to apply it to himself, Who has given his very best to the Cross ? Who has spent every possible moment of time in the service of Christ ? Who has not spared some one indulgence or possession for his own gratification ? These are questions sharper than any two-edged sword, and they are not to be brandished about by any official hand, they are to be whispered rather than thundered, and every man is to make his own reply to the solemn and inevitable inquiry.

" When ye be come into the land of Canaan."—Levit. xiv. 34.

The people were far enough from Canaan at this moment, yet a law of regulation was laid down for their conduct when they came into possession of the land. This is another revelation of the method of divine government.— Laws are made in advance.—The law is not always given merely from day to day ; the details of that law may be, so to say, announced morning by morning ; but the great law itself is laid down from eternity, and therefore it covers all times and occasions, never altering in its spirit though continually adapting itself to varying conditions and institutions without losing one spark of its righteousness.—This is the great law of God.—The moment a man comes into the world the whole law is prescribed for him. There is a law of childhood, full of forbearance, pity, and hopefulness; a sublime accommodation of the Infinite to the helplessness of earliest years; there is a law of youth, having in it a touch of discipline and even severity, passion being curbed, and impatience being restrained greatly to the trial of the restricted spirit; there is a law provided for times of prosperity, so that every man knows what to do with his gold, and how to deport himself in plentiful harvests; there is also a law for the time of poverty, affliction, pain, and sorrow of every kind and name.— In this way a man is permitted to look a long period in advance.—He may not anticipate providences, but he can study the whole law which involves and determines every aspect and issue of human life.—It is beautiful, too, to notice how an instruction of this kind acts as a stimulus upon human thought and conduct.—It was well again and again to mention the very name of the promised land.—So now it is well for us amid the cloud and tumult of life to hear about heaven and rest, about the pure land of eternal noon and the tender music of supernal harmony.— We need great words mixed up with our little terms; as we need a great sky over-arching and blessing our little earth.—It is wonderful how near the words of comfort are laid up side by side with terms of law and discipline. —The Bible is a book of solaces.—It does not give comfort for the sake of enervating men but for the sake of stimulating and strengthening them;

every time Canaan is mentioned it is to stir up the soul to nobler duty and harder service : so every time we hear of heaven and its ineffable rest we should spring at earth's duties and toils with a new energy and a deeper determination.—The laws of heaven are fixed.—Its law is a law of righteousness, and because of the perfectness of its purity is the absoluteness of its rest.—God never allows us to suppose that entrance upon a higher state of life means exemption from law or rioting in the wantonness of licence. —Heaven contains the fuller law, and because of our enlarging capacity and sanctified will, the amplitude and grandeur of that law will not deter us from heavenly service or cause us to become weary in all the solemn study of eternal thought.—Let us cheer one another with these words.—Again and again at the close of the weary day let us say to one another, "When we come into the land of Canaan."—Hymns about the heavenly land may be so used as to rouse us to completer service in the field of battle or in the quieter field of unknown but needful suffering.

"*. . . a scapegoat.*"—LEVIT. xvi. 10.

We must be very careful in the application of this term. It is one of the terms liable to abuse. The image has always been accepted as one symbolical of the work of Christ in bearing away the sins of the world. Considered strictly as a figure, it is full of beauty and helpful suggestiveness. It has, nevertheless, been open to the most mischievous perversion. We use the term now too freely in describing the action of a man who wishes to lay upon another the blame of actions which he himself has done We speak of certain men as being "mere scapegoats"; as if they had been dragged in to meet the necessities of a situation and to relieve others from the burden of just penalties.—The figure is not the less appropriate that it is open to perversion.—Sometimes the value of an analogy depends upon the fineness and even subtlety of its relations. We are never at liberty to abuse an analogy. Jesus Christ comes before us in the aspect of one who voluntarily takes upon himself our sins and bears them away so that they never can be found again.—Notice that he accepts the position voluntarily. —Notice that he himself actually proposes to become, in this sense, the Scapegoat of the human family.—Notice also that the sinner must be a consenting party to this most mysterious arrangement.— The Scapegoat does not come into the world and carry away the sins of mankind in any arbitrary fashion.—Every sinner must put his hands, as it were, upon the Christ of God, and by that act intimate his desire that Christ would bear his sins away.—Do not make a mere convenience of Christ.—Do not consider the presence of the Scapegoat a licence to sin.—The deceitful heart may say, —Take your own course, do just what you please, and at the end of the sinful day place all your iniquities upon the head of the Scapegoat, and he will bear them away into the wilderness of oblivion.—This is perversion; this is more than perversion, it is unpardonable blasphemy.—Blessed is the thought that the sin is borne away where it can never be found any more.—To have the memory of sin, to be for ever reminded of the commission of sin, to suffer all the inflictions possible to imagination in connection with sin, would be to destroy the very heaven which is connected with forgiveness.—In some mysterious way, not to be measured by human words or even conceived by human thought, sin is cast away where even the accuser cannot find it, or the enemy bring it back to fling it in our burning face.—This is a divine dispensation. It is therefore not to be explained or made easy to the comprehension of mere reason. It is rather to be accepted by faith and by love, and being so accepted, the heart is aware of its certainty of preciousness by the sweet peace which steals into it and rules it into profound repose.

———

" *And when ye reap the harvest of your land, thou shalt not wholly reap the corners of thy field, neither shalt thou gather the gleanings of thy harvest. And thou shalt not glean thy vineyard, neither shalt thou gather every grape of thy vineyard; thou shalt leave them for the poor and stranger; I am the Lord your God.*"—Levit. xix. 9, 10.

Here is a marvellous distinction of classes. That distinction is carefully preserved throughout the whole record of Scripture. At first sight, it is not only a marvellous but an incredible thing that one man should be rich and another poor.—Poverty is more than a merely incidental condition of life.— There is a moral mystery about poverty, relating alike to the poor man and to the rich man.—It may seem heartless to speak in this way, and it would be heartless but for the consistent record of time and testimony of experience.—Here is a distinct recognition of the right of property.—We read of "thy field," and "thy vineyard," and "thy harvest."—Yet though property is distinctly recognised, beneficence is also made matter of law. The command is "thou shalt not " in every case. This shows that the harvest is God's before it is man's, and that it is only man's that it may be used according to the law of God.— Something was to be left in the field and in the vineyard for the poor and stranger.—The poor and stranger are ministers of God, when rightly viewed. —They are not to be used as butts or objects of scorning and contempt; but as opportunities for the exercise, not of sentimental, but of lawful and divinely-regulated charity.—Nor are the poor and the stranger to consider themselves as ill-used on account of their position. There is a poverty that is wealth. Only the mean in spirit, or the imperfectly trained, or the ridiculously vain, can object to receive the assistance or the comfort of the stronger classes of society.—If some men are poor and strangers, they must remember that they are exempt from many of the responsibilities which attach to higher station. —Besides, riches and poverty are simply relative terms.—What is wealth to one man is poverty to another; and what is poverty to one man is wealth to another. There is no line at which contentment is absolutely and certainly reached, and apart from which contentment is an impossibility.—It is a profound mistake to imagine that the rich are exempt from pain, sorrow, loss, and that there is no serpent in their paradise.—Nor must the rich man imagine that he is exceedingly good and generous because he leaves something for the gleaner, or because here and there he has left a grape upon the vine. He is bound to do this. It is one of the divine taxations of property. What is left may be comparatively small as to its bulk and value, but the very fact of its being left establishes a divine claim and begins what may, under proper conditions, develop into a splendid scheme of social philanthropy. To be compelled to think about the poor even to the extent of leaving a few gleanings in the field or a grape or two in the vineyard is a part of human education which can hardly be too highly valued.—In

various ways God·draws the attention of rich men to the presence and the need of the poor; and he is indeed a man who has wasted his larger opportunities who has not eaten his own bread with fuller content and tenderer piety because of his endeavours to elevate the lot of the poor.—All these doctrines may be abused, or misunderstood, or even turned into ridicule; nevertheless, the wise in heart will so use them as to minister to the solid development of the best forms of character.—The Bible is the book of the poor.—From no other book in the world could so many injunctions be culled as bearing upon the rich in relation to the claims of poverty.— These grand philanthropic lines running from end to end of the Bible will always secure for the Bible a place in the highest thinking and best affections of all lands.

———

"Just balances, just weights, a just ephah, and a just hin, shall ye have."—LEVIT. xix. 36.

A book which talks in this language is a book which ought to be carefully preserved by the people.—The Bible is not a sentimental book, dealing with abstract emotion, or confining itself to metaphysical mysteries.—It has its deep places which cannot be plombed, and its great heights which dazzle the most daring eye, but again and again it comes upon the common ground and insists that everything between man and man shall be done healthily, honestly, and lovingly.—A religion that examines the balances and weights is a religion that may be trusted to attach a true value to praise and prayer.—This is the strength of Biblical doctrine.—Many a man would be glad to accept the metaphysical mysteries of the Bible if he could escape its practical criticism.—There would be no difficulty in making theologians if they could be allowed to do as they liked with the common practices of daily life.—The Bible will not allow of any trifling with right and wrong, and therefore it is the terror of the bad man, and not likely to be a favourite in any circle whose worship is bounded by compromise or calculation.—Just balances and just weights can only come out of a just *creed*.—For a man to adjust his balances and his weights for fear of the penalty of the law is by no means to be honest. His care simply implies that he is afraid of punishment, otherwise he would gladly avail himself of the wages of unrighteousness.—All these strict moral demands on the part of the Bible should make the acceptance of the spiritual mysteries, and even of miracles the more easy.—We need not begin with the miracles, and because we cannot understand them reject the morality ; we should begin at the other end, saying thankfully : A book which is so true, upright, and wholly just in all its views of social relations is a book which will not trifle with profounder mysteries and more distant truths, and though we cannot now understand these we will begin, by the grace of God, at all accessible and practical points.—The just balances were not to be used only as amongst the children of Israel themselves. The Israelites were to be just to all men. When Christian nations are just to Pagan people, the Pagan people may begin to inquire the more carefully into the religion of such honest nations.—We may astound men by our metaphysics ; we can only conciliate them by our temper and conduct.—Whilst it is well to reject the doctrine of works as between ourselves and God as constituting in any sense a ground of justification, we should cultivate that doctrine as between man and man and prove the

reality of our faith by the genuine goodness of our actions.

"*I . . . have severed you from other people.*"—LEVIT. xx. 26.

It is useless to cavil about such separations, because there they are, as a matter of indisputable fact in human history. Whoever made the differences, we have to acknowledge their existence, and to consider how best to treat them.—There are highly-civilised nations, and there are nations absolutely without formal language or written records. There are nations living upon land which brings forth abundantly, and seems to be but too eager to respond to the efforts of the cultivator : there are other people living, as it were, in barren wildernesses, to whose toil the inhospitable earth makes no reply. There are nations distinguished by the most brilliant intellectual genius, and other peoples who have scarcely the faintest notions of rational life. These differences must have had some origin. The shallowest of all ways of accounting for them is to refer them to mere chance.—It requires more faith to believe in chance than to believe in God, —that is to say, faith in the sense of mere credulity.—Whatever may be the differences in mere ethnology— that is, differences as between one race and another,—it is certain that in the Biblical conception of society a very broad distinction is made between the people of God and all other people.—This again is not arbitrary ; it comes out of the very nature of the separating God himself.—It is only because God is different from all other gods that his people are different from all other people.—This gives a new and elevated view to the whole conception of human differences.—When the nations accept God as revealed in

Jesus Christ, they invariably approximate to the same level.—Christianity does not drag down its believers to the level of other nations, it lifts up other nations to the level of its own elevation.—There is no encouragement to moral pedantry in such separations. —The difference is to be one of quality, and the higher the quality the less disposition there is to exult in it in the sense of feeling contempt for other people.—When the mind of Christ is fully in the minds of those who believe in him they will make themselves of no reputation and take upon themselves the form of servants that they may do good to others.—The morality of Christ is different from all other morality. It is not mere morality in the sense of calculation and adjustment to times and circumstances, it is spiritual morality, it is inspired conduct, it is full of divine passion as well as solid with divine righteousness.—Whatever might be the limitations imposed upon the Jews for temporary and local purposes, it is certain that no restrictions are placed upon Christians for the evangelising of the world.—The express command of Christ is that the Gospel should be preached to every creature.—The grand revelation made to the narrow mind of Peter was that in every nation he that feareth God and worketh righteousness is accepted of him.—Christianity would separate itself from other peoples, in order that it might raise other peoples to a higher platform.—Its elevation increases its leverage.—The withdrawment of Christians from other people is so conducted, when rightly conducted, as to show the other people that no contempt is involved in the severance, but rather a profound and unquenchable desire to turn the whole world into a Church of the living God.—The separation is not to be one of merely outward conduct; it is to be a severance of spirit,

of moral sympathy, of the very essence of life. It would be quite possible to draw up a programme of conduct which should be marked by mere eccentricity; but such a programme would never commend itself to the judgment of fair-dealing men : we do not want a nicely balanced programme, but a new heart, a purified conscience, and a spirit charged with the passionateness of Christ.—Christ was in the world, yet not of the world.—Christ could eat with publicans and sinners, and yet not be defiled by the association.—Monasticism is not taught by this text.—Men are to move up and down in the world, transacting all its usual business, and yet so to do the work of life as to exert a benign influence, and fill other men with encouragement to move in an upward direction.

_____

"*I will be hallowed among the children of Israel.*"—LEVIT. xxii. 32.

Reverence is the very basis of lofty character, and is the guarantee of the purity of society.—When our worship falls our conduct will go down along with it.—The loftier the prayer, the tenderer will be the common speech of the day.—If the children of God do not hallow him, the enemy never will.— God, so to say, depends for his position in the world upon the loyalty of his own people.—If we are ashamed of God, God will be ashamed of us.— "Them that honour me I will honour, and they that despise me shall be lightly esteemed."—We cannot love our neighbour until we love our God —The commandments, which are now but two in number, are really set in philosophical relation to one another. —In this sense theology is the great philosophy of life.—We cannot revere a redeeming God, and yet be careless about the moral condition of the people.—We cannot pray to a throne of mercy, and then seat ourselves upon chairs of judgment.—Our intensest solicitude should be expended upon the idea of true worship.—To have a small conception of God is to have a small conception of life.—To be irreverent in any degree towards Heaven is to be flippant in all our social relations.—When a man has come away from long and profound communion with a God of purity and tenderness, it is impossible for him to either sympathise with iniquity, or to be impatient with weakness. As a debtor himself to the mercy of God, he is bound to be a creditor to the infirmities of his fellow-men.—When the intellect of the Church supersedes the worship of the Church, Ichabod may be written upon its doors.—The tendency of the times may be to magnify preaching above prayer, or genius above meditation : this may be to pay a flattering tribute to the spirit of so-called progress, but it is to lose the very bloom of godliness.

" For unto me the children of Israel are servants."—LEVIT. xxv. 55.

This is a remarkable expression as connected with the fact of which God is always reminding the children of Israel, namely, that he brought them out of the house of bondage and out of the land of Egypt. He appears to acquire his hold upon their confidence by continually reminding them that at one period of their history they were bondmen.—Now he insists that the men whom he has brought into liberty, have been brought only into another kind of service.—This is the necessity of finite life. Every liberty is in some sense a bondage.—Christians are the slaves of Christ; they are burden-bearers and yoke-carriers, specially under the supervision and sovereignty of the Son of God.—All depends upon the nature of the service which is rendered.—Where the service is arbitrary and compulsory, it is of necessity reluctant, and by so much vicious and worthless.—The glory of Christian service is that such bondage is considered sweeter than any other freedom : those, indeed, who have known most about it have not hesitated to describe it as the glorious liberty of the children of God.—Where our love is, there is our service.—In the best sense of the term, we are the slaves of those whom we love.—Christians are called into the sweet bondage which gives them liberty.—They have seen that the mastery of Jesus Christ is a sovereignty which reason can accept, and love can joyfully obey.—It is not because of the grandeur of the mastery or the superlativeness of celestial dignity, it is because the sovereignty of Christ is in harmony with all that is best and purest in human nature itself; filling up every void in the life, and giving full development and scope to every faculty of the being.—The earth is glad to be the slave of the sun.—The folly of rebelling against the Christian religion because it requires the subjugation of the will ought to be obvious to every unprejudiced mind.—The subjugation of the will is a phrase, the meaning of which wholly depends on circumstances which have to be explained. To subjugate the will to an inferior is to disennoble human nature; to subjugate the will to an equal because of some temporary advantage is the deepest injustice to one's self. But to subjugate the will to the eternal God is really to acquire a still higher will, and to enter into the mystery of the peace of the God whose will we have accepted.—No analogy can be drawn as between the subjugation of the will of man to man, and the subjugation of the will to God.—This is the foundation principle of the true theocracy.— We are taught to say,—" Thy will be done on earth as it is done in heaven"; and again,—" Not my will, but thine, be done."—If Christ could say this in his human relation, we need have no difficulty in repeating it in our condition.—When did the will of God ever interfere with the broadest and deepest human progress? When did it turn aside noble aspiration? When did it enclose the soul in selfish narrowness, and forbid the outgoing of sympathy towards the outcast and the weary?— By these signs and tokens should the divine will be examined and judged.— Christianity does not shrink from such examination, but rather challenges it, knowing that they who know most of God will be most ready to accept his gracious dominion.

" *I have broken the bonds of your yoke, and made you go upright.*"—LEVIT. xxvi. 13.

God will have no slavery of a social kind.—He is against all bonds and restrictions that keep down the true aspirations of the human soul.—God has always proceeded upon the principle of enlargement and the inheritance of liberty.—We know how much God has done for a man by the degree of that man's uprightness.—That is an excellent and undeniable standard of judgment.—God has no crouching slaves cringing around his altar and afraid to look up to the Cross which has given them forgiveness.—In proportion as we are carrying bands and yokes, have we not known the Spirit of the living God.—This relates to all conduct and religious observances, to the keeping of times and seasons, and the offering of all manner of sacrifices. —Whatever is done through a sense of servility and humiliation is wrongly

done, and is in no sense done in obedience to the command of Christ.— When all is right within we run in the way of God's commandments, we sing at our work, we turn the very statutes of God into songs in the house of our pilgrimage.—What God has been doing for man in the first instance has been the breaking of yokes.—God has had much negative work to do for fallen humanity.—We do not know how much of our progress is due to the breaking of cruel restrictions,—the whole course of human history has been a course of enlargement and freedom in matters of education, knowledge, and the possession and exercise of personal and social rights. —This is in accordance with the very spirit of the New Testament.—Some men may not have made great progress in positive liberty, who yet have made some advance in the sense of having thrown off many restrictions and yokes, such throwing off being due to the operation of a gracious providence, which providence, indeed, is not always understood or gratefully appreciated; nevertheless, it works in human history with an undeviating and generous aim.—There is an hereditary principle involved in this arrangement; it is impossible that the children of upright men can fail in some sense to partake of the advantages arising from parental uprightness; those conditions may not amount to personal righteousness, and, indeed, may have no necessary relation to such righteousness, but the whole atmosphere is the purer and healthier for our relation to fore- fathers who have been upright and wise and generous.—More is expected of us, and the expectation is founded in reason and justice.—We are the greater debtors to society on account of the liberty into which we were born, and the uprightness under whose blessing we were reared.—**Always** acknowledge the divine hand in human history.—Always see that theology is indeed the larger history.—He knows nothing about history who is merely conversant with outward facts and the succession of measurable incidents : history lies in its spirituality : there is a genius of history,—a religion of liberation and progress.

"And I will bring a sword upon you, that shall avenge the quarrel of my covenant."—LEVIT. xxvi. 25.

It may be reverently said that God does not deal carelessly with his own covenants. He does not throw them away, and take no further heed of their operation. In the sense of looking after his word and observing its issues he may be described in Old Testament language as a "jealous" God.—This great principle operates in nature as well as in grace.—We see it in agriculture as certainly as we see it in what may be termed spiritual human conduct. We are not only punished because we do not pray, we are just as much punished because we do not plough.—If a man will not sow in the seedtime he shall not reap in the harvest, and not having anything to reap, or any fruits to garner, he will know the meaning of the mystic words, "I will bring a sword upon you, that shall avenge the quarrel of my covenant."—If a man will not gather water in the time when the river is full he shall surely die of thirst in the season of drought.—Who quarrels with this law of nature? Who says this is partial or unjust? We feel that the operation of such a law in nature is one of the guarantees of society.—The covenant is here represented as a living thing having a quarrel against those who trifle with its spirit and claim.—The covenant does not seem to avenge itself, but a sword from heaven is

let down to smite those who have dealt unkindly and unjustly with the angel of God.—This is a very solemn but a very grand and ennobling view of life.—We know how true it is that the spirit of love cannot be outraged without the whole life suffering evil consequences.—We also know that the spirit of honesty cannot be offended without a great fear and shaking passing through the whole constitution and framework of human relations.—It is by such aids as these that we raise ourselves into a conception of spiritual realities and issues.— Peace can only come by righteousness. "There is no peace, saith my God, to the wicked."—Discard theology, deny every proposition which theologians have ever asserted, and turn away from all prescribed religious forms, yet still there remains the indisputable fact that evil-doing is followed by tumult and pain, or if not so followed, a state of heart is revealed which is simply past feeling, and under whose judgments and actions human society is no longer safe.—Whenever a sword smites us we should inquire how we have been dealing with God's covenant. —Whenever the grave opens at our feet we should put solemn questions to ourselves regarding our treatment of the covenant of life.—Whatever helps to deeper religious consideration is a true agent in the education of mankind.

"And upon them that are left alive of you, I will send a faintness into their hearts in the lands of their enemies : and the sound of a shaken leaf shall chase them ; and they shall flee, as fleeing from a sword ; and they shall fall when none pursueth."—LEVIT. xxvi. 36.

So wrong-doing is never blessed.— Even when men appear to succeed and to save themselves alive, their success is partial, and may only create an opportunity for further divine judgment.— Do not suppose that men are successful simply because they are living.—A man may have escaped the sea only to die a more terrible death on land.— Marvellous are the judicious resources of God.—We have an indication here of a law to whose subtle force many men can testify.—Fear takes away all power, and turns the most dauntless soldier into a coward.—We cannot account for faintness of heart; it has no history; it cannot be cross-examined; it is something sent into us by a higher power, and is permitted to work miracles in the spirits of otherwise brave men.—We are surrounded by mystery.—The sound of "a shaken leaf" is magnified by the imagination into the sound of a rushing army.— Shadows are ministers of Heaven.—Unexplained noises come to do the work of judgment.—It is not enough to describe these things as superstition, or fancy, or nightmare: there they are, operating directly and energetically in the whole administration of life, and it is more rational to accept a spiritual interpretation of them than to regard them as mere dreams without purpose or force.—By so talking of them we disprove our own argument by the very fact that we are ruled by them, and cannot resist their effect.—God crushes some men as by a great weight: other men he beclouds so that reason cannot find its way through all the conditions of life's necessities: the memory of other men is taken away: men who never feared the face of man have fled before a shaking leaf, as if they were fleeing from an infinite sword.—It is a fearful thing to fall into the hands of the living God.—Our God is a consuming fire.—It is gracious on his part that he should be so revealed.—

His severity is but an aspect of his love.—We read of the wrath of the Lamb.—Can any wrath be so terrible? Can any surprise be so startling? Was ever such a change contemplated by the boldest imagination of man? When love becomes wrath, how hot is that perdition!—Yet God is always willing to turn, anxious to be conciliated, prepared to readopt the wandering child.—When we take out the element of fear from the Christian ministry, we deprive that ministry of one of its most useful auxiliaries.— Christ never failed to avail himself of the uses of fear.—There was a "hell" even in the gracious speech of the Saviour of the world.—He did not conceal the sword; he revealed it in its strength and keenness.

"*. . . whatsoever passeth under the rod.*"
—LEVIT. xxvii. 32.

This passage brings under our attention the fact that many passages of Scripture have been misinterpreted.— The misinterpretations of Scripture have been full of mischief.—Men should make sure of the interpretation before they assert the doctrine.—This has always been understood to refer to punishment, the figure being that God is smiting every one of his flock, and is only approving of them according to the measure of stripes which that flock lovingly accepts. No such meaning is to be attached to these words.— Instead of being severe they are gentle: instead of pointing to chastisement they point to proprietorship.—The idea is that the flock are passing into the fold, and that the shepherd is causing each of them to be numbered by the rod.—The sheep that pass under the rod in this sense have passed from out of the field into the security of the fold. They have been numbered. They have been safely housed.—The idea is that the flock does not go in as a whole without regard to individuality.—Sheep by sheep enters the sacred enclosure. —We are saved one by one.—We die one by one.—We are to be judged one by one.—Every man shall give an account of himself to God.—Those who have passed under the rod have been acknowledged as the sheep of the Shepherd; no mistake has been made as to the identity of the sheep; no other shepherd can come and claim any sheep that has so passed.—There is but one Shepherd who can identify each member of his flock, and cause each to pass into the fold from which there shall be no more going out. —Do not let us turn sweet words of grace and promise into bitter words of chastisement and penalty.—There is more sweetness in the Bible than we have yet discovered.—Do not let us be afraid to go up to many passages of which we have heretofore stood in terror; instead of being avenging angels they may be loving friends, waiting to deliver to us some new and larger message from heaven.

NUMBERS.

So called from the two numberings (ch. **i.** and ch. **xxvi.**) or the people at the beginning and end of the wanderings. The book relates to a period of thirty-eight years and three months, from the completion of the Law-giving, "the first day of the second month of the second year" of the Exodus, to the first day of the fifth month of the fortieth year. Its contents have been thus summarised:—(1) The breaking up of the encampment at Sinai; arrangement of the army, and the service of the priestly tribe, with an inventory of their charge; the parting service and blessing. (2) The march upon Canaan and its repulse. (3) Rebellions; confirmation of Moses and Aaron in authority; condemnation of the people to death in the wilderness. (4) Various events in the forty years' wandering. (5) Events of the last year, *e.g.*, the deaths of Miriam and Aaron; Balaam's mission; the corruption of the people by the Midianites, and its consequence laws of inheritance, etc.

From the death of Aaron to the opening of Deuteronomy there is a space of exactly six months. The first month of the six was passed t the foot of Mount Hor mourning for Aaron. Next ensued the journey to the brook Zered, accomplished within four weeks. Then came the two battles at Jahaz and Edrei. During the next two months the Israelites were engaged in completing and consolidating their conquest of Gil ad and Bashan.

Numbers i.

THE CENSUS AND ITS MEANING.

HOW long is it since the Tabernacle was set up? From some points of view it would seem to be years at least. Time is variously estimated : it is long,—it is short,—it is a flying wing,—it is a mountain of lead,—according to the circumstances under which we view and reckon it. Just *one month* has elapsed since the Tabernacle was set up, and during that month the whole ritual of Leviticus has been wrought out. Leviticus was not a manual for a year ; it was a ritual for a month. It would wear some of us out ; we have lived ourselves into shortening days. What a busy month ! Read the whole Book of Leviticus, from the first chapter to the last, and then remember that every word of it was to be carried out in critical detail within the compass of a single month, and when the month was over the ritual was to be begun again. All life was one Sabbath then. In very deed the days were well-filled in with labour—pressed down, heaped up, running over. Life meant something then. Poor are our services,—poor to begin with, run through perfunctorily, leaving behind not so much a thought as a faint impression—not an unconquerable inspiration, but a memory of partial weariness.

"And the Lord spake—." He was always speaking in the olden times ; he never speaks now. How foolish is such reasoning ! how vicious and degrading such a sophism ! We first misinterpret the terms, and then declare the conditions are never repeated. We bar out good things from ourselves not only by sin but by impious ignorance, by narrow-mindedness, by superstition meant for veneration. God is always speaking wherever he can find a Moses. Surely, he will not speak to stocks and stones, and deaf men and callous hearts : he will call up a child at midnight to whisper in his ear. It is the hearer that is wanting, not the speaker. He that hath ears to hear, let him hear what the Spirit saith. "And there came a voice out of the cloud, saying—." It is our consciousness that is dull—afflicted, indeed, with incurable stupidity; it is our will that is ironed in unholy obstinacy; otherwise, we should write down in plain ink, in open letters, in our mother tongue,—"The Lord spake unto me, saying—." We have to fight the ghost of superstition; we have lost spiritual health; we are in a diseased condition of mind and heart. To set up the Lord in ancient history, or exalt him into the inaccessible heavens, is mistaken for veneration. How suddenly the subject is changed! We have been reading about the tabernacle, the ark of the covenant, the shedding of blood, the consecration of priests; and our whole mind has, so to say, been steeped in religious thought and sacred phraseology, and now, by the overturning of one page, we come upon the divinely-appointed and divinely-directed census of Israel:—Number the people: mark them out in their families and tribes: arrange them according to a plan, and let us know the sum-total of the war force of Israel. We have been thinking, if not talking, of prayer,—suddenly the word *battle* is put into the history. Thus the chapter of life changes; the Author is the same, the writing continuous, with the same noble fluency, the same intellectual dignity, the same imaginative vividness, the same marvellous dramatic change of point and colour; but the subject is organisation for battle, a call for soldiers,—words that might have been spoken through a trumpet; yet the speaking God, the hearing Moses, the obedient Israel, are the unchanged quantities of the story. The Lord could have counted the people himself: why did he set others to do the numbering? It is part of his providence. He could do everything himself; but he trains us by criticism, by the use of our faculties, by the discharge of manifold duties and responsibilities. We need not pray to God as the mere necessity of informing him of our wants, because he knows every one of them better than the suppliant can know his own necessities; but this is educational: our prayer is part of our schooling; to project our heart's necessity into words is a marvellous thing to keep the tongue in balance of the heart, so that the speech shall not run out the need, or the argument be in excess of the conviction; so God cleanses the tongue and subdues it, bringing it into harmony with the whole movement of his own purpose and will. Reluctant, lying tongue! double-speaking tongue! how canst thou be turned and chastened into noble service but by being charged with prayer? This is God's wise way. How was the numbering to proceed? Every man was of consequence. We think we honour God by speaking of him only as the Lord of Creation, the God of Hosts, the Ruler of incalculable armies stretching over spaces infinite; it is our poverty of thought that so strains itself as to lay hold of what to us are great numbers;—God rather seeks to glorify himself in counting men one by one. " The very hairs of your head are all numbered." Looking round his banqueting-table, he says,—Yet there is room. He seems to notice the vacancies as certainly and as clearly as he notices the occupations. To us, numbers are alone of consequence; to our Father, the one child is of great importance: saith he,—One is wanting : go fetch him; call more loudly for him : the next appeal may strike his ear and elicit the response of his heart; go out again, and again, and rather blame the darkness of the night than the unwillingness of the child; give him one more opportunity. This is the philosophy : that the little is always striving to make up for its littleness by conceptions of infinite numbers; and the great—the divinely and essentially great—shows its quality by lighting a candle and sweeping the house diligently till it finds the piece that was lost. We owe ourselves to God's condescension. The men were to be registered for battle according to "the number of their names . . . from twenty years old and upward." Do we begin life at twenty? Are the nineteen years gone, forgotten, unreckoned? "Twenty years old" is the harvest time of preparatory education. At twenty a man should be able to give some account of himself; he ought to have read some books; he ought to know the figure of the world, and to have acquired, at least, a general outline of the little scheme of things within which he lives—a little fluttering wing of a world—just one little tuft of smoke whirled by infinite rapidity into an earth, a school-house, a preparation-place ; yea, "the great globe itself" is but a handful of smoke whirled into rotundity and made use of, until we become "twenty years old and upward." Let us have no frivolity even in the nineteen preparatory years. Every man is getting ready for war; every boy at school is a soldier in possibility. The children will be greater than we were: otherwise, they will have lost their foot-hold upon the line of progress, and have dropped out of the noble traditions of their species. Some men are long in beginning; they are not wholly to be blamed: men ripen in various degrees of rapidity; "Soon ripe, soon rot," is the old proverb, not wanting in wisdom. Others come to maturity slowly, but having reached maturity no wind can shake their deep roots.

There are some remarkable things about the census: for example, what high titles we find here! Following the first list of names, we read in the sixteenth verse: "These were the renowned of the congregation, princes of the tribes of their fathers, heads of thousands in Israel." So Egyptian bondage did not stamp out Israelitish pedigree and claim upon the past. Our bondage need not destroy our manhood. Israel recovered its noblest memories and reclaimed divine purposes and covenants which had fallen into desuetude and into the formality of a dead letter. We may go back over the period of our banishment and humiliating captivity and claim to bear the image and likeness of God; we, who went astray, may return unto the Shepherd and Bishop of our souls, and may become kings and priests unto God and the Father. Why should the mind plunge itself into the despair of guilt, rather than avail itself of God's ministry and mediation in Christ to project itself to earlier times and original policies and begin with the purpose and intent of God? There are, too, some singular fulfilments of prophecy in the numbering of the tribes. Judah had the most to set in array. Was this a mere accident? Not according to Genesis xlix. 8: "Judah, thou art he whom thy brethren shall praise." So we find, in the numbering, Judah stood first—the largest of the host. We find, too, that Ephraim had a number larger than Manasseh. Was this a mere incident, hardly to be accounted for? There are no such incidents in life: everything is accounted for, or to be accounted for, by those who search into roots, beginnings, motives, and divine intentions. In Genesis xlviii. 20, we find how Israel blessed the sons of Joseph,—"And he blessed them that day, saying, . . . God make thee as Ephraim and as Manasseh: **and he set Ephraim before Manasseh,"**—Joseph said, No; but the old father said, Yes !—Manasseh "also shall become a people, and he also shall be great : but truly his younger brother shall be greater than he,"—and now that the census is taken Ephraim stands at the head of Manasseh ! The details are given critically from verse to verse : " the tribe of Reuben were, forty and six thousand and five hundred "; " the tribe of Simeon were, fifty and nine thousand and three hundred "; " the tribe of Gad were, forty and five thousand six hundred and fifty " ; " the tribe of Judah were, three-score and fourteen thousand and six hundred." These are petty details, — what is the sum-total ? " . . . all they that were numbered were six hundred thousand and three thousand and five hundred and fifty " ! *That* is what we wanted to ascertain ! The tribes might exchange friendly challenges and criticisms as to their varying numbers as between and amongst themselves, — a little boasting might be permitted, a little religious pride ; but leaving the details as amongst the tribes themselves we come to the broad and grand truth that in relation to any enemy, rise where he might, there were six .iundred thousand men ready to dispute the ground with him inch by inch. To-day the Christian denominations are talking to one another about their various thousands : they take a melancholy pride in saying that one denomination has made five per cent. more progress than some other denomination. This is what they have to suggest in place of love and in place of prayer ! Simeon takes his census, and Gad reports his figures, and Issachar reminds the other denominations that he has fifty-four thousand enrolled under his banner, and Zebulun tells Issachar that his fifty-four are not equal to Zebulun's fifty-seven. These figures are interesting up to a certain degree and within given boundaries ; but how many men can Christ put on the field against the devil and his angels ? Do not be chaffering to one another and boasting as between fifty-four thousand and fifty-seven thousand ; but stand together, shoulder to shoulder, and say : All for Christ ; the enemy must not fight one tribe, but the consolidated hosts of God. It was but detailed and vexatious reading up to the forty-fifth and forty-sixth verses . we longed to know the sum-total of the strength on which Christ could reckon ; that is what we want to know to-day. A little friendly emu'ation, as between the various Christian communions, may relieve the monotony and inactivity of our modern piety; but what Christ would know is on what military strength he can reckon when he is challenged to the battle of Armageddon. These men whose names and tribes are given were men qualified to be sent forth to war. At that period of history war was an unhappy necessity : it was the school in which men were trained. We must read history in its own light and grow with its growth, if we would understand its philosophy and its purpose. If we deny the writing that is before us as an inspiration, we have still to confront the fact that social classes are precisely divided to-day as they were dis-tributed in the pages of the Bible; when we have denied the inspiration, we have still to deal with the fact. What is the distribution of society to-day ? Military, commercial, educational ;—these classes could not be interchanged. The true soldier can be nothing but a soldier : to bind him down to anything else is to invert his destiny. Men have the call of God in them. No man is at liberty to say what he is going to be and going to do. He has nothing "to do" but to obey. It may please him to talk about his "freedom," but it is the freedom of a cage. "Train up a child in the way he should go,"—in the way of God's purpose, according to the predestination of his life,—" and when he is old, he will not depart from it "—he will know at the end that all his life-pulses have been throbbing in harmony with the infinite music of the divine purpose. The true merchant could never be a soldier : he *must* buy and sell, he *must* make a little profit if he would sleep well at night ; it is in his blood ; he cannot retire to rest until he has bartered, discounted, added up, and given and taken receipts in full. If you suggested to him to go out to battle you would but distress his timid soul ; men of his temperature of blood were meant to buy and sell and to live in the awful tumult of a controversy across the counter. The scholar could never be a merchant; he must inquire and he must communicate ; a book is a treasure to him ; a new thought drives him well-nigh mad,—it may be true : if true, it would set back the horizon, heighten the dome of heaven, and make all things new ; he does not want to buy and sell, but to peruse, to examine, to criticise, to compare, to amass information, and to communicate his intelligence to others ; he is a philosopher and a teacher, not a bagman or a banker. There is the fact. Why quarrel with the Book of Numbers and raise a noisy discussion as to whether Moses wrote it ? The Book of Numbers is being written to-day : a million hands are doing the clerical work ; we are standing yet in this grand organisation and distribution of labour.

But some were not permitted to go to battle ;—who were they ? They were the Levites : " . . . the Levites after the tribe of their fathers were not numbered " among the warriors. They were appointed to be near " the tabernacle of testimony," and were set " over all the vessels thereof, and over all things that belong to it " ; they were to " bear the tabernacle, and all the vessels thereof " ; and they were to " minister unto it," and to " encamp round about the tabernacle " ; and when the tabernacle was set forth, the Levites were to " take it down " ; and when the tabernacle was to be pitched in a new place, the Levites were to " set it up " ; " and the children of Israel " were to " pitch their tents, every man by his own camp, and every man by his own standard, throughout their hosts." Then the Levites were not soldiers ? Not in the narrow construction of the term ; but all truly religious men are soldiers. " The weapons of our warfare are not carnal." The Sunday-school teachers of the land are its most powerful constabulary ; the truly Christian ministry is the very spirit of militancy — not urged against flesh and blood, visible substances, and nameable human enemies ; but against the whole spirit of perdition and against the whole genius of darkness. " Soldiers of Christ, arise, and put your armour on ! " That is the heroic call,—may every man stand up and say,—Here am I : send me !

PRAYER.

THE Lord reigneth, let the earth rejoice. To us there is but one Goa Thy will be done on earth as it is done in heaven; not our will but thine be done. Thou hast wrought in us this grace. We own thy power; thy law to us is liberty. We have no will: thy will be done—is the cry of the heart made right. It is well. Thou knowest all things; thou seest the end from the beginning. We cannot tell what a day may bring forth; we have no ground of evidence or argument, or reckoning; we are shut up in the darkness. Thou knowest all eternity. Thy will be done. This is the Lord's prayer; this is the prayer he taught us in the time of his bloody sweat, in the agony intolerable. We would hear the prayer; we would adore the suppliant; we would endeavour to repeat the glorious utterance; but thy Spirit alone can enable us to do this; we want our heart to say it—our whole spirit—without keeping back one feeling, one word, one reserve. This would be the sacrifice preceding resurrection, triumph, heaven. Thy will be done. Thou dost raise up men from the dung-hill, and set them among princes. It is the Lord's doing; it is marvellous in our eyes. Thou dost make the first last and the last first, and fix the places at the banquet-table without consulting any guest; thy will be done. One dieth in his full strength, being wholly at ease and quiet; another in the bitterness of his soul, who never eateth with pleasure, whose days are nights and whose nights are wildernesses ;it is the Lord: let him do what seemeth good in his sight. Thou dost permit the old man to live until he becomes a burden unto himself; thou dost pluck the young blossom when it is the chief beauty of the garden: the Lord gave and the Lord hath taken away, blessed be the name of the Lord. We would stand in the assurance that the Judge of all the earth will do right; that the very hairs of our head are all numbered; that the steps of a good man are ordered by the Lord, and though he fall he shall rise again. Herein is peace; herein is eternal Sabbath day. Give us this confidence in larger measure until it shall consummate itself in heaven's own peace. Thou knowest our impatience, our wildness of impulse, the difficulty we have in stopping to reason well—the Lord pity us! This is the pressure of the time which is so very short: we see the descending sun, and we want to do so much before the twilight of evening. We know not what we do; we are poor at the richest, weak at the strongest, ignorant in our utmost knowledge. We will rest in the Christ of God; labouring and heavy laden, we will come to him, and he will give us rest; his peace he will give unto us: not as the world giveth will he give, but otherwise—an eternal and infinite donation. Keep us in the love of God, always seeking for truth, welcoming wider knowledge, enjoying the enlargement of our liberty; but knowing always that Christ is first and last and midst, the dawn and the day, the star of the evening, the hope of the midnight; on the Cross, on the throne; suffering, praying, teaching, reigning; the Son of God, the Saviour of the world. O, Lord Christ Jesus, take us closely to thyself, and speak to us words which will make us live! Amen.

Numbers ii.

DIVINE APPOINTMENTS.

THIS chapter deals with the order of the tribes in their tents. Though at first we may seem to have no relation to this order, at last it may be perceived that we are in vital relations to it. Let us first set before the mind vividly the literal exactness of the case. The camp of Judah was to set forth first; the camp of Reuben was to set forth in the second rank; the camp of Ephraim was to go forward in the third rank; the camp of Dan was to go *hindmost* with their standards. Who arranged this order? The answer is in the first verse: " And the Lord spake unto Moses and unto Aaron, saying, . . the camp of Judah . . first; . . the camp of Reuben . . second; . . the camp of Ephraim . . third ; . . the camp of Dan . . hindmost." It was a military tone; there was nothing suggestive in its music; it was imperative, complete, final. Keep positiveness of speech quite vividly before the mind, even at the expense of some tediousness in words. Judah first, Reuben second, Ephraim third ;—these terms are arithmetical and may be accepted without murmuring ; but the next term is more than arithmetical : the camp of Dan " hindmost." That seems to be a word of stigma and of inferiority and of rebuke. Had the numbers been, —first, second, third, *fourth*, the arithmetic would have been complete ; but to be *hindmost* is to be further behind than to be merely fourth ; it is to have the position marked so broadly as almost to amount to a brand of tribal degradation. All this was to be done ; it never could have been done but by divine appointment. A third party may arrange a controversy, or a position as between two men ; but come to handle hundreds of thousands of men—nations, solar systems, constellations innumerable, and we can have no compromising, temporising, giving and taking on a small scale, so as to balance the pride of all parties ; there must be sovereignty, fiat,—the " let it be " out of which all smaller imperatives are struck, like sparks from an infinite flame.

Faith in the divine appointment could alone secure religious contentment under such circumstances. This is as necessary to-day, in view of the distribution of men, with their various gifts and their endlessly varied vocations. What is that mystic, subtle, nameless power that keeps society together, with its diversities, antagonisms, and contradictions? What is the astronomical force that so whirls society around an invisible centre as to sink the mountains into plains and lift up the valleys to a common level? Have we not to-day precisely this order in society intellectually,—Judah first, Reuben second, Ephraim third, Dan hindmost? This is not ancient history: it is the military rule and law of the passing time. Men cannot alter it. Ambition attempts to change relations and positions, and ambition dies in the abortive effort. The Lord will have his way in the whirlwind and in the fire and the storm. To deny it is to waste words; to contend against it is "to kick against the pricks"; to say "We will not have this Man to reign over us," is to utter an empty gasconade—a brag that bursts with its own swelling. We are standing in the region of law; we are bounded on every side. Every man has his gift, into the use of which the King will inquire when he comes back from the far country. How is it that men, being first, second, third, and hindmost in the matter of circumstances, are still knit together by a mysterious bond? The rich man cannot do without the poor man; the palace has its kitchen; the throne has its retinue of attendants, and if one be absent the harmony of the service is impaired. We, being many members, are one body; the hand cannot say to the foot—"I have no need of thee"; nor can the ear say to the eye, nor the eye to the ear—"I have no need of thee." Yet some parts are honourable, and some dishonourable; some comely, some uncomely. How is this? Marvellous if society made itself!—requiring quite a miraculous infidel to believe that it invented its own harmony. "The Lord reigneth; let the earth rejoice."

Order is but another word for purpose, or another word for mind. This mechanism was not self-invented or self-regulated; behind this military table of position and movement is the God of the whole universe. He is behind everything. It requires the whole Trinity to sustain the tiny insect that trembles out its little life in the dying sunbeam ; even that frail heart does not throb by having some small portion of the divine energy detached to attend to its affairs. Were there but one man in all the universe, he could only subsist by the omniscience, omnipotence, and omnipresence of the Triune God. The Cross was not built for millions, but for the sinner, though he be the solitary offender in creation. We see in everything that the amount of order which is represented suggests the extent and quality of the mind behind it. Acknowledging this in things earthly and human, why should we deny the doctrine in relation to things not local, not human, and not transient? Singular, if order means so much in little things, but means nothing in great affairs ! A marvellous thing, we say, is a book. There are in an English book but some six-and-twenty letters ; a most marvellous thing if some skilled printer, shaking the six-and-twenty letters out of his box, let them fall into the shape of "Paradise Lost" ! Might such a miracle occur? The world is amazed by the majesty of the poem ; the world devotes monumental brass and marble to bear to other ages the name of the poet who so arranged the letters. A most wonderful thing, then, if six-and-twenty letters cannot shape themselves into a poem, or be shaped by some magical toss of the mechanician's hand, that man, woman, and child, of all grades, and classes, and varieties of tongue, gifts, genius, and all stars and systems and constellations, should have rolled themselves into position and kept together in their magnificence without any mind, reason, or purpose, being above, below, or around, to account for and interpret into higher meanings the massive consolidation! The more exquisite the mechanism, the more valuable the result of its working. What a mechanism is the world ! How the earth rolls on in the midst of all its revolutions and burials and tragedies ! The same world, yet not the same two moments together, having a permanent quantity centralised in the very heart of changing phenomena. The wise man looks for the permanent quantity ; he is not a mere grubber amongst details and appearances and fleeting thoughts and complexions : he says,—Under all this is something that abides. To find out the eternal quantity is the philosophy of history and the philosophy of religion. We may know much about details, and yet

know nothing about the very thing which brings them into order and flushes them with the colour of moral purpose and meaning. Who knows most about the history of England : the man who has been in every market-town, who knows the market day of every borough, the name of every village, the departure and arrival of every train, the name of every mayor in every municipality ; or the man who knows England by its conquests, its sovereigns, the philosophy of its legislation, the measure of its progress, its relation to other kingdoms, the general set and purpose of its civilisation, but who knows nothing of any market-town in the whole country ? We assign the superiority at once. A country is not an affair of market-towns, and comings and goings of trains, and changes of local officers; it is a genius, a spirit, a purpose, and to find that is to find out the true history of the land. It is so with Providence, with the Almighty Ruler-ship that is above us and around us. We are affrighted by details, pained by cases of personal suffering, and are at a loss to reconcile individual anecdotes with the beneficence of a universal Providence ; but we must look for the central and eternal quantity—and that is plainly written in all history and in all enlightened consciousness : the sum of it was never so grandly expressed as by the Pauline eloquence—" All things work together for good to them that love God "—that are in the rhythm and majesty of the divine music. Let us not be traders in details, puzzle-makers amid the little occurrences of the parish, but students in the temple of wisdom, worshippers at the throne of light, recognising eternity amid the fluctuation and the tumult of time.

Dan was to go hindmost. The hindmost position has its advantages. It is a rule in the higher criticism that a critic, on looking at a picture, shall first look for its beauties. That rule we have not yet introduced into the Church ; but that is the rule in all the higher life of civilisation. The critic, looking at the picture, first inquires into the beauties, the fascinations, the marks of ability, the signature of genius ; and then reluctantly suggests the drawback or the point of inferiority, and submits it rather for consideration than for judgment. We ought, surely, to look so upon the picture of Providence, the map of human life, the marvellous academy of society. We ought oftentimes to pity the foremost men. The greater the statesman, the greater the responsibility he has to sustain ; the greater the genius, the more poignant its occasional agonies ; the more sensitive the nature, the more is every wound felt, the more is every concussion regarded with fear. The foremost soldiers will be in battle first ; we who are hindmost may have only to shout the hosanna of victory. Judah is first, and may have first to fight ; Dan is hindmost, and may take some pride in Judah's victories. The pioneer traveller has the hardships to undergo ; he was first in honour, but he was first in suffering. We travel on the road he made. This age is the hindmost in procession of time ; is it therefore the inferior age ? The nineteenth century comes after all the eighteen ; but it therefore comes on the firmer ground, with the larger civilisation, with the ampler library, with the more extended resources ; it comes with a thousand-handed ability because it is the hindmost of the days. Take this view of all circumstances, and life will become a joy where it has long been a pain ; our very disqualifications in one direction may become qualifications in another. If you had been fit for more field work, you could not have read so much ; if your health had been more robust, your spirit might have been coarser ; through the feebleness or the restraint of the body you became acquainted with processes of chastening and limitation and refinement which have made you your noblest self. There is no lot that has not in it some point of light ; if, indeed, we except men who have sinned away their day and are now in the wilderness of despair, still enough remains to justify the reassertion that in every human lot there are points of advantage. Let no man glory over another ; God has set everyone in his place, and every man must accept the divine appointment. But this was Old Testament ; we have supposedly outlived the venerable record. Is there anything to correspond with this order of the camps in the New Testa-ment ? Read 1 Corinthians xii. 28–30 : "And God hath set some in the Church, first apostles, secondarily prophets, thirdly teachers, after that miracles, then gifts of healings, helps, governments, diversities of tongues. Are all apostles ? are all prophets ? are all teachers ? are all workers of miracles ? Have all the gifts of healing ? do all speak with tongues ? do all interpret ? " This is the Old Testament translated into later language. So is this : "Now there are diversities of gifts, but the same Spirit. And there are differences of administrations, but the same Lord. And there are diversities of operations, but it is the same God which worketh all in all. . . For to one is given by the Spirit the word of wisdom ; to another the word of knowledge by the same Spirit; to another faith by the same Spirit ; to another the gifts of healing by the same Spirit ; to another the working of miracles ; to another prophecy ; to another discerning of spirits ; to another divers kinds of tongues ; to another the interpretation of tongues : but all these worketh that one and the selfsame Spirit, dividing to every man severally as he will." Paul, then, was but Moses evangelised ; the God of both Testaments is the same. The great mischief is, that one man is so often expected to be all men. This is particularly so in the Church. Outside the Church we have some little tincture of common sense in these matters ; but inside the Church we have another kind of sense. We thus declaim : The minister is an excellent visitor, but he is a very poor preacher. A marvellous thing it would have been, now, if the same man had been both a preacher and a visitor ! Or we say : No doubt he is a very learned theologian, but he has no gift in the relation of anecdotes. A marvellous thing if he had been great in the theological metaphysics of the fathers, and profound in his knowledge of anecdotes that never transpired ! Or : He is very solid, but not entertaining. Marvellous if he had been as solid as a Quarterly Review, and as great a liar as an evening newspaper ! In the Old Testament and in the New Testament there was some regard to specialty of gift, to definiteness of position ; having lost that regard we have lost power. You do not say, The clock is an excellent time-keeper, but no use at all as a musical instrument. You do not take up a trumpet and say, A finer instrument was never made to call men to feast or to battle, but it is utterly useless if you want it to tell you the time of day. Every man in his own place, in his sphere. The great question is not in what regiment we are, but rather, Are we in the army of Christ— whether with Judah first, with Reuben second, with Ephraim third, or with Dan the hindmost tribe ? To be in the army is the great consideration. There are no inferior positions in the Church ; there are no inferior clergy. There may be valleys ;

but the valleys are in the Alps—even the depressed places are on the high mountains; to be on those mountains at all is to be in an elevated position. We have the same reg, lation in the New Testament, as Paul has just proved. We need not have gone to Paul, for Paul was but an echo, not a voice; the Voice is Christ. The Son hath revealed the Father as a King who has gone into a far country, and before going divided to his servants, severally as he would, to one five talents, to another two, to another one, saying to each "Occupy till I come." So the Book of Numbers is but an earlier edition of the book by which Christian conduct is regulated and Christian education is completed. So the Bible has many writers, but only one Author. The hands that shaped its letters are many; the Spirit that revealed its truth is One.

NOTE.

THE Book of Numbers is rich in fragments of ancient poetry, some of them of great beauty, and all throwing interesting light on the character of the times in which they were composed. Such, for instance, is the blessing of the high-priest (vi. 24-26) :—

> " Jehovah bless thee and keep thee :
> Jehovah make his countenance shine upon thee,
> 　And be gracious unto thee :
> Jehovah lift up his countenance upon thee,
> 　And give thee peace."

Such, too, are the chants which were the signal for the Ark to move when the people journeyed, and for it to rest when they were about to encamp :—

> " Arise, O Jehovah ! let thine enemies be scattered :
> Let them also that hate thee flee before thee."

And,

> " Return, O Jehovah,
> To the thousands of the families of Israel ! "

In chapter xxi. we have a passage cited from a book called "The Book of the Wars of Jehovah." This was probably a collection of ballads and songs composed on different occasions by the watch-fires of the camp, and for the most part, though not perhaps exclusively, in commemoration of the victories of the Israelites over their enemies. The title shows us that these were written by men imbued with a deep sen:e of religion, and who were therefore foremost to acknowledge that not their own prowess, but Jehovah's Right Hand had given them the victory when they went forth to battle. Hence it was called, not "The Book of the Wars of Israel," but "The Book of the Wars of Jehovah." Possibly this is the book referred to in Exodus xvii. 14, especially as we read (v. 16) that when Moses built the altar which he called Jehovah-Nissi (Jehovah is my banner), he exclaimed, "Jehovah will have war with Amalek from generation to generation." This expression may have given the name to the book.

Numbers vi. 22-27.

22. And the Lord spake unto Moses, saying,

23. Speak unto Aaron and unto his sons, saying, On this wise ye shall bless the children of Israel, saying unto them,

24. The Lord bless thee, and keep thee:

25. The Lord make his face shine upon thee, and be gracious unto thee:

26. The Lord lift up his countenance upon thee, and give thee peace.

27. And they shall put my name upon the children of Israel; and I will bless them.

BENEDICTION.

WE have need of some such message as this; we needed a Sabbath day in the weary week of detail and mechanical arrangement and service of the hand through which we have been steadily passing. We know the Sabbath when it comes; we feel the Sabbatic air of this tender benediction. We dare not trifle with these words, were they anonymous; had we found them in some out-of-the-way place, when our hearts were weary and our eyes were red with tears, we should have blessed the unknown writer of music so sweet and tender. In some high mood of strength and passion we might not have heeded the words; but with a broken spirit, strength nearly exhausted, hope just expiring, the clouds closing thickly upon life, we should have pressed the writing to our lips and kissed back our thanks for the blessing which it brought. This is how the Bible appeals to us; it waits for our moods; it does not force food upon the sated appetite; it keeps back the bread until the hunger claims it, and then its hospitality is as great as our necessity. Reading the sweet passage, we seem to have come into a new clime. Now and again in the Old Testament there are surprises of beauty; there are words of gentleness in it not touched in their exquisite sublimity by anything in the New Covenant. Would you cull and gather into floral groups.

sweet words, tender expressions, gracious solaces, syllables
that find their way into the heart's night and bitterness ?
For this you must go to the Old Testament. The Hebrew
tongue was made for comfort, for a great redundance of solace ;
there is wine in the grape of every syllable ; he who presses
most in the agony of his need will drink most abundantly and
most refreshingly of the wine of God's love. It is right that the
Old Testament should have its supremacies ; it should not always
be a cumbrous ritual, an intricate and expensive mechanism ;
now and again, it should, so to say, overtop even the New
Testament, and claim to be the inspired Book of God, by the way
in which it speaks to the heart's wounds and all the agonies of
human life. We have waited for this blessing ; we felt there was
something coming to us when we saw God marking out the land,
laying down the plan of the hedges, fixing the gates and swinging
them on golden hinges ; when we noted what we may call his
anxiety that the garden should be properly laid out according
to the best geometry, we said in our hearts,—he means to grow
sweet fruit here ; all these pains and cares about hedges, and
gates, and paths, and positions must be interpreted into the
purpose to grow such fruit on this soil as never grew beyond the
lines of paradise. So the very detail has been to us prophetic ;
the mechanism has had a flush about it which told that love
was not very far away. We come fully into the sanctuary at
this moment : here is " blessing," " keeping," " shining,"—the
uplifting upon our poor life of all heaven's glad morning. We
expected it ; when we saw God troubled, if we may so say,
with such anxiety about the frame, the shape, the overlaying
with gold, the loops by which it was to be hung, we said in our
hearts, he means to put into this frame such a picture as there
is not to be found outside the galleries of heaven. Here is the
picture : a picture of benediction, and joyousness chastened into
peace ; say if on all the walls of the world there gleams a
picture charged with such suggestion of colour, such vitality,
such expressiveness, such mute eloquence. The heart knows
when the Bible is completed ; the spirit that is in man—part
of the Spirit of God—knows when to say, with grateful content,
" It is finished." This is the end at the very beginning ; much
history has yet to be evolved, worked out in intricate detail

revealed in perplexing contradiction, made evident by agonising tragedy; but when the tumultuous music has ceased, it will express itself in this very benediction. In God, in heaven, in all the solemn eternity, there is no word greater than *peace.* It was Christ's gift; it is a peace which "passeth all understanding"; it seizes for its explanation all figures that suggest light, beauty, comfort, strength, security, completeness; it is not a single element, it is the combination of all forces, their final and infinite reconciliation.

This is the Lord's prayer. We have by some means, not always easy of explanation, fixed upon another formula and clothed it with the dignity of being the Lord's prayer. The Lord's prayer occurs early in the Lord's Book. This is not a human invention; we do not read that Aaron spake unto Moses saying, I have conceived a formula of benediction which will please the hosts of Israel. It is the Lord himself who brings this flower out of the upper paradise; it is the Lord's own dear self that brings this bar of music from heaven's infinite anthem. This is the Lord's doing, outshining the sun, outvaluing the gold of the tabernacle, and coming into the heart with a sanctity that turns the whole life into one long Sabbath day.

Being the Lord's prayer, it is a *complete* prayer. God works by the circle; he is not satisfied with the abrupt straight line, or even with its endless monotony. He completes in geometric as in moral beauty what is needed for the comfort and inspiration of human life. "The Lord bless thee." Explain the word *bless.* You cannot; it explains itself. It will not condescend to be broken up into words capable of being totalised into its exact value; it floats about the life like a perfume; it touches the weak, weary life like a great soft hand, lifting it up into new strength; it whispers its messages into the soul's ear when other voices could not reach the attention of the spirit. A child knows what the word *bless* means, in effect, though it cannot explain the term : in other words, it knows the touch of love, it knows the coo of pleasure that enters into the congratulatory or encouraging tone. There is a masonry of hearts; there is a "touch of nature." Who does not know when the voice is charged with gospel, and when it is choked with thunder

and judgment ?   Magnify the word *bless* : it will stretch over
the whole firmament; gather around it all jewels symbolic,
suggestive, invaluable, and it can wear them all, and call them
trifles when compared with its own sublimity : they sit well
upon it, for nothing can overpower that word by external decoration.   " The Lord . . . keep thee,"—another word of one
syllable.   " Keep thee,"—what means the expression ?—gather
thee to his heart, put his arms around thee, keep the gate of
thy city, watch the fountain of thy pleasure, take care of thee
altogether, watch thy down-sitting, thine up-rising, thine outgoing, thine inccming, as if these were matters of profound
concern to his heart.   Surely this is the New Testament in the
Old ?   The very Christ of God, when he cometh, can have no
speech to make deeper than this.   History has verified this
forecast, for when he came the song was, " Peace on earth,"
and when he left the valediction was, " Peace, I leave with
you."

   This is an answer to prayer.   Being a prayer inspired, it is
answered by the very fact of its inspiration.   God never teaches
a prayer that he may deny its petition.   All true prayer is its
own answer.   Therein profound mistakes have been made, and
angry and useless controversies have raged amongst men.   We
do not wait for answers : we at once receive them, as Daniel
did, " while we are yet speaking."   True, we offer many words
that are not prayers, and for answers to such clamour we may
have long to wait, for God has no purpose of replying to them.
Other prayers are refreshing to the intellect, stirring to the best
ambitions of the soul, satisfactory to many of the instincts and
impulses of life ; but they begin and end within the suppliant
himself.   True prayer is answered before it is uttered.   True
prayer is the Lord's prayer, and the Lord answers none but
himself : herein is that saying true—" God cannot deny himself."
If we will pray our own prayers, we must be content without
divine replies ; if we will wait for the prayer, we shall never
have to wait for the answer.   The Lord's prayer is a simple
and loving desire to be lost in the Lord's will.   We do not pray
for fine weather for harvesting—nor for fine weather for the
voyage—in any sense that interposes our supposed goodness
between heaven and earth, as if we were more careful about the

harvest than God is, or as if we cared more for the voyager's life than does the Creator of that life and the Redeemer of it. Even such prayers as these—for bright sunshine, for south-west winds to dry the ripening corn,—we conclude with this part of the Lord's prayer,—"Nevertheless not our will, but thine, be done." No man learns that prayer on the first day of his regeneration, or in the early experiences of his life. Every man must pass through a period of impulse, impatience, vehement desire for some decision which he supposes will bring tranquillity; but after long travail, after a million disappointments have stung the soul, after experiences whose dominating colour is the blackness of utter night, after one hour in sad Gethsemane,—then a man prays and gets answers to prayer. As soon as we can say, "Not my will but thine be done"—doubling up our strength in humiliation and weakness—an angel will appear, strengthening us, and setting us up in the posture of dignity and in the attitude of conquest. Still, do not stop the flow of other speech; it does us good to talk up to heaven, to say what our requests are, to name them one by one; and that will become prayer if finished properly; in itself it is mere clamour—a noise of words with irreligious and ineffective fluency; but when ended with "Nevertheless not my will, but thine, be done"—through that exclamation comes the Divine benediction.

This is a prayer that suits all life. The universality of doctrines proves their inspiration. We cannot have a local gospel; we could not tolerate a book that could only be translated into one language. Ritual, tabernacles, colours, jewellery for the inner place of the sanctuary, and priestly robings,—all must fall off as local and temporary, and, by so much, worthless. But here is a benediction that can go all the world over and fill the ages with its tenderness, and can give all the time without being itself impoverished. Every heart may utter it. "The Lord bless thee, and keep thee,"—why it is the music of farewells to-day. Did ever parent send the child out from home without saying, if not in words, yet in feeling, "The Lord bless thee, and keep thee"? Did ever friend speak to friend, ailing and sick unto death, at night time, without saying, "The Lord bless thee, and keep thee: the Lord make his face shine upon thee, and be gracious unto thee . . . and give thee peace"? Amend the

terms! you who are gifted in speech, you who have learning in
the use of phrases,—amend these sentences, displace them by
purer music! To that challenge there can be no reply. This
is refined gold: all other speech is gilded; this is the pure lily:
all competing flowers are made of pliable wax. This is the
speech of God; every letter may conclude with it; every day
may begin with it; every night may be sanctified by it. Grammatical difficulty there is none; criticism has no place here; the
rudest soul is at least silent in the presence of this holy image,
and the most stubborn unbeliever almost wishes the words might
speak to his own weariness.

This is a mysterious prayer. The sacred Name occurs three
times. Without being unduly anxious to found any doctrine
upon the threefold repetition of the sacred designation, is there
not a suggestion here of the Great Tri-Unity? Are not all the
Christian benedictions founded upon these three lines? Do we
not invoke the Father and the Son and the Holy Ghost, in our
own words of blessing when we close the day spent at the
sanctuary? Do not seek texts, or force passages of Scripture
beyond the lines and boundaries intended by the Holy Spirit;
yet do not shrink from finding suggestion where you can find it
rationally, obviously, without straining—where the suggestion
comes to you, rather than you carry some stern dogma to the
words themselves. Is not all blessing threefold? Is there not
some kind of even rhetorical magic in the number three?—an
odd number; yet does it not come with evenness of rhythm,
when rightly applied in human speech? Does it not fall into
unity, as drops plash into the river as if they belonged to that
flowing stream? Has not the Father a blessing of his own, and
Christ a tender word that none but he can speak, and the Holy
Spirit a breathing more eloquent than articulate language?

But the light suggests the shade: Is there an unblest life?
Is it possible that there can be humanity without the divine dew
resting upon it? Not in the purpose of God. "God is no
respecter of persons: but in every nation he that feareth him,
and worketh righteousness, is accepted with him." But the
possibility is that a man may exclude himself from the blessing,
and live an unblest life. It is possible to outlive even the
blessing of human love—possible so to vitiate all purity, desecrate

all sanctity, violate every obligation, as that our steadiest friend is kept back by an intelligent reluctance from breathing any blessing on our name. Who will live the unblest life? None need do so. Let every one say,—Bless me, even me also, O my Father. Let the man farthest away say,—I will arise, and go to my Father,—and his first returning step means benediction, release from the past, an unburdening of the soul, an adoption into the redeemed and sanctified family. Let all hearts seek a blessing; let every man say,—Unless thy blessing go with me, carry me not up hence; give me God's blessing, and my poorest day in the market-place will make me rich in heart at least; and my most successful day on the battle-field of life, in the controversies of time, in the competitions of commerce, in the rivalries of literature, will be made the richer by an incalculable addition; let me live the life of the righteous, then shall I die the death of the righteous, and my last end shall be the beginning of my immortal youth.

Numbers ix. 15-23.

15. And on the day that the tabernacle was reared up the cloud covered the tabernacle, namely, the tent of the testimony : and at even there **was** upon the tabernacle as it were the appearance of fire, until the morning.

16. So it was alway : the cloud covered it by day, and the appearance of fire by night.

17. And when the cloud was taken up from the tabernacle, then after that the children of Israel journeyed : and in the place where the cloud abode, there the children of Israel pitched their tents.

18. At the commandment of the Lord the children of Israel journeyed, and at the commandment of the Lord they pitched : as long as the cloud abode upon the tabernacle they rested in their tents.

19. And when the cloud tarried long upon the tabernacle many days, **then** the children of Israel kept the charge of the Lord, and journeyed not.

20. And so it was, when the cloud was a few days upon the tabernacle ; according to the commandment of the Lord they abode in their tents, **and** according to the commandment of the Lord they journeyed.

21. And so it was, when the cloud abode from even unto the morning, and that the cloud was taken up in the morning, then they journeyed : whether it was by day or by night that the cloud was taken up, they journeyed.

22. Or whether it were two days, or a month, or a year, that the cloud tarried upon the tabernacle, remaining thereon, the children of Israel abode in their tents, and journeyed not : but when it was taken up, they journeyed.

23. At the commandment of the Lord they rested in the tents, and at the commandment of the Lord they journeyed : they kept the charge of the Lord, at the commandment of the Lord by the hand of Moses.

THE JOURNEY OF LIFE.

A VERY noble life ! a wonderful sense of comfort and security in it; a marvellous childlikeness of spirit and trust, expectation and hope ! We have not advanced beyond this. We may, in a sense, be cleverer, abler,—the production of a more intricate civilisation ; but we have not advanced beyond **this** sweet trustfulness, this calm of heart, this religious and sacred tranquillity. There is no strain upon the imagination in thinking of life as a journey. That is one of the simplest and most beautiful figures by which the action of life can be represented, We are travellers; we are here but for a little time; on our feet are sandals and in our hands are staves; here we have no continuing city, and we are called upon to testify to the age that we seek a country out of sight. So then, we are familiar with the figure; it commends itself to us, as life enlarges, as quite expressive of the reality of the case;—every day a milestone, every year so much nearer the end. At first the miles appear so many and so long; then, at a certain period of life, the miles are but a handful, and as for their length, it is the one dimension of which they are destitute. To the child, the year is a life—a quite immeasurable quantity; to the man in mid-life and passing beyond a certain point, the year is a breath, a shadow, quickly flying,—it will be gone whilst we are talking about it; and in that mood of mind, how pensive and tender, how solemn and rousing, the music : " Whatsoever thy hand findeth to do, do it with thy might."

Regarding life, then, as a journey, according to the pattern of this text, is there not a mysterious presence or influence in life which really affects our action ? In the text that influence is spoken of as a cloud by day and a fire by night,—two striking natural images. Our controversy is not about the image, or the metaphor : behind it is there not this ever-abiding solemnity, that in life there is a mysterious action—a ministry we cannot comprehend, an influence we cannot overrule ? At this moment we need not determine its name : at the outset of the inquiry there is no occasion to perplex the mind by a choice of religious terms; let us first admit that in life there is a mystery—a movement we cannot reckon in its totality, or fix in given boundaries; something that is greater than our thought, and that yet comes into it with illuminating and ennobling energy. We speak of " impression." When we think of changing our position in life, we say we have an *impression.* What is an impression ? Who created it ? Who determined its meaning ? How do you account for the impression ? Upon what is the impression made ?—upon the mind, upon something subtler than itself, upon the conscious-ness, the soul, the spirit—the innermost man. That is a mystery ! We will speak the non-religious language for the moment and talk of "impression." There you have a riddle, a difficulty ; you cannot explain it. You have a consciousness of its presence ; but how it came to be what it is, and how it came to act when it did, you cannot explain in words. Or we speak of "circumstances." We say that *circumstances* seem to point in this direction or in that. What are circumstances ? Where do they begin ? How do they sum themselves up into influence, or into definiteness ? How many of them are required to constitute a determining presence in human life ? Do we first make the circumstances and then worship them ?—then we are but idolaters. De we create the conditions which we suppose are favourable to our thought and our destiny, and then, having created the conditions, regard them as significant of the course which we ought to take ? In proportion as you create the circumstances, you must, in your inmost soul, distrust them. You know you shaped the course you follow ; you know you first created the conditions, and then construed them so as to affect beneficially certain selfish issues. The reasoning is sophistical ; the reasoning is, indeed, immoral. Having spoken about "impression" and "circumstances," we speak about another mysterious thing which has come to be known by the name of "tendency." We say the *tendency* of things is— ; or the *tendency* of life seems to indicate—. We have created a species of rhythm, or harmonic movement, falling into which we say,—This is the sweep of tendency, and to resist tendency is impossible. How anxious we are to get rid of religious names ! Men who will speak of impression, circumstances, and tendency, will hesitate before saying,—Providence, God, Father in heaven. Who is ashamed to speak about impression, circumstances, tendency ? These are words we can use everywhere without committing ourselves to anything definite in the way of religious faith. Let the Church beware how it gives up the grand old names—God, Providence, heavenly direction, spiritual influence ! We have exchanged these terms for a meaner currency. We must go back to them and not be afraid of the noble utterance. It may bring us into criticism from the other side, which has nothing kind to say about the noblest truth ; but when we utter such language, being at the time faithful to our convictions, we shall find satisfaction in our own hearts—r deep, rich, generous satisfaction, knowing that we have not been ashamed of him who is our Shepherd and Guide and Friend, saying,—"God is our refuge and strength, a very present help in trouble."

Why shrink from the definite religious testimony of the eighteenth verse: "At the commandment of the Lord the children of Israel journeyed, and at the commandment of the Lord they pitched"? We speak of definite testimony: here it is. When a man rises in the morning in God's strength, lies down at night in God's blessing, walks all day in God's energy, he lives and moves and has his being in God; he is lost in God; God is in his inmost thought, and every word upon his tongue is an implied or actual confession of childlike trust in God. We need not be ashamed of this definite testimony. It exalts human life. What is the meaning of it? Evidently that our life is recognised by God, our movements are of some consequence to him; he knows our downsitting and our uprising, our going out and our coming in; and there is not a word upon our tongue, there is not a thought in our heart, but, lo, it is known wholly in heaven. Realise that idea; you are not degraded by it, or servilely limited by it: on the contrary, you are lifted up into a nobler self-hood; life becomes a daily sacrament, and the sacrament a daily revelation. A conviction of this kind destroys superstition. The only destroyer of superstition, in any profound and lasting sense, is real religion—a simple, strong grasp of realities. I call the non-religious man superstitious, if he is the victim of impressions, circumstances, tendencies,—if he is always trying to piece together the accidents of the day, and to shape them into some guiding presence and meaning. Where is his point of rest? He is lost in petty details; he has no altar—that is to say, no grand centre of life, the point where he is his noblest self because most humbled before the Living God. Have no fear of the suggestion of superstition in your religious life. The only true rationalism is true religion; it is reason sanctified, reason glorified, reason taken into communion and friendliest fellowship with God. They are superstitious who know not where to build their altar, how to pray when it is built; who have no way into the Infinite opened up and marked by precious blood. They who consult oracles of their own creation, and are looking wistfully and vaguely round for signs of the times or signs of the spaces—these astrologers are superstitious ; but the man—great, strong, noble, healthy man—who clasps his hands, closes his eyes, and says in childlike tones—" Father, guide me every day," is not a superstitious man but really healthy in soul,—a man to be trusted, a man whose quality at the last will prove itself to be all gold. This consciousness of divine guidance in life, divine care of life, divine redemption of life, necessitates prayer. The man who seizes this view of things must pray. In no long words may he pray ; in no connected sentences flowing through hours need he importune the heavens ; the uplifting of an eye is prayer, the falling of a tear may be prayer, a sigh for which there are no fit words may be prayer ;—this is praying without ceasing, having that readiness and instancy of mind which flies into heaven when the cloud threatens, when the enemy is at hand, when the perplexity thickens into a baffling mystery ; then prayer is sweet. Prayer is natural to the child of God ; it is a touch, a smile of the heavenly face, a written revelation inscribed upon the tablets of the heart which the soul can read and understand and the will gladly obey. To be without that is to be in perpetual darkness and in continual pain.

This religious view of life brings the spirit into the restfulness and blessed joy of obedience. The children of Israel simply obeyed. If the cloud tarried long, they rested long ; if the cloud were taken up suddenly, they moved without surprise ; when the cloud abode from the even unto the morning, then they abode with it ; when it rose, they rose with its ascension ; " whether it were two days, or a month, or a year, that the cloud tarried upon the tabernacle . . . the children of Israel abode in their tents, and journeyed not." Theirs was not a life of controversy ; ours, unhappily, is. We have made it a life of controversy when we need not. We are always arguing with our orders ; we are trying to construe them into different and inferior meanings ; we are wasting life by discussing in idle words, which can settle nothing, the gravity and authority of our marching orders. If we accept God's Book, do let us accept it with full trust, not as a field for criticism, but as a code of life—the word, or the testimony by which every thought, feeling, and action is to be determined. Live that life and risk your destiny. If that life will not at the last overthrow the enemy, extract his sting and taunt the grave in rapturous triumph, nothing known to me can meet that final and tremendous necessity. To obey is to live. To look every morning for the marching order of the day is to be master of the day. He who opens the gate of the day with the key of prayer is master of the situation; though the day be full of difficulty, the spirit's rest will not be disturbed; though there be many things to make the day cloudy and turn it almost into a black night, yet in the soul there will be a light which nothing can dim, a fire which no sea can quench, a deep, holy, unmurmuring, expectant trust in the Living God. Where then is fear—fear of man? There is none. Where is anxiety? There is none. The soul is in heaven, rather than upon earth, in all matters which concern its deepest necessities and its final meanings. Have no marching orders, have no Living God, have no trust in Heaven; and then fear will occupy the mind, anxiety will be like a canker in the heart, a mysterious expectation of something distressing will disennoble every faculty, and life will be turned into a jugglery, a species of gambling, not knowing what will occur. Who will accept that policy of life? Not one, surely, but the fool. Rather let it be ours to look up, to hope on: for in so doing we are not spending our time in foolish contemplation; or in a mental absorption which admits of no practical expression; we are gathering strength for the daily fight, wisdom for the daily mystery, and contentment for the daily lot. Let me live the life of the righteous, let me die the death of the righteous; my last estate will be like his. The "last end" we must face; we can come to it in one of two ways: self-idolatrously, self-trustingly, having the fearlessness of mere boasting, mere defiance; or we can come to it trusting that things are larger than they look, deeper than they seem, believing that our sin was answered by the Lamb of God even before it was committed—for he was slain from before the foundation of the world. We can come to our last end believing that God knows us altogether, remembers our frame, knows how frail we are, has seen our loving trust in his Son Jesus Christ; and I should say that the man who comes to his last end in that spirit is not only a Christian but a philosopher—that he need not take rank amid the inferiorities of his age, but may stand at the front, having seen, by the grace of God, the meaning of life,

the mystery of sin, the grandeur of redemption, the certainty of
the fatherhood of God. Suppose we rise to that spirit—what
then ? Is the world of no consequence to us ? The world is of
all the more consequence to us ; we can be in the world, and yet
not of it ; we can handle it with a steadier mastery, because we
come down upon it from the highest heights of spiritual communion. Only he who really knows the Spirit of Christ can be
a true lover and helper of mankind. Others may try to help
and to love; others will invent theories and try new schemes
and set up various institutions ; but they will perish in their
own action, because there is no fountain sufficiently copious to
feed the current of their motive. But he who stands back in the
consciousness of Christ's personality, reality, and Christ's love of
the world—a love that shrank not from death ; he who has the
mind of Christ will live the helpful life ; he will feel that nothing
has been done while anything remains to be accomplished ;
every fatherless child will be his, every weak and deserving
cause will belong to his care ; the whole world will be too small
for a love kindled by the love of the Son of God. We have
committed ourselves to this policy. We know the other way of
life ; we know we can attempt to do without the religious
principle ; we can attempt to do without prayer or the recognition of divine ministries and influences ; we have deliberately
and for ever left that side. Do not speak to us as if we had no
experience of the atheistic way of living ; do not regard us as
innocent and simpering inquirers who have not yet known the
mystery and the grandeur of atheism. We know what it is to be
in a temple without a God, to pass by an altar without a sacrifice,
to take our own life into our own keeping ; we have done it, and
to-day we return, saying, each for himself,—How many servants
in my Father's house have bread enough and to spare, and I
perish with hunger ! I will arise and go to my Father, and tell
him all the tale of sin and sorrow, and if he will admit me into
the lowest room in the house, it will be better than being outside
amidst all this deprivation, weariness, emptiness, sadness, guilt.
We have left the other way of living ; we tried it, and found it
false ; we were allured by its fascinations, and found they were
mocking voices ; we tried to do without God, and our life
withered at the roots. We have now returned to the Shepherd

and Bishop of our souls, by the grace of God and the ministry of God the Holy Ghost; and having come back, we say to every man who is yet outside,—Ho, every one that thirsteth, come, we have a Gospel to preach, and we are not ashamed of its simplicity or of its glory.

PRAYER.

ALMIGHTY GOD, lead us in thine own way, and the end will be rest. We know nothing of the way ourselves, except that it is often long and weary, and much trying to every failing power; but thou knowest the road— all of it; it is not one mile too long. Lead thou us, and we shall be safe; carry us when we are weary, and give us rest according to thine own will and the measure of our need. We bless thee for the way out of time, out of all its perplexities and sorrows; and we bless thee for all the grace, day by day, whereby we are enabled to bear every perplexity and find in it a mysterious joy, and pass under all thy varied discipline and find in it holy meaning and gracious intent—a very mystery of love. We will not go without thy presence; without thy presence there is no light, there is no joy, there is no peace; except thy presence go with us carry us not up hence. Thy will be done on earth as it is done in heaven. Chasten our impatience; show us that we are blind and cannot see afar off, that we were born yesterday and to-morrow we die, that it is ours to rest in the Lord and wait patiently for him. This we have learned of Jesus Christ thy Son; we knew it not until we received his Spirit into our hearts; we were brought to this resignation by way of the Cross; we have learned in all things to rest in God, through Jesus Christ our Lord. So now, we stand still, and see the salvation of God; we are in no haste, in no fever of anxiety; in our hearts is the peace of God, which passeth all understanding, and our life is a long waiting, or a glad service, for Christ. We can do all things through Christ which strengtheneth us; he hath done all for us: we are his debtors: we have nothing that we have not received. We would live unto him who died for us and rose again. Amen.

Numbers x. 1-10.

1. And the Lord spake unto Moses, saying,

2. Make thee two trumpets of silver; of a whole piece shalt thou make them: that thou mayest use them for the calling of the assembly, and for the journeying of the camps.

3. And when they shall blow with them, all the assembly shall assemble themselves to thee at the door of the tabernacle of the congregation.

4. And if they blow but with one trumpet, then the princes, which are heads of the thousands of Israel, shall gather themselves unto thee.

5. When ye blow an alarm, then the camps that lie on the east parts shall go forward.

6. When ye blow an alarm the second time, then the camps that lie on the south side shall take their journey: they shall blow an alarm for their journeys.

7. But when the congregation is to be gathered together, ye shall blow, but ye shall not sound an alarm.

8. And the sons of Aaron, the priests, shall blow with the trumpets; and they shall be to you for an ordinance for ever throughout your generations.

9. And if ye go to war in your land against the enemy that oppresseth you, then ye shall blow an alarm with the trumpets; and ye shall be remembered before the Lord your God, and ye shall be saved from your enemies.

10. Also in the day of your gladness, and in your solemn days, and in the beginnings of your months, ye shall blow with the trumpets over your burnt offerings, and over the sacrifices of your peace offerings; that they may be to you for a memorial before your God: I am the Lord your God.

THE TRUMPETS OF PROVIDENCE.

MOSES was commanded to make two trumpets of silver. They were to be used in calling the assembly, and for the journeying of the camps. The trumpets were to be sounded in different ways. When one trumpet was blown, then the princes were to gather themselves unto Moses; when an alarm was blown, the camps were to move; when the congregation was to be gathered together, the trumpets were to be blown, but so blown as not to sound an alarm. The trumpets were to be blown by the sons of Aaron, the priests. Whether in war or in festival, the trumpets were to be to Israel for a memorial before God. Where are those trumpets? The sacred trumpets are still sounded; they still call men to worship, to festival, to battle. If we have lost the literal instrument, we are still, if right-minded, within sound of the trumpets of Providence. We do not now go out at our own bidding; we are, if wise, responding to a Voice, wherever we may be found. We impoverish ourselves by imagining that God does not now call the people to worship, the camp to war, the family to festival, the Church to victory. Look at the men who are pouring forth in all directions every morning; stand, in imagination, at a point from which you can see all the stations at which men alight; so present the scene to the fancy that you can see every little procession hastening to its given point of departure; then bring on all the processions to the various points of arrival; read the faces of the men; take in the whole scene. What action; what colour; what expression of countenance! And if we had ears acute enough to hear, what various voices are being sounded by every life; what tumult; what desire; what intersection of paths; what imminent collisions!—and yet the whole scene moves on with a kind of rough order all its own. What has called these men together— and yet not together?—the trumpet! That it was not a literal trumpet does not destroy the high poetry of the occasion; the trumpet is the more wonderful that it is not material. These men are not in a trance; they are not night-walkers; they have not been seduced by some dream to come out all at once, wandering hither and thither, not knowing destiny, purpose, or intention. This is a scheme; there is a mind behind all this panorama; it never could settle itself into such order and effect and issue if it were the mere sport of chance. Watch the scene : it is full of pathos, it is loaded with manifold sorrow. An awful sight is a crowd of men; the bustle, the rush, the apparent hilarity cannot hide the tragedy. To what are these men hastening? Explain the scene. Some have heard the trumpet calling to controversy. Many of these men carry bloodless swords; they are well equipped with argument; they are about to state the case, to defend the position, to repel, to assert, to vindicate righteousness, and to claim compensation for virtue outraged ; they are soldiers; they have mapped out the battle-field in private ; all their forces have been disposed within the sanctuary of the night, and presently the voice of genius and of eloquence will be heard in high wrangling, in noble contention, that so the wicked may claim nothing that is not his own, and the righteous have the full reward of his purity.   They are going to the political arena to adjust the competing claims of nations, or causes ; war is in their eyes ; should they speak, they would speak stridently, with clear, cutting tone, with military precision and emphasis ; they would hold no long parley with men, for they mean the issue to end in victory.   Others have heard no such trumpet: they have heard another call—to peaceful business, to daily routine, to duty, made heavy often by monotony, but duty still, which must be done according to the paces and beatings of the daily clock.   They cannot resist that voice without resist-ing themselves.   Sometimes they long to be in more active scenes, to vary the uniformity by some dash or enterprise, to startle the blood into a quicker gallop by doing something unusual and startling ; but they are not so called by the trumpet ; they are moved in that direction by some mean passion or unholy rivalry.   The trumpet has called them to the culture of fields, to the exchanges and settlements of merchandise, to the business without which the world, in its broadest civilisation, would stand still ; having heard the trumpet, they obey.   And other men, in smaller bands,—more aged men,—men who have seen service in the market field, in the political field, in the field of literature, —how go they ?   Away towards sunny scenes, quiet meadows, lakes of silver, gardens trimmed with the patience and skill of love.   They are men of leisure, men in life's afternoon.   The sunbeam has been a trumpet to them ; hearing it, they said,— Who would remain at home to-day ?   All heaven calls us out, the great blue arch invites us to hospitality in the fields and woods and by the river-side.   All men are obeying a trumpet ; the call is addressed from heaven to earth every morning.   We may have outlived the little, straight, silver trumpet, turned up at the ends ; but the trumpet invisible, the trumpet of Providence, the call of Heaven, the awakening strain of the skies,—this we cannot outlive : for the Lord is a Man of war, and must have the battle continued ; the Lord is a Father, and must have the family

constituted in order; the Lord is a Shepherd, and must have the
flocks led forth that they may lie down in the shadow at
noonday.

There are other men going forth. Fix yourselves again, in
imagination, at a point from which you can see nations moving
on as if to some great conference; they move from the east and
from the west, from the north and from the south;—fair men,
men of darker hue; men speaking our own language, men talking
an unknown tongue; stalwart men, trained, every muscle having
been under the touch of culture; men carrying arms of various
names, all meant to be steeped in blood. Have these men come
out in some fit of somnambulism? Are they sleep-walkers?
Is all this an illustration of nightmare? What is it? These
men have heard a trumpet. Many trumpets have been sounded,
and yet in the midst of all the blare and stormy blast there is
one clear note. What is the meaning of all this movement of
the camps? Strong nations are called to go out and support
weak ones. It is a policy of insanity which says, Take no heed
of other people; let them fight their own battles and settle their
own controversies. That is not the spirit of Christ. Every
weak nation belongs to the strong one; every fatherless child
belongs to the man who can keep it, and teach it, and guide
it. Were nations equal and causes equal, then the foolish talk
of leaving men alone might have some point in it. We must not
leave the slave and the slave-holder to settle the controversy;
the slave-holder will soon settle it, if it be so left; it is not an
equal fight. Freedom must plant all its soldiers on the field,
and strike for weakness and beat down the oppressor and grind
him out of existence. Who will speak one word in favour of
war? No Christian man. War can have no purely Christian
defence as war. It sometimes becomes a dire necessity;
it is, in very deed, the last appeal. As war, it is not only
barbarous and irrational, it is infernal, altogether and inex-
pressibly deplorable. Yet we cannot read history or study events
without seeing that the Lord has not scrupled to call himself
"a Man of war," and the sword has had a place in the history
of freedom and the development of progress. What Christian
men ought to see is, that the cause is good; that war is the only
alternative; that having exhausted all the pleas of reason, all

the entreaties of persuasion, all the claims of righteousness, all the appeals of pathos, nothing is to be done but to fight the tyrant with his own weapons. The Lord go with the right; the Lord support the weak; the Lord comfort those who are suddenly and tragically bereaved. But there is a call to difficulty, a call to battle, a call to sorrow. We must not delude ourselves into the notion that we are only called to Sabbatic calm, and the security of the sanctuary, and the delights of the mead, and the summer holiday of the verdant woods filled with sweet music of birds; we are called to battle, to loss, to die far away from home; and, rightly accepted, obedience to such a call means heroism upon earth and coronation in heaven.

The trumpets were to be sounded by the priests. The priests are not likely to sound many trumpets to-day. Ministers have been snubbed and silenced into an awful acquiescence with the stronger party. The pulpit should be a tower of strength to every weak cause. Women should hasten to the Church, saying, —Our cause will be upheld there. Homeless little children should speed to the sanctuary, saying,—We will be welcomed there. Slaves running away should open the church door with certainty of hospitality, saying,—The man who stands up in that tower will forbid the tyrant to reclaim me, or the oppressor to smite me with one blow. It was God's ordination that the trumpet should be sounded by the priests—interpreting that name properly, by the teachers of religion, by the man of prayer, by the preachers of great and solemn doctrines; they are to sound the trumpet, whether it be a call to festival or to battle. We dare not do so now, because now we have house-rent to pay, and firing to find, and children to educate, and customs to obey. Were we clothed in sackcloth, or with camels' hair, and could we find food enough in the wilderness—were the locusts and the honey sufficient for our natural appetites, we might beard many a tyrant, and decline many an invitation, and repel many an impertinent censor; but we must consider our ways, and balance our sentences, and remember that we are speaking in the ear of various representatives of public opinion and individual convic- tion. The pulpit has gone down! It has kept its form and lost its power; its voice is a mumbling tone, not a great trumpet blast that creates a space for itself, and is heard above the hurtling storm and the rush of hasteful and selfish merchandise. Were ministers to become the trumpeters of society again, what an awakening there would be in the nation! Were every Sabbath day devoted to the tearing down of some monster evil—were the sanctuary dedicated to the denunciation, not of the vulgar crimes which everybody condemns, but the subtle and unnamed crimes which everybody practises, the blast of the trumpet would tear the temple walls in twain! We live in milder times—we are milder people : we wish for restfulness. The priests wish to have it so also,—like priest, like people The man who comes with a trumpet of festival will be welcomed ; the man who sounds an alarm will be run away from by dyspeptic hearers, by bilious supporters, and by men who wish to be let alone—to creep into heaven, and to be as unnoticed there as they were unknown here.

There are trumpets which call us in spiritual directions. They are heard by the heart. They are full of the tone of persuasion—that highest of all the commandments. The heart hears the trumpet on the Sabbath day. The trumpet that could sound an alarm is softened in its tone into a tender entreaty, or a cheerful persuasion, or a promise of enlarged liberty. Everything depends upon the tone. The trumpet may be the same, but the tone is different. We cannot take up the trumpet of the great player and make it sound as he made it. What is it, then, that plays the trumpet ? It is the soul. If we knew things as we ought to know them, we should know that it is the soul that plays every instrument, that sings every hymn, that preaches every discourse that has in it the meaning of God and the behest of Heaven. No man can deliver your messages ; no man can preach your sermon. Never trust any man to deliver a message for you if you can by any possibility deliver it yourself. The words may be the very words you used, and yet what from you would have been a persuasion, from the lips of another may become almost an insult. Who can put the proper tone into the instrument—make it talk lovingly, soothingly ? Who can make the trumpet pronounce a benediction ? Only the skilled player whose lessons have been begun, continued, and consummated in heaven. We perish for lack of tone. We have the right doctrine but the

wrong expression; the words are the words of God, but the
voice is an iron one—a tongue heavy, and without the subtle
emphasis which makes every note a revelation and every tone
a welcome.   Hear men read what you have written, if you would
really see in it some other meaning than what you intended to
convey.   Ask another man to read the writing for you.   Whilst
you read it, you read it, with your soul's sympathy and with a
purpose in your heart, and the words answer something that is
within you, and therefore you imagine that the speech is sphered
off into completeness and is resonant with tones of music.   Hand
it to your friend; let him stand up and read your sermon back
to you, and there is no humiliation upon earth equal to the agony
of that distress,—every word misunderstood, the emphasis put
in the wrong place, words that you shade off to a vanishing point
are brought to the front and made to be principal actors upon the
scene; and you, with a wounded heart, turn away and say that
your word has returned unto you void.   But hear some man read
who has entered into the very music of your soul, and he brings
back a larger sermon than you gave him; he has heard every
word; all the minor tones, all the shades of thought have
impressed themselves upon his heart, and when he reads you
say—" Would God he had first made the speech!   Surely the
people would have risen and then bowed down and said,—The
Lord, he is God; the Lord, he is God."   The same trumpet
called to festival and to war; so the Gospel has two tones : it
calls lovingly, sweetly, tenderly; and it sounds an alarm,
making the night tremble through all its temple of darkness,
and sending into men's hearts pangs of apprehension and unutterable fear.

There is another trumpet yet to sound : " Behold, I show you
a mystery ; We shall not all sleep, but we shall all be changed.
In a moment, in the twinkling of an eye, at the last trump :
for the trumpet shall sound, and the dead shall be raised incorruptible, and we shall be changed."   The trumpet is not lost,
then ; it is in heaven, where the Ark of the Testimony is, where
the Shekinah is, where the Tabernacle of God is.   The Apocalypse has taken charge of all the things which we thought were
lost.   Reading on through the history, we say,—This is evolu-

tion : see how we have dropped off all these elementary, initial, temporary things, and how we have risen up into spirituality and idealism and the freedom of an air which has no boundary lines, no foundations, no beginning, no ending. And as we are talking this religious licentiousness, behold, the Apocalypse comes, and puts before us all the things we thought we had grown away from. Without the Apocalypse, the New Testament would have come to a deadlock ; with the Apocalypse, the whole Bible is reunited, consolidated into a massive consummation, and in the Apocalypse we have tribes—ay, of Judah, and Asher, and Simeon, and Zebulun, of Joseph and Benjamin ; we have censers and altars and significant blood, great lights, mighty voices, marvellous exhibitions of all kinds of strength. It seems as if all the Levitical ritual had been transformed and glorified into some sublimer significance. This is the Book of God. We thought the silver trumpets were lost, and we read,—And at the last, a great trumpet was sounded in heaven, and announcements were made to earth by the trumpet sounded by an angel, and the last battle was convoked by the trumpet of a spiritual trumpeter. He that hath ears to hear, let him hear. Speak, Lord, for thy servant heareth !

Numbers x. 29-36.

29 And Moses said unto Hobab, the son of Raguel the Midianite, Moses, father-in-law, We are journeying unto the place of which the Lord said, I will give it you : come thou with us, and we will do thee good : for the Lord hath spoken good concerning Israel.

30. And he said unto him, I will not go; but I will depart to mine own land, and to my kindred.

31. And he said, Leave us not, I pray thee ; forasmuch as thou knowest how we are to encamp in the wilderness, and thou mayest be to us instead of eyes.

32. And it shall be, if thou go with us, yea, it shall be, that what goodness the Lord shall do unto us, the same will we do unto thee.

33. And they departed from the mount of the Lord three days' journey : and the ark of the covenant of the Lord went before them in the three days' journey, to search out a resting place for them.

34. And the cloud of the Lord was upon them by day, when they went out of the camp.

35. And it came to pass, when the ark set forward, that Moses said, Rise up, Lord, and let thine enemies be scattered ; and let them that hate thee flee before thee.

36. And when it rested, he said, Return, O Lord, unto the many thousands of Israel.

GOSPEL INVITATIONS.

THE standards were all in motion. In the first place there went the standard of the camp of the children of Judah ; immediately following came the standard of the camp of Reuben ; then followed the standard of the camp of the children of Ephraim ; and last of all came the standard of the camp of the children of Dan. When the camps began to move, Moses said unto Hobab, his father-in-law,—We are going now ; everything is set in order for the march ;—"We are journeying unto the place of which the Lord said, I will give it you : come thou with us, and we will do thee good : for the Lord hath spoken good concerning Israel." It was a speech of nature. There is a gospel in human feeling. If we could abolish all written gospels, all doctrinal methods of welcoming and persuading men, there would still remain the gospel of love, sympathy, tenderness, all that is involved in the noblest meaning of the term *nature.* The gospel of heaven is in harmony with this gospel of the heart; it lifts it up to highest meanings, interprets it into broadest, brightest hopes, sanctifies and purges it of all selfishness and narrowness. This is the hold which the Gospel will always have upon human attention. It appeals to the heart; it addresses the pain of necessity; it answers the often-unspoken interrogatories of the soul. Thus it can never fail. Our conceptions of it will be changed; our methods of arguing it will be done away, being superseded by nobler methods; but the innermost quantity itself —the central spirit of redemption, love, hospitality—this will remain evermore, because, though we pass away, Christ is the same yesterday, and to-day, and for ever. Our years fail, and with them go all methods and plans and schemes of work; but Christ is the same, and his time is eternity.

A beautiful picture this! full of modern questioning—a very pattern of inquiry and invitation in a gospel sense. Can we honestly invite men to join us on our life-march? Consider the question well. Do not involve others in grievous and mournful responsibilities. Do not entreat men to leave what is to them at least a partial blessing, unless you are sure you can replace that enjoyment by purer and larger gladness. Can we honestly, with the full consent of judgment, conscientiousness, and experience, invite men to join us in the way which we have determined to take? If not, do not let us add the murder of souls to our other crimes. Do not let us, merely for the sake of companionship, involve in ruin innocent men. What is our life-march? To what place are we journeying? Who laid its foundation? Who lighted its lamps? Who spread its feast? What is its name? Are not many men wandering without a destiny? Is it not too usual to have no map of life, no definite end in view, no location that can be named to pursue day and night until we reach its golden streets? There is too much of haphazard in our life—not knowing where the night will land us, going forth day by day at a venture, not sure whether it is a mountain or a valley, a garden or a wilderness, with which the day shall close. This is not living; this is adventure, empiricism,—the very quackery of wisdom, the very irony and sarcasm of knowledge. Moses knew whither the camps were going ; they were all set in one direction. The divine flame was seen through the immediate cloud, and with eyes fixed upon the glowing point, away went the standards, the confidence of the leaders being in God, and the hope of the people being in the wisdom of the Most High. What is our destiny ? Towards what place are we journeying ? Are we surprised when we see an angel ? or do we say,—This is the satisfaction of expectation ? Sad, to tears and veriest woe, is the life that has no map, no plan, no purpose,—that is here and there, retracing its steps, prying, wondering, experimenting, frittering away its energy in doing and undoing, in marching and remarching. All wisdom says,—Determine your course ; have one object in view ; be ruled by one supreme purpose ; and make all circumstances, incidents, and unexpected events, fall into the march and harmony of the grand design. Be careful how you ask people to go along with you. First lay down a basis of sound wisdom. " We are journeying unto the place of which the Lord said, I will give it you." If that be the first sentence, or part of it, the sentence may end in the boldest invitation ever issued by love to the banquet of grace and wisdom. But let us have no adventuring, no foolish or frivolous speculation in life ; let us speak from the citadel of conviction and from the sanctuary of assured religious confidence.

Have we such a view of the end as may make us independent of immediate trials ? Was it all, then, such plain sailing, or easy marching, or garden-tramping, that Moses could invite any stranger to join the march ? Was he not exchanging one wilderness for another ? To what was he inviting his father-in-law ?—to great palaces immediately in front of him ? to a smoking feast ? to rivers of heaven's own pure wine ? He was inviting the man to march, to the incidents of battle, to the discipline of the day, to circumstances often fraught with trial and pain, disappointment and mockery ; for there were birds in the wilderness that were hooting at Israel, voices in the air taunting the leaders and mocking the priests. When we invite men to join us on the Christian pilgrimage, it must be on the distinct understanding that we are ruling the present by the future. This is precisely the logic of Moses :—" We are journeying unto the place." The end was indicated—the goal, the destiny of the march ; and that was so bright, so alluring, so glowing with all hospitable colour, that Moses did not see that to-morrow there was to be a battle, or seeing it, already passed the warfield like a victor. This, too, is the Christian logic as laid down by Paul ; the great apostle said,—" For our light affliction, which is but for a moment, worketh for us a far more exceeding and eternal weight of glory ; while we look not at the things which are seen, but at the things which are not seen : for the things which are seen are temporal ; but the things which are not seen are eternal." He brought " the power of an endless life " to bear upon the immediate day : he quieted to-day's tumult by a sure anticipation of heaven's peace. This is right reasoning ; this is practical philosophy. There is nothing pleasant in the process : " No chastening for the present seemeth to be joyous, but grievous : nevertheless afterward it yieldeth the peaceable fruit of righteousness unto them which are exercised thereby." Truly we have no special invitation that commends itself by the immediate rest and quiet and release and Sabbatic tranquillity which may be enjoyed. The Christian does not call the world to what the world understands by peace and luxury, rest and enjoyment ; these terms are indeed true in the Christian acceptation, but the world has not been educated to receive that acceptation, and to speak in those terms to a world not understanding them, may be to tell lies under the very banner of the Gospel. He who accepts the invitation to march with the Christian camp, accepts a call to service, duty, discipline, pain, disappointment, varied and continual chastisement,—self-consideration put down, passion destroyed, self-will rooted out, pride and vanity crushed down under a heavy weight. To join the Christian camp is to begin a process of self-mortification, to undergo all the discipline of self-contempt, and to accept much strain and distress of life. Is this Gospel-preaching ? It is so. Will not this repel men ? It will at first,—it must at first. It is Christ's method : " If any man will follow me, let him take up his cross." How, then, did Jesus Christ encounter the opening difficulties of the road and pass the trial of the cross ? In the same way—for the wisdom of God is unchanging :—he " had respect unto the recompense of the reward." " For the joy that was set before him he endured the cross, despising the shame, and is set down at the right hand of the throne of God." Moses had respect unto the recompense of the reward. Christ saw the end from the beginning; in the very conduct of the battle, he was wearing the conqueror's diadem. We must draw ourselves forward by taking firm hold of the end,—in other words, we must have such a conception of life's destiny as will invigorate every noble motive, stir every sacred passion, and make us more than conquerors in all war and conflict. This was the reasoning of Moses, this was the reasoning of Paul, this was the practice of Christ; and we are not yet advanced enough in true wisdom to modify the terms or readjust and redistribute the conditions.

Moses did not invite Hobab to join merely for the sake of being in the company; he expected service from Hobab, the son of Raguel the Midianite. He said,—" Leave us not, I pray thee; forasmuch as thou knowest how we are to encamp in the wilderness, and thou mayest be to us instead of eyes "—in other words,—Thou knowest the ground so well that thy presence will be of service to us; experience will assist devotion; we are willing to march : we know nothing of the processes of the way : thou understandest the whole country : come with us and be as eyes unto us. Moses showed leadership even there; it was the invitation of a soldier and a legislator and a wise man. Eyes are of inexpressible value in the whole conduct of life; to be able to see, to take note of, to recognise—the man who can do this is rendering service to the whole Church. So we invite men to come with us that they may render service according to their opportunity and capacity. To some men we say,—If you will come, you will supply the music. To others,—you will furnish the inspiration. And to others,—If you come with us, we shall feel the stronger in the security of your presence; there is such massiveness in your character, such solidity in your judgment, such ripeness of experience in your life, that if you will join this march, we shall be your debtors; you will give as well as take; you will bless as well as be blessed.

Did Moses make a mistake here ? I fancy so. Could Moses make mistakes ? He often did. What then becomes of his inspiration ? It is untouched; but Moses often acted in his own name and strength. He is weak here. When he gave the invitation he was noble: he intended to do the man good; but when he put in the reason, he showed the incompleteness of his faith. What did he want with Hobab's eyes? Had he forgotten the Eye that struck off the iron wheels of Egypt's chariots? For a moment, perhaps, he had. Who can be always his best self? Who can every day stand on the rock of the Amen of his own great prayers? Who is there amongst us—prince or priest or strongest man—that does not want some little local assistance? We are broken down by the wants of the place, by the necessities of the occasion, by the small difficulties of the road. Moses had no difficulty whatever as to the end of the way; and it is possible for us to have very definite conceptions of heaven, and yet to be asking help on the road from men to whom we should never come in suppliant attitude; offer to give them something, to do them good, to take them to the place of rest and security; but who can patronise the camps of Israel? Who can come in saying,—I am necessary to the march of the Church, to the triumph of those who war in the name of the Lord of hosts? Abram showed a better mettle; he said to the king, who offered him hospitality and bounty,—No; "lest thou shouldest say, I have made Abram rich." Moses wanted the eyes of a local man to help him, forgetting that God had been to him all eye—a fire by night, a cloud by day,—a veiled eye with the fire trembling under the filament. We all forget these things, and we want a crutch, forgetting the sword is enough; we want the help of magistrate, or important man, or local celebrity, or wise resident, forgetting that we are in charge of God, that his Spirit is the one fountain of inspiration, and that when we ask for human help, we distrust the Providence of God. But this is like us: we do wish the magistrate to help us just a little. We are not altogether independent of the spirit of local respectability: we will go to the little when we might go to the great, to the human when we might go to the divine,—to Hobab when we might go to Jehovah. Take care when you go to men that you ask no favour of them for God's camp; do not beg for patrons. Die of divinely-appointed starvation—if such discipline there be—rather than accept help which interferes with the completeness of faith in God.

The Church should always offer great invitations. The Church is not a Church if it be inhospitable. Christ's Church should always have its table spread, its flagons of wine full, and its bounty ready; and it should always be saying,—Still there is room: bring in the hungry guests; inquire not into littlenesses, peculiarities, infirmities, dressings and decorations; but go out into the highways, and the hedges, and compel them to come in. Has the Church lost its power of invitation—sweet welcome, boundless hospitality? Is it not now putting up little toll-gates of its own, and asking questions of approaching guests which Heaven never suggested? Is it using the eyes of Hobab when it might avail itself of the omniscience of God? If you are not giving Christian invitations, other people will give invitations of another kind. Men will not go without invitation; it is for us to say what shall be the quality and range of that invitation. " My son, if sinners entice thee, consent thou not. If they say, Come with us, let us lay wait for blood, let us lurk privily for the innocent without cause : let us swallow them up alive as the grave; and whole, as those that go down into the pit: we shall find all precious substance, we shall fill our houses with spoil : cast in thy lot among us; let us all have one purse : my son, walk not thou in the way with them; refrain thy foot from their path : for their feet run to evil, and make haste to shed blood." Who is to issue invitations to the young? Who is to be boldest and first in the offer of hospitality to the hungry life? The Church ought to be first; the Christian Gospel ought to have the first claim upon human attention. The Spirit and the bride say, Come; let him that is athirst come, and whosoever will. The Gospel is not a mere argument, a petty contest in dubious words; it is a great speech to the sore heart, a glorious appeal unto the broken spirit; an utterance of love to a world in despair. Let us, then, go back to the old methods of welcoming men. With all newness of scheme and method and plan in the conduct of Christian service, never drop out of your speech the tone of invitation, the music of welcome, the broad and generous call to ample—to infinite hospitality.

Numbers xi. 1-3.

1. And when the people complained, it displeased the Lord : and the Lord heard it ; and his anger was kindled; and the fire of the Lord burnt among them, and consumed them that were in the uttermost parts of the camp.

2. And the people cried unto Moses; and when Moses prayed unto the Lord, the fire was quenched.

3. And he called the name of the place Taberah : because the fire of the Lord burnt among them.

COMPLAINING OF PROVIDENCE.

THE people complained—and the Lord set fire to them! That seems rough judgment, for what is man's speech as set against the divine fire ? We must all agree that this was harsh—utterly and unwarrantably severe, out of all proportion to the temper and intention of the people. The people complained : they were in pain, in distress, in weariness—and the Lord burned them! Who can defend the procedure ? Who can so subordinate his reason and his sense of right as to commend the justice of this tremendous punishment ? So they might say who begin their Bible reading at the eleventh chapter of Numbers. There is only one place at which to begin the reading of the Bible, and that is at the first chapter of Genesis and the first verse ; and there is only one place at which the reading of the Bible can be completed, and that is the last verse of the last chapter of the last book. The difficulty of the Christian argument is that people will begin to read the Bible wherever they please. The Bible has but one beginning and one ending, and only they are qualified to pronounce judgment upon it who read the book from end to end, omitting nothing, setting everything in its right place, and causing the whole to assume its proper perspective and colour. It is easily conceivable that many a man, opening the Bible at this point and beginning his acquaintance with the sacred record at this incident, might exclaim—How harsh the divine action! how devoid not of reason only, but of justice! Who can worship a God who sets fire to people who, living in a wilderness, venture to complain? Who says so?—the man who does not understand the case. Who complains against God?—only he who does not know the meaning of the divine mcvement, the scope of the divine outlook, the purpose of the divine beneficence. Was this the first time the people had complained? Was the voice of whining quite new in the camps of Israel? The Bible does not begin with the Book of Numbers. Read the Book of Exodus, notably the fourteenth and following chapters up to the time of the giving of the law, and you will find complaint following complaint; and what was the divine answer in that succession of reproaches? Was there fire? Did the Lord shake down the clouds upon the people and utterly overwhelm them with tokens of indignation? No. When the Israelites first complained of the pursuing Egyptians, and asked if there were not graves enough in Egypt that they should have been dragged out into the wilderness to be buried, what was the answer?—Stand still and see the salvation of God. When the people complained at Marah, saying,—This water is bitter, and we cannot drink it,—did the fire descend? No spark fell from the angry heavens, but the waters were sweetened, every tang of bitterness being taken out of the pool. When the people complained of their wilderness life and having nothing to eat, what was the answer? Contempt? A storm such as fell upon Sodom and Gomorrah? No such reply was given; but the Lord said,—I will rain down food upon the sandy places, and all you shall have to do will be to go out and gather it. The people complain again—and the Lord burns them! To some murmuring there is but one reply that can be appreciated. The Lord is full of tenderness and compassion,—yea, infinite in piteousness and love is he; but there is a point when his Spirit can no longer strive with us, and when he must displace the persuasions of love by the anger and the judgment of fire.

But this is not the whole case. The people were not complaining only. The word *complaint* may be so construed as to have everything taken out of it except the feeblest protest and the feeblest utterance of some personal desire. But this is not the historical meaning of the word *complaint* as it is found here. What happened between the instances we have quoted and the instance which is immediately before us? Until that question is answered the whole case is not before the mind for opinion or criticism. What then had taken place? The most momentous of all incidents. God had said through Moses to the people of Israel,—Will you obey the law? And they stood to their feet, as it were, and answered in one unanimous reply, —We will. The spirit of obedience having been, as we have seen, thus created, the law was given in detail. You remember the criticism passed upon this circumstance. The law was not given, and then obedience demanded; obedience was promised, and then the law was given. The Ten Words are an answer to a pledge; the pledge committed the people to the Ten Words. What had they said in their pledge? They had uttered a vow which is seldom realised in all the fulness and pathos of its meaning; they had said,—We will have none other gods beside thee. So the people were wedded to their Lord at that great mountain altar; words of fealty and kinship and Godhood had been exchanged, and now these people that had oft complained and had then promised obedience, and had then sworn that they would have none other gods beside Jehovah, complained—went back to their evil ways; and the Lord, who takes out his sword last and only calls upon his fire in extremity, smote them— burned them. And this will he do to us if we trifle with our oaths, if we practise bad faith towards the altar, if we are guilty of malfeasance in the very sanctuary of God. To criticise Providence—who is fit for that high judgment? Providence is a large word; it is like the horizon, encompassing all things with a line that cannot be touched, including all things, yet without bond or token of humiliation. Who can criticise the Providence of life—that marvellous power that lights up the world in the morning, curtains it off with a veil of darkness night by night, blesses its soil with fertility, fills its channels with streams and rivers, feeds the roots of its tiniest flowers, paints the wings of its frailest insects, leads like a cloud by day and like a fire by night, that numbers the hairs of the head of every child living in the Father's house? Who has mind enough, penetration enough, judgment enough, to call God to his bar and pronounce sentence upon the Infinite? We are vexed by details; we are blinded by the immediate dust of the road. We are not called to judgment, but to acquiescence, to acceptance, to gratitude, to hope. To criticise God is to usurp the divine throne. Let who will pass their insane judgments upon the infinite scale of life; let it be ours, where we cannot understand, to believe; where we cannot direct, to accept, and in all things to kiss the rod and bless the Hand that lifts it. This is not the surrender of reason; it is the baptism and consecration of understanding.

Were the people content with complaining? They passed from complaining to lusting, saying, " Who shall give us flesh to eat? We remember the fish, which we did eat in Egypt freely; the cucumbers, and the melons, and the leeks, and the onions, and the garlic: but now our soul is dried away: there is nothing at all, beside this manna, before our eyes. . . . And the people went about, and gathered it, and ground it in mills, or beat it in a mortar, and baked it in pans, and made cakes of it "—and grumbled the while because Egyptian appetite was excited within them. There is a philosophy here. You cannot stop short with complaining. Wickedness never plays a negative game. The man who first complains will next erect his appetite as a hostile force against the will of God. A marvellous thing is this, to recollect our lives through the medium of our appetites, to have old relishes return to the mouth, to have the palate stimulated by remembered sensations. The devil has many ways into the soul. The recollection of evil may prompt a desire for its repetition. Worldliness has, no doubt, its pleasant memories. Let us be just to all men. The worldly life is not without its sensations of pleasure and gratification. We do not expect men to enter the sanctuary and forget all the old days as if they had had no pleasure in them. Old tastes will revive; the tongue will be stirred to new desires; an odour in the air will remind you of the feast you have abandoned; the sight of an old companion may drive you to wish for just one more day in the old house of bondage, in the old sensual relations. We live a very delicate life. We are not far from the enemy at any one point in our history. The sight of a face may awaken within us influences which we had supposed to be dead; the resonance of an old song may bring back the memory of black nights consecrated to the service of the devil with a will. We must not be harsh upon those who remember the pleasant side of Egyptian life. *We* may now think of the old days with some pleasure :—how free the riotous dance was; how eager our appetite at the feast; how we relished the ardent poison; how we enjoyed the exchange of passionate looks and words! And if a longing sometimes steals in upon the heart, putting back its prayer and threatening its overthrow, this may not be sin, it may be a severe temptation, a call to a tremendous struggle; and if in that struggle the poor soul may fall for a moment, yet, if its uppermost desire be true, though it fall it shall not be utterly cast down. If any man has escaped the snare of drunkenness, or the snare of evil indulgence of any kind, and yet now and again feels as if, after all, the old days had charms and pleasures, that transient feeling is not necessarily a sin on the part of the man who experiences its pain; it is a temptation of the evil one, and is only to be put down by nobler prayer, by a sharper, keener cry for omnipotent defence.

The public complaint affected the bravest spirit in the camp. Moses was utterly tired out. I wonder that all leaders are not occasionally driven to extremity by sheer disgust at public ingratitude. Moses said, " Kill me . . . out of hand." Moses was not a man who naturally longed for extermination; he was a soldier; he was born to be a leader and a commander of the people; but continual friction, daily exasperation, eternal misunderstanding, and implied insult, wrought in him a state of mind which expressed itself not only in a desire but in a prayer that he might die. Was the leader paid? Was the leader pampered? Was a separate table provided for Moses in the wilderness? Did he not throw himself into the common lot and live the life of the common people of the desert? Yet, notwithstanding, he was the subject of daily reproach and bitterest criticism. Who knows what it is to carry a thousand lives in his heart? Who knows the difficulties of the shepherd's life? Who understands the daily pain of the pastor's heart? What has he to do? To sympathise with all kinds of experiences; to understand all the varied qualities of human life and human desires; to transfuse himself into conditions and relations apparently far remote from his own central gift and call of God; **to make prayer for a thousand suppliants. It is no easy task.**

We should be gentler with men who have given themselves to be our pastors, and to carry us somehow in their great hearts. A bitter word is easily spoken, but it is not easily dislodged from the memory of love. Neglect is easily shown—coldness, contempt, disregard, want of appreciation; but all the time you are bringing the pastor, the shepherd, the leader, the Moses, to desire to die. There is another manslaughter than the vulgar shedding of blood; there is a heart-murder: there are crucifixions without visible crosses. People do not always come to the assault with the avowed purpose of killing or injuring; but for want of consideration and the simplest instincts of justice, they tear men to pieces; they say, in ghostly throngs around the good man's bed, —You shall not sleep to-night; we will tear the sleep from your eyelids and vex you with a thousand tormenting memories. Let us cease from the number of those who criticise the ways of Providence and kill the messengers of Heaven.

God found assistance for Moses,—the only answer Moses could understand at the time. God's answers are accommodated to the state of our intelligence and our moral feeling. To have seventy men moved by a spirit kindred to your own is an answer which can easily be understood. Divine and spiritual replies had been given to Moses again and again; but God says,—The poor soul wants something more visible and substantial this time; I never saw him so borne down,—a man's heart so stout of will, so faultless in its sacred obstinacy; but his bold face looked blanched to-day, his commanding voice hesitated and struggled in utterance to-day; I must give him a new reply. So seventy men were called out who were filled with a kindred spirit, and the Lord said, in effect, to Moses,—I have multiplied thee by seventy : now play the man. Wondrous are the answers of God! They who have studied them most are the most assured in their Christian faith; such men do not need wordy arguments to convince them as to the utility of prayer : they found the answer to the argument on the prayer itself.

What did Moses do ? He took heart again. When he heard of the fire at the outside of the camp—burning, singeing, scorching —he said,—Lord, put the fire out! He prayed for the very people that had very nearly killed him. Herein, he anticipated Christ. John said—"Lord, wilt thou that we command fire to come down from heaven, and consume them?" The Lord said: "Ye know not what manner of spirit ye are of." Two irregular men in the camp began to prophesy; and the message was taken to Moses that another kind of fire had broken out—a species of spiritual and official insanity. Moses said,—Let them alone; good water comes from good fountains, wise words flow from wise minds; do not feel envious on my account; "would God that all the Lord's people were prophets!" That is the philosophy of progress—not dragging down the one prophet to the level of those who might prophesy, but lifting up the common camp until it is moved by divine inspirations. The great preacher has no fear of other preachers arising; the greatest preacher would say,—Put all the churches in a row, and let him who knows most of God prove his knowledge. Have no fear of inspired men, no fear of the multiplication of their number, and do not be jealous of their success; when they succeed, we succeed. The Church is one, and every minister should claim brotherhood with every other minister; to insult one of the brethren ought to be felt to be an insult to the entire fraternity. Joshua thought that Moses would feel rather angry that other people were beginning to usurp his function. Would to Heaven there were fewer Joshuas of this kind and for this purpose! for such tale-bearers work no end of mischief in every circle into which they enter, and none the less mischief that they say— Our motive was pure, our intention was good; we heard these irregular persons exercising an irregular ministry, and we were concerned for the traditional unity of the Church. Have no such concern. The one man the Lord does not need is the tale-bearer. If he must speak, let him go out into a wide and solitary place, in the deepest darkness of the night, and speak his insanity to the unheeding winds. "Would God that all the Lord's people were prophets!" If they were all preachers, they would sympathise more with preachers than they do; if they were all commanders of armies, they would long for some army to command; if they had greater trials, they would have tenderer patience.

How did the Lord treat Moses? He asked him one question, "And the Lord said unto Moses, Is the Lord's hand waxed short?" We always forget the divine element. Moses says,—

"Who am I?" And the Lord says, in effect,—"Yes; who indeed?" It is not a question for you; the battle is not yours, but God's. "Is the Lord's hand waxed short? Thou shalt see now whether my word shall come to pass unto thee or not." The people got their way. The Lord said,—You shall have flesh enough to eat; I will find it: I will send out the winds to bring it, I will command the clouds to shed it; you shall have flesh enough. And whilst they ate the flesh—ate it to satiety—the judgment of the Lord fell upon them,—"And the Lord smote the people with a very great plague," and in that wilderness a great cemetery was dug. The Lord could not be harsher to us sometimes than to answer our prayers. Pray for fine weather, pray for the rain of manna, pray that flesh may be given in the wilderness and fowls in places out of the way; but having so prayed, say, "Nevertheless not my will, but thine, be done," and to that prayer God always sends an angel in reply.

NOTE.

The Israelites murmuring over their heavenly food looked back with regret to the melons and cucumbers, which they had eaten so freely even in Egypt, the land of their captivity. So plentiful are these fruits and vegetables in this and other hot and sandy countries, that they grow luxuriantly either with or without cultivation, climbing up the trees and shrubs, shading the roofs of the native dwellings with their broad green leaves, or covering the ground, which would otherwise be a desert, making it as a garden in fertility and beauty. The weary traveller pauses on his way when he sees from afar the vine-shaped leaves of the water-melon in the Indian cornfields, and he turns aside to seek with eagerness for the delicious fruit, which he is sure of finding cold and refreshing in the hottest season. The cucumber is also most grateful to the taste; cooling to the over-heated frame, and an incentive to more substantial and supporting food than would otherwise be desired ir these tropical countries. The God of love seems so lovingly to have provided for the inhabitants of these and all climates the food most suitable for nourishing and refreshment. Now the Israelites had heavenly food, and they needed none other, but (it is the story of a human heart) they must look back to the cucumbers and melons of Egypt.—C. W.

PRAYER.

ALMIGHTY GOD, thou hast set every one in his place. There is one God. We desire to accept thy will as complete and final. May every man know the calling wherewith he is called of God, and standing therein with all gratitude and patience, may he do his day's work as unto the Lord and not unto men. We accept the appointments of Heaven, saying,—Even so, Father: for so it seemeth good in thy sight. Thou art the Husbandman, and thy will in the vineyard who may question? The garden is thine, and the field, and all the growths of the earth spring out of thy goodness, and are blessed with thy smile. All souls are thine. Every living thing derives its pulse from God's eternity. We will then say,—This is the Lord's world, and God is the Sovereign of the earth, and the Most High controls all life and time. The Lord's will be done. God's blessing be our only heaven. Then we shall be always contented, and our soul shall live the life of peace, because of harmony with purposes divine. Thou dost fix the measure of our days; thou drawest the line and sayest,—This is the end. There we lie down at thy bidding seeing only thy purpose, hearing only thy voice, and being filled with thy Spirit; we know no shame or fear. Thou dost send us upon our errands, and thou dost fix the time of their completion. It is not in man to add one inch unto his stature, to make one hair black or white. Thou hast given us liberty, but thou hast enclosed that liberty within boundaries of thine own measurement. We are still thine—bound to thy throne, working out thy will in this way or in that, and certainly bringing to pass the purposes of eternity. Show us that all the house is ordered from heaven. Deliver us from the vain idea that we can extend our boundaries and inheritances in our own name and strength. May we know that God lives and rules and directs all things, and that he means to judge the earth in righteousness by that Man whom he has ordained, even by Jesus Christ, a Priest for ever and unchangeable. Then we shall have rest in the soul: a broad sunshine will make the whole life glad: the valleys shall be lifted up to the levels, and the mountains shall be brought down and made plain before our feet, and life shall be a harmonious movement towards the blessedness of immortality. We desire thus to reap the harvest of great faith; we would no longer be merely in the seed-time, but, thy will consenting, we would thrust our sickle into the golden harvest and make our souls fat and prosperous on the bounty of Heaven. We would live the life of strong men; we would be confident in faith, assured in sanctified hope, resolute in holy consecration of heart; and thus our life, though long will be short, though short will be long; we shall not know where the common time ends and the Sabbatic hour begins, where the human ceases and the divine interposes. We would be in God, in

Christ; we would be ruled by the Holy Ghost, we would live the upper life; we would see God in our disappointments and acknowledge the grace of Heaven in our humiliaticn, and would be brought to know that there are no inferior places in the Church, that to be a servant of Christ is to be as an angel of God, and to be a doorkeeper in the sanctuary is to be engaged in the highest of human service. Work in us these holy feelings; comfort us with all needful promise; stimulate us by such inspiration as our necessity or exhaustion may require; and, at the end—not knowing it as the end, but hailing it as the beginning—may we know that Christ hath made us more than conquerors. Amen.

Numbers xii.

CLAIMING EQUALITY.

THE question which Miriam and Aaron put to one another is quite a proper one. They said,—"Hath the Lord indeed spoken only by Moses? hath he not spoken also by us?" The inquiry, standing within its own four corners, is one which might be legitimately and reverently propounded. But what question stands thus? Perhaps hardly any that can be put by human curiosity. The interrogation must be determined by the atmosphere surrounding it. The question would take its whole quality at the particular time from the tone of voice in which it was put. Everything depends upon tone. Herein is the weakness of all writing and of all representation of thought by visible symbols. We cannot put into letters our own spirit and purpose; the tone determines the quality, and the tone can never be reported. We are, therefore, driven, if we would form sound judgments upon events, to look at issues and results; and having looked at these, we are by so much qualified to return to the question and judge it as to its real intent. Many persons inquire, with a simplicity too simple to be genuine, whether there was any harm in the question which was put. In the written inquiry, certainly not; but in the spoken interrogation the tone was full of virulence and evil suggestion and unholy design. It will not do to write the question with pen and ink and to submit it to a stranger for judgment. The stranger knows nothing about it, and when it is submitted to him for judgment it is submitted with so finely-simulated an innocence that the man is already prepared to accord a generous judgment to the terms. God is judge. We read that "the Lord heard it." To hear it was everything. It was not reported to the Lord. We cannot report anything to him in the sense of extending his information. The terribleness of his being judge and the graciousness of his being judge, is to be found in the fact that he *heard* it—balanced the tones, adjusted the emphasis, marked the vocal colouring, and interpreted the words by the speaker's tone and temper and attitude. The final judgment is with him who " heard " the cause during its process and during its consummation.

If the Lord did speak by Miriam and Aaron, what then ? The Lord himself acknowledges that he speaks in different ways to different men. To some—perhaps to most—he comes in vision and in dream ; things are heard as if they were spoken beyond the great mountain ; they are echoes, hollow soundings, wanting in shape and directness, yet capable of interpretations that touch the very centres and springs of life, that make men wonder, that draw men up from flippancy and frivolity and littleness, and write upon vacant faces tokens of reverence and proofs that the inner vision is at the moment entranced by some unnameable and immeasurable revelation. To other men God speaks " apparently "—that is, in broad and visible figure. He is quite near ; it is as if friend were accosting friend, and if mouth were speaking to mouth, as if two interlocutors were mutually visible and speaking within hand-range of one another. There is nothing superstitious about this ; it is the fact of to-day. This is written in the book that was published last week, and will be written in the book that is to be issued to-morrow. This is not a ghost story ; this is not some little cloud brought from Oriental skies, never seen otherwhere, and never beheld since it was first looked upon thousands of years ago ; this is solemn history, contemporaneous history—history of which we ourselves form vital constituents. Take a book of science—what do you find in that rational and philosophical bible ? You find certain names put uppermost. The writer says it is given to but few men to be a Darwin or a Helmholtz—they seem to sweep the whole horizon of knowledge. The Right Hon. W. E. Gladstone has said that it seemed to him as if Aristotle comprehended the entire register of the human mind. Why should not every boy that has caught his first fly, or cut in two his first worm,

say,—Hath not the Lord spoken unto me as well as unto Darwin,
or Cuvier, or Buffon ?—who are they ? But it does so happen
that outside the Bible we have the Moses of science—the chief
man of letters, the prince of song. Take the history of music,
and we find names set by themselves like insulated stars—great
planetary names. What would be thought of a person who
has just learned the notes of music, saying,—Hath not the Lord
spoken unto me as well as unto Beethoven ? He has ; but he has
not told you so much. There is a difference in kind ; there is a
difference in quality. We are all the Lord's children, but he
hath spoken unto us in different ways and tones and measures ;
and to found upon this difference some charge or reproach, or to
hurl against the chiefs of the world some envious questioning,
is to go far to throw suspicion upon the assumption that the Lord
has spoken to us at all. We must learn that all these differences are as certainly parts of the divine order as are the settings
and movements of the stars. " One star differeth from another
star in glory," yet no asteroid has ever been known to blame
the planets because of their infinite largeness and their infinite
lustre. Men must accept divine appointment. Every man must
stand in the call wherewith he is called, and encourage a religious
pride and sacred satisfaction with the position which he has
been called to occupy. Light is thrown upon these ancient
stories by reading them in the atmosphere of modern events.
We have this twelfth chapter of Numbers, as to its broadest
significance, enacted amongst us every day we live. There are
great men in all lines and vocations, and there are men who
might be great in modesty, if they would accept their position, and
might turn their very modesty into genius, if they would acknowledge that their allotment is a determination of the hand of God.

"And . . . Miriam became leprous, white as snow." That
is the fate of the sneerer in all times and in all lands. The
sneerer is not a healthy man ; though he be sleek in flesh and
quite bright with a foxy brightness of eye, there is no real health
in the man : for health is a question of the soul ; it is the soul
that lives. The sneerer is always shut out. For a moment his
sneer provokes a little titter, but the sneer has marked the man,
and he will not be invited again. Society cannot do with so
much bitterness. There is a spirit in man, and the inspiration

of the Almighty giveth him understanding; and the result is that the bitter cynic, who always tries to tear the clothes of the great man, knowing he cannot tear his character, is shut out of the camp, for no man wants him.   What is wanted?   Gentleness, tenderness, sympathy, appreciation, encouragement,—these will always be welcome; these shall have the chief seat at the table; these shall return to the feast whenever they show any inclination to come; the father and the mother and the children down to the least, and the servants of the household—yea, all, bid them loving welcome.   But the critic is not wanted—the sneerer is in the way; he closes the lips of eloquence, he turns away from him the purest cheek of child life; he is a blight like an east wind; and he never is permitted to repeat his visits in any family that respects its order, or cares for its most religious and heavenly progress.   A heavy penalty was leprosy for sneering. It is impossible for any penalty to be too great for sneering. Sneering is of the devil; sneering is a trick of the Evil One.   No man can sneer and pray; no man can sneer and bless: the benediction will not sit on lips that have been ploughed up by the iron of sneering.   Blessed be God for such judgments.   God thus keeps society tolerably pure.   There are men standing outside to-day whom nobody wants to see, whom no child would run to meet, for whom no flower of the spring is plucked,— simply because they are always challenging the supremacy of Moses, and thus obtruding their own insignificance, and bringing into derision faculties that might otherwise have attracted to themselves some trifling measure of respect.

We find this same law operating in all directions.   There are books that say,—Are not we inspired as well as the Bible? The answer is,—Certainly you are.   The Lord had spoken to Miriam and to Aaron as certainly as he had spoken to Moses, —but with a difference; and it is never for Moses to argue with Miriam.   Moses takes no part in this petty controversy. He would have disproved his superior inspiration if he had stooped to this fray of words.   So some books seem to say,— Are not we also inspired?   The frank and true answer is—Yes. Is not many a sentence in the greatest of dramatists an inspired sentence?   The frank, Christian, just answer is—Yes.   Is not many a discovery in the natural world quite an instance of inspiration? Why hesitate to say—Yes; but always with a difference? The Bible takes no part in the controversy about its own inspiration. The Bible nowhere claims to be inspired. The Bible lives—comes into the house when it is wanted, goes upstairs to the sick-chamber, follows the lonely sufferer into solitude, and communes with him about the mystery of disappointment, discipline, pain of heart; goes to the grave-side, and speaks about the old soldier just laid to rest, the little child just exhaled like a dewdrop by the morning sun. The Bible works thus—not argumentatively, not seeking an opportunity of speaking in some controversy that rages around the question of its inspiration. It lives because no hand can slay it; it stands back, or comes forward, according to the necessity of the case, because of a dignity that can wait, because of an energy that is ready to advance.

Some books claim to be *as* inspired as the Bible. Then they become leprous, and all history has shown that they are put out of the camp. Many books have arisen to put down the Bible; they have had their day: they have ceased to be. We must judge by facts and realities. The glory of the great Book is that it will bear to be translated into every language, and that all the changes of grammar are but changes of a mould, which do not affect the elasticity of water : the water of life flows into every mould and fills up all the channels, varying the courses and figure of the channels as you may. The Book is not an iron book, whose obstinacy cannot be accommodated to human requirements or progress : this is the water of life—a figure that indicates all qualities that lay hold of progress, development, change. The Bible is a thousand books—yea, a thousand thousand books, to a number no man can number, making every heart a confidential friend, whispering to every eager and attentive life some tender message meant for its own ear alone. When a man who has no claim to the dignity asserts that he is upon an equality with the great musician, the great musician takes no part in the fray; when the competitor has played his little trick, one touch of the fingers regulated by the hand divine will settle the controversy. By this token we stand or fall with our Christianity, with our great Gospel. If any man has a larger truth to speak, let him speak it; if any man can touch the

wounded human heart with a finer delicacy, a more healing
sympathy, let him perform his miracle. To be spoken against
is no sign of demerit. We are too fearful about this matter.
Put your finger upon any name in human history that indicates
energy of a supreme kind, influence of the most beneficent quality,
that has not been spoken against. The mischief is, as ever, that
timid people imagine the charge to bring with it its own proof.
The Church is wrecked by timidity. The fearful man is doing
more injury to-day than can be done by any number of assailants.
The man who treats his Christianity as a private possession, and
who is afraid lest any man should challenge him to combat, is a
man who is a dead weight upon the Church, and if we could get
rid of that man it would be the happiest event in our Church
history.

How did Moses prove his superiority ? By prayer. In effect,
he said,—Lord, let her alone ; be gentle to her, poor fool ; she is
moved by unworthy impulses—a little feminine jealousy because
of a marriage she cannot understand ; pity her ; wipe off the
white blotch, and allow her to come out again ; perhaps she will
never do it any more :—" Heal her now, O God, I beseech thee."
There he proves that his inspiration was of a quality most noble.
We are strongest when we are weakest ; we are sublimest when
we whisper our prayer under the load that would have oppressed
and destroyed us. Judge your inspiration by your devoutness.
Never be content with any inspiration that can merely ask
questions, create suspicions, perform the unworthy performance
of sneering ; but know that you are a great soul and a valiant
and most royal man and crowned prince, when you take the
large, bright view, which you are bound to do by noble charity.

All this would be of social consequence, and by no means to
be undervalued in the education of the world ; but it acquires its
most appalling solemnity in view of the fact that questioning and
sneering of this kind about prophets, preachers, books, churches,
means to go forward and to challenge the supremacy of Christ.
Sneering cannot stop short at Moses. We cannot draw a line,
saying,—Having overthrown the servant, we shall be content.
There is an impulse in these things, hurrying and driving men
on to issues which perhaps at first they never contemplated.
Beware of beginnings and resist them. To curtail our best

reading is to begin a process that will end in mental darkness. To give up the Church once a day means, being interpreted, that the time will come when the heart will relinquish the Church altogether. A sad and terrible thing it is when men suppose that they can do with less Bible, less Church, less public testimony. They plead weariness, distance, difficulties of a family kind; they are fertile in excuses when the heart is reluctant to go. Let us face broad meanings, final issues. The meaning is that men who challenge Moses will endeavour to dispossess Christ, saying,— "We will not have this man to reign over us." Was not Socrates as pure a man? Have we not found some morality in old Indian books quite as pure as the morality of the New Testament? Did not Marcus Aurelius approach very nearly to the sublimity of Christian ethics? Have there not been many men in all history who have been entitled to sit with Christ in the temple of purity and wisdom? These are not the questions. Christianity does not bring into disrepute any beautiful sentence found anywhere in heaven or in earth. Christ never said,— This is a beautiful thing spoken by a fervid fancy, but you must take no heed of it. He said,—"I am the light of the world," wherever there is a sparkle of brilliance, it is a jet of my own glory; wherever there is a wise word, it is God's word; wherever a beautiful song is sung, it is a snatch of heaven's music. Whoever speaks a holy, pure, comforting word must be permitted to go on with his ministry. If you call down fire from heaven against such an one, ye know not what manner of spirit ye are of.

Numbers xiii., xiv. 1-25.

IRRELIGIOUS FEARS.

GOD gives no speculative commands. When he said—"Send thou men, that they may search the land of Canaan, which I give unto the children of Israel," he meant that the land of Canaan was to be given to Israel whatever difficulties or delays might occur in the process of acquisition. There is no *if* in the commandments of Heaven that may mean either of two courses or either of two ways. God says,—You shall have this, if you are faithful. But the *if* relates to the human mind and to the human disposition, and not to the solidity and certainty of the divine purpose or decree. This is true in morals. Along the line that is laid down in the Bible, which is called, happily and properly, the line of salvation, heaven is found —not the mean heaven of selfish indulgence and selfish complacency and release from mere toil and pain, but the great heaven of harmony with God, identification with the Spirit divine, complete restfulness in the movement of the infinite purpose. There will be difficulties on the road; these difficulties will assume various proportions, according to the dispositions of the men who survey them; but the Lord does not propose to give the end without, by implication, proposing also to find the grace and comfort necessary for all the process. We are not at liberty to stop at processes as if they were final points; we have nothing to do with processes but to go through them; the very call to attempt them is a pledge that they may be overcome. But these processes test the quality of men. It is by such processes that we are revealed to ourselves. If everything came easily as a mere matter of course, flowing in sequence that is never disturbed, we should lose some of the highest advantages of this present time school. We are made strong by exercise; we are made wise by failure; we are chastened by disappointment; driven back again and again six days out of the seven, we are taught to value the seventh day the more, that it gives us rest, and breathing time, and opportunity to consider the situation, so that we may begin another week's battle with a whole Sabbath day's power. To some the processes of life are indeed hard ; let us never underrate them. Men are not cheered when the difficulties of the way are simply under-valued. No man can sympathise with another until he has learned the exact weight of the other man's trouble and the precise pain of his distress. There is a rough and pointless comfort which proceeds upon the principle that you have only to underrate a man's trials—to make them look as little i nd contemptible as possible—in order to invigorate his motive ind to increase his strength. That is a profound mistake. He can sympathise best who acknowledges that the burden is heavy and the back weak, and the road is long, and the sky dull, and the wind full of ominous moaning ;—granted that the sympathising voice can say all this in a tone of real appre-ciation, it has prepared the listener for words of cheer and inspiration—healthy, sound, intelligent courage. This is just the way of the Bible ; it recognises the human lot in all its length and breadth ; it addresses itself to circumstances which it describes with adequate minuteness and with copious and pathetic eloquence.

Here you find a number of men, such as live in all ages, who are crushed by material considerations. They report that the people of the country which they were sent to search were "strong," their cities were "walled and very great," and the population was made up of the Anakim—the "giants," the towering and mighty sons of Anak ; they reported that some dwelt in "the south," and some "in the mountains," and some "by the sea, and by the coast of Jordan." This was a mean report, it was hardly a report at all,—so nearly may a man come to speak the truth, and yet not to be truthful, so wide is the difference between fact and truth. Many a book is true that is written under the name of fiction ; many a book is untrue that lays claim only to the dry arguments of statistics and schedules. Truth is subtle ; it is a thing of atmosphere, perspective, unnameable environment, spiritual influence. Not a word of what the truth says may have occurred in what is known as literal fact, because it is too large a thing ever to be encompassed within the boundaries of any individual experience. The fact relates to an individuality; the truth relates to a race. A fact is an incident which occurred; a truth is a gospel which is occurring throughout all the ages of time. The men, therefore, who reported about walled cities, and tall inhabitants, and mountain refuges, and fortresses by the sea, confined themselves to simply material considerations; they overlooked the fact that the fortress might be stronger than the soldier, that the people had nothing but figure, and weight, and bulk, and were destitute of the true spirit which alone is a guarantee of sovereignty of character and conquest of arms. But this is occurring every day. Again and again we come upon terms which might have been written this very year. We are all men of the same class, with an exceptional instance here and there; we look at walls, we receive despatches about the stature of the people and the number of their fortresses, and draw very frightsome and terrible conclusions concerning material resources, forgetting in our eloquent despatches the only thing worth telling, namely : that if we were sent by Providence and are inspired by the Living God and have a true cause and are intent to fight with nobler weapons than gun and sword, the mountains themselves shall melt whilst we look upon them, and they who inhabit the fortresses shall sleep to rise no more. This is what we must do in life—in all life— educational, commercial, religious. We have nothing to do with outsides and appearances, and with resources that can be totalled in so many arithmetical figures; we have to ascertain, first, Did God send us ? and secondly, if he sent us, to feel that no man can drive us back. If God did not send us, we shall go down before the savage ; if God is not in the battle, it cannot and ought not to succeed, and failure is to be God's answer to our mean and unrighteous and untimely prayer. Who is distressed by appearances ? Who is afraid because the labour is very heavy ? What young heart quails because the books which lie upon the road which terminates in the temple of wisdom are many in number and severe in composition ? We are called to enter the sanctuary of wisdom and of righteousness ; therefore we must take up the books as a very little thing and master them, and lay them down, and smile at the difficulties which once made us afraid.

But one man at least spoke up and said,—We must go; this thing is to be done :—"Caleb stilled the people before Moses, and said, Let us go up at once, and possess it ; for we are well able to overcome it." Was Caleb, then, a giant—larger than any of the sons of Anak ? Was he a Hercules and a Samson in one ? Was his arm so terrific that every stroke of it was a conquest ? We are not told so ; the one thing we are told about Caleb is that he was a man of "another spirit." That determines the quality of the man. Character is a question of spirit. It is an affair of inward and spiritual glow. Caleb had been upon the preliminary search ; Caleb had seen the walls, and the Anakim, and the fortresses, and he came back saying,—We can do this, not because we have so many arms only or so many resources of a material kind—but because he was a man of "another spirit." In the long run, spirit wins ; in the outcome of all history, spirit will be uppermost. The great battles of life are not controversies of body against body, but, as far as God is in them, they are a question of spirit against body, thought against iron, prayer against storming and blustering of boastful men. While the cloud hangs over the field, and the dust of the strife is very thick, and the tumult roars until it deafens those who listen, we cannot see the exact proportions, colours, and bearings of things ; but if we read history instead of studying the events of the day which have not yet settled themselves into order and final meaning, we shall discover that spirit is mightier than body, that " knowledge is power," that "righteousness exalteth a nation," and that they who bear the white banner of a pure cause ultimately triumph because God is with them.

How little the people had grown ! They hear of the walled cities, and the great towns, and the tall men—the Amalekites, and the Hittites, and the Jebusites, and the Amorites, and the Canaanites, and they lifted up their voices and wept—and wept all night ! You have only to make noise enough in the ears of some men to make them afraid ; you have simply to keep on repeating a catalogue of names, and they think you are reciting the resources of almightiness ; mention one opposition, and possibly they may overcome the suggestion of danger : but have your mouth well-filled with hostile names and be able to roll off the catalogue without halt or stammer, and you pour upon the fainting heart a cataract which cannot be resisted. The people had grown but little : they were still in the school of fear ; they were still in the desert of despair; they were childish, cowardly, spiritless; they had no heart for prayer; they forgot the only thing worth remembering, the pledge and covenant of God. Let us not condemn them. It is easy to condemn ancient Israelites and forgotten unbelievers. How stands the case with us ? Precisely as it stood with the people of whom we are now reading. We are not an inch ahead of them. Christians are to-day just as fearful as the children of Israel were thousands of years ago : they have only to hear of certain bulks, forces, sizes, numbers, in order to quail as if they had never heard of the Eternal God. Would to Heaven we could make an exchange as between such people and some so-called infidels we know ! The infidels would make better Christians. There is more reality in them, more firmness, more standing right up to the line of conviction. He who prays, and then fears, brings discredit upon the altar at which he prayed ; he who talks of the promises of God, and then lives in subjection to the devil, is worse than an infidel.

What wonder that God himself was filled with contempt towards the people whom he had thus far led ? He would slay them ; he would " smite them with the pestilence, and disinherit them " ; he would root up the root of Abraham and begin a new people in the spirit and life of Moses ; he would start from a new centre ; he would obliterate the past : he would begin afresh to-morrow.

"And Moses said unto the Lord, Then the Egyptians shall hear it, (for thou broughtest up this people in thy might from among them ;) And they will tell it to the inhabitants of this land : for they have heard that thou Lord art among this people, that thou Lord art seen face to face, and that thy cloud standeth over them, and that thou goest before them, by day time in a pillar of a cloud, and in a pillar of fire by night. Now if thou shalt kill all this people as one man, then the nations which have heard the fame of thee will speak, saying, Because the Lord was not able to bring this people into the land which he sware unto them, therefore he hath slain them in the wilderness" (xiv. 13-16).

What book but the Bible has the courage to represent a man standing in this attitude before his God and addressing his Sovereign in such persuasive terms? This incident brings before us the vast subject of the collateral considerations which are always operating in human life. Things are not straight and simple, lying in rows of direct lines to be numbered off, checked off and done with. Lines bisect and intersect and thicken into great knots and tangle, and who can unravel or disentangle the great heap ? Things bear relations which can only be detected by the imagination, which cannot be compassed by arithmetical numbers, but which force upon men a new science of calculation, and create a species of moral algebra, by which, through the medium and help of symbols, that is done which was impossible to common arithmetic. Moses was a great leader; he thought of Egypt : what will the enemy say ? The enemy will put a false construction upon this. As if he had said,—This will be turned against Heaven ; the Egyptians do not care what becomes of the people, if they can laugh at the Providence which they superstitiously trusted; the verdict passed by the heathen will be :—God was not able to do what he promised, so he had recourse to the vulgar artifice of murder. The Lord in this way developed Moses. In reality, Moses was not anticipating the divine purpose, but God was training the man by saying what he, the Lord, would do, and by the very exaggeration of his strength called up Moses to his noblest consciousness. We do this amongst ourselves. By using a species of language adapted to touch the innermost nerve and feeling of our hearers, we call those hearers to their best selves. If the Lord had spoken a hesitant language, or had fallen into what we may call a tone of despair, Moses himself might have been seduced into a kindred dejection ; but the Lord said, I will smite, I will disinherit, I will make an end ; and Moses became priest, intercessor, mighty pleader,—the very purpose which God had in view—to keep the head right, the leading man in tune with his purposes. So Moses said, "Pardon"; the Lord said, "Smite"; and Moses said, " Pardon "—that is the true smiting. The Lord meant it ; the Lord taught Moses that prayer which Moses seemed to invent himself. The Lord trains us, sometimes, by shocking our sensibilities ; and by the very denunciation of his judgments he drives us tó tenderer prayer.

How stands our own case in relation to this ? We deserve divine contempt : we are frail and spiritless and mean ; we shun

danger; we are afraid of the damp night; we want to be let
alone; if it is possible to die without fighting, let us die in the
wilderness; if we can escape danger, we prefer to turn over
upon our couch and to slumber away into death and oblivion.
Where is the aggressive spirit amongst Christians? Men have
gone out to search the land, and they have brought back this
report : that the land is a land of darkness : the land is a land of
shame : there are thousands upon thousands of people dying of
starvation, perishing for lack of knowledge, contemning the
sanctuary, shut up in avenues and alleys and back places into
which the daintiest civilisation dare not go : rough men given to
drunkenness, bestiality and cruelty : women who are concealing
their beauty under distress and poverty and manifold shame :
children who have never heard the divine name or been invited
to the divine table. Christians are few in number; the devil's
army is an infinite host, dwelling in great cities walled and very
strong, and the devil's men are of heroic proportion; their language is strong and definite; their habits have in them no touch
of fear ; they are valiant in their master's cause : they care not
whether they swear, whether they drink, whether they do the
foul and forbidden deed of unrighteousness and untruthfulness.
The Church says,—Let us sing an evening hymn and go home
by the quiet way, and sigh ourselves into any heaven that may
be ready to take us; do not be sensational; do not attempt
anything novel or unusual; let us be quit of all things; and if
we can get home by sneaking along the eaves of the houses and
in the shady part of the road so that nobody may see us, do let
us sing the evening hymn and go to rest. Is there no Caleb?
Is there no Joshua? Is there no man of "another spirit" to
say, Let us go up at once, when we are well able to overcome
it ? In whose strength ? In God's. By whose armour ? God's.
The battle is not yours, but God's. The one thing we have
dropped out of our calculations is—Almightiness.

Numbers xiv. 26-45.

26. And the Lord spake unto Moses and unto Aaron, saying,

27. How long shall I bear with this evil congregation, which murmur against me? I have heard the murmurings of the children of Israel, which they murmur against me.

28. Say unto them, As truly as I live, saith the Lord, as ye have spoken in mine ears, so will I do to you:

29. Your carcases shall fall in this wilderness; and all that were numbered of you, according to your whole number, from twenty years old and upward, which have murmured against me,

30. Doubtless ye shall not come into the land, concerning which I sware to make you dwell therein, save Caleb the son of Jephunneh, and Joshua the son of Nun.

31. But your little ones which ye said should be a prey, them will I bring in, and they shall know the land which ye have despised.

32. But as for you, your carcases, they shall fall in this wilderness.

33. And your children shall wander in the wilderness forty years, and bear your whoredoms, until your carcases be wasted in the wilderness.

34. After the number of the days in which ye searched the land, even forty days, each day for a year, shall ye bear your iniquities, even forty years, and ye shall know my breach of promise.

35. I the Lord have said, I will surely do it unto all this evil congregation, that are gathered together against me: in this wilderness they shall be consumed, and there they shall die.

36. And the men, which Moses sent to search the land, who returned, and made all the congregation to murmur against him, by bringing up a slander upon the land,

37. Even those men that did bring up the evil report upon the land, died by the plague before the Lord.

38. But Joshua the son of Nun, and Caleb the son of Jephunneh, which were of the men that went to search the land, lived still.

39. And Moses told these sayings unto all the children of Israel; and the people mourned greatly.

40. And they rose up early in the morning, and gat them up into the top of the mountain, saying, Lo, we be here, and will go up unto the place which the Lord hath promised: for we have sinned.

41. And Moses said, Wherefore now do ye transgress the commandment of the Lord? but it shall not prosper.

42. Go not up, for the Lord is not among you; that ye be not smitten before your enemies.

43. For the Amalekites and the Canaanites are there before you, and ye shall fall by the sword : because ye are turned away from the Lord, therefore the Lord will not be with you.

44. But they presumed to go up unto the hill top : nevertheless the ark of the covenant of the Lord, and Moses, departed not out of the camp.

45. Then the Amalekites came down, and the Canaanites which dwelt in that hill, and smote them, and discomfited them, even unto Hormah.

DIVINE SOVEREIGNTY.

IS this ancient history ? Is there no inquiry of this kind propounded in heaven to-day ? Has the generation ceased to be evil ? and is God no longer made angry by repeated and aggravated disobedience ? Because the thing was once written, we must not conclude that it was only once done. There are some things we cannot keep on writing, and we cannot continue to speak ; we write them once, and the words must stand for ever as our one testimony ; other things we say once for all : we could not bear to re-utter the complaint, so bitter, so trying, so destructive to the utterer : we pass from words to signs ; sometimes we do not even make the sign, unless it be found in some broken sob or sigh, full of unutterable meaning. We shall put ourselves in a right relation to this inquiry, if we make answer that the generation is still evil, the Lord is still forbearing, the attitude of Heaven is a posture expressive of wonder and sorrow, and the answer of the earth to that posture is a repetition of rebelliousness and disobedience. A tender word is this word *bear*—" How long shall I bear with this evil congregation ? " And yet the word *bear* is put in by the English writer ; it seemed to him to express the divine meaning most fully. But another word might have been inserted here, and is inserted by the best commentators upon the sacred text. "How long shall I *forgive* this congregation ? " Forgiveness itself becomes a kind of weariness ; the repetition of pardon becomes a bitter irony and most vexatious mockery of the man who pardons ; an awful thought, verified by our own experience, needing no long and wordy argument to establish it. There does come a time in heart-history when the utterance of another pardon would seem to dispossess the man himself of judgment, responsibility, or sense of rightness ; he is driven to say,— No, the pardons have all been lost, the noble words have been thrown into the sea, or they have died upon the idle wind, and I will say them no more. So there comes a day of withdrawal, even in human relations: a time when we say, We cannot repeat our supplication for pardon addressed to Heaven on the part of one who has seen a thousand pardons trampled under foot. Is this ancient history? It is the story of this present day; it is a line from every man's biography. Could we rid ourselves of the distance of mere time and look with eyes cleansed and strengthened from on high at this passage, we should feel that it set before us the very agony of God in relation to our own accumulated and intolerable guilt.

What is the great all-determining thought arising out of this reasoning on the part of God and this determination to judge and destroy the men who have so long defied him? That thought is, that it is impossible to resist God and live. Were it possible to live in a spirit of resistance to God, that very possibility would dethrone the God who is defied. He is not God who can be resisted, and yet the rebel enjoys all the delights of immortality and all the security of heaven. This is not fatalism. Fatalism can play no part in the distribution and action of men who are morally constituted. It is a contradiction in terms to assert that a man who is morally constituted can be fated. · Wherever moral purpose asserts its presence and influence, fatalism is impossible. By the very circumstances of our nature God has rendered predestination, of the narrow and selfish kind, impossible. We cannot predestinate moral beings. By the very act of predestination, narrowly construed, we take out the moral element which we are supposed to have fatalised and predetermined. To have a moral constitution is to have rights. God made of one blood all nations of men—not in any merely physical or animal sense; but he made of one kind all men—one kin, one fellowship, one soul—one central and unchangeable relation to himself. That is the full meaning of the declaration that men are one, that humanity is one. But is there not a difference amongst men with regard to genius, force, capacity,—all kinds of accent and individuality? Certainly; but all these bear no relation whatever to the eternal destiny of the soul. There is a difference in the things of nature,—the little flower, the great tree; the tiny insect, and the sun-darkening eagle that lives at its gate ;—but all these have a common centre : all these are, so to say, gravitated around the one centre : all these plants, trees, flowers, grasses, are rooted in the same soil, are baptised by the same cloud, are warmed by the same sun. The difference is a difference of expression and relation ; but the root is fed by the same great bounty. So differences of capacity and of influence, and differences of all kinds must be regarded within other boundaries than those which men attempt to set up as describing the fatalism of life. God makes no experiments upon his creatures. God did not create a man with the view of satisfying the divine wonder as to how that man would work out the mystery of life. The purpose of God is one. The Bible reveals the unity of that purpose. It never changes. It is one of two things in relation to the ages : salvation or destruction, complacency or judgment ; heaven or hell. We are not justified in making experiments even upon one another in any sense that involves the possibility of an awful destiny. When we inflict pain, when we occasion disappointment, when we subject our nearest and dearest ones to all kinds of suffering,—we can only justify ourselves by saying that the process will be consummated in a result that will repay all the trial of the road, and glorify it, and make its memory sweet, so that our very sufferings shall add to the richness and intensity of our joy. You have no right to subject anyone to the pain of travelling—its disappointment, its humiliation, and its sorrow,—say to all the agony of the sea—merely for the sake of watching the sufferer writhe under the torment ; but knowing that all the heaving billows and stormy winds, and all the evils incident to such travel, mean final escape, the attainment of a desired haven, the hospitality of a new world, the liberty and progress of ennobled conditions, you say,—Bear up ; cheer thee ; be brave ; to-morrow there will be land ahead, or presently you will see those whose faces you have desired, and one glimpse of them, one clasp of united hands, and the sea is forgotten, and your enjoyment of your escape is none the less because of your recollection of many a discomfort and your memory of many a pain. So God is conducting this congregation of Israel through the wilderness ; but he will have his own way. If it were an exercise of merely arbitrary judgment and wisdom, we might feel unable to accept the story; but the purpose of it is liberty, enjoyment, progress,—a great Canaan, a place of summer and fruitfulness and home.   Where the purpose is beneficent the process must partake of its nature, and the process is justified by the beneficence of the end.   Who could justify God, even within the narrow boundaries of this earth, if our present experience were to end in itself?   The days so few—a handful at the most —so troubled, so storm-darkened, so shaken by a thousand alarms; the body so ailing, so frail, always cowering under the fear of approaching death; disappointments thick as thorns upon the tree; who could justify even God himself, who set us in this life, if this life were all?   Who then could refrain from the cry,— " If in this life only we have hope, we are of all men most miserable," because our standard is wrong, and our expectation is a deception?   Take in the whole horizon; embrace the whole purpose of God; then you will be enabled to say,—" All things work together for good to them that love God."   We must not interrupt the process saying,—We will judge God here, or there; we must wait until he says,—It is finished,—and then give our judgment.

It is impossible to obey God and die.   Those who went out to spy the land and brought back a whining report filled with trouble and discontent died.   The divine contempt killed them; God's laugh drove them away like a bitter wind.   But Caleb and Joshua lived.   Why did they live?   Because they wrought in harmony with the divine purpose.   They brought back the gospel—not a gospel of sensuous ease and indulgence, calling upon men to fold their arms and wait in slumbrous tranquillity until heaven descended into their hearts; but the braver gospel: Let us go up at once and possess it, for we are well able to do this; the Lord's hand is mighty enough to win this battle for us. Such men cannot die.   God will protect their immortality.   Our cheerful singers cannot perish; their songs belong to the ages; their words of joy and stimulus and inspiration are at once taken in by every heart and are welcomed into every home.   Analyse human history: go into origins, and roots, and central springs, and fountains, and you will find that the gospel spirit of Caleb and Joshua is the victor spirit; the cheerful spirit, is the spirit immortal.

All fear tends to death; it darkens the mind; it shuts out complete views of things; it distempers all colour; it disqualifies a man for using his own resources. " The fear of man bringeth a snare." Wherever there is fear, there is not a sound mind or a perfect will or a united strength. This is well known in all circles. If the speaker utters his discourse under fear either of criticism or misunderstanding, by so much that fear binds the wings of his mind, puts out the eyes of his genius, shears the locks of his strength, and throws him down in humiliation and helplessness; but when he is himself in very deed, living in the joy of the hearer, answering with gracious response the appeal of radiant faces, at home in the mystery of his subject,— then he wins : every sentence is a victory, every argument a conquest, the closing of every paragraph the waving of the white banner of entire victory and success. Fear cannot read the Bible; fear cannot hear the Gospel; fear cannot understand the darkness. Let us beware of the spirit of fearfulness; nor let us distress ourselves by imagining that fearfulness arising from physical conditions is a sin before God. Your fearfulness may not be the result of unbelief but of some subtle trouble in the body. God will understand that difficulty. He knoweth our frame, he remembereth that we are but dust—a wind that cometh for a little time and then passeth away. He will not plead against us with the thunder of his power; he will comfort us in the day of our weakness. But whilst this word of tender solace is spoken to some, it must not be taken as a justification of fearfulness or timidity arising from partial belief; under such circumstances Christ's question is " Why are ye so fearful? how is it that ye have no faith?" We wound him by our unbelief; we break in two his miracle by our want of perfect trust in wisdom and truth.

The men who brought the report died, and their children had to wander in the wilderness a year for every day that their fathers were away searching out the land. The children had to bear the burden. If there were no Bible, this would still be the case. This is the Bible of fact, not the Bible of speculative theology. We see this every day : that we are bearing the burdens left us as a heavy inheritance of trouble. The lines upon your face would not have been so deep but for the sin you may not name. You would not at five-and-forty years of age have been an old man, out of whose voice all tones of joy have been taken, but for the sins of those now dead whose names you will not even mention aloud, lest the utterance of them should double the sorrow already too much. This mystery is in life. The Bible does not invent a fanatical Providence or set up some wonderful scheme built upon the baseless fabric of imagination. We have facts occurring around us : experiences of our own : a consciousness that cannot be destroyed in our own hearts ; and all these gather themselves up into a poignant and firm corroboration of what is found written in the Holy Scriptures. The children *do* suffer for their forefathers' misdeeds. The battles of one century are occasioned by the misrule of centuries long forgotten. We carry our dead about with us in many forms day by day. Are we, then, to content ourselves with this retrospective contemplation, saying,—My diseases are due to my forefather, my sorrow is a black inheritance, my weakness has a history stretching far back through my ancestors? We may indulge in that retrospect, but only for a moment. It is a selfish retrospect if pushed too far. It becomes gracious, Christian,—a noble stimulus—if coming out of it we say,—Then by so much as I have been injured by the past, I must take care in God's grace and strength to do what I can for those who are to come after me ; I will prevent their carrying a burden if I can possibly do so, in the strength and grace of God ; I will try to live so wisely, simply, purely, obediently, as not to leave any great black cloud resting over my house and name. If the retrospect lead to that noble decision, then it is of the quality of prayer, and belongs to the holy class of the most spiritual and sacred oaths. Beware of sentimentalism. Recognise the reality of history and turn it into an inspiration in view of all the untravelled and unknown future.

The people were like ourselves. Having heard from Moses what the Lord had resolved upon—for " Moses told these sayings unto all the children of Israel "—" the people mourned greatly. And they rose up early in the morning, and gat them up into the top of the mountain, saying, Lo, we be here, and will go up unto the place which the Lord hath promised : for we have sinned." But Moses said,—No. Men cannot work out of time. There is a providence of time; there is a providence of opportunity. The people, smarting, perhaps, more in consequence of the effects of sin than in consequence of a thorough perception of the nature of sin, said,—We will now go up. But Moses said,— Do not be foolish; if you go, the Ark of the Covenant will not depart out of the camp and go with you; you are out of time; you are too late; you had the opportunity and neglected it. Men cannot create opportunities after this fashion. There are prayers that become idle cries; there are religious services that become, because untimely, mere mockeries. There is a reading of the Bible which gets nothing out of the sacred Book; you let the hour of light pass by, and now in these dark troubled clouds you can read nothing of truth, of grace. Redeem the time! "Whatsoever thy hand findeth to do, do it with thy might." Work while it is yet day, for the night cometh wherein no man can work. You will pray by-and-by? There is no by-and-by. You will go up presently? There is no presently. You mean one day to shake off the devil and be free? There is no promise of such day,—"now is the accepted time .. now is the day of salvation." "To-day if ye will hear his voice, harden not your heart, as in the provocation in the wilderness." Be wise! be wise in time!

PRAYER.

ALMIGHTY GOD, show us that we are living under thy rule, and that thy rule is best because it is thine. God is love; God is light: in him is no darkness at all. God knoweth the end from the beginning, and every step of the long road; therefore will we take our marching orders from thyself, going as thou dost command, halting where thou dost please, and going quickly, or slowly, or standing still, as we may receive word from God. We never thought we should have said this; it is not natural to us. We love our own way; we think our wisdom quite divine; we are obstinate and self-regarding; but thou hast wrought upon us directly and indirectly, by light, by opening of the mind, by bitter portions, by stinging disappointment, by showing us that the road we thought led to liberty led nowhere. So we have come back again, humbled, much enlightened, conscious of our own folly, and modestly desiring to be taught of God. We thought we were mighty, until we lifted our arm and found it was but a straw; we said we would run all the way and know no weariness, and, behold, in one hour we were laid down in fatigue and pain and distress. Thus thou dost teach men, not always by doctrine and argument and exhortation in words which men can answer again with vain impertinence of mind, but by overthrow, confusion: night suddenly encroaching upon day, and all things set upside down in bewilderment that cannot be ordered into straight lines. So are we taught, and taught of God. We call it experience, because we are afraid to use some noble and truer term. Yet even here thou art patient with us, so that now many men who once spake of experience venture to speak of God. We would be found in the number; we would not be of those who are afraid to give the right names to things. Open thou our mouth that we may show forth boldly our testimony on thy behalf. It will do us good to speak the word that fills the mind. If we could once speak it, we could speak it again, more easily, with more familiarity and even tenderness. Help us to say,—God did thus for me; God led me in this wise; God is my Maker, my Portion, my Redeemer, my All; God is his name, and God is love. We bless thee for this use of words; we are the better for it; we feel as if we had opened a channel through which purest water had streamed from fountains in heaven the very words purify the channel through which they flow. Thou hast led us all our days. We see it now; it is perfectly clear to minds that once could see nothing because of spiritual blindness; we see now why the message came in the night time and not in the morning, why the flower was plucked in the bud before it opened the secret of the mystery of its beauty ; we see now how, though the night was crying, the tears were morning dew,

We understand things better than we did. Time has altered itself to us; it is nothing: it is a breath—a wind; sometimes a mere mockery of duration, without substance—flying, dying, whilst we speak of it. So now we take our stand upon thy word. We are sure, through Jesus Christ thy Son, that thy purpose concerning us is full of mercy; thou hast no pleasure in the death of men: thy delight is in life, in liberty, in immortality. Life and immortality are brought to light in the Gospel by thy Son, our one Saviour, almighty in power, infinite in love. We give thee thanks for all the mercies of our little life. If we have escaped the sea and are again on firm land, we say,—The earth is the Lord's, and the fulness thereof, the sea and they that dwell upon it;—and we bless thee for nightly protection, daily care, for family reunion, and the incoming of the hopes which make our life worth living. Accept the praises of those who in reunion bless the Lord in family rejoicing and sacred song. If we have been brought through perplexity, business difficulty,—if controversies have been settled,—if the dark cloud has been lifted,—if the pain at the heart has been somewhat lessened,—if the sorrow-flood has assuaged a little—we bless thee: it is God's doing, it is the Father's revelation of himself in the night of our distress, and we will rejoice and be glad, and with instruments of music will heighten the song which our own voices cannot fully express. Tell the old man that he has hardly begun to live: that the ages in the flesh are not in the soul. Take up the little child, and show it wonders in all the blue heaven, and bid it be glad whilst it may, and to know nothing of the mystery of tears. Whisper to the dying that death is the gate of immortality. Speak to the lonely; startle his solitude into mystic and solemn communion. Bring back the bad man; we cannot reach him; he is to us as hell: no water can drown the flame; no speech of ours can be heard by badness so wicked. The Lord hear us, pity us, spare us a little while; and then, the shadows thickening, lengthening, darkening, may there be beyond a glint of light, which means dawn, morning, heaven. Amen.

Numbers xiv. 43.

". . . because ye are turned away from the Lord, therefore the Lord will not be with you."

RELIGIOUS EXPLANATION OF FAILURE.

EVEN that is a word of comfort. The comfort is not far to fetch, even from the desert of this stern fact. The comfort is found in the fact that the Lord will be with those who have *not* turned away from him. The law operates in two opposite ways. Law is love, when rightly seized and applied; and love is law, having all the pillars of its security and all the dignity of its righteousness to support it in all the transitions of its experience. The reason why we fail is that God has gone from us. Putting the case so, we put it wrongly. God has not gone from us : we have gone from God. What we want is more plain speaking to ourselves. Until a man can see the word CRIMINAL written in capital letters upon the very centre of his heart, and can spell the word, pronouncing each letter with tremulous deliberation, and uttering the whole word with broken-heartedness, he does not begin to touch the gate which opens upon the kingdom of heaven. He must not apply the word *sinner* to himself too familiarly, because it is a common name ; it is an appellation written upon the whole belt of the world, and can therefore be used with vague generality. The term is right enough : it is a necessary term ; but it must be so personalised and accentuated and driven home that there can be no mistake about the individuality of its application. When we *see* the sin, we will cry for the Saviour. The Church is nothing without its godliness ; it is less than nothing : it is not only the negation of strength, it is the utter and most helpless weakness. Israel was the Church in the wilderness, and Israel was nothing without its God. The number might be six hundred thousand fighting men, and they would go down like a dry wooden fence before a raging fire, if the Lord was not in the midst. They were not men without him. The Church lives, moves, and has its being in God—not in some high or deep metaphysical sense only, but in the plain and obvious sense of the terms : that it has no being or existence outside God. When it forgets to pray, it loses the art of war ; when the Church forgets to put on the beautiful garments of holiness, though it be made up of a thousand Samsons, it cannot strike one fatal blow at the enemy. Let us understand this with some clearness. The Church is assembled, say, a thousand strong; but if every man in that thousand has turned from the Living God, what does the thousand account for in battle ? For nothing ! Ceasing to be godly, they cease to be men, in any sense significant of devotion, energy and successful application of resources. They were only made men by their goodness; it was only while they prayed that they stood upright; whilst the hymn was singing in their hearts and outpouring itself from their grateful lips, they were men who could fight and win, every stroke being a victory, but when they left off their religion, or their religious loyalty, they did not become as other men ; it is impossible to fall back into the common quantity of human nature after having been in heaven : the fall is deeper than that. When Lucifer fell, he fell into a bottomless pit : wherever he is, he is falling *now.* So the Christian professor, having turned aside from God, does not become an ordinary man and take his old place in society, and be just as he used to be in the old times when he never prayed or confessed the holy Name. We do not fall back upon our old selves : we fall into perdition. The Church is not a club, nor is it so much physical force, nor is it, in any technical sense, a mere army of men drawn up in battle array, equal to the fight, whatever their principles may be. Again and again let it be said, till the densest heart responds to the tremendous appeal, the Church has no existence apart from its godliness. It is constituted upon divine foundations ; it is animated by divine impulses ; it is inspired by divine motives ; it is protected by divine security. A Church that has lost its faith has lost *itself.* You cannot have an unbelieving Church, a faithless Church : when the faith has gone, the Church has gone. Were there not, then, a thousand men of Israel against a thousand men of Amalek ? No ; the thousand men of Israel had no existence but for God. They represented an idea, a kingdom, a divine purpose, a theocracy,— a wholly new thought in the universe ; and apart from that, they became minus quantities. A thousand men of Israel were a thousand men *plus* God. Men cannot lose their godliness and keep their character. A man who has once really prayed can never go back to the common speech of men and be as if he had never prayed when he goes back ; the common speech becomes profanity in lips which have forsworn their own oath. You cannot take the statistics of the Church. You cannot be number-ing men and saying,—The Church is thus and so, as to quantity, force, and influence. The Church lives upon bread the world knoweth not of. Count the Church by the volume of its prayer ; register the strength of the Church by the purity and complete-ness of its consecration. If you number the Church in millions, and tell not what it is at the altar and at the cross, you have returned the census of a cemetery, not the statistics of a living, mighty, invincible host. Genius is nothing, learning is nothing, organisation is a sarcasm and an irony,—apart from that which gives everyone of them value and force—the praying heart, the trustful spirit. The Church conquers by holiness. There is an answer to grammar; there is no reply to self-sacrifice. Men may smite theology of a formal and scientific kind, or may render its existence a perpetual risk; but there is no answer to the love which hopeth all things, endureth all things,—love which is mightiest when the clouds are darkest, and most redeeming when the sin is most complete.

We shall conquer the Amalek world when we have conquered our own hearts. God does not fight for nominal believers. Israel represented nominal religion. The Amalekite and the Canaanite would be represented as peoples of heathenish relations and conditions, and Israel would be represented as the people of God. But the Lord will not fight the battles of nominal believers. By the very righteousness which makes him God he prefers an honest idolater to a dishonest nominalist. That is a thought which should make us consider our position. An idolater may be honest; but a professing Christian, if not faithful to his profession, is not merely unfaithful: there is no term that can describe the turpitude of his wickedness. The Lord will make Amalek conqueror and send down the Canaanite to burn the dry stubble of prayerless Israel :—"the Amalekites came down, and the Canaanites which dwelt in that hill, and smote them, and discomfited them, even unto Hormah"—men that might have been beaten back by a hand that was true to Heaven. It is right that the heathen should conquer when the Church is unfaithful. It is solemnly right that the heathen should mock the land that sends out missionaries one day and doers of all evil the next, if not in the same ship. What wonder if the heathen laugh at the missionary when they see immediately behind him the man who is to undo all that the Christian evangelist attempts to accomplish? It may be rough logic—it may be reason in which many a flaw can be found by penetrating minds; but it is not to be wondered at, considering the nature of heathenism and the intuitions of common sense. You have no right to ask God to go with you merely as a convenience. Amalek is in sight, the Canaanite is on the alert, the walls are thick with the enemy—Lord help us! —that is a coward's prayer, and Heaven will be empty to that cry ; the shout will dissolve in echoes, because the heart is not faithful towards God. Who does not make a convenience of his religion ? What coward is there who does not pray when he wants fine weather for the wedding at which he will make a sot of himself ? Or who does not pray because a spirit—dim, spectral, black—is in the air, and may any moment alight upon the roof or quench the household fire ? But the prayers of the wicked are an abomination unto the Lord. The air is vexed with cries of atheistic distress which want to ennoble themselves into momentary prayer.

Moses told the people of Israel exactly how the case stood, "and the people mourned greatly" ; and afterwards they said they would go up, and Moses replied, "Go not up, for the Lord is not among you ; that ye be not smitten before your enemies. For the Amalekites and the Canaanites are there before you, and ye shall fall by the sword "—your only safety is in not going up ;—but the people " presumed to go up unto the hill top." They thought they were still men, though they had turned away from God. Not one of us could live a moment but for the mercy of Heaven. We have no " selves " in any sense significant of independence and self-invigoration and self-renewal ; we are God's offspring. As well let the little grass-blade leap up out of its green bed and say it will live, without rooting itself in the earth or warming itself at the sun, as for us to say we will live, in any profound and immortal sense, without dependence upon the mercy and redeeming help and grace of God. We are in danger of living lives of presumption. Surely, we think, God will not remember that we have not paid him our tribute of prayer. Surely, in all the streams of praise continually flying towards his throne as towards the centre of the universe, he will not miss our little rill of adoration and confession. So we deceive ourselves. We presume : we say we will take our chance : we will go out under all circumstances, and see what can be done,—and, behold, we have put our sickle into a field of darkness, and if we bring back aught with us, we bring back sheaves of fog. There is no life without God, no true fighting without faith, no lasting conquest that does not express the righteousness that accomplished it.

The picture is most graphic. There was only a hill between

Israel and the land of promise. One stony mountain or range of hills. Surely, the space being so small some concession will be made to Israel? If God could concede one inch to the bad man, he could concede all heaven. No concessions are made to unbelief. This religious life is not a matter of proportions; we do not come into fraction and decimal here, and throw things in as if they were of no consequence. A ship may go down within ten feet of the shore; the vessel that has come proudly over the main may be wrecked in the channel. There is to be no intermission of service; no space is to be accounted trifling; no action is to be regarded as of but secondary consequence. There are no days off duty. May not a man pray six days and do what he will on the seventh? It is morally impossible. The law is one, goodness is one, loyalty is one. This is not a theological mystery: this is a simple matter of daily experience and personal proof. We cannot love our friend six days out of the seven and disregard him on the seventh. If it is impossible in human relations, how can it be possible in divine relations? Love makes all the week into a Sabbath day. Faithfulness accounts that every moment of time is due to those with whom we have covenanted as to its duties and its remuneration. Find a man who can say,—This is but one hour taken from the service which I have pledged and for which I have been paid—and you find a thief. Find a man who will take ten minutes to do a piece of work which he could easily have done in five, and will receive payment for it, or set up a right founded upon it, and you find a felon—the deadlier that the magistrate cannot lay hold upon him. These are the truths we must trust; this is the standard by which we must measure ourselves. Measuring ourselves by ourselves, who is not respectable—passable at least?—who is not upon something like an equality with his brother? But measuring ourselves by the divine standard, who would not run away into the darkness, finding his heart-ache intolerable, and his self-reproach like a scorching fire? "What I say unto one I say unto all," said Christ, "Watch!" "Be sober, be vigilant; because your adversary the devil, as a roaring lion, walketh about, seeking whom he may devour." After a long life of devoted labour, see that ye be not lost at the very last by a remission of discipline, by lightening of duty, and by the curtailment of prayer. Having come proudly, as to divine reliance, over a thousand miles of water, see that there be no collision at the last for want of watchfulness, no breakdown for want of self-criticism. We must complete the journey; we cannot get off a few miles before the appointed landing-place. We are called to discipline. We can keep our learning, our genius, our intellectual energy, our marvellous mental capacity, and can do all kinds of conjuring with the imagination and with the tongue, and may appear unto men to be as we have ever been—(society is easily deceived)—but if we have put out the altar fire which no eye can see—if we have let the temperature of love go down —if we begin to calculate where once we were delighted to serve —if we begin to set up an argument where once we built a cross,—we may go out to fight Amalek, but the heathen will laugh at us, and the men against whom we are pitted will have us in derision. We are nothing without God; but we can do all things through Christ, which strengtheneth us.

PRAYER.

ALMIGHTY GOD, we cannot do the whole law. We have tried. One man said unto thee,—All these things have I done from my youth up. We have not done one of them; we have spoiled the whole law. We have done what we liked, and we have left undone that which we disliked. We have been partially good, but not good in the root of us, in the inner heart, in the place where the true life lives. We have a chamber of imagery in our hearts; we know the way down to it, though no other man knows of its existence. The whole head is sick; the whole heart is faint; both hands are criminals; and as for our feet, they have been swift to run in the evil way. We are clever in wickedness: we have great ability in serving the devil; but to serve God rightly, truly, constantly—who hath found it possible? God be merciful unto us sinners! Yet it is something to know that we have been ill-behaved, it is worth knowing that we have done the things we ought not to have done. We would be contrite—really broken-hearted; we would come without plea, defence, excuse—extenuation of any kind and say,—We have done the things we ought not to have done; we have left undone the things we ought to have done, and there is no health in us. Have mercy, thou living Christ of God! Thou hast shown us how we may begin again; thou art always giving the soul new opportunities. If we confess our sins, thou art faithful and just to forgive us our sins, and to cleanse us from all unrighteousness. We will try to confess—not with our lips, for that is worthless, but with our hearts; we will let our souls talk; we will call upon our spirits to accuse themselves, and to deny their claim to any virtue, or comeliness, or beauty. There is none righteous, no not one. All we like sheep have gone astray: we have turned every one to his own way. We have been mistaken altogether; we have lived in ill-reasoning, and we have perpetrated innumerable mistakes. Beside all this, our heart is wrong: we are rotten at the core. The heart is deceitful above all things, and desperately wicked. The work must be done in the heart, and thou alone canst do it. We will not marvel that thou sayest,—Ye must be born again. We know it; that is right; we answer thy declaration with a great shout of acquiescence, full of tears and sobs. Lord, give us the Holy Ghost! spare not the gift divine! Not by works of righteousness which it is possible for us to do, but according to thy mercy must thou save us, by the washing of regeneration and the renewing of the Holy Ghost. This is God's doing; this is the miracle of the Holy Spirit. Encourage us. Thou couldest overwhelm us with despair, and so the enemy might get great advantage over us; but even in our far-away wandering, and in our obstinacy of heart, send some message after us saying the house-door is still open and Christ is mighty to redeem. Amen.

Numbers xv. 30-36.

30. But the soul that doeth aught presumptuously, whether he be born in the land, or a stranger, the same reproacheth the Lord; and that soul shall be cut off from among his people.

31. Because he hath despised the word of the Lord, and hath broken his commandment, that soul shall utterly be cut off; his iniquity shall be upon him.

32. And while the children of Israel were in the wilderness, they found a man that gathered sticks upon the sabbath day.

33. And they that found him gathering sticks brought him unto Moses and Aaron, and unto all the congregation.

34. And they put him in ward, because it was not declared what should be done to him.

35. And the Lord said unto Moses, The man shall be surely put to death: all the congregation shall stone him with stones without the camp.

36. And all the congregation brought him without the camp, and stoned him with stones, and he died; as the Lord commanded Moses.

PUNISHMENT FOR SABBATH-BREAKING.

THIS incident has been the occasion of a good deal of jeering. It has often been quoted as an instance of extreme and intolerable severity, and has been cited against those whose reading of the Scriptures leads them to propose to keep the Sabbath day. The mocker has found quite a little treasure here. The incident is altogether so monstrous. The appeal made to common sense and human feeling is so direct and so urgent that there can be no reply to it. The poor man was gathering sticks on the Sabbath day, and he had to forfeit his life for the violation of the law! If he had been gathering anything else, the fancy of the reader would not have been so suddenly struck; some grand phrase would have helped him through the difficulty; but when it was known that the poor man was only gathering "sticks," it seemed to be out of all proportion that he should lose his life. Many an amateur commentator has so spoken. No wonder. Men are the victims of phrases. Had the man been found gathering golden wedges out of other people's caskets, there might have been some proportion between the theft and the penalty; but to be gathering "sticks" and to die for it, does shock the pious fancy of heathen mankind with a sense of disproportion. No artist would have taken this course. A man who had painted the most beautiful picture ever produced by the human fancy and the human hand, would not of course be severe with anyone who had punctured the picture with a needle all over; though he might be a little irritated with any man who set fire to his work of art. A noble-minded artist would have said,—Take no heed: it is only the puncture of a needle; if the picture had been ripped up with a knife I should have been angry, but seeing that it was but the point of a needle, perhaps it is as well done as not done; no notice should be taken of this, and no penalty shall be inflicted.—No engineer would for a moment have allowed any such sense of disproportion to occur in his plans; when he sends a locomotive whirling at lightning pace across the land, he will say to it,—If a fly should alight upon the rails you will pause; if an elephant should be there, or some mighty bird of prey, do what you will; but if a fly should be on the rail, you will stop, and in a spirit of pity, if not in a spirit of respect, you will allow the little trespasser to resume its wing. But law is impartial—terrific yet gracious. It does not work along one line only: it is a guarantee, as well as a penalty; it brings with it in one hand a crown of righteousness, as certainly as it brings in the other a sword of judgment. It is here that we get wrong: we will not grasp the idea of sovereignty, law, order, progress according to divinely-philosophical methods; we will clip, and niggle, and compromise, and patch the universe where we have injured it, and think no one will see the seams we have made. Had the text read,—And a certain man was found in the wilderness openly blaspheming God, and he was stoned to death,—we should have had some sense of rest and harmony in the mind: the balance would seem to be complete. But that is the very sophism that is ruining us. We do not see the reality of the case. We think of huge sins;—there are none. We think of little sins; there are none. We live in a region of fancy; we picture possibilities of sin. We play at the great game of jurisprudence, setting this against that, weighing, measuring, balancing, and telling-off things in definite quantities and relations. It is the spot that is ruin; it is the one little thing that spoils the universe. God cannot drive on his mighty

chariot until something has been done with those who have
committed, so-called, "little sins," and have perpetrated small
and almost nameless trespasses. The whole conception is wrong.
We are not fallen because we have committed murder in the
vulgar sense of the term. When a man commits murder, there
may be some palliation for the crime; there may be a stronger
defence for murder than for one evil word. It is easy to
imagine how eloquence could warm up into a noble speech on
behalf of the man who, carried away by a sudden gust of passion,
had perpetrated some dreadful deed; but there is no eloquence
that can expand itself for one moment and keep its own respect
in defence of backbiting, whispering, evil-thinking and all the
miserable pedantry of righteousness; on that side no advocate
can be found: an advocate disdains the fee that would bribe his
speech; it is mean, contemptible, indefensible. Yet we who
reason so in ordinary affairs become quite amateur divinities in
relation to the poor man who went out on the Sabbath day
to gather a bundle of "sticks." We will look at the "sticks"
and not at the Sabbath. We say,—It was but a drop of blackness;—but we forget that the robe on which it fell was a robe
of ineffable purity. A drop here or there upon a garment already
stained will count for nothing; but who could not see even
one ink-blot on the white purity of the Jungfrau? Every eye
would seem to be fastened upon it; no notice would be taken
of it in the murky valley; but on that shining whiteness—on
that snowy purity—it is an offence that cannot be forgiven;
the man who wantonly flung that blot on such purity is a base
man in his heart. Why not look at the reality of the case—
of every case—of our own case—and, instead of trying to reduce
the enormity by dwelling upon the relative smallness of the
offence, fix the imagination and the judgment and the conscience
upon the thing violated?—for only in that way can we establish
the balance of righteousness and begin to understand the movement of God.

Obedience can only be tested by so-called little things. It is
in relation to little things that a character stands or falls as to its
wholeness and reality of good purpose. We are all prepared for
state occasions. There is not a man in the world, surely, who

has not some robe of respectability he can wear on festive days and notable anniversaries. That arrangement gives no indication of the real substance and tissue of the man's character. We are all prepared to be heroic ; but a man cannot live in ostentatious heroism all his days. We are only too glad of an opportunity to play the hero ; it is an hour's work, or a day's endurance, and its history will be written in large letters, and men will speak about it, and fame will come to us,—we only long for the occasion and we will provide the man. It is quite easy to join in a great demonstrative procession to show on which side we are. Human nature does not altogether dislike processions ; there is something in the human heart that inclines it towards display. To be part of a great host, marching to the blare of trumpet and the touch of drum, all to show on which side we are, is quite an easy piece of display and is no test of obedience. Who is not ready to watch by the death-bed of the most loved one ? The night will bring no weariness—the day and the night shall be run into one common time, and no heed shall be taken of the exhaustion of the flesh; it will be a proud delight; the sacrifice will bring its own heaven with it. We long to show in some such crisis how loyal is our love. It is not so that life is measured by the Living One who is the Judge of all the earth; he does not look at state occasions, at heroic opportunities, at processional displays, at death-bed attendances ; he looks at the little things of daily life. Where one man is called to be a hero on some great scale, ten thousand men are called to be courteous, gentle, patient ; where one has the opportunity of being great on the battle-field of a death-bed, all have opportunity of being good in hopefulness, charity, forgiveness, and every grace that belongs to the Cross of Christ ; where one has the opportunity of joining a great procession, ten thousand have the opportunity of assisting the aged, helping the blind, speaking a word for the speechless, and putting a donation into the hand of honest poverty. Let us realise the truth of the doctrine that we are not called upon to display our obedience upon a gigantic scale within the theatre of the universe and under the observation of angels,—but to go out into the field and work with bent back and willing hands and glad hearts, doing life's simple duty under Heaven's inspiration and encouragement. The man who gathered sticks on the Sabbath day might have been quite a great man on festival occasions when all Israel had to be dressed in its best; he might have been one of the foremost of the show. You discover what men are by their secret deeds, by what they do when they suppose nobody is looking, by what they are about when they are suddenly pounced upon. Give a man notice that his obedience is to be inquired into, and then how prepared he is! But the man is not what he is at that particular moment, but what he was a few moments before, and what he will be a few moments after. It is only by so-called little things—minor moralities, punctuality, civilities, penny honesties,—that we can understand what we are and estimate the quality of the character of others.

People will always be more willing and ready to punish than to obey:—" all the congregation . . . stoned him with stones." The congregation was glad of the opportunity :—anything for a new sensation; anything for a change from the intolerable monotony of the wilderness. Stoning a man made a little bubble on the quiet river of the day's sluggish life; moreover, it looked well to be stoning somebody else; there is a kind of indirect respectability about it. What a heroic people! You would not judge from this verse what a history we have read through up to the time of its being written in the record. These are not the people who mourned, and murmured, and complained, and rebelled against Moses and fought against Heaven, and turned away from righteousness and forgat the Living God ? They are unanimous in stoning the Sabbath-breaker; they would have been equally as unanimous in stoning Moses. A word has no sense when it comes to decision and distinctions of this kind. We are all, perhaps, more ready to punish than to obey; when we condemn the action of another, we seem to add to our own piety in public estimation. Herein we do not live in the Mosaic day. Is there no stoning under the Christian dispensation? Yes. By what rule is that stoning determined? A very easy one and most equitable. Christ laid it down, and Christ is our one Law-giver—the true Moses of the Church. We bring a man to him, saying,—Lord, we found this man gathering sticks on the Lord's day,—what is to be done to him? Stone him. How? " Let him that is without sin cast the first stone." And beginning at the eldest, right away down to the youngest, they all slink out

and leave the sabbath-breaker to face the Founder of the day.
That is the right law of stoning—may it never be changed!
Jesus, Son of God, thou wast never so dear to human hearts,
conscious of their guilt and burning with shame, as when thou
didst say to the pious hypocrites of thy time,—" Let him that is
without sin cast the first stone " ;—thou art Saviour ; these words
will keep thy crown above all other crowns, long as the ages of
time shall breathe, or the larger ages of eternity roll on in infinite
duration. " The law was given by Moses, but grace and truth came
by Jesus Christ." There must be punishment, but let us take care
how it is administered. If there be no stone-throwing until pure
hands begin, no stones will be thrown. We are speaking now
within the boundaries of the Church, within the sanctities of the
holy place,—not of political and municipal life, but of that inner
and spiritual existence and relation explained in the person and
priesthood of the Son of God.

We must not delude ourselves with the notion that there are
sins which are of no consequence. We say that the man in
question may be guilty of telling a lie, but he was never guilty of
committing a murder. What is the difference ? There is none.
You say,—He may be a little unforgiving, but he never murdered
anyone ;—therefore we invite him to dinner, we travel with him
on the road, we recognise him in public, we cheer him when he
rises to address a Christian assembly on Christian topics. We
say,—Such and such a man may be a little censorious in speech,
but he was never known to be drunk. What is the difference?
There is more said in the Bible against pride than is said against
drunkenness ; there is more said in the Bible against censoriousness than is said against unchastity. We are wrong. We are
back among the beggarly elements ; we have not come into the
sanctuary in which we see spiritual doctrine, spiritual judgment,
heart-work ; and until we enter that holy place and read the
smallest print of the divine record, do not let us suppose we can
rival the kingdom of God or annotate with our pointless comments
the wisdom of Heaven. The kingdom of heaven is within. Piety
is not abstinence from vulgar crime : it is consecration to spiritual
purpose and perpetual aspiration after spiritual ideals. Whoso
hateth his brother without a cause is guilty of murder. He who
has told a lie will break the Sabbath. He who has broken God's

Sabbath—understanding that term in its amplest meaning and intention—has violated to the measure of his power the purity and sanctity of Heaven. The law is one; the universe is one; God is one. He that offendeth in the least offendeth in all. But we cannot have new works till we become new workers, and we cannot become new workers except by the mighty power of the Holy Ghost. Said the Son of God,—" Marvel not that I said unto thee, ye must be born again."

NOTE.

The Seventh Day in every week was " set apart " as a day in which no work was to be done ; the seventh year was " set apart" as a year in which no seed was to be sown ; and at the end of seven times seven years, there was a great festival during which the whole land was to rest, and when debts were to be cancelled, alienated estates to return to their owners, and slaves to be set free.

Consecrated Men, consecrated Property, consecrated Space, consecrated Time, declared that God still claimed the world as his own, and that in all the provinces of human life he insisted on being recognised as Lord of all.

The separation of the Sabbath from the common uses of other days was an essential part of a vast and complicated system for the assertion and maintenance of certain great spiritual ideas. I do not wonder at the severity of the penalty attached to the crime of Sabbath-breaking. The high-priest himself was forbidden, under the penalty of death, to enter the Holy of Holies on any other than the Day of Atonement. To violate the sanctity of that mysterious chamber was a profanation of the Space which God claimed as his own ; to violate the Sabbath was a profanation of the Time which God claimed as his own. The defence of the sanctity of the Sabbath was exceptionally necessary in the early times of Jewish history. Before synagogues were built and public worship was celebrated in every part of the country, the vast majority of the people, but for the institution of the Sabbath, would have been seldom reminded of God, except when they went up to Jerusalem to keep the great feasts. The weekly rest from their common labour was a constantly recurring appeal to them to remember the God of their fathers.— DR. DALE'S *Ten Commandments.*

PRAYER.

ALMIGHTY GOD, when thou dost hide thyself from us the time is long and weary even to intolerableness; when thou dost light up the horizon with the spring time then all things are beautiful and full of joy, and the whole earth is a beautiful sanctuary. We love thee to be near us; when thou art near we are safe; when thou art near we are without timidity or distress of any kind. We say,—The Lord hath called us up, therefore will we be safe, though the enemy press upon us with a heavy hand and threaten us with deadly frowning. Our confidence is in God, not only in his almightiness, but in his eternal, immeasurable affection for us; his great heart, his perpetual love—the love that died that we might live. We will count upon God; he shall be the centre of our calculation. When we think of the future, we will think of the great future, eternity; and not of the little fretful future, to-morrow—full of vexation and noise and angry tumult. We bless thee that we have the foresight that sees eternity, whilst our eyes are holden that they may not see to-morrow. Thou dost give long sight to thy Church. Thou wilt not permit us to pry into the next day, but thou hast given us revelations concerning the next world. This is thy wonderful way. Thou dost move by vast lines. Thou wouldest draw us forward by a wondrously-comprehensive education . We bless thee for the largeness of the wisdom by which we are governed, as well as for the depth of the love by which we are saved and redeemed for ever. Thou dost look upon us; thou dost watch us body, soul, and spirit; no part of us is exposed to the divine neglect; thou dost see our hand, our foot, our heart; thou lookest into us altogether, and if there is any evil way in us thou art troubled by its wicked presence. Do thou give us to feel this, and to say, morning, noon and night,—Thou God seest me—not lookest upon me only, but seest me in every thought, feeling, motive, purpose,—in the whole interior mystery of our being. Thus our life will be spent in heaven's light, and all our days shall be numbered and shall be regarded from on high. All the way is thine. Such a varied way it is : sometimes all sward, green and soft and velvet-like, with hedges on either side, rich with blossom, musical with song; and sometimes it is all gates, and stiles, and difficult places : the roads are many, and large, and rough, and the way altogether is without hospitality or comfort; still it is part of the long mileage—part of the way ending in the brightest land. May we accept all the road, even through the churchyard, and through the desert, and across the river, and up the steep hill, and believe that the way is all regulated and determined for us by the wisdom of the infinite Father. We bless thee if we have any hope in this direction, for it is natural to us to be frivolous, superficial, living in the present moment, and if we can extract a laugh from it, accounting our life a happy one—such fools and empty in head and heart are we; but if thy kingdom has touched us with its glory and ennobled us by its sublimity so that now and again even we have larger thoughts, nobler purposes, wider outlooks, behold, we thank thee for this increase of life; and now we understand in part what Jesus Christ meant when he said,—I am come that they might have life, and that they might have it more abundantly—like wave upon wave of life, a great river of life, pure as crystal, beginning in God's throne, and winding its wondrous way back to its own origin. We would be wise—sometimes we think so at least; we would live the noble life, free from all canker, care, and distress; we would dwell in God; we would say in the time of thirst,—The river of God is full of water,—and in the time of famine,—The wheatfields of heaven are never exhausted. Thus living in the upper liberties—in the very heavens of the divine presence—we would do to-day's work with a clear head, a loving heart, and a willing hand, and count all life a sacrifice that it may become a joy. Thou hast brought thy people together from varied homes into one house. This is a hint of the great meeting,—the eternal fellowship: men shall be brought from all lands, and with all accents shall sing one song. We hope in this: we would not have this sacred forecast overclouded; it makes time easy, and labour light, and suffering but a momentary pang. We give ourselves, our houses, our businesses—all into thine hands. We want to succeed, we are determined to succeed, we are ashamed of failure, and we will resolve again and again to make life a solid success; but when we have made this resolution, if our idea of success be wrong, we are willing that it should be foregone, and that we should die without house, or friend, or helper, if it be better for our soul's health that our body should thus decay. We will put ourselves into the Father's hand, without wish, or will, or thought, or desire, that we cannot subordinate to his purposes: we will utter our little prayer, and then leave God to give what answer he may. But to one prayer thou wilt return the answer which we need. God be merciful unto us sinners; wash us in the atoning blood of Christ; speak out of the mystery of eternity to this guilty time, and say to every soul,—Son, daughter, thy sins, which are many, are all forgiven thee. Amen.

Numbers xv. 37-41.

37. And the Lord spake unto Moses, saying,

38. Speak unto the children of Israel, and bid them that they make them fringes in the borders of their garments throughout their generations, and that they put upon the fringe of the borders a ribband of blue:

39. And it shall be unto you for a fringe, that ye may look upon it, and remember all the commandments of the Lord, and do them; and that ye seek not after your own heart and your own eyes, after which ye use to go a whoring:

40. That ye may remember, and do all my commandments, and be holy unto your God.

41. I am the Lord your God, which brought you out of the land of Egypt, to be your God: I am the Lord your God.

THE FRINGES AND THEIR MEANING.

THE word *garments* is used with a special direction. The Lord was very careful about the raiment or garment of his people. The Lord's eyes are upon his people's apparel. We want to make him simply a Figure in theology—to confine him within the radiant lines of what to us is an invisible heaven. But God will not so be treated. He lives with us in the house ; he will make our bed in our affliction ; he will turn the house round that it may catch the morning light, if the morning light is best for us. He will keep our books, and watch all our steps ; he will conduct the blind man across the busy thoroughfare, and he will set a singing bird in the poor man's little house. "The very hairs of your head are all numbered." Why make a theological fancy of God ? That is practical blasphemy. It is not worship ; it is ill-treatment of the divine idea and the divine personality. God would have a seat in our house, a desk in our business, a pen in our library ; he would rule our whole life, and make us his companions and friends. From the first he took an interest in the raiment of the people ; he knew that poverty was no transient distress, but a part of the general life of the human family ; so he made arrangements even about pawnbroking, saying, "If thou at all take thy neighbour's raiment to pledge, thou shalt deliver it unto him by that the sun goeth down" (Exod. xvii. 26.) Pawnbroking was to be but for a few bright hours of the day ; as soon as the chill evening came down the pledge was to be restored. Why ? The garment referred to was a large four-square cloth ; in the middle of it a hole was cut through which the head could pass, so that the whole cloth fell round the body of the wearer. That garment was both a day garment and a blanket for the night. Allowing, therefore,—such would seem to be the divine reasoning—that a man can do without his outer cloth for a few hours whilst the sun is shining —for the sunshine is a kind of cloak—yet remember that the nights are cold and thy neighbour must not be allowed to lie down to sleep without being properly covered. This is what the Lord says in so many words in Exodus xxii. 27 : "For that is his covering only, it is his raiment for his skin : wherein shall

he sleep ? and it shall come to pass, when he crieth unto me,
tnat 1 will hear ; for I am gracious." Let us understand the
meaning of this gospel tone.   When the cold man cries because
for want of his raiment he cannot sleep—when he had to pawn
his raiment for bread,—" I will hear " his cry.   What is the
reason for hearing the cry ?—" for I am gracious "—I care
for men who cannot sleep because of the cold ; I care for
children who cannot sleep because they are hungry ; the foxes
have holes, the birds of the air have nests, how then can I forget
my own image and likeness ?—my heart hears : my heart
responds.   At the four corners of this cloth were four tassels
or fringes.   The tassels or fringes were called *Craspeda.*   Great
sanctity was attached to these tassels by the Jews : hence the
poor woman's declaration : " If I may but touch a *Craspedon* I
shall be healed."   We miss the whole meaning of the passage
by thinking of the hem of the garment in the ordinary sense of
the term.   The garment was four-square ; the head was put
through it ; at each of the corners there was a fringe or a tassel ;
each tassel was called a *Craspedon;* each tassel was regarded with
great seriousness by the Jewish mind ; it represented great
thoughts, and even the divine presence itself : hence the poor
woman, knowing this, said within herself—" If I may but touch
one of the tassels—if I may but touch one of the fringes, I shall
be healed."   So these *Craspeda* were not mere ornaments in
dress : they were full of typical ideas, if not of moral virtues.
Speaking of the scribes and Pharisees, Jesus Christ says
(Matthew xxiii. 5)—"They make broad their phylacteries, and
enlarge the borders of their garments "—they are great in tassels
and fringes : they enlarge them that they may in some way write
upon them words from the law, and appear unto men, not only
to be very learned in wisdom, but to be excellent patterns of
virtue.   The ordinary tassel was not enough for the Pharisee ;
the customary fringe is too small for the pedantic scribe, therefore the fringes must be enlarged, the writings must be multiplied,
and a more ostentatious display of virtue must be made to the
public eye.

   Is all this passed and done with ?   It can never be obsolete so
long as human nature is human nature.   If the Lord permit us
to wear a fringe or a tassel, or any outward and typical sign of

adoption and sonship, we are by so much exposed to insidious and mighty temptation. Yet we must have something to look at and something to touch, for we ourselves are in the body, and all the creation that we can see is a creation tangible, substantial, full of allegorical writing, it may be, which only skilled eyes can read. Still this visible creation must have some correspondence in the invisible creation into which we are called through Christ, the Keeper of the kingdom. We cannot be trained according to divine purpose except we have the outward, the material, and the visible. These gifts are of divine appointment. God recognises our need of them, and he supplies them, and names them, and specifies their uses. But who can be trusted with line or image, with tassel or fringe, with book or censer,—with anything that appeals to the eye and the touch, without misunderstanding God and exaggerating the purpose of the thing visible and tangible, and thus passing through into all manner of superstition and idolatry ? God has given us tassels and fringes to the great garment of the spiritual gift in Christ Jesus his Son, and we have misunderstood them, and what were divine gifts to begin with have been turned into temptations by which our worship has fallen into a species of feeble or contemptible idolatry. God has given us the Sabbath day. A most beautiful gift if we could have regarded it within the divine intention, and have accepted God's sweet purpose implied in the great donation ; but we must needs meddle with it and enlarge the tassel, and make broad the phylacteries and the borders, and write upon God's spring day all manner of narrow-minded and evil writing of our own invention ; or we must needs make hard what God made soft with pity, and gracious with love ; we must make the day into the sourest of the week, instead of the smile of the passing time ; we must be pedantic, stern, iron-bound, exacting in a most narrow-minded and despotic degree ;—and this we do to show our noble piety ! This is Pharisaism. We condemn ancient Pharisaism the more vehemently that we do not understand what we are condemning, for ignorance has no bounds. But let us be careful whilst we recognise the divine tassel, fringe, or ribband of blue, that we accept it in God's sense, and with God's limitation and purpose ;—then it shall be unto us Heaven's own sign—a visible thing by which we enter into invisible meanings and invisible liberties. But Pharisaic virtue will be meddling ; it will add one hour to the Sabbath day : it will begin a little earlier than was at first intended ; it will make its face sour and its fingers hard, and it will lay upon people exactions intolerable, whilst it, by some way unknown to the people, will sneak off to the enjoyment of its own wicked luxuries. In this way the fringe of the Sabbath has been enlarged by Pharisaic impiety and ostentation, and the sweet idea of sleep, rest, renewal, reinvigoration,—worship, psalm, sacrifice of a spiritual kind,—all these have been subordinated or lost. He does not keep the Sabbath who merely talks about it. Sabbath-keeping is an affair of the heart. You cannot keep the Sabbath by Act of Parliament ; you may close every business in the kingdom by imperial statute, but when you have done so, unless there be a consenting heart, every place devoted to business in the kingdom is more open on the Sabbath than it was on the common week day. We must cultivate love of the Sabbath spirit before we can have obedience to the Sabbath law ; we must recall the idea of Christ's resurrection and believe in its historical reality, or we cannot have a day to celebrate what never took place. We do not keep the birthdays of people who were never born. The birthday represents a historical reality in the family—an advent, a sweet epiphany, an incoming of a stranger who shall never be stranger more. Lose the idea of the birth, and the birthday must go ; lose the idea of the resurrection of Christ, and the Sabbath will come only to be misunderstood, and will pass away in contempt or in violation of its claims.

The Lord has given us two tassels called the Sacraments. Look at the Sacrament of the Lord's Supper. It was meant as a memorial ; it was a sublime appeal to the memory of the heart. Said the dying Son of God,—"This do in remembrance of me." A simple feast : a Supper which the poorest man can have at his own little deal table, if so be he will drink one little drop of water and taste one crumb of bread,—nay, he can even do without these things if he eat and drink with the Spirit. Into what enlargement of priestly pomp and meaning has that Sacrament been brought ! What magic has been used over the bread and the cup ! What with transubstantiation and consubstantiation, and all the polysyllables of the theologues, we have lost the

Supper. Memory has now next to no function to perform in connection with that Sacrament. The priest must operate upon the elements, some mysterious process must take place in the bread and in the cup; and not until such priestly pranks have been played may the common people touch these things,—nay, in some churches, they may not touch them at all, especially one of the elements : it is enough if the priest drink in some kind of representative capacity. They have enlarged the borders of their garments. The blue ribband was right, the fringe was of divine appointment, God meant the robe to have its tassels; but we have enlarged and vitiated and perverted and played all manner of tricks, and exercised every possible species of invention. "God made man upright ; but they have sought out many inventions "—and God does not know the tassels he appointed because of the enlargements and the discolourings invented and accomplished by depraved human genius.

God has given us another tassel in the Bible. He knew we could not do without a book : he made the Bible as small as possible ; never book had so much matter crushed into it—every line a living stem of a living vine ; the very punctuation seems to be part of the common vitality. But it is possible to make a fetish or idol of the Bible ; it is possible to make it a mere gathering of isolated texts to be fingered by men as they may be pleased to manipulate the thousand beads of heaven. So we have the Bible misunderstood—little detached texts thrust into wrong perspective and relation. We have lost the Biblical spirit in pedantic reverence for the Biblical letter. We have never yet seen in all its fulness that the letter is trying to tell something which it can never tell in all the amplitude of its meaning, and we have been afraid lest we should lose the spirit by not properly regarding the letter. Believe me, God's Book is a revelation. Everything is contained in it. The Book cannot be enlarged by human hands : it enlarges itself. You can enlarge the loaf of bread by your hands whilst that loaf is in process of formation, but you must keep your fingers off the growing blade and ear of wheat ; let the baker deal with the dough—he may not touch that living, golden thing which, through great agony and travail down in the darkness, has pierced the sod and come breathingly and lovingly up into the mellowing and ripening light. It is even so with God's Book. It needs no vindication. Your manufactured bread may need to be announced and weighed and justified to the public examiner and the public taste; but God's wheat is not to be so regarded. How it grew he has never told us; in all the information he has conveyed to the human family, he has never told us where the wind is, how the wheat grows; he has kept these things—so palpable and obvious in their appearances—to himself, as to the secret of their origin and movement. The vindication which the Bible asks for is to be seen, to be read. The Bible does not begin at the Book of Kings, or in the middle of the volume; the Bible—simple as the statement may appear—begins at the beginning, where so few people have ever begun; they have used the Bible as if it began nowhere, and could be opened promiscuously and understood in the most casual manner. The Bible has its own beginning, its own line of evolution, and it must be begun and perused according to its own genesis and law if its music is to be heard, and if human life is to fall into rhythm with its majestic purpose. Nothing is easier than to pervert the Bible. More mischief can be done by incompetent persons talking about the Bible and in its favour than ever can be done by the most skilful and obstinate assailants of its inspiration. The Bible has more to fear from its friends than from its enemies. I will vary the phrase and say, the Bible has nothing to fear from opposition; sometimes even it may tremble under the shadow of patronage.

All these—the Sabbath, the Sacraments, the Bible, the Sanctuary—are divine institutions, tassels ordained and declared in heaven; but we must be careful to ascertain where the divine ends and the human begins. The Pharisees have meddled with the fringes; the scribes have performed magical tricks upon the tassels. It is so with the ministry of the Gospel. The ministry of the Gospel is a divine institution; but how we have meddled with it and made it less in trying to make it larger! The ministry of the Gospel is a ministry of brotherhood, sympathy—great human love. It has been made into a priestly trick and has been invested with sacerdotal sanctions, and men—constables of their own appointment—have stood at the pulpit stairs to keep away persons who were supposed not to be authorised. The

great authorisation of the preacher is first of God, and next of
the common people. The common people will soon tell you
whom God has called to the ministry. The congregation is
judge. You cannot deceive the great common heart; it knows
the elect man : the very first sentence he utters is recognised as
genuine or as counterfeit. The people, the common people, all
the people,—they stand next to God in this matter :—" *Vox
populi, vox Dei."* The question has sometimes been asked—Do
the common people hear us " gladly " ? That question ought
not to be asked until another has been answered : Do we preach
to the common people—in great human words, in tears of
compassion, in genuine, manly, Christian sympathy ? Blessed
be God, the common people will never listen to theology, to
polysyllables, to wordy refinements. The common people can
understand the sunshine and respond to its sublimity; but they
cannot understand many of the lights which men have invented
and patented and heavily charged for. So with truth. The
great fringe truth has been enlarged by opinions. Opinion has
been enthroned. Not until we distinguish between truth and
opinion can we distinguish between God's fringe and the Pharisee's
phylactery. When any man has spoken—whatever his name,
intellectual capacity, moral pith, or rhetorical eloquence—he has
only announced a series of opinions. He can so announce them
as to make himself ridiculous, offensive, as to usurp a divine
position. But the truth underlies opinion, is different from
opinion, admits of great variety of opinion. As the sun will
grow all kinds of flowers, and the good old mother earth will let
all flowers grow within the bounds of her hospitality, so truth
will admit of all shades of opinion, all varieties of expression.
Why can we not recognise this, and clasp hands in spiritual
brotherhood, every man having a right to his own opinion and
being bound to society in nothing but in the reality and sincerity
of his soul ?

We must not go the other extreme, and do away with profession—tear off the ribband of blue, and the fringe on the
borders of the garment, and say,—We will have nothing more to
do with these things. They are all divine appointments. The
sanctuary is God's; the coming together of men to worship is
itself a holy act. You cannot worship individually, in the fullest

sense of the term. What is an individual? There is no such thing; society has rendered that impossible. God is the Author of society; God is the Author of humanity. Only in some narrow or limited sense can a man offer any worship in solitude. He is part of a band—a great organisation built for music. In some sense it may be true that a man considerably under six feet high may take hold of a gun and sword and say he will go out and fight as an individual wherever the war may be; but such an action needs hardly to be named to bring upon itself the contempt which it deserves. The individual is part of a larger individuality; the person is part of the larger person called the army. To your ranks! To your regiments! When the trumpet-blast sounds, it sounds an appeal and an instruction to the whole body of men. Forsake not the assembling of yourselves together, as the manner of some is. A man who is not a church-goer is a bad man, in some sense, or an incomplete man in others; he has fallen below a right comprehension of human relations and social connections and reciprocations. Behold the solitary wanderer who has gone away by himself on the holy Sabbath morning!—he is going to "hear the birds sing" and "the brooks ripple and gurgle," and "see the hyacinths and the violets"—behold him there! Was ever irony more complete? He has missed the divine idea. He should have said,—No; to the centre! to the meeting-place! to the rendez-vous!—together, all together,—common prayer, common song, common study; and then radiate as you please, carrying the public personality with the narrow individualism, and enlarging the little unit by the infinite completeness of human nature. We need some outward help. We love to hear somebody pray when we are very lonely and dyingly sick. To hear another human voice is a hint of fellowship, a hint of consolidation, a hint of heaven. We could pray by ourselves, mayhap. Not alto-gether. It will do us good if some man has force enough to pray aloud; the very audibleness of the speech will bring a kind of society into the chamber; we shall feel the larger by hearing some sympathetic voice arguing, pleading, with God; the walls of the chamber will be broken down and the boundary line will be a horizon, the roof will be removed and the blue ceiling will be heaven. We need the Sabbath day, the memorial

Sacraments, the Holy Book, the preaching man, the fellow-suppliant, the congregation ; but let us take care not to make more of these tassels than God intended. Let us take care lest by enlarging the fringe we destroy its meaning.

NOTE.

THE LAW OF FRINGES.—According to Herodotus, the dress of the Egyptians consisted of a linen garment, over which was worn a white woollen cloak or shawl. The former, which seems to have been often, if not generally, worn without the other, was fringed at the bottom. Concerning the form of this fringe perhaps nothing positive can be determined. Some endeavour to ascertain its character by examining the two Hebrew words by which it is expressed, צִיצִת *tzizith*, in the present text, and גְּדִלִים *gedilim*, in Deut. xxii. 12. The former of these words elsewhere (as in Ezek. viii. 3) means a lock of hair ; and the latter a rope, such as that with which Delilah bound Samson (Judges xiv. 11, 12) ; and it is hence imagined that these fringes consisted of many threads which hung like hair, and were twisted like a rope. The " ribband " probably was either a blue *thread* twisted with a white one through the whole fringe, or a lace by which the fringe was fastened to the edge of the garment. Many commentators of authority think, from the explanation in Deut. xxii., that the " fringes " were no other than strings with tassels at the end, fastened to the four corners of the upper garment, the proper use of these strings being to fasten the corners together. Of this opinion are the modern Jews. What *they* understand by the direction of the text appears from Levi's description of the tzizith or robe in question. It is made of two square pieces with two long pieces like straps joined to them, in order that one of the said pieces may hang down before upon the breast, and the other behind ; at the extremity of the four corners are fastened the strings, each of which has five knots besides the tassel, signifying the five books of the law. The rabbins, under whose instruction this profound analogy has been established, further observe that each string consisted of eight threads, which, with the number of knots and the numeral value of the letters in the word *tzizith*, make 613, which is, according to them, the exact number of the precepts in the law. From this they argue the importance of this command, since he who observes it, they say, in effect observes the whole law ! The law seems to require that the fringes should be constantly worn ; but as it would not consist with the costume of the countries through which the Jews are now dispersed to wear the fringed garment as an external article of dress, every Jew makes use of two—a large one which is used only at prayers, and on some other occasions, and is then worn externally, and a small one which is constantly worn as an under-garment. The principal denomination of this article is *Tzizith*, on account of the fringes, in which all its sanctity is supposed to consist ; but the proper name of the vestment itself is Talith, and by this it is commonly distinguished.

There have been various conjectures as to the object of this law. The most probable is that the " fringe " was intended as a sort of badge or livery, by which, as well as by circumcision and by the fashion of their beards, and by their peculiar diet, the Hebrews were to be distinguished from other people. Be this as it may, much superstition came in the end to be connected with the use of these fringes. The Pharisees are severely censured by our Saviour for the ostentatious hypocrisy with which they made broad the " border " of their garments.—*Pictorial Commentary.*

PRAYER.

ALMIGHTY GOD, to thy throne we come as if by right of love. Surely we have no right of conduct. Our behaviour would turn us away from places of light, but because of a love thou hast created in the heart we cannot be content with darkness; we yearn towards the morning; we would stand up in places full of glory and take part in every hymn of praise which celebrates thy pity and thy grace. This is the Lord's working in our hearts, this is the seal divine, this is the signature of Heaven; there is none like it, there is no mistaking it. We feel what we cannot explain—that we have been born into a new life, have laid hold of a new relation, and are now standing in the strength and comfort of a covenant that cannot be broken. If for a moment we doubted this, we should be as men who think the clouds have put out the sun; we should reason wrongly, and make perverted use of thy promises and ministries in the soul. Yet it is difficult sometimes not to think that the sun is dead, that the clouds have conquered at last, and that the air is mightier than light. Thou wilt pity us herein, for our ignorance is our commendation as well as our infirmity. If we own it, thou wilt displace it by wisdom; if we obstinately cling to it, we may suffer the penalty of our folly. We are of yesterday and know nothing. We will not reason before thee; we will that thou wilt reason with us; so there shall be no argument on our side, except the argument of listening well, fixing upon thee the attention of our love and looking at thee with eyes of hunger. With this thou wilt be satisfied. Thou delightest in our upward look; to thee it is a great speech without words, a longing of the heart, a quick beating of the pulses. Behold, thou art worshipped by all the world in this form or in that; but it is after thee the nations yearn. They do not all know it, nor could many of them explain it, and some might even deny it; but, Lord, the earth groaneth for thee, and the peoples of the world are looking wistfully for thy coming. This day we all worship thee: some through the moles and the bats, some through hideous images; those of broader and livelier imagination through the sun and moon and stars, the dawning east and the purpling west; and some in this way and in that: some truly, wisely, by way of revelation, grasping the Cross, seeing the propitiatory Blood, owning the mighty Name, and sealing every prayer with the name of Christ; but the whole earth is thine. In our littleness we reject and classify and distinguish, but in thy greatness thou dost see the inner meaning of things—the spiritual purpose, the ultimate design, and thou wilt judge righteous judgment and save many whom we would lose. We come before thee with different forms and conceptions of worship, but thou wilt interpret the motive and answer the heart's desire. Hear the little child. who can but say, FATHER, and then wait in troubled silence because other and equal words will not come; tell him it is the greatest prayer—the unfinished cry, and the cry that never can be finished. Hear the sinner—broken, shattered, and confounded, who can but sob,—God be merciful to me a sinner. Stop him there as thou dost stop men who have built a whole tower; there is no need for further word, or speech, or plea; thou wilt stop it with an infinite reply, and come with much of blessing, yea, with festival and banqueting of soul to those who are alive at every point, who commune with thee in high imagining, in gracious fellowship, in tender yearning, through every form possible to the human mind, through all the mediums open to the access of the creature; and thus give a portion of meat to each in due season, and make us all forget the difference of way, and speech, and degree, in the enthusiasm of a common thankfulness, the burning of a unanimous love. We put ourselves into thy keeping. They are well kept whom thou keepest. Stand by the gate; watch the way to the heart; set a burning word near the tree of life to keep it from all trespass. Help us to do our duty bravely, wisely, tenderly, as strong and trustful hearts should do it. May we walk through the night as if it were a new form of day, may we plunge into the sea assured that the plunge will divide the waters, and may we face the wilderness as if it were a garden planted from on high; and when the way is beauteous and summer-lighted, full of song and sweetness and manifold delight, keep us from its fascinations and help us to make it but a dim, poor symbol of the paradise and the heavens which we have yet to realise. Amen.

Numbers xvi.

EVERY MAN IN HIS PLACE.

THIS is strikingly modern in its temper. This ancient democracy has steadily kept pace with the ages and is at this moment as lively and audacious as ever. It is hard for men to keep their places; it is hard because the next higher place appears to be so near and so accessible. It is always difficult for the heart to be quiet, contented, restful in God; it is fertile in plan, ambitious in spirit, conscious of great power, and not wholly unconscious of great deserts. But men fritter away their strength by finding fault with their positions. We can only work really and deeply, and therefore lastingly, as we have the blessed consciousness of being where God has put us, and doing the kind of service God has indicated. The appointment may be an inferior one, but it is divine, and, therefore, if we answer it with faithfulness and obedience, we shall find in the discharge of its duties sweet comfort and a continual re-invigoration of our best motive and purpose. The people who rebelled against Moses had inferior appointments in connection with the tabernacle; but they were not content with these: they actually sought not only the priesthood, but, according to the literal translation, the high-priesthood. They would have censers such as Aaron himself used; they would try what they could do on the throne; they did not see any reason why they should be excluded from the very pontificate of Israel. Who ever did see any reason why he should not be a great man? It is expecting much of human nature to expect it to be just what it is, and to accept the position simply, loyally, gratefully;—but only in such acceptance of position can men be their best and do their best. Let a preacher once get it into his mind that he ought to move in a larger circle and have a pulpit twice the size of his present pulpit, and the ambition which moves his mind in that direction, takes away from him much of his working strength, so that, instead of filling the little sphere, or the sphere comparatively small, he shrinks within it and becomes for all effective service a smaller man than he really is. Let us accept our position whatever it be, saying,—God put me here, he takes care of me while I am here, and when he wants me in some larger place he will send for me, and until the message comes I will serve him with both hands diligently, and my heart shall be as a fire burning up towards him in aspiration and sacrifice.

What a picture life is with regard to personal position and social gradation!—and we cannot alter the picture; do what we may, still the graduated lines are plainly written, and they constitute a kind of unnamed but verily inspired Bible. There are men who are as Moses and Aaron amongst us, and there are men who are as Korah, and Dathan, and Abiram. Outbreaks of temper do occur in regard to social position and influence. The question will arise,—"Who is greatest in the kingdom of heaven?" —but all complainings arise and perish without touching the settled and determined lines of personal function, and social gradation, and ecclesiastical and other relationships. There is a tide in these things, as in the sea, and no Canute can roll back the advancing water. It is not enough to assent to these propositions; the aim of their statement is to constitute itself into a noble persuasion to adopt them and to make them part of the rule and guide of life. Moses said,—If this is the case, meet me to-morrow; bring your censers, put fire therein, and put incense before the Lord to-morrow; and whom the Lord chooses, let him be pontiff. That is the only appeal. The battle has been settled ten thousand times, and still the war of ambition rages in the human heart. The morrow came; the competitors were there; what became of them we know. It would be difficult to believe the letter of this ancient history if we did not see the same fate happening to every Korah, Dathan, and Abiram in our own day. Modern facts help us to receive the testimony of ancient history. In all the departments of life there are men who are as Moses and Aaron. Take any department of life that may first occur to the imagination. Shall we say the department of commerce? Even in the market-place we have Moses and Aaron, and they cannot be deposed. Where is the man who thinks he could not conduct the largest business in the city? Yet the poor cripple could not conduct it, and the greatest punishment that could befall the creature would be to allow him to attempt to rule a large and intricate commercial concern. But it seems to be hard for a man to see some other man at the very head of commercial affairs whose word is law, whose signature amounts to a species of sovereignty, and to know that all the while he, the observer, is, in his own estimation, quite as good a man—a person of remarkable capacity, and he is only waiting for an opportunity to wear a nimbus of glory—a halo of radiance —that would astound the exchanges of the world. But it cannot be done. There are great business men and small business men: there are wholesale men and retail men, and neither the wholesale nor the retail affects the quality of the man's soul, or the destiny of the man's spirit; but, as a matter of fact, these distinctions are made, and they are not arbitrary: in the spirit of them there is a divine presence. If men could believe this, they would be comforted accordingly. Every preacher knows in his inmost soul that *he* is fit to be the Dean of St. Paul's, or the Dean of Westminster,—every preacher knows that; but to be something less—something officially lower—and yet to accept the inferior position with a contentment which is inspired by faith in God, is the very conquest of the Spirit of heaven in the heart of man, is a very miracle of grace. Even the Apostle Paul required education in this matter—"for," said he, "I have learned,"—referring to a process of daily education—"in what-

soever state I am, therewith to be content." Shall we take the
department of poetry? As a matter of fact, even in that
department there are some men higher than others. It is an
astounding thing that there should be in the department of
poetry some men who can make poetry, and some men who
can only read it. How difficult to believe that the man who has
made two lines rhyme cannot write the "Idylls of the King"!
There is always the secret hope that the development may come
late; it is an ineffable comfort to know that some men reached
their highest influence at a very remote period of life. Who
made these men different? Who made one man able to make
paper and another man able to write upon it as the great poets
have written? We cannot be atheistic in presence of such facts.
We may differ about the name to be applied, but there is the
absolute fact—that even in the region of poetry, some men can
make it and other men cannot. When it is made, there is no
mistake about it; the heart answers the appeal; the world waits
to see where the fire will fall, and when it has fallen there is no
mistaking the answer of the human observer. We know the
Bible by the reading of it; we know inspiration by the sharing
of it; we feel that the stranger beside us is a guest from heaven,
because he makes our heart burn within us. We did not make
ourselves; we must not attempt to appoint ourselves. We must
remember that we are not our own: that we are the flock of
God—the sheep of his pasture: that he formed us, and not we
ourselves: that the very hairs of our head are all numbered, and
that in the Father's house there are many mansions. "O, rest
in the Lord, and wait patiently for him; and he will give thee
thine heart's desire,"—or, if not, he will give thee some larger
blessing, showing the capacity of the heart is not the measure of
the divine bounty.

Moses took the only course that was open to him. It is no use
arguing with men as to greatness: let the appeal be to experience; let us come to the testimony of fact. This applies to the
pre-eminence of the Cross of Christ. Many a Korah, Dathan,
and Abiram has said to the Cross,—Thou dost take too much
upon thee. The Cross says,—Let the appeal be to history, to
fact, to power. The Cross never claims to be accepted without
examination, and testing, and competition in some sacred and

noble sense of that term. Philosophy has said,—I can save the world, and as for thee, thou grim Cross, thou takest too much upon thee; thou art broad in sentimental appeal, but I am subtle in all my researches and fundamental in all my relations and my instructions. The Cross is willing that philosophy should be tried. It has been tried. It has a beautiful voice, a delicate touch, an eye that sees in the darkness. The Cross does not despise the love of wisdom—which is the true definition of philosophy;—but philosophy cannot touch the whole life : it touches certain men, appeals with great effect to certain qualities of men : it speaks to men of large capacity or of ample leisure, to persons who have time to give to the study of philosophy proper attention; but philosophy, as ordinarily understood, does not get into the universal heart, does not cover the universal experience, does not rejoice with them that do rejoice, and weep with them that weep; it lacks what the Cross has—the patience, the sympathy, the long hand that reaches into the heart's innermost necessity and ministers to the life's profoundest need. Morality says to the Cross,—Thou dost take too much upon thee; I can make the world what it ought to be. And the Cross says,—Let the appeal be to history ; let the appeal be to facts ; let us abide by the arbitrament of reality. So morality comes with small recipes and nostrums and codes of behaviour, and bills of disci pline, and insists upon registering human behaviour according to certain more or less pedantic laws ; but morality never touches the world's deepest wound ; morality is, according to its own verbal definition, a manner, a posture, a calculated attitude, a providence based upon a species of arithmetic. So philosophy, morality, imagination, new schemes, new books, have all arisen to challenge the supremacy of the Cross. Is the Cross not a philosophy? The Cross is the profoundest of all philosophy, though it does not come to the world under that name, but under some tenderer designation. Is not the Cross a morality ? The Cross insists upon righteousness ; it will have nothing to do with wickedness ; it seeks to purge human nature of its depravity. It does not begin with codes of behaviour, but with regeneration—with the new or second birth of the heart, and out of that will come clean hands, a pure tongue, a noble speech, a charitable disposition, and a sacrificial service of the world. So we do not separate Christianity from philosophy, morality, imagination, great and intellectual speculation; but we put these things all in their right places and relations, and the appeal of Christianity is an appeal to sinners, to lost men, to hearts that cannot heal themselves, to a ruin complete and absolute; afterwards we come to high thinking, brilliant speculation, a very apocalypse of vision and wonder and gracious delight. So Christianity asks for no quarter upon any arbitrary or superstitious grounds; it is willing that to-morrow every Korah, Dathan, and Abiram shall meet it, and let the contest be settled by experience. Christianity can call upon a thousand men to speak in its name and ten thousand times ten thousand more day by day. Let the question be—What has most deeply touched your life? What has given you the surest and strongest hope under the pressure of a guilty conscience, the charges of an accusing memory? What has touched your tears most lovingly and healingly? What was it that sat up with you longest in the dark night time? What was it that found for you flowers in the snow, and summer among the winter ice? Speak out—be just; and the heart will say, whenever there has been any real experience,—The Cross of our Lord Jesus Christ has covered most of my life, most has healed my diseases, has spoken to me a larger language than I ever heard before—"God forbid that I should glory, save in the Cross of our Lord Jesus Christ."

The rebels were overthrown and a marvellous providence asserts itself immediately in connection with the overthrow:

"And the Lord spake unto Moses, saying, Speak unto Eleazar the son of Aaron the priest, that he take up the censers out of the burning, and scatter thou the fire yonder; for they are hallowed. The censers of these sinners against their own souls, let them make them broad plates for a covering of the altar: for they offered them before the Lord, therefore they are hallowed: and they shall be a sign unto the children of Israel" (xvi. 36-38).

So Christianity uses the weapons of its opponents: as David uses the sword of Goliath; so that which has been consecrated unto the Lord, even by men whose spirit and temper were not divine, must be claimed for the service of the altar. The altar was made of wood, yet it was covered with metal that the continual burning upon it might not injure the structure; and now "the censers of these sinners against their own souls," shall be

made into " broad plates for a covering of the altar."—Behold the
Cross—what changes it is undergoing in outward appearance !
What are these things which men are nailing to it now ?   Swords
taken in war, trophies brought from the battlefield, crowns once
erected in ignoble pride against the supremacy of Christ.   So
the process goes on.   What a Cross it is !   What a spectacle !—
nailed to it every weapon that has ever been raised against it ;
and in the very upbuilding of the Cross through the generations
we shall read a history which no pen could ever fully write.
Shall we join this process of nailing to the Cross that which we
have used against it ?   We have used our little genius—let us go
and nail it to the Cross.   We have opened our mouth in rude
eloquence in many a charge and objection against the Cross—let
us give our remaining breath to the praise of him who has never
looked upon us but with upbraiding or hopeful gaze.   We have
fooled away our money in helping those to propagate their views
whose object was to turn all earth into a flat plane confined
within the four corners of a definite boundary, and to shut out the
blue heavens, or to use them merely for the sake of convenience
—let us take what remains and say,—Thou wounded Lamb of
God, we know thou canst pardon sin, but canst thou forgive
folly ?—we know not the measure between the tragedy of thy
sacrifice and the turpitude of our guilt, but we are not only
sinners : we are fools—oh canst thou, Son of God, pity the fool
as well as forgive the criminal ?—we thought to fight against
thee : we meant to win : we accepted the challenge, and now
there is nothing left of our rebellious selves but our censers,—
Galilean, thou hast conquered !

Let us then accept our places in the divine providence ; let us
acknowledge a divine order in social relations ; do not let us
attempt to settle great social questions by the rule of thumb.—Do
not imagine that rich and poor can be levelled together all into
one plane by some easy democratic method ; do let us recognise
the presence of a marvellous providence in life.   On the other
hand, do not let us take such a view of that providence as to lead
us to tyrannise over our weaker fellow-creatures ; do not let us
imagine that we are gods and have a right to override all poor
and inferior persons ; the true line of wisdom lies between.
What hast thou that thou hast not received ?—that shoul I be the

question which every man should hear addressed to himself when he is counting his gold and adding fields to his estate and is most conscious of his commanding intellect and his imperial genius. And as for the poor, they should be taught that poverty is no disgrace. There is a rich poverty. There is a noble failure in life; there is a bankruptcy with extenuating circumstances. There are sufferings that have a divine meaning behind them. So we will have no boasting and no despairing. We are free— the rich and the poor, the leader and the follower. "The Lord reigneth; let the earth rejoice."

NOTE.

Korah was the leader of the famous rebellion against his cousins Moses and Aaron in the wilderness, for which he paid the penalty of perishing with his followers by an earthquake and flames of fire (Num. xvi.; xxvi. 9-11). The particular grievance which rankled in the mind of Korah and his company was their exclusion from the office of the priesthood, and their being confined—those among them who were Levites—to the inferior service of the tabernacle, as appears clearly, both from the words of Moses in ver. 9, and from the test resorted to with regard to the censers and the offering of incense. The same thing also appears from the subsequent confirmation of the priesthood to Aaron (ch. xvii.). The appointment of Elizaphan to be the chief of the Kohathites (Num. iii. 30) may have further inflamed his jealousy. Korah's position as leader in this rebellion was evidently the result of his personal character, which was that of a bold, haughty, and ambitious man. This appears from his address to Moses in ver. 3, and especially from his conduct in ver. 19, where both his daring and his influence over the congregation are very apparent. Were it not for this, one would have expected the Gershonites—as the elder branch of the Levites—to have supplied a leader in conjunction with the sons of Reuben, rather than the family of Izhar, who was Amram's younger brother. From some cause which does not clearly appear, the children of Korah were not involved in the destruction of their father, as we are expressly told in Num. xxvi. 11, and as appears from the continuance of the family of the Korahites to the reign at least of Jehoshaphat (2 Chr. xx. 19), and probably till the return from the captivity (1 Chr. ix. 19, 31). Perhaps the fissure of the ground which swallowed up the tents of Dathan and Abiram did not extend beyond those of the Reubenites. From ver. 27 it seems clear that Korah himself was not with Dathan and Abiram at the moment. His tent may have been one pitched for himself, in contempt of the orders of Moses, by the side of his fellow-rebels, while his family continued to reside in their proper camp nearer the tabernacle; or it must have been separated by a considerable space from those of Dathan and Abiram. Or, even if Korah's family resided amongst the Reubenites, they may have fled, at Moses's warning, to take refuge in the Kohathite camp, instead of remaining, as the wives and children of Dathan and Abiram did (ver. 27). Korah himself was doubtless with the two hundred and fifty men who bare censers nearer the tabernacle (ver. 19), and perished with them by the "fire from Jehovah" which accompanied the earthquake.—SMITH's *Dictionary of the Bible.*

PRAYER.

ALMIGHTY GOD, thou art our Father. God is love. We live in God; without God we cannot live. Thou hast made us, and not we ourselves. The lot is cast into the lap, but the whole disposing thereof is of the Lord. Thou hast given unto us a time of birth and a time of death, and no hand can alter the record. We stand in God's eternity. As the mountains are round about Jerusalem, so the Lord is round about his people. Not a sparrow falleth to the ground without our Father; the very hairs of our head are all numbered. Behold, in what a way hast thou led us these many years in the wilderness! When there was no water, thou didst find streams in the rocks; when the pool was bitter, the healing tree was nigh; when thou didst send upon us a great judgment, in the whirlwind we heard a tone of mercy. In wrath thou dost remember mercy; in judgment thou art compassionate. The mercy of the Lord endureth for ever; and this will we say with the passion of great love. The way of man is not in himself. The Lord giveth, the Lord taketh away, and the Lord's way is always right. Even so, Father: for so it seemeth good in thy sight—would we say in every event of time, how much soever we may be disappointed, and how heavy soever may be the burden we have to bear. This is the time of endurance; this is not the season of explanation. What we know not now we shall know hereafter, and thy answer shall be greater than our question, and where we were much pained we shall be mightily delivered and glorified from on high. Thou art the Father of our life. We are thine, not our own. If we have aught that is our own, it was thine first and will be thine last, for we ourselves are bought with a price. Make us tender, loving, sympathetic, always living in others and for others; and watch over us with Christly solicitude, even though it become aggravated into pain of mind and sorrow of soul because of ingratitude and because of rebellion. May our love be measured by the divine love, and not be changeful, fickle, and uncertain; may it be a great love, originating in the Cross, sustained by daily grace, made larger and more intelligent by the constant inspiration of the Holy Ghost. Bless the orphan, the sad, the lonely, the friendless. Why these miseries should come upon us we cannot wholly tell in words, though there is a voice in our heart which tells us that the way of the Lord is right. Where thou hast given heavy burdens, thou wilt give needful strength; where the tears are many and hot, thy hand will be present in its gentleness. The Lord succour those who need continual help; be a light to the blind, a staff to the weak, a Guide to the perplexed, and the Saviour of all. We commend to thee the children who have no earthly father, those whose homes have been desolated by sudden death, or other invasion of distress. Thou dost anticipate our prayer: and, behold, the infinite answer of thy pity is uttered upon the earth before our prayer is heard in heaven. We pray in the name of Jesus Christ, Son of man, Son of God, God the Son, who loved us and gave himself for us, and who, being our Saviour and Priest, is not ashamed to be called our Brother. Amen.

Numbers xx. 14-21.

14. And Moses sent messengers from Kadesh unto the King of Edom, Thus saith thy brother Israel, Thou knowest all the travel that hath befallen us:

15. How our fathers went down into Egypt, and we have dwelt in Egypt a long time; and the Egyptians vexed us, and our fathers:

16. And when we cried unto the Lord, he heard our voice, and sent an angel, and hath brought us forth out of Egypt: and, behold, we are in Kadesh, a city in the uttermost of thy border:

17. Let us pass, I pray thee, through thy country: we will not pass through the fields, or through the vineyards, neither will we drink of the water of the wells: we will go by the king's high way, we will not turn to the right hand nor to the left, until we have passed thy borders.

18. And Edom said unto him, Thou shalt not pass by me, lest I come out against thee with the sword.

19. And the children of Israel said unto him, We will go by the high way: and if I and my cattle drink of thy water, then I will pay for it: I will only, without doing anything else, go through on my feet,

20. And he said, Thou shalt not go through. And Edom came out against him with much people, and with a strong hand.

21. Thus Edom refused to give Israel passage through his border: wherefore Israel turned away from him.

UNEXPECTED RETRIBUTION.

ALL these things have an explanation. The judgment of things does not lie upon the bare surface, nor is our life a quantity constituted between four visible and measurable points. Life is a mystery—sometimes distant, shapeless and measureless as a cloud, and sometimes a veil so thin we can almost see through it, yet when we touch it, it is a hard wall built by hands invisible, and rising up with darkening height to the very clouds from which we expected revelations of morning and summer. Why do we whine and complain, and say we are ill-used and Edom is unkind and ungenerous, wanting in hospitality, and in all the tenderest attributes of human nature? It is an ill speech; it is as wanting in honesty and self-recognition as it is in sound reasoning. Israel was not the poor little innocent wanderer that it appeared to be from the plaintive, suppliant speech of Moses. Nothing is self-contained. We must go into yesterday to find the explanation of to-day. To-day!—What is it? An up-gathering and sharp, yet transient, representation of things that happened in the centuries dead but never forgotten and never inoperative. Who pleads? Israel. To whom is the plea addressed? To a brother. How did the word *brother* come into the narrative? It came historically. We have here Jacob and Esau. Edom is the name by which Esau was known. Wherever we find the term Edom, our minds may instantly associate with it the history of Esau, and an action of divine sovereignty in relation to that history. Jacob supplanted Esau, ran away in the night time, met his brother at some distance of time afterwards, the brothers fell upon one another's necks, kissed each other, and seemed to sink the infinite outrage in grateful and perpetual oblivion. Nothing of the kind. Life cannot be managed thus; things do not lie between man and man only. Herein is the difference between crime and sin. Crime may be an affair open, visible, measurable, to which adequate penalty may be measured out; but sin hurts the heavens, insults and stains the sceptre of the universe—pains the heart of God. Can men shake hands over it, sponge it out by some act of transient generosity, and say,—Let it be forgotten, as though it had never been? We cannot treat our own sin. The answer to the sin of men must come from the God against whom the sin was committed. Do not let us imagine that sin is a breach of etiquette, a perversion of social custom, an eccentricity of personal taste, a mere outrage of a conventional kind. If we talk thus flippantly and superficially about sin, we shall be astounded when we behold the Cross that was erected for its obliteration and pardon. We must know the sinfulness of sin before we can know the compassionateness of mercy. So Jacob and Esau come face to face throughout the ages. The supplanter cannot sponge out his miserable cunning and selfish deceit and unpardonable fraud. Jacob the individual dies, Esau the individual dies: but Jacob and Esau, as representing a great controversy, can never die : to the end of the chapter Edom will encounter Israel with deep and lasting animosity. We cannot always explain the animosities which burn in our excited hearts;

examined and cross-examined as to their history, we may be quite unable to give any exact account of genesis and growth and culmination. Man cannot explain himself to himself; he only knows that inexplicably he feels an animosity which cataracts cannot quench—a burning, blazing scorn which seas cannot drown. There is a mystery in human development. Things are larger than they seem to be. Awkward, perplexing, distressing, is the fact we are bound to recognise, that we come up against ourselves day by day, and our ghostly history follows us from wedding to burial, from feast to battle, from day to night; and when we would be gladdest it thrusts in its sting the furthest. Let us take care of this life. The day is more than twelve hours long; invisible threadlets pass through the dark night and connect themselves with the next day.—Our life is not a thread like a line; it is a web moving in various directions, and thickening itself into substance not always easy to handle, and sometimes wrapping itself round us like a robe that burns off our skin, and sometimes lifting itself above us to shut out the fire and blessing of the sun. Fools are they who live from hand to mouth,— yea, fools inexplicable and unpardonable and wholly undesirable as to companionship, who live a flippant life, thinking that things are in no wise related, and forgetting that to-morrow brings the harvest of to-day.

Influence is not limited by personal action. What is a "person"? There is no such thing, in any narrow and limited sense of the term. A man stands up and says,—Am I not a man?— ; and I say,—No, you are not— ; there need not be any long and wordy discussion about that. What is an "individual"? There is no such thing, in the sense of a quantity that can be measured, weighed, and set down in exact figures, and as having no relation whatever to anything past or to come. When the little child stands up, generations beat in his pulse. When a man asks if he is not a "person," an "individual," he forgets that all his forefathers gather up mysterious influences in his breathing, his attitude, and his action. We are more than we appear to be. We do not bury the past and shut it out as an operative factor in the daily ministry of being. This makes life solemn even to awfulness. When the young life coughs and heaves under the influence of internal pain, what is it that happens?

Whole generations of weakness gather up in that sense of distress and powerlessness. When a young and apparently lovely character suddenly deflects from the straight line and goes away into forbidden places, what has happened? Generations of criminals have asserted their ascendency over the individual will, and the wanderer may have run off to meet in invisible council more than two or three generations of men.

Jacob must meet Esau again and again. There is no easy escape for wrong-doers. The eternal distrust which subsists between man and man, family and family, race and race, has a moral explanation. It is not all whim, fickleness, mere passion and selfish excitement. We must be philosophical in our quest for causes and motives. Far back in time almost immeasurable we shall find the seed was sown which comes up in unexpected places. The children must suffer for the fathers. We cannot help it. We would complain of it were there not a supplemental and completing truth : for as certainly as the children suffer for their fathers, are they benefited by their fathers' nobleness and beneficence—as certainly do they come to reap golden harvests because of the good seed sowed by the generations that are gone. The way of the Lord is equal. We perhaps cannot understand why we are not allowed to pass through this land, to have right of passage down this country, to navigate certain rivers, and to cross particular provinces ; and we take offence : our sensibilities are easily wounded ; we say,— This is hard. But you cannot set aside the " divinity that shapes our ends "—the Providence that looks now and again upon us with a face of solemn judgment and transfixes us with a look full of spiritual accusation. What then ? Instead of complaining and moaning and reproaching other people, let us search into the reality of the case, and we shall find, perhaps to our surprise— and our surprise may be turned to our instruction,—that whatever occurs to us in the way of disappointment, humiliation, and subordination, is explained by sin done long ago. Is there any consolation in that explanation of the mystery? None; but there is what is better. Why do you always seek for consolation and soothing ? Who are we that we should cry out in moaning terms for perpetual consolation ? Stand up and say,—This is God's law, and by it we will work ; we suffer hurt, damage, loss, because of what went before us; we cannot remedy that, but, by the help of God, we will see that our posterity shall reap sweetness where we have gathered only bitterness. The lesson is before you; the application relates to those who are coming afterwards. We can make their burdens lighter; we can already open gates through kingdoms for men who are coming fifty and a hundred years and more after this very day; and as the gates fly open, and hospitality is offered in the time of their wandering, they will remember that this day good men sowed good seed, mighty men fought battles with Heaven, great suppliants won great answers which *they* will enjoy in the fulness of their noble fruition.

So Esau had his turn. We pitied the hairy man as he was driven away portionless, without a blessing, his great big heart full of sin no doubt, quivering with agony, for which there was no adequate expression in words; but in so far as he has been wronged he will see satisfaction and himself be satisfied. The supplanted family had a land when the supplanter's descendants had only a wilderness. This is the law of Providence. Events are not measured within the compasses of the little day. The cunning man or the strong man, the oppressor or the wrong-doer, may have his victory to-day, and may smile upon it, and regard it with complacency, and receive the incense of adulation from persons who only see between sunrise and sundown. But the heavens are against him; he has to encounter the eternities, long time after his victory shall wither, and in his descendants his humiliation shall be consummated. Suppose, however, that he should not care for his descendants? Then he is not a man to be trusted now. Have no companionship with him. Do not put your hand into his hand, for he will wrong you and you will come out of the grasp with a stain upon your palm. Do not laugh with the fool when he says that he cares not for his descendants. A man who does not care for his descendants, cannot care for you, cannot care for his contemporaries; he writes his own condemnation in his flippant neglect. My son, have nothing to do with such a man; he will take thee into dark places, strip thee, wrong thee, and to suit his purpose may kill thee. Is it not wonderful how the wheel goes round? "Dearly beloved, avenge not yourselves, but rather give place unto wrath : for it is written, **Vengeance is mine ;** I will repay, saith the Lord." Events translate themselves into punishment swiftly and suddenly. A shut gate means you are historically connected with a great wrong. Israel adopts the affectionate style of entreaty and says " thy brother Israel." But wrongs are not thus to be obliterated ; complimentary speeches do not restore inheritances that have been turned away ; eulogiums cannot repossess men of the blessings forfeited by the fraud of others. Live the larger life, the nobler life. Ye are not yourselves : you represent others, and you prepare for others to represent you ; and he only handles life wisely who takes hold of both its ends and who remembers the law of cause and effect, seedtime and harvest, action and influence.

Here is the wrong-doer brought to his knees. That always happens. The wicked man has a short day. The deceiver must face his own deceits. Nothing prospers long in the bad man's hands. The money which he gets wrongfully he cannot spend to his own satisfaction : it is gone whilst he counts it ; it vanishes as he admires it ; there is no stay in the gold, no abiding in the substance ; it is money put into bags with holes in them. If a bad man could succeed, in the large, deep vital sense of the term, he would by so much dethrone God. He cannot, therefore, succeed ; with Heaven against him, with eternity against him, with God against him, when he apparently succeeds, it is but the flash of a little flame that dies in the effort which it makes.

Notice what is termed the solidarity of human life. The human family is one. If one member suffer, all the members suffer with it. The wrongs that were done ten generations ago are being re-asserted as to their moral claim to-day. The controversies of the world are not controversies which began this morning—fights that surprise the combatants ; their beginnings lie far back in the gone centuries, and in proportion to the distances from which they come may be the judgment which they will demand.

We live, then, in a scheme of Providence. Life is not atheistic. Our sufferings have an explanation ; our weakness is not an accident, but the outcome of a series of processes often lying beyond the line of imagination. The lesson is that we should accept life solemnly, pass through all its processes circumspectly, do nothing at our own bidding or for the gratification of our own will or fancy, but should always say,—My God, thy will be done. Let no man undertake to be God for himself; let him occupy his definite position as servant, errand-bearer, worker in the vineyard, and let his spirit express itself substantially thus: Lord, at thy bidding I would go, at thy bidding I would stay; give me understanding of my time; give me the noble Christly heart, and inspire me by thy Holy Spirit that I may be enabled so to succeed as to ripen into a harvest of satisfaction and gladness in the coming days. No man can live in that spirit without being in heaven as to all the substance and quality of heaven's meaning. That is what is meant by praying without ceasing—namely, living in the prayerful spirit, always being in touch with God, ever having God's throne in view, God's law at heart, God's will the inspiration and direction of life.

Viewed from this altitude, what is sorrow? what is loss? what is disappointment? All these things may be sanctified: orphanage may come to have a special sanctity; loneliness may be surprised into fellowship by visitants bearing no earthly name; and difficulty in living may become the inspiration and enlargement of noble prayer. If we live within the day, if history be nothing but a series of unrelated anecdotes, if seed-time has no reference to harvest,—then the joy of life is dead, the inspiration of labour has ceased, hope no longer plays its heavenly part in the movement of life and in all the gladness of being. "Be not deceived; God is not mocked: for whatsoever a man soweth, that shall he also reap." Clever Jacob, designing Jacob, supplanter of the absent brother, stealer of blessings, will one day have to knock at that brother's gate and say,—If it please thee, my lord, may I be permitted to hasten through thy land? —and believe me I will touch nothing. Touch nothing! thou thief of the ages, thou simulator of honesty,—nay, thou wilt touch nothing! How the thief can prate of honesty! How the designing supplanter can say he will "go by the king's high way," and no vine will he touch, and not a drop of water will he drink!

We may have acquired such a reputation that people will not believe us even when we intend to be good for a moment. We may sin away our social standing; we may so act towards men that when we go before them, as it were, on bended knees and say we will touch nothing, hurt nothing, drink no water out of the wells but hasten through, they will laugh at us and say,— Mocker ! liar ! thief ! remember the past, and then ask if we can be foolish and trustful enough to believe thee. Take care of your character, take care of your soul's honesty ; one day it will open gates, which will secure the hospitality of princes ; and they who serve the Lord—mightily labour for him, and put their whole trust in him, shall go through by the king's highway, and be permitted to eat of the vineyards and drink of the wells, and the longer they stay the more welcome will they be. Let me live the life of the righteous, let me die the death of the righteous, let me cast in my lot with the true and the wise and the divine—I would live and move and have my being in God.

PRAYER.

ALMIGHTY GOD, in wrath thou dost remember mercy. What are thy judgments but calls upon the compassion of thy people? By thy threatening thou dost bring forth men who will pray. Behold, when thy judgments are abroad in the earth, men take censers and fill them, and pray more mightily unto God than before. Such is thy wondrous way. We, who will not pray in calm time when no wind is abroad shaking the forest, fall to and pray most vehemently when the tempest shakes the heavens and the earth seems to tremble. We, who will not wait upon thee at the altar or care for thy sanctuary in any way when all things flow serenely around us, hasten to the Lord's temple when the air is tainted with death. Thou wilt lay hold upon us either here or there, in this way or in that: but surely thine hand shall find us, and we must face the living God. Thou hast given us a Gospel which is a savour of life unto life, or of death unto death. We cannot escape it or deny it: behold, we must account with it; it is the Lord's voice, it is the testimony divine, and we have to make some answer to its great cry of pity and offer of redemption. Thou dost take away the preacher: but the Gospel remains; thou dost change the congregation: but the sanctuary abides for ever; other hands pile the altar fire: but the altar itself is of thy founding and cannot be removed: it is the Lord's appointed meeting-place; there his name is recorded and there his glory shines. Enable us to remember how little we are. We are but the creatures of yesterday and the victims of to-morrow, with a little time of tumult and anxiety between; and instead of attempting to solve the great mysteries of being—to set up an answer to the awful problems of the universe,—may we learn to pray, to love, to cry in penitential cries over our sin, and to hope in the living God, and thus may we be enabled to leave all mystery and great wonder and miracle of thought to be revealed and solved in the eternal world. Meanwhile, make us industrious in all things practical; give us a heart to feel for human want, a hand willing to help all human weakness; heighten our reverence for things divine; put into our voices the tone of noble solemnity; work in us the spirit of resignation; turn our eyes away from all saviours and redeemers but One; and, fixing our vision upon the central Cross, may we behold the Lamb of God that taketh away the sin of the world, and give ourselves to him, asking him to have mercy upon us and apply to us all the virtue of his priesthood. Prepare us for all events. We never know what shall be on the morrow: we will rest in God and trust in truth, and make a sanctuary of the divine righteousness, and would have God find for us a hole in the side of the rock in which we may stand in perfect security until all calamities be overpast. Amen.

Numbers xx. 29.

"And when all the congregation saw that Aaron was dead, they mourned for Aaron thirty days, even all the house of Israel."

CONNECTING LINKS.

WE have seen the earth open and swallow up the rebels; now we may expect to have peace. A great judgment has fallen upon Israel, and from this time there will be no more murmuring and complaining. An earthquake will settle everything. If one could rise from the dead and visit the living, one sight of the dead man would cause the mind to think, the heart to dissolve in tears, and the whole will to consecrate itself to perpetual obedience. We have often invented methods of evangelising the world. Were an angel to stand in the very centre of the mid-day sky so that every one upon the earth could see him, and were he to preach some brief sermon to the sons of men, all the populations upon the face of the globe would instantly hail Jesus Christ, Son of man, Son of God, Saviour of the world. If during some great outrage or crime of nations the earth were suddenly to tremble, shaking down tower and temple here and there, as if about to shake down all cities, men would begin to think, and repent, and pray, and believe. How long shall we forget that history is full of miracles and wonders and signs intended to convey moral instruction to the nations and to bring the peoples to sobriety of mind and religiousness of purpose? All these inventions which we suppose ought to accompany a divine administration of affairs have been tried and they have all failed. The earthquake is useless, and the great flood, the drowning deluge, and the storm of fire and brimstone;—these things are exploded as arguments for the purpose of pointing in the direction of the right method of converting the world. An instance in point is now before us (Numbers xvi. 41). "But on the morrow all the congregation of the children of Israel murmured against Moses and against Aaron, saying, Ye have killed the people of the Lord." When did this murmuring occur? The very day that the divine judgment was inflicted. Earthquakes have no abiding moral; great physical demonstrations seem to perish in the using. An earthquake becomes a familiarity; a plague becomes a topic of common gossip; darkening heavens and shooting lightnings are remarked upon by the people who pass under the tempestuous canopy. The world is not to be sobered as we thought—to be steadied and brought into prayerful mood and temper; it is not by miracle, nor by earthquake, nor by fire, but by some other way subtler, farther off, apparently less effectual, and a method requiring long time to develop itself and apply itself to the whole line of human action and human need. It would be difficult to believe all this if we could not corroborate it by our own experience. When was the great sin committed in your case? "On the morrow" after the judgment. Can men sin so suddenly and immediately after the divine chastisement for wrong-doing? As an argument we should say, No, they cannot do so; but we are forced back upon facts, realities, solid and personal experiences, and all these combine to say: Hardly will the night pass to separate men from the great judgment before they are back at the forbidden altar, drinking the forbidden cup, and lifting up their hand in obstinate challenge to Heaven. It is so everywhere. Men see the evil results of wrong courses of behaviour, and they repeat those wrong courses as soon as their energy is recruited; men feel the ill effects of wrong living, and they will repeat that wrong living to-morrow. Daily we see what comes of evil practice, ignoble purpose, unholy thought, and yet we no sooner look at the punishment than we go away to do the very thing which involved the judgment of God. Account for this. There is no accounting for it argumentatively. If this were a mere matter of words, it could only be settled in one way. Were it possible for any human fancy so to forget all the history of the world as to stand up and say what men would do under such and such circumstances, detailing the very facts of life as we ourselves know them, we should resent the suggestion, we should declare it an exaggeration, an expression of an absurd impossibility. The witness is in ourselves: our conscience condemns us. Why is it important to dwell upon this? To show that human nature is one, to show that the Bible deals with one kind of humanity, and that one kind of humanity is found in all lands, in all ages it never changes ; and it is important also as aggravating a condition to which some reply must be made from Heaven. We mass ourselves up into one terrific solid, and God must find some answer to the tremendous consolidation which we present. He must answer it with judgment, or he must answer it with mercy. The answer must come from above, be it what it may ; and it can only be one of two answers : destruction—salvation ; anger—pity ; an assertion of sovereign and majestic power, or a condescension of divine majesty to the low condition and awful apostasy of human nature. Reading the Bible through thus, page by page, steadily and patiently, one may come upon the Cross with a feeling which would be utterly impossible under any other conditions of Biblical perusal. The Lord is angry with the people ; he says he will destroy them after all : he will send a plague upon the camp which shall utterly burn it up. Is the Lord not sometimes tempted to fight us with our own weapons ? Is not the divine patience apparently exhausted ? Does it not seem as if only in one way can God get hold of us, and that by the way of destruction ? So often is his hand lifted up and so often does it fall without inflicting the penalty. This is a holy vacillation ; this is a glorious hesitancy. Looking at history we say,—Now the arm will fall and nothing can prevent it ;—and suddenly as by a breath—soft as the breath of prayer—that great arm is turned aside, and the blow is not struck. This is divinity. It would be fickleness but in God ; it would be an incertitude of mind but in the Most High. God knows that the way of salvation is the best way,—not the readiest, not the directest—destruction always lies handiest to the law that has been outraged ;—but salvation may be so conceived, wrought out, and applied as to vindicate itself in the long run. Any time in relation to eternity must be a quantity infinitesimal. We store up our millenniums and call them long periods ; we pile one thousand years upon another thousand years and multiply the double thousand by ten until our poor imaginations stagger under the vastness of the result; but the accumulated millenniums are but the flicker of a pulse, coming, going, dying, in the twinkling of an eye, compared with the duration of the divine throne. It will be seen, therefore, in Heaven's by-and-by, that the method of salvation, though ap-

parently so indirect and so remote in its influence and effect,
is a divine method—the only method, the method that alone can
vindicate itself by its sublimest issues.

So Moses and Aaron turned aside the divine wrath, and the
Lord took to another course. He said,—This matter of rulership
and guidance must be settled once for all. If the tone of
impatience could enter the divine voice, it would be under such
daily and vexatious provocation. So he will appeal to the eyes
of the people ; he would have the rods laid up, according to the
statement in the seventeenth chapter,—he would have every
one of them take a rod according to the house of their fathers,
of all their princes according to the house of their fathers : twelve
rods ; and every man's name was to be written upon his rod,
and the man whose rod budded was to have the rulership and
the primacy of Israel. So God will become an infant to us,
because we are infants. This is the great method of human
education. The philosopher has to become a child if he would
teach a child ; the mother can only charm the baby as she herself
becomes a baby ; God can only help man as he becomes a man.
Great is the mystery of godliness, because always great is the
mystery of love. Great is the mystery of condescension—infinite
is the miracle of stooping to the lowest condition. Now Israel
shall see a sight,—it is the stoop of God. The rods were laid
up, in due time they were examined, and there was one rod
budding and blooming like a living thing, and nor bud nor
blossom could be seen upon the other rods. Whose rod budded
and blossomed ? It was Aaron's rod. Henceforth it was to be
a sign of power and divine election, and the sight of that rod
was to settle all conflict, all controversy. Did that succeed ?
Nothing can succeed that is outward, visible, typical, or even
miraculous. The miracles have all been tried, and they have
all failed. Christ laid them down as useless tools. He knew
from the beginning that they were useless; but he must adapt
his plans to the condition of the scholars who are supposedly
attending his school. So he leads us to drop miracle and sign
and wonder and judgment, and causes us to cry out,—What then
is the strength of God ? what is the method of Heaven ? and
when our judgment and imagination have been purged of false
conclusions and vain imaginings, then he says—and he could

have said it at no earlier period, " God so loved the world, that
he gave his only begotten Son, that whosoever believeth in him
should not perish, but have everlasting life." To have said so
at the beginning, would have been to puzzle the human mind,
and distract the human imagination. First of all man must be
cleared of the sophism that judgment can work wonders, that
rising from the dead can convert families and nations. The
miracle delusion must be destroyed. Yet the purpose of the
miracle remains; when the mere miracle drops off, the spirit
which animated it abides for ever—a spirit of compassion, condescension, gracious and tender appeal to men, willing in any
way, if by any means the human heart can be touched with
religious and ennobling emotion. This miracle in its great
moral purpose is still wrought amongst us. The Bible is the
rod that buds. We have laid up all other books along with it :
we have given them plenty of time together, and now when we
open the place where they were put together, we find that only
one Book has upon it bud and blossom, and sign of satisfying
fruit. Our appeal is to facts. Many books have arisen to
dispute the supremacy of the Bible ; many plans have been
invented for overturning Christ's method of saving the world ;
the mocker has laughed, the vain imagination has invented its
fancies, and the troubled conscience has wrought miracles in
casuistry and in the base use of language with double and triple
meanings, and men have invented noises for the purpose of
destroying spiritual and moral voices and appeals; but after all
the experiments there is one rod that buds, one Book that
blossoms, one tree whose leaves are for the healing of the
nations. We must, therefore, go through miracles to facts,
through spaces which daze the mind by their mystery or their
vastness, to the simple realities of life ; and the Bible this day
and every day calls men to any Carmel they may choose, and
on the height of the solemn hill it will settle the controversy by
appealing to the influence exerted upon human life, to mastery
of human affairs, and to the power of giving solace under all the
exacerbations and infinite distresses of human life.

Now the history passes on, and we find, presently, that the little
company of leaders becomes less. In the twentieth chapter and
the first verse we have one line which says,—" And Miriam died

there, and was buried there." You could scarcely say less about a dog! She began bravely and musically did this woman, but she was full of thought; she inspired her feeble brother Aaron that they might together challenge the pontificate of Moses. She began with timbrel and dance, with a thrilling soprano; she was first among those who sang the Song of Deliverance, and we thought then she would do well; but hers was a poor course— a bright promise that never came to any solid effect. She murmured against Moses, she found fault with his marriage, she disputed his supremacy, she inspired the most fickle and feeblest of all great men, namely, Aaron her brother, that he might take share in the cowardly attack upon Moses; and now history— solemn, impartial, awful history—avenges the cause of righteousness and gives Miriam but one line:—" Miriam died there, and was buried there." We may so live as to be so characterised ourselves. It is possible for us so to live that nobody may miss us when we die. Of course we must have a grave: the earth must be scarred in some few inches to let us into its impartial bosom; but it is poor work; and there lies here a man over whose grave no child ever wept, over whose resting-place no heart ever beat with unusual quickness as if stirred by grateful emotion; here lies a man who took up room that a better man might have occupied, and he is thrust in here without any memorial. It is possible to live so. There is a happier possibility: we may live so that our grave shall be a sacred spot, a kind of altar inscribed to the honour of the mercy and goodness of the living God, so that men passing it may say, He was a brave soul; he had a noble heart; no suspicious thought ever vitiated that man's thinking; no mean desire or purpose ever warped and depraved his career, in relation to the cause of weakness and poverty and pain. Such men cannot die, except in the narrowest sense of that term; when they are laid away they seem to be more with us than ever. We multiply our dead: we magnify our good ones; we create a little heaven in our own imagination and heart, and we remember little words, quiet tones, and gentle touches, subtle references, and sum up all these things into the judgment of goodness, and the record of gratitude. That the sweet singer—that the sister of Moses— that a woman with the spirit of leadership in her, should simply have "died" and been "buried" is a lesson to us. How are the mighty fallen! how have the sons of the morning lost their light!

Was Moses, then, perfect? The two brothers are left alone now,—was Moses a perfect man? Let us thank God that he was not. The perfect man is a most discouraging influence in any community. He repels rather than attracts, being simply a man and perfect as such, first because perfection is impossible, secondly because its appearance, assumption, or attainment, discourages men who feel that they cannot advance with its pace or attain to its pre-eminence. So Moses falters; Moses will become in some degree one of us. When the people murmured for want of water, the Lord said,—Go forward; show them the rod, and quiet their murmurings. But this was never done. Moses went forward, and in a moment of rage or impatience—not to be wondered at—he struck the rock; and because of that stroke God struck him. We must not do things in our own way; we must show the rod, not strike with the rod. By such fine distinctions are men judged. The difference between men is not the difference between black and white—great broad issues,—but often becomes a distinction between full obedience and partial obedience, continual sacrifice and occasional sacrifice; a difference of tone—too loud, too low; too emphatic, too hesitant. So critical—so minute—is the vision and the judgment of God. Then we come to the time when Moses was left alone.

"And when all the congregation saw that Aaron was dead, they mourned for Aaron thirty days, even all the house of Israel" (xx. 29).

They took the nobler view of the man. After all he was God's priest. We must have some regard to the men who have thrown even the censer of the sanctuary. He was sometimes feeble to contemptibleness, sometimes perhaps a little vain, though he would not have been half so vain but for the prompting of his ambitious sister; he made the calf of gold, he did things which he ought not to have done; still for him the ephod was made, on him the sacerdotal robes were set as by the very hands of God; he was Aaron after all. So when he died there was a thirty days' mourning for him, "even all the house of Israel." They remembered the old man's best qualities: they said,—

he was always valiant : he seemed—he was—a good man in the soul of him : the rotten places were all outside : the core of the old priest was a sound and healthy core. The people have the spirit of judgment ; the people know the true from the false. There is hardly any bar of judgment out of heaven so exact in its decisions as the bar of the common opinion of the nations. So Aaron was mourned for by all the house of Israel. We shall—said they in effect—see the old man no more; he had a noble speech : he was the rhetor of the wilderness : he was chosen because of his eloquence : he was to be a mouth unto Moses and Moses was to be as God unto him. So they complemented one another : what the one had the other had not : what the one had not the other had ; they were brothers indeed, and the mourning was touched with a deeper pathos when Israel caught sight of Moses. Miriam gone, Aaron gone—who next can go but the great chief himself? So wondrously are the events of life related to one another, touched by one another, coloured by one another, and so profound and subtle is the mystery of pathos itself. Who remains? The Lord abideth for ever—Jesus Christ, the same yesterday, and to-day, and for ever. The singing Miriam dies, but the music still flows on ; priestly Aaron passes away, but our Melchizedek abideth a Priest for ever ; the great Moses dies with the only pomp possible to the majesty of his career—in the solitude of the divine companionship, but the God of Moses lives. This must be our confidence in the day of fear, when we ask,—What shall Israel do when Miriam ceases to sing, when Aaron ceases to pray, when Moses ceases to lead ? What shall be done when the prophets drop their mantle and the fathers say Adieu ? Our confidence must be in God : his heaven is full of angels, his ministers are without number in their host, and never yet sang human voice, never yet resounded human eloquence, never yet went forth the champion of human liberties, whose place God could not supply with an ampler abundance. There is no searching of his understanding. The Church does not stand in the song of its singers, in the eloquence of its preachers, in the prayers of its priests ; the Church stands in Christ. When he dies, the Church dies. He abideth for ever ; the Church is, therefore, assured as to its duration by the eternity of its Lord.

PRAYER.

ALMIGHTY GOD, thou dost lead us by the right way. Its length is determined, and all the influences which operate upon it are under thy control. We did not begin the way, nor do we know one turning that is upon it, nor can we determine the length thereof. It is not in man that walketh to direct his steps; the way of man is from the Lord which made heaven and earth, and he will sustain the traveller, he will bring the weary pilgrim to the heavenly rest. Thou hast led us these many years in the wilderness, and thou hast made a garden of the desert, and thou hast found for us orchards amongst the rocks; thy course towards us has been a daily miracle, a surprise of love, a new revelation of light. So now we begin to see somewhat of God's meaning in what to us has been so long confusion and bewilderment. Thou dost work secretly, so that we cannot see thee; thine hand is not always visible to us so that we can say,—This is the Lord, and this is his work, and, behold, he doeth it in his own way and time. We cannot see much; we can hear but a little; we must, therefore, live our larger life—the life of faith, the noble, eternal life of trust in the living God; saying daily, until our very voice becomes musical by the exercise,—The will of the Lord be done: it is best; thy will be done on earth as it is done in heaven. When we can speak this prayer with our hearts, we shall know that the pinnacle is being put upon the temple, that the topstone is being set upon the tower, and that our life's education upon earth is nearly completed. Do thou take us, by thine own way, to the city which hath habitations built for the sons of men. We think we see the shorter road; but our life is full of mistakes of our own making: so we will judge nothing before the time, but wait in the spirit of trust and in the meekness of patience. We will leave all the way to God. We will not take our life-course from our passion, our imagination, our selfishness; we will have nothing to do with it, except in God and through the ministry of the Holy Spirit. Then our thirst shall be a blessing, our hunger shall be a means of grace, our difficulties shall be elements of delight, and the strain that is put upon our weakness shall be the beginning and the assurance of power. Bring us into the inner places of God's house; take us from chamber to chamber until we see the innermost centre possible to earthly vision; give us to feel the warmth of the sanctuary —its tender, hospitable glow; give us to feel assurance of God's nearness and God's love and God's almightiness to save. Protect us from impression made through the senses only, and undertake for us that we shall learn wholly from thy Spirit, disregarding appearances which we can neither understand nor control. Enable us to trust thee, and love thee, and serve thee: and when the enemy's hand is mighty upon us, may the hand of God be mightier still; and when the discouragement of the way is very severe, may our gift in prayer be greatly enlarged, and our souls see an open gate to the throne of the heavenly grace. We bless thee for thy Son Jesus Christ, our Saviour. We love him because he first loved us. Whilst we were yet sinners he died for us, much more now that he is raised and throned in heaven will he mightily succour us by his consolations and ennoble us by his promises. Comfort thy people; say unto them their iniquity is pardoned, and grant unto them assurance that the enemy hath no more power over them, seeing they are bought with a price and are marked by the sign of God and are guided by the Spirit Eternal. We remember our loved ones everywhere, praying for them with all prayer and supplication, that they, with us, may enjoy the common blessings of the sanctuary, and, having happiness of home, may have triumph in the house of God and great success in the market-place; the Lord bless them in basket and in store, in property, in children, in all manner of business and avocation, in travelling by sea and by land; and show us all that there can be no distance from one another, where there is no distance from the common centre; if we love God, we shall be near one another, though mountains intervene and seas roll between us; we touch a common Cross, we look at a common Light, we breathe to the One, the Universal, Father; and in this sweet, noble fellowship we are conscious of living union. Make the sick thy care. In many cases they are quite beyond us; our gentlest touch is roughness, our whispered affection is a loud voice; but thou canst speak to souls nearing heaven, thou canst comfort those whose feet are touching the last cold river, thou canst trim the light when we cannot touch it. So we hand over our sick chambers and all our suffering loved ones to the Physician and Healer of the universe, willing to be his servants that we may work as he bids us, and wait all the time until our patience is completed. The Lord hear us in these things; the Lord send us answers more than we have capacity to receive; the Lord show us that he is able to do exceeding abundantly above all that we ask or think: that in our mightiest prayer we have not begun to touch the infinity of his reply. Amen.

Numbers xxi. 4.

".... much discouraged because of the way."

DISCOURAGEMENTS.

THE people wanted to take a straight course through the land of Edom, and the people of Edom said they should not pass through their provinces—even though Israel promised to "go by the king's high way," and not to enter the vineyards, and not to take a drop of water out of the wells, or if they did take any water to pay for it. But Edom was resolute. The people, therefore, had "to compass the land of Edom"—to take a roundabout course ; and it was so long, so wearisome, so heavy with monotonousness, and altogether so unlike what the other way would have been, that "the soul of the people was much discouraged because of the way." Discouragement is a kind of middle feeling ; it is, therefore, all the more difficult to treat. It does not go so far down as cowardice, and has hardly any relation to a sense of triumph or over-sufficiency of strength ; but the point of feeling lies between, deepening rather towards the lower than turning itself sunnily towards the higher. When that feeling takes possession of a man, the man may be easily laid down, thrown over, and may readily become the prey of well-nigh incurable dejection. Discouragement is not far from despair. The feeling, then, is : Let us return,—why did we come out at all ?—the short way is the way backward : let us undo the journey and return to the origin whence we started. That is a human feeling ; that is the feeling of every man at some point in his education. You take up a new language : you say you will certainly master this tongue. But the way is circuitous. For a little while it is bright enough and easy enough, and we think we might take children with us along a way so broad and sunny ; suddenly we come to irregularities, exceptions, endless variations and shadings ; we confuse moods with tenses, and tenses with moods ; we ask for things we do not want, and we name things by names that are all but comical mistakes ;—and we say at this point of our progress,—Let us return to the Egypt of our ignorance : this task is too heavy this penalty is a burden ;—would we had never started from Egypt, where we could speak what little language we needed quite fluently and could ask in it for more things than we were ever likely to get ! The student is discouraged,—yea, much discouraged because of the way. Let him persevere a month or two, or six, or twelve ; let him get beyond the middle point and begin the joy of acquisition, and taste the sweetness of liberty, and know the magic of thinking in another tongue than that in which he was born ; and nothing can take him back to the Egypt of ignorance, to the captivity of intellectual darkness. What wonder, then, if in learning a language, or science, or any other complicated lesson, we come to a point of discouragement, that there should be kindred discouragements in all upward ways? The right way is uphill. It is easy to go downhill: we think we are not tired in going downhill; yet it is most weary work to climb the steep ascents. But the temples are all on the top of the steep; the heavenly cities are away above the valleys. We have, therefore, to consider one of two things: whether we will succumb to an innate indolence that simply wants to be let alone and to be amused or gratified without expense; or whether we will clear the valleys, leave all the lower levels behind us, and go up with ever-increasing vitality and ever-brightening hope, until there comes into the soul a sense of joy which can never permit the soul to go back to the places where the fog thickens, where the damps choke, and where there is nothing broad, grand, eternal. But we have to be very careful with the discouraged soul. When the young student feels his eyes moistening because he cannot subdue the unruly irregulars and exceptions, we must not shout at him or speak to him roughly, but tell him that once we were exactly at that very point, and we cried our eyes out for very vexation that these unruly things would not be set in order and would not do just what we wanted them to do; then the little learner, the young soul, remembering that we fought a battle just there, may take heart again, and come up to-morrow with reinvigorated motive and strength. Power is rightly used when it is employed to sustain and inspire the discouraged; it ceases to be power—it becomes a merely exaggerated strength and an unruly despotism —when it is employed to threaten, to distress, and to grieve the soul that is already too much troubled.

There are necessary discouragements. How awful it would be if some men were never discouraged!—they could not bear themselves, and they could not act a beneficent part towards other people. It is well, therefore, for the strongest man occasionally to be set back half-a-day's travelling and have to begin to-morrow morning at the point where he was yesterday morning. If he could go on with continually enhancing strength, he would become a severe critic of other men, and would himself be turned into the severest discouragement which could be inflicted upon competitors. It is well, therefore, that some supposed baragins should turn out mistakes; it is best that some strokes that were going to cleave the rock right in two should strike the smiter himself that he may tremble under the force of his own blow. Otherwise, who could live with some men ? They would be so outblown, so self-flattered ; they would be so conscious of their superiority as to fill the whole street in which they lived and the whole city which they plagued by their presence. It is of God that the strongest man should sometimes have to sit down to take his breath. Seeing such a man tired, even but for one hour, poor weak pilgrims may say,—If he, the man of herculean strength, must pause awhile, it is hardly to be wondered at that we poor weaklings should now and then want to sit down and look round and recover our wasted energy.

We must not forget that a good many discouragements are of a merely physical kind. We do not consider the relation between temperament and religion as we ought to consider it. We are apt to be too abstract and spiritual, and therefore exacting and tyrannous in our judgments of one another. Many a man would have been abreast with the foremost of us to-day but for some physical peculiarity of temperament over which he has no control. His sunny moments are but brief and very few in number; when a ray of light does strike him, he can smile with the merriest and play with the most free-handed ; but suddenly the clouds shut, and then he is as blank and cold and fear-driven as ever. We ought to speak gently to such a sufferer. Your inability to pray to a bright heaven arises entirely—if you could see your own physiology—from a little pressure here, and a little congestion there, or some imperfect action yonder ; this trouble is not in the soul of you, and it has nothing to do with your standing before God and your citizenship in heaven : it is a physical disturbance, it is a purely temporary affair ; and if you can seize that thought, and accept the assurance which it involves, you will pray as gladly into a thick cloud as into a radiant morning, because you will know that the cloud is not in the heavens, it is only a covering before your own disordered vision. These views are needful to a right judgment of life. Sometimes, too, men's physical strength is utterly exhausted, and therefore their intellectual energy and their spiritual vitality may be by so much impaired. The wheel cannot go on for ever. The strongest giant begins to totter, Hercules asks for a staff, and

Samson begs to be allowed to retire awhile, promising to come up as bravely as ever to-morrow, if he can but steep his soul in one short night's oblivion. Consider, therefore, that you are not necessarily unfaithful, disloyal, unworthy, because, for the moment, you have lost your gift of vision, your faculty of prayer, your priestly standing which men have so often recognised as being full of power—the power of prevailing sweetness; your soul has not gone down, your spirit is not impoverished, but the poor flesh gives in; you have been working too many hours: you thought you would make six days almost into seven, and that is a miracle you cannot perform; you have said you would light the lamp and keep it aflame an hour longer than usual; and the lamp got the better of you. In your very soul's soul you are just as good as you ever were, and just as true to God and as anxious to serve him and follow all the way of his finger; but your body is being overworked, and you must stop to get the candlestick repaired, or the candle may drop out of it, and there may be a destructive fire in your premises. Examine yourselves, whether the discouragement comes out of some spiritual fault—some inner secret which no eye can see but your own; or whether it is accidental, physical, and therefore transient. Be rational in your inquiry into the origin of your discouragement, and be a wise man in the treatment of the disease.

There are exaggerated discouragements. Some men have a gift of seeing darkness. They do not know that there are two twilights—the twilight of morning, and the twilight of evening; they have only one twilight, and that is the shady precursor of darkness. We have read of a man who always said there was a lion in the way. He had a wonderful eye for seeing lions. Nobody could persuade him that he did not see a ravenous beast within fifty yards of the field he intended to plough—not there only, but absolutely in the street, so that you do not find him half-way to the field, but peering out of his own side-window and beholding a lion in the very middle of the way. That is an awful condition under which to live the day of human life. But that lion is real to him. Why should we say roughly,—There is no lion,—and treat the man as if he were insane? To him, in his diseased condition of mind, there *is* a lion. We must ply him with reason softly expressed, with sayings without bitterness;

we must perform before him the miracle of going through the very lion he thought was in the way; and thus, by stooping to him and accommodating ourselves to him, without roughness or brusqueness, or tyranny of manner and feeling, must bring him round to the persuasion that he must have been mistaken. We read of a man who would not sow because he had been observing the wind. That man still lives. He is sure the wind is in a cold quarter. It is absurd on your part to attempt to prove to him that it is breathing from the warm south-west;—upon you it may be so breathing, if you like to feel it so; but he says,—I know by my own sensations that the wind is breathing from the north-east, and if I go out the seed will be blown into some other man's field, and my own life will be sacrificed to the cruelty of the wind. So we have men much discouraged by lions that do not exist, by winds that do not blow, by circumstances that are purely imaginary; but we must recognise these facts, and address ourselves to them with the skill of love, as well as with the energy of conviction.

Discouragement does not end in itself. The discouraged man is in a condition to receive any enemy, any temptation, any suggestion that will even for the moment rid him of his intolerable pressure. Through the gate of discouragement the enemy wanders at will. The gate of the mind is not open, the gate of a sacred purpose is not open; every gate of entrance into the mind's inner life is shut but one,—the gate of discouragement swings back and forward and seems to wave a welcome to any thought that will prey upon the mind and to any enemy that chooses to desolate the heart. Therefore be tender with the discouraged, help them to swallow their tears, tell them that you have had kindred experiences with their own, show them how you were led through that gate out of the bondage into the sweet liberty, and say you will stop with them all night. The discouraged man likes to feel himself in the grip of a strong hand. Some men cannot stop up all the night of discouragement by themselves; but if you would sit up with them, if you would trim the light and feed the fire, and say they might rely upon your presence through one whole night at least, they might get an hour's rest, and in the morning bless you with revived energy for your solicitude and attendance. If the prophet had bidden thee do some great thing, thou wouldest have done it : the prophet bids thee do some little thing, some act of gentlest patience and love, and to do it as if not doing it—to do it as if by gracious necessity, to do it as if conferring an obligation on thyself. Not the thing done but how done, is often the question which must be determined by the doer.

Discouragements try the quality of men. You cannot tell what some men are when their places of business are thronged from morning until night, and when they are spending the whole of their time in receiving money. You might regard them as really very interesting characters ; you might be tempted to think you would like to live with them : they are so radiant, so agreeable, so willing to oblige ; they speak so blithely that you suppose you have fallen upon some descendant of the line of angels. That is quite a mistake on your part. If you could come when business is slack, when there are no clients, customers, patrons, or supporters to be seen, you would not know the lovely angels, you would not recognise the persons whom you thought so delightful. Look at the face, how cloudy ! Hear the voice, how husky ! Observe the action, how impatient ! Mark the eye, how furtive and angry ! Now you see what the man really is. Adversity tries men. We are in reality what we are under pressure. The year is not all summer; the year has long rains and heavy snows and biting frosts, and the entire year must be taken in if we would make an accurate survey of the whole land. Do not let us deceive ourselves. We have times of a little excitement and triumph and gladness, when people think us kind and amiable and delightful; but we know we are saying within ourselves,—If these people could only see us at other times when we snap like mad dogs, when nothing pleases us, when feathers are hard, when summer is winter, when our best friends are burdens to us, they would not form such judgments of our delightful qualities. The meaning of all this is that the Christian has to show, whatever other men have to do, that Christianity is a religion for night, and winter, and ill-health, and loss, and discouragement; a religion that sits up all night, a religion that does not run away when the dogs of war are let loose, but that comforts, and sustains, and animates under deprivations of the severest kind.

What is the cure of this awful disease of discouragement ?
Men are not to be laughed out of their discouragements as if
they were merely illusory, or as if they were assumed for the
purpose of affectation. Let us repeat to ourselves again and
again, that discouragement is positive and actual to the man who
suffers from it. The very first condition of being able to treat
discouragement with real efficiency is to show that we know its
nature, that we ourselves have wandered through its darkness,
and that we have for the sufferer a most manly and tender
sympathy. What is the discouragement? Loss in business?
We have all lost in business. Ill-health? We have all suffered
from ill-health. Bereavement? Where is there a hand that has
not dug a grave? Temptations from hell? Who lives that has
not felt the devil's hot breath upon his soul? We must be one
with the discouraged man. Identification is the secret of sympathy, and sympathy spoken tremblingly that realises the meaning
of the apparently contradictory words,—" When I am weak, then
am I strong."

Then are there no encouragements to be recollected in the
time of our dejection ? Do the clouds really obliterate the stars,
or only conceal them? The discouragements can be numbered,
—can the encouragements be reckoned—encouragements of a
commercial, educational, social, relative kind,—encouragements
in the matter of health or spirits or family delights? Is it rough
in the market-place? Possibly ; but how tranquil is it at home !
—and what is any market-place when home is quiet with the
peace of heaven? Are there losses and trials? Possibly ; but
are there no spiritual gains, acquisitions, subtle accretions of
moral power, so that a receding earth means an approaching
heaven? Do the papers bring you bad news this morning?
What about the letters that are lying in your lap—letters from
children at school, from children in business, from friends who
are giving you thanks for assistance lent years ago ? Why, all
these letters are like the gathering up of sunbeams. God forbid
I should say to you,—Do not write down your discouragements.
Take slate enough and pencil enough to put down the whole
black list ; but God forbid I should forget to say,—Now write on
the other side your encouragements, your sources of happiness,
your springs of strength, your inspirations, and your hopes ; put

them down with a firm hand, and you will have to turn the slate over to accommodate the growing list.

The great cure for discouragement is a persuasion of being right. We have really very little to do with mere circumstances; we are not masters of the weather, we cannot control the atmosphere, nor have we any magical wand by which we can do things which are of a supernatural kind. The eternal consolation is in the fact that the purpose is right, the heart is sound, the suppliant means his prayer, the student grasps the truth;—all other changes are atmospheric, climatic, transitory,—damping enough and discouraging enough in the meanwhile, but forgotten to-morrow. The devil has but a short chain, and he cannot add one link to its length. This is eternal life, to know thee the only true God, and Jesus Christ, whom thou hast sent.—The clouds do not throw down the house : the house is founded upon a rock; think of the rock, not of the falling snow; think of the eternal foundation, and not of the changing clouds. "The foundation of God standeth sure, having this seal, The Lord knoweth them that are his."

Then the chief cure, the master remedy, the sovereign assurance, must be found in the example of Christ. *He* was much discouraged because of the way. "He marvelled because of their unbelief;" "he did not do many mighty works there because of their unbelief;" but when he was come nigh the city, he wept over it, and said : "O Jerusalem, Jerusalem, how often would I have gathered thy children together, even as a hen doth gather her young under her wings, and ye would not!" They went out against him with swords and staves as against a thief; but for the joy that was set before him he endured the Cross, despising the shame. It is worth waiting a whole winter night to behold the brightness of the coming summer. A little rain, a high wind, a fall of snow, unexpected frost, a little bitterness in the cup;—these things come and go, but we, being in Christ, seek a kingdom which cannot be moved. If we are seeking nothing, then discouragements will prevail; in the absence of definite purpose, distinct assault will have a tremendous effect upon us; but if our eye be single and our whole body be full of light, and if our vision be set upon a given destiny, and that destiny be a city which hath foundations whose Builder and Maker is God, then apostles will shake off the viper into the fire, lions will shake the dewdrops from their manes, sleepers will throw back the garments in which they have been slumbering, and brave men will find in the end more than compensation for the way, and one glimpse of heaven will cast into eternal forgetfulness all the little troubles of earth.

NOTE.

Crossing the Arnon, we reach in succession, *Rabbath Moab,* still called *Rabba,* in the midst of a wide plain, where we find more broken cisterns, fallen columns, and ruined heaps, betokening former greatness and importance. Farther on is *Kerak,* the Biblical *Kir-Moab,* or *Kir-hareseth,* on the brow of a hill which juts out from a yet higher range in the form of a peninsula, flanked by stupendous ravines on three sides. It is a position of great strength, as seems intimated by the Scripture references; and it was here that in desperation at the long siege by Jehoram and Jehoshaphat, the King of Moab offered his firstborn son as a sacrifice upon the walls. During the Crusades, Kerak became again famous, and the Crusaders castle still remains. The population of the modern town is between seven and eight thousand, of whom nearly one-third are reckoned as Christians belonging to the Greek Church. Their bishop takes his title from Petra, probably because, when the see was founded in the twelfth century, the place was mistaken for the great " rock city " of ancient Edom.

The journey now assumes a new character; and while more desolate and even dangerous, from the bands of roving Bedawin, has a wonderful interest. For, in Bible language, we have passed from Moab to the confines of Edom. The Dead Sea is left behind, on our right is Mount Seir, a range of hills, averaging two thousand feet in height, on this side chiefly of limestone, swelling gradually upwards from the desert, and crowned by ridges of a reddish sandstone, through which crop up masses of basalt. The mountain wall is broken by deep clefts clothed with every variety of herbage, while on every level terrace, and on all the less precipitous slopes, shrubs and flowers luxuriantly grow. "It is indeed the region," remarks Dr. Robinson, "of which Isaac said to his son, 'Behold, thy dwelling shall be the fatness of the earth, and of the dew of heaven from above.'"

On the left hand stretches the wilderness in which the last months of Israel's " wanderings " were passed—the dreary arid waste to which they were driven by the inhospitality of Edom; in which "the soul of the people was much discouraged because of the way," the wilderness of the fiery serpents, and still the most dreaded part of the pilgrim's road to Mecca. It is not, however, necessary for the traveller to descend into this fearful desert. Strongly escorted, and paying due tribute to the Bedawin tribes along his route he may pursue his way in safety, on the skirt of the hills, passing through several large villages beautifully placed upon the heights until he reaches Petra --DR. GREEN's *Pictures from Bible Lands.*

PRAYER

ALMIGHTY GOD, thou art always healing men; thou healest all their diseases. Thou knowest our frame; thou rememberest that we are but dust. Thou dost not send affliction willingly upon the children of men, nor grieve them for thine own pleasure; thou dost chasten men for their profit, and thou dost mean affliction to lead to the throne of grace. We would not accept affliction rebelliously, but would endeavour to receive it even thankfully, that, in the long run, we may say,—It was good for me that I was afflicted : before I was afflicted I went astray. Thou dost send punishment upon the evil-doer, and we are called upon to say with our whole heart,—This is a judgment that is righteous. Thou dost pain the wrong-doer; thou dost baffle the evil-minded man; thou dost turn to confusion the council of thine enemies. This is the Lord's doing; in it we find rest, security, and eternal hope. The wicked shall not prevail against thee; all his bows shall be broken, and his sword shall be turned upon his own heart. The good man shall live before thee because he is good; the gracious soul shall have more grace, and the praying spirit shall be enriched with great replies. This is thy government, thy purpose, thy way in the hearts of men and among the nations of the earth. We accept it; we do not only submit to it, but receive it with open hearts, with thankfulness of spirit, knowing that the Lord reigneth and in the end his throne shall be established and there shall be no rebellion. Thou hast set up a great vision for men to gaze upon : thou hast erected the Cross; upon it we behold the Lamb of God that taketh away the sin of the world; we hear thy voice saying,—Look unto him, all ye nations of the earth, and be ye saved : believe on the Lord Jesus Christ, and ye shall be saved. We look: we behold the amazing scene. We cannot understand the mystery,—we feel its solemnity, we answer its pathos; but the miracle of the righteousness, and the law, and the mercy, and the divine intervention, we cannot understand. Help us to look steadfastly to the Cross; enable us to keep our eyes evermore upon the one Saviour of mankind; may we be found in that posture living, dying, throughout all our days;—then shall our sin have no power over us, and our guilt shall lead us into deeper acquaintance with the mystery of the love of God. We bless thee for the Cross :—God forbid that we should glory save in the Cross of our Lord Jesus Christ. We find in it all that the soul needs—an answer to a mystery, help in the time of distress, joy in the night of sorrow, balm for every wound. So do we rejoice in the Cross; we will not turn away our eyes from it; it is the Tree of Life, the leaves of which are for the healing of the nations. May all eyes be fixed upon it; may all hearts be moved to great expectation; may we know that the Cross is the way to pardon, that the Cross receives the crown, that there can be no peace until there is forgiveness. May forgiveness be granted unto every one of us according to the measure of our sin—yea, and beyond it, that in the abundance of the pardon we may begin to see that sin is swallowed up. Amen.

Numbers xxi. 5-9.

5. And the people spake against God, and against Moses, Wherefore have ye brought us up out of Egypt to die in the wilderness? for there is no bread, neither is there any water; and our soul loatheth this light bread.
6. And the Lord sent fiery serpents among the people, and they bit the people; and much people of Israel died.
7. Therefore the people came to Moses, and said, We have sinned, for we have spoken against the Lord, and against thee; pray unto the Lord, that he take away the serpents from us. And Moses prayed for the people.
8 And the Lord said unto Moses, Make thee a fiery serpent, and set it upon a pole: and it shall come to pass, that every one that is bitten, when he looketh upon it, shall live.
9. And Moses made a serpent of brass, and put it upon a pole, and it came to pass, that if a serpent had bitten any man, when he beheld the serpent of brass, he lived.

MURMURING PUNISHED.

ABOUT the extreme probability of the whole story of the wandering of Israel there can be no doubt. Nothing occurs out of time in the story, nothing out of place; nothing is in false colour or tone. Looking upon the story from a merely literary point of view, there is not one line of improbability discoverable in it. Not a single decade, much less a century, is anticipated in the speech of the people. They are children always, with children's whims, faults, desires, amusements, hopes, fears. It is the story of children overgrown, often too much indulged, not knowing the meaning of the thong of chastisement, and not measuring the process by the end. It is a child's life, shut up within the present day and receiving no glory from the promised land. What was the talk of the children of Israel? It was always about the body—want of food, want of water, fear of death, inconvenience, sudden alarm, and pain of body. It was, therefore, just the talk for the age. There is no soul in it, no immortality, no aspiration after liberties immeasurable as infinity. The whole speech is of the earth, earthy. It never throbs with noble passion; it beats fiercely with the excitement of selfishness, beyond that it never goes into the region of vital and solemn tragedy. Is there any improbability in such a statement? We cannot conceive the improbability because we ourselves too frequently literally repeat the experience. Examine any speci men of modern talk : let it be written down and set before the eye in plain print, like the story of Israel, and say what better is much of it. It is the talk about the body, the weather, the state of business, the income and the outgoing ; it is a mean speech about balances and counter-balances, and the politics of the day, and who is to be first, and who will win, and who will lose ; the talk is about bullocks in the field, and about balances in the market-place, and about health at the fireside. Is not much human talk now going on around us about trials and circumstances, want of bread, want of water, want of enlargement of domestic comfort, pining for further fields and larger resources ? Where is the altar ? Where is the harp ? Where is the vision that divides the clouds and pierces beyond them, and sees that this little earth is but a help towards some vaster universe ? We do discover it in our case ;—did we not, shame would be ours more burning than fire, for then the centuries would have been wasted upon us and we should have neglected the plainest revelations of Providence ; but an inquiry into our own methods and experi-ences, and analysis of our own conversation will show the extreme probability of every line that occurs in the portraiture of the wilderness life of Israel. Where do you find the children of Israel in rapture about the tabernacle ? Where is there any noble speech about it ? Where the wonder that after becomes religion ? Where the solemn amazement that stands next in rank and quality to prayer ? The same question might be asked in modern days. If we were careful to take the lowest view of current life, we might establish an analogous case to-day, but we are bound to take in other elements and circumstances which illuminate and colour and enlarge the spectacle and give it some charm and dignity of divinity ; still there is enough in ourselves and about us to establish beyond all successful disputation the probability of the story as it is written in the Pentateuch.

The children of Israel complained because their soul loathed the light bread, they wanted change of food. We do not complain perhaps along the same line ; but are we quite sure that we have lost the spirit of murmuring, with regard to all the sustenance by which the mysterious human life within us is sustained and nourished? Let it be granted that we have of bread enough and to spare for the body—abundance, even to luxury, so that we never complain : we are thankful for a loaded table : we bless Providence for an abundant supply of all necessaries for the body; but does the speech end there? Is there not one within who requires food and whose hunger must be attended to if death would be averted? Are we all body? Is our little life now dwarfed into the measure of such hunger as can be felt by the flesh? Have we no mind to feed, no soul to nourish, no inner nature to brace and strengthen, to inspire, and to complete in strength and perfectness of moral beauty? If we examine the outer man, he expresses himself in terms of contentment; but what if we subject the inner man to cross-examination? What is the tone of *his* reply? It is pungent with reproach, it is bitter with complaining ; it is the utterance of a dissatisfied and morbid spirit. Who is content with the spiritual food which God has been pleased to supply for the nourishment and culture of the soul? Is there no complaining in the Church? Is there no disposition amongst the spiritual children of Israel to rise and say,—We are tired of this food, or of that? Where is the spirit of genuine contentment—heart and soul satisfaction? If the food is solid, partaking of the nature of scriptural exposition, full of instruction, solid in thought, noble in knowledge, ample in intelligence, demanding attention, constraining the soul to take heed or it will miss the luminous point, then do not many fall away saying that during the week they are so vexed by difficulties and so strained in their attention that on the Sabbath day they have no appetite for such solid provision? If it is light, moving, not with fluency only, but with some glibness from point to point, digging nowhere, building nowhere, flying like an uncertain bird in the air ; then is there not complaining from the other side of want of solidity, and depth, and rock-like massiveness? If the teaching is historical, going far back to find out the way of God in the ancient time, then is there not a voice which says,—All that is dead and gone ; the ages have had their turn,—they have lived, flourished, died,—why exhume the centuries? And if it be of the nature of current criticism, referring to living men, contemporaneous events, the immediate fever and passion of the time, then is there not a voice saying,—All this we can read during the week; we can keep abreast with this to-morrow; on this one brief day called Sabbath day be nobler, grander, deeper, vaster in intellectual reach, and keener in spiritual perception? Surely an assembly of contentious and unruly guests! There is nothing right. The host's attention has been stretched to the utmost, and behold the viands are rejected! How few remember that they need not eat the whole of the viands! How few remember that a little here and a little there may be enough to satisfy the hunger of the mind! One line may be a revelation; one little jewelled sentence may be perfectly sufficient; one cry to Heaven in opening or concluding prayer may be equivalent to inspiration. The contented soul will always find enough to be contented with; that soul will say,—This is better than I deserve; I have not earned this by my own strength or wit or industry; this prey has been taken for me by the mighty hunter on the mountains of the Lord, and I will bless the Giver in heaven, and I will bless the provider on earth for venison which the soul may relish. The discontented man never can be satisfied do not attempt to please him; have no connection with or relation to him; ignore him; pass by him and turn away. He hinders all growth, he disturbs all serenity, he is a plague in the feast. We must not, therefore, set ourselves against the children of Israel as if we had come to a larger manhood altogether. It is perfectly certain that we have an abundance of food; we are not confined to the eating of this light bread which caused the soul of Israel to experience a sensation of loathing; we have enough, we say, and to spare, and there is no complaining about earthly abundance. Stop! you must not steal even the meanest heaven. What about your soul's food? What about the mean whine—There is no food for the soul? What about weariness with the Book? What about the desire to add some other book to it? Who would not rather hear some other publication read than the inspired volume? Who is not best pleased by snatches of verse from some human singer? Who would not suspend the harp of David to listen to some instrument of modern invention? Let these inquiries stand in that impersonal form, and let each take up the interrogation and test himself by it; and may God give sound judgment to all!

Did these people desire knowledge? Did they ever gather

around their leaders and say,—Give us a brighter revelation from heaven; we feel that we are more than mortal: we are too large for this wilderness; within us there is a voice which says, Give; but let the donation be knowledge, light, revelation? When did they ever utter large prayer, noble desire, and express the kind of discontent which is pleasing to Heaven—that is to say, discontent with present acquisitions, discontent with intellectual darkness, discontent with the prison of earth, longing for the liberty of heaven? When do we hear that expression now? Who cries out for more Bible—a larger reading of the holy volume? Who would be content to read through one whole book of the inspired volume, taking it in its entirety and enjoying the reading as men might enjoy honey brought from the very garden of heaven? Who would not weary were the leader of public worship to read through the whole of the Epistle to the Romans? What man would stand up and say,—Begin again: no music like it; repeat its rolling thunder, its tender persuasion, its triumphant anthem, its connected and culminating reasoning? Judging ourselves by false standards, we have made great progress; but judging ourselves by the standard of the Sanctuary, who stands? There is none righteous, no, not one. When did the children of Israel pray for likeness to God, expressing, in some indirect way, almost jealousy of Moses that he should have seen more of the divine personality, that he should have been nearer than anyone else the very throne of God? Who called upon him to show how this mortal might put on immortality and this corruptible put on incorruption? If it could not be done at that time of day, it can be done now; and the question is still pertinent—Where is the soul that longs for transfiguration, that desires above all things holiness, likeness to God, the exact reproduction of the divine image, and the very brightness of the eternal glory? It is not enough to long for instruction; instruction may be but a load of knowledge. Knowledge is not enough; it may but puff up. Knowledge has to become wisdom, wisdom become inspiration, and inspiration become almost identification with God—a mysterious ascension of the soul, but not beyond the experience which the divine education contemplates.

The people complained. The complaint was heard. When we complain, we complain against God. It is God's universe, not man's. Man did not make a single blade of grass in all the earth's green crop ; man did not light a single jet in all the sky burning with stars. When we complain, therefore, we touch the Head of the house, we lay our finger upon currents which report the pressure to the very Heart of creation. We forget this solemn view of things. We treat life as a mere game of chance ; we think it is all of our own handling, or of the handling of other men ; whereas written upon the earth and inscribed upon the heaven is this declaration :—" The earth is the Lord's, and the fulness thereof." To complain is to be atheistic, to murmur is to throw down the altar, to adopt a reproachful tone regarding the necessary education of life is to challenge divine wisdom. The complaint was punished as complaining must always be. Fretfulness always brings its own biting serpent along with it. Charge what improbability you may upon the particular account of serpents in the text—get rid of them if you can from the historical record,—there remains the fact, that the fretful spirit burns itself, the discontented soul creates its own agony, the mind wanting the sweet spirit of contentment stings itself night and day and writhes continually in great suffering. Discontent never brought joy, peevishness never tranquillised the home-life, fretfulness in the head of the house, or in any member of the house, creates a disagreeable feeling throughout the whole place. Complaint punishes itself. Every complaint has a corresponding serpent, and the serpent bites still. The people complained of the light food— then God sent them fiery serpents. There is always something worse than we have yet experienced. The children of Israel might have thought the bread was the worst fate that could befall them. To be without water, and to be continually living upon manna—surely there was nothing worse ? We cannot exhaust the divine resources of a penal kind. There is always some lower depth, always some keener bite, always some more painful sting, always some hotter hell. Take care how you treat life. Do not imagine that you can complain without being heard, and that you can be heard without punishment immediately following. This is the mystery of life ; this is the fact of life. We cannot reason ourselves out of it. Whatever metaphysical universe we may construct, we have to lie

down at night in the concrete universe which the almighty God
has made and is governing. It is not enough to find fault with
marvellous things in the Holy Book, as if they never could have
been real in the narrow sense in which we define reality,
because, when our peddling criticism has done its utmost, there
remains the fact, that complaint means suffering, peevishness
means agony, discontent means the failure of every sanctuary
of rest and every refuge of confidence. "Go : sin no more," said
Christ, "lest a worse thing come upon thee." There is always
a worse thing to come. Do not press God ; do not challenge the
Most High. Do not say,—If there is anything worse than this,
I cannot imagine it. Things are not limited by our imagination.
The chariots of God are twenty thousand, and as for the number
of his weapons, no man has been in his armoury to reckon up
the sum-total of the weapons. God is a consuming fire. God's
wrath cannot be directed by the futile hand of man. How, then,
is the fire to be extinguished ? How is the wrath to be turned
aside, or to be pacified, or to be brought into the harmonic
movement of the universe ? To that human riddle there is no
human answer. He who sent the serpent must remove it ;
he who inflicted the punishment must lift his hand, for we
cannot turn it aside. So we find God not only the Punisher
of Israel but the Saviour of his Church and people in the
wilderness. Moses was commanded to make a serpent of brass,
to put it upon a pole, to set up the symbol ; and whosoever
looked towards it, having been bitten of the fiery flying serpent,
was healed because he looked. In wrath God remembers mercy :
he will not impose severe efforts upon those who have been
punished by the fiery flying serpent ; he will have but the turned
eye, the significant look, the glance that means the soul. His
terms are easy ; his burden is not heavy ; his yoke is not
oppressive. The great condition is—Believe, and thou shalt be
saved. Look unto him, all ye nations of the earth—the look
of the heart—and the answer will be redemption, salvation,
pardon, heaven. This is very easy,—and yet it is not so easy
as it appears to be. The look must not be merely a glance
of distress ;—it must be the expectancy of faith, the eager look
which means God will give salvation to the eyes that are
directed towards him. To adopt a Christian term, this vision

means "faith"; to preach a Christian gospel my words must be brought from the Scriptures themselves : "This is a faithful saying, and worthy of all acceptation, that Christ Jesus came into the world to save sinners. For the Son of man is come to seek and to save that which was lost." How ? By reasoning? by argument ? by high controversy ? by some pitched battle of words ? No; but by self-renunciation, and by the look that means prayer, and by the expectation that expresses the trust of the soul. Why preach on this ancient incident? It is not so ancient. Why now refer to a brazen serpent ? Because Christ referred to it, because Paul referred to it. The New Testament records the story. Christ believed it, Paul believed it—I will not separate myself from them and create some instance of unbelief or rejection ; I will rather say with Paul,—Take care : do not murmur as some of the Israelites murmured in the wilderness and were bitten of fiery flying serpents. I will use the incident as a warning. I would rather say with Christ— " And as Moses lifted up the serpent in the wilderness, even so must the Son of man be lifted up : that whosoever believeth in him should not perish, but have eternal life." If Paul believed it, if Christ applied it, I know enough of them to know that they did not avail themselves of myths, of incidents that never occurred, of imaginary instances. I know enough of their general character and temper and spirit—I know what they did for the benefit of their race and day, and for the benefit of the whole world, to be fully aware that where they adopted a history it would be unwise upon my part to reject it. Let us, therefore, gather around the incident as a solemn warning ; and, having been all but overpowered by the awfulness of the example, let us turn in the upward direction, see the descending God, listen to his instructions to his servants, look upon the brazen serpent as a symbol ; let us pass from the symbol to the reality—the uplifted Son of God. One look of the soul, and we shall be healed ; one expression of deepest trust, and the load of guilt shall be removed ; one vision of the meaning of the Cross, and all the pain and shame and death, consequent upon guilt, shall be done away ; and we shall know the meaning of Christ's own words : "I am come that they might have life, and that they might have it more abundantly."

PRAYER.

ALMIGHTY GOD, we bless thee for great gospels, wondrous speeches of love, revelations of mercy, mysteries which astound the imagination, and appeals which seek and secure the deepest confidence of the heart. We come to thee, in the name that is above every name, as through a wide open gate, set open on purpose that we might be admitted to the throne of the heavenly grace, there to sing our psalm, charged with joy and adoration, and there to breathe our thanksgivings and utter our desires. We love the name of Jesus Christ. We love it most when we are most heart-broken; we cling to it with the greater tenacity when we know that there is no redeeming help in ourselves, and that our salvation is of God and not of man. We bless thee for a sweet gospel that can wait—that will wait, that will come to us in the darkness as if we had not affronted it, and offer again its great offers of mercy and pity, love and help, and will seek to win us to the light and to the truth. We cannot have peace until we have God's pardon—and is not abundance of pardon succeeded by a peace that passeth all understanding? Is not the blessing equal to thy great speech of love? When thou dost release us, thou dost seal the release with a calm like thine own tranquillity. Regard all worshipping spirits, all up-looking and mightily-praying hosts, and astonish thy Church by the brightness of thy rising, and set upon every believer the stamp of thy personal majesty. Thus shall we be known in our day and generation as not of this world, but always seeking a country out of sight. May we, with sandals upon our feet and staves in our hands, be constantly moving on to the city which hath foundations whose Builder and Maker is God, doing all the work of the present little space with the eager haste which tells how the heart longs to be at home in the fuller liberty and in the larger service. Amen.

Numbers xxi. 9

"And Moses made a serpent of brass, and put it upon a pole, and it came to pass, that if a serpent had bitten any man, when he beheld the serpent of brass, he lived."

THE SYMBOLICAL SERPENT.

HAS not the serpent bitten every man? We come, thus, by our questioning, into larger meanings and ultimate truths. These alphabetic incidents did not terminate in themselves. An alphabet was never created for its own use as a

mere set of unrelated and incoherent symbols. He who makes
an alphabet makes, in purpose, a library in the language which
that alphabet represents. The early people in the Bible lived
the alphabet life, the symbolic and significant life; and in after-
ages we come to consolidation and consequence, to profound
and eternal meanings. The serpent of brass was but a poor
invention if it began and ended in itself. By the very necessity
of the case it means more than the mere letter expresses. So
we return to the opening question,—Is not every man bitten by
the serpent? If this were a question to be determined by
argument, into what high and fruitless words and controversies
we might enter, coming out of them with nothing but sense of
tumult and weariness! Every man knows that he has been
bitten through and through. The appeal is not to merely
grammatical expression and critical definition of letters and
words: the solemn appeal is to consciousness—not the consciousness of any one particular moment—it may be, as when the life
fritters itself away in some vain frivolity, or is engaged in
admiration of some vain symbol or object, or when it is excited
by transient controversy, or momentary challenge and appeal of
any kind, relating to earthly experience, which can be terminated
by temporal adjustments and compensations;—consciousness
is not set up within that small excitement. Take the consciousness right through the whole life, and, though we may avoid
theological expressions, religious terms, and turn our back upon
Biblical symbolism and allusion, yet right away at the core is a
throb, a spasm, an accusation, a sense of restlessness which,
perhaps, the theologian with the Bible in his hand can better
turn into words than can any other man. Your life is not a
plain surface, without wound or bruise or mark of cruel tooth;
it is a torn thing, crumpled up by great forces, punctured by
sharp bodkins, made sore by many a keen stroke. Things will
turn themselves upside down. Prayer does not go up like
untroubled incense to the sun. Things do get out of place;
words will come wrongly both as to time and as to setting;
temper will rise; bad blood is fast made in the moral system.
What is this? Having heard what men say about it in explanation, we have come to the conclusion that no terms so correctly
express our consciousness, so thoroughly satisfy our own sense

of reality, so completely fill our capacity of imagination, as the old words which are found in Holy Scripture. We change them or modify them, or perform upon them some magical rearrangement; but they are best let alone. Their very setting seems to be of God; they are not loose jewels to be set haphazard as any man's fancy may dictate : each is set in its right place by the finger of God. We know this serpent; we have been associated with its history. If we cannot see it, we can see the tooth-mark it has left. We know that we are wounded men. As the poet, then, has well said,—"To know one's self diseased is half the cure."

There are, as a matter of fact, incurable physical diseases. The doctor looks, and says,—They are beyond my reach. He looks at all his resources, and, shaking his head significantly, he says, I have no weapon with which I can fight successfully this assailant; there is no hope; but a few days may come and go, and then—the last deep sleep. Why, then, may there not be incurable spiritual diseases—that is to say, incurable by any remedy known to men? We have no hesitation in confessing that some physical diseases are incurable, why should we falter over the case of spiritual disease and trouble? Why hesitate to say—We are lost men; there is no health in us; we are dead men before God; the law we cannot answer; conscience we cannot appease; our own small imagination has no poem or dream by which it can cover up this sense of guilt and absolute unworthiness? Why not put our hand upon our mouth and our mouth in the dust, and say,—Unclean; unprofitable; unworthy; undone! That word must be spoken if any better language is ever to be set in the soul as fit speech of a new liberty and a recovered and assured sonship. What word can better express the sense of loss and helplessness than the Bible word "unclean," or "unpardonable," or "unworthy," or "undone"? The soul says—That is the right word; that sacred term is no human invention; it touches with exquisite precision the very meaning I have been toiling to express. So long as we imagine that we can cure ourselves, we shall not look in the right direction for healing. We are not ashamed to go to others for bodily healing, why this reluctance or hesitation to go out of ourselves and beyond ourselves for spiritual healing? No sick man apologises

for going to the physician. Do we not sometimes lament the
obstinacy of men saying,—They will not take advice; they will
persist in their own course; they become the victims of their
own ignorance; if they would only call in adequate advice they
might be well presently? What is the full meaning of such
expressions? We speak that we do not know in all the fulness
of its possible meaning and force. That is the complaint of the
motherly universe over her child that will try to cure himself:
she says,—Poor sufferer! why turn in upon thyself, and waste
thy supposed cleverness in attempting to do impossibilities?—the
secret of restoration is not in thee: in thee alone is the writing
and condemnation of death; life is otherwhere; look for it; I do
not say, Go for it, for that might imply impossible effort; but thou
canst at least move an eye-lid in the direction of the remedy,
thou canst at least turn a languid eye in the direction to which
I point; the meaning of that turned eye will be that thou hast
given up all thought of saving thyself or finding health where
there is none; look! look! look up and be saved! It is a gentle
force; it falls into the harmony of our daily experience and action
in relation to other things; it has upon its side what controversial force there may be in the fact of harmony, rhythm, sound
rational analogy. The reason is not suspended: it is elevated,
it is touched with a higher glory, it is summoned to a nobler
attestation of its supreme and divine function. "Come now, and
let us reason together," saith the Lord. Who is not pleased to
say that he has in time of illness taken the very highest advice
which the latest science can supply? Is he not somewhat proud
of so explaining his position? He has not called in some inferior
doctor; or availed himself of cheap advice; he has not turned
in the direction of inexperienced wisdom; but has gone with
plentiful gold in his hand and knocked at the highest medical
prophet's door, and the prophet has condescended to come down
to him and treat him with marked distinction. He decorates his
dreary tale by such small and vain allusions as these. Even
here we may find some point of suggestion, rather than of
analogy. Who calls us? Anyhow, the call is from God, even
in the poetry and idealism of the case. This is no infant deity
that asks to play with the soul's malady, and by spiritual vivi-
section learn something of which he is now ignorant. Even in

the poetry, in the dream, it is the Eternal God that calls for the wounded men. We are not handed over to inexperience, to mere sympathy or pity on the part of fellow-sufferers ; it is the Physician of the universe that asks us to be healed.

So, if in the terms of Scripture we are humbled, crushed, set back with such contempt as holiness may feel for iniquity, yet, on the other side, it is God who calls us to be healed, it is the Eternal who stoops to us, it is the Mother of the universe that cries for the child-earth. If we cannot rise to theological awe, we are bound to respond to poetic harmony and completeness. We go out of ourselves for consolation—why hesitate to go out of ourselves for the greater blessing salvation ? We are thankful when some friend who knows the secret of the low tone and the gentle speech, quiet as dew, sweet as honey, calls upon us in the dark time, when the heavy load is crushing the whole strength ; we say we will never forget the call ; we treasure the words that were spoken ; memory says,—I will never forget the sweet prayer, the noble supplication ; the holy pleading ; it was a visit as of an angel, full-robed, charged with special messages. If we can speak so about consolation in the time of sorrow, bereavement, pain, loss,—if we say we owe the solace to another—why this pitiful reluctance to say salvation is of God ? It is no human devising : it is the thought of the Eternal. There is no salvation in the self-destroyed man : his help cometh from the hills of heaven and from the throne of eternity. Are we not dignified— yea, even glorified—by the fact that our salvation is of God and not of man ? If we would see what human nature really is, as to its dignity and grandeur and possible destiny, we must go to the very Book which humbles it with the severest reproaches. God did not send his Son to recover other than his own image : when the Son came, he spoke the native language of the race he came to redeem : he is not ashamed to be called our Brother. The very fact, therefore, that we are not saved by man but by God reveals the value of the nature which God stooped to redeem.

The great thought of all is, that the cure, as well as the disease, in the case of ancient Israel, came from God. The God who punished was the God who saved. Find an instance in the whole Scripture in which healing or preservation is connected with the name of the enemy of man, Satan—that old serpent, the devil. This is a marvellous thing. If all the Bible writers had lived in the same age and held common consultation as to the structure and form of their book, they might have made a mechanical arrangement which would have secured an artificial symmetry and unity; but they were separated by centuries; they were sundered, in some instances, by thousands of years; in many instances they did not know what would be written or what was written in its completeness;—yet, when all the fragments are brought together, in no case do I find that the devil is ever credited with having attempted really to do man substantial good, to heal him, to help him. The help which the Bible dwells upon, whatever it may be, is uniformly and consistently connected with the divine name. It is God who is mighty to save. He that cometh up from Edom with dyed garments from Bozrah, arrayed in his apparel, is red with his own precious blood.

Suppose we treat all this in the meantime symbolically, poetically,—is there not still a grand moral suggestion arising out of this perfect harmony and absolute unity? and do not the lines so interlace and co-work in all their outgoing as to suggest a noble argument? God only can wound. Injury of a certain kind is said to be inflicted by the devil; but even that is not the permissible tone. In the profoundest sense of the term all punishment for wrong-doing is from God; all trials of our spiritual quality are from God. Can there be evil in the city and the Lord not have done it? In the letter, that is a mystery; in its innermost meanings and most comprehensive bearings and issues it is a fact attested by religious consciousness. The enemy himself is but a permitted disgrace in the universe. Do not let us magnify the devil into co-partnery as to the division of the universe. He—the starry leader of the seven—is but allowed to live—the ages will tell us why. The Lord reigneth: wherefore comfort one another with these words.

What is the New Testament use of the incident recorded in the Book of Numbers? Jesus Christ took up this text, and from it preached himself. " Beginning at Moses "—he could not begin earlier as to the letter—he preached himself. Hear his words :—" As Moses lifted up the serpent in the wilderness, even so must the Son of man be lifted up : that whosoever believeth in him should not perish, but have eternal life." Jesus Christ having quoted the passage, we need not hesitate to receive it. If Jesus Christ had passed it by, we might also have turned away from the sacred symbol or have classed it with some obsolete mythologies. Where Jesus Christ rested, we too may sit down. Jesus sat upon the well—would God we could have sat around his feet and looked up into his heaven-shining eyes! Where he lingers, I would gladly stay. He lingers here : he saw in that serpent a worse foe of the human race than ever bit the flesh of man ; he saw in that pole, or standard, a cross; he saw in that uplifted serpent of brass the symbol of himself; and said he,—" I, if I be lifted up, . . . will draw all men unto me." We believe in Christ; we are not ashamed to utter his name; we do not adopt all that has been said about it by ignorance, inexperience, and perverted ingenuity ; but putting aside all these things, we go straight to him and say each for himself,—" My Lord, and my God!" We come to the uplifted Man, we come to the crucified Christ, not to talk, but to look, to pray without words, to begin to speak and to be choked by our own speech. Look unto him and be ye saved, all the ends of the earth. Lord, to whom can we look, but unto thee ? We have gone to many, and have only received riddles for replies, enigmas in exchange for mysteries, and contradiction where we begged for peace. Wilt thou take us in ? We have come to thee last : we have knocked at every door like cringing beggars, and only because we could not find satisfaction we have come to thee. If we could have eaten bread elsewhere, we would have stayed ; but when we asked for bread, they gave us a stone. Jesus, Son of David, have mercy on us ! If last of all God sent his Son, last of all the sinner accepts the Son, coming without price in his hand, without defence in his heart, and casts himself in living, loving, hopeful faith upon the Son of God. It may be delusion—it may be some horrid nightmare ; but in the meantime nothing gives such rest, such peace, such sense of union with God. In this faith we live, and in death will test the mystery,

PRAYER.

ALMIGHTY GOD we cannot live without thee. Thy smile is heaven. To know that thou art looking upon us is a judgment. We can answer it with a good heart, if so be thy Christ be in us, our Saviour and our Priest. We can bear the light when he is with us—yea, a light above the brightness of the sun. He himself is light, and in him is no darkness at all; and if he is in us, and we are in him, behold, in thy light we see light, and we love the light because of its revealing power. Give us more light. We die if we have not light enough. Thou hast made us to live in light and not in darkness. We wither away, as if struck with ice and chilled through and through, if thy light be not in us,—a brightness and a warmth, a continual blessing, an eternal hope. Once we loved darkness rather than light, but now thou hast brought us out of darkness into a marvellous light. All light is marvellous, but thy light most marvellous of all. It shows the reality of things; it finds its way into the soul; it reveals and discloses what is excluded from every other ministry. We, therefore, ask for light, more light, and more still, until the night be driven away and life become one eternal morning. Thou dost comfort us with light; yea, a pleasant thing it is for the eyes to behold the sun. We seem to be akin to that sun of thine: we claim one another; the heart answers the gospel of light, and we would go forth and see all the wizardry which thy sun works in the grandness of the field and the beauty of the garden. But thou dost work still more wondrously within us. Thou dost make all things new; old age is driven away; death is taken up, as by a giant's hand, and abolished by infinite strength: death is swallowed up in victory, and life has become immortality. These are wonderful things to say to a man. Thou hast said them: they are all written in thy book. We do not understand them—nor would we: for what we understand we come at last to contemn. We would live in wonder—in the continual appeal to our noblest imagination; we would live in the certainty that we do not know all things, and never can know them, and that to know God is to be God. Therefore do we stand afar off, without shoe upon our foot or staff in our hand, with bowed head, listening if in the warm wind we may hear at least some one tone that will tell us of wider places, infinite liberties, glorious heavens, days without night. Thou art visiting us constantly with visitations that are meant to be instructive. Thou dost take away the old traveller, so that in the morning we miss the pilgrim who has companied with us these many days—only the staff is left behind, the traveller is gone forward. Blessed are the dead which die in the Lord. Comfort those who are feeling the chill of death, the encroachment of the graveyard upon their household hearth; speak comfortingly to them, and show them that light is above, that home is on high, that here we have no continuing city, that permanence is beyond the clouds. The Lord make up for losses of this kind in so far as they can be made up, for great vacancies in the heart—the eyes looking with expectancy and beholding nothing, the ear listening for accustomed appeals, and no more appeal addressed to the hearer. We need the Lord's comfort: some warm word, some gracious speech,—yea, some great trumpet sound, that shall swallow up the mean noises of earth, and rule into harmony and order and sacred and ennobling thought all tumult and fear, all apprehension and pain. Save us from folly! We are prone to it; we like it: we roll it under our tongue as a sweet morsel. We sometimes feel as if we were the children of fools, and were born to be fools greater still. We think the earth is all: the blue sky is an exclusion not an inclusion; to our mean thought, the lights that glitter in it are but points of amber—not flaming gates falling back upon radiant heavens; we gather up things with both hands, and hide them and cover them up so that nobody else may see them, and this we call prosperity; yea, we put our money into bags with holes in them; we sow plentiful seed, and others reap the harvest; we build our tower that is to reach unto heaven, and whilst we are putting on the topstone, builder and building are thrown to the ground. The little child dies, and the old man, business withers, health gives way, the house totters without our being able to find out why; we live in uncertainty; we are walking upon the edge of a precipice; we know not what will happen to-morrow—so near a time as that. God pity us!— for God made us—and send us the messages we need. Revive our hope; establish our confidence; bind us to the infinite meaning of the Cross; there we see with the heart that thy Cross is greater than our sin, that thy grace is infinitely more than our guilt. The Cross is the place of vision. Amen.

Numbers xxii.

BALAAM.

B ALAAM comes into the narrative most suddenly;—but he will never go out of it again. Other men have come into the Bible story quite as suddenly; but they have only remained for a time. Balaam will never disappear: we shall read of him when we come to the Book of the Revelation of John the Divine. There are some historical presences you can never get rid of. It is useless to quibble and question. The same mystery occurs in our own life. Some persons, having been once seen, they are seen for ever. You cannot get away from the image or the influence, or forget the magical touch of hand or mind or ear; they turn up in the last chapter of your life Bible. You

cannot tell whence they come : their origin is as great a mystery
as is the origin of Melchisedek ; they come into your life-lines as
quickly and abruptly as came Elijah the Tishbite ; and they
take up their residence with you, subtly colouring every thought,
and secretly and mightily turning speech into new accents and
unsuspected expressions, full of significance, and revealing that
significance in ever-surprising ways and tones. Why sit down
and look at the story of Balaam as though it were something that
occurred once for all ? It occurs every day. God teaches by
surprise.   He sets the stranger in our life, and while we are
wondering, he turns our wonder into some sublimer mystery.
Who would have a life four-square, in the sense of limitation,
visible boundary, tangible beginning and ending ? Who would
not rather be in the world as if he had been in some other
world, and as if he were moving on to some larger world ?
We lose power when we lose mystery. Let us not chaffer
about words. If the spirit of mystery is in a man, the spirit
of worship is in him ; and if the spirit of worship is in him, it
may detail itself into beliefs, and actions, and services, which are
accounted right, and whose rightness will be proved by their
beneficence. Balaam comes as suddenly as Melchisedek, as
unexpectedly as Elijah ; but we shall find him at the very last
an instructive historical character. He is called Balaam the son
of Beor, and he is located at Pethor on the river Euphrates. At
that time the king of Moab was called Balak, and when Balak
saw how Israel had destroyed the Amorites, he said,—Fighting
is out of the question ; if we have to come to battle, we may as
well surrender before we begin ; the numbers are overwhelming.
"Moab was distressed because of the children of Israel" (xxii. 3).
Balak said,—"Now shall this company lick up all that are round
about us, as the ox licketh up the grass of the field " (xxii. 4).
You can hear the lick and the crunch, and be present at the
destruction. It was a day of fear and much sorrow in Moab.
What, then, was to be done? Herein came the wisdom of Balak.
He also lives to the end of life's chapter, for to the end of that
chapter we shall find the touch of superstition in the human
mind. Balak would have recourse to supernatural help. He
had heard of Balaam the soothsayer of Pethor—a man of divina-
tion, a person who had power to bless and to curse—the Simon

Magus of his day ; so he took advantage of his superstition, and thought to sow the air with curses which would work where his little sword could not reach. That is not a mean thought. Call it perversion, or superstition, you do not touch the inner and vital mystery of the case. The great agonies of life are not to be explained by calling them perversions, or labelling them superstitions, or denouncing them as nightmares or dreams : they are there. Man must obey voices which are not always articu-late and reportable as to words and tones. It may be more superstitious to deny the supernatural than to affirm it. Never forget the cant that is talked against cant. Do not believe that they are the heavenly, pure, brilliant souls who have no Church, no religion, no altar,—who live under the dome of their own hats and walk on the marble of their own boots. Whose prophets, pray, are they ? They must be accounted for, as well as the Melchisedeks, the Balaams, and Elijahs of old time. What is their history ? Where have they made their mark ? What marvels of beneficence have they performed ? Or do they only live in the very doubtful region of sneering at other people's piety ? Balak's was a great thought. We do not adopt its form, but we should perhaps do unwisely to reject its spirit and intent. Balak said,—Numbers are against us ; if it is to be a mere con-tention of army against army, Moab will be destroyed at once ; the thing to be done—if it can be done—is to enlist the service and action of the supernatural. Quite right. We say so now. If that can be done, any other thing that can be done is contemp-tible in comparison. All the little inventions and tricks and arts of man, in arranging and rearranging and adjusting and adapting, are beneath contempt compared with the discovery of the spring of life, the spring of thought. If one could read the heart of man and understand his thought afar off, that—if possible—would throw all other acquisitions into the shade, and reduce them to puerility and nothingness. If it cannot be done, still the auda-cious imagination that it *might* be done is a force that might play a very beneficent part in human thinking and human service : it might ennoble the mind, it might create a holy impatience with all little and transitory things, it might enlarge the soul's whole outlook, and constrain all life into an attitude of prayer and expectation. That, indeed, is prayer. The words are not the prayer. Herein we make the continual blunder of supposing that the sentences are the prayer. As well say the body is the man ; as well say the house is the tenant. The prayer is in the sentences—wrapped up in them ; a spirit impatient with the sentences, frowning upon them because so empty, so short, so inadequate. Prayer is the very mystery of breathing. Balak's thought, therefore,—let us say again and again—was an anticipation of the greatest of all thoughts, namely, that the spiritual is mightier than the material. The man who lays down that proposition commits no crime against reason. Suppose it to have entered into some man's mind—altogether apart from what is known in Christian countries as revelation—that a thought is mightier than an arm. It is a sublime conception, whoever conceived it in his own imagination. The man seems to be going upon the right line ; he is not a man to be jeered at. He suggests that "knowledge is power." Take down the sentence ; write it in a book ; on hearing it, we feel as if we might be ready to die for its exposition and vindication. Some bold man has said—let us suppose,—Could we get at the Ruling Spirit of the universe and enlist that Spirit upon any given side of a controversy, that would be the winning side. Now you say so, we feel the possible wisdom of the reasoning ;—nay, more, of course it must be so. Your argument is, that were it possible—about which we do not dogmatise—were it possible to get hold of the Force, whatever it be, that made all things, that holds all things, that rules all things—that would be getting hold of omnipotence and securing the soul within the walls of a sanctuary that cannot be violated. Yes, we admit it, if—. But that *if* does not destroy the reasoning ; that *if* does not turn the reasoner into a mere dreamer, or sentimentalist, or fanatic ; he stands behind his *if* as a great man. To have driven up to that *if* is some progress in human thinking. Better die behind that *if*, with great tears of disappointment in your eyes, than live the narrow, superficial, selfish life. It would seem to be a mile nearer home. It would seem as if any spirit that may be behind things must answer the reverent audacity that says to the universe,—This is not all : I fling it from me, and hope. "Such a thought," the heart says, "cannot be turned to disappointment ; it must evoke any fire of Deity that may be burning

behind the visible stars." The idea has occurred to Balak that
if he can enlist the services of a man who is a spell-binder—a
man who can curse or bless, *if* he can enlist the supernatural
on his side, then Israel may be ten times as many as Israel is,
yet they shall be but a multitude of grasshoppers. Balak in
his superstition is not a man to be smiled upon as if he had
committed some act of harmless lunacy.

So Balak sent for Balaam, who made answer that he would
not go. By-and-by, Balak sent other princes more honourable
still, with offers of promotion and honour and abundant wages.
Balaam said he would ask God. He asked God, and angered him
by so doing. Some second prayers are worse than superstitions.
So God said,—" If the men come to call thee, rise up, and go
with them "—take thine own way; no secondary use shall be
made of me, but go—" yet the word which I shall say unto
thee, that shalt thou do" (xxii. 20). " God's anger was kindled "
against Balaam. " And God's anger was kindled because he went:
and the angel of the Lord stood in the way for an adversary
against him. Now he was riding upon his ass, and his two
servants were with him. And the ass saw the angel of the Lord
standing in the way, and his sword drawn in his hand : and the
ass turned aside out of the way, and went into the field : and
Balaam smote the ass, to turn her into the way. But the angel
of the Lord stood in a path of the vineyards, a wall being on this
side, and a wall on that side " (xxii. 22–24).

When Balak heard of Balaam's arrival he was glad. Gold
went for nothing, now the soothsayer had come. Riches were
as water poured forth. In those days the supernatural went for
something in the market-place. It is the cheapest of all things
now. Ideas are without value; religious thoughts are mere
breath. But Balaam remembered that he was only to speak
what God told him ; so he began to play the priest. He would
have altars put up. "He took up his parable, and said, Balak
the king of Moab hath brought me from Aram, out of the mountains
of the east, saying, Come, curse me Jacob, and come, defy
Israel" (xxiii. 7) ;—and he would have altars put up and sacrifices
rendered; and the answer was,—No, Israel cannot be cursed.
So Balak took him to another point of view, where, perhaps,
the multitude looked greater or did not look so great. " And he

took up his parable, and said, Rise up, Balak, and hear; hearken
unto me, thou son of Zippor" (xxiii. 18); and again the people
were to rise like a lion, and lift up themselves as a young lion;
and the people were not to lie down until they had eaten of the
prey and drunk of the blood of the slain. Well, then,—Balak
said—if that be the case, this thou must do for me, neutralise
thyself: be nothing: act as if thou hadst not come at all—
"Neither curse them at all, nor bless them at all" (xxiii. 25).
But Balaam said,—No; you cannot treat God's messengers in
that way; as a matter of fact, they are here: you have to account
for them being here, and to reckon with them whilst they are
here. We cannot quiet things by ignoring them. By simply
writing UNKNOWABLE across the heavens, we really do not
exclude supernatural or immeasurable forces. The ribbon is too
narrow to shut out the whole heaven; it is but a little strip;
it looks contemptible against the infinite arch. We do not exclude God by denying him, nor by saying that we do not know
him, or that he cannot be known. We cannot neutralise God,
so as to make him neither the one thing nor the other. So
Balaam was the greatest mystery Balak had to deal with. It is
the same with the Bible—God's supernatural Book. It will not
lie where we want it to lie: it has a way of getting up through
the dust that gathers upon it and shaking itself, and making its
pages felt. It will open at the wrong place;—would it open at
some catalogue of names, it might be tolerated, but it opens at
hot places, where white thrones are and severe judgments, and
where scales are tried and measuring wands are tested. It will
speak to the soul about the wrong-doing that never came to
anything, and the wicked thought that would have burned the
heavens and scattered dishonour upon the throne of God.

"Would to Heaven"—Balak said, in effect—"I could get rid of
this man!" He took Balaam to another point of view, and Balaam
"set his face toward the wilderness, and took up his parable," and
sang a sweet and noble song:—"How goodly are thy tents, O
Jacob, and thy tabernacles, O Israel! As the valleys are they
spread forth, as gardens by the river's side, as the trees of
lign aloes which the Lord hath planted, and as cedar trees
beside the waters. He shall pour the water out of his buckets,
and his seed shall be in many waters, and his king shall be

higher than Agag, and his kingdom shall be exalted. God brought him forth out of Egypt; he hath as it were the strength of an unicorn: he shall eat up the nations his enemies, and shall break their bones, and pierce them through with his arrows. He couched, he lay down as a lion, and as a great lion: who shall stir him up? Blessed is he that blesseth thee, and cursed is he that curseth thee." Balak made a bad bargain that day. He had added to his troubles instead of diminishing them. If we invite Christ into the house merely to do our bidding, he will burn the house and he will burn the host that invited him to break bread. We cannot trifle with these mysteries. The Gospel is a savour of life unto life, or of death unto death; the truth is a stone to be fallen upon, or it is a stone which will fall upon those who invoke it. We cannot get rid of these spiritual presences and influences. We seem to do so for a time—I admit it. We are so broad in physical dimensions, so healthy in physical functions, so radiant in physical life, so successful, too, in the market-place; we walk over the course, and bring back the prize; we smile with gracious contempt upon unsuccessful persons, who are labouring all day and bringing back nothing but a handful of wind; we name them by sneering names; we use them as typical instances whereby to excite our own laughter and the laughter of other men. Why, we could not do with a God under those conditions. But all human life is not enclosed within such limited boundaries. Not in any one mood can we determine these great questions. Life, in its sum-total, with all its variations, rapid changes, and increasing responsibilities, must be taken into account.

Balak would gladly have parted with Balaam, but he could not get rid of him; and Balak was wroth. It became a king to become angry. "And Balak's anger was kindled against Balaam, and he smote his hands together: and Balak said unto Balaam, I called thee to curse mine enemies, and, behold, thou hast altogether blessed them these three times. Therefore now flee thou to thy place: I thought to promote thee unto great honour; but, lo, the Lord hath kept thee back from honour" (xxiv. 10-11). And Balaam spake a great speech to Balak: he said,—Is this not precisely what I said to the king's messengers? Did I not say, "If Balak would give me his house full of silver and gold, I cannot go beyond the commandment of the Lord, to do either good or bad of mine own mind ; but what the Lord saith, that will I speak " ? (xxiv. 13)—now I will tell that which I see. And then came the parable of the man whose eyes are open :—"And he took up his parable, and said, Balaam the son of Beor hath said, and the man whose eyes are open hath said : He hath said, which heard the words of God, and knew the knowledge of the most High, which saw the vision of the Almighty, falling into a trance, but having his eyes open : I shall see him, but not now : I shall behold him, but not nigh : there shall come a Star out of Jacob, and a Sceptre shall rise out of Israel, and shall smite the corners of Moab, and destroy all the children of Sheth. And Edom shall be a possession, Seir also shall be a possession for his enemies ; and Israel shall do valiantly. Out of Jacob shall come he that shall have dominion, and shall destroy him that remaineth of the city " (xxiv. 15–19). Then the parable is continued, Balaam looking Balak full in the face ; and last of all " Balaam rose up, and went and returned to his place, and Balak also went his way " (xxiv. 25). You cannot carve your God into any shape that will please your fancy. You cannot send for any true faith and bribe it to speak your blessings or your cursings.

Balaam was a man of noble sentiments. Look at some of his words, " Let me die the death of the righteous, and let my last end be like his ! " (xxiii. 10). And again :—" God is not a man, that he should lie ; neither the son of man, that he should repent " (xxiii. 19). And again : " I shall see him, but not now : I shall behold him, but not nigh " (xxiv. 17). Then take the grand word he spake to Balak as reported in the prophecies of Micah. Say, did ever man preach a nobler sermon than this : "He hath shewed thee, O man, what is good ; and what doth the Lord require of thee, but to do justly, and to love mercy, and to walk humbly with thy God " ? (Micah vi. 8). Who can amend that speech ? Who can refine that gold ? Who dares touch that lily with his mean paint ? Who taught Balaam that great speech ? We sometimes say we find scattered up and down in ancient literature morals as beautiful as any we find in the Bible. Possibly so. Who wrote them ? Whence did they come ? Is God the God of one corner of the creation ? Is God

a parochial Deity ? Is there not a spirit in man—universal man
—and doth not the Spirit of the Most High give him understanding ? Wherever there is a line of beauty, God wrote it;
wherever there is a sentiment which is charged with the spirit
of beneficence, that may be claimed as a good gift of God. The
Apostle Paul never uttered a nobler sentiment than is uttered by
Balaam, as reported in the prophecies of Micah. This is the
Sermon upon the Mount in anticipation. That is the vicious
Church, built on the wrong foundation, aiming at the wrong
heaven, which does not recognise in every literature and in every
nation all that is good, noble, wise, prophetic.

Balaam's convictions and wishes disagreed sometimes. Therein he was most human. He knew he ought not to go, yet he
wished to go. He would ask the second time ; he would doubt
his own convictions, or he would adjust them according to the
shape and temper of circumstances. Wherever he came from,
he claims herein to be quite a near neighbour of ours. Doubts
may exist as to the exact relation of Pethor to the river upon
which it was built, but there can be no doubt whatever of the
blood relationship between Balaam and our own age. Speaking
impulsively from the centre of his convictions, he said,—No !—
nothing shall tempt me to go; you speak of gold and silver—if
Balak were to give me his house full of gold and silver, I would
not go ; I am the Lord's servant, and the Lord's work alone will
I do. Then the thought occurred to him—a second message
coming, borne by more honourable princes,—Perhaps I might go
and obtain this wealth and honour, and still do my duty. He is
on the downward road now. A man who thinks to do forbidden
things and spend the bounty for the advantage of the Church is
lost ; there is no power in him that can overcome the gravitation
that sucks him downward. He says,—I will bring back all
Balak's gold and silver and add a transept to the church or
another course of marble to the altar. He will never return.
God will not have his house so patched and bungled ; nor does
he want Balak's gold for the finishing of his sanctuary. A
nobler spirit was Abram, who said to the King of Sodom,—No,
" lest thou shouldest say, I have made Abram rich." Thus do
we poison our consciences, pervert our judgment, hold a veil
before our eyes ; thus do we attempt to look up to heaven and

clutch the advantages of earth. This cannot be done; the whole
spiritual gravitation is against it; the law of the Lord is against
it. This miracle of evil he never permits his creatures to
perform.

NOTE.

Dr. Cunningham Geikie says:—"The whole story is intensely Oriental
and primeval. The first deputation is dismissed in obedience to a divine
warning: but, so far as we know, "the wages of unrighteousness" which
Balaam "loved," are carefully retained. A second embassy of nobler
messengers, carrying richer gifts, succeeds. He does not at once dismiss
them, as God had required, but presses for permission to go with them,
which at last is granted. He would fain earn the wealth and honour
apparently in his grasp, yet knows that when the prophetic afflatus comes
on him he can only utter what it prompts. With a feigned religiousness,
he protests that if Balak were to give him his house full of silver and gold,
he could not go beyond the word of Jehovah his God, to do less or more;
but he also bids them wait overnight to see if he may not, after all, be
allowed to go with them. If his ignoble wish to be allowed to curse an
unoffending nation be gratified, he has the wealth he craves: if it be refused,
he can appeal to his words as proof of his being only the mouthpiece of
God. That he should have been allowed to go with Balak's messenger,
was only the permission given every man to act as a free agent, and in no
way altered the divine command, that he should bless and not curse. Yet
he goes, as if, perchance, at liberty to do either, and lets Balak deceive
himself by false hopes, when the will of God has been already decisively
made known."

Dr. Samuel Cox says:—"One of the sins brought home to Balaam with
extraordinary force and bitterness in the New Testament Scriptures is his
venality. And it is impossible to study his career, and to note his ardent love
and admiration of righteousness, yet not be struck with surprise and shame
at discovering that he loved the wages of unrighteousness, and was capable
of prostituting his rare and eminent gifts for hire. Still, do we not find this
same strange and pitiful combination of piety and covetousness in Jacob,
who was surnamed Israel, 'the Prince with God,' and from whom the
whole seed of Abraham have derived their name, and perhaps something
more than their *name?* No candid student of his history can deny that,
even from the first, Jacob showed a singular appreciation of spiritual things,
a singular ambition for spiritual primacy and honour. Nor can any man who
accepts the Bible record of him doubt that dreams and visions of the most
ravishing beauty, pregnant with the most profound spiritual intention and
promise, were vouchsafed him; or that, at least when he blessed his sons
from his dying bed, his eyes were opened to behold things that were to
befall them and their children years and centuries after he himself had been

gathered to his fathers. Even the oracles of Balaam do not surpass the long series of dooms and benedictions which Jacob was then moved to utter. Yet what was his whole life but, on the one side, a constant endeavour to enrich or secure himself at the cost of others, by superior craft or superior force; and, on the other side, a divine discipline by which that worldly and grasping spirit was chastened out of him, in order that his genius for religion might have free play?

"And, again, who can deny that this love of money, this covetousness which is idolatry, this selfish and grasping spirit, is of all sins that which always has been, and is, most common and prevalent in the Church, and even among sincerely religious men? It clothes itself with respectability as with a garment, and walks often unrebuked, often flattered even and admired, in almost every assembly of the saints. How many of *us* are there who, if we love righteousness, also hanker after the wages of unrighteousness, after the opulence, the gratifications, the success which can only come to us through a selfish and worldly, *i.e.*, a sinful life! No transgression is more common than this among spiritual men, though none is more fatal to the spiritual life, since none renders a man more impervious to the rebukes of conscience or the warnings of the Word and Spirit of God.

"Or take that other and grosser crime which we have seen brought home to Balaam, the sensuality that made the foul device by which the early innocence of Israel was debauched, familiar, or at best not impossible to him. Is it difficult to find a parallel to that? It would not be fair, though many would think it fair, to cite the example of David's well-known sin; for no sin was ever more deeply repented than his, as few have been more terribly avenged. But think of Solomon; think of the beauty and promise of his youth. Recall his choice of a wise and understanding heart above all the luxuries of wealth and all the flatteries of power. Read his wonderful prayer when he dedicated himself and all the resources of his kingdom to the service of Jehovah, and invoked a blessing on all who at any time and from any place should turn to the Temple and call on the name of the Lord. And then remember that this most religious king, this great prophet who 'spake three thousand proverbs and whose psalms were a thousand and five,' to whose heart God gave a largeness like .that of the sea, sank into the very sin of sensual idolatry with which Balaam betrayed Israel, suffering his wives and concubines to turn away his heart from the Lord his God, till at last he fell from his harem into his grave, an unloved tyrant, a jaded voluptuary, and probably a believer whose faith was shot through and through with a pessimistic scepticism."

22. And God's anger was kindled because he went: and the angel of the Lord stood in the way for an adversary against him. Now he was riding upon his ass, and his two servants were with him.

23. And the ass saw the angel of the Lord standing in the way, and his sword drawn in his hand: and the ass turned aside out of the way, and went into the field: and Balaam smote the ass, to turn her into the way.

24. But the angel of the Lord stood in a path of the vineyards, a wall being on this side, and a wall on that side.

25. And when the ass saw the angel of the Lord, she thrust herself unto the wall, and crushed Balaam's foot against the wall: and he smote her again.

26. And the angel of the Lord went further, and stood in a narrow place, where was no way to turn either to the right hand or to the left.

27. And when the ass saw the angel of the Lord, she fell down under Balaam: and Balaam's anger was kindled, and he smote the ass with a staff.

28. And the Lord opened the mouth of the ass, and she said unto Balaam What have I done unto thee, that thou hast smitten me these three times?

29. And Balaam said unto the ass, Because thou hast mocked me: I would there were a sword in mine hand, for now would I kill thee.

30. And the ass said unto Balaam, Am not I thine ass, upon which thou hast ridden ever since I was thine unto this day? was I ever wont to do so unto thee? And he said, Nay.

31. Then the Lord opened the eyes of Balaam, and he saw the angel of the Lord standing in the way, and his sword drawn in his hand: and he bowed down his head, and fell flat on his face.

32. And the angel of the Lord said unto him, Wherefore hast thou smitten thine ass these three times? behold, I went out to withstand thee,—because thy way is perverse before me:

33. And the ass saw me, and turned from me these three times: unless she had turned from me, surely now also I had slain thee, and saved her alive.

34. And Balaam said unto the angel of the Lord, I have sinned; for I knew not that thou stoodest in the way against me: now therefore, if it displease thee, I will get me back again.

35. And the angel of the Lord said unto Balaam, Go with the men: but only the word that I shall speak unto thee, that thou shalt speak. So Balaam went with the princes of Balak.

BALAAM STOPPED BY AN ANGEL.

ONE of the most pious and profound commentators has suggested that all this was seen in a vision; in other words, the narrative may be taken as Balaam's report of a very marvellous dream. Any suggestion will do when men want to get rid of the supernatural. Under such circumstances, the very indifferent man may become an important personage. Anything that will rid us of lines beyond our own personal experience, and give us a sense of comfortable snugness within four visible points, will be received with gratitude by the natural heart. We like insulation. We are pleased with a clock that we can see, every tick of which we can hear, and every indication of which we can read. But the clock is not the time. The time is invisible, impalpable, in many regards incalculable; quite a ghost, a very solemn thing, always talking, and yet talking in a way that is not always clearly apprehended or understood. People like to be comfortable, and nobody can be comfortable with the supernatural who is not in harmony with it. If a certain miracle has not been wrought in the soul, the supernatural becomes a kind of ghost, a spectral presence, an uncanny possibility in the life, and had better be got rid of; and when the mind wants such riddance, any suggestion that will aid in that direction is received with effusive thankfulness. In this instance, we had better, perhaps, in the first place, endeavour to find out what are those things in the story which do lie within the limit of our own experience—an experience which we are in danger of exaggerating into a kind of instinct and claim of infallibility. First of all, therefore, instead of troubling the mind with vexing questions which never can be settled, let us collect the lessons which are obviously within the circle of our own observation and experience; after that, we may be in a position to look at certain miraculous aspects and ascertain their import and their divine intention.

It lies quite within our experience that we do get our own way, and yet have a sense of burning and judgment, of opposition and anger all the time. Balaam was invited to go to Balak's country and he said,—No. He said No with some emphasis. He was a man of fine impulse, and his first impulse was generally healthy and strong in a right direction. Instead of giving a hesitant No he gave a bold round thunderous NO! Then Balak tried again; he also believed in importunity. He doubled the bribe,—nay, he may have multiplied the bribe by ten. He sent more honourable princes; men who in their own country were accustomed to command, and they assumed the obeisant attitude with great grace and humility. Balaam said,— No. But all the thunder had gone out of that No; it was a No which a mean man might have said. However—he said—I will pray about it, I will consult the Lord—when he need not have consulted the Lord at all. Men forget that there is a time when they need not ask the Lord any questions. Never trouble the Lord to know whether you cannot do just a little wrong; he is not to be called upon in relation to business of that kind. He does not pray who palters with moral distinctions, who wants to make compromises, who is anxious to find some little crevice or opening through which he can pass into the land of his own desire. Whimpering hypocrite! miserable miscreant! thou wilt pray in order to get leave to go in the direction pleasant to the imagination or profitable to the pocket and call it prayer! —wilt consult the oracle, wilt look to heaven, wilt inquire diligently in the Scriptures, wilt endeavour to find out some sign indicating what God means thee to do, whilst before thou didst pray thou hadst fashioned the answer. It was a mocker's religion. Balaam got his own way so far. The Lord has a method of his own in this particular. Providence does shape itself curiously in some instances. The voice said to him,—Go! —you want to go; you have made up your secret mind to go,— go; only the word that I bid thee speak, that shalt thou say; and Balak, who sent for an ally, shall find himself confronted with a missionary. These things lie quite obviously within our own experience. We need not describe them at all as theological; we have seen this in a score of instances,—perhaps, in some instances, we ourselves have been the chief actors and sufferers. So far then we are upon the line of experience.

Men are stopped in certain courses without being able to tell the reason why. That also is matter of experience. The wind seems to be a wall before us; the road looks quite open, and yet we can make no progress in it. Our eyes deceive us, because surely this is a highway—the king's broad road—and yet, scheme as we may, promise what we may, we can make no progress along that road. If an army met us, we could run home, and say,—Lo! a host beset us, and we have fled before the furious opposition. But there is no army. If some beast of prey had rushed out from the hedge, we could have turned back and explained to our comrades in life that we were stopped by a threatening beast. But there is no such difficulty on the road that is at all visible to us. We lift up our hand, and say we will go in this direction, oppose us what may,—and there is nothing to strike at. Again and again do we say,—How is this? —we came the first two miles easily, pleasantly, as if galloping over a flowery land at bright summer time, and we said in our hearts,—This journey will be a right pleasant one all through ; and suddenly we can go no farther. This is matter of experience. Let us constantly say to ourselves : We cannot account for the impossibility of progress. The business stands still ;—we have risen at the same hour in the morning, carried out the usual arrangements, been apparently on the alert all the time; and yet not one inch farther are we permitted to go. Suppose we have no God, no altar, no Church limitations, no ghostly ministry exerting itself upon our life and frightening us with super-stition and spectre—we are healthy reasoners, downright robust rationalists,—men who can take things up and set them down, square-headed men,—yet there is the fact, that even we—such able-bodied rationalists, such healthy souls that any society would insure us on the slightest inquiry—there we are, puzzled, mystified, perplexed, distracted. We will not use theological terms : we fall back upon the second grade of language ; still there remains the substantial and abiding fact, that progress along this road is impossible. So far, this story affords no ground of serious difficulty, even to the reason and the mind in its soberest mood.

It also lies within the region of experience that men are rebuked by dumb animals. That is odd ; but it is true. The whole Scripture is charged with that statement, and so charged with it as to amount to a practical philosophy in daily life :— "But ask now the beasts, and they shall teach thee ; and the fowls of the air, and they shall tell thee "—" The stork in heaven knoweth her appointed times"—"The ox knoweth his owner, and the ass his master's crib "—" Go to the ant, thou sluggard ; consider her ways, and be wise." Dumb creatures are continually teaching us. They keep law with wondrous obedience. The poorest brutes are really very faithful to the rude legislation under which they live. If men could only be as drunk as a beast, they would never go far from the paths of sobriety. It is a foul slander upon the beast for a man to set himself beside it and say that he is as oblivious of law, as negligent of divine intention, as the brute that perishes. In temperance, in acceptance of discipline, in docility, I know not any beast that is ever used by man that may not teach some men, very distinctly, helpful and useful lessons. That the beast does not speak is the very smallest and poorest objection that can be taken to the teaching. It is putting speech in a false position, it is altogether altering the relations and perspective of things. What is speech ? How is speech delivered ? Is speech confined to the tongue ? We must define the word *speech*, if we are to enter into the particulars of a controversy which can never be settled. But we cannot allow rude definitions to be given as if they were philosophical. There is the substantial fact, that the beasts of the field do teach us, rebuke us, humble us ; and that they do not do all this through the medium of articulate speech—as that term is understood by us,—is a frivolous objection, and ought not to be taken account of in any court in which the presiding disposition is to find out substantial and eternal truths. So far, I see nothing in the story to disturb the sobriety of experience.

Then, again, it does lie within our cognition that men do blame second causes for want of success. Balaam blamed the ass. That is what we are always doing. There is nothing exceptional in this conduct of the soothsayer. We want to get on—it is the beast that will not go. Who ever thought that an angel was confronting him—that a distinct ghostly purpose was against him ? Who ever imagined that he, a rationalist with a healthy digestion, was stopped on his course by some beneficent providence ? He naturally feels that he *ought not* to have been stopped ; he is a healthy-minded man, there is no nonsense about him,—a practical man, shrewd, with eyes well-set in his head and that can see one colour in its distinction from another—an

eye skilled in proportion and distance and expression ; he *ought
not* to have been stopped. Yet he is arrested. He blames his
surroundings, his assistants, his colleagues, his " stupid partner,"
his "reluctant people." He would have been miles ahead—he
might have been back by this time, but he was stopped by
second causes. How much nobler the health of the man who says,
—I am but of yesterday, and know nothing ; I cannot tell what
a day may bring forth ; it is good to be disappointed ; it is
beneficial for my soul's health not to have my own way always ;
I wanted to go along this road, and to go at a very quick rate,
but I am mysteriously arrested, and I cannot move through an
invisible wall ; but God built it—I fall down before it as before
an altar, and thank God for the stoppage ! To some men, that
appears to be the true reasoning. They have such self-distrust
—they have seen the consequences of leaning to their own
judgment so frequently, they have tested life at so many
points and find what a mystery it is—that at last they have come
to say,—We see nothing as it really is ; we know nothing as it
really is ; we are in the hands of the divine Father ;—not our
will but thine be done. To some imaginations, that appears
to be fanaticism ; to others—not altogether ridiculous in mental
capacity, nor altogether unworthy of credit—really genuinely-
learned and cultivated men—it seems to be the finest rationalism,
the noblest sobriety, the most substantial conviction.

Does it not also lie within the range of our experience that men
do want to get back sometimes but are driven forward ? Did
not Balaam want to return when he said, "If it displease thee,
I will get me back again"? We cannot. Life is not a little
trick, measurable by such terms. A man cannot make a fool
of himself, and instantly turn round as if nothing had happened ;
we cannot drive a nail into a tree and take it out without leaving
a wound behind. It does not lie within the range of our arm—
pontiffs though we be in the shabby church of reason—to break
the vessel of glass, and put it together again as if it had never
been dashed to pieces. This is not in harmony with the mystery
of the universe as we know it. This proposition of Balaam's is
the ridiculous imagination of men who suppose that they can
sin against God and say,—Now we will turn back ; we will not
do it again ; we have blasphemed God—now we will go to

church. To get that sophism out of the human mind is the difficulty of God. It appears so easy to commit a sin, and then to say we are sorry that we committed it, and to go back home as if nothing had been done. What has been done? The universe has been dishonoured; the snowy purity of God has been stained; the great creation in all its harmonies has been shocked and distressed with a great pain. We ought not to infer anything to the disadvantage of God from such a method of providence. It means that we are more than we thought ourselves to be. Conduct is of greater consequence than we imagine. Humanity is a sublime mystery, as well as God; and there is no way backward, unless it be in consent with the Mind that constructed and that rules creation. Balaam would go back and remain at Pethor as if he had never left his native village; but the Lord said,—No; go forward;—only now be the representative of holy truth to the heathen king.

But there is a difficulty about the dumb ass rebuking the perverse prophet? So there is. I would be dismayed by it if I were not overwhelmed by greater miracles still. This has come to be but a small thing—a very momentary wonder, a riddle which a child might guess,—as compared with more astounding circumstances. A more wonderful thing than that an ass should speak is that a man should forget God. If you challenge me to the consideration of both the subjects, and take them in the order of their importance, in proportion as I am a sound reasoner and in a healthy condition of conscience and imagination, I cannot hesitate which to assign the overwhelming importance. That a man should forget deliverances—that a man should be delivered from the jaws of the lion and the bear and should forget the deliverance—that is a more astounding circumstance than that all the beasts of the field should open their mouths in articulate and impressive eloquence. Why do we vex our little selves with little questions, instead of exciting our greater selves by greater problems? The miracle that astounds the Lord is that we should have forgotten that he had nourished and brought up children and that they should have rebelled against him. We—childish, foolish, vain,—are busy with little puzzles in the history of miracles, whilst the infinite impeachment is uttered by all the thunders of the universe, that we have forgotten

God, turned away from the fountain of waters, and have hewn out to ourselves cisterns—broken cisterns—that could hold no water. Riddle-loving, easily tickled and amused, excited by miracles of the smallest quantity and the feeblest quality, we are wondering if the ass *did* speak to Balaam; whilst all the angels of God might stand appalled in looking on any sinful man who ever lifted his hand against the majesty of Heaven. There are historical miracles, there are miracles of a physical and material kind, there are mysteries to which we have no immediate answer; but there are other mysteries which involve destiny, and to these miracles we think it best to address ourselves in the first instance. The miracles of a physical and historical kind may admit of postponement as to their consideration; but that men should have forgotten God, and insulted law, and done unrighteously,—these are mysteries which must not be delayed in their explanation and settlement.

So we come again and again to the great practical inquiry,— Being on the wrong road, how shall we get back? There is no answer in man. If Balaam could have retraced his steps, put up his ass in the stable and gone about his business as if nothing had occurred, it would have been but a paper universe. That he could not do so, that he was under the pressure of mightier forces, indicates that the universe is itself a tragedy, and that the explanation of every character, every incident, and every flush of colour, must be left for another time, when the light is stronger and the duration is assured. Meanwhile, we can pray, we can look up, we can say, each for himself,—"I have sinned."

PRAYER.

ALMIGHTY GOD, receive us everyone in the name of thy Son Jesus Christ, we humbly beseech thee. There is room in thine heart for every one; thou dost miss the least. Teach us the minuteness of thy care that we may give to thee the keeping of our whole life, reserving nothing for our own regard, but delivering the whole space of life, great and small, to the rule and blessing of Heaven. We will do nothing without thee; though the temptation be strong to arise and move on and begin the battle and seize the gate, yet will we stand still until we are sure of thy bidding to move. Thou hast made one star differ from another star in glory; thou hast set one man above another; thou hast made one life the ruler of many lives. The distribution is entirely in God's hands; we would accept it and adore the sovereignty which it represents. But thou hast a place for every one: thou hast omitted nothing from thy reckoning; to every man thou sayest,—Why stand ye idle in the market-place? thou wilt find a position for every life. We bless thee for this confidence; it delivers us from care; it helps us patiently to wait. Thou hast marked our life by many a sign we cannot mistake. It is thy life: it was thy life before it was ours; it is only ours because it is thine. Thou dost close the door upon us suddenly and open another door that we did not know to be in existence; thou takest away from us our staff and thou puttest into our hand a still stronger one. We cannot tell what thou doest. Thou sendest winter in the midst of summer, and a glow of heavenly light amid the clouds that darken the heavens. Thy will be done evermore. As for our sin, if it is not always present to us, it is always in our heart, a reckoning to be settled, a guilt to be pardoned; but if the sin is there, behold, the Cross of Christ is still within the vision of our faith, and the blood of Jesus Christ thy Son cleanseth from all sin. We will not fall into despair: we will not turn our imagination into the plague of our life; but looking to the heavens and to thy revelation in the Holy Book and to the Cross of our Lord Jesus Christ, even in the deep pit we will take heart again and our hope shall be strong in God. Let a morning light be in our hearts; let a gracious blessing make us glad; may the Spirit of the Living One destroy all death within us and make us now joyous and rich with the assurance of immortality. Amen.

Numbers xxii.-xxiv.

BALAAM'S MANŒUVRES.

BALAAM'S was a manœuvring life: very truthful, and yet very false; very godly, and yet very worldly;—a most composite and self-contradictory life; still a most human life.

Balaam never breaks away from the brotherhood of the race in any of his inconsistencies. When he is very good, there are men living to-day who are just as good as Balaam was; when he is very bad, it would not be difficult to confront him with men who are quite his equals in wrong-doing ; when he is both good and bad almost at the same moment, he does not separate himself from the common experience of the race. He was always arranging, adjusting, endeavouring to meet one thing by another, and to set off one thing over against another. It was a kind of gamester-life—full of subtle calculation, touched with a sort of wonder which becomes almost religious, and steeped in a superstition which reduces many of the actions of life to a state of moral mystery wholly beyond ordinary human comprehension.

In the first instance, he poses as a very pious man. So we read : " And Balaam said unto Balak, Lo, I am come unto thee: have I now any power at all to say any thing ? the word that God putteth in my mouth, that shall I speak " (xxii. 38). We may take these words as equivalent to saying,—I am a very pious man ; nothing in myself, wholly destitute of intellectual vigour and brightness, and laying no pretension to any conspicuous altitude of a personal kind ; I am simply an instrument : I am a mere machine ; thou hast sent for me, but in sending for me thou hast but brought to thy side a trumpet through which God must deliver his own message. There was self-consciousness about his piety : he knew that he was a most religious man. We may be too well acquainted with our own religiousness ; it may form quite a large object on which our vision is fixed in a kind of trance and adoration. Were we more pious, we should be less conscious of our piety. When we really pray, with all the fulness of divine inspiration, keeping strictly to our necessity, and yet allowing the soul full play as to spiritual communion with God, when the exercise is closed we cannot tell what we have said in mere words : our speech will run to this effect,— Whether in the body or out of the body, I cannot tell ; I saw things without shape, I heard voices without articulation, I felt upon me the ministry of light ; and as to all the influence exerted upon my soul, that must report itself in the nobleness and beneficence of my life. Self-conscious piety is often impious.

We should know more about Christ and less about ourselves. Yet in any endeavour to avoid self-consciousness, we certainly fall into it. Self-consciousness is not to be escaped by effort, as directed against itself: it is only to be absolutely escaped by growing in grace and in the knowledge of our Lord Jesus Christ, and by such enlargement of faith and multiplication of religious resources as shall cause us to be more occupied with divine things than with our own immediate and measurable relation to them. When we are filled with God, we shall be emptied of ourselves. But let no man judge his brother herein. Some are too keen in finding in others self-regard, self-conceit, and self-consciousness; and refinement vulgarises itself when it fixes upon the vulgarity of other people.

Then Balaam represented, consistently with this first view of his character, a most ostentatious religion. Having come to the field of action, he begins demonstratively. He would have everything done upon an ample scale. The Oriental mind itself shall be satisfied with the gorgeousness of the theatre within which the little magic is to be wrought. So, in the opening of chapter xxiii., we read,—"And Balaam said unto Balak, Build me here seven altars, and prepare me here seven oxen and seven rams." Balak did as Balaam had spoken; Balak and Balaam offered on every altar a bullock and a ram. In the same chapter we read,—"And he brought him into the field of Zophim, to the top of Pisgah, and built seven altars, and offered a bullock and a ram on every altar" (v. 14). Again, we read : "And Balaam said unto Balak, Build me here seven altars, and prepare me here seven bullocks and seven rams" (v. 29). There was to be no mistake about the preparation. The scaffolding was to portend a magnificent erection. All this lay at an immeasurable distance from the divine purpose and the divine simplicity. This was conjuring : these were the little tricks of a well-paid priest; these were accommodations to the Pagan mind. When we leave simplicity, we leave power. When we build after the fashion of earthly architecture, we forget that the true Builder is God, who builds invisibly but builds for eternity. The prophecy which we are called upon to represent to the age is not a prophecy of demonstration, or show, or spectacle. Balaam wandered from the first principles with which

God had charged his soul. Nothing was said in the original instructions about building altars and slaying bullocks and rams. Word was given to Balaam, but instead of thundering that word at the very first and never changing it and repeating it until it deafened the very men who heard it, because of its resonance and majesty, Balaam betook himself to altar-building and to the keeping of perfect numbers—to the insistance of seven, so that everything might be complete in an outward and mechanical way. Balaam should have made shorter work of it. He had a message to deliver, and the message seemed to be kept back until all the pomp and demonstration had played its little part before the astonished gaze of the king and princes of Moab. That very same thing may be done now. It is possible now to put the Gospel last, and to leave it but small space for its expression. We may elbow out the message by doing things which are but introductory at best, and some of which were never prescribed by directing Heaven. What we want is the message, the great speech, the mighty judgment, the holy revelation. What does God say ? What does the Lord require of us ? To that inquiry there should be instantaneous, emphatic, and persuasive reply.

Still, consistently with the first and second positions thus discovered in his character, we find upon further inquiry that Balaam displays a highly poetical and sentimental religion. Six times we read the words,—"And he took up his parable." He spake like an oracle. The parables are marked by nobleness of thought, grandeur and massiveness of expression. There is genuine poetry in the utterances of Balaam ; but, so far, the religion which Balaam represents is of a poetic and sentimental and histrionic character. The age needs more than parable. We may be so poetical as to convey a wrong impression as to the message we have to deliver. Poetry has its place. Parable was an instrument well-worked by the divine hand of Jesus Christ himself ; but the moral purpose of the parable was never hidden : the meaning of the message was vividly written upon its whole face. The age wants direct speech. There is a kind of poetry that is harmless : it is delightful to the ear, it flows through the organ of hearing and leaves no impress behind ; those who hear it say—How lovely! how beautiful ! how exceedingly pathetic !—but the whole impression is only for a moment, and never goes in the direction of rousing men to action, to sacrifice, to complete and costly obedience. Balak did not want all these altars and all these parables,—why does Balaam resort to them? Because he did not accept and realise the policy of God. A clear policy would have rendered all altars and parables unnecessary. We should have fewer apologies for our Christian service if we had a distincter conviction of its divine inspiration and absolute human necessity. Why try to decorate our message of judgment? Why these vain endeavours to paint the commandments of God? If we begin to decorate and adorn and garnish and parabolise, so as to miss the point, let us take care lest all this persiflage be so much reckoned against us in the final judgment. The altars were many, the parables were grand, the courtesy, as between prophet and king, was a courtesy perfect in dignity and in grace; but where is the message? It may be right to fold the sword in velvet, but let us beware lest we so enclose the sword in velvet, as practically to deprive it of edge. Beauty we will never exclude, parable we must always welcome as highly illustrative of the truth : we can never forget that parable has been used for the representation of the kingdom of God; but let us, at the same time, beware lest the beauty of the parable should conceal the righteousness of the kingdom, and the splendour and exquisiteness of the decoration should hide in fatal darkness the tremendous Cross of Christ. Balaam was not sent forth to make poems for the Moabites : he was sent forth with one clear errand, and that he ought to have delivered instantly, and not have resorted to conjuring tricks, and to the small devices of a calculating magician.

Balaam represents but too vividly those who build many altars but build no character. How possible it is to be always *near* the Church without being really in it ! How possible it is to preach *about* the Gospel without preaching it ! This is the infinite danger of all spiritual service. We may be so wearied by things external and visible as to suppose we have rendered the sacrifice, when we have only kindled the coals. The altar is not built for coal-burning but for man-burning. The fire of coals is merely an instrument—part of a process,—but the leaping flame

is an impious irony, if it be left to burn itself out without consuming the human will and the human self-idolatry. It would
be easy to say, watching Balaam in all his course,—How particular he is to build altars!—he will insist upon the perfect
number; truly, he is a most exact and religious man in all his
appointments; even the number must be right, and the beasts
must be fit for sacrifice. It is easy to be mechanically right.
There is no drain upon a man's life in getting out programmes of
service and outlines of effort. It is easy to build the altar and to
run away from it; it is not difficult to build an altar and burn a
beast upon it. The difficulty is to go to God's altar—an altar
built by God's hands, burning with God's fire, and to lie down
upon it with the grace of absolute self-surrender.

Is Balaam far from any one of us in the peculiarity of his
character which displayed itself in keeping up an open correspondence with heathen persons? He never quite closed the
correspondence : even when he refused to go he would have the
way open for renewed communications. He might have sent
a message to which Balak dare not have replied; but he did not.
He would rather seem to have said,—Who knows what may
come of this ?—we had better not foreclose all communication;
in the meantime, I must stand upon my dignity as a wizard or
prophet : I must send a message indicating that my services are
not to be cheaply or easily engaged; I will say clearly that God
will not permit me to go, but I can so say it as to suggest the
idea that perhaps even God's commandment may be trimmed and
modified; we never can tell what may occur : I will, therefore,
give such an answer as will not shut up the correspondence. Is
that ancient history? Are not men in precisely that position
to-day, in relation to many old associations or tempting opportunities or half-abandoned habits? They know the right, but
they cannot speak it with a final emphasis. They are not
untruthful, nor are they unfaithful in a degree which involves
final apostasy or which ought to be visited by minor excommunication on the part of the Church; still they are in a mood
which, being expressed in words, signifies that even yet something may come from the Moabite quarter that may be turned
to account,—it will be better, therefore, not to repel with too
severe an answer; let the appeal be renewed, or come under

some modified form, and then we will see what can be done. Such action is what we have termed a manœuvre—a work of the hand, a clever manipulation; it is not righteous in its soul; the fire may have singed the outside and given a kind of sacrificial colouring to the man, but it has not burned the inner core and wrought in the soul the miracle of burning out the evil spirit. It is possible to be on the right side hesitantly. It is easy to be so far committed to the Church as to be able on occasions to shake off the connection and " deny the soft impeachment." We are prone to say, when the answer will suit the company,—We often attend the church; we are pleased to be there; attendance upon the service is a season of refreshment and edification. And when it will suit the company we can modify that assertion : we can represent ourselves as being occasionally there, and as having had our wonder partially excited concerning the service; and we can talk truth and tell lies; we can stand back in a manner which, though not chargeable with visible apostasy, means, in the soul of it, treachery towards God. We have nothing to do with Moab; Christ has no companionship with Belial; light never enters into partnership with darkness. "Ye cannot serve God and Mammon."

Balaam is as one of us when we regard him as not clearly perceiving the motive by which he is actually impelled. Our motives are not always clear to our own minds; or we can so trifle with the motive as to vary its expression and modify its claim and suppress its inspiration. We lose sight of the motive in the operation of secondary causes, and these secondary causes we endeavour so to manipulate as to represent the real purpose of life. There are a thousand ways of lying; even falsehood may be turned into a fine art. Balaam did not perhaps fully know his own mind in this matter; and sometimes we have to be revealed to ourselves by others; and the apostolic pen was inspired to write the real motive which urged Balaam forward in his remarkable career. In one suggestive sentence we have the explanation. Balaam is described in the New Testament as a man who "loved the wages of unrighteousness." He did not know it. It does not become us to charge him with this perfidy in any broad and vulgar sense. Balaam was not a bad man through and through; he was marked by many noble features;

there comes out again and again in his whole speech a distinct
and valiant courage ;—but he "loved the wages of unrighteousness." He did not altogether long for them, yet he did not resist
the bribe; he wanted to be good, but he heard the chink of
Balak's gold; he loved preaching, he was a born preacher—but
a spark, and his soul flamed into poetry and noble rhetoric—but
he heard of promotion and honour and dignity, and what
amounted almost to the kingship of Moab : for Balak said,—All
that thou biddest me do, I will do. It was a fierce temptation ;
it was a terrific agony. To stand beside a king, to move the
springs of the royal mind, to dictate imperial policies, to curse
invaders and repel encroachments, to have gold as the dust of
the ground and honours like showers of rain, and to stand there
firm, impeccable, resistant to every appeal—to be in a far off
country without a friend, and yet to be as good as we might now
be in our own blessed homes—who could expect it ? When we
condemn Balaam, we condemn human nature ; when we praise
any feature in his character, we praise the grace that wrought
that mystery in his soul.

PRAYER.

ALMIGHTY GOD, thy Church thou hast redeemed with blood. Thou wilt keep thy Church in eternal security. The foundation of the Lord standeth sure, having this seal,—The Lord knoweth them that are his. We can hide nothing from thee. The smallest of thy children is still thine. They shall be mine in that day when I number up my jewels, saith the Lord. Thou dost not lose any jewel. God cannot lose anything. Hold thou us up, and we shall be safe. Show us that we may lose ourselves : that if we are sons of perdition we are sons of waste, and even Christ's wounded hand cannot save us from ruin. Establish us in the confidence of thy Fatherhood ; and may we not live in it as in a doctrine only, but exhibit it in daily trust, in noble spiritual sacrifice, in continual and beneficent industry. Thus shall the Lord's seal be confirmed by our loyalty, and no man shall curse what God the Lord hath blessed. We stand in thy blessing : thy benediction is our heaven, thy smile our perpetual light. This is our joy ; and this holy confidence brings amongst us the shout of a king, so that all thy princes are greater than Agag, and the smallest of thy children is more than the kings of the earth. Fill us with holy delight ; drive away all temptation and evil importunity, and extinguish every baleful fire ; let our bodies be the temples of the Holy Ghost ; may our souls be inspired, and our whole hearts know the mystery and the joy of sacrifice. Thou regardest us according to our need. Thou art twice Father to some. Thou art the God and Father of our Lord Jesus Christ, and to us who are in Christ thou art Father ; but to those who have no father on earth and are yet children redeemed thou art Father upon Father : thy Fatherliness rises into the passion and mystery of love. This is our confidence and our delight and our sure hope. The Lord regard those who are in peculiar circumstances of loneliness, or pain, or fear, or weakness; spread the table of poverty, and make the one loaf into many; draw water for those who are thirsty, and may it be unto them as the wine of heaven; make the bed of affliction, soften the pillow of pain ; send into the hearts of the people a spirit of love and generosity and beneficence ; and may we know that life is only noble as it gives, and lives in others, and delights in spreading sunshine and joy. Let the Book of the Lord be a flame of fire in the night-time and a pillar of cloud in the day season ; in our right hand may there be a rod, in our left hand a staff. Thy rod and thy staff shall comfort us, and the valley of the shadow of death shall have in it no evil or darkness because of the Lord's presence. Help us to sing again loudly, sweetly, lovingly ; and whilst we tarry in God's house, may we feel the nearness of the Lord's hand. Amen.

Numbers xxii.-xxiv.

BALAAM'S VISION OF THE CHURCH.

LET Israel, as gathered within sight of Moab, be regarded as representing the Church of the living God : let Balak, king of Moab, be regarded as representing all the forces which encounter the Church of the living God with suspicion or hostility : let Balaam be regarded as the prophet of the Lord standing between the Church and the kingdoms of heathenism, and declaring the divine purpose, and dwelling in sacred and rapturous eloquence upon the condition, the forces, and the destiny, of the Church of Christ. Such are the conditions which are now before us :—Israel the Church, Balak heathenism and every manner of hostility, Balaam the voice of Heaven, the prophet of God. Such being the picture, what are the doctrines which underlie it and breathe through it and appeal to our confidence and imagination ?

First of all, the Church is represented as being "blessed." We read,—"And God said unto Balaam, Thou shalt not go with them ; thou shalt not curse the people : for they are blessed " (xxii. 12). To repeat that word is best to explain it. Some words refuse to pass into other terms, for they are themselves their best expositors ;—*blessed* is one of those words. We are not taught that Israel was in a state of momentary enjoyment—passing through some transient experience of gladness ; but Israel is represented as sealed with a divine benediction : Israel is blessed—not merely to be blessed, or reserved for blessing ; but through eternity is blessed—set in sureness in the divine covenant, created and made a people by the divine knowledge and purpose and love. Here is no small contention as between momentary complacency and momentary hostility : we are in the eternal region, we are standing amid the august certainties of divine purpose, recognition and determination. The Church is, therefore, blessed—sealed, gathered around the Lord, set in his sight,—an inheritance, a possession, a sanctuary. That the Church does not rise to the glory of its election according to the divine purpose has no bearing whatever upon the argument. All things are in process ; nothing is yet finished. Is it a temple ?—the walls are being

put up. Is it a tree ?—the tree is yet in process of growing, and
we know nothing yet of its magnitude or its fruitfulness. Is it
a character?—time is required, and we must read destiny—not
in immediate appearances, but in the divine decree and in the
inspired revelation. A man is not in reality what he appears to
be at any given moment : man is as to possibility what he is in
the divine thought. Until we have seen that thought in clearest
realisation, it little becomes us to sneer at the meanest specimen
of human nature, or to mock the handiwork of God. Let this
stand : that there is a family, a Church, an institution—describe
it by any name—which is "blessed ";—in other words, there
is a spot on the earth on which the divine complacency rests
like a Sabbath-light; we may well consider our relation to that
place ; it would not be unbecoming even the dignity of reason to
ask what its own relation is to that sacred and ever-blessed
position.

This being the case, the negative seems to become the positive
when we read that the Church of the living God is beyond the
power of human cursing. Said Balaam,—" How shall I curse,
whom God hath not cursed ? " That is a great principle.
Balaam might use the words of cursing, but there would be no
anathema in his impotent speech. The curse of man cannot get
within the sanctuary of God. The Church is hidden within the
pavilion of the Most High : the Church is beyond " the strife of
tongues " : the curses are all outside noises—like the wings of
night-birds beating against the eternal granite. " No weapon
that is formed against thee shall prosper";—the weapon shall
be formed, the weapon shall be lifted up, the weapon shall
apparently come down ; but it shall miss thee, and cut nothing
but the vacant air. Unless we have some such confidence as
this, we shall be the sport of every rumour, exposed to every
wild alarm, without peace : in the whole week there will be no
Sabbath day, after the day's tumult there will be no time of
repose : the house will be open to the encroachment of every
evil. We must, therefore, stand in great principles, and take
refuge in the sanctuary of divine and revealed appointments.
You cannot injure the really good man : you may throw many
stones at him, but you will never strike him ; much speech may
be levelled against him, but the speech will be without point. A

good man is the Lord's jewel; a soul in harmony with the
Christian purpose is a soul hidden in the security of God's
almightiness. That we do not realise this is to our shame and
not to the discredit of the inspired testimony. When a Christian
is in alarm, he is doing more injury to the Christian cause than
can be done by any outside assailants; when the good man
interrupts his prayer by some expression of fear or doubt, he is
doing more to invalidate every argument for the sufficiency of
prayer than can be done by the most penetrating intellectual
criticism or by the most audacious unbelief. Our religion is
nothing if it does not make us feel our security and turn that
security into a temple of living and daily praise. It still lies,
therefore, with the believer to injure his cause, to bring discredit
upon God's temple, and to expose the Eternal Father to human
suspicion. Let us beware of this, lest the enemies of God should
be found in his own household.

Is there not something in the condition of the Church that
might excite—shall we call it ?—the envy—the religious envy of
the world ? Read chapter xxiii. 10 :—" Who can count the dust
of Jacob, and the number of the fourth part of Israel ? " The
Church grows upon the attentive vision ; at first it does not seem
to be what it really is, but as the prophet looks the little one
becomes a thousand and the small nation becomes a great
empire, and those who were of little account from a physical
point of view rise into immeasurable proportions of force and
possibilities of service. The Church is—let us repeat—what God
sees it to be : God sees it to be the power of the world, the light
to illuminate it, the salt to preserve it, the city to be as a beacon
in relation to it. The Lord has said that the Church shall overcome all opposition. The time in which it is about to do this is,
by our reckoning, very long—so long, that our poor patience
almost expires and our faith sharpens itself into an almost
doubtful inquiry, saying,—O Lord ! how long ?—the wicked
are robust, evil-minded men are many in number, and virtue
seems to be cast out upon the street and to be exposed to a very
precarious fortune—O Lord ! how long? It is a natural question,
full of reasonableness from a merely human point of view, and
it never can be suppressed except by that increase cf faith which
makes our life superior to the death-principle that is in us—that

fills us with a sense of already-realised immortality. Balaam saw Israel to be an innumerable host. Numbers played a great part in the imagination of the Eastern mind, and the Lord, touching the imagination of Balak along the only accessible lines, makes Balaam speak about the great host. Why, the dust of it could not be counted; no reckoning could sum up the fourth part of Israel; and as the numbers increased and came down in threatening countless multitudes upon the imagination of Balak, he was staggered by the vision of the majesty of Israel. That is the view we must take of the case. Let God number his Church. He teaches us by all these allusions that numbering is impossible on our part. We do but vex ourselves by taking the statistics of the Church : only God can take them, and he so represents them as to dazzle the imagination—to throw our power of reckoning into absolute despair. From the beginning, he spoke thus about numbers : he would never entrust us with the exact numerical secret ; when he told one man how many children he should have, he said,—More than the stars, more than the sands upon the sea-shore,—innumerable. God's arithmetic is not a pronounceable quantity ; it touches the imagination and excites the wonder, until imagination and wonder consent in their intellectual impotence to fall down like white-robed worshippers and say,— Thine is the kingdom and the power and the glory, thou Father in heaven!

According to Balaam, the Church is named in an unchangeable decree : " God is not a man, that he should lie ; neither the son of man, that he should repent : hath he said, and shall he not do it ? or hath he spoken, and shall he not make it good ? " (xxiii. 19). This is not a God that can be changed by temptation or whose decrees can be varied by circumstances. We do not surprise him by our sin. He does not alter the will because the younger son has gone away contrary to his expectation : when he made the will he foresaw the apostasy. There is nothing omitted from the divine reckoning. He saw the sin before he called me his child ; he knew every time the arm of rebellion would be lifted and every time the voice of unbelief would challenge the integrity of his promises. The will overrides all these things : the Testator foresaw them, and

the covenant was made in view of them. Herein is comfort,
but not licence; herein is a great security, but no permission
to tempt the living God. The view which the divine eye took
of the whole situation was a complete view; reckoning up
all sides, all forces, all possibilities and issues, the decree went
forth, that out of this human nature, come whence it may—
straight from God's hands, in one form or the other, it must
have come—this human nature shall be the temple of the living
God, and out of those human eyes shall gleam the fire of divinity.
If we believed anything short of this, our testimony would not
be worth delivering—at best, it would be but a happy conjecture,
or a fanciful possibility, wanting in lines of solidity, and in
characteristics of certainty—wanting in the absoluteness which
alone can give a steadiness of position to the human will and
the destiny of the human career. Were all these covenants,
arrangements and promises open to mere criticism of a verbal
kind, we should have no inheritance—we should be but beggars
to the last, living upon appearances and exhausting the unsub-
stantial fortune of illusory hopes; but our Christian position is,
—God is unchangeable, the covenant is unalterable, the good
man is the accepted of God, and the almightiness of God is
pledged to see the good man through river, sea, wilderness,
and the battle, being God's, can only end in one way.

According to Balaam's vision of the Church, Israel is guiltless
and royal. This is proved by chapter xxiii. 21 :—"He hath not
beheld iniquity in Jacob, neither hath he seen perverseness in
Israel : the Lord his God is with him, and the shout of a king is
among them."

Herein is the mystery of love. Already we begin to see the
meaning of the marvellous expression—"Where sin abounded,
grace did much more abound." "He hath not beheld iniquity
in Jacob, neither hath he seen perverseness in Israel "—whilst,
from the human point of view, he has never seen anything else.
The whole history up to this point has been on the part of Israel
or Jacob a disclosure of meanness, selfishness, complaining,
perfidy, and perverseness. Both the statements are perfectly
true. They may not be open to the cheap reconciliation of mere
verbal adjustment, but they are strictly in harmony with the

great central line which unites and consolidates the universe. God does not judge in great and final senses by the detailed slips, losses, mistakes, misadventures, follies, and sins of his people ;— what a life would be God's eternity could it be vexed by these details ! We are lacking in the divine charity which sees the " man " within the " sinner "—which sees behind the iniquity the divine seed. We are lacking in the divine benevolence which distinguishes between the action of the hand—which sometimes does not express the motion of the will—and the inward and set purpose of the sanctified soul. We count ourselves clever if we can trip one another up in discrepancies of speech, in small or great shortcomings,—if we can but record a heavy score against some brother, as to a lapse here and a mistake there, and some evil deed yonder. God does not measure the man or Church according to that standard and method : he sees the purpose, he reads the soul, and he sees that nowhere is there a redder blush of shame for anything evil which the hand has done than in the soul of the man who has been convicted as the trespasser. So there are two views to be taken of the Church—the small view, the magisterial criticism, the estimate which is formed by the ingenuity that is most successful in fault-finding ; or the view which is taken by God's purpose, by divine charity, by eternal election and decree. God's purpose is to have the uttermost parts of the earth for an inheritance and a possession ; and already the earth may be called his :—" The earth is the Lord's, and the fulness thereof "—not looked at here and now and within given lines—so looked at it is the devil's earth, it is ripped and seamed by ten thousand times ten thousand graves ;—little children's bones are rotting in it, bad men are building their thrones and palaces upon it. The devil's hunting-ground is this earth within a narrow or limited point of view ; but in the divine purpose, in the great outcome of things, this earth is verdant as the upper paradise, pure as spotless snow,— a sanctuary of the Lord ; all lands and languages, all seas, all thrones, all powers, are baptized in the Triune Name, and the whole earth is a worthy annexe of God's own heaven. Take any other view, and you become at once unsettled, unsteady, depleted of all enrichment arising from confidence and hope and promise. This is the true view, for it is the view given in the Scriptnres of God.

Balaam recognises the operation of a miracle in all this. He describes Israel as a supreme miracle of God. He says,— ". . . according to this time it shall be said of Jacob and of Israel, What hath God wrought!" (xxiii. 23). Thus the Church becomes the uppermost miracle. From the first it did not seem such workmanship was possible : the material was rough, the conditions were impracticable,—everything seemed to be as different as possible from the grace and purpose of Heaven; but years passed on, and the generations and the ages, and still the mighty Worker continued with patient love to carry forward his purpose, and already chaos seems to be taking shape, already some notes harmonious are heard through all the harsh discord, already there is the outlining of a horizon radiant with the silver of rising day, already God seems to be subduing, overruling, controlling, and establishing things; and looking further on the prophet says,—" According to this time it shall be said of Jacob and of Israel, What hath God wrought!"—how wondrous the transformation; how sublime the moral majesty; how gracious the complete deliverance! That, again, is our standing ground. "Not by might, nor by power, but by my Spirit, saith the Lord." It is not within our little ability to establish the divine kingdom upon the earth ; but God will bring in an everlasting kingdom : he " will overturn, overturn, overturn, . . . until he come whose right it is." So we wait on in patience—patience often sorely troubled, patience that is vexed by many a question from the hostile side : men say,—" Where is the promise of his coming? for since the fathers fell asleep, all things continue as they were from the beginning of the creation "—not seeing the invisible Hand, not having that sharp vision which perceives the rectification of lines so fibrous and so delicate, not knowing that God's transformation is being worked from the interior; that it is not a case of external painting but a case of spiritual regeneration, and according to the majesty of the subject within whose life this mystery is to be accomplished is the time which even God requires for the outworking and consummation of his miracle.

Then Balaam paints a picture—such a picture as would appeal to the Eastern imagination. He compares Jacob and Israel to the most beautiful of all spectacles ; he says,—" How goodly are thy tents, O Jacob, and thy tabernacles, O Israel! As the valleys

are they spread forth, as gardens by the river's side, as the trees
of lign aloes which the Lord hath planted, and as cedar trees
beside the waters.   He shall pour the water out of his buckets,
and his seed shall be in many waters, and his king shall be
higher than Agag, and his kingdom shall be exalted" (xxiv. 5-7).
Why speak so much about streams and rivers and waters?—
because nothing appealed so vividly to the Oriental imagination.
To have plenty of water was to be rich in the days of Balaam
and in the country of Balak.   So Balaam, taught by the Lord to
speak the music of truth and of heaven, speaks of Jacob and
Israel as being "valleys" where the water rolled, "as gardens
by the river's side, as the trees of lign aloes . . . and as cedar
trees beside the waters."   In other parts of the Old Testament
those same cedar trees are spoken of with the rapture of poetry:
—they put out their dark roots towards the river, they suck up
the streams, and they report the success of the root in the far-
spreading branches which seem to have lifted themselves up to
the very clouds of heaven.   Every country has its own standards
of success, its own signs of prosperity, its own symbols which
most vividly appeal to the imagination of the inhabitants; and
water constituted the great object of admiration and of thankfulness in the Eastern mind.   And then the King that was
coming was to be "higher than Agag" (ver. 7).   The word
"Agag" means "high"; the word "Agag" is the name of the
Amalekite kings, as "Pharaoh" was the name of the kings of
Egypt, and "Abimelech" the name of the kings of the Philistines ;
so Agag is not any one personal king but the *you* or *I* of the
Amalekite nation ; and when Balak and his hosts looked upon
their mighty Agag, Balaam said,—He is a child compared with
the coming King—a mere infant of days compared with the
crowned One of Jacob ; when He comes whose right it is to
reign, all other kings and princes will acknowledge his right,
and fall down before him, and pay their crowns as tribute to his
majesty.

    This, then, is the position of the Church of Christ.   We believe
a great future is in store for the Church.   Were we to look at
the Church within given lines, we should say,—Great is its
poverty, very questionable its intellectual stand-point; a very
troubled community is the Church—vexing itself by divers

theologies and conceptions and theories and speculations. But
we must not look at the question in that way. Call for the
Lord's prophet : let " the man whose eyes are open " be called
to stand on the hills of Moab, and his speech will be :—

> " Jesus shall reign where'er the sun
> Doth his successive journeys run;
> His kingdom stretch from shore to shore,
> Till moons shall wax and wane no more."
>
> " Kings shall fall down before him,
> And gold and incense bring;
> All nations shall adore him,
> His praise all people sing " :—

they shall come from the east and from the west, and from the
north and from the south, to increase the hosts of the divine
army. He shall have the heathen for an inheritance and the
uttermost parts of the earth for a possession ; he shall rule the
enemy with a rod of iron. This shall be the end. He shall
reign till all enemies are put under his feet; and the whole
universe, complete in its intermediate education, shall shout
in thunder-psalm : HALLELUJAH ! HALLELUJAH ! the Lord God
Omnipotent reigneth ! It is in that forecast we work ; left to
ourselves, we should give up the battle to-day, saying,—The
enemy is too many for us ; but a Voice says,—The battle is
not yours, but God's; then we reply,—They that are for us
are more than them that be against us.

PRAYER.

ALMIGHTY GOD, the way to thee is a broad way. We may come boldly to a throne of grace. The access which thy Son has wrought out for us is a great access. We will approach thee by the way which he has marked out. So we advance without fear, and can even venture to lift up our eyes unto heaven. At the very moment when we smite upon our breast, we have confidence in God, through our Lord Jesus Christ. We think we could now bear to look upon the shaded glory of the Lord of hosts. We have been with Jesus, and have learned of him. At first we were afraid of the great fire, saying, Behold, it burns like an oven, and is hot as the wrath of justice. But now we know thee. God is love. Thou dost wait to be gracious, thou dost live for thy creation. We feel as if thou thyself wert praying for us in the very act of answering our petition. Thou dost make our prayer for us ; it is the inditing of thy Holy Spirit in the heart. It is a speech we never invented, but which we receive and adopt as the good gift of God, relieving our heart as it does of the pressure of its pain and expressing happily all the desire of its necessity. Thou dost teach us how to pray. Thou wouldest have us praying always and never faint. Help us, then, to pray without ceasing, as we live without ceasing. We live whilst we sleep, we live in our unconsciousness ; the life still keeps beating on ready for the morning of expectation and service and sacrifice. So may we pray in our very unconsciousness—yea, when we do not know we are praying in form and in set petition. May our life so acquire the sacred habit of the upward look and the heavenly expectation that without a word we may mightily cry unto the Father-Heart. We bless thee that we have experience of this kind. We are ashamed of our words : they are wings that cannot fly far ; our souls must of themselves, in all the speechlessness of enraptured love, seek thee, find thee, and hold long and sweet communion with thee. We would live and move and have our being in God. This prayer thou dost never deny. Thou dost keep wealth from us, and prosperity, and renown, and riches, and honour, and ease ; these things thou dost drive away with a sharp wind ; but never didst thou say No to the soul that longed to be purer, to the heart that desired to be cleansed. May we find great answers to our petitions. They are addressed to thee in the appointed way, they are sealed with the name of Christ ; every syllable is sprinkled with the blood of reconciliation ; we say nothing out of our own name, or because of our own invention ; we speak the Lord's prayer in the Lord's name, and we are sure of the Lord's answer. We cannot tell thee what thou dost not know ; yet thou dost love to hear us talk ; thou delightest in the speech of man ; there is something in it which we ourselves cannot hear ; thou art carried back to thine own eternity. Even in our poor attempts to speak thou hearest a music which no other ear can detect in the utterances of man.   What is that music ?   Is it a cry of pain ?   Is it the note of a voice of one who is lost in a wild night and cannot tell the east from the west, or where the sweet home lies warm with hospitable welcomes ?   Thou knowest there is divinity in it—a strange pulsing of the eternal music.   When we speak thus to thee, in the name of Jesus, our music becomes a mighty prayer, and thine answer encompasses the heavens like a cloud too rich with blessing for the very heavens to contain.   Lead us on.   We do not know where the grave is, nor do we care.   It may be one foot off, or many a mile away, hidden among the years that are yet to be numbered by tens and twenties.   Whether it is already dug, or is not to be dug for many a day, what care we ?   Being in Christ we cannot die ; rooted in the Life Eternal, death can but touch the outer frame.   We ourselves are already in heaven.   Amen.

Numbers xxvi.

DIVINE ENUMERATION.

IN the second verse we read,—" Take the sum of all the congregation of the children of Israel."   We have had that instruction before.   God is a God of numbers.   He numbereth the stars ; and as for those who hold sweet counsel together respecting him and his kingdom, he says,—" They shall be mine in that day when I make up my jewels."   " The very hairs of your head are all numbered "—not counted only, but singled out as if each particular hair bore its own number.   Whatever will assist the imagination in the direction of recognising the exquisiteness and minuteness of the divine care may be employed in this service of exposition.   As we said when the census was first taken, God could have numbered the people himself, but instead of undertaking the work himself he appointed others to carry out his purpose.   God is always numbering.   He may number to find out who are present, but in numbering to find out who are present he soon comes to know who are absent. He knows the total number, but it is not enough for him to know the totality : he must know whether David's place is empty, whether the younger son has gone from the father's house, whether one piece of silver out of ten has been lost, whether one sheep out of a hundred has gone astray.   We are all of consequence to the Father, because he does not look upon us through the glory of his majesty but through the solicitude of his fatherhood and his love.   Take heed that ye despise not one of these little ones; it were better for a man that a millstone were hanged about his neck, and that he were drowned in the depths of the sea, than that he should offend—wound the heart of—one of these little ones. So, everywhere we find God concerning himself with individuals, with single families, with solitary lives,—stooping in marvellous condescension, sweeping the house diligently until he find the one piece that was lost. We need this kind of thought in human life : living would be weary work without it. If we do not need the thought every day in the week, we need it twice over some days, and so we make up the average of necessity. The earth needs the sky. Even in the larger world of thought, history, science, it is not enough to have mere facts, measurable as to their magnitude and numerable as to their succession. Even literature has its poetry, its fiction, —its noble imagination. There is a great philosophy in all this. The human heart will not be caged within small bars ; if it must be caged, it will be bounded only by the infinity of God. So the hardest mind has its religion ; it calls that religion " poetry," " imagination," " fiction " ; but it has its larger world. This same thought runs through all time, all life. Even the day has its night of dreams. So, we need the comforting thought that God looks after us, numbers us, and makes a register in which the meanest name is written down with palpable and infinite care.

This chapter reads very much like the other chapter in which the census was first taken. The same great and noble names recur. Who could distinguish between the first chapter of Numbers and the twenty-sixth if they were read in imme-diate succession ? Who would not declare that the chapters are identical ? Yet they are not the same. The vision that mistakes them as being identical is a clouded eye; the ear that thinks it hears the same music in the enumera-tion of the names is an ear not trained to the discrimination of the finer sound : it is a rough ear—a mere highway of sound, not critical, watching, balancing and understanding the minuter tones and the tones that are subdued and so finely-coloured as to seem to be without flush of light. So roughly do we read the Bible, that we imagine that every chapter is like every other chapter. We do not number after God's critical method, but

after some rude and coarse way of our own, by which we miss
all finest lines, all tenderest suggestion of life and mystic presence.
But are there not many names just the same? Yes, the generic
names are the same. Still we read, even in the twenty-sixth
chapter of Numbers, of Reuben and Simeon, of Judah and
Issachar, of Zebulun and Joseph, of Manasseh and Ephraim, of
Benjamin and Dan, and Asher and Naphtali. The historic names
are the same, but what a going-down in the detail! We must
enter into this thought and follow its applications if we would be
wise in history: generic names are permanent, but the detail of
life is a panorama continually changing. It is so always and
everywhere. The world has its great generic and permanent
names, and it is not enough to know these and to recite them
with thoughtless fluency. Who could not take the statistics of
the world in general names? Then we should have the wise and
the foolish, the rich and the poor, the faithful and the faithless,
the good and the bad. That has been the record of life from
the beginning; and yet that is too broadly-lined to be of any
real service to us in the estimate of human prayers and human
moral quality. What about the detailed numbers, the individual
men, the particular households, the children in the crowd? It
was in these under-lines that the great changes took place. The
bold, leading names remained the same, but they stood up like
monumental stones over graves in which thousands of men had
been buried. So with regard to our own actions: we speak
of them too frequently with generic vagueness: we are wanting
in the persistent criticism that will never allow two threads of
life to be intertangled, that must have them separated and
specifically examined. God will have no roughness of judgment,
no bold vagueness, no mere striking of averages; but heart-
searching, weighing—not the action: any manufactured scales
might weigh a deed. He will have the motive weighed, the
invisible force, the subtle, ghostly movement that stirs the soul;
not to be found out by human wisdom, but to be seized, detected,
examined, estimated, and determined by the living Spirit of the
living God. That is how a man's actions, motives, and whole
inner life must be weighed and estimated.

The sin of the individual does not destroy the election of the
race. Israel is still here, but almost countless thousands of

Israelites have sinned and gone to their doom. With all this individual criticism and specific numbering, do not imagine that it lies within the power of any man to stop the purpose or arrest the kingdom of God. There is a consolatory view of all human tumult and change, as well as a view that tries the faith and exhausts the patience of the saint. Balaam could not curse Israel, but Israel cursed himself. That is always so. No man outside of us can do us any permanent harm, though his tongue be set on fire of hell and he have the wit of Beelzebub in the invention of evil and malignant accusations. Balaam brought Israel to curse himself. What highest prophet cannot do externally the meanest tempter may do internally and spiritually. Balaam brought Israel into entanglement with the Midianitish women, and in one day four-and-twenty thousand Israelites fell— suicides!—not blasted by an external curse of priest or prophet or magical conjurer, but lapsed in heart, devoted to things forbidden,—self-damned. What wonder if God would have the people renumbered—not only that he might take some account of life but make a solemn registry of death? It is well to number the dead, to tell of what diseases they die, and to have our attention directed to the silent cemetery as well as to the tumultuous city. How stands the kingdom then? The kingdom still stands. Did we suppose that four-and-twenty thousand Israelites all caught in sin and all smitten with a common plague would arrest the kingdom of God? What a mischievous imagination! What a shallow and foolish sophism! The kingdom is decreed, the covenant is made, and none can hinder. We bewilder ourselves by looking at individual sinners, or by fixing our wondering attention upon individual saints or believers, and saying,—What progress can the kingdom of heaven make when prominent Christians are so faulty in character or in spirit? We then talk as foolish people talk. The kingdom of heaven is an everlasting kingdom: it moves on through city and cemetery, up steep hills and down dark valleys, and nothing can arrest its progress. It is not in the power of the individual—let us say again—to stop the upbuilding of the theocracy. We lament that a man here or there should have done wrong,—why, if four-and-twenty thousand men were all to do wrong to-day and die, the kingdom is not touched: the four corners of it stand to the wind and defy the tempest. The counsels of eternity are not exposed to the irregularities of time. God has decreed that man shall bear his image and likeness and shall be beautiful with ineffable comeliness, and Philistine, or Canaanite, or Moabite, cannot keep back the purpose from ultimate fulfilment. We live in a sanctuary ; we are bound to an infinite thought. It is pitiful for any Christian man to talk about individual instances of lapse or faithlessness, as though they touched the infinite calm of the mind of God and the infinite integrity of the covenant of Heaven. It is so in all other departments of life—why not so on the largest and noblest scale ? The nation may be an honest nation, though a thousand felons may be under lock and key at the very moment when the declaration of the national honesty is made ; the nation may be declared to be a healthy country, though ten thousand men be burning with fever at the very moment the declaration of health is made. So the Church of the living Christ, redeemed at an infinite cost, sealed by an infinite love, is still the Lamb's Bride, destined for the heavenly city, though in many instances there may be defalcation, apostasy,— yea, very treason against truth and good. Live in the larger thought ; do not allow the mind to be troubled and distressed by individual instances. The kingdom is one, and, like the seamless robe, must be taken in its unity.

Individuals must not trust to ancestral piety. Individual Israelites might have quoted the piety of many who had gone before ; but that piety goes for nothing when the individual will is in rebellion against God. No man has any overplus of piety. No man may bequeath his piety to his posterity. A man cannot bequeath his learning,—how can he bequeath his holiness ? It does not lie within a testator's power to leave wisdom to any child of his ; how, then, can he leave to any child of his character, good standing before the heavens ? Nor must the individual trust to the divine covenant in the time of his evil-doing and in his devotion to the Baal of Midian ; the covenant will not save him ; he cannot break the covenant, for the covenant relates to larger lines, to further issues ; and though he be left like a dead dog in the wilderness, the army will go on and the Church will be admitted into heaven. A wondrous conception is this thought that human detail does not interfere with divine purpose ; and a marvellous thing it is to fix the mind upon the intention of God to create in the long run a humanity that cannot die. When theology, in its boldest propositions, comes to be restated in the light of the completest research and experience, the mind will be projected to points of issue, and will be enabled to take in such comprehensive views of divine thought and purpose, as shall reconcile, in their vastness and their harmony, things which at present assume the sharpness and the vexatiousness of contradiction. We will look too near the dust. The artist will not allow us to go too near his canvas; but we thrust our very faces into the painting of God;—what wonder if it should appear rough and wanting in the mystery of perspective? Stand back; give God time; let the relations of survey and criticism be wisely adjusted; and when God's processes are complete then say whether he hath done all things well.

A mournful line is this:—"But among these there was not a man of them whom Moses and Aaron the priest numbered, when they numbered the children of Israel in the wilderness of Sinai"—except Caleb and Joshua (verses 64, 65). But there are always two old men left, blessed be God! We need not make a mournful line of it wholly. There are always some left who keep up good traditions, who link us to a noble past, who remind us of altars where men prayed with vehement strength and prevailing persuasiveness. The congregation changes year by year, but new men succeed to vacant places; and yet in every congregation there are old Caleb and Joshua, rich with years and experience; and we say that if two such old men could join hands, they might stretch back a hundred-and-fifty or two hundred years and touch some good man's hand in the centuries dead and gone. Not a man left,—yet Israel was left, more than six hundred thousand strong. True, the census had decreased by some eighteen hundred since it was taken in Sinai; but Israel remained. True, many had gone down through living their days in vanity and spending their nights in the service of the evil one; but Israel, the chosen of God, remained—a mighty host, a great and blessed people. Not a man save two,—but God lives, God remains; Jesus is the same, yesterday, and to-day, and for ever. Preachers die, but the ministry continues; sermons are ended, but the Christian pulpit stands from age to age;

congregations change, but the Lord's Gospel has never wanted a hearing people, an attentive host, crying for the word of the Lord. So we have the permanent and the transitory—the eternal God, and the changing host; and yet amid the changing host we have a central quantity : the details change, the great columnar line abides, and none can touch it. "The foundation of God standeth sure, having this seal, The Lord knoweth them that are his";—and no false soul can pass the gate and elude the criticism of Omniscience.

NOTE.

Moses laid down the law (Ex. xxx. 12, 13) that whenever the people were numbered, an offering of half a shekel should be made by every man above twenty years of age, by way of atonement or propitiation. A previous law had also ordered that the firstborn of man and of beast should be set apart, as well as the first fruits of agricultural produce; the first to be redeemed, and the rest with one exception offered to God (Ex. xiii. 12, 13 ; xxii. 29).

Many instances of numbering are recorded in the Old Testament. The first was under the express direction of God (Ex. xxxviii. 26) in the third or fourth month after the Exodus, during the encampment at Sinai, chiefly for the purpose of raising money for the Tabernacle. The numbers then taken amounted to 603,550 men, which may be presumed to express with greater precision the round numbers of 600,000 who are said to have left Egypt at first (Ex. xii. 37).

Again, in the second month of the second year after the Exodus (Num. i. 2, 3). This census was taken for a double purpose: (*a*) to ascertain the number of fighting men from the age of twenty to fifty. The total number on this occasion, exclusive of the Levites, amounted to 603,550 (Num. ii. 32), Josephus says 603,650 ; each tribe was numbered, and placed under a special leader, the head of the tribe. (*b*) To ascertain the amount of the redemption offering due on account of all the firstborn, both of persons and cattle. Accordingly the numbers were taken of all the firstborn male persons of the whole nation above one month old, including all of the tribe of Levi of the same age. The Levites, whose numbers amounted to 22,000, were taken in lieu of the firstborn males of the rest of Israel, whose numbers were 22,273, and for the surplus of 273 a money payment of 1,365 shekels, or five shekels each, was made to Aaron and his sons (Num. iii. 39, 51).

Another numbering took place thirty-eight years afterwards, previous to the entrance into Canaan, when the total number, excepting the Levites, amounted to 601,730 males, showing a decrease of 1,870. All tribes presented an increase except the following :—Reuben, of 2,770 ; Simeon, 37,100 ; Gad, 5,150 ; Ephraim and Naphtali, 8,000 each. The tribe of Levi had increased by 727 (Num. xxvi.). The great diminution which took place in the tribe of Simeon may probably be assigned to the plague consequent on the misconduct of Zimri (Calmet, *on Num.* xxv. 9). On the other hand, the chief instances of increase are found in Manasseh, of 20,500 ; Benjamin, 10,200 ; Asher, 11,900 ; and Issachar, 9,900. None were numbered at this census who had been above twenty years of age at the previous one in the second year, excepting Caleb and Joshua (Num. xxvi. 63, 65).—SMITH'S *Dictionary of the Bible.*

PRAYER.

ALMIGHTY GOD, let the words of truth sink into our hearts and abide there like roots planted by thine own hand which shall spring up into beauty and strength in days to come. We know the right way in all things; our hearts by thy grace point it out and say to us in plain words, This is the way: walk in it. Yet there is another voice in our hearts which bids us walk another path which seemeth right, but the end whereof is death. So we are set between these two voices, each of which is strong and clear and full of persuasion; and now we walk the right road, and now the wrong one; now we sing like children going home, and now we bow down the head and cry like prodigals whose sins have blotted out the light. This is our life: it is indeed our own—not some other man's, which we may speak about and feel for, approve or condemn; but it is our own spirit, our very self. We see it, know it, own it, and are lost between conflicting and tremendous emotions. Thou dost know us altogether—the quantities in which we are made, the forces which constitute our energy, all the weak points in our character, all the infirmities of our constitution, all the peculiarities of our circumstances; the very hairs of our head are all numbered. We can, therefore, find rest in the infinity of thy knowledge, and in the infinity of thy compassion. We have no answer; justification we have none. We could plead weakness, temptation, and suddenness of trial; but in all these things we should answer and condemn ourselves without the opening of thy mouth in judgment. Verily, our mercies are more in number than our difficulties; thy Cross is infinitely in excess of our necessity, thou art near to help, if we were but ready to pray. We have all things in God as revealed to us in Christ Jesus his Son, and yet we go hither and thither like men doomed to want, elected to perish under cold, and storm-clouds, and fated to die in darkness for whose gloom there are no words. Thus we belie thee; we falsify thee to ourselves and before men, and we bring the Cross of Christ into disrepute, because having seen it and felt its power, we still talk of our sins as of an unlifted load, we still point to our iniquities as if they had not been dissolved and destroyed by thy forgiveness. Pity our piety; forgive the poverty of our worship, and see in the incertitude of our religious action how pitifully weak we are at the very centre of our being, how wanting in faith, how ungrateful for the promises of God. Still we hover about thy Book as if even yet we might find honey in the flower; still we inquire meekly for the house of God, if haply we may there see an outline of his image and hear some tone of the music of his love. We would hope in these things and because of them—yea, we would multiply them into assurances of thy nearness, goodness, and purpose to save; because we are so near the altar we feel we cannot die. We have brought our mercies to our memory, that we might carry them up into songs of praise, and express our feeling in loud psalms of reverence and adoration. Our bodies are the temples of the Holy Ghost. Thou hast satisfied our hunger; thou hast drawn water for us when the well was deep, and we had nothing to draw with; thou hast made our bed in our affliction; and as for our friends who are not with us in the body, thou hast so quickened our imagination and our sympathy, that they are with us in soul, and we are in fellowship with them at the throne of grace. Thou hast given us views of life which have abolished death: so now we triumph in solitude and in pain; we know that we are separated by the thinnest of clouds, the flimsiest of veils, from that which is now invisible and eternal. Here we stand; in the strength of this faith we struggle; in the inspiration of this confidence we move onward from day to day, writing what we can of good upon the record whilst the sun lasts, and confident that it is good in Christ Jesus thy Son to fall into the hands of the living God who knows us better than we can know ourselves, whose mercy exceeds our sin and whose great heaven makes our earth look so small. Amen.

Numbers xxvi. 11.

"Notwithstanding, the children of Korah died not."

THE PROGENY OF EVIL.

WE read that "the sons of Eliab" were "Nemuel, and Dathan, and Abiram. This is that Dathan and Abiram, which were famous in the congregation, who strove against Moses and against Aaron in the company of Korah, when they strove against the Lord: and the earth opened her mouth, and swallowed them up together with Korah, when that company died, what time the fire devoured two hundred and fifty men: and they became a sign. Notwithstanding, the children of Korah died not." This statement is pregnant with conflicting inferences and suggestions about some of which at least we can be definitely and instructively certain. I wished in reading the verse to be able to find in it an expression of mercy, but in this quest I had rather to force my desires than to follow the lead of my understanding. I wanted the "notwithstanding" to be a gracious word indicative of a sparing and discriminating mercy on the part of the Destroyer. Then the text might have run in some such melody as this: The father was a bad man, but the children were spared; notwithstanding the judgment that righteously fell upon him, God said,—The children need not fall in their parent's apostasy : they shall be kept from harm and danger; they shall be succoured, and defended, and cherished, and all the grace of Heaven shall be their security; the father was, indeed, a bad man : he outraged the sanctity of all the solemn relationships which he sustained : the earth opened and swallowed him and his company and fraternity ; but his children love me, serve me, go in the right roads, and they are this day spared because of the pureness and the love of their heart and life. I wanted to rest there, and pass on into the next verse. It would have been a happy adieu to the children of Korah, it would have satisfied the poetry of the occasion ; but the reason of it—the steady, stern, sober lesson of it—so to say, laid its grip upon me and said,—You have not got the meaning of that verse yet : read it again ; be faithful to what you yourself know of life, and experience, and judgment, and fail not to beat out the solemn music from this judicial record. We cannot read things as we would like to read them. There is not a man in the world who likes to stoop over the cradle and think of original sin. It is repugnant in every aspect and in every inference, and seems to be contradicted by the whole appearance of the occasion, and to be one huge black lie, not against the child only, but against God. The question is,—How shall we read life ? Shall we read it with intent to find out its meaning, or with the hope of smoothing down its rough sentences, escaping its penalties, and hiding ourselves from its judgments ? We had better have a little rough reading at the beginning. Nothing stands but real truth, that which is perfectly transparent in its moral beauty ; and we had, therefore, better bring ourselves to critical and definite reading. Better have the roughness at first than at last ; better be wise in the morning and have the whole day to work in, than begin as fools who, having wasted the light, fall to praying in the darkness.

"Notwithstanding, the children of Korah died not." May we not read it,—that though the sire dies the progeny lives? There is a continuity of evil in the world. We only cut off the tops of iniquities : their deep roots we do not get at ; we pass the machine over the sward, and cut off the green tops of things that are offensive to us ; but the juicy root is struck many inches down into the earth, and our backs will hardly be turned, and the click of the iron have ceased, before those roots are asserting themselves in new and obvious growths. Iniquity is not to be shaved off the earth—ironed and mowed away like an obnoxious weed,—it must be uprooted, torn right up by every thinnest, frailest fibre of its bad self, and then, having been torn out, left for the fire of the sun to deal with—the fire of mid-day is against it and will consume it. And thus only can growths of evil be eradicated and destroyed. Is Cain dead? Not he! Is not Cain a historical character? Not he!—in any sense that excludes his being a member of a Christian congregation, and, it may be, a tenant of our own hearts. There is some danger in making little children cry over the story of Cain and Abel. We put a great block of time between them and the murder of the sweet Abel, son of Adam and Eve : we never give them the impression that this happened this morning, and that Cain's strong arm is lifted up at this moment and is about to descend in murderous stroke upon weakness and innocence. There is no reason to deny the historical antiquity of the literal event; but we shall lose the meaning of it, and all the wholesomeness of its moral instruction, if we do not tell the child to ask whether he himself is Cain or Abel—the one of them he must be. Only in this way can the Bible keep pace with the ages and look in upon every modern window as the day's dawning light. Is Achan the thief dead, as well as Cain the murderer? Long ago he stole the wedge of gold and the Babylonish garment—yet he stole them this morning—he is stealing them now! A poor thing to say that Achan lived three thousand or four thousand years ago! He is now with leering eye looking round to observe who is watching him; he has got the wedge of gold secreted, and he is now folding the Babylonish garment quietly, noiselessly; he will be off presently, he will hide them whilst other eyes are shut in prayer! How pleasant to talk of him as "he"! What a relief to speak of him as an outside person,—another person! What a cruel criticism that turns the sword point right round towards our own heart, saying, —Your name is Achan! Do not run away because the merely literal incidents do not fit the occasion. The Bible is within the Bible; the meaning is within the meaning. Search into spiritual intent and purpose, and let the man who thinks he is not an

Achan stand up in God's house if he dare. It is understood that he may bluffly deny the charge in conversation, that he may add lies to his knavery in protesting his respectability; but the rudeness of his self-defence is only an additional proof of his spiritual culpability. Is Judas the traitor dead, as well as Cain the murderer and Achan the thief? No: Korah is dead, Cain is dead, Achan is dead, Judas is dead—notwithstanding, the children of these men died not. I have heard an English audience, made up presumably of Christian men, laugh quite audibly when told that in heathen countries it is possible to tempt an idolater to sell his little god; I have heard a Christian assembly laugh when told that some heathen priests have even sold rosaries and sacred things out of the temple courts, but especially laugh when told that some poor idolater has sold his idol for silver or gold. Do Christians know what they are doing when they laugh at such infirmity? Is there no selling of gods in this country? Is there no selling of the Son of God for any number of pieces of silver—even less than thirty—that he will bring? O lying Christian, laugher at poor heathen dupes and at heathen worshippers of vain idols! ours may be a deadlier crime. The man who sells his principles, who keeps quiet in critical times, lest he should bring himself into difficulty or subject his business to loss—it shall be more tolerable for the heathen man in the day of judgment than for that Christian traitor! Every day we are selling Christ, every day we are crucifying the Son of God afresh and putting him to an open shame; and yet at a missionary meeting how some men gather themselves together and chuckle with pious hypocrisy over the poor deluded idolater who parted with his stone god for gold! Men do not think of these things. When you smothered your convictions you sold your God. When, instead of standing square up, and saying, "I will not," that you might save your situation, or your family from starvation, you bartered your God for gold. I cannot sit quietly and hear the heathen laughed at because they take off their little rosaries and sell them for money. They know no better. That very parting with the rosary may be a step in an upward direction when the whole solution is before us. But as for us, to be dumb in the presence of evil, to turn away lest we should bring ourselves into scrapes and difficulties because of standing up for the

oppressed—for us to smooth down the accusation of our Chris·
tianity by saying that the church we go to is the most respectable
in the neighbourhood—that is a lying which the blood of Christ
itself may hardly be able to expunge! There is an unblottable,
an unpardonable sin. Is Ananias the liar also gone? No.
Literally and historically, Yes—notwithstanding the children of
Ananias died not. Lying is a fine art; lying is now a kind of
oral legerdemain. What with keeping back and silently or
expressively suggesting; by reversing, qualifying, parenthesising,
it is now difficult for some men to speak the truth, the whole
truth and nothing but the truth. Herein men must judge themselves; every heart must go in upon itself and say,—Am I a
truth-speaker and a truth-looker? How seldom it is that Korah
thinks he will have any children; that a parent realises that he
is going to live again in his child's life! I have heard of men
boasting that since a very early period in life they have pursued
such and such habits and no harm has come of them. I have
been able to see the harm when they have not detected it. In
the tremulous tone, in the uncertain hand, in the failing memory
falsely attributed to old age, I have seen how the black seed has
come to black fruit. But, apart from that, I have traced the issue
of certain practices in the constitution and habits of the children.
You are not living to yourself and in yourself: you cannot help
living in and for other people. Twenty years after this your son
will bring you to judgment. Yes, when you have passed away
from the earth, he will exhume you, try you, and condemn you at
his judgment-bar. You may now be ruining his constitution,
disarranging his nervous system : you may be making a hell for
him; in all your buoyancy, and hilarity, and worldliness, and
thoughtlessness, in all your so-called holiday life, you may be
lighting a perdition for your sons and daughters. It is an awful
thing to live! You cannot tell where influence begins, how it
operates, or how it ends. The boy sitting next you is partly
yourself, and he cannot help it. You cannot turn round and say,
"You must look after yourself as I had to do." That is a fool's
speech. You can never shake off the responsibility of having
helped in known and unknown ways and degrees to make that
boy what he is. Life is not a surface matter, a loose pebble
lying on the road that men can take up and lay down again

without any particular harm being done. When the boy drinks himself into madness, he may be but expressing the influences wrought within him by three generations. When the young man tells a lie, he may be surprised at his own audacity, and feel as if he were rather a tool and a victim than a person and a responsible agent—as if generations of liars were blackening his young lips with their falsehoods. When this youth is restive and will not go to the usual church, do not blame the modern spirit of scepticism and restlessness, but go sharply into the innermost places of your own heart, and see how far you have bolted the church doors against your son, or made a place which he would be ashamed to be seen in.

Then there is a bright side to all this view. I can, now that I have got my rough reading done, turn this "notwithstanding" into a symbol of hope, a light of history; I can make high and inspiring uses of it. I will blot out the word *Korah*, and fill in other names, and then the moral lesson of the text will expand itself into gracious meanings, rise above us like a firmament crowded with innumerable and brilliant lights. In days long ago they killed the martyrs,—notwithstanding, the children of the martyrs died not. There the light begins to come; there I hear music lifting up sweetest voice of testimony and hope. The murderer could never get everybody into the fire; there was always some one little boy that could not be got hold of, and he was made of the old family stuff—a grand old heroic quality that could not lie, that could lay down its poor bodily weakness to the axe, but could never lay down its soul to the murderer. That is the testimony of all history. We are not now dealing with opinions, or imaginations, or sentiments that we should like to be true; but we have before us plain history written in our mother tongue in which this truth is declared with an emphasis that cannot be modified. The tyrant has said, "I will make an end of this mischief." He has laid his hand upon every man accessible, and has supposed that he has bound all into one bundle of death—notwithstanding there was one child wanting, one family missing, one line of action not involved in the oppressors' evil success; and no sooner had the martyrs' fire died out than the surviving martyrs went forward, took up their places, followed in their train and mocked the destroyer.

> " We're the sons of sires that baffled
> Crowned and mitred tyranny;
> They defied the field and scaffold
> For their birthright : so will we "—

is but turning into rhyme the sternest of prose, and expressing in melody that which was first written in heroic blood. So, in all the ages, and, thank God, so now, one generation passeth away and another generation cometh, and still Christ's following enlarges ; on the whole, he sums up into higher figures year by year. Not that I care for census-religion, not that I would number people for the purpose of ascertaining Christ's position in the world. The kingdom of heaven cometh not with observation ; is not a matter of census-reckoning or statistic-returns ; it is a matter of spiritual quality, inner manhood, meaning and attitude of the soul; and amid all sin, struggle, doubt, difficulty, darkness, the kingdom moves. " Thy kingdom come. Thy will be done in earth, as it is in heaven."

PREACHING THROUGH THE BIBLE

BY
JOSEPH PARKER

VOL. 4

NUMBERS XXVII—DEUTERONOMY

Originally printed
under the title,
The People's Bible

CONTENTS.

THE FOURTH BOOK OF MOSES

CONTINUED.

PRAYER.

ALMIGHTY GOD, we need thee; our hearts cry out for thee as for the living God. Sometimes we do not care for thee, nor think of thee, much less seek thee with earnest determination; but again we feel that without thee we are nothing and can do nothing, and that we need thee above all other needs; then thou art our Father, Redeemer, Shepherd, Friend. These are the better times in the soul's history: they are full of joy and tenderness; and though the great gladness sometimes touches tears, yet the very tears help the gladness which they endeavour to express. We need thee now; we would see a light above the brightness of the sun; we would stand very near to God and feel his breathing upon our hearts and his gentle touch upon our whole life; and we would answer that conscious nearness by new vows of service and new oaths of loyalty. We would say again, with new strength of words and thought, that the Lord shall have all we are: for we are his: not our own, but bought with a price; therefore, to glorify God shall be our one work, our one delight,—the immediate beginning of heaven. We bless thee that we can say this with our hearts. Once it would have been a strange tongue to us, and we should not have understood any one of the terms; but now, being born not of corruptible seed but of incorruptible, these words have become the tongue of our second nativity; we speak them with the familiarity of love; they express the soul's desire, they utter the inmost wish of the life. Sometimes we are tempted away, but it is only to return with more eager haste to the life we have deserted. There is no house like thine—so large, so secure, so full of light; the very air a living song. We would feel its nearness and warmth and comfort now; we would see written upon it everywhere—our Father's house—great welcomes of love bidding us eat and drink abundantly at our Father's table, that we may forget the weariness of the week and prepare for the battle of to-morrow. We bless thee for the first day of the week, when Mary Magdalene, and the other Mary, came to see the sepulchre. We have come to see the risen Christ; we have filled up the sepulchre with our joy, and gladness, and triumph: it is a garden of flowers. We would with our heart's vision see the risen Christ, throned now, King of kings, Lord of lords, with the wounds in his hands, but his hands the mightier for the wounds. Grant us this vision, O Lord! Let us see heaven open. We know it is there; our faith sees it, our hope hovers around it like a bird that would enter into its nest; but we want to see heaven open,—just one rent, one glimpse, one gleam of light; then we shall be glad: we shall laugh in the valley, climb the mountain steeps with young feet, and there shall be no difficulty in our way that shall not tempt us to nobler strife and yield us deeper joy. We bless thee for those who have gone up nearer the light, nearer the throne, nearer the love that casts no one out who will put forth one trembling hand towards its great security. May we follow them as they followed Christ; may we have no fear of death: may we welcome it; though clothed in black and coming stealthily at midnight, yet may we know that the blackness and the stealth are but parts of the great plan written down in the ink of heaven. We are here but for a little time: we shall soon be told to go up into the mountain of Abarim, and there look and wait, and there fall back on the breast of God and die. May we so live that we may be missed: that people will look round for us, and say,—Where is the smile? where the strong hand? where the tender ministry? where the noble prayer? And yet may we so live as to ascend into nobler service and leave behind so strong an assurance of this ascension that friends will rise from their inquiry to complete their praise, giving thanks unto God for his crowned ones who have escaped the river of trouble. We thank thee for all tender comfort; though others may not seize it with gladness, we rejoice to be of the number of those who count such comfort necessary to the strength and the peace of life. "Comfort ye, comfort ye my people, saith your God. Speak ye comfortably to Jerusalem, and cry unto her, that her iniquity is pardoned." This voice we would hear. We could hear it only at the Cross; and at the Cross we now delight to find ourselves. O Saviour, have mercy on us! Risen Christ, pray for us! Advocate with the Father, forget not the name of the least of these little ones! May we hear thy prayer in our hearts; then shall we receive the Father's answer. Let thy blessing be round about us, a morning within a morning, a morning above a morning,—a light that makes all other glory pale. Amen.

Numbers xxvii. 1.

"Then came the daughters of Zelophehad, the son of Hepher, the son of Gilead, the son of Machir, the son of Manasseh, of the families of Manasseh the son of Joseph: and these are the names of his daughters; Mahlah, Noah, and Hoglah, and Milcah, and Tirzah."

MAHLAH, NOAH, HOGLAH, MILCAH, AND TIRZAH.

THESE are the names of five women; the five women were five sisters; the five sisters were daughters of a man called Zelophehad. This man had five girls, but no boys. He was a quiet man, and took no part in a certain great rebellion against the Lord, in which Korah and his company justly perished

This man Zelophehad died in his own bed; he had committed
no public sins; he had only sinned in the usual way, and died in
the usual way, and so far there was an end of him. One day
these five women put their heads together on a family subject.
There was something that disturbed them, took away their sleep,
and made them grievously discontented. The result of their
deliberation was that they determined to make a public speech,
and a great audience they had, viz., Moses, and Eleazar the priest,
and the princes, and all the congregation of Israel, and they
stood by the door of the tabernacle of the congregation and
made their statement. They said, with wonderful conciseness of
manner, keeping themselves strictly to facts, and coming to the
point with admirable brevity :—Our father died in the wilderness: he was not one of those who took part in the sin of Korah;
he died quietly, not tragically ; he had no sons, and according to
the present law of Israel the name of our father dies, and it is
just as if he had never lived, though he has left five girls who
bear his name and love his memory ; now we ask you to look at
this case ; it is peculiar ; see if anything can be done under such
extraordinary circumstances ; and give us, women though we be,
give us a possession in Israel, give us property in the land,
create a legal status for us amongst the brethren of our father.
It was a practical speech, and, as our judges say, it started quite
a novel point. It was for Moses to say what should be done, but
he could not speak on the spur of the moment, so he took time
to consider, and "brought their cause before the Lord." The
answer from heaven was,—Certainly: the women ask only for
that which is right; thou shalt cause the inheritance of their
father to pass to them, and out of this particular instance there
shall arise a new law of succession in Israel, "If a man die,
and have no son, then ye shall cause his inheritance to pass unto
his daughter, and if he have no daughter, then ye shall give his
inheritance unto his brethren, and if he have no brethren, then
ye shall give his inheritance unto his father's brethren, and if his
father have no brethren, then ye shall give his inheritance unto
his kinsman that is next to him of his family, and he shall
possess it: and it shall be unto the children of Israel a statute
of judgment, as the Lord commanded Moses." These are the
circumstances which furnish us with our subject, and it will be

for us now to discover what there is in them to instruct and comfort us.

1. The rectification of things that are wrong sometimes seems to come from man and not from God. Look at this case. It was the women themselves who began the reform. Providence did not stir first. The five women gave this reform to the economy of Israel. So it would seem on the face of the story, and many people look at the face and go no farther, and so they blunder and lie. Suggestions are from God. The very idea which we think our own is not our own, but God's. " Every good gift and every perfect gift . . . cometh down from the Father of lights." He inspires the prayer which he means to answer. He says, Arise, when he is prepared to meet us. An idea occurs to you, and you think it admirable, and call it your own; you will change your policy; enlarge your business; go to another town; strike out another line : you will alter the machinery, patent an invention, introduce yourself to a firm, and you think this is all your own doing. That is the fatal error. "We are fellow-workers with God." "He is Lord of all,"—of all good ideas, noble impulses, holy inspirations, sudden movements of the soul upward into higher life and broader liberty. This is his plan of training men. He seems to stand aside, and to take no part in some obviously good movements, and men say, "This is a human movement, a political movement, a non-religious movement," not knowing what they are talking about,—forgetting that the very idea out of which it all sprang, came down from the Father of lights, that the very eloquence by which it is supported is divinely taught, that the very gold which is its sinew is his: they do not go far enough back in their investigation into the origin of things, or they would find God in movements which are often credited to human genius alone. We do not see all. The finest threadlets are hidden from us. Now and again, in a dream, we may catch a sight of the ladder connecting heaven and earth, but it is always there, the highway of angels, the path into the skies.

2. Everywhere the Bible is full of the very spirit of justice. It is the Magna Charta of the civilised world. This is the spirit that gives the Bible such a wonderful hold upon the confidence of mankind. Look at this case as an example. The applicants were women. All the precedents of Israel might have been

pointed to as the answer to their appeal.   Why create a special
law for women?   Why universalise a very exceptional case?
Why not put these people down as sensational reformers?   Yet,
the case was heard with patience, and answered with dignity.
O women, you should love the Bible!   It is your friend.   It has
done more for you than all other books put together.   Wherever
it goes it claims liberty for you, justice for you, honour for you.
Repay i.s service by noble endeavour to make it everywhere
known.   Not only were the applicants women, they were *orphans.*
Their father dead, no brother to take their part, nothing left them
but the memory of a man dead and gone.   Yet the God of the
Bible is their friend.   He says, "They are right."   He will not
break the bruised reed.   The weak are as the strong before
him, and the friendless as those who are set in families.   A
God so just, so pitiful, so mindful of individual cases and special
desires, is the God who will save the world!   This God of justice
is the God of love.   We shall see more of him as we go from
page to page of his book; one day we may see him on a Cross
dying for man!   Give any nation the Bible, and let that nation
make the Bible its statute book, and every class in the community will have justice: masters will be just to their servants;
servants will be just to their masters; family peace will be
protected; social relations will be purified; common progress
will be guaranteed.   This spirit of justice is the social strength
of the Bible.   No life is to be tampered with; the small
cause as well as the great is to be heard; no kid is to be
seethed in its mother's milk; no fruit tree is to be cut down
even in time of war; no bird's nest is to be wantonly destroyed;
all men are to be honoured, helped, and saved.   A book with a
tone like this should be protected from the sneers of persons who
have never actually studied its ennobling pages.

3. Every question should become the subject of social sympathy and matter of religious reference.   These women were
heard patiently.   It is something to get a hearing for our
grievances.   Sometimes those grievances perish in the very
telling; sometimes the statement of them brings unexpected
help to our assistance.   This case is what may be called a
secular one; it is about land and name and inheritance; and
even that question was made in Israel simply a religious one.   It

was not political. It was not an outside question. The Lord
was King of Israel, and to the King the appeal must be made. Is
Christianity farther from God than was Judaism? Are there
some questions which we now take into our own hands? Does
God take no interest in our merchandise, in our land, in our
professions? Can he not still tell the physician what to do, the
merchant what to buy, the mariner how to go, the lawyer how
to plead? In ancient Israel, with its priestly system, men had
to go to the leader and the priest first; in Christianity we can go
straight to God; we have no priesthood but Christ; the way to
the throne is open night and day. O wronged and suffering
woman, tell thy case to the Father! O man, carrying a burden
too heavy for thy declining strength, speak to God about the
weight, and he will help thee with his great power.

SELECTED NOTE.

In no history can there be found, save in the Bible, an equal number
of charming female portraits. But the formative influence of female character
as seen in the Bible must be referred to the pure and lofty religious ideas
which the Biblical books in general present. If woman there appears as the
companion and friend of man, if she rises above the condition of being a
bearer of children to that noble position which is held by the mother of a
family, she owes her elevation in the main to the religion of Moses and
that of Jesus. . . . Bringing to bear on the domestic ties his own doctrine
of immortality, our Lord made the marriage bond co-existent with the
undying soul, only teaching that the connection would be refined with the
refinement of our affections and our liberation from these tenements of clay
in which we now dwell (Matt. v. 32; xix. 3, *seq.*; xxii. 23, *seq.*). With views
so elevated as these, and with affections of the tenderest benignity, the
Saviour may well have won the warm and gentle hearts of Jewish women.
Accordingly, the purest and richest human light that lies on the pages of the
New Testament comes from the band of high-minded, faithful, and affectionate
women who are found in connection with Christ from his cradle to his
cross, his tomb, and his resurrection. These ennobling influences have
operated on society with equal benefit and power. Woman, in the better
portions of society, is now a new being. And yet her angelic career is only
just begun. She sees what she may be, and what under the gospel she
ought to be; and ere very long, we trust, a way will be found to employ in
purposes of good energies of the finest nature, which now waste away from
want of scope, in the ease and refinements of affluence, if not in the
degradations of luxury—a most precious offering made to the Moloch of
fashion, but which ought- to be consecrated to the service of that God who
gave these endowments, and of that Saviour who has brought to light the
rich capabilities, and exhibited the high and holy vocation, of the female sex.

PRAYER.

ALMIGHTY GOD, teach us that a man must first come to himself before he can come to thee. Give us a considering mind. Help each of us to look at himself as he really is, and to spare no searching into his condition, so that he may come to know that from the crown of the head to the sole of the foot all is wrong. We are only driven to prayer by hunger; we are turned towards heaven by pain and sharpness of discipline; for wherein we tread green pastures and rich wheatfields we soon become foolish, waxing fat and kicking against God. We are arrested by poverty; we are made to think by sickness; when the pain and fear of solitude seize the soul, then we begin to grope for thee. All this has meaning in it. Thou hast many servants; thy ministry is an incalculable host; fire, and sword, and vapour, and hail, and thick cloud, and all the beasts of the field are thine, and the stars in their courses fight against evil men, and the whole creation sets itself upon thy side. Thou hast made all things to wound the evil-doer. Thy universe becomes a serpent to bite the man who thrusts himself through a hedge. This is glorious;—it is security; it is a proof of eternal defence. Thy throne is set in verity and judgment, and cannot be overturned; and they who set themselves against thee shall at last be flung down in mortal defeat. No man can fight against God and conquer. Thou art the Lord of hosts, the God of battle,—a man of war; and to thy thunder there is no reply. But how good thou art to those that show themselves towards thee as children! Then thy grace is higher than heaven, more beautiful than summer, more persuasive than all we have ever known of music; then all things support and comfort them, and promise them immortality and heaven. May we be found in Christ; may we be found at the Cross; may our attitude be one of adoration and expectancy; and may our souls be satisfied with the words of heaven. We bless thee for a hunger which earth cannot appease, for a thirst which can drink up the rivers, and still be mad with the sensation of fire. This is our immortality; this is the declared image and likeness of God. Pity us wherein we are weak and foolish, and vain and self-considering; and pardon us wherein we are guilty before God of the breach of the whole law, and let the ministry of the Cross avail to redeem and reinstate, and to rekindle in the heart the lamp of hope. Be merciful unto us—yea, so condescending as to touch us, to sit beside us, to breathe upon us, to explain secretly the word to our attentive hearts; and may we know of a surety that the Lord is near by a burning heart, a glowing love, an irrepressible desire to ascend into heavenly places, and a deep and sacred contempt for everything that would draw us downward, and fix our vision on perishable things. Amen.

Numbers xxvii. 12–23.

12. And the Lord said unto Moses, Get thee up into this mount Abarim, and see the land which I have given unto the children of Israel.

13. And when thou hast seen it, thou also shalt be gathered unto thy people, as Aaron thy brother was gathered.

14. For ye rebelled against my commandment in the desert of Zin, in the strife of the congregation, to sanctify me at the water before their eyes: that is the water of Meribah in Kadesh in the wilderness of Zin.

15. And Moses spake unto the Lord, saying,

16. Let the Lord, the God of the spirits of all flesh, set a man over the congregation,

17. Which may go out before them, and which may go in before them, and which may lead them out, and which may bring them in; that the congregation of the Lord be not as sheep which have no shepherd.

18. And the Lord said unto Moses, Take thee Joshua the son of Nun, a man in whom is the spirit, and lay thine hand upon him;

19. And set him before Eleazar the priest, and before all the congregation; and give him a charge in their sight.

20. And thou shalt put some of thine honour upon him, that all the congregation of the children of Israel may be obedient.

21. And he shall stand before Eleazar the priest, who shall ask counsel for him after the judgment of Urim before the Lord: at his word shall they go out, and at his word they shall come in, both he, and all the children of Israel with him, even all the congregation.

22. And Moses did as the Lord commanded him: and he took Joshua, and set him before Eleazar the priest, and before all the congregation:

23. And he laid his hands upon him, and gave him a charge, as the Lord commanded by the hand of Moses.

MOSES ORDERED TO ABARIM.

HERE is a man receiving notice to prepare for death. We need not stumble at this reading as if it involved any impossibility, for if we were keener in vision, and more sensitive in response to providential intimations, we ourselves should know that it is quite common on the part of God to give men notice to quit this dark and narrow scene. The notice comes in various ways; but it certainly does come. We have the condemnation of death in ourselves. We know what we cannot always tell to other people. We are conscious of influences and actions which point in the direction of decay. Some men begin very early to die. That is wise. Dying should not be an act of closing the eyes in one little moment which is beyond the range of our reckoning. We may begin so soon to die as not to die at all. We should be familiar with death, and so reverently and religiously familiar with it as to abolish it. Marvellous wonders can be done by expectation, by preparation, by accustoming the mind to certain issues and facts, so that when they transpire in the one critical moment which marks our history, we shall be superior to the event; the event which was expected to strike us on the head will sweep beneath our feet and pass on without leaving mark of wound or defeat upon us.

When we read these words we could amend the providence. It is marvellous how God exposes himself in Providence to adverse criticism. Only he could do this. Wooden gods make mechanical arrangements, and in their clockwork no flaw must be found, or down goes their deity. Never was any government so open to adverse comment as the government of the human family. Where is there a man so dull of mind that he could not amend the ways of God ? God lets little children die before they can speak—poor little speechless things that can only look their pain or smile their love. He allows good lives to pass away in the night time, so that in the morning they cannot be found. He permits vice for a time to ascend the highest places in the State, and to exercise the largest influence in human affairs, when he knows all the time that virtue is standing outside shivering with cold, wet with the dews of night,—homeless, breadless, friendless. We cannot improve the sky, but who could not improve the earth ? We cannot paint a lily without spoiling its beauty, but who could not raise into finer expressiveness of strength almost any human life ? Things are so roughly huddled together. The men that ought to live a thousand years die before they touch the maturity of their strength; and gates that creak, creak on for ever, and lives destitute of fire and genius and nobleness, seem to be immortal. Why should Moses die ? How we shall miss that man ! It will be a sunset full of trouble. We do not want *him* to go,—let Balaam die, if the heavens must needs look down on death. Balaam is a mighty man, a man of genius, of avarice and sensuality, combining the passions,—why should not *he* die ? He has been slain with the sword; but why might not he have been taken up to a mountain and made a specimen of in some grander way ?

Not only does the Lord expose himself to adverse criticism, but he offends us morally. "For ye rebelled against my commandment in the desert of Zin, in the strife of the congregation, to sanctify me at the water before their eyes : that is the water of Meribah in Kadesh in the wilderness of Zin" (v. 14). This makes us impatient. The punishment is out of proportion to the sin. These are little words ; they take out of the occasion all its dignity. We are shocked. If the sin was so great, it should have been visited at the time. We ourselves being witnesses are bound to say Moses has deserved any Canaan under heaven. We must not allow our brother man to be run thus to earth. How, then, can we rid ourselves of the moral offence—the pain of soul—which afflicts us ? By remembering that the fourteenth verse is really not in the history at all. The *Speaker's Commentary* very justly says this appears like a gloss. Even those who are not scholars feel that these words have no right to be here. We read on as if God were about to crown the man and to give him rest, saying,—Noble soldier ! thou hast done valiantly : come home and partake of the feast and enjoy the security of the immortals ;—instead of which, we begin to read about rebellion that happened long ago, and passions that had died out of the human heart, if ever they raged there. The words were written on the margin. We go back to find reasons for things, and with our blundering pens we often write on the margin our own condemnation. We will insert marginalia ; we like to account for events. So, when some scribe had heard that Moses had been ordered into the mount of Abarim to see the land and hear the message of God, he began to wonder why ; and then, going back in history, he found out the occasion of the rebellion in the desert of Zin, at the water of Meribah in Kadesh in the wilderness of Zin, and accounted for the order to Abarim by that historical event. Do not let us attempt to account for everything. It is unprofitable work. Our great sphere of service, duty, and suffering is in the future. We shall find, in the long run, that those things, even in the divinest books, which have shaken our confidence, or offended our conscience, were only scribblings on the margin made by some ill-guided hand. Yet Moses himself might have written those very words, —as we ourselves have done, on lower scales and on meaner occasions. When we have been driven into isolation, or had some heavy loss imposed upon us, or have been brought into very critical and bewildering situations, we have sat down to find the reason why, and in many a diary we have written this spiritual nonsense. We have thought of reasons, and magnified them, and fixed dates for events and causes for effects; and in the midst of our wisdom we have played the fool. The way of the Lord is right, and his judgment is good; verity and grace are the pillars of his throne.

All these things, which we mourn as untimely events, suggest that this life cannot be all. We are driven to that conclusion by events when we endeavour to resist it by logic. When the great preacher died at thirty-seven years of age, in the very act of retranslating the Bible into the latest speech of religious civilisation, we said,—This is very hard. When the great missionary was just about to put on the top-stone of the temple he had built, and was taken away before he saw it finished, we said,—This is cruelty, whoever did it. When the great leader has been smitten down just when the occasion became insufferably critical, and he alone seemed to have the power to overcome every difficulty, our hearts have sunk within us, and we have been too sorrowful to pray. Then we have had forced upon us the suggestion that this life cannot be all: there must be a place of explanation, there must be a time of enlightenment, there must be a heaven of reconciliation.

See how much out of place the fourteenth verse appears to be when Moses himself speaks :—"And Moses spake unto the Lord, saying, Let the Lord, the God of the spirits of all flesh, set a man over the congregation, which may go out before them, and which may go in before them, and which may lead them out, and which may bring them in; that the congregation of the Lord be not as sheep which have no shepherd " (vv. 15–17). That prayer vindicates the character of Moses,—a shepherdly prayer, an unselfish desire. He will not appoint one of his own family; he will have nothing to do with the thing personally and directly; it shall be God's action—for it is God's Church, and he alone can make the bishop, the minister, and the guardian of the redeemed. In this very prayer Moses shows how appreciative he was of the difficulties of the situation. The only man who could undertake the work must be a divinely-selected and a divinely-appointed man. We cannot raise our leaders out of the ground : we must receive them from the opening heavens. If they can pray, they are God's gift to us; if they can speak the Word in small syllables so that little children may pick up somewhat of heavenly wisdom, they are God's great donations to the race. Herein is that word true,—" I proceeded forth and came from God "; and herein, also, is that word true of the lesser servant,— " There was a man sent from God whose name was John." Moses held his office from the Lord. Every man must hold his appointment from the same hands, or he will be a hireling, tiring very early in the day, discontented with the service, stung by its disappointments, and overwhelmed by its responsibilities. Only Omnipotence can sustain a ministry of redemption.

Look for the consolations. They are abundant, but they can only be indicated by one or two examples. This interview took place between the Lord and Moses. Even if the sin was mentioned, it was mentioned in a whisper. Moses is not dragged forth before the whole congregation of Israel and condemned as an evil-doer. It was a secret interview. Jesus Christ had a secret interview with Simon Peter, who had denied him ; they talked together on the lonely sea-shore, and what they said no man can tell. Moses was then honoured in the sight of Israel. " The Lord said unto Moses, Take thee Joshua the son of Nun, a man in whom is the spirit, and lay thine hand upon him " (v. 18). This does not read as if the sin were the active cause in the premature removal of Moses. The Lord recognises the whole ministry of his servant, and connects him with the past and with the future of Israel. " And set him before Eleazar the priest, and before all the congregation " (v. 19). Joshua was not called as Moses was called. Moses had his commission direct from the Most High ; he was priest before Aaron prayed ; but all other leaders are to be appointed otherwise, and have to pass the priestly recognition and receive the priestly touch. The Lord adds : " and give him a charge in their sight." This is not pouring contempt upon Moses ; this is not visiting a sin upon the great and chivalrous leader ;—this is giving him crown upon crown, honour upon honour. This is the reading that the heart answers ; the spirit of man says,—This is the work of God. " And thou shalt put

some of thine honour upon him, that all the congregation of
the children of Israel may be obedient. And he shall stand
before Eleazar the priest, who shall ask counsel for him after
the judgment of Urim before the Lord" (vv. 20, 21). So
Moses was still the leader of Israel. Good men are not cut off
ruthlessly. Such a sun as this is not allowed to set amid
thunder-clouds and tokens of trouble. The man who thus closed
his history did not die;—let him go with his Lord somewhere,
and let him pass upward without first going downward. It was
the right end. The very mystery was part of the goodness;
the concealment enlarged the dignity. They go well together,
these two—even the Lord and Moses; it is right that Moses
should thus pass away. Do we ever hear of him again? We
read of him in the account of the Transfiguration of Christ in
another mountain. Moses and Elias appeared unto the Son of
God to talk of the Exodus which he should accomplish at
Jerusalem—another Exodus. Moses had written one Exodus,—
Christ was to accomplish the spiritual decease or outgoing—
leading forth into liberty those who were held in the bondage of
death. Do we ever hear of him at a remoter period of history?
You will find the answer in the Revelation of John the Divine.
When the seer listened to what was proceeding in heaven, he
heard there the song of Moses and the song of the Lamb. There
is no speech about the sin in the desert of Zin, or the waters of
Meribah in Kadesh in the wilderness of Zin. "Where sin
abounded, grace did much more abound." God does not name
their sins to his servants when they are about to die; He speaks
to them of immortality, of heaven and higher service, of perfect
and imperturbable rest. There is only one kind of forgiveness
impossible, and that is self-forgiveness. God can forgive, but
man cannot forgive himself; and it will be no wonder if
in the dying time even what may be called the least sins
should blot out the light of heaven: they will appear to be
so great when looked at in contrast with the purity of God.
Moses may have written the fourteenth verse, some scribe may
have written it,—it is not in the flow of the text, it is upon the
margin of the book—a suggested reason, rather than a divine
visitation. If God were to mark our sins in this way, who could
live? If man were to die for one sin, what man would be

living ? Read the whole passage together in its noble scope, its broad and urgent flow of thought and sentiment and sacred consolation, and you will find how God dismisses his servants : he gives them honour in the sight of the people ; he crowns them on earth before he crowns them in heaven ; the testimony they are enabled to leave behind them is an ascription of praise to him who sustained their life and energy. " What thou knowest not now thou shalt know hereafter." We wanted Moses to remain ; we would have made him king of Canaan; we would have had a glad day when we touched the promised land together; the old man should still have been chief: we would have chaired him and throned him and gathered round him, and shouted acclaims of recognition and thankfulness and delight. That is the little heaven we would have made for him; and because God meant him for a greener Canaan, a fairer paradise, a larger sphere of service and worship, we complain, or wonder, or suspect. Have we lost dear friends ? Let us weep for ourselves, not for them. Have we stood at the grave, wondering how deep it is and how dark and awful ? Let us rather look up into the blue heavens, rich with morning glory, and say concerning dearest loved ones,—They are not in the grave, they are risen. " Risen " is a height which has no measurement, an altitude that may go up for ever,—a word of poetry rather than of literal definition. Risen !—always rising—still ascending. Inquire for the liberated soul at any moment, go back to the point where last you left him, and some angel will say,—" He is not here. he is risen " ;—a speech worthy of an angel.

PRAYER.

ALMIGHTY GOD, thou hast called us to the tent of meeting. We heard thy voice in the night time, and it spake of morning—morning life, and morning hope, and morning hymns of praise. We were not disobedient to the heavenly trumpet; we heard its call, we answered its peal; we are here in the appointed place, and we wait the revelation of thy presence. Thou wilt not disappoint the expectation of love; thou wilt hasten to meet us; and whilst we are crying for thee to come, thou wilt prove by some touch, or glance, or odour of unknown flowers, that thou wert in the place before us, and waiting for those who supposed they were crying for thee. Thou art the first alway; no man may be in front of God. Thou art in the tent of meeting night and day; our coming is thy coming. Thou knowest our thought afar off, and before it is shaped into a purpose, behold, thou art standing at the altar. Thou hast called us all our life long: sometimes suddenly, always graciously, yea, though it has been along thorny ways, and up steep roads, and down amongst the stony places. Judging by these things, we have said,—Surely the Lord hath not called us to these difficulties and burdens; he hath no pleasure in tears, and can find no delight in the distress of weakness. So our ignorance spoke; we knew not what we said: how could we? We know nothing; we are affrighted at the sound of our own voices: we feel as if in the company of someone unknown, when our own voice smites the ear. But we have lived to know that thy trumpet calls in all directions: to festival, to battle, to wedding banquets, and to mournful scenes. The trumpet is God's, the tone is God's, the tone is full of meaning—varied according to thy purpose. We know all the meaning, though we cannot put it into words: we know the thunder, and have no pleasure in the sullen storm; we know the falling of the rain, and we bless thee that thou givest drink to the thirsty land; we know the sound of young voices, and take heart again under their silvery music. Speak, Lord, thy servants hear. If thou hast aught to say that the mid-day may not hear, and only the midnight can receive, call us up, that in the silence of eternity we may learn some lesson for the days of time. If thou canst speak to us in the great city, amidst tumult and roar, thy voice shall find its way to our heart, and we shall learn lessons of wisdom in the place of tumult and noise. We want to hear no other voice; we know thine by wisdom of our heart; we answer it as we answer none other—with a glowing love, a spontaneous and vehement affection and trust. In this response we know that the joy of heaven begins. To answer thee is to gather strength for the duty which is imposed; to put forth the withered hand at thy bidding is to see it fully restored. We would do all thy bidding;

we would carry out thine instructions to the letter; in all our ways we would acknowledge God, that our paths may be directed. We bless thee for this consciousness that thou art always speaking to us. We will listen for thee; we will hush almost the beating of our heart, lest we miss one tone of thy gospel. When we do not know which way to go, let us hear a voice in our ear saying,—This is the way, walk ye in it. And when the roads are many in number, crossing one another in thick perplexity, let a light shine upon the road we ought to take, and we shall know that light to be the finger of God. We have walked upon wrong roads, but thou hast brought us back again. The wrong road is the heavy one; there is no rest in it: it does not go towards gardens, and still waters, and green pastures; but towards widening deserts, great wildernesses, and mockeries of stone. But thou hast called us home, and thy call has been an infinite persuasion. In obedience to it we stand before thee, claiming the name of Christ, trusting in the Cross of Christ, cleansed by the blood of Christ, made free by the Spirit of Christ. This is not our own doing; that we are here at all is God's miracle. Our hearts love the darkness and the tumult, and the altar of self-idolatry; and now that we find ourselves in God's house, and at Christ's Cross, we know that the victory is Heaven's. Regard all for whom we ought to pray. Thou needest not to be reminded of them, but by allowing us to think of them in prayer, thou dost ennoble and refine our love. Be with those who are in difficult places. Look pitifully upon men who cannot find the key of the high iron gate, or scale that gate—who are standing outside barred against progress and liberty. Look upon those who are fighting ill-fated battles, to whom the morning brings no hope and the night no rest —baffled, disappointed, sorely stricken. The Lord grant unto the soldier in the day of battle, and of fear, and of death too certain, confidence in right and truth and God. Pity those whose homes are battle-fields, though the war be fought many a mile away, for at home men die over again, and still worse death is died because of distance, imagination, and aggravated trouble. Comfort those to whom men may not speak, because of the sacredness of sorrow. Regard those who are on the sea, as if pursued by the winds, as if the storm were wreaking vengeance upon them, and tearing their frail ship to pieces; the Lord plant his footsteps on the sea, and make the storm a trumpet softening into gospel tones and filled with meaning which the heart alone can comprehend. Bring back the traveller; make his face radiant with joy; take the age out of his limbs, and let him run with the vigour of youth. Speak to the dying, and they shall not die. Touch the old man, and he will forget his earth-age in the hope of heavenly youth. Pardon our sin; it will make thy heaven higher if thou dost pardon penitent men—yea, thine own Sabbath shall have a deeper calm because of this miracle of love. Bind our hearts together—man and wife, parent and child, employer and employed, friend and friend; consolidate the people; fill them with the Spirit of Christ, in which Spirit there is neither Jew nor Gentile, bond nor free, circumcised nor uncircumcised; but an infinite life of pureness, and love and hope. Amen.

Numbers xxxii. 1-5.

1. Now the children of Reuben and the children of Gad had a very great multitude of cattle : and when they saw the land of Jazer, and the land of Gilead, that, behold, the place was a place for cattle ;

2. The children of Gad and the children of Reuben came and spake unto Moses, and to Eleazar the priest, and unto the princes of the congregation, saying,

3. Ataroth, and Dibon, and Jazer, and Nimrah, and Heshbon, and Elealeh, and Shebam, and Nebo, and Beon,

4. Even the country which the Lord smote before the congregation of Israel, is a land for cattle, and thy servants have cattle :

5. Wherefore, said they, if we have found grace in thy sight, let this land be given unto thy servants for a possession, and bring us not over Jordan.

REUBEN AND GAD.

THIS is too often the prayer of prosperous men. They find upon the earth what they regard as heaven enough. Having found plenty of pasturage and deep wells of water, they say,—This is enough,—why not build here, and here remain during the rest of our lives? This has, sometimes, quite a religious look ; it seems to breathe the spirit and to bear the image of a serene and pious content. They would leave whatever is beyond Jordan to other people ; they are quite willing to let well alone ; give them grass enough, cattle enough, water enough, and who will may pass beyond the river and realise the mystery of the unseen. Is it not so written in the history of nearly every man to whom a considerable measure of prosperity has been accorded? Yet how he soliloquises and lets out the bitter truth in his mournful talk ! Says he,—If I could be rid of this pain, I should be quite content to toil year after year and age after age upon the green and sunny earth ;—if I could extract the sting of this one disappointment, I should be in all the heaven I need ;—if I could see the prodigal return, and so complete the circle of the family, so that there might be no vacant chair in the house, I should order music and dancing and fatted calf, and enter into the inheritance of all the joy I shall ever require. So, when he talks over the *matériel* of his estate, we find everywhere the slimy line, the touch of weakness, the signature of guilt ; and the whole speech, which was meant to be so musical, is broken up, to the ear which can hear its inner sounds, into dissonances that distress the soul. We will not let God alone : we will punctuate him by our mischievous suggestions. He is writing a long book,— there are hundreds of pages yet to be added to it ; yet, when we come to some little amusing paragraph, or some grand and solemn period, we arrest the divine pen and practically say,— Write no more : put the full stop here. This is so profoundly human as to constitute a continual temptation to many men. If they could but double their income, they would sigh for no bluer heaven ;—if they could but have health without increasing the income—simply increase of physical energy,—they would desire no better paradise than they can find on earth. Who likes to cross the Jordan that lies before every man ? It is a black river, so deep and so cold, and altogether so mysterious ;— better be content even with a little hut on this side than plunge into that awful stream. There is a point at which it becomes very difficult to say to God,—We are still ready to go on ; whatever next may come—great wilderness, or cold river, or high stony mountain,—we are still ready to go on ; thy will be done, and thy way be carried out to its last inch. ' Yet, until we reach the resignation which becomes triumph and the triumph which expresses itself—not in loud sentiment, but in quiet and deep obedience, we have not begun to realise the meaning of the kingdom of heaven.

What was the answer of Moses ?—" Shall your brethren go to war, and shall ye sit here ? " (v. 6). It was a soldier's taunt; it was a tremendous retort to those who could read between the lines and to those who understood the lower tones of human suggestion and reproof. It was not a question put for considera-tion ; it was a question and an answer in one—an interrogative tone, a query,—long, sharp, terrible as a sword forged in heaven. The matter was not put before Reuben and Gad for purposes of consideration and debate and the statement of reasons on the one side or the other. " Shall your brethren go to war, and shall ye sit here ? " What suggestion there is in the colour of every tone! What sublime mockery! What a hint of cowardice ! What an infliction of judgment upon meanness ! Sometimes the only way in which we can put a rational rebuke is in the form of an inquiry. We remit the case to its original propounders, and by putting the case into the form of an interrogation we confound their counsels. It is well to hear how other men can put our case. We may talk ourselves into sophistical conclusions; we may become so accustomed to our own voice as to be quite enamoured with it, and to regard it as the dual voice of the plaintiff and the defendant. It is good to hear how other men take up our words and send them back with new accent and new colouring. The answer of Moses was instantaneous; it was a quick, sudden spark; it was a question which revealed his own mettle, as well as tested the quality of Reuben and Gad; it never occurred to his martial soul that any man could sit down whilst a battle was to be fought—whilst a conquest was to be won; so, he expressed his amazement, and perhaps his contempt, in the form of a martial inquiry.

But there was more to be considered. "And wherefore discourage ye the heart of the children of Israel from going over into the land which the Lord hath given them?" (v. 7). Take the word "discourage" in any sense, and it is full of meaning. Perhaps a stronger word might have been inserted here—a word amounting to aversion and utter dislike to the idea of going forward. Our actions have social effects. There are no literal individualities now; we are not separate and independent pillars;—we are parts of a sum-total; we are members one of another. Consider the social effects of certain actions. It is possible for men to say,—We will not go to church; we have really outgrown the whole idea represented by the Church;—not that it is a vicious idea, but by culture, by reading, by progress of every kind, we have practically outgrown the Church;—we will sit down outside in the wood where the birds sing, by the stream where the wild flowers grow, clear out in the blue morning; and there we will be glad with a kind of mute religiousness. Does the matter end there? Finding you sitting outside, what are those who have not outgrown the Church to do? It is easy for you to say they should go on; but you have miscalculated your own influence: you have undervalued your own social importance. When men like you do certain things, your doing of them must have an effect upon inferior minds. It might be well, perhaps, to sacrifice yourselves somewhat, lest you discourage other men, or avert their attention from those

things to which you, may be, owe more of your own manhood
than you are at first disposed to acknowledge. A great deal is
assumed in this reasoning—namely, that a man *can* outgrow the
Church. Personally, I have never known a man outgrow the
sublimity of prayer; I have never seen a man who need no
longer sing God's praise; but for purposes of argument, assuming
that outside the Church you can find room for your cattle, pasture
for your flocks, water enough for all the purposes of your life,
remember that you are not all Israel or the sum-total of
humanity, and that sometimes even persons who have outgrown
the Church—at least, in their own estimation—would show the
better side of their nature by sacrificing themselves and passing
through a process which may amount to tedium, rather than
repel, discourage, or avert men who have not yet attained that
sublimity of mental altitude or moral compass. The answer of
Moses was not only military but shepherdly. At first, he taunted
Reuben and Gad with being cowards, and then, with a shepherd's
solicitude, thinking of the larger Israel, he said,—How can ye
discourage the hearts of your brethren, and hinder them morally
from going over into the land which the Lord hath given them?

Then Moses utilised history. Beginning at the eighth verse,
and going to the thirteenth, Moses brings to bear upon Reuben
and Gad a tremendous historical impeachment, commencing—
"Thus did your fathers, when I sent them from Kadesh-barnea
to see the land" (v. 8). They belonged, therefore, to an
ancestry not only physically but morally akin. Who can tell the
origin of the desires, ambitions, propositions, and programmes of
his life? The past speaks in the present. Our fathers come up
in a kind of resurrection in our own thinking and our own propositions. Meanness of soul is handed down; disobedience is
not buried in the grave with the man who disobeyed. This is
a broad law; were it rightly understood and applied, many a
man's conduct would be explained which to-day appears to be
quite inexplicable. Appetites descend from generation to generation; diseases may sleep through one generation, and arise in
the next with aggravated violence. Men should take care what
they do. The great scheme of life—whether it be a scheme
invented by chance or originated and governed by God—asserts,
in the soul of it, a principle of criticism and judgment and

penalty, which makes the strongest men afraid. Argument is, of course, lost where the heart is predisposed to evil. There are men who would drink wine if they knew by a writing of heaven that all their progeny would through that act go to the devil ; argument has no relation to such men : the fire that is within them consumes all reasoning, as the open volcano might consume a shower of rain. Still, there may be some who have not gone so far along that ruinous line, and to them this word of caution may be fittingly addressed : What you do will reappear in your posterity. No man liveth unto himself ; no man dieth unto himself. In the name of an unborn generation ; in the name of children who may be born and may live to curse you, beware, be wise ; you are sowing seed which will bring forth a disastrous harvest.

Then Reuben and Gad said they would fight :—they would build sheepfolds for their cattle, and cities for their little ones : but they themselves would go ready-armed before the children of Israel, until they had brought them unto their place : and then their little ones should dwell in the fenced cities because of the inhabitants of the land. They said, in these plain words,—" We will not return unto our houses, until the children of Israel have inherited every man his inheritance. For we will not inherit with them on yonder side Jordan, or forward ; because our inheritance is fallen to us on this side Jordan eastward " (vv. 18, 19). Moses said, in effect,—So be it : if you complete the battle, you shall locate yourselves here : but you must complete the battle, and when the conquest is won, you may return and enjoy what you can here of green things and flowing water ; but, let me tell you, " if ye will not do so, behold, ye have sinned against the Lord ;" this is not a covenant between you and me— between man and man ; but your sin will be against the Lord, " and be sure your sin will find you out." The matter was not easily arranged ; Heaven was invoked, tones of judgment were employed, a covenant was entered into which bore the seal eternal. That law still continues. Supposing there to be no Bible, no altar, no invisible judgment-seat, no white throne,—as has been conceived by sacred poetry—there is still, somehow, at work, in this mysterious scheme of things, a law of a constabulary kind, which arrests the evil-doer, which makes the

glutton sick, which makes the voluptuary weak, which stings the
plotter in the very time which he had planned for his special
joy.   There is—account for it as we may—a ghostliness that looks
upon us through the cloud, so that we feel the blood receding
from the face, or feel it returning in violent torrents, making the
face red with shame.   But there is the law, give it what name
we may, shuffle out of religious definitions as we like: the
wrong-doer lays his head on a hard pillow; the bad man stores
his property in unsafe places.   This may not seem to be so
to-day, or to-morrow, or the third day; but that it is so in the
long run and summation of things, history has too clearly
testified to leave the matter open to wordy disputation.

The relations were thus settled; Reuben and Gad and the
half-tribe of Manasseh would locate themselves as inhabitants
of cis-Jordan, Israel might become inhabitants of trans-Jordan.
We remember Lot having made a very fortunate choice.   With
a sharp keen commercial eye he saw the country was well-
watered; so he said he would locate himself there, and his
uncle Abram might go where he pleased.   Lot seemed to have
the best of it.   Reuben, Gad, and the half-tribe of Manasseh
seem to have escaped very considerable possibilities of misadventure,—they had a bird in the hand, and they thought
that bird better than any two that might be in the trans-Jordan
bush.   There was no mistake about the land—its greenness,
its fruitfulness, its plentiful supply of water and its favourable
conditions generally.   It was indeed a very excellent bargain.
As to fighting, by this time they had become so accustomed to
it that fighting itself was a kind of recreation; they would soon
complete what was required in the way of battle; then they
would come back to the cis-Jordan heaven.   Listen!   Reuben
and Gad and the half-tribe of Manasseh were among the very
first that were taken captives by the king of Assyria!   Separate
not yourselves from the Father; do not set up little heavens
of your own; fall into the great harmony of things; be part
of "the whole family, in heaven and on earth;" and the end
will justify the wisdom of the choice.   "Wisdom is justified of
all her children."   What is God's plan?   Where would he have
me located?   If I can receive an answer to that inquiry, that
answer shall determine my policy and course.   There may be no

individual reply; we may have to study the history of the Church and acquaint ourselves with the direction of a certain grand historical line, and we may have to learn to hold our tongues in moments of temptation and to keep down our ambition, when we think we see the throne which we could easily seize and permanently occupy. The solemn lesson—yet a lesson full of sacred and tender joy—is, that the bounds of our habitation are fixed; the place of our feet is appointed : the very ground in which the grave shall be dug is already outlined. We have nothing to do with things which offend, vex, and harass our attention and our noblest faculties. " Seek ye first the kingdom of God, and his righteousness; and all these things shall be added unto you." We have one business ; and when we are consecrated to it, devoted to it; when we have settled down to it with concentrated energy, and men ask us to explain our " fanaticism," our reply is prepared, our reply is divine,—" Wist ye not that I must be about my Father's business ? "

SELECTED NOTE.

The Reubenites, like their relatives and neighbours on the journey, the Gadites, had maintained through the march to Canaan, the ancient calling of their forefathers. The patriarchs were "feeding their flocks " at Shechem when Joseph was sold into Egypt. It was as men whose "trade had been about cattle from their youth " that they were presented to Pharaoh, and in the land of Goshen they settled "with their flocks and herds and all that they had." Their cattle accompanied them in their flight from Egypt, not a hoof was left behind. The tribes who were destined to settle in the confined territory between the Mediterranean and the Jordan had, during the journey through the wilderness, fortunately relinquished their taste for the possession of cattle, which they could not have maintained after their settlement at a distance from the wide pastures of the wilderness. Thus the cattle had come into the hands of Reuben, Gad, and the half of Manasseh, and it followed naturally that when the nation arrived on the open downs east of the Jordan, the three tribes just named should prefer a request to their leader to be allowed to remain in a place so perfectly suited to their requirements. When the Reubenites and their fellows approach Moses with their request, his main objection is that by what they propose they will discourage the hearts of the children of Israel from going over Jordan into the land which Jehovah had given them. It is only on their undertaking to fulfil their part in the conquest of the western country, the land of Canaan proper, and thus satisfying him that their proposal was grounded in no selfish desire to escape a full share of the difficulties of the conquest, that Moses will consent to their proposal.

PRAYER.

ALMIGHTY GOD, thou art the God of our life. Our life is hidden with God in Christ. In God we live and move and have our being. Without Christ, we can do nothing: we can do all things through Christ which strengtheneth us. As the branch cannot bear fruit of itself, except it abide in the vine; no more can we bear fruit except we abide in Christ. Did he not say,—"I am the true vine, and my Father is the husbandman"? We are but branches, —thank God, we are branches. No man can pluck away the branch; it abides by its fruitfulness, and, being fruitful, it is eternal. Prune us, if thou wilt, that we may bring forth more fruit. Do with us as thou pleasest, for we are not husbandmen; we will submit intelligently, lovingly, hopefully. We know thy purpose: thou dost not wound even the branch merely to give pain: thou dost cut that we may be improved; thine object is purification, enlargement, health, immortality. God's will be done; thy will be done on earth as it is done in heaven. Then shall we be fruitful branches, and the Lord shall have pleasure in our abundance. We thank thee for this life. Now and again we find a fountain in it, and we sing gladly. Sometimes we find no well, and there is nothing but hot sand, and a disappointing sky without cloud or hint of rain; and then we are gloomy, sad of heart, and apt to be rebellious of will. Then the old man dies, and we say,—The head of Israel is cut off, and the remainder must decay. So, we are led on from station to station, from point to point, in all the curious way;—may we ever see the lamp of fire by night, and the pillar of cloud by day; then no matter where we are, we are still on the right road, under God's guidance, and, at last, we shall find house and home and welcome in heaven. The Lord's light be on us a perpetual summer, our Father's blessing be upon us a continual delight, and the Cross of Christ ever magnify itself above our sin, and the blood of Jesus Christ thy Son ever show its preciousness as applied to the sins of the soul.

This is our prayer, our psalm of adoration and thankfulness, our anthem of triumph and hope; whilst we say, on earth, Amen, do thou, in heaven, say Amen.

Numbers xxxiii. 1-49.

1. These are the journeys of the children of Israel, which went forth out of the land of Egypt with their armies under the hand of Moses and Aaron.

2. And Moses wrote their goings out according to their journeys by the commandment of the Lord: and these are their journeys according to their goings out.

THE JOURNEYS OF ISRAEL.

THIS chapter gives a very graphic and instructive picture of a much larger scheme of journeying. The local names may mean nothing to us now, but the words "departed," "removed," "encamped," have meanings that abide for ever. We are doing in our way, and according to the measure of our opportunity, exactly what Israel did in this chapter of hard names and places mostly now forgotten. Observe, this is a written account :—"And Moses wrote their goings out." The life is all written. It is not a sentiment spoken without consideration and forgotten without regret : it is a record—a detailed and critical writing, condescending to geography, locality, daily movement, position in society and in the world. It is, therefore, to be regarded as a story that has been proved, and that will bear to be written and rewritten. Who would write again a mere dream ? Who would spend ink upon so vapoury a thing as a nightmare ? If Israel had passed through the Red Sea in some distorted dream, would Moses have cared to make actual history of it—at least, in form and expression, for there is no hint in all the story that the man is parabolising or drawing upon a vivid and masterful imagination ? The whole experience has been long past, and here it is recalled and set down with a firm hand, without hesitancy or staggering. Here it stands like stern history, plain fact,—something that did actually and positively occur. Men may write about miracles so frequently as to divest them of the element which first touched surprise and awakened suspicion through the medium of the imagination. We may read of miracles until we lose their pomp and their meaning. But life is a miracle : every day is a sign from heaven. We have outgrown the infantile mind which could only see miracles in form and hear them in noise and be amazed at them in tumult and earthquake and varied violence, and now we see the meant-miracle, the ever-intended wonder, of life coming out of death, light springing upon darkness and chasing it away with victorious power, as if one bright beam could slay a million nights. So now, in the absence of startling phenomenon and tumult and vision apocalyptic, we see in quietness itself a miracle, in light a token, in summer the wonder-working power of the loving God. Life is twice written. We have amongst us what are termed, by some stretch of imagination occasionally encroaching upon the impossible, "biographers." It is a complimentary term. Biography is, in the deepest and truest sense, impossible. A man cannot write his own life : he can but hint at it, and the only surprise he can feel, when he has finished the page, is amazement at its emptiness. Yet it is good for a man to put down the facts of his life. His birthplace should be dear to him, as also the place where he fought his early battles, and won his first victories, and opened his first gates, and saw his first chances, and struggled in the agony of his first prayers, and seized with the hand of faith the first blessings of heaven meant for his soul's nurture and strengthening ; and it is good to continue the page, fill it up, turn it over, and to go on to the new page, and charge the whole book with memories intended to express amazement and thankfulness. The one perfect Biographer is God. Every life is written in the book that is kept in the secret places of the heavens. All things are naked and opened unto the eyes of him with whom we have to do. Nothing is omitted. The writing is plain—so plain that the blind man may read the story which God has written for his perusal. Who would like to see the book ? Who could not write a book about his brother that would please that brother ? Without being false, it might yet be highly eulogistic and comforting. But who would like to see his life as sketched by the hand of God ? " Enter not into judgment with thy servant : for in thy sight shall no man living be justified." " Have mercy upon me, O God, according to thy lovingkindness : according unto the multitude of thy tender mercies blot out my transgressions."

What a monotony there is in this thirty-third chapter. This will be evident to the eye. The reader sees but two words or three, and all the rest are difficult terms or polysyllables unrelated to his life. The terms are " departed," " removed," " went." It is almost pathetic to see how the writer tries to vary his expressions and cannot. Verse after verse he uses the word " departed ; " then verse after verse he uses the word "removed;" here and there he said "they went," but back again he comes to "departed," and then to "removed," and back to "went." "They removed . . . and pitched,"—that is the little story. Is it not so with us too? How dull the days are. How full of tedious similitude is the succession of events. We want variety; we cry for amusement; we sigh for change; we propose re-arrangements and re-combinations that we may at least please the eye with what seems to be a varying picture. Very few words are needed for the record of most lives; as to outward and actual event, very few words are needed at all. If you have in any language, say, five thousand words, you can really conduct the business of life upon about five hundred of them. There are great stores of words that are locked up in the prisons of lexicons: they are only wanted now and then, and they are, therefore, but occasionally liberated. The language of actual life is a narrow language which may be learned in a very brief time. So with our daily life: we rise, we sit, we retire; we eat and drink, and bless one another in the name of God; and go round the little circle, until sometimes we say,—Can we not vary all that—and add to it some more vivid line? Has no friend of ours the power of flushing this pale monotony into some tint of blood? Then we fall back into the old lines: we "depart" and "remove" and "pitch;" we "pitch" and "depart" and "remove;"—we come and go and settle and return; until there comes almost unconsciously into the strain of our speech some expressive and mournful sigh. "Few and evil have been the days of thy servant."

Yet, not to dwell too much upon this well-ascertained fact, we may regard the record of the journeys of Israel as showing somewhat of the variety of life. Here and there a new departure sets in, or some new circumstance brightens the history. For example, in the ninth verse we read —"And they removed from Marah, and came unto Elim: and in Elim were twelve fountains of water, and threescore and ten palm trees." Sweet entry is that! It occurs in our own secret diaries. Do we not dwell with thankfulness upon the places where we find the waters, the wells, the running streams, the beautiful trees, and the trees beautiful with luscious fruitage? It is a dull life that has nothing in it about the fountain, and the palm tree, and the beautiful day that seemed to throw its radiance upon a hundred other days and give them some glint of celestial beauty. The pleasant lines are not many, but when they do come they are the more pleasant because of their infrequency. We all remember the beautiful garden in the May-time, when the whole scene was one blossom. How we hastened home to write the story of the garden-day, when everything seemed to be in vernal glee, in high spirits,— bird outvying bird in sparkles of music,—note after note shot out like star after star into the willing and hospitable space ;— and the birth-day and the wedding-day, and some holy time, quiet like an anticipated Sabbath ; and the time of victory in prayer, when we received the answers in the very act of offering the supplications,—times of enlargement and vital communion with God. Then comes the fourteenth verse :—" And they removed from Alush, and encamped at Rephidim, where was no water." Such are the changes in life. We have passed through precisely the transitions here indicated. No water ; nothing to satisfy even the best appetences of the mind and spirit ; all heaven one sheet of darkness, and the night so black upon the earth that even the altar-stairs could not be found in the horrid gloom ; if there was water, it had no effect upon the thirst ; if there was bread, it was bitter ; if there was a pillow, it was filled with pricking thorn. When we were at Elim, we said we should always be glad : the plash of the fountain and the shade of the palm tree would accompany us evermore ; and yet, behold, at Rephidim there "was no water for the people to drink." How singular is Providence !—apparently, so contradictory ; apparently, so wanting in consistency. Why is there not one great deep river flowing all the globe around— a belt of blessing ?' Why these arid places—the wildernesses without fountains, these deserts unblest with a flower ?—Why ? In that " Why " there is no suspicion, nor is there one accent of distrust, but there certainly is an expression of wonder. It is so in all departments of life—say, even, in life intellectual. Sometimes the mind has it all its own way ; it can see heaven opened and the Son of man standing at the right hand of God ; as for language, it knows all the languages of the earth—claims them, absorbs them, repeats them so as to astound every man with the music of the tongue in which he was born. At other times, that same life seems nothing, has no language, no vision, no touch of God's presence or hint of God's blessing. We go from Elim to Rephidim in that department of life. There is another variety of the story; the thirty-eighth verse presents it:—" And Aaron the priest went up into mount Hor at the commandment of the Lord, and died there." Is that line wanting in our story? All men do not die on mountains. Would God we may die upon some high hill! It seems to our imagination nearer heaven to die away up on the mountain peaks than to die in the low damp valleys. Granted, that it is but an imagination. We need such helps: we are so made that symbol and hint and parable assist the soul in its sublimest realisation of things divine and of things to come. There is a black margin upon every man's diary,— here a child died, there a sweet mother said good-bye, there a strong father—the man who was never tired, the tower of strength—said he must go home.

This, also, presents a focalised life: all the lines are tending to one point. So it is in our own story. What is that point? the modern teacher might say. It is a grave. That is only intermediately so; that is but atheistically so. We are moving to the tomb—to the one black gate that keeps us out of the city of light; and we will, in God's strength, unlock it, break it, triumph over it and all the strength it represents, and join the blood-washed throng of holy victors on the other side. We will not finish the song with the word "tomb," it is no poetry whose ultimate syllable is in the grave. We are moving—if in Christ, washed by his blood, pardoned through his propitiation, to the land of light and summer and blissful immortality. "Every beating pulse we tell leaves the number less;" every night we "pitch our moving tent a day's march nearer home." Whilst we look at the various localities and their relation to one another upon the map—now moving north, now south, now east, now west, we say,—What is the meaning of this tumultuous movement? It is only so broken up within a small compass, measured by heaven's meridian, the direction is in one line, at the end of which burns all the warmth and light of heaven.

And yet, there is an unwritten life. This cannot be all: there must be some reading between the lines. Life was never an affair of such grim and unfamiliar polysyllables: between the lines, there must have been loving, praying, weeping, suffering, rejoicing, wedding, dying, fierce word, and word of benediction. This is but a river-map : all the cities have to be filled in and all the city-life to be created. Still, wherein it is but an outline it is like our own story as we ought to tell it or represent it to others. No man knoweth the spirit of a man but the spirit itself that is within the man, and that spirit has revelations for which there is no language—visions that cannot be syllabled and printed to the eye and apprehension of outside observers and critics.

SELECTED NOTE.

A visit to Mount Hor (*Jebel Harùn,* "Mount of Aaron "), or at least a distant view of its wild precipices and ravines, helps to make the visit to Petra memorable. Here it was that Aaron, the priest laden with years and weary with the toil of the desert-wandering, was " gathered to his people." Even Scripture has few more solemn and majestic pictures than this of the two aged men—brothers in heart and sacred service—ascending with the youthful Eleazar to this wild mountain-top. " In his full priestly dress " walked Aaron to his burial. He knew it; and so did all in that camp, who now, for the last time, reverently and silently looked upon the venerable figure of him who these forty years had ministered unto them in holy things. There were no farewells. In that typical priesthood, all depended on the unbroken continuance of the office, not of the person. And hence on the mountain-top, Aaron was first unclothed of his priestly robes, and Eleazar his son formally invested with them. Thus the priesthood had not for a moment ceased when Aaron died. Then, not as a priest, but simply as one of God's Israel, was he "gathered unto his people." But over that which passed between the three on the mount has the hand of God drawn the veil of silence. And so the new priest Eleazar came down from the solemn scene on Mount Hor to minister amidst a hushed and awe-stricken congregation. "And when all the congregation saw that Aaron was dead, they mourned for Aaron thirty days, even all the house of Israel." The traditionary tomb of the high-priest is shown to visitors in a vault below a small chapel, which evidently occupies the place of a more imposing structure, and is built out of its ruins. The Bedawîn still holds the name of Aaron in great veneration. A singular custom of theirs is to sacrifice a kid or sheep to his memory, in sight of Mount Hor, raising a heap of stones where the blood of the animal has fallen. These heaps are seen all through the neighbouring valley.—*Pictures from Bible Lands,* by Samuel G. Green, D.D.

PRAYER.

ALMIGHTY GOD, kindle a light in our hearts that can never go out: the light of Christian confidence, the glory of Christian hope; may we walk amidst its beauty, and enjoy its nourishment and warmth. We need the comfort of heaven: we pine for a blessing from on high; we shall know it when we receive it, for none can resemble it in all-tenderness and sufficiency and inspiration. Withhold not thy regard from us, and let thine attention be the outlook of love. We may not say this in our own name, for it is valueless in heaven. We have fallen: we have done the things we ought not to have done; we have forfeited all right of speech with the throne. But Jesus is our Daysman: he is able to lay his hands upon both of us, and to bring us together in happy communion. There is one Advocate with the Father, and he is the Son of man. He pleads our cause; he bears our name as well as thine; and he will plead for us with all the agony of blood, and with all the tenderness of love. He is able to save unto the uttermost all that come unto God by him, seeing that he ever liveth to make intercession for us. We are strong in confidence: we are bold at the Cross. The Cross has turned the throne of judgment into a throne of mercy, and now we come before the King, clothed with the righteousness of his Son, and there plead for such blessing as our poor life continually needs. We thank thee for the sacred Book, and that it is written in many places in our mother-tongue. We know it here and there; sometimes we are quite familiar with it: it falls upon us like a remembered song of youth, which made us glad and hopeful in the early time. Here it is a mountain we cannot climb, a cloud we cannot penetrate, a deep river we dare not touch; but oftentimes it is a hill covered with flowers, a cloud bright with chastened light, and a screen that makes glad the city of our life. Help us to read it with the heart, to answer it with the will, and to be found always commenting upon it with the eloquence of an obedient life. Pity us wherein we are weak; have mercy upon us wherein we have forfeited our lives; continue thy blessing unto us wherein we have begun to do right under the guidance of thy Spirit; and, at last, give us an abundant entrance among the heroic band who fought thy fight, O Christ, in thy strength, and won their every victory in thy name. Amen.

Numbers xxxiii. 50-56.

50. And the Lord spake unto Moses in the plains of Moab by Jordan near Jericho, saying,

51. Speak unto the children of Israel, and say unto them, When ye are passed over Jordan into the land of Canaan;

52. Then ve shall drive out all the inhabitants of the land from before

you, and destroy all their pictures, and destroy all their molten images, and quite pluck down all their high places :

53. And ye shall dispossess the inhabitants of the land, and dwell therein : for I have given you the land to possess it.

54. And ye shall divide the land by lot for an inheritance among your families : and to the more ye shall give the more inheritance, and to the fewer ye shall give the less inheritance : every man's inheritance shall be in the place where his lot falleth ; according to the tribes of your fathers ye shall inherit.

55. But if ye will not drive out the inhabitants of the land from before you ; then it shall come to pass, that those which ye let remain of them shall be pricks in your eyes, and thorns in your sides, and shall vex you in the land wherein ye dwell.

56. Moreover it shall come to pass, that I shall do unto you, as I thought to do unto them.

THOROUGHNESS.

THE subject is evidently *thoroughness.* Do the work completely—root and branch, in and out, so that there may be no mistake as to earnestness ; and the result shall be security, peace, contentment ;—Do the work partially—half and half, perfunctorily ; and the end shall be disappointment, vexation, and ruin. Causes have effects ; work is followed by consequences. Do not suppose that you can turn away the law of causation and consequence. Things are settled and decreed before you begin the work. There is no cloud upon the covenant, no ambiguity in its terms. He is faithful who hath promised—faithful to give blessing, and faithful to inflict penalty. Faithfulness in God is not a one-sided quality or virtue. Do not fear to call God " Judge." We mistake and misapply the term when we think of it only in its vengeful aspect. To " judge " is to do right. God will "judge the fatherless and the widow," God will "judge" every worker. He will come into the Canaan which he has appointed to us, and see whether we have done the work thoroughly or only partially ; if thoroughly, Canaan will be as heaven ; if partially and selfishly, then the very land of promise shall become the land of disappointment. It is well the words were spoken before the work began. There is no after-thought with God. Hell is not a recent invention of Omnipotence : it is as old as right and wrong. Let us have no affectation of surprise, no falling-back as from uncalculated violence ; the covenant is written in plain ink, uttered in distinct terms—so written, so uttered, that the wayfaring man need not err.

There was so much to be undone in the Canaan that was promised. It is this negative work which tries our patience, and puts our faith to severe tests. We meet it everywhere. The colonist has to subdue the country, take down much that is already put up, root out the trees, destroy the beasts of prey, and do much that is of a merely negative kind, before he begins to sow corn, to reap harvests, and to build a secure homestead. This is the case in all the relations of life. The weed is not the green thing on the surface; that is only the signal that the weed is underneath. The work that has to be done is a work of eradication. The weed must be torn up by its every fibre. We are apt to lop off the top, and think we have completed the work of destruction. We must learn the meaning of the word eradication—the getting out of the root, the sinking right down to the very farthest point of residence, and then having no pity, but pulling out the weed, not for the sake of destruction, but to make room for a flower that shall please the very vision of God. But the colonist is a character of whom we know little. The illustration by being so remote does not immediately touch our life; but an illustration can be drawn from our own experience and conduct. In the work of education, for example, how much has to be undone! When the first thing the teacher has to do is to destroy a man's supposed wisdom, he encounters the most obstinate hostility of the man. The student comes with lines that have pleased him, with conclusions which he thinks established, and with processes of accomplishing results which he regards as perfect. Solemn is the work of the teacher, even to pathos and tears, when the first thing he has to do with the young man is to tell him that he cannot speak his mother-tongue. At home he was quite an idol in the family; they considered him a paragon; they called upon him to recite his poems and to display his talents, and he answered the challenge in gay response; and now some learned chief in the temple of wisdom tells him that he does not know how to utter the alphabet of his mother-tongue; he battles with him over the very first letter: he will not have it so pronounced but quite otherwise; he will have the alphabet reconstructed as to tone, colour, fire; and, in the end, he who thought himself so excellent in speech will deliver himself in a tongue which will be foreign to those at home. This holds good in nearly every department of education. There is so much to be undone: so many prejudices have to be conquered, so many evil habits have to be eradicated, like the weed we would not spare; so that, at the end of a few months, when idolatrous friends ask how the young student is advancing, they find that he is actually worse at the end of six months than he was when he went to be taught. So he is, in a certain sense. But we must not punctuate processes by our impatience: we must await the issue; and when the educator says, "It is finished," we may pronounce the word of judgment.

The theory of the Bible is that it has to encounter a human nature that is altogether wrong. It is not our business, at this point, to ask how far that theory is true. The Bible itself proceeds upon the assumption that " All we like sheep have gone astray; we have turned every one to his own way;" " There is none righteous, no, not one;" " God hath made man upright; but they have sought out many inventions;" there is none that doeth good, no, not one; the whole head and the whole heart are not righteous or true before God. That being the theory of the Bible, see what it proposes to do. What iconoclasm it must first accomplish! How it must swing its terrific arms in the temples of our idolatry and in the whole circuit of our life, breaking, destroying, burning, casting out, overturning, overturning! What is it doing? It is preparing; it is doing the work of a pioneer; it is uttering the voice of a herald. Mark the audacity of the Book! It speaks no flattering word, never uncovers before any man, bids every man go wash and be clean. A book coming before society with so bold a proposition must expect to be encountered with resolute obstinacy. If we suppose we are ready-made to the hand of God, to be turned in any direction he is pleased to adopt, we begin upon a false basis; our theory is wrong, and our conception will lead us to proportionate disappointment. God has to do with a fallen intelligence, an apostate heart, a selfish will; and, therefore, he undertakes much negative work before he can begin constructive processes

What a temptation there is, however, to reserve something. Point to one instance in all the Biblical history in which a man actually and perfectly accomplished the divine will in this matter of destruction. A good deal of destruction was accomplished, unquestionably; but was there nothing left? " What meaneth then this bleating of the sheep in mine ears, and the lowing of the oxen which I hear?" The temptation to reserve something is very strong. Take it as a matter of old companionship. It does seem to be ruthless to cut off the old comrades as with the blow of a sword. They do not understand the process of excision; they say,—We can still be friends; you have changed your theological convictions and your religious standpoint : you attend church, you pay respect to the altar, you read the Bible with a new attentiveness,—let it all be granted ; but surely there is neutral ground : there are occupations that are not directly touched by the religious sanctities; surely we need not wholly separate one from another, as if we had never seen each other's face? Such a plea is not without tenderness : there is a touch of humanity in it; but to the man who is earnestly religious before God there is no neutral ground, there is no secular occupation, there is no non-religious relation; the dew of the heavenly baptism has fallen upon all life, all duty, all suffering. "If any man be in Christ, he is a new creature : old things are passed away; behold, all things are become new." We cannot clutch time with one hand and eternity with the other, in any sense of dividing them into secular and religious; we cannot serve God and Mammon. Then take the thought in relation to old places, where we used to spend the happy evening, where the recreation was innocent and, in a sense, helpful, reinvigorating jaded faculties, and giving a new start to weary or exhausted impulses. Why not look in just once more, or now and then, —say, annually, on particular occasions, when the men are at their best and the institution is in state? It will look friendly; in fact, we may do good by some such arrangement, because we shall show that we are not Pharisees and pedants; we have not betaken ourselves to a monastic life, but we can return to old places and old associations, and breathe upon them a new spirit. The reasoning is specious: there is no doubt about its plausibility ; but take care how you carry a naked candle into a high

wind ; take care lest the battle should go the other way. It
is dangerous for immature experience to expose itself to rooted
prejudices and established habits.   There is a time in the growth
of some lives when a loud laugh may blow out the trembling
light of a young profession.   Our language, therefore, must
be that of caution ; the exhortation, charged with tenderness,
must begin with the words, "My son," and flow out in most
sacred and persuasive emotion.   It is not enough to adjure, to
hurl the bolt of avenging judgment : we must wrestle and reason
and pray.

The words of the text are complete in their force and range.
In many a life, great improvement takes place without eradication
being perfected.   We are not called in the Bible merely to
make great improvement.   That is what we have been trying
to do by our own strength and wit, and which we have always
failed in doing.   Nowhere do the sacred writers encourage us
to make considerable advance upon our old selves.   The exhortation of the Bible is vital.   Suppose a man should have been
addicted to the meanest of all vices—the vice of lying, the vice
that God can hardly cure,—that last deep dye that the blood of
God's own Christ's heart can hardly get at, that defies the very
detergents of heaven ;—suppose such a man should lie less, is
he less a liar ?   Suppose he should cease the vulgarity of falsehood and betake himself to the refinement of deceit, has he
improved ?   Rather, he has aggravated the first offence—multiplied by infinite aggravations the conditions which first constituted
his character.   Suppose he should neither lie nor deceive on
any great scale, but should betake himself to the act of speaking
ambiguously—that is to say, using words in two senses, meaning
the hearer to accept the words in one sense, whilst he construes
them in another ; he then becomes a verbal trickster, a conjurer
in speech ; he has mental reservations ; he has a secret or
esoteric backway by which he interprets to his own conscience
the language which he uses in public and which he intends to be
construed by public lexicography.   Has he improved ?   He has
gone to a deeper depth of evil.   The vulgar criminal may be
hopefully encountered ; but the man who has twisted language,
coloured and flushed with new significance terms which ought to
have been pure in their meaning and direct in their intent ; the

man who trifles with the conscience and intelligence of his fellow-creatures, and does so in cold blood, is no black criminal : he is a skilled artist in the devil's pay, and so far in that the divine finger can hardly touch his supposed security. So, we are not called to great improvements, to marvellous changes of a superficial kind : we are called to newness of birth, regeneration, the washing of the Holy Ghost, the renewal—the re-creation of the inner man. "Marvel not that I said unto thee, Ye must be born again." There is a great work of destruction to be done which we dare not undertake. You can never reason down many of the institutions of Christian countries which are at this moment mocking the sanctuary, and secretly laughing with jeers and bitterest sarcasm at Christianity. We must use force in relation to some institutions—not the force of the arm, which is the poorest of all strength, but the force of reasoned law, righteous legislation, laws made at the altar and sanctified by the very spirit of prayer. There are institutions in every nominally Christian city that can burn up any number of tracts, blow away any force of eloquence, turn aside any dart of argument. Nothing can touch them but the mighty arm of rational—that is to say, intelligent and righteous—legislation.

Thoroughness gives confidence in all things. Take it in the matter of language. How many men know just enough of any language not to dare to speak it! How many persons know the first syllables of a word, but dare not commit themselves to a precise termination! The grammar lies where the sting lies, at the tail of the word. So, how we huddle up our terminations, broaden, or sharpen, or blur the final vowels, so that men may not know whether we have used the one vowel or the other, coming out with tremendous emphasis on the syllables about which there is no doubt. Thoroughness gives confidence. The man who understands the language in and out, through and through, speaks off-handedly, freely, with dignified carelessness ; he knows that he is fully master of the language, and can speak it with a master's ease. That is true in theology. If we do not believe our theology, we cannot preach it; if we do not believe the Gospel, we can only preach *about* the Gospel,—make complimentary references to it, set it in a very dignified place in the lyceum of intellect; but knowing it, we breathe it like a great healing, purifying wind over the whole earth, saying, -"One thing I know: once I was blind,—now I see." Where are the Pharisees that can frighten us, or the critics that can displace our crown? Do not go beyond your own knowledge; keep strictly within the line of experience and living testimony; and then you will be Herculean in strength, Job-like in patience, Paul-like in heroism and courage.

If not, punishments will come. If you will not do this, "those which ye let remain of them shall be pricks in your eyes, and thorns in your sides, and shall vex you in the land wherein ye dwell;"—they will tease you, excite you, irritate you; they will watch for the moments of your weakness, and tempt you into apostasy. What keen eyes the spared enemies have! Looking upon our life, they say,—Now a malign suggestion might be effected—try it; behold, he halts,—Now speak to him, and tell him that just near at hand is a place to which he may resort for the recruiting of his strength; listen! the old emphasis has gone out of his voice: he does not speak as he used to speak: his convictions are halting, faltering,—now say unto him, but gently, —"Where is thy God?" Take him up to an exceeding high mountain: show what he might be under given conditions. Lift him to the pinnacle of the temple, and show that it is possible for a man to hold churches and temples under his feet—to stand above them and to be more than they;—but speak it quietly, softly, as if you had *his* interest at heart, and, who knows? you may prevail. Has it, then, come to a battle of skill against skill, faculty against faculty? Nothing of the kind. On the Christian side it comes to a question of character. How is that character created and established? By the Spirit of the living God. We cannot explain the process. "The wind bloweth where it listeth, and thou hearest the sound thereof, but canst not tell whence it cometh, and whither it goeth: so is every one that is born of the Spirit." If we are to meet temptation by cleverness, it is impossible for any cleverness to rival the ingenuity of the devil; whenever it was a battle of words, the devil won; he is mighty in conversation, he is most excellent in speech. We can only oppose him by the higher Spirit—the divine Spirit, living in the heart, breathing in the soul, established in the character; so that when he cometh, he findeth nothing in us,—altar everywhere, prayer in all the spirit, righteousness at the foundations, and the whole man burning with the presence of the unconsuming fire. When Satan cometh, may he have nothing in us ! Let us begin the work of destruction—tear the enemy out, cut him in pieces, and never repeat the habit. Do not say you will touch with the tips of your fingers the Old Canaanitish idols and temptations : say,— Lord of heaven and earth, make me a sword, and give me an arm to wield it ; may I go forth as thy warrior, sparing nothing that is impure and unlike thyself. Do not attempt to build a Christian character upon rotten foundations. That is a miracle you cannot accomplish. Do not suppose you can heap up a great pile of noble theological dogmas upon rottenness and bog. The work is foundation work, vital work, work in the heart ; and until that negative, iconoclastic work is done, we cannot begin to build. Overturn ! overturn ! overturn !—then He will come whose right it is.

SELECTED NOTE.

The Israelites were delivered from Egypt by Moses, in order that they might take possession of the land which God had promised to their fathers. This country was then inhabited by the descendants of Canaan, who were divided into six or seven distinct nations. These nations the Israelites were commanded to dispossess and utterly to destroy. The destruction, however, was not to be accomplished at once. The promise on the part of God was that he would "put out those nations by little and little," and the command to the Israelites corresponded with it ; the reason given being, "lest the beast of the field increase upon thee."

The destructive war commenced with an attack on the Israelites, by Arad, king of the Canaanites, which issued in the destruction of several cities in the extreme south of Palestine, to which the name of Hormah was given (Num. xxi. 1-3). The Israelites, however, did not follow up this victory, which was simply the consequence of an unprovoked assault on them ; but, turning back, and compassing the land of Edom, they attempted to pass through the country on the other side of the Jordan, inhabited by a tribe of the Amorites. Their passage being refused, and an attack made on them by Sihon, king of the Amorites, they not only forced their way through his land, but destroyed its inhabitants, and proceeding onwards toward the adjoining kingdom of Bashan, they in like manner destroyed the inhabitants of that district, and slew Og, their king, who was the last of the Rephaim, or giants. The tract of which they thus became possessed was subsequently allotted to the tribes of Reuben and Gad, and the half-tribe of Manasseh.

PRAYER.

ALMIGHTY GOD, thou hast set us in our places, and we would not change them but at thy bidding. We want to sit, when we are ambitious and left to our vain selves, one on the right hand and the other on the left; but now, being taught of the Spirit and being chastened by daily providence and touched into new sacredness of service and hope by grace divine, we are willing to go as thou dost point the way,—to run, to stand, to serve, to wait; —only give us some foothold within the living circle. Thou wilt not thrust us out into the darkness immeasurable. God is light, God is love; his eyes are full of tears; his hands are loaded with gifts for men. Comfort us with these words, for our hearts sometimes give way, and we think the lamp of our hope is going quite out, and we never can light it again. We know we are wayward, for we are of the earth : we are rooted in the soil; we carry the clay in our whole form, and every feature is charged with the dulness of the dust. Yet we carry something more : we are filled with the presence of God : we have the divine treasure in an earthen vessel, and the divine treasure burns through the crust and makes it glow with immortal flame. We are made in the image and likeness of God. Sometimes we are all but in heaven : now and again the life-tide rises within us so high that it plashes against the very throne of God ; sometimes we say we cannot be kept out of the inner places much longer. Then we come down again to darkness, and strife, and disappointment, and weariness; but, though we may sigh our impatience, we cannot utter our unbelief, for our hearts are still saying, each in its own way,—Lord, I believe; help thou mine unbelief. So, we are still on the right side : our life is still lifted up in prayer, our souls are not without hope. So, we can bear the jeer and folly of frivolous men ; they know not what they say, and they say it for no purpose. We would be found in the tabernacle, in the holy place—just on the borderland that hardly separates earth from heaven ; and, being there, we catch occasional warmth and occasional glimpses of better things, and we hear voices that touch our inmost spirit by their subtle music ; and we hope, nor spend our hope in unprofitable sentiment, but receive it as an inspiration, and return to heal the sick and help the blind across a busy thoroughfare, and teach ignorance its alphabet, and break bread to the hungry ; this is the proof of our hope ; were it a merely coloured vapour, we should cast it away, but it is an inspiration: it rouses us to endeavour, it compels us to transfer ourselves into other people, and to carry, where we may, part, at least, of their heavy burdens. We bless thee for this Christian hope ; it lives when all things fail ; it goes upstairs with us when we go for the last time—never to come down again until we are borne out by devout men ; it is the Christian's inheritance, his immediate and blessed paradise. Help us all according to our need. Speak to the aged pilgrim, and say the last mile is the very sunniest of all the road —quite an eventide blessing resting upon it, a tenderness of light, a kind of opening door in the sky, showing how grand the prospect is. Help the young to measure their days, count them and allot them, setting them down in columns and adding them up, and dividing them wisely, to see which is day and which is night, which is the young time, with all its blood, and which is the old time when the blood becomes pale and languid ; and then let them set themselves to work out, like wise economists and devotees of God, the whole purpose of life's little day. As for the prodigal, we send after him ; our letters are left unanswered—perhaps our prayers may be responded to. We will still think and love and hope, not knowing but the next knock on the door may be the announcement of return. Comfort the sick ; they are very ailing and frail and all but breathless ; may we give their looks large interpretations of love : may we spare them the trouble of speaking by knowing in looking at them just what they want ;—for we, too, shall be sick, and must be waited on. The Lord's blessing be upon all families : unite them in the holy fear of God ; upon all business : purify it from all evil and meanness, and pitiable selfishness. Look upon all kinds of honest life, giving them force and breadth, daily reinvigoration and continual blessing.

We speak our prayer in the sweet name of Jesus, crucified once, crowned for evermore. He died for us—the just for the unjust ; he rose again for us to show that death can snatch but a momentary triumph, the final and eternal victory being on the side of life. God be merciful unto us, and bless us, and cause his face to shine upon us ; and in the shining of that face, we shall forget all the pale and mocking glory which once made us glad. Amen.

Numbers xxxiv. 1-12.

1. And the Lord spake unto Moses, saying,

2. Command the children of Israel, and say unto them, When ye come into the land of Canaan ; (this is the land that shall fall unto you for an inheritance, even the land of Canaan with the coasts thereof :)

3. Then your south quarter shall be from the wilderness of Zin along by the coast of Edom, and your south border shall be the outmost coast of the salt sea eastward :

4. And your border shall turn from the south to the ascent of Akrabbim, and pass on to Zin : and the going forth thereof shall be from the south to Kadesh-barnea, and shall go on to Hazar-addar, and pass on to Azmon :

5. And the border shall fetch a compass from Azmon unto the river of Egypt, and the goings out of it shall be at the sea.

6. And as for the western border, ye shall even have the great sea for a border : this shall be your west border.

7. And this shall be your north border : from the great sea ye shall point out for you mount Hor :

8. From mount Hor ye shall point out your border unto the entrance of Hamath and the goings forth of the border shall be to Zedad :

9. And the border shall go on to Ziphron, and the goings out of it shall be at Hazar-enan : this shall be your north border.

10. And ye shall point out your east border from Hazar-enan to Shepham :

11. And the coast shall go down from Shepham to Riblah, on the east side of Ain ; and the border shall descend, and shall reach unto the side of the sea of Chinnereth eastward :

12. And the border shall go down to Jordan, and the goings out of it shall be at the salt sea : this shall be your land with the coasts thereof round about.

BOUNDARIES.

LIFE is marked all over with boundary lines. Two different views may be taken of such lines,—that is to say, in the first place they may be regarded as limitations and partial impoverishments, or, in the next place, they may be regarded as defining rights and liberties, possessions and authorities. Thus, the low view or the high view may be taken of everything in life. Men will work according to their imagination—their noblest faculty. Where that is dull, everything will be dull ; even God could not sow stars in the leaden firmament of a dull imagination. Where that noblest faculty is alive, bright, daring, devout, all labour will be rest, all pain will be a pledge of reward nobly won. So, we may make the boundaries of life cages, prisons,—very serious and depressing limitations ; or we may accept those boundaries as a pledge, a seal of inheritance,— standards and lines to be appealed to when our claim to stand in the lineal sonship of God is questioned or disputed. Very subtle and delicate things are boundaries oftentimes. They are invisible. Are not all the greatest things invisible, as well as the best and most delicate and tender ? Show the line of love. There is no line to show. It is at this point that conscience comes into active play. Where the conscience is dull, or im- perfectly educated, or selfish, there will be much dispute about boundaries ; but where the conscience is sanctified by the power of the Cross and is alive with the righteousness of God, there will be no controversy, but large concession, noble interpretation, willingness to give, to take, to arrange and settle, without the severity of the law or the cruelty of the sword. Sometimes we say,—Let a certain line be imagined. We put imaginary lines upon the very globe itself ; the points of the compass cannot touch the lines, yet they are there, present to the spiritual sight, quite open and intelligible to the sanctified conscience. And rights of an imperial and enduring kind are based upon what may be called imaginary lines. Sometimes we are brought very near to the territories of others; it requires more than the naked eye to distinguish between *mine* and *thine* in some cases; the approach is very close; the naked eye could see no difference. There are men who have nothing but a naked eye, nothing but a naked hand; they have not the lens of heaven, or the touch that breaks the few loaves into a great feast; rough, heartless men, seizing everything, but enjoying nothing,—slaves of their own cupidity. Many a controversy may arise as to boundary in this matter, because the lines do appear to run into one another: a sword could not divide them; the finest edge ever made by most skilled workers in iron could not part them asunder; but there is a sword that can do so—not iron or steel, but the sword of the Spirit, which is the Word of God, written in the book and set in the heart,—a wonderful tone that gives vision to conscience, the marvellous perception which is a miracle of God in the intellectual and moral constitution of human nature.

What differences there are in boundaries! We read of one, in the seventh verse, whose boundary was "from the great sea"; in the twelfth verse, "the goings out of it shall be at the salt sea." There is so much sea in some people's limited possession. What a boundary is the inhospitable sea! We cannot cut it up into acres, and lay it out; we cannot sow it with wheat, and reap the harvest, and enjoy the bread; it is to most of us but a spectacle—great, melancholy, unresponsive, pitiless; a liquid emblem of cruel death. Is not this the case with many men? They know they have great possessions, but their greatness is not the measure of their value. A little garden-plot would be to some men more valuable, for purposes of living, than the freehold of the Atlantic. Sometimes men are born to great estates that have nothing in them—boundless nothings; a proprietorship of infinite bogs and wastes and unanswering sterilities; sand that cannot be ploughed, water that cannot be sown with seed, and bogs that cannot be built upon. Contrast with such allotments the words of music which you find in the fifteenth verse: "toward the sunrising." That is an inheritance worth having! The morning sun blesses it: early in the morning all heaven's glory is poured out upon it with the hospitality of God; whatever is planted in it grows almost instantly; the flowers love to be planted there; all the roots of the earth would say,—Put us in this place of the morning sun, and we will show you what we can do in growth and fruitfulness; give us the chance of the sun, and then say what we really are.   We cannot all have our estates "toward the sunrising"; we cannot wholly cut off the north and the north-east—the shady side of the hill: somebody must be there.   Does God plant a tabernacle in such sunless districts? Is there any temple of God in the north-lands, where the storm blows with a will and the tempests seem to have it all their own way, rioting in their tumultuous strength, and, as it were, accosting one another in reduplications of infinite thunderings and roarings of whirlwinds?   Even there God's footprint may be found.   Even a little may be so held as to be much.   Quite a small garden may grow stuff enough for a whole household. Gardens like to be cunningly handled, lovingly arranged, quite embraced with love;—then the least plot of land looks up smilingly, and says,—You have treated me to the best of your ability; if there had been more sun, we should have been as good as any other land in the world; still, let us be friends; till me, culture me, sow me with seed,—do what you can for me, and my answer shall be the brightest answer of love that is in my power to return.   Yield not to dejection.   Some must live in the north; some must be towards the bleak quarter.   Is it not possible for us to have joy in the recollection of the fact, that brothers of ours are living in the south, and that on their gardens, if not on ours, the morning looks with benediction and heavenliness and approbation?

We cannot get rid of boundaries.   Never listen to those who talk about equality—simply because you have no time to waste. Equality is impossible.   If we were all equal one day, we should all be unequal before the sun went down.   Let us listen only to the truly reasonable in this matter.   There is something better than outward and nominal equality, and that is an intelligent appreciation of the fact that there must be differences of personality and allotment and responsibility, and that in the end the judgment will be divine in its righteousness.   We find boundaries in gifts of all kinds.   "Why do you not paint a

picture for the Royal Academy ? " Suppose a great artist put
this inquiry to me, I should reply,—" Nothing would give me
much greater pleasure that is of an intellectual kind." Then the
artist may say,—" Why do you not realise your ideal of high
enjoyment ? " I answer interrogatively,—" How can I ? " He
replies cordially,—" I will find the canvas, I will mix the colours,
I will supply the brushes—now what hinders you to be baptised,
and to rise an artist ? " Why talk about equality ? I would rise
an artist in a moment, if I could, but it is impossible ; my brother
must be artist : enough for me I may be but preacher. So I say
to him,—" Why do you not preach ? " He says,—" I would like
to." " Then why do you not ? I will find the church and a
pulpit and a Bible—why not be baptised, and rise a Voice ? "
He cannot : it is not born in him ; another good gift of God is
his, and it is a great gift ; and it is not becoming in us that we
should put our gifts in hostile opposition to one another, as if one
were a gift of God and another a gift of some lower power. All
boundaries and divisions and distributions are divine, and the
acceptance of them is itself a religion. Why not write a book of
exactly the same quality as *Paradise Lost?*—here is ink enough ;
what hindereth me to be baptised for poetic honours and Miltonic
renown ? I have as much right to the six-and-twenty letters of
the alphabet as any poet whose brows were ever covered with
bays and coronals. That is true. The poorest man is born to
own as much of the sun as he can get hold of; the feeblest
cripple may wave his crutch in the face of the heavens, and claim
all the landscape ; but we are limited, distributed, set in our
places. One star differeth from another star in glory : one man
differeth from another man in mental scope and force. Why
rebel ? Why call God's attention to the fact that my boundary
on the one side is nothing but a great sea, and I have not a piece
of south-looking land in all my little estate? And why aggravate
my discontent by pointing to the largeness of my brother's
inheritance, and the sunniness of the aspect which his dwelling-
house commands ? There is a better policy—a noble and devout
emotion—which says,—Not my will, thou great boundary-maker,
thou God of allotment and distribution, but thine be done. The
tortoise may beat the hare ; the poor widow may do more
excellently than all the rich men in the city. As for being little,

Jesus took a "little child," and set him in the midst of the
disciples and said,—This is the standard of greatness; it were
better for a man that a millstone were hanged about his neck,
and that he were drowned in the depths of the sea, than that
he should offend one of these little ones. Look for the bright
spots; add up all the excellences; totalise the attractions of the
situation; and it is wonderful how things add up when you
know how to add them.

So we have boundaries in general character. Sometimes, one
man is *nearly* as good as another. Sometimes the son is almost
mistaken for the father, in point of genuine excellence, benevolence, and thorough goodness of soul; still, he is not his father;
he never will be so princely and so good, because there is not
so much of him to work upon; he is a less man altogether.
Why are not men equal in good, equal in power of prayer, equal
in willingness in the direction of self-sacrifice? Why is it hard
for some men to pray? Why do they fall down in some pitiable
fit if they try to pray aloud and in the hearing of others? That
miracle never can be wrought. Suggest to some men that they
should pray in public, and instantly they reply in expressions of
wonder too profound for words. Who made these differences?
Are all these things indications of chance, haphazard, mere
experiment, without reason for a centre or probability for an
issue? What if the attentive eye should see the divine hand in
all these appointments, and, recognising that hand, should touch
it reverently and say to it,—O hand of the Lord, arrange everything for me: be my hand: when I write, take hold of my hand
with thine, and let us write together; and when war comes upon
me, let thine hand be outstretched in my protection and defence!

Boundary is disciplinary. Who would not like to add just
one more shelf to his library, and could do it if he were at
liberty to take the books from another man's study? Who does
not desire to have just the corner plot to make the estate geo-
metrically complete, and would do it if the owner of the plot
were not looking? But to retire within your own boundary!—
to have nothing but a ditch between you and the vineyard you
covet! Who is stopped by a ditch? To have nothing but
one thin, green hedge between proprietorship actual and proprietorship desired! Why not burn the hedge, or transfer it?

" Whoso breaketh an hedge, a serpent shall bite him,"—saith the proverbs, of Solomon. To be kept within our own lines, to build our altar steadily there, and to bow down at that altar, and confess that " The earth is the Lord's, and the fulness thereof," and that, whether a man has much or little, he may be God's child, God's servant, and Christ's apostle ;—that is the highest discipline, and it is possible to every man.

Boundaries are suggestive. Every boundary, rightly-interpreted, means : Your last estate will be a very little one—a grave in the cemetery, a tomb in the silent place. Does it come to this, that the man who wanted acres a thousand in number doubled lies down in six feet, or seven, by four ? Can a carpenter measure him for his last house ? Does there come a time when a man steals quietly upstairs with a two-foot measure, and afterwards hurries out to build for him in the eventide his last dwelling-place ? It is impossible to exclude this thought from all our best reasoning. There is no need to be mawkish, sentimental, foolishly melancholy about it ; but there is the fact, that there is an appointed time to man upon the earth, as well as an appointed place to man upon the earth, and that he is the wise man who looks at that certain fact and conducts himself wisely in relation to it. Men have the power of closing their eyes and not seeing the end, but to close the eyes is not to destroy the inevitable boundary. Even the grave can be made beautiful. A man may so live that when he is laid in his grave other men may go to see the tomb, and bedew it with tears, and even stoop down and touch it with a loving hand as if it were a living thing.

Then comes the other thought immediately upon this gloomy one, saying,—The man is not there : he is risen ; he has entered the boundless land, where every man may have as much as he can receive, and still feel that he has not begun to realise the infinite possibilities of immortal life. Our Christian contention is, that any man who lives under the inspiration of all these thoughts is living a wise life ; he can defend himself by reasoning without a flaw, by eloquence noble, persuasive, dignified. There is the difficulty of living up to this ideal ;—there is the blessed satisfaction of knowing that we never can live up to it. Let us take comfort in our inability as well as in our ability.

Who can overtake his prayers? When the mocker says,—
Could the suppliant live his prayers, he would be a noble man,—
it is he, not the suppliant, who talks irrationally and foolishly.
Our prayers are our impossible selves : our prayers are the
selves we would be if we could. To have our life set in their
direction is itself a conquest; and that conquest is possible
to all of us. Poor life! Some seem to have nothing; they
wonder why they live; their bread is bitter; and as for the
water they drink, there is hardly enough of it to touch the fire
of their thirst; they think they do not want much, and they
suppose they could do with a good deal more than they have.
Who is right—the distributing God or the receiving man? In
whose hand does all this business lie? The Christian doctrine
is, that it lies in the hands of God, and that he will withhold
no good thing from them that walk uprightly; and the motto
he has written upon his broad heavens is this : " Seek ye first
the kingdom of God, and his righteousness ; and all these things
shall be added unto you ; " and they are the mighty preachers—
voices sent from eternity—who can read that writing, pronounce
it accurately, and so utter it as to bring men to thought, to
reason, to prayer.

"HANDFULS OF PURPOSE,"

FOR ALL GLEANERS.

"In the wilderness of Sinai, in the tabernacle of the congregation."—Num. i. I.

The wonderful conjunction of names and situations in life.—Here we have "wilderness" and "tabernacle."—We cannot be blind to the "wilderness"; sometimes a teacher is required to point out the "tabernacle."—The "tabernacle" is always to be found by the earnest searcher.—The wilderness, as to mere space is incomparably larger than the tabernacle, but the tabernacle as to its quality and radiance destroys the unhappiest aspects and influences of the wilderness.—The wilderness may represent what nature can do for man; the tabernacle is the peculiar and distinctive work of God, showing how the supernatural subdues and glorifies everything with which it comes in contact.—Sometimes the tabernacle is in the man's heart; if indeed its spirit is not there no outside building can supply its place or offer such security as either reason or feeling can really enjoy.—Be afraid of no wilderness in which there is a tabernacle.—By setting up his tabernacle God means to make the wilderness blossom as the rose.—Life itself may often assume the desolation of a wilderness; this it must do in the absence of supernatural influences; decorate it as we may, scatter upon it all the wild flowers that hands can gather, it is a wilderness still: in such circumstances the traveller must cry out for the living God, and yearn for a dwelling place not made with hands.—The tabernacle may be some quickening thought, or sacred memory, or inspiring promise, or the companionship of a kindred soul; the tabernacle of God has a thousand aspects, and is consequently different in its representation according to the circumstances in which every man looks upon it.—The tabernacle is never so beautiful as when seen in contrast with the wilderness.—As the weary night makes the dawn doubly welcome, so the great wilderness develops in the tabernacle a beauty and a splendour which would be otherwise unrecognised.—As in darkness we see the stars, so in the wilderness we ought to see the spiritual glory of the tabernacle.

"Able to go forth to war."—Num. i. 3.

Then there are differences amongst men; some being able, and others unable to go forth to war.—Forgetfulness of these differences leads to indiscriminate and cruel criticism.—There is always a war in life.—Sometimes a real battle is only known to the man himself.—In all solitary conflicts the man himself is of course alone responsible.—Even in such conflicts the warrior needs inspiration and encouragement from without.—There is a solitude that leads to despair, and in the darkness of that solitude the war goes against the soul.—The words of the text refer to open or public battle, in which every man is expected to appear in the fulness of his strength. —The statistics of the army are kept in heaven.—The spirit of this text forbids every man to look only at his weakness.—Every man is ca'led upon to make the most of himself in the presence of the enemy.—Sometimes the very going forth to war develops the power of battle.—Let every man take a *hopeful* view of his capacity.— The wars to which men are called in this day may be of the nature of controversy, testimony under difficult circumstances, consistency in the midst of subtle and persistent temptation; because we do not wrestle against flesh and blood, it does not follow that we have no conflict with principalities and powers and innumerable enemies out of sight.—The spirit of Christianity is a spirit of war.—The Christian is at war with every form and action of evil.—There can be no doubt as to the side which the Christian will take in every moral conflict.—The suggestion of the text is that some men are not called upon to engage in public strife. —They may be soldiers, nevertheless, suffering heroically, illustrating the majesty of patience, and proving by joyful resignation how possible it is to wait without complaining, and to sing in the darkness and weariness of night. —Cowardice is nowhere commended in the Bible.—The distinguishing feature of Christianity in relation to all the forces of life is heroism.—Let imagination picture the scene; the Christian is not afraid to go forth where ignorance is densest, where rebellion is most violent, where cruelty is most desperate, and even where in-

fection is most contagious; the picture is always vivid with heroic colour, and expressive of consecration, which can neither be daunted or discouraged.— " The Son of God goes forth to war." —It is too commonly supposed that Christianity is a bed of roses, a new variety of luxury, a sentiment which, while it excuses, also aggravates the natural selfishness of the heart.—Every man should put to himself the question, Why am I not at the war?—Every wound that testifies to honourable battle is a sign of true soldiership.— Do not be ashame of wounds and scars that tell o suffering only see that they are on the breast, and thereby indicate fearlessness, and not on the back, and thereby prove fear and faithlessness.

" *Every man . . . shall pitch by his own standard.*"—NUM. ii. 2.

Order is necessary to success.—Men cannot be allowed to run from standard to standard.—Obedience to this precept would reconstruct the Christian army.—There is a natural fondness in the human heart in the matter of changing standards.—Such changing represents action without progress.— It is to be especially noticed that there is a standard for every man.—Individuality is the gift of God.—Individuality does not destroy the social bond; while contributing to its strength it adds much to its variety.—Denominationalism in the Church has its uses.— As no one standard is the army, so no one denomination is the Church.

There is a psychology of denominationalism.—Moral or intellectual constitution renders it impossible that all men should be content with the same ecclesiastical conditions.—Every temperament has its own standard.—No man should say that another is not in the army because he does not belong to some particular standard.—Loose-mindedness which supposes that it is a matter of indifference as to whether any special standard should be chosen is strongly discouraged by the spirit of this text.—Observe, every man is not called upon to direct the army.— Some men have simply to pitch by their standard, and wait for orders.— " Blessed is that servant who, when his Lord cometh, shall be found watching."—"Choose ye this day whom ye will serve."—Enemies of Christ are sometimes bolder in the avowal of their standard, than his friends.— Boldness in the faith when regulated by intelligence and chastened by patience is a sign of progress in the highest life.

" Every one to his service and to his burden."—Num. iv. 19.

Another aspect of individuality.— This is the individuality of endurance as the former was the individuality of service.—As a matter of fact every man has a burden of his own.—" Bear ye one another's burdens."—The burden is adapted to the man who bears it.—It is easy to exhort another man to carry his burden, but here as everywhere example is better than precept.—There is no limit to the influence of example in this matter.— People are looking on and drawing their conclusions as to what can be done under circumstances of distress, and sometimes they are shamed into greater resoluteness by the bravery which they note in others.—A difference is always to be marked between the burdens which we make for ourselves, and the burdens which are appointed by God. It is profane to create a burden by our own wickedness and then to speak of the mysteries of divine providence.—Let a man examine himself carefully: to live is to

endure trial; to be in the world is to feel somewhat of its cruel pressure; but besides this there may be the special burden of infirmity, temper, appetite, or some form of selfishness. —How jealous are some hearts ! how peevish are some spirits ! how narrow in conception are some minds ! how resentful are some tempers ! Every man must examine himself in the light of such suggestions and determine the magnitude and weight of his own burden.—But the text speaks not only of burden but of service.— Every man has his own gift of God.— The service is one, although the servants have different work to do.— Each man must find out what he can do best.—For want of this definiteness of conception much energy is misspent or utterly wasted.—Infinite mischief arises from the supposition that all men should serve alike.—" Every one of us shall give account of himself to God."—The doorkeeper will not be blamed because he was not high-priest; the least of the brethren will not be overlooked because he did not hold high office.—The spirit of the Bible is thus just to human nature in all its variety of gifts and opportunity.—There is no indiscriminateness or confusion in Bible judgments.—Of one it was said, " She hath done what she could."—This is the spirit by which the judgment of all workers will be determined.

" Is the Lord's hand waxed short ?"— Num. xi. 23.

The question which will bring all other inquiries into right relation.— The inquiry is based on history. The history of the world is the history of the divine hand.—The question points to the fact that the Lord's hand has hitherto always been equal to the occasion.—If the hand of the Lord could wax short the throne of God would be destroyed by that very fact.—Providence continues only so long as Godhead continues; to be God is to be Almighty; to be other than Almighty is to be less than God.—The person making the inquiry is supposed to have had personal experience of the power of the divine hand.—Let every devout man put this inquiry to himself in all the varying circumstances of life; in perplexity, in extremity, in the agony of doubt, in the experience of bereavement, and, in short, at every point in the circle of life.

To be strong theologically, that is to say, to have a clear conception of God's presence and action in life, is to be strong morally and socially.—The inquiry certainly suggests that some circumstances wear the appearance which justifies the very solemn and awful fear.—We gain nothing by ignoring such circumstances.—The wicked are often highly exalted and invested with disastrous influence; the righteous often seem to be left to themselves, and made to feel that their godliness is the reason of their poverty or pain.—The bad man may put this inquiry in a tone of mocking and contempt, and may have some justification for his tone.—Take the case of Jesus Christ himself when he suffered upon the cross: bad men challenged God to appear on behalf of their victim, and no response was made from the darkening heavens.—From this great case of agony lessons may be drawn suitable to every form of unhappy experience.—" Consider him who endured such contradiction of sinners against himself."

" Enviest thou for my sake?"—Num. xi. 29.

We often justify our worst actions by pleading that they are done on account of others.—The thief may say that he steals in order to save life with the money.—We may claim to be so jealous for the Lord of hosts as utterly to misrepresent his Spirit.—We may be so anxious to honour the institutions of Christianity as to violate all its charities and benedictions.—Infidelity may be opposed in an unchristian spirit.—The great leaders of the Church never feared what is termed competition, simply because their power is not merely official, but is personal and ennobling.—Instead of desiring that the voices of prophesying should be silent Moses expressed a desire that all the Lord's people were prophets.—Greatness does not depend upon surrounding littleness where moral influence is in question.—Mont Blanc may be the greater because of the depressions which surround it, but this can afford no analogy in the estimate of moral majesty.—When other people become prophets they will more appreciate the prophetic dignity of Moses.—Envy of the kind which is deprecated is a subtle expression of selfishness.—The men who burned with this envy wished their leader to suffer no loss of official supremacy, not knowing that Moses was part only of the great commonwealth, and that the prophetic power of others illustrated and confirmed the prophetic energy which had marked the great legislator.—It is indeed part of the function of a great prophet to make prophets of other people.—Not only was Christ the Light of the world, he invested his disciples with the same character.—Instead of deprecating any possible increase of their light he called upon them to let that light shine before men, and demanded that no light, even though but the glimmer of a candle should be hidden under a bushel.—It is right to protect the authority of great men, but this is best done by excluding every hurtful passion.—Make great men standards of measurement, not discouragements to holy ambition. —Christ, we may reverently say, may put the same inquiry to his Church when men arise with proposals to help the world.—They may call themselves philosophers, reformers, rationalists, or what they please, Jesus Christ is willing that they should work out all their purposes and that they should be tested by the results of their action. —The Church should be generous to all competitors.—Let every man do what he can and he will find in the long run that experience is his best teacher. —There are of course ameliorations which teach the service of influence and which are on no account to be undervalued; in so far as they are helpful Christ will accept the service, and in the degree in which they are genuine they will point to influences beyond themselves.—Call down fire upon no man who does not walk with you. —Instead of envying on account of God's supremacy, acknowledge the good that is in every man and exhort him to increase it.—Moses would not be an idol to be superstitiously regarded; he would be a leader to be followed, a teacher to be obeyed, an example to be imitated; let us be careful lest our religion amounts to no more than an expression of official envy; when new lights arise let us give them scope; when new voices are heard speaking good things let us listen attentively; our duty is to try the spirits whether they be of God.

" *And Caleb stilled the people before Moses, and said, Let us go up at once, and possess it; for we are well able to overcome it.*"—Num. xiii. 30.

" The Lord said to Moses, Send thou men that they may search the land of Canaan which I give unto the children of Israel."—Men were accordingly sent, being told to "see the land, what it is; and the people that dwell therein, whether they be strong or weak, few or many; and what the land is that they dwell in, whether it be good or bad; and what cities they be that they dwell in, whether in tents or in strongholds."—In a word, they were to make a full survey of the land and its inhabitants, and to report to Moses.—"So they went up, and searched the land from the wilderness of Zin unto Rehob, as men come to Hamath."—After forty days' search they returned, bringing with them a branch with one cluster of grapes, and also a specimen of the pomegranates and the figs.—On the whole, their report was very gloomy.— They had, of course, some good things to say about the productiveness of the land, but they gave a very alarming account of the people : " All the people that we saw in it are men of great stature—we were in our own sight as grasshoppers, and so we were in their sight."—Caleb was a man of another spirit : he stilled the people before Moses, and said, "Let us go up at once, and possess it; for we are well able to overcome it."

This incident sets forth vividly some of the difficulties which lie in the way of the higher kingdom, the kingdom of our Lord Jesus Christ; and it is in this view that we shall regard the graphic narrative.

1. *The kingdom of heaven challenges the inquiry of all men.*—It addresses an appeal to human reason, and to human trust.—Though itself a revelation, and therefore not to be handled as a common thing, nor to be tested by common instruments, yet Christianity invites the most careful inquest.—It does not seek to rest upon the human intellect as a burden, but to shine upon it as a light; it does not fasten itself upon the

human heart as an excrescence, but blesses and enriches it with a new and mightier life.—If Christianity may be represented under the image of a land, such as ancient Canaan, then it is fair to say of it, that it offers right of way over its hills and through its valleys, that its fruits and flowers are placed at the disposal of all travellers, and that he who complains that the land is shut against him speaks not only ungratefully but most falsely.

There are not wanting men who say that Christianity forbids inquiry.

The kingdom of heaven is the highest revelation of the mind of God to the mind of man.—The mind must be at its highest possible point of energy in order to lay hold of the doctrines which constitute that revelation.—To get the mind to this point requires the excitement of the *heart;* for mind is never fully alive whilst the moral powers are dormant.—When the heart is moved in its deepest passions, and the mind is set in its highest key, the man is prepared to enter upon the great studies to which he is invited by the Gospel.

It is certainly true, and ought to be taken account of in this connection, that some people have peculiar notions of what is meant by inquiry.—In the first instance, they dismiss everything like reverence; in the next place, they make themselves the standard and measure of all truth; and in the third place, they seek to materialise and debase everything that is spiritual and heavenly.—This is not inquiry, it is insolent self-sufficiency; it is not the spirit of a student seeking light; it is the spirit of a braggart who thinks the sun inferior to his spark.—The tone of mind must be in harmony with the subject considered; in every department of intellectual life it is required that a student be self-controlled, patient, docile; that his temper be subdued, and that his conclusions be

reached through long and earnest watching of processes.—This is required in all sciences, why not in the science of sciences—the knowledge and worship of the true God?

2. *Different reports will, of course, be brought by the inquirers.*—It was so in the case of the spies: it will be so in all inquiry.—The result of the survey will be according to the peculiarities of the surveyors.—As streams are impregnated by the soils over which they flow, so subjects are affected by the individualism of the minds through which they pass.—Thus Christianity may be said to be different things to different minds.—To the speculative man it is a great attempt to solve deep problems in theology; to the controversialist it is a challenge to debate profound subjects on new ground; to the poet it is a dream, a wondrous vision many-coloured as the rainbow, a revelation many-voiced as the tunes of the wind or the harmonies of the sea.—Each inquirer will have his own way of reporting the result of his inquiry.—Christian testimony is not of one unchanging sort.—One Christian will report his experiences in highly intellectual phraseology, as if God had entered his heart through the shining chambers of his mind; another will show that he has reached peace through many a stormy conflict with doubt; another will speak the language of music as though he had been taught it in intercourse with the angels; another will stammer by reason of sobs and tears.—Yet the subject is the same, the result is the same—this is the diversity that is unity—

"Ten thousand thousand are their tongues,
But all their joys are one."

(1) Some inquirers will see *all the hindrances.*—(2) All will confess that there is *something good* in the land.—(3) Those who hold back by reason of

the difficulties will come to miserable end.

;a) We don't escape by *false reasoning.* — (b) We don't escape by *fear.*

Application :— 1. Some have shown the spirit of Caleb—*what is your testimony ?*—2. Will you resolve, in divine strength, to follow the Lord fully ?

Observe that it is the *spirit* of Caleb which is commended.

" As truly as I live all the earth shall be filled with the glory of the Lord."
—NUM. xiv. 21.

No bolder word was ever uttered even by a Christian apostle. — This prediction is founded upon the philosophy of the principles which it represented ; that is to say such is the adaptation of divine thought to human need, that it must in the long run put down all competition, and prove itself to be the one thought which is full of rational satisfaction. — It is not to be supposed that one set of principles is to get the better of some other set, as the result of a kind of pitched battle in which the one side has been cleverer than the other.— Christianity is to triumph by virtue of its adaptation to every necessity of human need.—By addressing itself to the experience of mankind, by waiting with long patience for a full reception into the heart, and an honest trial in the life, by answering questions which no other religion can settle, and in every way to the ministry of thought, Christianity will show itself to be the one religion which abundantly covers the whole space of human necessity.— Other religions address themselves to races or kingdoms, to particular climates and modes of life ; Christianity looks abroad upon the whole earth and proposes one blessing, the blessing of adoption and pardon for every member of the human race.—The promise

seems to be founded upon the very constitution of God : the terms are, "As truly as I live " ; this is not a mere exclamation, or a varied form of oath, least of all is it a rhetorical embellishment ; it would seem to be that the filling of the whole earth with the glory of God is a necessity of the very nature of God.—God is love ; God is light ; love and light have undertaken to fill the whole earth with beauty and splendour.—This is not the God of a mechanician who does so much work for so much reward, and who is willing to do a directly opposite work for higher compensation ; it is the ministry of love, the energy of light, and the pressure of eternity.—God will have all things like himself.—He is holy, he is good, he is wise, and what he is he means all responsible creatures to be in their degree.—The Christian worker is to conduct his service under the inspiration of this prediction.—He is not to look at temporary discouragements, or vexatious details, or personal infirmity, or the supposed strength of an enemy ; he is to stand upon the rock of divine promise, and daily sustain his confidence by the pledge of God.—Love and light must always succeed.—They are the forces which give energy to the Christian ministry in all its forms and activities, and because they are of the very nature and quality of God they cannot ultimately fail of their purpose.

" How long shall I bear with this evil congregation, which murmur against me ? "—NUM. xiv. 27.

This is really a parental inquiry.— The proof of this is in the very agony of the terms.—A tyrant could have crushed the difficulty, a mere ruler might have been haughtily indifferent to it, but where tyrants and rulers are exhausted fatherhood begins to put its most anxious inquiries. — God has never been readily received into the human heart.—His rejection has in some cases been grounded upon the mystery of his nature; in others, on the difficulties of his providence; and in others upon the love of self-indulgence which characterises all human affections.—The terms of the inquiry assume that the forbearance has been long continued.—God does not ask such a question at an early period of his attempts to subdue the heart and will of man.—The inquiry, which is here put as to a congregation, is addressed to every human creature in his individuality. — Every man has justified the inquiry.—No man can satisfactorily answer the inquiry.—Every man is witness in his own case that the forbearance of God has been continuous and tender.—It is evident that forbearance has only been equal to the occasion created by human rebellion. — This circumstance having been amply proved, we come upon the discovery that forbearance has been completed by redemption.—The cross is not only an expression of forbearing love, it is the mystery of pardon wrought by righteousness. — If the cross should fail, God has no other resources so far as revelation can guide us.—Our forbearance expresses our love.—Where there is little love there will be little forbearance.—Where there is much love the anxious inquiry will often arise, How can I give thee up?—This is the inquiry which is culminated in the cross of Christ.

" *Consumed the two hundred and fifty men that offered incense.*"—Num. xvi. 35.

No man is indispensable to God.—Better that incense be not offered than that the censer be swung with unworthy hands.—Officialism does not necessarily involve personal fitness.—Incense does not disinfect corrupt hearts.—The man, not the censer, is the standard of determination.—Officialism in the Church often destroys the sensitiveness of the heart.—What is true of officialism is true of any repetition that ends in familiarity.—Mechanical religion is easily acquired; it is merely a trick of the hand, it is not the sacrifice of the heart.—God's anger burns most hotly against unfaithful leaders.—He may be more angry with parents than with children, with preachers than with hearers, with the experienced than with the inexperienced.—God relies not upon the number but upon the character of his servants.—The removal of two hundred and fifty men was a serious numerical loss, but as to character, quality, and spiritual effectiveness, there was no loss whatever.—The tree is the better for the cutting off of the dead branches.—That which has ceased to be useful should cease to be cumbersome.—When God looks through all his hosts that he may number and value them, he will cut off no man whose spirit is true, whose purpose is noble, and whose thought is steadfast.—An awful picture presents itself to the imagination as we look back upon blighted ministries, unworthy characters, dishonoured servants, and the whole line of disaster and wreckage. — Many who started well have brought upon themselves the consuming anger of God.—The comforting thought is that in all this judgment and desolation God reveals his kingdom as a kingdom of righteousness, truth, and purity.—"Be ye clean that bear the vessels of the Lord."

" *Sinners against their own souls.*"— Num. xvi. 38.

This is the tremendous hold which God has upon us, namely that we cannot sin against God without committing direct wrong upon ourselves.—All experience proves this to be the case. All the lower analogies tend to the confirmation of this doctrine : he who sins against cleanliness sins against his own health; he who sins against social honesty sins against his own advancement; he who sins against social truth deposes himself from the seat of honour and divests himself from all healthy influence.—We are physically so constituted that a bad thought lowers the health of the brain; and unregulated passion devastates the nature in which it rages; neglect of discipline means loss of force.—Carry up these analogies to the highest level; to cease to pray is to contract the outlook of the soul; to cease to do good is to diminish the power of doing it; to turn away from the heights of heaven is to impoverish the veneration which did homage to old age and bowed itself in the presence of genius and worth.— To go down religiously is to go down in every point and line of life.—If a man can resist God and yet maintain health of soul, without wound or scar, he would in effect be God himself.—If the branch could bear fruit without the vine it would in reality be the vine.— If mortality could overcome death it would prove itself to be immortality. —It is necessary to the unity of all things that Right should be the fountain of health, harmony, and all that is necessary to spiritual progress.— Following the line of this thought, Christians should be living exemplifications of the law which is exceeding broad; they should be men of lofty mind, able to take wide and generous views of all questions, willing to pardon offences and render assistance to weakness; their souls being right with God, their hands should be outstretched in every form of charity.— Christianity is infinitely more than a

set of theological particulars; it educates the soul, it strengthens the mind, it ennobles all impulses, it increases and consolidates all the forces of manhood.—The soul that sins is in a state of ill-health.—Sin is a positive wrong done to the quality and function of the soul.—It is an insult to the better nature.—It is as if a man should strike loveliness in the face, or lay his hand upon the throat of living music.—Sin is murder.—We must not look upon sin as a mere mistake for which ample apology can be made; it is blasphemy against all right, health, beauty, music. —It is all this because it is an offence against God.—When night descends upon the earth, it does not darken one room only, it fills the whole house with darkness. So when. sin is committed it is not simply one faculty that is impaired, or one impulse that is discouraged; the whole man goes down and is made the slave of conquering evil.—The prodigal son was made to feel that in leaving his father he lost his property, his companions, his brother, his friends; and all these he lost because he first lost himself.

"*I am thy part and thine inheritance among the children of Israel.*"— NUM. xviii. 20.

The reference is to Aaron and the priesthood.—The priests were not to be landed proprietors, or in any sense a territorial aristocracy.—Aaron had his position in spiritual enlightenment and spiritual honour.—"Man's life consisteth not in the abundance of the things which he possesseth."— This spiritual allotment is symbolical. —The idea is that the last result of education will be comparative contempt for all material things.—Material things must of course be owned and governed and turned to good uses; still whatever is material is of necessity temporary; and that which is temporary should never engross the attention of men who are immaterial. —He lives the great life who lives in thought, high feeling, and beneficence.—The expression of high intellectual passion is marked by the truest disregard of all things related to time and space.—The Son of man had not where to lay his head; yet he had bread to eat that the world knew not of.—He who lives this inner life does not see when drought cometh, neither can famine threaten his strength. —No matter what inheritance a man has, it is only valuable in so far as it is made the means of helping spiritual culture.—"Jeshurun waxed fat and kicked."—How ennobling the thought that we may have our inheritance in God! —This is the distinct promise of the text, and it applies not only to priests but to all who live and move and have their being in God.—The humblest Christian can say, "The Lord is the portion of mine inheritance and of my cup: thou maintainest my lot."— Even in the midst of distresses of the acutest kind, the prophet was enabled to exclaim, "The Lord is my portion, saith my soul; therefore will I hope in him."—This text will, as to its spirit and sublimest meaning, be addressed to the Christian in the hour and article of death, and the soul, answering the promise in the spirit of thankfulness and assurance, will exclaim, "My flesh and my heart faileth: but God is the strength of my heart, and my portion for ever."

'*And this your heave offering shall be reckoned unto you, as though it were the corn of the threshingfloor, and as the fulness of the winepress.*"—NUM. xviii. 27.

Thus does love magnify all human offerings.—Love does not content itself

with the letter, or with weights and measures; it looks at spiritual intention, and according to the purity and scope of that intention is its recognition.—The two mites were valuable beyond gold because of the motive which prompted the gift.—The cup of cold water is to be regarded as a cup of choice wine.—The purpose of David to build the temple was accepted as if the temple had been actually built.— Not the work of the hand which may be imperfect, but the purpose of the heart is recognised and accepted by the loving God.—Interpret all the service of life in the light of this method, and see how the first may become last and the last may become first.—Work is not to be estimated by mere bulk, but by the motive which constrained its performance.—What is easy to one man may be difficult to another; it is easy to some men to give, to serve, and to pray; all these signs may be performed without their being spiritual miracles.—He who has great ideas concerning the kingdom of Christ, but who cannot carry them out for want of strength or opportunity, will be accounted to have done the very things which he intended.— Our life is what we most solemnly mean it to be.—If any man can accept this suggestion as warranting release from toil and sacrifice, he is not entitled to the comfort and inspiration of this holy doctrine.—The divine magnifying of our acts is never meant to discourage our efforts, but rather to increase and ennoble them.—Many who are not now recognised as great workers may in the end be honoured with bright crowns.

"*A serpent of brass.*"—NUM. xxi. 9.

Physical objects may be made the medium of spiritual suggestion.—The true use of material objects is to find out their spiritual suggestions.—The sown seed, the growing corn, the fields white unto the harvest, are all instances which may be turned to spiritual advantage.—So may all growth, all life, all beauty, all force.—It is very significant that the word "serpent" should be identified in the Bible with its sublimest remedial activities.—It would seem as if God intended even in this way to humble and punish the tempter who ruined our first parents.—It was the "serpent" that was more subtle than any beast of the field.—In the last book of the New Testament the enemy is referred to as "the great dragon, that old serpent, called the Devil, and Satan, which deceiveth the whole world."—Images and relics are to be strictly limited in their use.—Nothing is to stand between the soul and God but the priesthood of Jesus Christ.—Hezekiah "brake the images, and cut down the groves, and brake in pieces the brazen serpent that Moses had made."—Why did Hezekiah take this course?—Because the children of Israel had become image-worshippers, and had a superstitious veneration for an institution which had served its purpose and was no longer needed.—The only eternal institution is the work of Jesus Christ himself.—It is nothing less than wickedness to go back to the symbol when the reality is before us.—Men are not at liberty to judge themselves by the commandments when they can adopt the more penetrating criticism of the Beatitudes.—The whole meaning of the serpent of brass was realised in the uplifting of the Son of man.—The proof of this is found in John iii. 14, 15.—The uplifting is an action as remarkable as is the name of the serpent.—Jesus Christ referred to it repeatedly, thus: "Even so must the Son of man be lifted up";—again: When ye have lifted up the Son of

man." The lifting up is an act equivalent to manifestation; the lifting up is highly symbolic; it means separation, elevation, exposure to the whole world, welcome to all mankind. "For this purpose the Son of God was manifested, that he might destroy the works of the devil."

"*Am I not able to promote thee to honour?*"—Num. xxii. 37.

Balak had no other inspiration than worldly honour to offer.—He could not understand any man being unmoved by such an offer.—Herein Balak fitly represents the spirit of the whole world.—Who can resist gold? or distinction? or influence? or a throne? The whole spirit of this temptation culminated in the attempt of the devil to win the homage of Jesus Christ by offering him the kingdoms of the world, and the glory of them.—The world is making this very speech to every young man to-day.—This, too, is the speech which many a man is addressing to the woman who is unworthy of his love.—He will give her a name, a social status, and abundance of domestic comfort; he addresses no appeal to the companionship of the heart, the masonry of the mind, the desire for mutual growth in all sacred life and power.—The man who can accept a bribe for his service proves that he will oppose that very service if a higher bribe be offered.—He who will accept a bribe will give one.—He who will tell lies for you will also tell lies to you.—The spirit of Balak was reproduced in Simon Magus.—He offered the apostles money if they would give unto him the Holy Ghost.—There is no relation between material gifts and spiritual powers. They belong to different spheres.—Even when material treasure is offered in recognition of spiritual benefit it must cover itself with contempt in the presence of the majesty it seeks to recognise.—Ministers ought not to be bought for money.—The poet should not abandon his harp because the money-spender is not listening to him.—The princes of this world are never so thoroughly humbled as by the citizens of heaven. —Alexander could do nothing for Diogenes.—Abram would receive nothing from the King of Sodom, lest the king should put a wrong construction upon the deed.—The living water is to be had without money and without price. —True honour cometh from God only. —"Them that honour me I will honour."—To receive honour from men is to blind the understanding, and shut out the true judgment.—" How can ye believe which receive honour from one another?"—If we are in quest of spiritual light and security we must bring a broken and a contrite heart, a spirit bowed down with humbleness, and a self-disposing soul.—"Blessed are the poor in spirit : for theirs is the kingdom of heaven."

" *My covenant of peace.*"—Num. xxv. 12.

Phinehas, the son of Eleazar, the son of Aaron, the priest, was a type of Christ.—The covenant of grace is described in Isaiah liv. 10, and in Malachi ii. 5, as the covenant of peace.—Peace must be the result of harmony with God.—God is the God of peace.—He blesses his people with peace.—Speaking to his servant, he said, " My covenant was with him of life and peace." —The converse of this is true ; " There is no peace, saith my God, to the wicked."—Peace does not represent a grace so much as a virtue.—Great misunderstanding prevails as to the true meaning of peace.—True peace represents the highest energy, controlled and sanctified.—Never represent spiritual peace by death or the grave, or by anything that is inert, or passionless.—

He only is at peace who in full possession of every faculty feels that there is no power in his soul that does not aspire towards God in loving obedience.—Peace of this kind does not exempt from daily trial and daily sorrow.—The presence of peace in the soul takes the right view of such discipline, and is sure to find stars in the darkness. — The peace that is spoken of is not a temporary arrangement ; it is a matter of covenant signed and sealed.—The blessing of God is a covenant ordered in all things and sure.—Judge spiritual progress by the depth of spiritual peace.—" Perfect love casteth out fear."—The great gift of Christ to the Church is a gift of peace. — The apostle describes the peace of God as passing understanding, —an enjoyment beyond analysis, and beyond criticism : passing understanding as flying passes walking, as the light of the sun passes all the sparks man can kindle upon earth, as the ocean passes the little rills that trickle over the surface of the earth.

" *Famous in the congregation.*"— Num. xxvi. 9.

This is a necessity of human life.— In every assembly diversity of position and influence must be recognised.— The evil to be guarded against is jealousy.—Aaron and his sister envied Moses, because of his pre-eminence.— Men who are truly famous have restraints enough to keep them within proper limits ; restraints which are often unknown to the very people who envy them.—Fame is an element of moral power.—To have fame, is to have opportunities innumerable for profitably addressing public attention. —Jesus Christ's fame went throughout all Syria.—The more his fame extended the larger became the number of applications for healing.—It is right to have high spiritual ambitions.—Men who work solely to acquire fame, will be disappointed.—" He that saveth his life shall lose it."—We have simply to do the work and let fame come or go as it may.—The motive of fame is contemptible vanity; but fame as an honest result of beneficent life may become the beginning of new and large advantages.—There were famous men amongst the disciples of Jesus Christ. —Peter, James, and John were admitted to privileges which other disciples did not enjoy.—Jesus Christ laid down the great doctrine : " He that is greatest among you, let him be the servant of all."—Eminence is not to be a justification of tyranny.—There is a bad fame as well as a good one.— " Diotrephes loveth to have the pre-eminence."—Simon Magus gave out that he was some great one.—Character is of infinitely greater importance than reputation.—It is of no importance how much fame a man may have, if he has not self-respect.—A man must, so to say, confirm his own fame, if it is to be of any service to him or to others.— The approval of a good conscience is the fame which every honest man supremely desires.—We know not who may be famous at the last, for then many an undiscovered worker will be revealed and crowned.—The "well done" of the Lord, is the fame after which every labourer should aspire.

" *They became a sign.*"—Num. xxvi. 10.

So even the worst actions may be turned to public utility.—Let the word " sign" be considered equal to the word " example," and then every drunkard, liar, thief, becomes a sign.—A sign was attached to Cain, and that sign is attached to all his progeny.—In the language of the prophet, " the shew of their countenance doth witness against them."—A very solemn purpose is thus served, by all persons who have been faithless or wicked.—"Remember Lot's wife."—New periods are dated from the commission of great crimes.— Some names cannot be mentioned without sending a shudder through the hearers.—We may well say of such names that they have become " signs." —Whole histories may be summed up in a name.—All present examples of evil may be traced to a definite source. —There is a family or kinship of evil, the very household of Satan.—The other side of this text is happily true, for good men are examples stimulating in noble directions.—" Ye have heard of the patience of Job."—The eleventh chapter of Hebrews vividly illustrates the power of brilliant examples.—One of two things is certain, men either leave a name that degrades or a name that elevates.—It is in our power to say which name we shall leave.

" *A man in whom is the spirit.*"— Num. xxvii. 18.

The spirit is the man.—As a man thinketh in his heart so is he.—" If any man have not the Spirit of Christ, he is none of his."—There is no mistaking the true spirit.—It is one of ardour, purity, self-sacrifice, unquenchable earnestness.—We only know the true spirit by the effects which appear in the life.—It is in vain to say we have the Spirit unless we bring forth the fruits of the Spirit.—" If ye then, being evil, know how to give good gifts unto your children : how much more shall your heavenly Father give the Holy Spirit to them that ask him ? "—Genius is the gift of God.—The spirit of poetry is a gift sent down from heaven: "Every good gift and every perfect gift is from above, and cometh down from the Father of lights."—The spirit was given to Bezaleel and those who worked with him in connection with the tabernacle.—

The spirit we are to cultivate is the " spirit of judgment and of burning "; we are not to judge the spirit exclusively by what may be called romantic effects; the spirit may be shown in love, tenderness, simplicity, unselfishness: whatever effects may be displayed that are not accompanied by these graces are mere fireworks, utterly destitute of spiritual value.— Here again another side is suggested by the text.—We cannot disguise the evil spirit.—That spirit is noticeable in the very tone of the voice, and in every manner and action of the life. It is a spirit of sneering and repulsion, mistaking rudeness for frankness, and even in its most reckless manifestations planning its own safety and honour.—As for the indwelling Spirit of God, we have often need to adopt the caution not to judge by appearances, but to remember that God looketh on the heart.—It is everywhere taught in the New Testament, that if we really desire the Spirit it will be granted unto us.—The great and solemn prayer which should begin every day is, " Create in me a clean heart, O God, and renew a right spirit within me."— Blessed are they who, without renown, riches, genius, have yet the spirit of a sound understanding and a devout loyalty to the doctrine and life of Christ.

" *Beside the continual burnt offering.*" —Num. xxviii. 10.

What can there be beside or in addition to that which is " continual " ?— The burnt offering is declared to be " continual," and yet something is to be added to it.—Is not that simply impossible ?—For an answer to this inquiry we must turn to actual life, and there the mystery is being constantly illustrated.—Beside the continual sustenance of household life, there is a festive occasion when neighbours and friends come to enlarge the family circle, and enhance its occasional joys. —The birthday is an event " beside " the continual love and interest lavished upon the child.—The continual exercise on road, or in field, and garden, is supplemented by the annual vacation when larger excursions test the strength and appeal to the imagination. —The continual regard shown between friend and friend accentuates all particular recognitions, presents, and signs of peculiar love.—The answer to all such mysteries is to be found in the deeper mystery of love, that is pure and intense.—Love is inventive.—Love is self-forgetful.—Love sees where another flower will grow, hears where another bird is singing, sees where a still purer stream is flowing.—The mother who writes to her child at stated intervals, is quite capable of creating special occasions upon which to express her solicitude and affection. —The doctrine of love is that nothing has been given whilst anything has been withheld.—Life would sink into a dreary monotony, were not provision made for outbursts of enthusiasm.— The monotonous line of life must be flowered here and there with acts which are not expressed by the letter of the law.

The continual is always held to be the principal life.—That is a fact of vital consequence.—Many persons are ready to be affectionate on occasions, to indulge the eccentricities of attachment and regard, and to be heroically ready for the crisis which seems to appeal to their pride of strength and resource.—Such affection is not to be relied upon.—It is as the morning cloud and the early dew ; the occasional is indebted to the continual for its whole value. It is to the continual that the occasional owes its power of surprise, because when love is so con-

stant as to exclude the apparent possibility of addition, the amazement is
the greater that love itself has invented
a new delight.—Christianity is a "continual" service; it claims all strength,
time, resource, and when all has apparently been done, it stretches forth
its hand for something " beside."—This
seems to be a contradiction in words,
and the contradiction may indeed be
real, but there is reconciliation in the
passion and vehemence of sanctified
affection.—Let nobody begin with the
additional or exceptional, until he has
honestly completed that which is continual.

"*The Lord's tribute.*"—NUM. xxxi. 37.

The association of the words is remarkable.—Who can give anything to
the Lord, when the earth is his and
the fulness thereof?—This again, as in
the former instance, is a mystery of
spiritual love.—It is indeed because
all is his, that we are expected to give
him part of it.—What is ours is ours,
for convenience, comfort, for passing
necessity of any kind, and never ours
in the sense of proprietorship.—This
is vividly set forth in the words, "Ye
are not your own."—When the hand
does not belong to the man, it is easy
to see that what the hand contains
cannot be his.—Paul said, "I seek not
your's, but you;" and the Christians to
whom he spoke discovered that, in
securing themselves, he had in
reality secured all they had.—The
Lord has his tribute of harvest, viz., the
firstfruits; his tribute of time, the
Sabbath day; his tribute of land and
the sanctuary: his tribute of love,
worship. — "Will a man rob God?
But ye say, Wherein have we wronged
thee?" The answer is, "In tithes and
offerings."—The withholding of the
tribute thus becomes felonious.—The
tribute is not spontaneous, in the sense

that the character is as complete without the oblation as with it.—The Lord's
tribute and money appropriated to
ordinary uses will not exist together,
no more than the ark could stand
peacefully side by side with Dagon.—
To spend the Lord's tribute in self-
gratification, or for any purpose not
included in its original dedication, is to
expose all other money to the risk of
defilement and loss.—No man is the
poorer for paying the Lord's tribute.—
It is a mistake to suppose that the payment of the tribute must always relate
to work carried on at a great distance
from customary action and association.
— Sometimes charity may justly both
begin and end at home.—He does not
please the Lord, who allows his own
children to go without spiritual culture
and illumination.—It will be found,
however, as a rule, that they who do
most for objects that are near at hand
do most in response to appeals which
come from afar, and also that those
who are most interested in the conversion of the ends of the earth, are
most deeply engaged in the evangeli-
sation of the localities in which they
reside.—A sanctifying influence seems
to follow the setting aside of the Lord's
tribute.—The whole house is the
sweeter for the place in it where
prayer is most constantly offered.--
The whole library is made select by
the presence of the Bible, which will
not keep unholy or unworthy company.—The whole commercial account
is turned into a spiritual record, by
lines here and there, which record the
dedication of property to charitable
uses.—Men are often left wholly at
liberty to find out for themselves the
best way in which to spend the Lord's
tribute; some give it to the young,
others to the aged, others to Christian
apostles and missionaries, others to
the circulation of pure literature; every
man must discover for himself what he

thinks to be the worthiest field on which to expend the tribute of the Lord.

" Their names being changed."—Num. xxxii. 38.

Many persons live in names.—This is fatal to the grasp of complete truth and relation.—The poet asks, " What's in a name?"—The name of a friend may be necessary to his identification, but the name is not the man.—Character is to be studied, motive is to be understood, purpose is to be appreciated, then whatever changes may take place in the mere name, love and confidence will be undiminished. —The change of names, both in the Old Testament and the New, deserves careful study.—The name of Abram was changed, so was the name of Jacob, so was the name of Saul of Tarsus. — Those changes of name symbolise changes of trust and vocation in life.—The name should enlarge with the character, but the character should be always more highly valued than the name.—The solemn application of this text is to the matter of great evangelical truths and doctrines.—For want of attention to this matter, bigotry has been encouraged, and men have been separated from one another.—Some persons do not know the gospel itself, except under a certain set of names, words, and stereotyped phrases.—This is not Christianity, it is mere literalism; it is, in fact, idolatry, for there is an idolatry of phrase as well as of images.—It is simply despicable, when men trickle about names, or details of any kind, in other words when they pay tithes of mint, anise, and cummin, and forget the weigh tier matters of the law.—Literalism was the sin of the scribes.—The truth is not in the letters which print it, the letters but stand to express the inexpressible.—All life is symbolic.—God has spoken in little else than parables. —Revelation addresses the imagination, when imagination is used in its highest senses.—It is not the faculty of mere cloud-making, but the faculty of insight into the largest meanings and the innermost relations of things. —Many persons have less difficulty with the miracles than with the parables, simply because the one requires unquestioning assent, and the other continually discloses new aspects, colours, and suggestions of meanings. The parable will be found to be at once the hardest and pleasantest reading of the spiritual future.—The parables represent the kingdom of heaven, and in proportion to the dignity of that which they represent, is the rapture of following all their suggestion.—Your child is not a mere name to you; see that you be not a mere name to God.—The letter in which you endeavour to express your love, is a poor substitute for the living voice, and the living touch; it is indeed invaluable in the absence of the living personality; but what letter was ever written that quite satisfied the writer when love was the subject and devotedness the intention?—There is a change of names that inspires the soul with hope.—God is to give his servants a new name in the upper world; their name is to be in their foreheads; but, in the changing of the name, there is no changing in the burning love, and the rapturous adoration.

DEUTERONOMY.

DEUTERONOMY, or the repetition of the law, is a book extending to thirty-four chapters. In the beginning of the book Moses is in the fortieth year of his leadership, and at the close of the book he is succeeded by Joshua. Moses speaks clearly of God's promise, and strengthens himself by its quotation in view of the great work which was yet to be accomplished. He then proceeds to instruct the people in the appointment of officers, and directs the sending of the spies, pointing out with his accustomed severity God's anger at unbelief and disobedience, and restrains the people from meddling with the Edomites, the Moabites, and the Amorites. The venerable leader desires to enter the Land of Promise, and is permitted but a prospect of it from a distance. His memory dwells with grateful delight upon all the wonderful disclosures of the divine presence and government as beheld within the compass of his personal leadership. The old story of Horeb and the ten commandments is told with a glow of thankfulness. Moses still persists in the recital of all details connected with foreign alliances and the taint of idolatry, assuring the people all the while that their enemies will be conquered, yet mingling the glad recital with recollections of Israel's rebellion ; thus chastening an expectation which might grow into an unholy presumption. As Moses becomes older he seems to become even graver in his moral tone, constantly recommending obedience, showing how God is worthy of it because of his work amongst the children of Israel and because of the promise of blessing which he has attached to all willing service, not forgetting that threatenings are associated with disobedience : thus the great exhortation of Moses may be taken as the pattern of a truly evangelical sermon ; knowing the fear of the Lord, he endeavours to persuade Israel : when persuasion would seem to be carried to a point tempting almost to laxity of discipline, Moses suddenly turns round and reminds his hearers that God presides over the tabernacles of lightning and thunder and storm, and that it is a fearful thing to fall into the hands of the living God. Singularly, with an evident intent towards broader issues, comparatively little things are forbidden along with things that are manifestly important ; as, for example, the use of blood is forbidden in food, and holy things must be eaten in the holy place ; these would seem to be but matters of detail, yet along with them idolatry is not so much as to be inquired after, and enticers to idolatry are to be avoided and destroyed by stoning, however near and dear they may be. Then again there is an elaborate statement of what may be eaten of beasts, of fishes, and of fowls. Yet these comparative trifles are also associated with distinct instructions to destroy cities which are given to idolatry. Special attention is devoted to the question of tithes in the fourteenth chapter, and instructions so minute are given that there can be no possible misconception as to their range and purpose; yet amidst all this rule and enactment the sabbatical year of release dawns like a summer above the snows of winter, and sounds of jubilee are heard throughout the ranks of Israel. We even hear of the voluntary slave in the fifteenth chapter—a name which would seem to involve a contradiction of terms, yet the gracious anomaly is reconciled by the very spirit which conceived it. It is most instructive to notice the alternation of subjects which are indicated as from the seventeenth chapter onward : thus things that were sacrificed were to be sound, and yet idolaters were to be slain,—where is the line of connection between points so remote? Then the election and duty of a king are set forth specifically, and whilst the local sovereign is to be respected and honoured a mysterious prophecy is announced concerning a Great Prophet who is to be heard and obeyed as the representative of God (xviii. 15-19). In the nineteenth chapter the matter of detailed obedience is kept up in all its vigour : the landmark is not to be removed ; two witnesses at the least must testify in a disputed case : the false witness is to be punished ; and then, quickly following these instructions, it is shown that "trees for meat" are to be preserved in siege ; the sex is to be distinguished by apparel ; the dam is not to be taken with her young ones ; the house must be built with battlements; and attention must be paid to the fringes upon the vesture. Rapidly succeeding these comparatively trivial matters are found instructions regarding physical uncleanness and moral perversion of the most loathsome kind ; then suddenly attention is directed towards usury, and vows, and the exemption of a newly-married man from war ; stripes are not to exceed forty ; the ox is not to be muzzled ; and every weight is to be just. What a system of law was that in which Israel was trained ! On every side was to be found prescription, authority, limitation, and all the apparatus of personal and social drill ! Now and again we hear of the sabbatical year of release, and of the treatment of slaves at given periods, and in the twenty-fourth chapter we even read of charity ; but the general tone of the book is that of legal restriction, criticism, and penalty. Hastily reading the whole book, it may be described as a book of law and little else ; yet reading it more attentively, it will be found that even in Deuteronomy there are evangelical lines full of the very love and tenderness of God. The cities of refuge may be described as gospel cities ; the protection of the birthright is an interposition of mercy; the very battlement upon the house is the law respecting the neighbour exemplified rather than merely uttered in words; the protection of the dam (xxii. 6-7) is full of evangelical suggestion; and the measuring of stripes so as not to exceed forty shows that the law itself was restrained by wisdom and mercy. Unquestionably the curses pronounced upon disobedience in the twenty-eighth chapter are like a very storm poured down from the heights of heaven; but in the same chapter the blessings pronounced upon obedience show that high above all law there reigns the spirit of love and pity. In the thirty-first and following chapters Moses prepares to give up his leadership, and in doing so he tenderly encourages the people to persevere, and in paternal tones cheers the heart of Joshua in view of the tremendous task about to be assigned to him. Then Moses begins to sing, and soon after is sent up to Mount Nebo, whence he views the land. There Moses died and was buried, and no man knoweth of his sepulchre unto this day. This is a bird's-eye outline of the marvellous book of Deuteronomy. Let us now turn and consider the whole book chapter by chapter.

"Ye have dwelt long enough in this mount."

REMARKABLE THINGS.

THIS is the first remarkable thing in the opening chapter of the fifth book of Moses. God knows, then, how long we have been here or there. Our downsitting and our uprising, our going out and our coming in, are of consequence to him who made us. He keeps the time : he knows when we have been "long enough" in one place. He does not always consult us, saying, in terms of affectionate inquiry,—Would you desire to tarry longer here?—would it suit you to remain another year? Sometimes God seems to come down upon our life ·with a precision and an imperativeness which make us feel how little, after all, we have to do with what we call our own concerns. A blessed life, surely, and most sweet, and altogether tender and restful, is it when we wait patiently upon God and tarry until we receive his reply, and then go out and do his bidding with both hands and with the unbroken consent of the entire mind. From the way in which he speaks to us, God seems to take it for granted that no question will arise upon his instructions. Surely in the very method of approaching us, a tribute is paid to our noblest qualities. The Lord comes with an instruction as if we had been waiting for it ; he tells us when to move and when to rest, as if our eyes were continually directed unto him in attitude of attention and expectation ; his speeches are answers, not to questions but to prayers; his commands are not merely edicts, but translations of the spirit which he assumes to be in us. Infinite is the wisdom of God.

"Ye have dwelt long enough in this mount." We may get tired even of mountains. Wherever we live, we need change.

The first happy impulse often commits itself to the doctrine that
we could live here or there alway. God does not take us at our
word, because he knows that our word is but a speech of ignorance or of impulse : it does but give utterance to the emotion of
the moment ; so, he allows our little speech to plash round about
our life as if it were a river of his own creating ; but we soon see
how it is dried up by the sun, and we are left in a thirsty and
barren place. Expect the answer from Heaven when you are in
wonder as to your residence and pilgrimage, or action of any
kind. There need not be any communication of audible speech
between your soul and God : the communication will be in the
spirit—in its profound and loving obedience, and in its positive
readiness to give up mountain and castle, and palace and crown,
without one moment's querulousness, or suggestion that another
day would be another day of good fortune. That is the attitude
of the pious spirit—the heart that is really healthy towards God,
the soul that has in it constancy and loyalty without speck or
flaw.

We are ordered down off the mountain. Soon after we have
said, It is good to be here, the Leader proposes that we should
go down again. He will not have any heaven built upon earth ;
he will never allow us to build permanently upon foundations
that are themselves transitory. Who can build straightly upon a
crooked foundation ? Who can build for ever upon a basis that
may succumb in a moment? Who would rear a supposedly
eternal palace upon foundations that are doomed to be burned ?
So, we are told to descend the mountain, though the sky be at its
bluest, and though the air be full of health, and though our vision
and our general senses be so quickened that we can almost detect
the presence of spirits and angels. There are many mountains
to come down—mountains of supposed strength, when the very
robustest man must lie down and say : I am very weary, tired to
exhaustion ; mountains of prosperity, when Crœsus himself
must come down saying : I am a poor man ; let the meanest slave
serve me, for I cannot longer serve myself. Then there is the
coming down that is inevitable—the time when God says to every
one of us : You have been long enough on the mountain of time:
pass through the grave to the hills of heaven, the great mountains
of eternity. Sometimes, we think we have been too long on the

mountain, and wonder when he will come, whose right it is to bring the sheep into the fold ; we say in our peevishness—not always impious, but rather an expression of weakness : Surely we have been forgotten : by this time we ought to have been with the blessed ones ; the night is coming on quickly, and we shall be drenched with dews.—So long are some men kept outside, on the very top of the hill, where very little grass grows,—bare, rocky places.   But God cannot forget : we must rest in his memory ; he puts himself even before a mother who may forget her sucking child, but he has pledged himself never to forget his redeemed Church.

But, having ordered his people away from the mountain, where can they take up their abode ?   We find the answer in the seventh verse.   God has many localities at his command, so he disperses the people, setting them " in the plain," " in the hills," " in the vale," " by the sea side," and " unto the great river, the river Euphrates."   What space God has !   " In my Father's house are many mansions,"—in my Father's house are many localities.   Do not say God has done with you because he has driven you from one pulpit, one church, one business, one very happy engagement in life, where you were making honest bread, and where you could sleep the night through untroubled by a single bitter memory. God has places enough for us all.   We did think it hard when that last door was shut as if in our very face : when we turned away that day our faces were pictured all over with sorrow and grief and disappointment : agony was written upon the countenance ; we went home saying : The end has come, the cloud has gathered : there is no more hope ;—and, behold, whilst we talked thus atheistically and foolishly, the cloud opened, and we caught such glimpses of morning as our weary eyes had never caught before.   The old mount had become a kind of home to us : we knew the short ways up the mountain : we knew the long, grassy slopes that led to the summit ; we had some little property on the very top ; we had begun, before getting full orders about anything, to lay just two or three courses which we meant to raise into a tabernacle ; we did stand upon the mount, and, looking upon those who dwelt in the plain, said we would not live down there : we would always live up among the blue skies, the white clouds, and at the very gate of morning.   So, it was hard to leave the old homestead : that morning we drained the cup of bitterness, and, when half-way down the hill, oh what a look we gave at the summit we should never re-ascend !—the old business, the old pulpit, the old happy relations in life, the mountain that had become a sweet home to us, and on whose steeps there was not one weary league. It did cost us much to leave the sweet place, haunted by ten thousand tender memories, and blessed by the recollection of many an answered prayer. But God has more places : instead of mountains, hills—little mountains ; not the great bulging mountains that seem to vie with heaven itself in majesty : still, little mountains—undulating mounds having green valleys on their tops which are still valleys in highlands, then plains, vales, sea-side, rivers. Who would not see all God's places ? Is it not wiser to take the longer lines, and to say to the heavenly One : Show us all the inheritance of thy power, and lead us hither and thither as thou wilt : it is thy world,—how green in the spring-time ! how rich in blossom ! how richer still in fruits !—If thou wilt lead us, the vale shall be as the mountain, and the mountain shall be as the plain ; and the sea shall be without a storm, and the river shall flow like a gospel of refreshment and hospitality. Why do we choose our own places ? Did ever man dispute the divine sovereignty without regretting his encounter with the Eternal will ? Why have any will ? Were we serving wooden gods, mechanical deities, divinities of our own creation or invention, we might dispute with them, point out what possibly they may have overlooked, suggest happier expressions, and draw bolder programmes ; but if God is the only-wise, if God is love, if God is light, if God died for us in the person of his Son, why not say : Not my will, but thine, be done : take me to the mountain or the plain, the hills or the vale, the sea-side or the river ; the taking itself shall be as a vision of heaven ?

Happy days were those of Deuteronomy !—God the Lawgiver, Instructor, Guide ; Israel receiving the speeches of heaven, and instantly striking the tent, and marching gladly, with hymns of thankfulness, to the music of the divine movement. Was this the case ? We find the exact contrary was the reality. When men brought back "the fruit of the land," which they had been sent to search out, "and brought it down unto us, and brought us word again, and said, It is a good land which the Lord our God doth

give us. Notwithstanding—" These are the words we read in
the twenty-fifth and twenty-sixth verses. What is their meaning?
Evidently, that eye-witnesses were disbelieved. Caleb's word
went for nothing; Joshua's testimony was ignored. That is
precisely what we are doing to-day; that is literally what is
being done with regard to Christian testimony in our own
generation. What are Christian speakers saying? They are
saying that they themselves have tasted, and handled, and felt
the good word of life; and we give them the lie. Do not be
hard upon ancient Israel, for, if inclined to a temper of severity,
we may well inflict upon ourselves the severest chastisement.
Do Christian speakers draw pictures, and appeal to the imagination, and suggest material for happy dreams? If so, then
we commit no breach of decency or courtesy in subjecting their
testimony to close cross-examination; but when men say, each for
himself,—I was blind, but now I see; I was cruel, but now I am
kind; I was a devotee of all evil and wrong, of every form of corruption and mischief, but, by the grace of God, I love truth and
light, and grace and beauty;—if the living men themselves are
there—not the words, not the logic, not the argument, not the
rhetoric, but the men—we must first destroy their character
before we can touch their testimony. This, then, puts the whole
controversy in a very serious light. Christianity has not only sent
messages to us, but messengers—not messengers who can repeat
sentences, but messengers who incarnate the doctrine they preach,
—or they have forced themselves into a service for which they
have no qualification. Let the life speak : let the sweet temper
be its own argument; let the invincible charity bear down with
celestial strength the bitter opposition. " Charity suffereth long,
and is kind;" it "beareth all things, believeth all things, hopeth
all things, endureth all things. Charity never faileth." Were
this controversy an antagonism between two hostile camps of
words, then let his be the palm who wins it : let cleverness enjoy
the prize, and let the wordiest speaker have the triumph due to
his efforts. But it is not so : this is a matter of life and death, of
reality or of unreality. The Christian speaker is not an argument
only, but an incarnation ; and before we can impugn his message,
we must assail the character which he declares that message to
have wrought in his own case. Good Christians would be good

servants : splendid lives would be splendid works ; yet Caleb and
Joshua were disbelieved. Eye-witnesses go for nothing in the
pressure of an inveterate and unreasoning prejudice. Christ himself was disbelieved : he was " despised and rejected of men."
Purity is a noble argument, but not one that inevitably secures
victory and triumph : otherwise, the Son of God himself would
but have required to show his life in order to win and subdue the
ages.

What did Israel say ? Notwithstanding the beautiful messages
and the cordial welcomes, they went into their " tents, and said,
Because the Lord hated us, he hath brought us forth out of the
land of Egypt " (v. 27). That is human nature. Do not suppose
that human nature is incapable of baseness so complete.
Whatever can be imagined can be done. The fiction is often the
larger truth. We say, on reading sundry books,—These are inventions. So they are; but inventions are possibilities: inventions
may be the larger facts. We must see in others where we are
ourselves. We cannot separate ourselves from others, saying,—
We should not have done so. Said a lady in the hearing of
Thomas Carlyle,—" Do you think, sir, that we should now act
towards Jesus Christ as the Jews acted in their day ? We should
receive him with love and enthusiasm." " No, madam," was the
answer, " if he came a rich man, without touching any of our prejudices or habits or customs, I might receive a card from you to
be at your house at a given hour, and on the back of it might be
written, ' To meet the Saviour ; ' but if he came back as he first
came—the same poor man, the denouncer of all Pharisaism and
evil,—you would say, ' Send him to Newgate, and hang him ! '"
Certainly. It was human nature that did it—not the Jews. The
Jews acted but incidentally : the Jews happened to furnish the
historical point which gave vividness to the tragedy ; but when
the Cross was set up, it was human nature that crushed it into the
rock : when Christ was jeered, it was the civillest of genteel
persons that mocked him to his face : when he was in agony, it
was the purest unchristian civilisation that added bitterness to
his cup. We must not allow ourselves to imagine that the Jews
disbelieved Jesus, and that if he came now we should welcome him. No : the human heart can never welcome Christ :—
' No man can come to me, except the Father which hath sent

me draw him." It is a mystery : we cannot explain the profound
enigma ; but the human heart never had anything for Christ but a
Cross ; and from the Cross the miracle must be wrought which
constrains human nature to crown him with many crowns. We
may disbelieve Caleb and Joshua, we may turn our back upon
Moses and Aaron, we may even bring ourselves under the awful
denunciation of the thirty-second verse, in which we read—"Yet in
this thing ye did not believe the Lord your God." Now, seeing
that we must live by belief, who are we going to believe ? We
cannot get away from this faith-life. Who is to be leader ? Say
some,—" As for me and my house, we will serve the Lord ; "—
others,—" The God that answereth by fire, let him be God." Set
up what standard you will, fix the terms of your own appeal ; but
Christian men will never hesitate to stand forward and say :
Christ is my Lord and my God ; I cannot reach the sublimity of
his holiness, but I can aim in that direction; I cannot overtake my
own prayers, but I can hold my face towards the rising of the
sun ; I count not myself to have apprehended, but this one thing
I do—I press—I press ! The attitude is Christian, the attitude is
an argument, the attitude imposes a solemn and incommunicable
responsibility.

Deut. i. 19.

"That great and terrible wilderness."

MEMORABLE EXPERIENCES.

THERE are some things that are never to be forgotten in life. There are troubles whose shadow is as long as life's whole day. The troubles are past, but the shadow is still there; the victory is won, but the battle seems still to be booming in the ear. We are miles and miles away from the desert—yea, half a continent and more—but who can ever forget "all that great and terrible wilderness"? Yet life would be poor without it. The memory of that wilderness chastens our joy, touches our prayer into a more solemn and tender music, and makes us more valiant, because more hopeful, in reference to all the future. There cannot be two such wildernesses in the whole universe. If there were another like it, it would not be equal to it, because our experience in the first would enable us to go through the second with a firmer step and a more cheerful courage. We are the better for the wildernesses of life, and we cannot escape them. No evasion is possible here. Apparent evasions have been accomplished, but they have been apparent only. You cannot get your children through life without passing through the wilderness at some time and in some way; and you are foolish when you think you can pay for their passage by some other and happier road. There is only one road— rough, cavernous, uphill, where the wind has full scope for its roar and cold assault; and we are the better for passing through it patiently, steadily, and religiously. I know it may seem hard to you that that dear little boy should have to go through the wilderness; but he must go. I know how you take him into your arms and say that you have had to suffer and he shall not but you cannot help it; and if you postpone his suffering too long, he will suffer the more for the postponement. There is a chronology of discipline; there is a time-bill written in heaven, and hung down from the skies, by which all chastisement is administered, all discipline is undergone, all burdens are imposed, and all strength is given. It is folly, it is cruelty, to suppose that you can find out some road in which there is no wilderness—some method of education in which there is no chastisement. Oh, that great and terrible wilderness! It comes after us now like a ghost; it darkens upon our vision in the dream-time; we repeat the journey in the night season, and feel all the sleet and cold, all the dreariness and helplessness of the old experience. How many a joy we have forgotten, how many a glad laugh has left no memory behind it, how many a salutation has been but a beating of the air and an instant descent into oblivion; but we cannot play with "that great and terrible wilderness." The very pronouncement of the words makes us cold. It was "great," it was "terrible," it was a "wilderness." But, rightly trodden, its barren sand made us men; taken in the right spirit, we thought we saw in it the beginning of the garden of God.

Every man does not pass through exactly the same wilderness; it is not needful that he should do so in order to confirm this doctrine—viz., that in all lives there are great dreary spaces that we would gladly jump—great and terrible wildernesses that we approach with fear and traverse almost with despair.

There was that great business wilderness that you passed through—when all was loss and no profit; when your friends forgot you, or when their smile was not followed by any substantial blessing; when you dare not tell the tale to your wife at night, because you had no wish to make her cry and bear a heavier burden. You were not dishonest, nor deceptive; you were not guilty of a culpable secretiveness in keeping the state of affairs from her; you wanted to tread the wine-press alone. You said it would be better to-morrow, and then you would tell her all about it. You listened to her laugh and said, "Poor thing! did she but know how near the bankruptcy court is that laugh would be choked in her young throat." But you would not tell you were passing through a great and terrible wilderness. I am not prepared to blame men who wish to keep the length and the terribleness of the desert as secrets in their own hearts; that secretiveness may be born of love and tender sympathy and real manliness. You remember the time when you had no night, if night be time for sleep; when you had no day, if day be time for joy and triumph. You remember the time when you dare hardly look into your own books, they were such blanks. You have not forgotten your old companions—Poverty that walked on the right hand, and Friendlessness that walked on the left. It was a great and terrible wilderness. If you could have talked of it as a wilderness, you might have found some garden patches in it, but you dare not tell exactly where you were—everything was so dark, so hard, so sterile; no hint of green thing, no sound of bird-music, no glint of subtle and unexpected light. The wilderness was great and terrible; but it is past. You are in fairer lands now; your property is accumulating, your speculations are paying, your adventures are crowned with success. Do not forget the wilderness: other men are in it. The man sitting next to you now, with an apparently jocund face and bright eye, is in the very middle of the wilderness which you have escaped. "Bear ye one another's burdens, and so fulfil the law of Christ;" bear them prayerfully, sympathetically. It is not needful that you should know them in name and detail, in date and actual locality; you must fall back on the solemn and perpetual facts of human history, and always consider that your comrades, friends, companions, neighbours, are undergoing chastisements and bearing burdens the very memory of which is no small part of your own individual training and spiritual education. Let prayer be made for all men. Never offer a prayer without thinking of the heavy-laden, the broken-hearted, the wounded spirit, the tired wayfarer.

Yours, on the other hand, was no business trouble, it was a long and painful affliction—the more painful because of a conscious strength that could not assert itself. Oh, that is pain! to know that you have great strength and yet to be pinned down, as it were, at one point. It is humiliating, it makes one impatient. We could sometimes almost tear the pinned filament away and claim opportunity for the exercise of our conscious power. To stop there and to say : "It is right that I should so suffer, be so mocked ; Father in heaven, not my will, but thine be done"—that is the last accomplishment of our spiritual culture. When we can say so, we are on the very last page of Heaven's first lesson-book, and will soon be ready to begin the second volume in the ampler and clearer light. You remember the affliction—when everybody in the house was quiet; when no one could commence anything new, when to-morrow was to be a revelation of some sorer trouble, some deeper darkness, some heavier burden ; when you thought about yourself as about a life that was run out ; when you said—by that curious euphemy by which we deceive ourselves—"If anything should happen to me." It is so that men speak about their own mortality ; you remember the time when there were no joyful words in the speech of the house, when the morning was as night, and the night was sevenfold in darkness—that was "a great and terrible wilderness." The poor reason was reeling, the light was going out, the burden was increasing, because the spirit was chastened. It was a "great and terrible wilderness."

But yours was neither business nor affliction, it was a wilderness of temptation. You fought with beasts at Ephesus, you fought with yourself seven days a week, it was the hour and power of darkness, the hours were crowded and huddled into one rough midnight. You were without strength ; it was the day of helplessness. You were mocked and haunted by invisible and impalpable powers. If they had been flesh and blood you could have struck them, and that would have been some relief; but we wrestle not against flesh and blood, but against principalities, against powers, against the rulers of the darkness of this world. Oh ! could we but see our enemies, we might take measure of them ; we could fasten our eye upon their eye, and anticipate their purpose by a steady glance studious of their intentions. But we do not see the enemy—he is on the right hand and on the left, behind, in front, and everywhere—a ubiquitous foe. Like the wind we cannot seize him, like the darkness we cannot measure him, like our own life, feeling it everywhere, but unable to place it in any one exclusive locality. We cannot corner those spiritual foes, they never sleep, they give no notice of their approach, they have no Sabbath day in their long week, when they say—" We must give the hunted foe or prey a rest." Just now it is a "great and terrible wilderness." Recognise it as such, lay your account with it, and study the divine intention in its presence, and in its awful shadow.

What are the thoughts that such a review should excite? Can we look back upon that way, through all the great and terrible wilderness, without remembering the divine help which we received? God was God in the wilderness; God came walking upon the wings of the wind, and flying upon the pinions of the storm; God looked at us through the darkness, and there was no blaze of anger in his eye. Who can forget the touch that came upon our burning brow in the night-time? Who can forget the ever-branching tree, just by the side of the bitter pool? Who can forget the clump of palm trees where no palm trees were expected? Who can cease to remember the voice of leadership—the strong, authoritative man who came amongst us like a revelation from God, and spoke broad words in broad tones, and was a tower of strength to us in the time of our weakness, and wonder, and fear—the sympathetic pastor, the mighty preacher, the kind friend, the one who understood us wholly through and through? I know of no wilderness in which there were not mitigations of its dreariness and solitude; yet we could not map these out and say they will never occur to-day, and to-morrow, and a week hence, and in a year's time. Our blessings also come suddenly, unexpectedly, and, it may be, according to our reckoning, irregularly. But the "great and terrible wilderness" was the place where our great prayers were prayed. The darkness inspires an eloquence of its own; sense of loneliness makes a dumb man eloquent in intercession. You do not know what you said in that long night of wilderness and solitude; the words were taken down; if you could read them now, you would be surprised at their depth, richness, and unction. You owe your very life to the darkness which made you afraid.

Then, is there no divine purpose, the recollection of which may sustain us in traversing wildernesses and lonely deserts? Who made the world? Is the world a fatherless thing, an unmade world, a self-rounded thing that may split up at any moment, or is there method in it? Is there a God above it? Is there a throne anywhere? And the King, is he but a name ur an echo? I see purpose in my life; I see it now—"Thou hast done all things well." I did not think so at the time; I should have made the wilderness a mile shorter, but it was on the last mile that I saw the brightest angel. I would have come to honour and renown sooner; but I see now that the very movements were ticked off, and that a moment earlier would have been a mistake. "I would have come," says another Christian man, "to a sense of competency, and comfort, and household security ten years ago; but in my soul I see that ten years ago I could not have borne what I now carry gracefully." Thou hast done all things well. I would not have had seven graves in the cemetery, nor two, nor one; but I see now that I am the richer for the seven; I would not now have it otherwise. They are my best estate; I have property in them; I grow my choicest flowers there; there I meet with the angels that understand me. There is a method in all this: I will accept it; I will bow down before it; I will kiss the rod that lacerated me to the bone: it was in my Father's hand.

Then, is there to be no human gratitude springing out of all this? Is ours to be a false life—an unsympathetic existence? Ought there not to be a new power in the hand-grip? Ought not my hand to get round yours with a more cunning and expressive masonry, because of the wilderness through which I have passed and the sorrows which I have undergone, and which are now just beginning to fall upon you? You can never be wrong in regarding human life as having in it great gaps, great deserts, great and terrible wounds. The preacher should never forget this. When an assembly comes together, it does not convene as an assembly of philosophers and high thinkers and men who are thirsting for some special intellectual gratification. I care not where the assembly is, it is an assembly of broken hearts, burdened lives, blinded eyes, sorrow-laden souls. I will undertake, that he who speaks of God's infinity, eternity, spiritual majesty, deific magnificence and grandeur shall not touch one heart as compared with the man who speaks of fatherhood, pity, condescension, need of help, need of grace. He who so speaks to Heaven will take up a thousand hearts with him, and in his one voice there will throb the necessity of a multitude of souls. As we have received help of God, let us give help to others. If our help sometimes be imposed upon, no matter. I do not want the sagacity which never makes a mistake; I want the sympathy, the great motherly love that tells a prodigal that he is almost an angel. That will do more good in the world than your sharp criticism, your discriminating and penetrating judgment, that knows exactly who is good and who is bad. That is not my business; I have but one hand in this matter, and that is the right hand—the giving hand, the writing hand, the helping hand, the working hand, the sheltering and protecting hand. He only must have two hands who can discriminate with infinite penetration and justness between the good and the bad. We do not all come through the wilderness with equal strength. Some are far behind, they were very weak; they got sore tired; they said, "Comrade, how far is it now?" And all we could say was, "It is not so far to-day as it was yesterday." Do not count the miles, take the steps; do not say you have to travel fifty miles, but say you have to take the next step, and grace shall be equal to thy day. "My grace is sufficient for thee." And at the last he will say, "Thy shoes were iron and brass; and as thy day, so thy strength was." And we shall reply, "Even so, my garments were not worn, my shoes bore no travel stains, the mystery of endurance was equal to the mystery of trial; so, God be thanked for the great and terrible wilderness!"

Deut. ii.

PROVIDENTIAL LINES.

THERE is a remarkable expression in the fifth verse— " because." The same expression occurs in the ninth verse —" because." The same word occurs in the nineteenth verse— " because." Yet it is the infinite God who speaks and puts himself in the position of one who would explain to his creatures his reasons for making certain allotments. Instead of speaking as one might suppose the Eternal Majesty of the Universe to speak, he seems to place himself upon a level with men, and to tell them *why* they are not to do certain things. For example : The command was that Israel was not to interfere with the children of Esau :—" Meddle not with them ; for I will not give you of their land, no, not so much as a foot breadth ; because I have given mount Seir unto Esau for a possession " (v. 5). That mount belongs to another man. The law of proprietorship must be recognised. We must have social rights, or we shall not have social securities. Very particular is the direction. Read the words again,—" No, not so much as a foot breadth." It is upon such fine lines that such great rights are based. If Jacob, in the person of the children of Israel, could have put one foot upon Mount Seir, he soon would have put the other foot there too, and Esau might have been dispossessed. The only way for some men to keep themselves honest is to have nothing to do with the other side. A footprint may some day be turned into a boundary : a finger-print may one day be pointed to as a right. " Touch not, taste not, handle not,"—but keep away absolutely, in the very innermost thought of the mind, from the things that are not yours. The same law holds good in regard to the Moabites :—" Distress not the Moabites, neither contend with them in battle : for I will not give thee of their land for a possession ; because I have given Ar unto the children of Lot for a possession " (v. 9). The same law related to the children of Ammon :—"Distress them not, nor meddle with them : for I will not give thee of the land of the children of Ammon any possession ; because "—then comes the reason (v. 19). God has taken care of every one of us in life. There is a little portion for the very smallest of us—one little handful of bread for the poorest man, one little ewe lamb for every life ; and God knows what he has given and to whom he has given it, and he keeps the title-deeds in his own heavens; and he would look more after our property and rights if we would allow him to do so. Could we but give ourselves heart and soul to the kingdom of heaven, the doing of right, the continual education of the soul in truth, holiness, and nobility, God would see that every right was protected; and when we come to measure the estate which we thought to be but small, we may find that the boundaries have been enlarged and that we have more than we supposed we had. He is good unto all them that call upon him. He knows the measure of our hunger, and never did God send away from his table the unsatisfied appetite which he himself had created.

Contrast these commandments with the ten words which were given in Exodus—say, for example,—"Thou shalt not steal ;" "Thou shalt not commit adultery ;" "Thou shalt not bear false witness." Where are the reasons there ? Who can find a "because" following such laws ? Yet the Lord could not rear virtue upon a command. "Thou shalt not steal"—never made an honest man. "Thou shalt not" is a proper enough form of representation of the idea, if it be understood in its spiritual relations. The word is much grander than "shalt" or "shalt not." If a man were to say,—I do not steal because I have been told not to steal,—he is a thief in his heart, and he is stealing all day ; his meaning is :—Had I not been told not to steal, I would steal at once, but being told not to steal I do not steal. He does not know how much he is deceiving himself. Where is the honesty ? But change the form of expression, and light comes above all the lightning of Sinai :—"Thou *wilt* not steal ;" "Thou *wilt* not bear false witness;" and throughout the commandments, "Thou *wilt*," "Thou *wilt* not ;"—the meaning being, that if the spirit of obedience is in the heart and the spirit in harmony with God, the man *will* not do wrong, *will* do right,—

by no effort, not because a prize is before him, or a whip is being laid upon his back in cruel laceration ; but the man will be so m ıch like God, will live so deeply and truly in the Spirit of God, that he *will* not do things that are wrong, that he *will* do things that are right : he *will* keep the Sabbath day, and he *will* not covet his neighbour's goods. In our early education, we need the " thou shalt not " of verbal prohibition, because at a certain period we could not understand spiritual reasoning ; for a time, therefore, we live under what may be called arbitrary law— that is, law which vindicates itself solely by the majesty of the law-giver, and will not condescend to reasoning or explanation. In the progress of our education, crude words such as " Thou shalt " and " Thou shalt not " fall out of our commerce with heaven, and we know the meaning of the divine speech which says,—" Thou *wilt* honour thy father and thy mother ; " " Thou *wilt* remember the Sabbath day to keep it holy ; " " Thou *wilt* do no murder." So, commandment is turned into revelation : at last we come to see that God was not speaking arbitrarily, or laying down small boundaries without stooping to give us explanations, but was anticipating the greater word—" Thou *wilt*," " Thou *wilt* not." The good tree will bring forth good fruit.

A very tender word is found in the seventh verse :—" For the Lord thy God hath blessed thee in all the works of thy hand : he knoweth thy walking through this great wilderness : these forty years the Lord thy God hath been with thee ; thou hast lacked nothing." We may put down wordy debaters who have nothing to live upon but their own invention,—troubled by their own verbosity ; but we cannot put down witnesses who testify what they have seen, known, and handled for a period of forty years. Time has a good deal to do with testimony ; time enters very subtlely into all things human and mundane. Men may make a ladder in a very short time, but who can make a tree ?—and how constantly we are mistaking a tree for a ladder, or a ladder for a tree ! Time makes the tree ; time makes character ; time makes practical theology. Moses could say with emphasis at the end of forty years what he could only say with hopefulness at the begin-ning. The Christian witness is forty years old ; forty years have men tried the Christian doctrine and the Christian consola-tion, and at the end of forty years their witness is stronger,

tenderer, larger than at the first.   Possibly they may know much
or they may know nothing about theological terms and theological controversies ; but they know the vitality of the matter—the
inner grace and solace and inspiration,—and they are strong in
testimony that, but for a doctrine heaven-descended and heaven-
inspired, they would long ago have given up life in utterest
despair.   So we have to deal with facts now as well as arguments.   A man rises and says: But for this Christian doctrine
which is written in the Christian Scriptures, I should have been
the worst of men, the unhappiest of men : explain it how you
may, I am so constituted that I should have been a terror unto
many, a shadow upon my own house, a plague to my own consciousness ; but I have studied the Christian kingdom in its
doctrine, legislation, and solace, and I have been enabled to
receive Christ into my heart ; and now, by the grace of God,
I am what I am, and my life has in it the promise and the
seal of a blessed immortality.   Whatever did that for the man
who is bearing witness is to be spoken of with respect.   The
Christian testimony, doctrine, or example never made immoral
men.   The men who profess this Christian guidance through the
wilderness may not always have been what they ought to have
been—they themselves will be swiftest witnesses in this matter
as against themselves ;—but no man who has tasted of this
doctrine will be slow to confess that but for it his life would have
been without a centre, without restfulness, without a purpose
adequate to his faculties.   This side of the Christian cause must
never be neglected.   Many men can be strong only upon this
side, because they are not master of words, controversies, and
counsels : they know next to nothing of the processes of evolution through which Christian argument has passed ; but they say
they know that after prayer their hands are stronger, their eyes
keener of vision, their hearts tenderer in all sympathy.   Any
religion that will do that for any human creature is a religion
well-deserving the noblest church that can be built to its
genius.

The great leader who has lost so many of his followers
becomes pathetic in the fourteenth verse, wherein he says, "All
the generation of the men of war were wasted out from among
the host."   It is sad to live in a cemetery.   It is sad to be the

survivor of thousands of old comrades; the air is cold when they leave us; summer is itself but a cloud when our heart-companions are no more. To have lost them in noble strife is not the worst of the situation. We could bury them with honours : we could lay the colours of the army on their green graves and call the soldiers sleeping their last sleep " good knights of God ; " but Moses had to look upon a different spectacle. That many fell in honourable war might be true enough ; but four-and-twenty thousand of them were struck down by the javelin of God because of an outrage against the holiness of his law. God can do without his generals, captains, and leaders of hosts ; God can do without every preacher he has ; but he cannot do without his holiness, his purity, his infinite righteousness. God will handle the evil-doers : where all the opponents of Israel could do nothing, the Lord blew upon the host of the chosen, and by one plague four and-twenty thousand of them were swept from the land of the living. God does not want our patronage. Never does he say : They are generals of mine, great leaders, marvellous captains in controversy, and therefore I must spare them, though they be evil-hearted and their minds be filled with superstition and error. He can do without any creature he ever made, but he will not have the integrity of his throne impaired. But take the brighter view. Suppose all to have died in honourable conflict—brave, upright, honest men, gentle—as all strong men are, wise and good ; and still time bears them down and causes them to disappear. The Church is always suffering losses in this way. Some whom we wish to live for ever live but a handful of days ; men whom we thought essential to the Christian cause are taken away as if their presence upon earth were of no consequence. Herein is the wisdom of God and the righteousness of the Father. He will not encourage idolatry of any kind ; he will have the truth resting upon itself ; he insists that the Bible shall make its own way in the world. Whilst we are deeply thankful for annotation, we should be still more profoundly grateful for the Book which is annotated. We do not live upon the comments : we live upon the Book ; as we do not live upon opinions respecting the bread, but upon the bread itself.

How will God make up for all these losses ? He takes the

case into his own hand. He will not put four-and-twenty thousand more men in the field : he will double the influence—or multiply the influence indefinitely—of those who are already engaged in his cause, representing and vindicating his kingdom. The twenty-fifth verse supplies the explanation and the proof :— "This day will I begin to put the dread of thee and the fear of thee upon the nations that are under the whole heaven, who shall hear report of thee, and shall tremble, and be in anguish because of thee." He will work spiritually. Instead of working through the sword and the battle, he will work through fear. He promised this in the Book of Exodus ; in chapter xv., verses 15, 16, we read,—"Then the dukes of Edom shall be amazed; the mighty men of Moab, trembling shall take hold upon them ; all the inhabitants of Canaan shall melt away. Fear and dread shall fall upon them ; by the greatness of thine arm they shall be as still as a stone ; till thy people pass over." Thus God works through the medium of apprehension, wonder, curiosity ; thus God holds the eyes of men that they may not see the reality of the case ; and thus God touches the eyes of men that they mistake one man for a thousand. Clouds on the horizon God makes into oceans, the very vastness of which terrifies the observer. God makes noises in the air which men mistake for the sound of battle, as if the war were being led by an infinite host of skilled soldiers. Write the history of fear as known in your own consciousness ; put down exactly what fear has done in your case—how it has multiplied difficulties, how it has excited anxieties, how it has made you feel as if the little number you saw only came ahead of an infinite host ; and the result will be that you will discover that fear has done more in life than reality has ever done—that imagination has outrun literal realism. We have suffered more from the things we thought were going to happen than we ever suffered from the things which really did occur. The mind of man is in the hand of the Lord ; the heart of man is under the guidance of Heaven.

No Christian man can too strongly denounce the spirit and cruelty of war : there are no terms sufficiently expressive and emphatic with which to characterise the horribleness of the military spirit; but there are worse things than war : slavery is worse, oppression is worse, robbery is worse; war may become comparatively righteous and even holy, but slavery can never become so, or oppression, or robbery, or wrong-doing, or corruption. That war will ultimately cease is true; but we cannot "take Jesus by force and make him a King:" he must come in his own time, he must appear in his own way. It would suit our impatience and our often unreasoning and immoral rapidity to crown him now; but he is more careful about his crown than we could ever be. The ages are in Christ's own hand; God knows every tick of time, every pulse of life: all the centuries are upon the divine record and are under the divine administration. We cannot hasten things. To hasten peace is to imperil peace. The Bible is a book of wars; "the Lord is a man of war:" he has arrows that are "drunk with blood," a sword that has devoured flesh; but in the end he will bring in everlasting peace. We cannot have the Christian kingdom in the Pentateuch: Christ is not born in the historical books; the Bible itself is the standard by which all progress is indicated; and not until many a weary chapter has been read, and many a weary period survived do men see a star in the east. We did not make the stars: we cannot make them come and go: they are God's bright lights; and he will indicate the time in his own way. Meanwhile, we can live in a spirit of anticipation, in a spirit of peace; we can hold up the great, broad, solemn sentiment of peace. This we are bound to do; but as to how the great nations of the earth shall be reconciled and held in amity, that is a divine mystery for which we must await a divine explanation.

Deut. iii.

"Og the king of Bashan came out against us" (v. 1).

REVIEW AND PROSPECT.

IS it not remarkable that good causes and good men should meet with constant opposition? We are now perusing the history of a journey which was undertaken by divine direction, and again and again—almost on every page—we come upon the fact that the journey was from end to end bitterly opposed. Probably, if the people had started on a pilgrimage at their own suggestion, they could hardly have encountered severer hostility. We may even go further and say—Had the people gone out in direct opposition to the will of God, they could scarcely have been resisted with more obstinate animosity. Looking at the intensity of the hatred which the progress of the Israelites excited, one might say, not without plausible reasoning, that they had wholly mistaken the course which they ought to have pursued; it would be simply impossible to believe that God could lead any people into so many snares, antagonisms, battles, and cruel repulsions. The one part of the story thus appears to contradict the other. If we read the divine direction, we come to one conclusion; if we turn our attention almost wholly to social and national opposition, we come to a totally different opinion and judgment. What then is to be done? We must revert to facts which are known to ourselves and are vividly and completed attested by this day's bitter experience. Were this matter of ancient history, we might, in a happier condition of civilisation and in a happier mood of mind, dispute the theory that Israel travelled under divine direction and guidance; but this very thing is done to-day in our country, in all countries, in our own heart and life. Never man, surely, went to church without some enemy in the form of temptation, suggestion, or welcome in other directions, seeking to prevent his accomplishing the sacred purpose. Where is the good cause against which some modern Og king of some modern Bashan, does not arise? The argument can be set in so many angles and helped by so many illustrations known to ourselves that we need not have any doubt about ancient history. Does no enemy arise against honesty? Does cleanliness, the simplest of the virtues, pursue an uninterrupted way—men, cities, and nations welcoming her and blessing her with thankfulness? Is the cause of temperance an easy, broad, and sunny road on which to travel, and having simply to show a radiant face, and lift up a ringing and pure voice to make converts by the thousand and the million? Name a good purpose which ever arose in your heart that was not instantly resisted by some force, sometimes without a name and without definite measure, sometimes almost a shadow, now and then apparently a mere superstition; still there was the hostile force. There need be no marvel then that precisely this fortune befell the progress of the Christian kingdom even when that kingdom was led visibly by the very Christ of God in the days of his flesh. He was "despised and rejected of men;" men sent after him the message,—We will not have thee to reign over us. "He came unto his own, and his own received him not." At every heart he stands in a beggar's attitude and adopts a suppliant's tone. This is mysterious; this is bewildering; now and again it throws the heart into dejection akin to despair. The other course would have seemed so much more probable- - that men should have seen Christ and instantly bowed down before him and hailed him Redeemer—King. But this has not been the history of education, of the higher thought of man, even of science itself,—certainly not of the broader and nobler truths, certainly not of the purpose of Christ. He who would be good must fight a battle: he who would pray well must first resist the devil. This makes life very hard: the burden is sometimes too heavy; but the voice of history so concurs with the testimony of conscience and the whole is so corroborated by the spirit of prophecy that we must accept the discipline, and await with what patience God himself can work within us the issue of the tragic miracle.

Is there no compensatory consideration or circumstance? The

Lord himself must speak very distinctly in some conditions and relations of life. There must be no third party; the interview must be a face to face communion with God. There are times in life when we could not bear even a friend's voice, or a pastor's prayer,—when we must verily with the heart's eyes see the very God of heaven. How sweetly the divine voice mingles with the human story! How wondrously the low places are lifted up, and the rough places are made plain, and the mountains are brought low by words full of divine fire and love! The verses seem to alternate—now darkness, now light; now dejection, now hope; now the moan of the weary leader who longs to unyoke himself and take rest, now the inspiring voice of God—a new promise, or an old promise set in new terms—the old, old diamond in a new and beauteous setting. The words with which the second verse opens are familiar words, but their familiarity does not destroy their preciousness. "And the Lord said unto me." That is how the balance is adjusted. In the one verse, Og king of Bashan; in the next verse—Jehovah. Thus the story of our life alternates—now an enemy, now a friend; now the fight is going to be too severe for us and we shall certainly fall, and now the Lord of hosts is in the van, and kings are burned by his presence as stubble is burned by the fire. What was the divine message? It was a message adapted to the sensitiveness of the circumstances :—"Fear him not : for I will deliver him, and all his people, and his land, into thy hand." Get rid of fear, and you increase power. "The fear of man bringeth a snare." He who is touched by the cold shadow of fear is not himself in all the richness of his quality, in all the amplitude of his strength. This is a miracle which can be wrought only by divine energy. The demon of fear cometh not forth but at the Master's own bidding. Disciples may cheer one another, for a moment alleviate the acuteness of the distress, and for a period may suggest thoughts which lift up the mind below the level of darkness; but the demon of fear—the demon that makes a coward of a man—can only be expelled by the voice of God, at the very bidding of Omnipotence. This should give us comfort. Many men suffer from a spirit of fear who imagine they are suffering from a spirit of doubt, amounting almost to impiety and even blasphemy. Men are thus cruel with themselves because they do not distinguish between things that differ. All men are not equally valorous. We are not equal in intellectual energy and determination. Some men are in bondage all their life-time through fear—not always of death, but of all kinds of difficulty; the very air is full of spectres; every wind that blows brings with it a moan of despair rather than sounds a trumpet of hope. God must judge all men herein. Let us, at all events, try to take the upper and better view, and not allow the enemy to cheat us out of our prayer by the suggestion that we have lost the altar and forgotten the all-prevailing Name. This is Christ's word. " Fear not " is taken from the Old Testament into the New : " Fear not them which kill the body ; " " Fear not, little flock ; for it is your Father's good pleasure to give you the kingdom ; " " Fear God." We must pray for the fearless spirit. Observe, this is a purely spiritual inspiration. Israel is not equipped with a new set of armour, as of bows or arrows, or swords or instruments of steel, or, modernising the incident, with all that we now call weapons of war. What ally is this who comes to the head ? It is God himself. A promise is a victory. A seized and applied comfort of heaven lifts mean men into heroic proportions. How valiant would the Church be could she but realise and claim with thankfulness and energy the exceeding great and precious promises of God ! " The weapons of our warfare are not carnal,"—the armour is spiritual ; we live by thought, we fight by inspiration, we suffer in the spirit of hope ; and, glorified by the indwelling presence of God, no king that ever came out against us can effectively lift his hand to smite the Christian banner. He who is strong in spirit is strong all through and through his nature ; he who is only muscularly strong will fail in the fight. The brave heart, the soul alive with God—that will always conquer. Let us live and move and have our being in God.

What was the consequence ? We read the story in the fourth verse :—" And we took all his cities at that time, there was not a city which we took not from them, threescore cities, all the region of Argob, the kingdom of Og in Bashan." Opposition to God always means *loss.* No man ean fight God, and retire truly and lastingly rich. He can have a thief's store ; he can pillow his head upon heaps of gold ; but he will find it hard lying, and in the night-time his pillow may be stolen. Whoso opposes God comes to ruin in this way. There is no bad man who is successful. Do not let us interpret the word "successful" narrowly and partially, as if it were a term descriptive of mere appearances or momentary relationships. In the partial accepta tion of the term the proposition will not bear examination; but in discussing great spiritual realities we must take in the full view; and, fixing the attention upon that view, the proposition remains an indestructible truth—that no bad man is really prosperous. He has no comfort. He eats like a glutton, but he has no true enjoyment; out of his bread he draws no poetry, no thought, no fire; it is lost upon him, for he is an evil eater In his apparent wealth he is miserably poor. He has more anxiety than the penniless man. We suppose that anxiety is the portion of poverty; anxiety, in a still larger measure, is the portion of wealth, and especially of ill-gotten wealth—money that has a bad history behind it; the men who hold it will presently be coming in, setting down the money, and going out and hanging themselves that they may hasten after their elder brother Iscariot. If it could be proved that a man can oppose God and be truly happy, the whole Christian kingdom would be destroyed by that proof. The word of the Lord, as written in the Book, is against the possibility. If a man, therefore, can rise, whose word can be taken, who is of sufficient standing and station in society to have his word accepted, who can say,—I have broken all the commandments, I have defied the Spirit of the Cross, I have denounced the God of the Bible; and lived a bad man's life, yet I have purest enjoyment, a sense of sanctity greater than could be boasted by Christ and his Apostles;—if a man could bear that testimony, we should have brought into visible conflict the God of heaven and the spirit of earth. But, whilst we are waiting for that witness, we can call up an army, ten thousand times ten thousand strong, to testify that "the way of transgressors is hard"—that there is no peace to the wicked; that the mind of the wicked is like a troubled sea. The testimony upon that side is complete and invincible.

But what became of Og, the king of Bashan? We read in the eleventh verse,—"Behold, his bedstead was a bedstead of iron; is it not in Rabbath of the children of Ammon? nine cubits was the length thereof, and four cubits the breadth of it, after the cubit of a man." What an ending! How appropriate! How bitter the satire! Og king of Bashan came out to fight the people of God ; a few verses are written in which battles are fought and cities taken, and at the end the bedstead of Og is nearly all that remains of the mighty king of Bashan! This is worthless fame ; this is the renown that is pitiable. But there is no other renown for wicked men : they will leave a name in history, but a name the children will laugh at ; they will leave behind them a memorial, but the memorial itself shall be an abiding sarcasm. The Lord turneth the counsel of the wicked upside down ; the Lord will laugh at the wicked man and have all his devices in derision. His bedstead will be remembered when he himself is forgotten ; he will be spoken of in the bulk and not in the quality ; he will be measured like a log ; he will be forgotten like an evil dream. The righteous shall be had in everlasting remembrance. Who would be wicked ? Who would oppose God ? Who would not rather coalesce with the heavens, and pray that the Spirit of God would work in the human heart the miracle of reconciliation with things eternal and celestial ?

Now Moses has a desire. In the whole course of the Pentateuch he only spoke twice on his own account in the matter of desire, and in both instances he was refused. Moses said, first,—"Shew me thy glory ;" and God said, No : no man could see my glory and live : it would blind him and strike him dead ; but I will show thee my goodness. Now, towards the end, Moses says,— "And I besought the Lord at that time, saying, . . . I pray thee, let me go over, and see the good land that is beyond Jordan, that goodly mountain, and Lebanon" (vv. 23-5). And the Lord said,—No. This seems to be cruel. It occurs in our own life. We are sometimes so near, and, behold, the scene dissolves like a mirage—vanishes at our approach like a thing that mocks us. The child comes to the twenty-first year, but never completes his majority ; the dream is just going to come true, when some rude wind blows it absolutely away ; the blossom is beautiful, the fruit is forming, and whilst we are looking on the east wind comes and blights the tree ; now and again, in prayer, we are just going to lay both hands upon the answer and bring it back with us like a reaper returning with a sheaf from the harvest field, and before we can touch it we who were mighty in prayer become weak in unbelief; we see so many things come towards maturity which never ripen into the bloom of perfect life. Then what became of Moses? Here is an unanswered prayer. Blessed be God for many prayers that have never been answered! What if at the end we have to thank God more for the prayers he did not hear than for the supplications to which he replied? Let us picture Moses now as an old man : let us, in imagination, see his white hair, his wrinkled face, the fire of his eyes diminishing —nearly extinct; let us for a moment imagine a child's emotion swelling his old breast as he says,—" Let me go over, and see the good land ; "—and then imagine him doubling his age and falling into decrepitude as in a moment when the forbidding word falls from the lips of God. That is no romance : it is to-day's distressing story. But that is not the end. Moses wanted to see the lower Canaan—what if he saw the higher ? Moses uttered a little prayer—what if God denied a reply so small as the intercession and took him up without prayer into the region of eternal praise ? The prophets were cut off without seeing the culmination or fruition of their predictions; but what heavens blazed upon their opened eyes in the other and better world what sage may hear, what poet imagine ? There we stand. God denies only that which is little, earthly and mean, or miscalculated, or undesirable. He surprises us by the vastness of his answers. He "is able to do exceeding abundantly above all that we ask or think." Into that sanctuary of promise our souls would fly as into a refuge inviolable. You prayed for the child's life, and the child died—what if it were but transplanted from cold climes to the summer air of heaven ? You prayed for a certain kind of prosperity, and it was denied—what if your soul was enriched with a nobler largess—a greater proof of favour divine ? Do not interrupt God, or mischievously and narrowly interpret his promise. It is written upon the record, it was spoken by the voice of Christ—that God will always do some better thing for us than we have ventured to desire. If the little prayer is denied, it is that God may make room for a larger blessing—yea, for the new Jerusalem itself.

Deut. iv.

THE DIVINE FOUNDATION.

THIS book is a book of speeches. The man who delivered the speeches—three in number—said he could not speak. Aaron was chosen because he could deliver public messages and take charge of the appeals and commandments of God to mighty men. But, as in life, the first is last and the last is first. Who can quote anything that Aaron ever said ? Who does not know that the whole of the Pentateuch is alive with the eloquence of Moses from the very time of his coming into it ? Yet Moses said he could not speak : he was " of a slow tongue," and his lips did not move easily to music or eloquence. How God turns the counsels of men upside down ! How the slow mouth might become most eloquent, could the man but accept the will of God !— making his very weakness a reason for accepting, that God might be the more magnified and honoured and glorified. When did God choose a man for his ministry without intending to qualify him for it ? He does not accept the mighty man who says he is all but omnipotent. He accepts the trembling man, broken-hearted, his eyes full of tears, his tongue stammering because it cannot carry the burden of his thought and his emotion. Whom God has called to his ministry—be he a dumb man—he will qualify and he will crown. A book of speeches should have extraordinary fascination for us. There is a literature of speech as well as a literature of mechanical and exact composition. The difference is easily discernible and is often quickly felt. The world will surely neve· wholly dismiss its speaker. The speaker is so much nearer to us than the writer can ever be. He brings so much to his work which cannot be reported or reproduced— all the sympathy of presence, voice, tears, encouragement. The very utterance is itself an annotation ; the speech is made alive by the man. Let us .encourage one another in this ministry of speech—often broken, sometimes all but incoherent, yet singular in fascination because singular in sympathy and reality, not a lesson recited, but an appeal delivered; and not an effort accomplished with great outlay of strength and patience, but a new breathing of a wind from heaven. Moses appears, therefore, as a speaker in this book of Deuteronomy. His speech is solid with instruction, tremulous with appeal, grand with character. Yet Aaron was to have been the speaker. Aaron is dead,—Moses is quoted by Christ and is sung in heaven. Moses called upon Israel to "hearken" (v. 1). Who can hear? Who has ever met a man, in any congregation, that could listen? What is wanted to-day may be described as good hearers. It is not given to man to rush away from his business, place himself down suddenly in the sanctuary, and call for revelations that he can appreciate. Men must be prepared to hear as well as prepared to preach. To "hearken" is not a mechanical exercise. The word "hearken" is charged with profound meaning; it represents the act of acute, vital, profound, fervent attention. He who "hearkens" is in an attitude of eagerness—as if he would complete the speech, anticipate it, or elicit from the speaker a broader eloquence by the gratitude and expectancy of his own attention. Would that they who say much about speaking would learn the elements of good listening!—so learned, they would be dispossessed of themselves, their ears would be purged of all noises and tumults and rival competitions, and importunity being dismissed, anxiety being suspended, and the soul set in a posture of expectation, would receive even from slow-speaking Moses statutes and precepts solemn as eternity, and rich as the thought of God. "He that hath ears to hear,"—not for noises to please,—"let him hear." Such hearing is almost equal to praying; such listening never was disappointed. Moses had such grasp of his ministry and understanding of his holy function that he was strong even within supposed limitations. It is when men have no boundaries that they are vague in intellectual conception and indefinite in religious speech. Moses should be the teacher of teachers. Moses was under the impression, which is fast being got rid of, that God has begun the ministry, has actually pointed out the starting-place, has gone further, and prepared the speech, so that man now has only to deliver it, incarnate it, represent it.

It is not the word of man, but the word of God. About what other word could Moses have said—" Ye shall not add unto the word which I command you, neither shall ye diminish ought from it, that ye may keep the commandments of the Lord your God which I command you " ? (v. 2). Certainly, this puts human genius upon a severe trial. Men, having " sought out many inventions," would like to invent a Bible. What a Bible man could invent! There should be in it no dust of the ground answering to the breath of God, no trial-tree, no tempting serpent, no tragedy ; but a kind of minor heaven, a dull blue and pale light, and mechanical virtue, and regulation enjoyments,— no devil, no hell. Men are not compelled to accept the Bible ministry, but if they do accept it, they are bound by the record. Men may invent bibles, but they ought also to invent churches to preach them in, and invent the sacrifice which could bear the disappointment which always follows the criticism of disapproving Heaven. We are not forced into the pulpit, but being in the pulpit by the highest force—namely, the inspiration of the Holy Ghost—the one thing we have not to do is to invent either law or gospel. That is what is meant by limitation. The centre is given and the circumference is described, and within the circumference we have large liberty. We have no right of trespass or violation. Who can describe the moral contemptibleness of the man who invents bibles and gospels whilst he is standing on professedly Christian ground and surrounded by Christian sanctions and is enjoying the comfort of Christian recognition ? What is wanted is more Bible ; a fuller reading of the Bible, following a profounder understanding of the Bible. Who has exhausted all the truth of God's Word ? Who can get to the end of these five loaves and a few small fishes ? The feast grows with the appetite that enjoys it : the light increases upon the vision that can receive it ; until, at last, the Christian student says, lifting up his eyes : I see heaven opened, and the Son of man standing on the right hand of God. Add nothing, take away nothing, but give the Word opportunity of natural and proper development. The kingdom of heaven is like unto a grain of mustard-seed, the least of all seeds ; but when it is sown and grown, how ample its branches ! how hospitable its shelter ! So the Book is more than a letter ; it is a letter to begin with, but it must be sown, planted, watered from the clouds of heaven, shone upon by the light of the God who wrote it; and then it is not a Bible projected by the invention of man, but a revelation fully expanded, blooming with immortal summer, grand and rich with the joy of God.

But does not this require great faith? Most certainly it does; but that faith itself is sustained by vision. The law of God is confirmed by experience. It is not all faith, a merely intellectual or spiritual effort. It is marvellous how this inner action is sustained by outward facts; how God re-writes the Bible in human history and annotates it with a thousand facts day by day. So Moses said, "Your eyes have seen what the Lord did because of Baal-peor: for all the men that followed Baal-peor, the Lord thy God hath destroyed them from among you. But ye that did cleave unto the Lord your God are alive every one of you this day" (vv. 3, 4). Marvellous is this interplay of faith and fact, consciousness and experience, prayer and realisation. The world is an outside representation of many a sanctuary mystery. The book of Proverbs is not a book of apophthegms, of guesses at possibilities: every proverb is a history expressed in a proposition. The way, therefore, to read the proverbs is to select one, and say, What does human history reply to that proposition?—and a fair analysis of human nature and a fair induction of human facts will end in the confession that the proverb has anticipated in a marvellous manner, and generalised with massive eloquence, all that has been proved by human history. When the Sanhedrim laughed at Peter and John and said bitter things about them, they were merry up to the point of victory, but, "beholding the man," a sudden cloud fell upon their joy, and troubled them exceedingly; there is the man who was lame standing up, looking in the face the accusers of the Christian healers. A written miracle they could have smiled down—they had a gracious smile;—but—"beholding the man!" That is the proof to which Moses refers; that is the proof to which Christian teachers may always refer. " Beholding" the temper, the charity, the nobleness, the purity; "beholding" the miracle of the Holy Ghost, eloquence is dumb, and criticism commits suicide. But, if we have nothing to show, we may at once surrender. We must be able to refer to experience, and fact, and reality, and call up the witnesses a thousand at a time to bear testimony. All men cannot bear that testimony in logical terms or in high theological expressions : it is not given to every man to confuse the Word of God by terms which no other man can understand ; but who cannot take part in the testimony which is indicated by the words, "Once I was blind, now I see " ? In the last grand " Hallelujah ! " there is emotion as well as argument. The great thinkers and the great teachers say, " Hallelujah ! for the Lord God omnipotent reigneth : the kingdoms of this world are become the kingdoms of our Lord, and of his Christ." That is argument ; that is history ; that is eloquence. Now some can only take part in the emotion, and they say, " Hallelujah ! hallelujah ! " Do they contribute to the testimony ? Certainly. The testimony of God is a testimony that must have fire, emotion, soul. Great leaders, mighty sons of the morning, may speak about the king- doms of this world having become the kingdoms of God and of his Christ—may speak statesmen's language and utter imperial sentences ; but the mothers, and the broken hearts, and they who have had small chance in literary life can take part in the final testimony, saying, " Hallelujah ! hallelujah ! hallelujah ! "— a mere declamation to those who have never been touched by the emotion, but an argument in fire to those who know the mystery of the peace and joy of God in the soul.

This grand argument of experience is sustained by the grand argument of public criticism and public recognition. Thus, we read in the sixth and seventh verses,—" Keep therefore and do them ; for this is your wisdom and your understanding in the sight of the nations, which shall hear all these statutes, and say, Surely this great nation is a wise and understanding people. For what nation is there so great, who hath God so nigh unto them, as the Lord our God is in all things that we call upon him for " ? It would seem as if Moses represented the heathen nations as forming their estimate of what we now call Christian people and kingdoms. The picture is a vivid one, full of graphic suggestion. The heathen are looking on, observing the temper of so-called Christian communities and nationalities ; they see there what they can see nowhere else, and, gathering up all the evidence, they say, "Surely this great nation is a wise and understanding people " We always have that great possibility in front of us.

There may be those who could sneer at a nation praying in the face of imminent war. There is no need to sneer at such an act. Sneering men never did anything for the world; it is not in the power of a sneering man to help any noble cause. Impressions are made upon observing peoples by religious acts, by religious consecration, by Christian charity; and it may be—who can tell?—that even heathen nations may fear to approach in deadly hostility a nation that can truly pray. There is a wondrous power in innocence. Men have gone up to it at midnight to challenge and arrest it, and they have been struck to the ground by an arm unseen.

The appeal of Moses is the eternal appeal of the Bible :— " And what nation is there so great, that hath statutes and judgments so righteous as all this law, which I set before you this day?" (v. 8). That is the appeal to common sense and to common honesty. The commandments are not described as eloquent, marvellous intellectual conceptions, great advances in ethical thinking. Moses asks,—What other nation can produce a Bible so righteous? Any Bible must go down that is not righteous above all other things, how high soever the varied attributes by which any book may be characterised. What is the moral tone of the Bible? Pure, righteous, true, holy. What are the great commandments of the Book? " Love," " love,"—twice love. The first object?—" God ;" the second, " Thy neighbour." This is the strength of the Bible ; and we can all begin at this point to inquire into the remainder of the Book. The difficulty with many students is that they begin at the wrong point. The great duty of every reader of the Bible is to begin at any point he can. He may say, I understand the beautiful word, "Honour thy father and thy mother." Keep there : watch at that gate, for many an angel comes through it from heaven. Another reader says, Whatever there may be in the Bible which I cannot understand, I feel my whole heart going out towards the man who said, " The Lord is my shepherd ; I shall not want "—and all the music of the twenty-third Psalm. That is your Bible : stand there ; blessed is that servant who is found standing by that door, for out of it the Lord comes. Men may ask bewildering questions about the archæology and the so-called science of the Bible, and may even puzzle the uncultured reader with many a question relating to spiritual mysteries ; but taken from end to end the Bible is charged with righteousness : it will have the neighbour loved as the man himself ; it will have the harvest like the seed-time ; it will insist upon right balances and full weights ; it will have no concealed iniquities : it carries its candle of flame with fire never kindled upon earth into the secrets of the mind and the chambers of the soul and the hidden places of motive and purpose and ultimate, but unexpressed, intent. The Word of God is sharp, sharper than any two-edged sword, piercing to the dividing asunder of the joints and marrow. It is a righteous Word. The Bible has a thousand weapons in its armoury : not the lightest, not the weakest is its magnificent morality, its heavenly righteousness, its incorruptible integrity. It shakes off the wicked man ; it will have no communion with darkness ; it strikes the liar on the mouth ; it avoids the unholy follower. This is—let us repeat—the argument of Moses, and it is the eternal argument of Christianity.

SELECTED NOTE.

The Lawgiver here stands amidst Israel, warning and consoling, commanding and exhorting, surveying and proclaiming the future with marvellous discernment. The speeches begin with the enumeration of the wonderful dealings of God with the chosen people in the early period of their existence. Moses clearly proves to them the punishment of unbelief, the obduracy of Israel, and the faithfulness of Jehovah with regard to his promises, which were now on the point of being accomplished. Fully aware of the tendencies of the people, and foreseeing their alienations, Moses conjures them most impressively to hold fast the commands of the Lord, and not to forget his revelations, lest curses should befall them instead of blessings. The Lawgiver then expatiates on the spirit of the law and its reception into the hearts of men, both in a positive and negative way. Fear, he says, is the primary effect of the law, as also its aim. As Israel had once listened to the announcement of the fundamental laws of the theocracy with a sacred fear, in like manner should man also receive, through the whole system of the law, a lively and awful impression of the holiness and majesty of God. But as the essence and sum of the law is love to Jehovah, the only and true God, man shall by the law be reminded of the divine mercy, so variously manifested in deeds ; and this reflection is calculated to rouse in man's heart love for God. This love is the only and true source from which proper respect and obedience to the law can proceed.

Deut. iv.

MEMORY AND DUTY.

IN the ninth verse we have a very solemn possibility indicated. The words of Moses are :—" Only take heed to thyself, and keep thy soul diligently, lest thou forget the things which thine eyes have seen, and lest they depart from thy heart all the days of thy life : but teach them thy sons, and thy sons' sons." The solemn possibility is the possibility of forgetting God and God's providence in human life. We fail not always through sin or vulgar crime, as if with both hands we would smite the sceptre of God and the throne of righteousness : we may be far enough from any such exhibition of a rebellious kind ; but what is of equal fatality as to spiritual loss and consequent exposedness to every temptation of the enemy is the possibility of forgetting all that is worth remembering. We may not have endeavoured to expunge, as by an express and malicious effort ; but memory is treacherous : the faculty of recollection is otherwise than religiously employed, and before we are quite aware of what has been done, a complete wreck has been wrought in the memory of the soul. The accusation will not found itself upon the thought that we have learned a lesson and have allowed the lines to slip, but our attention will be called to the fact that we who were eye-witnesses can no longer bear testimony because of the vacuity of our minds. There will settle upon the intellectual faculties themselves, and upon the senses of the body, a stupidity amounting to sinfulness. We may have no memory for words : had we committed the lesson to an intellectual recollection we might have been excused for forgetting somewhat of its continuity and exactness ; the point is that we are called to remember things which our eyes have seen. The eye is meant to be the ally of the memory. Many men can only remember through the vision ; they have no memory for things abstract, but once let them see clearly an object or a writing, and they say they can hold the vision evermore. God's providence appeals to the eye ; God's witnesses are eye-witnesses—not inventors, but men who can speak to transactions which have come under their immediate and personal observation : they have seen and tasted and handled of the Word of life. What a loss it is to forget the noble past ! How treacherous is the memory of Ingratitude ! All favours have gone for nothing ; all kind words, all stimulating exhortations, all great and ennobling prayers,—forgotten in one criminal act. To empty the memory is to silence the tongue of praise ; not to cherish the recollection is to lose the keenest stimulus which can be applied to the excitement and progress of the soul. On the other hand, he whose memory is rich has a song for every day ; he who recollects the past in all its deliverances, in all its sudden brightnesses, in all its revelations and appearances, cannot be terrified or chased by the spirit of fear : he lives a quiet life, deep as the peace of God. Can Moses suggest any way of keeping the memory of God's providences quick and fresh ? He lays down the true way of accomplishing this purpose :—" Teach them thy sons, and thy sons' sons "—in other words, speak about them, dwell upon them, magnify them, be grateful for them ; put down the day, the date, the punctual time, when the great deliverances occurred, and when the splendid revelations were granted ; and go over the history line by line and page by page, and thus keep the recollection verdant, quick as life, bright as light. What a reproach to those Christians who are dumb ! How much they lose who never speak about God ! " Then they that feared the Lord spake often one to another : and the Lord hearkened and heard it, and a book of remembrance was written. . . And they shall be mine, saith the Lord of hosts, in that day when I make up my jewels." To speak of the mercies of God is to increase the power of witness at another point. We first see, then we teach. The teaching of others is not to come until there has been clear perception on our own part. The eye-witness is doubly strong in whatever testimony he may make : not only can he tell a clear story from end to end, he can sign it with both hands, he can attest it with the certainty and precision of a man who has seen the things to which he sets his signature. Our Christianity amounts to nothing if it is not a personal experience. We cannot preach Christ until we have seen

Christ. To preach salvation should mean that we ourselves have been saved.

Were all days alike, then, to the ancient Israelites—a great monotony of light: for even the summer may become a burden, and men may long for cloud and pouring rain? The days were not all alike : the monotony was broken in upon. So we read in the tenth verse : "Specially the day that thou stoodest before the Lord thy God in Horeb, when the Lord said unto me, Gather me the people together, and I will make them hear my words, that they may learn to fear me all the days that they shall live upon the earth, and that they may teach their children." There are " special " days even in the highest experiences ; there are great high-tides in the soul's emotion ; there are times of transfiguration, seasons when we see things as we never saw them before, glimpses of day, shootings, first, scarcely discernible, of bright lights across the whole firmament, which may be received by the soul as pledges of a whole heaven full of glory. Such moments may be few in number, but such is their quality that they require whole pages of our life-book for their clear and explicit writing. In all life there are " special " days :—the birth-day, the wedding day, the funeral day, the day when the letter came that brought a gospel of release from manifold and intolerable anxiety, the day when the epistle came from a hand which we thought would never write again. What is the day which Moses specialises ? It is the day that ought to be the most memorable in every man's experience : the day when the divine Word was heard—revelation day, conversion day, salvation day,—say broadly—resurrection day. The day when the soul first became conscious of its true relation to God, and answered the appeal of heaven, ought to be the all-absorbing day ; it should be as the day when the ear heard music for the first time. Can the man cured of almost total blindness forget the moment when he first saw the blue sky and the beflowered earth under his feet? No more can the soul forget the time when it first saw through the letter the meaning of the Spirit—when it first caught the music of heaven, when it first realised the meaning of life and duty and sacrifice. Whilst Moses would have nothing forgotten he would have a special remembrance made of the day when the word of the Lord was heard in the mount that " burned with fire."

A singular expression directly follows in the eleventh verse. Moses says:—"And ye came near and stood under the mountain." This is a new view of humanity. Probably the people themselves to whom Moses immediately spoke this word did not come near the mountain : most of them may have been born after the promulgation of the law from Sinai ;—because, indeed, of their not having heard that law in its original promulgation these great Deuteronomic speeches were spoken by Moses: it was a repetition of the law to men who had not themselves actually heard it in the first instance ; yet the people are spoken to as if they themselves in their own personality had been present, had come " near and stood under the mountain," and had felt the scorching of the fire which made that mountain unapproachable. This is the right view of human history. Human nature is one ; humanity is a solid. *We* were at Horeb, and we heard the law. There is no recognition of such time as separates ages and races and revelations in the matter of devolving the responsibility of witness wholly upon dead men. We who now live crucified the Son of God. When the world believes that, it will rise to a new conception of its relations to the whole race and to all the ages of time. We were not born and shall not die, in any sense that shall insulate us from all the currents and significations of human history. We are the poorest of the city : we are the richest of the land ; we who now live are great as kings, and are unknown as suppliants who hide themselves in darkness and speak their muffled prayers from obscurity. God " hath made of one blood all nations of men." We belong to one another. The child born yesterday was at Horeb, and will be present at the last great scene. Realise this thought, and instantaneously the true democracy is appreciated and valued—in no pedantic or narrow sense, but in the holy sense that all nations are one, that whether we be conventionally and socially high or low, rich or poor, is a matter of mere detail : we are alive with the same blood, and are hastening to the same arbitrament. There are narrow and partial and transitory senses in which men differ from one another, and are separated and classified ; but sinking down to proper depths we come upon a vital line which unites and consolidates the human family.

An extraordinary caution was addressed to the Israelites by

Moses in the fifteenth verse :—"Take ye therefore good heed unto
yourselves ; for ye saw no manner of similitude on the day that
the Lord spake unto you in Horeb out of the midst of the fire."
The people were not to make any image of God—"the similitude
of any figure, the likeness of male or female, the likeness of any
beast that is on the earth, the likeness of any winged fowl that
flieth in the air, the likeness of anything that creepeth on the
ground, the likeness of any fish that is in the waters beneath the
earth" (vv. 16-18). We must not touch God in the matter of
making similitudes of him at any point. It is quite true that God
fills his creation, and that any pebble taken up from the sea-shore
might be made a symbol of his presence ; but, seeing that no
object can represent him in his totality, there must be no attempt
to engrave the image of the Eternal. He is without shape, without gender ; he is in the beast of the earth ; he is in the
winged fowl that flieth in the air ; he is not ashamed of any worm
he ever made to wriggle in the meanest soil ; he is not ashamed
to hear the young lions when they cry, or to entertain the insects
at his bountiful table ;—they are his : every pulse is his, every
drop of blood is his ; but he will not be figured, represented, or
monumentalised in fragments and in detail. "God is a Spirit,"—
a marvellous revelation of that which cannot be revealed ! We
seem to have heard something, but we have heard nothing ; the
soul is enchanted by the music of a new expression, but not
helped by the carving of a new symbol. The soul delights in the
meaning, seizes the purpose of the revelation, and in repeating
the holy words brings itself into a sweet rhythm and harmony
with all the movement of creation, saying, again and again, as if
uttering the refrain of an eternal song,—"God is a Spirit."

Why forbid the creation of a similitude ? The answer is given
in the sixteenth verse :—"Lest ye corrupt yourselves." The
answer is also given in the nineteenth verse :—"And lest thou
lift up thine eyes unto heaven" and begin to worship sun and
moon and stars, and all the hosts of light. There is a reason for
the invisibleness of God. There is a reason for all the denials
which God has addressed to human curiosity. Who would not
know more of the future—not the mere future of time, but the
great future which we have learned to know by the name
"eternity" ? The answer is, "lest"—and there the curtain falls.

Who would not know more of the dead—the holy, sainted
crowned dead ? Why this eternal silence? Why not an occasional glimpse of the outline of the soul's figure? Why not an
occasional note of the individual voice to assure those who are
upon the earth that the loved one is uniting in the songs of light?
The answer is, " lest "—meaning that it is for our good, that this
denial is part of our education, that by the trial of our patience
we might rise to some higher perfectness of faith. Who would
not wish to have one moment's glimpse of heaven—one opening
of the cloud ? If we could see the green land of paradise—
unblighted, unsullied, bearing upon it the light of an infinite
blessing, responding to the smile of its Creator—we never could be
unhappy any more. So we think; it may be but mere supposition on our part. No good thing will God withhold from them that
walk uprightly ; if anything, therefore, is withheld, it is because
the granting of it would interfere with the divine cultivation and
perfecting of the soul. We are thus called to the rest of faith.
We are educated by silence, as well as by speech. To have our
liberty bounded may be to have our liberty perfected. There is
an *in*tension of spiritual life as well as an *ex*tension ; in the one
case, the spiritual life is deepened, enriched in every quality,
ennobled in all thought ; in the other case, information is widened,
multiplied, and so rapidly and unexpectedly that the soul is
almost affrighted out of the most solid and enduring peace. The
growth in grace and in the knowledge of our Lord Jesus Christ is
not always ostentatious—that is to say, an appeal to vision, to
sense of any kind ; much may be proceeding which no observer
can discern and of which the subject himself may be to some
extent uncertain. We are too much inclined to go by what we
can measure and totalise in augmenting figures, saying, with the
tone of a statistical inquirer,—We have grown thus and so much,
within a given period of time. How long shall we take that
childish way of measuring our soul's progress ? Let us remem-er
for our comfort that there is a deepening process going on in
silence, that providences may be so interpreted is to enter the
soul with new vitalising forces, which are not yet ripe for expression ; and when we open our whole being to the h ghest influences
of heaven, and keep earnestly holding ourselves in readiness for
light upon light and truth upon truth, instead of being able to

measure the increments, we shall know that they have taken place in the soul, by some day, suddenly to ourselves, breaking forth into new songs, surprising the soul by a music within itself which it had not hitherto realised. Our duty is plain; our duty is simple; our duty is to keep our minds and hearts open to the inspiration of God, to read the law of the Lord, and meditate therein day and night, to gather richly of the word divine, letting it dwell in the soul like roots planted in good ground by the Husbandman of the Church. The great thing is to keep a clean heart towards God, never to invite the Most High into a complete and furnished heart, the very elegance of which involves a subtle compliment to the heart itself and a subtle patronage to the God who is invited, but to ask God to come into a broken heart, a contrite, helpless heart, a sighing, self-complaining, sin-confessing, sin-detesting heart,—then the meeting will be a glad one, because it will be founded upon right relations; there will be no mockery on the part of the man, and there will be no interception of the whole almightiness of the living and redeeming God. Let us beware of materialising the spiritual. We must have the material, because we ourselves are not wholly spiritual. The senses need to be assisted that the forces which they represent may be sanctified; but it is one thing to have the house, and another to mistake the house for the tenant: it is one thing to keep the dead body in the house for a day or two before interment, another to keep it there as if the laws of nature could be set aside and a new economy established by the utter weakness of man. We must fall under the grand ideals which are everywhere brought to our attention in the Holy Book. The ladder we see is a ladder into heaven; the opened heaven is an opportunity of seeing the Son of man; and the written Book itself is God's nearest way of bringing his hand close to our life. We do not worship the built house, or the piled altar, or the living teacher, or the sculptured monument; in so far as we have these, we use them as lenses through which to see the furthest stars, the more distant lights, the very Shekinah of heaven.

In the twenty-fifth verse we find not only the possibility, but the disastrous influence of corruption in religious thinking. "When thou shalt beget children, and children's children, and ye shall have remained long in the land, and shall corrupt yourselves, and make a graven image, or the likeness of any thing, and shall do evil in the sight of the Lord thy God, to provoke him to anger: I call heaven and earth to witness against you this day, that ye shall soon utterly perish from off the land whereunto ye go over Jordan to possess it; ye shall' not prolong your days upon it, but shall utterly be destroyed." Out of what origin or fountain does this cataract of denunciation proceed? Moses sets before the children of Israel the possibility of their religion becoming irreligious, than which no greater curse can befall the human mind, or pervert the way of human progress. Wrong in your religion, you are wrong everywhere. Man is profoundly religious in senses that have not been altogether fully realised and applied. He not only worships instinctively—that is to say, turns up his eyes to the heavens to find an object greater than himself, or falls down before an object which he supposes to be greater than himself; but he is so religious that when he becomes wrong or mistaken—wilfully or unwilfully—in his religious conception, the influence is felt in every point of the circumference of his conduct. Men soon turn away from the right religious thought. It is a painful thought in some aspects; it must be so, because it imposes discipline; it educates a man by humbling him; it will accept nothing of his patronage; it will insist continually upon the doctrine that without Christ he can do nothing; that all he is an *i* has and does that is good is really a manifestation of the Son of God within him. Other religions might give him importance, might assign him a kind of superiority, might even deign to consult him, or to accept some addition from his hands; but the religion of the Bible is as unapproachable as the sun, and yet as friendly as the light. There is always a point gleaming in the infinite heights which can never be touched: a mystery in the clouds and above the clouds; and yet there is always a beautiful blessing round about the poorest life—an hospitable, re-invigorating and hopeful light beating upon the poorest man's one paned window, calling him to hope and energy and renewed prayer, and promising him still broader glory. It might suit our vanity to lay our hand upon the sun himself, but that is not permitted unto man; it is enough that he see the light, receive the light, walk in the light, toil in the light. His concern is not with the mysterious body out of which the light descends, but with the

light itself. Jesus Christ teaches this doctrine in words charac-
teristically his own; he says,—"If the light that is in thee be
darkness, how great is that darkness!"—in other terms,—If the
religion that is in thee be wrong, if thy piety be impious, if thy
prayers be profane, how profound the iniquity! how unutterable
the blasphemy! How false is the supposition that religion will
take care of itself in the human mind, that it will accept any
course of conduct and be equally at home with the drunkard and
with the pious man, with the thief and with the honest citizen;
that it resides almost exclusively in the intellect, and in the imagination, and never descends into all the practical walks and relations
of life! Say religion is a sensitive angel, shocked by evil conduct,
affrighted by temper not sweet or gracious, turned away in great
pale fear from all things unholy, unclean, undivine,—that would be
a right representation. We cannot keep our prayer and our profanity in the same heart. The final choice must be made. Allow
the mind a false conception of God, and what follows? Necessarily a false conception of all life, all duty, all sacrifice. Given a
profound and true conception of God, and what follows? Elevation of the whole character, an ennobling of the whole circuit and
range of the mind, out of which will come the testimony of good
temper, beautiful feeling, responsive sympathy, eternal charity.
So, rightly understood, in no narrow or pedantic sense, everything
really turns upon a true theology, by which is not meant a formal
science, a shaped and articulated doctrine, but a right conception
of the spirituality of God, the fatherhood of God, the invisibleness
and mysteriousness of God—ideas so received into the mind as to
create reverence, and never to debase intellectual action into mere
superstition. What becomes of those who corrupt religion and
turn away from the light? Is God indifferent? Never do we
find human conduct treated with divine unconcern. Our conduct
seems to make a kind of other heaven for God when it is right.
He loves to be with the soul when it prays, when it looks up
with expectancy, when it claims, how mutely soever, its kinship
with the Infinite and its association with the Eternal. "To this
man will I look, to the man that is of a humble and contrite
heart, and who trembleth at my word." In the heart of such a
man God finds an under-heaven, a sanctuary he delights to dwell
in,—a place sacred to his presence. By so much as this is true

on the one side there is a completing truth on the other. Let a graven image be set up instead of the spiritual Deity, and God will wither the life of the worshipper :—" ye shall soon utterly perish." As the branch cannot bear fruit except it abide in the vine, so a man cannot bear fruit except he abide in the true God, and he can only abide in the true God by a true spirit—a spirit of simplicity, trustfulness, burning sincerity, saying, in every look of his eye and every action of his hand : I would be like my Father in heaven. Let us never suppose that we can safely trifle with religious conceptions, thoughts, and disciplines ; we are only safe as we are in the sanctuary ; the outside seems inviting, the paths are full of flowers, the air trembles with the music of birds, and a thousand seductions endeavour to draw us forth into the open spaces and the boundless liberties, but we are soon taught that law alone is liberty, and that the sanctuary of right thinking and right conduct is alone exempt from the lightning and the tempest of judgment. No religion that is not true has ever come to anything in the world, viewed in the largest relations and in the amplest and clearest light of things. Great nations have had false religions, but what have the nations been great in ?—great in number, great in contemplation, great in poetry that never embodies itself in energetic and beneficent action. Only they— account for it as you will—who love the Lord God of heaven and earth, as revealed in the Bible, are found east, west, north, south, preaching gospels, seeking to reclaim human nature, to evangelise the world, and are prepared to suffer and to die for their faith. We are not unaware of the existence of stupendous idolatries and of great nationalities associated with false altars ; but judging religion by the spirit of sacrifice, by the desire to do good, by the inspiration of beneficence, by practical conduct of every kind, no religion can stand beside the religion of the Bible. God will soon cause those to pass away who displease him by graven images. Moses said in effect : You shall have enough of them, you shall be humbled amongst the heathen ; you, who have begun with speciality of name and function and destiny, shall dwindle away among the heathen whither the Lord shall lead you—" And there ye shall serve gods, the work of men's hands, wood and stone, which neither see, nor hear, nor eat, nor smell "—if you will have idolatry, you shall have it in fulness, yea, to repletion ; yea, until the soul mocks the divinity it began to adore. The way of wrong-doing is always downwards. Wrong has no radiant stairway up into heaven, its ways downward are more than a thousand in number, and easy is the descent of the way to the pit. It is easy to go downhill. There is something in wrong-doing that suits the complex nature of man : he goes to it so easily, as if he loved it ; when the iniquity is cleansed out of his hands and his countenance is purified from its more obvious stains, so cunning is he that he rolls iniquity under his tongue as a sweet morsel : but he lives a life of decay ; the sentence of death is upon him ; though he spread himself like a green bay tree he will pass away so that he cannot be found— yea, when men seek for him they shall obtain no intelligence of his destiny. Whom God wipes out who can find ? Hence the point of the exhortation and the value of the warning. We should take heed unto ourselves and unto the written Book which we hold, so that we depart not from the simplicity of spiritual worship. "God is a Spirit : and they that worship him must worship him in spirit and in truth"—often in silence— golden, precious, expressive silence ; the speechlessness which means that the thing cannot be spoken because of its majesty and sacredness and heavenliness. Do not trifle with religious convictions ; do not play with religious institutions. Everything that is solid and useful and beneficent in life springs out of a right sound, true conception of the nature of God and the purpose of his kingdom.

In the twenty-ninth verse we have what may be described as the eternal Gospel. Hear the sweet words ; say if in sweetness they do not make you forget the honey and the honeycomb :— "But if from thence thou shalt seek the Lord thy God, thou shalt find him, if thou seek him with all thy heart and with all thy soul. When thou art in tribulation, and all these things are come upon thee, even in the latter days, if thou turn to the Lord thy God, and shalt be obedient unto His voice. . . . . He will not forsake thee." We may go back to God. He will not look at our blushing shame. He will interpret the set of our countenance, saying,—Behold, they who went away have returned : their hunger shall plead with me : their necessity shall be their vindication ; having come back they shall come home. What a proposal is this! Verily, human life needs it, and is the better for it. To hear that we may go home again and tell the tale of our sins, and have it interrupted by the very tears of God—whoever dreamed that dream knew as no other man ever did know the deepest necessities of the human heart. The Old Testament is full of the word "return," "come," and other terms of welcome, and hailings, as of friendly expectation and assurance of hospitality. The Old Testament would almost seem to out-run the New in its broad welcomes and assurances of divine love. Nothing can stand against the Old Testament but Christ's own words. When the Apostles come to speak of these things, they seem to speak in a sterner language than did the ancient Hebrew prophets, psalmists, and leaders, as if the Greek tongue were edged, and sharp, and poignant, and the old Hebrew music were round and redundant in the amplitude of its love, having upon it no keenness, no hidden judgment concealed in all the harmonious roll of its musical thunder. Let us enter by some door. The Old Testament speeches may touch some hearts, the New Testament invitations may touch others,—both mean the same thing; all came from the same Fountain. Jesus Christ's words are very simple—" Come unto me, all ye that labour and are heavy laden, and I will give you rest." Jesus Christ knew all about this departure from the Father's house, and he represented the exodus by the parable of the prodigal son, who said,—"I will arise and go to my father, and tell him I have sinned;" and he who painted the prodigal in colours so true represented God in love infinite and ineffable, interrupting the penitential speech, and thrusting heaven upon the man whilst the prayer was yet trembling on his lips. Let us return unto the Lord. "Rend your hearts, and not your garments." We have to rid ourselves of many a corrupt thought, of many a debased course of conduct, and to return to simplicity, to the child's conceptions of God and to the child's sweet way of praying. Say, is there any picture known to the human imagination so expressive and tender as a little child upon its knees, with clasped hands, and eyes searching heaven with all the expectation of unsophisticated love? Except we be converted and become as that little child we cannot enter into the kingdom of heaven We must not have a theology which the people cannot understand; religion must not be one of the fine arts or the most recondite of the sciences. It must be a gospel, a piece of music, a heart-welcome, a cry outrunning the sinner, and sounding upon his ears in the wilderness, telling him of home and sacrifice, of the Cross and of forgiveness. These are words which never can be displaced by the enticing words of man's wisdom.

A wonderful pathos is given to the whole speech of Moses by the words of the thirty-first verse:—"For the Lord thy God is a merciful God." Who speaks this? A man who is about to die. This is a dying testimony. The man is old; no man of his time ever had such variety and range of experience; he is the principal man of his age;—in many respects he is the principal man who has yet risen in all the ages up to the date of his birth; —now his course is closing; he is to see the promised land from afar, but is not to cross the river; he is making a valedictory address, and this line comes into it—"The Lord thy God is a merciful God." How nobly the old man said it! How his grand voice trembled under the emotion! Moses was not a sentimentalist: Moses was a legislator, a leader, the very captain of the Lord's hosts; a man that could break the tables of stone, grind the golden calf into powder and scatter it upon the water and make offending Israel drink the water so empoisoned; and he—prince, king, mightiest man of his day—closes his course by saying, "The Lord thy God is a merciful God"—I know him; I have lived with him; I have been closeted with him in the secrecy of the mountain girded by light and by tempest; I know him; he has denied my desire to go and see the land flowing with milk and honey; all this is before me, and yet my dying testimony is—"The Lord thy God is a merciful God;" he gave the commandments, and I brought them to you; but, though Legislator, I have seen his tears; though he speaks commandments, I have been close to his heart; though one hand is judgment, yet in another is mercy; the Lord thy God is no mechanical deity, no infinite Jove, seated upon a throne of ivory, without sentient response to all the tragedy of life,—lifted high upon the circle of eternity, he "is a merciful God." Give me a man's dying testimony. We shall know the man's religion by what he says in the last extremity. When speculation can do nothing for him, when genius has blown out its flickering lamp, when the earth recedes, when time closes its dull days, when the cold river plashes suddenly against the approaching feet—tell me what the man said then, and I may touch the reality of his conviction and his hope. Blessed are they, with heaven upon heaven, who are enabled to say, when life is closing and heaven is nearing,—" The Lord our God is a merciful God."

PRAYER.

ALMIGHTY GOD, thy mercy endureth for ever. We have read of it: our fathers have told us concerning it; but, blessed be thy name, we ourselves have tasted and felt and handled the word of life. We know somewhat of its power in the soul; we know what the Holy Spirit hath done for us. Once we were blind: now we see; once this world was enough: now it is too small. We look up: we look beyond; we search the distant lines of the sky to see if any opening reveal itself to tell of further spaces. Once we knew not God, and our life was dark and very cold, without sympathy, without hope,—a great riddle without an answer; but now, having seen the Saviour with the eyes of our love, having been accepted in the Beloved, behold, all things are new, all nature is larger, written all over with messages full of holy suggestion; creation itself is an infinite altar at which we bow in holy, tender prayer. Behold, thou hast made all things new to us. If any man be in Christ Jesus, all things are new: old things have passed away; new heavens and a new earth, and a new future—these are the gifts of God in Christ Jesus our Lord; then the promise of heaven—heavenly study, heavenly service, heavenly progress. Our mind cannot follow the line of fatherly promise: we know not what it is in all its meaning; eye hath not seen, ear hath not heard, nor hath it entered into the heart of man to conceive what God hath prepared, laid up in store for them that love him. Truly, by the Spirit, we now see in part: we see through a glass darkly; but still thou dost hold before us the solemn truth that we have not yet begun to see or hear or comprehend as compared with our enjoyments of thy presence and thy light in the world to come. Help us to read thy Book with an understanding mind, with an acute and reverent attention; and may we hear all the tones of thy voice, and see in thy word some outline of thy shape, thine image, thy glory. Let thy mercy be extended unto us according to our need. We are the children of necessity: our life is one continual want; our eyes are unto the hills whence cometh our help. We bless thee for answered prayer and for prayer denied. We pray, and leave our prayers at the throne, sprinkled with atoning blood, made eloquent by the intercession of the Son of God; and thine answer, whatsoever it be, shall make us glad or content, or quiet us with the assurance that a denial is the most beneficent of answers. In this faith we stand; in this confidence we live. It gives us strength and light and hope evermore. Amen.

32. For ask now of the days that are past, which were before thee, since the day that God created man upon the earth, and ask from the one side of heaven unto the other, whether there hath been any such thing as this great thing is, or hath been heard like it?

33. Did ever people hear the voice of God speaking out of the midst of the fire, as thou hast heard, and live?

34. Or hath God assayed to go and take him a nation from the midst of another nation, by temptations, by signs, and by wonders, and by war, and by a mighty hand, and by a stretched out arm, and by great terrors, according to all that the Lord your God did for you in Egypt before your eyes?

35. Unto thee it was shewed, that thou mightest know that the Lord he is God; there is none else beside him.

36. Out of heaven he made thee to hear his voice, that he might instruct thee: and upon earth he shewed thee his great fire; and thou heardest his words out of the midst of the fire.

37. And because he loved thy fathers, therefore he chose their seed after them, and brought thee out in his sight with his mighty power out of Egypt;

38. To drive out nations from before thee greater and mightier than thou art, to bring thee in, to give thee their land for an inheritance, as it is this day.

39. Know therefore this day, and consider it in thine heart, that the Lord he is God in heaven above, and upon the earth beneath; there is none else.

40. Thou shalt keep therefore his statutes, and his commandments, which I command thee this day, that it may go well with thee, and with thy children after thee, and that thou mayest prolong thy days upon the earth, which the Lord thy God giveth thee, for ever.

THE SPECIALITY OF THE BIBLE.

THIS is the eternal challenge of the Bible. The appeal may be regarded as a call to the study of comparative religions. There are many religions in the world; gather them up into one view, extend the inquiry far and wide, through time and space, and see whether the Bible does not separate itself from all other books by miracles that cannot be rivalled and by excellences that cannot be equalled. Other miracles are not denied, other excel-

lences are not disputed ; the point is whether the Bible after
occupying common ground with many other religions does not
represent forces and qualities unknown to any of them. Let it
not be supposed that other good books are denied ; let it not be
imagined that idolatries are ignored ; let it not be supposed that
the Bible is afiaid of comparison or competition. God himself
inquires for all other gods; he will have them skilfully displayed :
the best of our artists may be engaged in arranging all the deities
that were ever named in mythology or philosophy, or the best
dreaming of the human mind ; God will have them well shown :
there shall be no attempt whatever to underrate values and
dignities, or to cover with the disadvantage of obscurity any
god who can do anything. The God of the Bible says concerning
gods, " Where are they ? " and awaiting the production of other
gods there is silence in the universe. If the Bible were a priest's
book, or a mere trick on the part of some incipient divinity, it
would keep all to itself : it would ignore the existence of all other
gods and religious claims and even revelations, and it would turn
darkness into an instrument of protection, and employ obscurity
to add to the accent of its claim. The Bible does nothing of the
kind. In the spirit of Moses it says, " Ask now of the days that
are past, which were before thee, since the day that God created
man upon the earth, and ask from the one side of heaven unto
the other, whether there hath been any such thing as this great
thing is, or hath been heard like it ? " (v. 32). Never forget
this challenge on the part of the Bible. It is a noble speech.
The Bible will not remain with us one day longer than it can
supply what no other book can furnish. The Bible awaits to be
displaced. As soon as any one can arise who can speak in a nobler
eloquence, ir a tenderer music, with a profounder wisdom,
the Bible is willing that its old pages should be closed for
ever. There are good men who have no Bible ; there have been
virtuous men who never heard of Christ ; there are good writings
which the world will not willingly let die that have not been
baptised in the triune name of God. This is acknowledged,
and must be broadly and frankly and gratefully confessed ; the
question still remains, Does not the Bible by some quality stand
out above all other books—the very pinnacle of the temple of
literature ? The inspiration of the Bible must be proved by the

quality of the Bible. For a considerable period other books may keep pace with the Bible, but at a certain point it bids them farewell and rises into heights they can never ascend. The Bible lives by its peculiarities. Individuality is a matter of speciality. Up to a given point all men are alike : in repose it might be very difficult to distinguish between one man and another : both claim to be men, both lay claim to certain dignities and honours of citizenship : there is, no doubt, a broad and indisputable democracy ; but in special circumstances, great national crises, in struggling with certain difficulties, and attempting the solution of special problems, men are distinguished from one another sharply, and the greatest man proclaims his ascendency not in words but in deeds, by giving the best answer, the largest reply to the necessities of the mind. This is substantially the case with the Bible in the first instance. When all other books have made their speeches, the Bible rises as though no voice had been heard, clears a space for itself, and by uniqueness of majesty and sympathy it claims the primacy of literature. If the Bible is merely held sacred as an expression of a superstitious feeling, it will daily lose influence, it will daily evaporate as to all the energies which have given it position and authority, and hence on it will do nothing but decay and die. The Bible simply wants to be heard, to be read, to be expounded, and to be understood. It asks nothing from its ablest teachers but a paraphrase true to its own spirit and tone. It will not have addition : it will have expansion ; it will not be decorated from the outside : it asks that its root may have full scope to express in leaf and blossom and bud and fruit all the bloom of its beauty and all the wealth of its uses. This is the position Moses occupies ; we cannot amend the position : we accept it.

Note the speciality which Moses fixes upon. He asks a question—" Did ever people hear the voice of God speaking out of the midst of the fire, as thou hast heard, and live ? "—if so, prove it. The challenge is not a lame one. The Bible awaits the evidences. We, if earnest men, should be in quest of the best book, without asking who wrote it or by what authority it was written. If it speak to us as no other book can speak, we are bound to accept it. Books must not be imposed upon us : they must consort with the soul, develop a latent and often unconscious kinship of mind and spirit, and so educate the whole man that at last the man will scarcely be able to distinguish between his own thoughts and the thoughts which are inspired : they are so alike in quality, in range, in purpose, in nobleness. How easily Moses speaks about " fire ! " How early he seized upon the right word ! the very key-word of the universe, for what is there in all the temple of space but fire ? Is not thought fire ? Is not spirit fire ? How did Moses come to speak so familiarly about hearing God out of the fire and living afterwards ? He came to do so because he himself had passed through this very experience : he said, I will turn aside and see this great sight, why the bush is burned with fire and yet is not consumed. And as he drew near a voice said unto him, " I am the God of Abraham, the God of Isaac, and the God of Jacob." Moses saw the fire, heard the voice, and lived. Personal experience is the great secret of preaching. If Moses had only heard of the fire as a possible vehicle of the infinite and eternal God, he might have spoken about fire in a very different tone ; but he himself had seen the fire, had been warmed by its glow, had watched the whole miracle, had heard the God of history, and yet he lived. Such men must lead the Church ; such men must preach to the world. Since the world began was it ever heard that God died, and yet faith in the existence of God was required on the part of man ? When a man can say, I have seen that very miracle ; I have watched at the Cross until it became a ladder reaching unto heaven ; I myself have seen the dying Christ, and felt the cleansing of his blood, such a man begins with power, grows in power ; age cannot wither him : and as for preaching, custom cannot stale its infinite variety, because the man himself lives in God. The appeal of Moses is so rational, so broad in its common sense, as to be wholly invincible by logic. That is true in its moral purpose. By asking a question you may outlive an argument. An inquiry may be a reply. Sometimes men have to express their wonder in interrogation ; simple affirmation would fall below the necessity of the case. Moses adopts this course : " Did ever people hear the voice of God speaking out of the midst of the fire, as thou hast heard, and live ? " The thing was historical : the argument was based upon facts, something had occurred that could be identified, and every assertion based upon that fact partook of the quality and strength of the fact itself. The pulpit cannot live upon dreams, impulses, or imaginations : it must be founded upon a rock, if it would survive the shaking wind, the tempest, the great rain. What was the gift of God ? It was the gift of a word. Call that word by such names as " statutes," " judgments," " commandments," it comes to the same thing ; it was the word of God, the speech of God, the mind, the will, and thought of God. What more can even God give ? He has given wondrous framework in the matter of suns and stars and great gleaming fires that have not yet received baptism at the hands of men who would describe the universe in parcels and in names ; but having set up all the framework, he must needs speak the word—or, in other terms, breathe the word, and give meaning and dignity to the works of his hands. We have received nothing until we have received the word—the word of wisdom and of grace ; the subtle, spiritual music that sings in the soul and charms the life out of its tumult and fever. They miss the king who only see the palace. It is something to be permitted to walk over the state-apartments when the monarch is absent,—then curiosity is touched, then vanity may in some degree be pleased ; but what is really wanted to be seen by the truly earnest observer and inquirer is majesty, monarchy, living sovereignty,—the I AM THAT I AM. Until we have heard the living word, we have but seen the exterior framework of the Most High.

Christianity adopts this challenge : Christianity says in effect, —What other religion is there that deals with *sin* as I deal with it ? I do not ignore it ; I do not hasten over it ; I do not treat it as a mere incident, or a cutaneous affection which superficial means may subdue and which proper attention may remove. What other religion, theory, philosophy, grapples with sin as Christianity does ? It will penetrate it, cleave it asunder, analyse it, search into it, and never rest until it gets out of the soul the last fibre of the bad root, the last stain of the fatal poison. Let us be fair to facts ; whether we are in the Church or out of the Church, whether we belong to this section or to that section, do let us in common decency acknowledge that Christianity, come whence it may, does grapple with infinite energy with sin. The appeal of Christianity also is,—" Ask now of the days that are past, which were before thee, since the day that God created man upon the earth, and ask from the one side of heaven unto the other," whether any other religion tries to make the same kind of men that Christianity makes? Let us judge the tree by its fruit. We are not superstitious or fanatical or narrow-minded; we do ask the question and insist upon an answer, Does any other religion make such men as Christianity makes? Here Christianity must be judged by its purpose, by its own written word and claim, and not wholly by the men themselves, because we are still in the land of bondage in many particulars : we are in the flesh : we suffer from a thousand weaknesses; Christianity, therefore, must be judged in its declared intention regarding the culture of manhood. What kind of men does Christianity want to make? Weak men? It never made one man weak. Strong men, valiant men, men of the keenest mind, men of the largest judgment, men of the most generous disposition ;—if that is the kind of men Christianity wants to make, where is the religion that can excel or equal Christianity in that purpose? Produce the *men!* Judge by facts. Where Christianity has entered into a life, what has it done with that life? Can it be proved that Christianity, fairly understood and thoroughly received, has soured the temper, narrowed the sympathies, dwarfed the noble ambitions of the soul? Has Christianity ever made unhappy homes, unrighteous parents? Let the challenge be thoroughly understood and frankly replied to. Christianity lives visibly in the Christian. Christianity wants to put away all other evidence, argument, and wordy encounter, and to be able to say : Judge me by my children ; judge me by my believers; I am what they are. Therefore, if the Church of the Living God could stand up complete in the purpose of its Redeemer and Sanctifier, the snowy pureness of its character, the lofty dignity of its moral temper would abash every assailant and silence every accuser. Do not be harsh, or point with mocking finger to some poor weak soul, and say : If this man represents Christianity, we do not want to know further what Christianity is. Christianity can only be judged by the Book which reveals it, by the Christ who founded it, and by the noble history which has surrounded it. So, we accept and repeat this challenge. Christianity has no reason to retire from the field if there is to be a thorough and impartial examination of the races which have been under its nurture and the races which have never known its influence.

The inference which Moses suggests is perfectly clear :—If there is a religion anywhere—for Moses gives the points within which the examination is to be completed—"ask now of the days that are past, which were before thee, since the day that God created man upon the earth, and ask from the one side of heaven unto the other "—if there is a religion with equal credentials, equal miracles, equal morality, equal grasp of the future, produce it. Can a challenge be more rational, more dignified ? We do not live in a corner, or perform the little miracles of Christian faith under the shadows of night. Christianity longs with eagerest solicitude to meet on an open field to contest any other religion that has ever touched the imagination or affected the will of man. We must, however, limit this matter of contest and comparison. Let us see whether the limitation be not reasonable. The challenge cannot apply to anything found in nominally Christian countries. Who can tell what Christianity has done even for countries that are not practically Christian ? How soon we forget our indebtedness to the influences which shaped our life and blessed us in times of unconsciousness ! No man can be permitted to rise in any Christian country and say he has a Bible which surpasses the Bible of Moses and the prophets, Christ and the Apostles. Why may not he arise and challenge ? Because he was born in a Christian atmosphere, he was trained by Christian parents ; there never was a moment of his life that was not influenced by Christian ministries of one kind or another ; he lived under the light of the Cross, enjoyed the liberties of Christianity, was educated in the civilisations of Christianity ; and, therefore, he cannot say,—This is original : this has been invented by me without any obligation to Christian teaching, and therefore I produce it in reply to the challenge of Moses and of Christ. We cannot tell how much we are indebted to the earliest associations of life. It is pitiful to see some broken-down, vain-headed infidel starting up with some theory of morality which, consciously or unconsciously, he stole from the Christ whom he is anxious to depose. I know of no object more hideous and contemptible than some weakling boy, who was prayed over morning and night, loved with all Christian love, indulged because of the very excess of that love, turning out to play the infidel and to be wiser than his parents were ; specially is he ineffable in contemptibleness when he wants to play off some other morality against the morality of Christ, saying he has found in Hindoo literature various beautiful proverbs, or seen in the Koran lines glittering with moral beauty, and has understood that long before Christ came into the world men spake morals and discussed ethics and set up philosophies of conduct. There is no speech permitted to well-regulated minds that can meet a case so morally contemptible. It is a cleverness that ought to be frowned down, an originality that ought to awaken the moral laughter and scornful derision of just men. We have been trained in a Christian country ; we learned to read out of the Bible ; one of our first little lessons on which we laid our young finger was—" God is love," and another, " The Son of man is come to seek and to save that which was lost," all words of one syllable, which our mother helped us to read. The child that learned these lessons, that uttered these syllables lispingly because of infantile weakness, can never rise to claim originality and to compete with Moses and the Lamb ; he drank in these thoughts with his mother's milk ; he was reared upon them ; they are part of him : sooner can he part with his blood and remain a living man than he can take out of his intellectual and moral nature all these influences, and pretend to have invented civilisation or discovered a religion.

"Know therefore this day, and consider it in thine heart, that the Lord he is God in heaven above, and upon the earth beneath : there is none else."

THE RELATION OF MAN TO GOD.

I SHOULD like it to be understood, that I occupy the position of a distinctively Christian teacher, with the Christian Scriptures open before me, and everything I say is to be judged by this fact. A pagan might argue for the existence of a Creator ; but the pagan and I would mean different things, though we might employ exactly the same words. Mine is a *Christian* faith ; therefore I seek to teach truth as it is in Jesus. This you must bear in mind if you would follow my meaning closely and correctly.

I can imagine a man of average education and intelligence, asking me some such question as this : *How is it that God does not show himself more clearly to us than he does, and so put an end to all uncertainty concerning himself?* I answer : Are we capable of understanding what is and what is not the proper degree and method of divine manifestation? Have we so proved our own wisdom as to be justified even to ourselves in saying that we are competent to judge how far God has manifested himself, and how much further he ought to have done so? Every day, as a matter of mere fact, we convict ourselves of making mistakes in the commonest affairs of life. Each day is marked by its own special sin. We are always going too far or not far enough. If we are just to ourselves, we shall apply the scourge of self-reproach to our hearts and understanding every day. Are we, then, with all these mistakes, like so many wrecks lying about us ; are we, after all, the men to say *how* God should manifest himself, and *when* he should do so? Is it decent that we should take upon ourselves this high task of dictation? Is it becoming in men, who cannot certainly tell what will happen in one single hour, that they should write a programme for God, and appoint the way of the Almighty?

These things cause me to say that religious questions, if they are to be profitably considered at all, must be considered in a deeply religious spirit. You can make no advancement in this learning unless you bring a right heart with you. That is the beginning. If my scholar escape me at this point he will flounder through all the rest of the lesson. What is your sincere desire? What is the condition of your heart? Are you really and truly anxious about this matter? Are you self-sufficient, boastful, confident in your own strength? Do you light the candle of your own wit and judge the universe by such little light as it can shed? Or are you reverent, humble, meek, and wishful to learn things as they really are? Everything depends upon the tone and temper of your spirit in entering upon any course of religious inquiry and instruction. If a man shall spring into the arena, where Christian inquirers and worshippers are assembled praying and considering these questions, and say, "Now then, look about, I am coming to see what the whole thing means. I shall set up this standard and lay down this rule; I shall put things round about and set them in the right way; I shall examine and cross-examine, and none will get over me"—if a man shall come into the arena talking with such vigour as that, he will one day certainly have an arena worthy of his incoherence. But God will not speak to him; the universe will be hushed, and the fool shall hear nothing but his own noise!

I shall not soon forget standing upon a lofty and magnificent hill, amidst some of the most romantic and impressive scenery in Britain. It was summer noonday. A spirit of rest seemed to be upon everything; the eternal hills were talking to me, and the great grey rocks, which might have been the tombstones of centuries, were standing there, witnesses of my youthfulness and comparative insignificance. I enjoyed the scene as if it had been the house of God and the very gate of heaven. But there came upon it half-a-dozen wanderers, laughing and jibing and exchanging their poor vulgar jokes with one another; and when they got upon the hill-top one of them said, "What have we come up here for? there's nothing up here." He was right; there was nothing for him there. He was a trespasser and ought to have been arrested as a criminal; he was out of his sphere; give such people sandwiches, and barrels of beer, and dancing bears, and brass bands, and then the scene would have been "worth going to." But the eternal hills spake not, and the grand old majesties of the rocks were silent! They have nothing to say to vulgarity, and rudeness, and boisterousness. Incline thine ear and they will speak to thee; be calm, be struck with wonder and reverence and intelligent admiration in their hoary presence, and the hill tops will tell thee many a story of the past, and the rocks will have sermons upon their rugged faces graven there by the hand of Time!

It is so in the consideration of great religious questions. A man is not to come into this school and say, "I have it; I will show you how it is; I have a measure in my pocket, and a plumb-line in my hand, and a pair of compasses; I will undertake to examine the whole thing for you and pronounce an opinion upon it." Never! "To this man will I look." When God looks, it is morning; when he does not look, it is midnight! "To this man will I look." The man that is going to square up every-thing—the man that uses contemptuous expressions—the man who says, "Hoity-toity," and takes the Bible and throws it into the fire, and tells his wife and children that "religion is all nonsense, you know"? No! "To this man will I look." Lord, to which man wilt thou look? To the man that is humble; to the man who is of a humble and contrite heart, and that trembleth at my word. This is a qualification for the religious school. A truly reverent and earnest desire to know what God's meaning is, and God's will. To the man who possesses these qualifications, every page of the inspired volume will bring messages of light and comfort and heaven.

I once heard a peculiar controversy or conversation in a garden; it quite entertained me. There were, after some heavy rains, two worms that had struggled out of the earth, and found their way upon the wet green grass; and they began to talk in a very decided and mocking manner about myself. One, the elder and better-to-do of the two, said, "Eh, eh, eh! we have been told that this garden has an owner, or somebody that takes care of it, that nourishes the roots of things, and that altogether presides over the affair. Eh, eh, eh! I never saw him. If there is such an owner why does he not show himself more clearly? why does he not come to the front and let us see him?" And the leaner of the two said, "That is an unanswerable argument. *I* never saw him. There may be such a being, but I care nothing about him: only, if he is alive, why does he not show himself?" They quite wriggled in contemptuous triumph; yet all the while I was standing there, looking at the poor creatures, and hearing them! I could have set my foot upon them and crushed them; but I did not. There is a way of wasting strength; there is also a way of showing patience. But the worms could not understand my nature. I was standing there, and they knew me not! What if it be so with ourselves in the greater questions? And if out of this homely illustration we may get a far-off glimpse of the fact that we who are talking about God manifesting himself, and asking him to come to the front,—what if one day we are compelled to exclaim, "Lo! God is here, and I knew it not! This is the house of God; this is the gate of heaven!" That, whilst we are discussing about God and calling his existence in question, he is listening to us. He could put the tip of his finger upon us and destroy our life. He could touch our reason and wither our intellect. Yet he spares us. For judgment is his strange work, and mercy is his supreme delight.

Proceeding with our statement respecting the revelation of God, I ask you to believe with me, as a matter of fact— First: That we stand to God in the relation of dependants. That is our actual position in life. "What hast thou that thou didst not receive?" Let a man begin his studies there, and he will become correspondingly reverent. Have you genius? Who lighted the lamp? Have you health? Who gave you your constitution? Do you find the earth productive? "Yes." Who made it productive? "I did. I till it; I supply all the elements of nourishment needful; I did." Did you? Can you make it rain? Can you make the sun shine? Come, I will set you a little task, mighty man, potentate! This: Change the quarter of the wind! Now, come, that is a very little thing for a great man like you. "Well," you say, "that is the sort of thing that I

really cannot do." Then, clear a fog off the hill. You can do
that. Look what a port you have, and what infinite impudence.
Come, clear a fog! Where would your tilling, and your manur-
ing, and your subsoiling, and your harrowing and rolling all be,
and what would they come to, if God were to say to the wind,
"Never leave the east;" if God were to say to the clouds,
"Stand still;" if God were to say to the sun, "Do not show
thyself for a year"? All these things show us that we are,
notwithstanding our resources, which are undoubtedly numerous
and great, dependants. There is a point at which we must give
up and stand still, and say, "We can do no more." That is a
matter of certainty in common daily life; and out of it will
come such reflections as these: I have nothing that has not
upon it God's signature and God's superscription. I can work;
but my work may come to nothing. I may sow my seed; but if
he withhold the baptism of the dew and the rain, and the
benediction of the sunlight, all my labour will come to nothingness, mortification and pain! This must have some meaning.
There must, in such a combination of circumstances as these,
be a purpose which I ought to know, and understand, and work
by. If a man once be started on that course of reflection, the
probability is, that he who begins as a reverent inquirer, will
end as a devout worshipper.

The very fact of being dependent should lead us to be very
careful how we measure the sovereignty and the government of
God. He has made us servants, not masters. We are little
children, not old beings, in his household and universe. We
are mysteries to ourselves. We need not go from home to seek
mysteries. Sometimes it seems to be supposed that we have only
to give up the idea of God and all will be light. There will be
no difficulty about anything. Life will then be a straightforward
course, and we shall have no enigmas to answer and no spectral
mysteries to affright us. It is a misrepresentation of facts. Oh
man, thou art thyself a riddle, but half answered! What is the
secret of thine own life? Explain the secret of thy desires, thy
restlessness, thy ambition, thy hunger which cannot be appeased
by the stones and the dust of this world! Hast thou seen thine
own soul? Where is it? What is its image, and what is its
nature? Are there not secrets in thine own blood and life which

have never spoken to thee ?   Are there not spaces in thy hidden
being on which the candle of finite knowledge has never thrown
its dim ray ?   Canst thou stop the throbbing heart that is within
thee, and say to it successfully, " Tell me thy secret, let me know
what it is in thee " ?   The heart has stopped.   Can you start it
again ?   You can touch it ; you can put your finger and thumb
upon it ; can you not start it into action again ?   You are very
clever ; you want to know all about God, and you have turned
your back upon the Almighty, because your little questions are
not answered ; why cannot you just take hold of that little heart
that has stopped its beating, and say, " Begin again " ?   There is a
man with blighted reason.   Why do you not go and breathe a
new summer upon the man's brain ?   There is a brain in
which reason has lost her way.   Why do you not find the poor
wanderer and set her in the right course again ?   If you cannot
do that—who are you, I ask, that you should determine the
measure and the method of divine manifestation, and pronounce
dogmatic opinions upon the sovereignty and the government of
God ?

The very fact of the mystery of our own life should be the
beginning and the defence of our faith in God.   Reason from
yourself upwards.   There is a way out of the human to the
divine.   It is a commendable course of procedure to reason from
the known to the unknown.   If you are such a mystery to your
own child, if the philosopher is such a mystery to the uninstructed
man, if you are such a mystery to yourself,—why may there not
be power around more mysterious still, higher and nobler yet ?
Reason from yourselves,—from your own capacities and your
own resources.   Is not the maker greater than the thing made ?
Will you show me the machine you have made, and say to me,
" I made that machine, and the machine is greater than I am " ?
Is it within the compass of any man's ability to make something
that is greater than himself ?   Does not the thing made prove
always to be less than the maker of it ?   It is so in our own
life.   The artist is greater than his picture ; the engineer is
greater than his viaduct, his tunnel, his railway, or his steam
engine.   The *man* is greater than the mere manual labourer.   If
it be so amongst ourselves, may we not carry the reasoning up
to its religious application, and say, he who made the sun and

the stars and the whole universe, what can he be but the sum
of all mysteries, even God blessed for evermore ! I am convinced
of this, that for men of a certain type of mind to become religious
—profoundly and truly religious—they must study this with
care ; they must work from the point of their own mystery, and
carry the wondrousness of their own nature up to its highest and
best applications.

Pascal said, " I am greater than the sun ! " How so ? " I am
greater than the sun." Show it. " The sun could fall and crush
me ; but I should be conscious of defeat, whilst the sun would
be unconscious of victory ! " Herein is the wondrous greatness
of man. Even his failures show the mystery of his being,—he
is majestic in ruin ; he is all but divine even in death !

Take away the idea of God from human thinking, and mark
the immediate and necessary consequences. This is a method
of reasoning which I commend to the attention of young
inquirers, who are earnest about this business, the method,
namely, of *withdrawment.* If a man doubts concerning God, I
shall withdraw the idea of God from human thinking, and see
the necessary result. If a man has any argument to adduce
against Christianity, take Christianity out of the country, and
see what will be left. Take out the doctrine, take out the
practice, take out, not only Christian theology, but Christian
morality, and see how many hospitals would be left, how many
refuges for the homeless and the destitute, how many peniten-
tiaries, infirmaries, schools, and asylums for the deaf and the
dumb and the blind and the idiotic. So take away the idea of
God from human thinking, and see the immediate and inevitable
consequences. There is no God : then there is no supreme
supervision of human life as a whole ; for none could have the
eye that could see the whole orbit of things. We see points, not
circumferences. There is no God : then there is no final judgment by which the wrongs of centuries can be avenged ; there is
no heart brooding over us to which we can confide the story of
our sorrow, or tell the anguish of our pain : the promise of a
cloudless morning, and a graveless world, is the bitterest irony
of human speech : the weak must die under the heel of the
strong : human culture is but the carving of so much dead wood :
poetry is but falsehood set to music : the shining heavens, in

whose every star we have seen a welcoming light to something higher, whose every golden morning has been to us as the gate of glory, instead of being the beginning of a better universe, those shining heavens are but the upper boundaries of a magnificent prison : and as for the mysteries of our own hearts, their hope, their pain, their struggles after something better, their dreams, their battles, ."their fond desires, their longings after immor- tality," what are these, but the refinement of cruelty, and the very torture of hell ! Set God again on the throne, and all that makes life worth having, even imaginatively, comes back again. Set God upon the throne, and all things take upon them a new, true, beautiful meaning ; there is hope of judgment, and a certainty that right will eventually be done.

Need I ask you to remember—that our little day has been too short to know the full mystery of God ? When an infant of yours has gone to school, do you expect the little one to come back at twelve o'clock on the first day and be able to read you a chapter even out of the simplest book ? When your little boy, six years of age, first looked at his arithmetic, did you expect him to come back, after two hours' teaching, and be able to reduce a certain set of fractions to a common denominator ? Did you expect him, after an hour's consideration of arithmetical questions, to be able to do the most advanced rules, and to throw the book up before your face and say, " No more of your arithmetic for me, let me go into algebra at once " ? You did not expect that, did you ? You would have said, " That boy, depend upon it, is half crazy ; he does not know what he is talking about ; " and you would probably consult the most prudent adviser about the prodigy. Yet we want to know all about God at once, and we cannot get the information ! How old do you say you are ? " Old ! why, threescore years and ten." "No ! threescore years and ten ! Why, there is a tree two hundred years old, which has seen generations of your family buried." " How old ? " " Getting on for fourscore years." " Are you ? There is a star ; look at it ; ten thousand years ago that star was shining ! You are an old man ; yes, but a young being, an infantile being. Very old indeed, if you think of insuring yourself, or buying another estate, or laying out a great sum of money,- very, very old indeed ; but if you are talking of the

universe, you are the insect of a moment—hardly born! But you
wish to read the book called the Universe through at one sitting,
like a cheap novel. You cannot do so! When you have concluded your school day here, you have only begun just to turn
over the first leaf,—hardly that indeed, perhaps. Put your
seventy years—an expression which fills your mouth so, and
which is intended to awe the human family into respect and
veneration for your person—put it down and look at it, multiply
it by ten thousand, and then by ten thousand more, multiply
the whole by millions of ages, and eternity has hardly yet
begun!"

We are of yesterday and know nothing; and the teacher, what
is he, but a man who having seen one ray of light amid thick and
terrible gloom, comes to say you may see the same beautiful
revelation? All this shows us what our spirit ought to be. All
this ought to put young men upon their guard respecting such
as suppose themselves able to answer every question, and to
settle every difficulty, and to determine every controversy. Is
there one of them can tell you what will happen in the next
five minutes? At the very beginning, therefore, we must
all agree that we are of yesterday, and of ourselves we know
nothing, and that we are dependent for the revelations of God
upon God himself. And this, let me say to you, young
men, The greatest men I have ever known have been the
most humble, docile, self-distrustful. If Isaac Newton likened
himself to a child on the sea-shore, gathering a few pebbles
brighter than the rest, and humbly said that the great ocean
of truth lay all undiscovered before him; who are we that
we should set ourselves up in mid-water and say, "We see the
other side of the sea"? We must begin at the beginning; we
must begin in a religious spirit; we must not come with any
preconceived conclusions and prejudices, and argue along our
own lines and in our own way. We must remember our ignorance, look our own mistakes fully in the face, and say: With
these things around me, I dare not be boastful, I cannot be
confident; I will say with my heart, "Speak, Lord, for thy
servant heareth." And the Samuel who shall put himself in
that attitude before God and his book, shall in due time become

a learned and able man in the school of Christ,—well controlled in his spirit and temper, charitable and noble in all his sympathies, gracious to the weak, a source of strength to those who have no helper, a very pillar and ornament of society.

PRAYER.

ALMIGHTY GOD, thou dost, by thy Son Jesus Christ, take away the sin of the world. Thou dost not cleanse the outside, thou dost purify the inmost life. Out of renewed and sanctified motive thou dost bring pure and noble conduct. Other gods tempt us, and mock us; but thou dost take away the sin of the world. Who but thyself, thou Christ of God, could lift the infinite load? What power but thine could dispel the infinite cloud? We cannot take away sin; but the blood of Jesus Christ the Son of God taketh away all sin. We cast our sins on Jesus. We do not understand his love, but we answer it with tears and faith and sacred hope. If this is not the way of salvation, then is there no other. We have hewn out unto ourselves cisterns—broken cisterns—that could hold no water, and we have attempted to build towers that should reach even unto heaven. But we stand before thee now, convicted, burning with shame, having utterly failed to do the thing which we set our hand to accomplish. Thou dost teach us in many ways: by fear, by poverty, by joy, by wealth; and by all the ministry of life, thou art teaching us the holy truth, and shedding upon us the upper light, and drawing us more nearly to thyself. Being in a school, may we not forget the lesson. Having an opportunity of learning wisdom, may we not live and die as foolish men. May we know the rod, and him who hath appointed it. Enable us to kiss the chastening hand. Lift upon us the light of thy countenance, and our tears shall be beautiful. Take not thy Holy Spirit from us in the night of sorrow, suffering, disappointment, and pain. Sanctify to us all trouble, distress, and fear, and sadness, and out of death itself may we see a springing of immortal life. Work before our eyes this wondrous mystery. Show us how thou dost bring beauty out of that which is unbeautiful; how the morning rises upon the night, and how summer comes swiftly after winter. Thus may we have hope, through Christ, in the living God. Teach us that all things work together for good to them that love thee. When the cup is very bitter, may we drink it in thy strength, and because thou hast given it unto us. Teach us to bring all prayers into one, saying, with full hearts, with unbroken, ever-hoping trust, "Not my will, but thine be done." In that spirit there is triumph; in that faith there is no overthrow. Lord, increase our faith. Then from the place of darkness shall we see the stars. In the night-time of solitude shall we have angel-like companionship, and up the steep hill we shall feel the sustaining hand of God. Amen.

Deut. vi. 1-12.

1. Now these are the commandments, the statutes, and the judgments, which the Lord your God commanded to teach you, that ye might do them in the land whither ye go to possess it:

2. That thou mightest fear the Lord thy God, to keep all his statutes and his commandments, which I command thee, thou, and thy son, and thy son's son, all the days of thy life; and that thy days may be prolonged.

3. Hear therefore, O Israel, and observe to do it; that it may be well with thee, and that ye may increase mightily, as the Lord God of thy athers hath promised thee, in the land that floweth with milk and honey.

4. Hear, O Israel: The Lord our God is one Lord:

5. And thou shalt love the Lord thy God with all thine heart, and with all thy soul, and with all thy might.

6. And these words, which I command thee this day, shall be in thine heart:

7. And thou shalt teach them diligently unto thy children, and shalt talk of them when thou sittest in thine house, and when thou walkest by the way, and when thou liest down, and when thou risest up.

8. And thou shalt bind them for a sign upon thine hand, and they shall be as frontlets between thine eyes.

9. And thou shalt write them upon the posts of thy house, and on thy gates.

10. And it shall be, when the Lord thy God shall have brought thee into the land which he sware unto thy fathers, to Abraham, to Isaac, and to Jacob, to give thee great and goodly cities, which thou buildedst not,

11. And houses full of all good things, which thou filledst not, and wells digged, which thou diggedst not, vineyards and olive trees, which thou plantedst not; when thou shalt have eaten and be full;

12. Then beware lest thou forget the Lord, which brought thee forth out of the land of Egypt, from the house of bondage.

PRINCIPLES AND DUTIES.

A WONDERFUL change has taken place in the tone of Moses. We can tell by his very voice that he is much older than when we first knew him, and much tenderer. When we first heard his voice, we noted how singularly wanting it was in mellowness, sympathy, kindliness, such as sore and wounded hearts may recognise and bless. Throughout the Book of Exodus the tone of Moses was very high, penetrating, and commanding. Then a change took place in the whole manner of the man : he was not less in stature, not less keen of vision ; yet somehow he was quieter, perhaps more indulgent, certainly mellower. In Deuteronomy all these qualities of the voice, being also qualities of the spirit, culminate ; Moses exhorts, entreats, wrestles with men, that they may be wise and good ; there is nothing wanting that is suggestive of ripeness of experience, depth and genuineness of sympathy. Moses becomes shepherd again, only now men and women and children, more wayward than any beasts of the earth, constitute his multitudinous and most trying flock. Read Deuteronomy immediately after Exodus, and mark, though the fire of his eye is not dimmed, the growth of the man in the softening of his voice, in the multitude of his tears, in his pastoral solicitude for the salvation of Israel. The sixth chapter of Deuteronomy is full of exhortation and expostulation. In the third verse we read,—"Hear therefore, O Israel, and observe to do it ; that it may be well with thee, and that ye may increase mightily, as the Lord God of thy fathers hath promised thee, in the land that floweth with milk and honey." This is not bribery. Moses must not be conceived of as holding up a prize, saying,—This donation is for the best-behaved amongst you. No man can be made good by such temptations. The very desire to have the prize may itself indicate a viciousness inveterate and ineradicable. Moses is not pointing out a reason, but indicating a consequence or issue : whoever observes and does the commandments of God shall enter into largeness of blessing, immeasurable depth of holy contentment, and every land shall be a land flowing with milk and honey. The man makes the land. When men everywhere praise the Lord, the earth shall yield her increase : the swelling psalm of honest thankfulness and the waving harvest of golden wheat shall be seen together upon the earth. No man can do right in order that it may be well with him, but no man can do right without its being consequentially well with every faculty of his mind, every emotion of his spirit, every outgoing of his life. Moses is already preaching the Sermon upon the Mount according to the measure of the light which made up his ancient day. What is he now doing but saying, "Seek ye first the kingdom of God, and his righteousness; and all these things shall be added unto you"? "Hear therefore, O Israel, and observe to do the commandment of God; that it may be well with thee, and that ye may increase mightily." Our business is with the "hearing" and the "observing," and God's business is with the other end, namely, the end of result, and issue, and blessing.

But Moses soon comes back to central principles. Moses is never less than a philosopher,—a philosopher with a broad streak of shepherdliness running all through his mental and moral constitution, but still a philosopher, a reasoner, a theologian. What could be more pregnant with meaning, more inexhaustible in suggestion and poetry, than the fourth verse,—"Hear, O Israel: The Lord our God is one Lord"? The sentence seems to be easy. There is no simplicity in the Bible that does not hold within its lines the very eternity of Jehovah. We must have a right view of God. The meaning of the exclamation of Moses is not that the Lord our God is one Lord as against some possible distribution of number in His own constitution, but He is one Lord in distinction from all the gods and idols, and all the claimants to human worship known in all the lands and peoples through which Israel has passed; the Lord stands apart from them; he is singular in relation to them; he has no relations with them, unless they be relations of contempt and mockery and disdain. Moses was not arguing a theological proposition: he was not laying down the doctrine of the unity of God as against the tri-unity of God; that sphere of thinking was not involved in this contemplation of the divine nature; Israel was called to monotheism as opposed to polytheism—the many gods that ruled the inferior thinking, and accounted for the debasing superstition of mankind.

Yet, though so lofty in his conception, Moses soon becomes tender in his tone. Hence we find in the fifth verse words which even Jesus Christ did not alter :—"And thou shalt love the Lord thy God with all thine heart, and with all thy soul, and with all thy might." God must never be set away from our love—that is to say, in some inaccessible region of intellectual contemplation or of high theological imagining. God must be kept quite near to the heart. Once let the heart lose touch of God, and God himself becomes but a distant and infinite idol.

Keep the heart right, keep the soul sweet, keep love unmixed and unembarrassed—a free, generous, undivided affection, and all the rest will flow out of that central conviction and attitude as a living stream out of a living fountain. The question which the soul should often put to itself should relate to love. There is a place for reverence—for the worship so awestruck as to be speechless; but we must always find room for simple, childlike, clinging love. Jesus Christ delighted to paint God as a Being full of love—so loving the world as to spare nothing for its redemption and salvation. The love of God culminates in the Cross of Christ. The Cross of Christ is not only the symbol of the Atonement, it is the eternal pledge of a beneficent Providence: not only does it include forgiveness of sin and the way into the liberty and peace of heaven, it includes a guarantee of daily bread and daily care, divine attention to all the details of human life. "If God spared not his own Son"—is the basis of Paul's sublime appeal on the matter of human providence and social government. God being the object of love, we ourselves must have the spirit of love in regard to God; we must love God. Love does not reason: love is a poor logician as to forms and symbols; love insists upon speaking its own language and finding its own prayers, and creating its own songs and setting them to its own music. Love will have liberty. Love could never live in prison. Love was made to fly in the open firma-ment of heaven, to beat its gracious wings against the very gates of the morning, to rise into the holy place of the light, and to come back to do earth's work with heaven's purity and tenderness. Children can love where they cannot understand. Love is before reason and after reason: love passes through the zone of reason, and ascends to the heaven where it was created in the heart and thought of God. Live in reason, and life will be cold; do nothing that cannot be defined and affirmed and indicated by consecutive reasons, and life may become mechanical. Rise into the very passion of love—the very sacrificial temper of consecrated affection—and the wilderness shall be a garden, and death but a messenger sent to bring the soul into some inner place in God's infinite sanctuary.

Is it enough to have a right conception of the unity of God in relation to the multitudinous idolatries of the world, and to

have a right view of the moral qualities of God as opposed to
an insensate and unresponsive deity ? Moses teaches that there
is no religious sufficiency in either or both of these things.
Moses will have more. What more he will have he tells us in
plain terms :—"And these words, which I command thee this
day, shall be in thine heart " (v. 6). We begin with words;
we begin with things and with pictures, with substances and
with commandments, visible and utterable; and from all these
we may grow away not by an act of separation but by an act
of the fulfilment which comes out of development. Christian
words are to be in our heart. The heart has a memory of its
own. Give into the custody of the heart some lesson, and it
will be retained. Men remember what they want to remember,
in all the highest relations of life. Intellectual memory is hardly
called into operation in this matter of religious communion.
The heart is kept alive; the fire upon the altar of the heart
never goes out; the heart hears every knock upon the door; the
heart sees every sign that is marked upon the spaces of the
firmament; the heart overhears all that is passing which has
relation to its own development and completion. We are what
we are in the heart. " As a man thinketh in his heart, so
is he."

Are the words of God to be kept in the heart as treasure
may be kept in some secret and inviolable place ? Is the heart
the only organ that is interested in this great matter of religious
information and culture ? Moses gives the reply :—"And thou
shalt teach them diligently unto thy children " (v. 7). He
who teaches out of his heart will be able to speak to children,
even in the simplest sense of that term. Children like teachers
who talk out of their hearts. The heart knows all the little
words because itself is a little word of one syllable. The heart
waits for the very slowest walker in this great quest of the
temple of wisdom : the heart says,—We must tarry for the
cripple. When the intellect would say,—Let us urge forward,—
and the imagination would step from mountain-top to mountain-
top, miles at a time, the heart says,—Wait ! here is a little child
who cannot go at that pace ; here is a poor old traveller who
wants to res a while ;—stop ! not one must be lost : every child

and every cripple and the meanest member of the flock must be saved. There is a way of teaching the words of God : they may be so taught as to repel or discourage or affright ; or they may be so taught as to allure, fascinate, entrance, and put out of view every competitive spectacle or seduction. God's word must be spoken in God's way.

Having delivered the words to the children, does the task end there ? Moses says it does not end at any such point ; he adds,--" and shalt talk of them "—not lecture upon them, not deliver superb and magnificent orations upon them, but " talk " of them. The very word is suggestive. The words of God are to be so thoroughly in our hearts as to become part of our life, and to mingle with our very breathing ; then we may talk about them with the ease of conscious mastery, with the familiarity —not only of intellectual intimacy, but of the heart's truest friendship. Religion is not to be introduced upon state occasions, or upon great days, or even upon the Sabbath day as an exclusive period of time. The word of God is to be talked about, is to come into conversation as if it had a right to be there, to elevate the speech of social man, to give grace and dignity and solemnity to all the transactions and covenants which make up the business of the day. To teaching we must add talking ; to the formal exposition we must add the informal and most friendly sugges- tion and the unexpected prayer, coming into conversation with the ease which belongs to perfect acquaintance with the Spirit of God.

Is the teaching to be conducted in the sanctuary, and the talking to be limited to holy places of public resort ? Moses gives an answer to these inquiries, and there is no escape from the comprehensive terms in which his response is couched :— " when thou sittest in thine house, and when thou walkest by the way, and when thou liest down, and when thou risest up " (v. 7). Here is a religion which covers the whole day, which belongs to every attitude of man, which condescends to flow into the mould of daily position and continual progress. The word of God can accommodate itself to every season and to every position and to all the circumstances of life. It is never there by force, or unaccountably there ; it belongs of right to

our whole life. It can be spoken in walking; it can simplify
itself so as to suit the position of one who is sitting in his house,
quietly and lovingly, in the very centre of the family; when the
man lies down, religion will consent to be spoken about in terms
and promises of restfulness and recruiting and the sleep which
brings youth back with it; and religion is so energetic that when
the man rises up a whole man, complete in strength, reinvigorated
in every faculty, it can leap forth into every expression of energy
and outrun every effort of the mind.

So the answer of Moses is very complete. The word of God
is to be in the heart, it is to be taught to children, it is to form
the subject of talk, it is to be talked about everywhere. Does
the matter end there? Moses has still further field for religious
activity. He is delighted to find the words of God in the heart,
and to hear them talked in the public assembly, and to hear
them spoken about with all the familiar ease of conversation:
he is delighted to meet men in the house and on the highway,
sitting down, rising up, and still talking about the goodness and
the judgment of God; but he will have more: Moses adds,—
"And thou shalt bind them for a sign upon thine hand, and
they shall be as frontlets between thine eyes" (v. 8). There
shall be no secret religiousness, no stealthy piety, no profound
consecration that wraps around itself garments which are so
used by itself as not to involve particularity of devotedness. If
the word is in the heart, it must also be written on the hand;
if the word is part of the speech, which only a few can hear,
it must be as frontlets before the eyes, that observers may note,
so that men passing by may be able to say,—This man publicly
acknowledges, and, perhaps, publicly worships, God.

Does Moses put a full stop here? Moses does not: Moses
still finds further space—"And thou shalt write them upon the
posts of thy house, and on thy gates" (v. 9). Moses would
have a broad religion, and would have a broad religion broadly
acknowledged. The heart, the tongue, the hands, the eyes, the
house,—this is most comprehensive. It is, in fact, absolutely
inclusive. There is no spot left on which the devil may play
his pranks. The heart all Bible, the speech all savour, the
hand all consecration, the eyes set in one direction, the posts

of the house and the very gates bearing inscriptions of heaven, this was the religious idea and this the religious programme of Moses.

Then comes a great caution :—" And it shall be, when the Lord thy God shall have brought thee into the land which he sware unto thy fathers, to Abraham, to Isaac, and to Jacob, to give thee great and goodly cities, which thou buildedst not, and houses full of all good things, which thou filledst not, and wells digged, which thou diggedst not, vineyards and olive trees, which thou plantedst not; when thou shalt have eaten and be full; then beware—" (vv. 10–12). Moses is growing old, but he is intellectually as astute as ever. It is not his soul that is growing old; it is not the perennial mind that is drying up or withering away. Mark the conception which Moses formed of all advancing civilisation. How much we have that we have not done ourselves! We are born into a world that is already furnished with the library, with the altar, with the Bible. Men born into civilised countries have not to make their own roads. We are born into the possession of riches. The poorest man in the land is an inheritor of all but infinite wealth, in every department of civilisation. In the very act of complaining of his poverty he is acknowledging his resources. His poverty is only poverty because of its relation to other things which indicate the progress of the ages that went before. Young men come into fortunes they never worked for; we all come into possessions for which our fathers toiled. We could not assemble in God's house in peace and quietness to-day if the martyrs had not founded the Church upon their very blood. Men to-day enjoy the liberty for which other men paid their lives. It is ungrateful to forget that every liberty we enjoy, every security we boast, is the result of suffering too poignant to be expressed adequately in words. Coming into a civilisation so ripe and rich, having everything made ready to our hands, the whole system of society telephoned so that we can communicate with distant friends and bring them within hearing, the table loaded with everything which a healthy appetite can desire,—all these things constitute a temptation, if not rightly received. Moses drew the picture, and then said—" Beware." In the time of prosperity, and fulness, and overflow—" then beware lest thou forget the Lord, which brought thee forth out of the land of Egypt, from the house of bondage" (v. 12). Prosperity has its trials. "How hardly shall they that have riches enter into the kingdom of God! For it is easier for a camel to go through a needle's eye, than for a rich man to enter into the kingdom of God." Poverty may be a spiritual blessing. The impoverishment and punishment of the flesh may be religiously helpful. There are anxieties connected with wealth as well as with poverty. The high and the mighty amongst us have their pains and difficulties as well as the lowliest and weakest members of society. Ever let men hear this word of caution—"beware." When the harvest is the best harvest that ever was grown in our fields, then—"beware." When health is long-continued and the doctor an unknown stranger in the house, then—"beware." When house is added to house and land to land, then—"beware." Many men have been ruined through prosperity.

SELECTED NOTE.

"*Frontlets between thine eyes*" (v. 8).—The practice of using phylacteries was founded on a literal interpretation of that passage where God commands the Hebrews to have the law as a sign on their foreheads, and as frontlets between their eyes. It is probable that the use of phylacteries came in late with other superstitions ; but it should be remembered, that our Lord does not censure the Pharisees for wearing them, but for making them *broad* out of ostentation ; and it is still uncertain whether the words referred to ought not to be taken literally. One kind of phylactery was called a *frontlet*, and was composed of four pieces of parchment, on the first of which was written Exod. xiii. 1-10 ; on the second, Exod. xiii. 11-16 ; on the third, Deut. vi. 4-9 ; and on the fourth, Deut. xi. 13-21. These pieces of parchment, thus inscribed, they enclosed in a piece of tough skin, making a square, on one side of which was placed the Hebrew letter *shin* (שׁ), and bound them round their foreheads with a thong or riband when they went to the synagogue. Some wore them evening and morning, and others only at the morning prayer.

As the token upon the hand was required, as well as the frontlets between the eyes, the Jews made two rolls of parchment, written in square letters, with an ink made on purpose, and with much care. They were rolled up to a point, and enclosed in a sort of case of black calf-skin. They then were put upon a square bit of the same leather, whence hung a thong of the same, of about a finger in breadth, and about two feet long. These rolls were placed at the bending of the left arm, and after one end of the thong had been made into a little knot in the form of the Hebrew letter *yod* (י), it was wound about the arm in a spiral line, which ended at the top of the middle finger.

Deut. vi. 20-25.

20. And when thy son asketh thee in time to come, saying, What mean the testimonies, and the statutes, and the judgments, which the Lord our God hath commanded you?

21. Then thou shalt say unto thy son, We were Pharaoh's bondmen in Egypt; and the Lord brought us out of Egypt with a mighty hand:

22. And the Lord shewed signs and wonders, great and sore, upon Egypt, upon Pharaoh, and upon all his household, before our eyes:

23. And he brought us out from thence, that he might bring us in, to give us the land which he sware unto our fathers.

24. And the Lord commanded us to do all these statutes, to fear the Lord our God, for our good always, that he might preserve us alive, as it is at this day.

25. And it shall be our righteousness, if we observe to do all these commandments before the Lord our God, as he hath commanded us.

QUESTIONS AND ANSWERS

QUESTIONS upon religious subjects will be asked, and we ought to be prepared to answer them in some degree at least. We are not called upon to be irrational—that is, without reason—even in our Christianity. We did not part with our reason when we were enabled to yield ourselves to the higher inspiration of faith. We ought to be able to say something in reply to inquiries addressed to us concerning the most important portions of our history. We ought, therefore, to be instructed in our own doctrine, and to have some clear conception of the way along which Christian doctrine has passed; and we ought, further, to be able to identify ourselves with that doctrine, and thus give sharpness and clearness to all our religious recitals and arguments. Moses told Israel that questions would be asked. The son would ask of the father the meaning of institutions, statutes, and judgments, and the father was bound to reply to the son's natural and rational inquiry. Such is our position now. Suppose that one wholly uninstructed as to Christian faith and doctrine and practice

should ask us,—What mean ye?—account for yourselves; what
are you doing? and why do you act as you do?—it would be
pitiful to the point of unpardonableness if in presence of such an
inquiry we were dumb; our speechlessness would show that
our piety is a mere superstition. It is surely, therefore, incum-
bent upon us to be able to give some reason or explanation for
the faith and the hope that are in us. We cannot adopt a better
reply than the answer suggested by Moses. No originality of
answer is required. The leader of Israel gave the only reply
that will stand the test of reason and the wear and tear of time.
All we need is in this paragraph.

Adopting this reply, what answer should we make to the kind
of inquirer now supposed? We should, first of all, make the
answer broadly historical. We are not called to invention, or
speculation, or the recital of dreams : we do not want any man's
impressions as a basis of rational and universal action; we call
for history, facts, realities, points of time that can be identified,
and circumstances that can be defined and have a determinate
value fixed upon them. We could enlarge the answer which
Israel was to give, and ennoble it. We, too, were in a house of
bondage. That must be our first point. The house was dark;
the life of the prison was intolerable; no morning light penetrated the dungeon; no summer beauty visited the eyes of those
who were bound in fetters. Human nature had gone astray.
The great cry of the ages was,—" All we like sheep have gone
astray; we have turned every one to his own way; " "There is
none righteous, no, not one." The Christian argument starts
there. All Christian doctrine is founded upon that one fact, or
bears direct and vital relation to it.

We, too, could add with Israel, human nature was divinely
delivered. The action began in heaven. No man's arm
delivered us; no man's eye could look upon us with pity that
was unstained and unenfeebled by sin. God's eye pitied; God's
arm was outstretched to save. Great was the compassion of
God and tender his love; and every action of his hand, though
an action of almightiness, was chastened, softened, mellowed,
by an indwelling and overflowing tenderness.

Then we could continue the reply, and say the divine deliverance was attested by many "signs and wonders." Christianity

has its miracles corresponding, according to time and speciality of need, to the miracles wrought in Egypt by the Jehovah of Israel. We do not surrender the miracles. Some of them we have seen. As we grow away from them we grow towards them, in their highest and most spiritual meaning. To-day miracles are wrought—miracles of the higher sort: an inner vision is opened, the ear of the soul is excited to reverent attention, the whole nature is transformed, changed, lifted up into new relations, and made glad with new and immortal hopes. The temple of God is a temple of miracles. The nature of the miracles may have undergone considerable change, but their inner meaning is an eternal truth : it abides through all the ages, for every purpose of God in the miracles which were wrought was a purpose of life, growth, holiness, transformation into his own image. The purpose is in reality the miracle. That being so, the miracles never cease, for to-day the Gospel performs nothing less than the miracle of making the dead live, and the blind see, and the dumb speak in new and beauteous eloquence. We, too, had a Deliverer, as Israel had ; the name of our Deliverer is Jesus Christ. He was born in Bethlehem ; he proclaimed himself the Son of man, the Son of God ; he looked upon the whole race with eyes filled with tears ; he tasted death for every man ; he died the just for the unjust that he might bring us to God ; he was crucified, he died and was buried, and on the third day he rose again, and now he is in heaven, our Advocate before the throne ; his wounds still upon him as historical marks, but the pain of the wounding is for ever gone. That is our answer in brief and imperfect outline. We, therefore, stand upon this historical ground. Right or wrong, here we are. We did not make the history, we may not modify it, we are not at liberty to introduce any new elements into it ; our position is historical : we continue a story, we are chapters added to a great narration. Never part with your history ; always go back upon the fact. We are not called upon, as has been said many times, to invent a Bible or to suggest a new form of revelation ; we stand upon history, and therefore give a broadly historical reply.

In the next place, still following the idea laid down by Moses, we must make the answer definitely personal :—" thou shalt say unto thy sor " (v. 21). Speak about yourselves, about your own vital relation to the historical facts. The history is not something outside of you and beyond you : it is part and parcel of your own development, and your development would have been an impossibility apart from the history ; let us, therefore, know what this history has done for you. The answer will be poor if it be but a recital of circumstances and occurrences and anecdotes,—a vague, although partially reverent, reference to ancient history. The man who speaks must connect himself with the thing which is spoken. Christianity, in its incarnations, is not the recital of a lesson : it is the embodiment and vitalisation of a truth. We may repeat the history all day long, and who will care ? But give it personality, show how it bears upon the individual life and the personal witness, include and involve your own integrity in the story which you recite,—then the man who hears it has two things to do : not only to disprove the history but to disprove your testimony. Suppose, then, we could speak thus in reply : We perused the history ; it seemed strange to us ; many a question was excited by the perusal ; sometimes our faith was in the ascendant, sometimes doubt seemed to break our wings so that we could not fly heavenward : we fell to the earth enfeebled and distressed ; but we returned to the history and considered it deeply ; in the first instance we felt our own need of something of the kind ; the miracles bewildered us, but when we came to the offer of salvation, when a Man called Jesus stood up before us and said, " I will give you rest "—we said within ourselves,— Rest is what we need : we are restless ; we are killed all the day long ; the burden of life is heavy over us, and the accusations of life bear down upon us like a final judgment ;—then we began to see that perhaps this Man is the very man we needed ; we trusted him ; we began shamefacedly at first : we were almost afraid to be caught in the company of the Man or listening to his doctrine ; but as he advanced we wondered at the gracious words which proceeded out of his mouth ; we turned aside and said to one another,—He knows us altogether : he has plumbed the depth of our necessity ; hear how he speaks !—with what wisdom ! with what grace ! with what sympathy !—he will cast none out ; now we begin to see a new light shining upon the miracles ; we could have doubted them ; we could have brought them altogether in one view and written our denial

across them ; but, becoming familiar with the Miracle-worker
himself, getting to know somewhat of his spirit, feeling in some
degree the fascination of his sympathy, we were enabled to go
farther, and we stood before the Cross : we watched the whole
tragedy; and as we looked upon him we said to one another,
"Truly this Man was the Son of God ; "—our reason could not go
much further, but a new faculty was called into operation, a faculty
called faith—trust, confidence, an outleaping of the heart towards
outstretched arms ; we were enabled to cast ourselves into the
arms of Jesus Christ, and having done so rest came into our souls,
a sense of pardon made us glad ; we entered into the mystery
of spiritual peace; then we were stirred towards beneficence of
ministry : we became eyes to the blind, and ears to the deaf, and
a tongue to the man that was silent ; and we followed Christ
step by step, doing as he did according to the measure of our
power ; and now we feel the energy of God in the soul, renewing
us every day, drawing us forward by gracious compulsion to
nobler life.   That is our answer to any man who asks us, What
mean ye by this Christian profession and activity ?

Thus the answer is, in the first instance, broadly historical—a
mere outline of facts, the facts being well-nigh innumerable, and
so striking in many instances as to be almost incredible.   Then
the answer is distinctly and definitely personal.   We had to
deal with the facts, to weigh them and consider their value.   We
adopted that course, and the outcome of the process was faith in
the Lord Jesus Christ,—a tender, vital clinging to the Saviour's
Cross.   So far we feel the solidity of our ground.   The ground
would not have been solid to us if the history had not been
personalised, vitalised, adopted by the individual man himself
so that he who went through the process of conversion becomes
an annotator upon the page of the history, and where there was
difficulty before there is light now.   The answer is still incomplete.   It is broadly historical, and therefore can be searched
into by men who care for letters and events and ancient
occurrences ; the answer is definitely personal, and therefore
the character of the witness has to be destroyed before any
progress can be made with his particular view of the history ;
now the answer must, in the third place, be made vitally ex-
perimental.   The twenty-fifth verse thus defines this conclusion :

"And it shall be our righteousness, if we observe to do all
these commandments before the Lord our God, as he hath
commanded us." One targum says, "it shall be our merit."
The general meaning would seem to be,—"it shall be accounted
unto us for righteousness:" the attention and the service shall
not be disregarded or put down into any secondary place, but
what we do in the way of attention and observance and duty and
service shall be reckoned unto us as a species of righteousness.
What is the meaning to us in our present state of education and
our present relations to one another? The meaning is that out
of the history and out of the personal relation to that history
there will come a quantity which is called character. God is all
the while forming character. His object has been to do us
"good always, that he might preserve us alive, as it is at this
day." Without the righteousness where is the history? Without the character what is the value of our personal testimony?
We may be speaking from a wrong centre—from mental invention, from intellectual imagination, from spiritual impulse, from
moral emotion; we may not be standing upon vital facts and
spiritual realities. The outcome, then, is righteousness, character, moral manhood, great robustness and strength, and reality
of life. The Christian man's history is to himself worthless if it
be not sealed by character. The speaker's eloquence is as
sounding brass or a tinkling cymbal if it be not followed by solid
and invincible character—not the kind of character that is
mechanically arranged, one part being beautifully consistent with
another but so beautiful as to be suspicious; it may be a rugged
character, but in the centre of it is a burning fire, a desire after
God and God's holiness. The character is not a neatly trimmed
and dressed arrangement: it is a spirit, a meaning, a high and
noble purpose in life; the word is a bond; the outputting of the
hand is an oath; an assurance is a pledge that cannot be broken.
The man who is thus righteous may die, but will never break
his word; he may suffer much, but he will never falter in his
testimony; he may be marked by a thousand defects as to
action, attitude, and temporary relation, but his soul is alive with
God and his life is consecrated to his Saviour. Who adds
righteousness to the good-doer? Not himself. If the man made
record of his own actions and totalised them into some nameable

virtue, his diary and his reckoning would throw suspicion upon his motive. God is not unrighteous to forget your work of faith and labour of love. It is God who imputes righteousness. It is God who says,—" Well done, good and faithful servant." It is the Father who says,—" Bring hither the fatted calf, and kill it ; and let us eat and be merry : for this my son was dead, and is alive again ; he was lost, and is found "—make the house thrill with music, for there is a birth in it of manhood and immortality. So, we must have no mongering in virtue, no dealing and tricking and arranging in nice little actions and pat little circumstances, having upon them the bloom of a bastard piety. We must keep up the history, relate ourselves personally to it, turn it into character, and leave God to count the righteousness and to number up our actions and to put a value upon them. Character involves solidity, hope, recompense, reality. A man cannot pretend to character who may lay some little claim to reputation. Reputation is but expressive of appearances, superficial estimates ; but character is the man, the man's very soul, the man's very self, without which he would seem to have no existence. So then, there is a doctrine of virtue, a doctrine of works, a doctrine of legal values. The fatal mistake upon our part would be if we set ourselves to its adjustment and determination. We have really nothing to do with it. We begin with duty, we continue with duty; we add nothing to God's Word : we obey it by the grace of our Lord Jesus Christ ; and at last we shall be startled and gladdened by finding that all our life long we have by the grace of God been building up into heaven.

PROHIBITIONS.

THIS chapter might be so read as to give great offence. There is in it a tone of pitilessness. The whole chapter is a vengeful speech. The chapter is charged with partiality on the part of God towards one nation, as though other nations were self-created or had been fashioned by inferior deities, and were worthy of nothing but contempt and destruction. Who made the Hittites, and the Girgashites, and the Amorites, and the Canaanites, and the Perizzites, and the Hivites, and the Jebusites,—seven nations greater and mightier than Israel? Were not they also the creation of God? Did they not live because " his mercy endureth for ever " ? Why this passion? Why this almost eagerness to get rid of them by violent means ? The putting of such questions reminds us that we are living in a different age. We do not read many portions of the Old Testament in the right light. Of course the great mental and spiritual difficulty is to think ourselves back to the exact condition of the time and circumstances under which certain parts of the Old Testament were written. There is a language of the time; there is an atmosphere of history as well as a detail of circumstances and events. This chapter, read in full recognition of that fact, assumes a totally different relation to our mind, and reveals a totally different purpose from that which at first we might suspect and condemn. People must be talked to in their own language. God himself must speak in terms which the people can understand. There is a providence of language. Language is daily changing in aspect and colour and accent; meaning is poured out from vessel to vessel, and many of the old word-vessels are either thrown away or have to be used by some carefully-guarded hand and application of thought and meaning. No ruthless hand must touch some of these vessels, and no untutored mind must undertake to discuss some of those lessons; otherwise God himself and his whole truth will be put in a false light, and will be so expressed as to draw upon themselves the anger and moral indignation of mankind. The language of this chapter is in some parts awful. It is not to be explained by mere criticism, but is rather to be expounded and revealed in its intentions by the New Testament spirit, by the larger providence by which God has revealed his purpose and discovered to the observation of man what all the time he has been endeavouring to do. We must avail ourselves of some such principles as these if we are to get through with any comfort many of the rough places and rocky roads of the ancient record. The language might be changed, and yet every principle remain in its integrity. This is the very lesson which revelation is endeavouring every day to teach us. The revelation is not a matter of mere words or unchangeable expressions, but of what is in the words: the words being the mere wrappage within which we are to find the contents of the divine mind and purpose. The chapter might be rewritten in modern language and yet not one or its principles would be for an instant modified or impaired. We could get rid of the passion and yet retain the justice; we could wholly strip off all vengefulness and yet retain the divine purpose which is to create a Church, a family, a kingdom pure as the purity of God.

Look a little at the detail. All marriages with the heathen peoples were forbidden :—" Neither shalt thou make marriages with them ; thy daughter thou shalt not give unto his son, nor his daughter shalt thou take unto thy son" (v. 3). The separation is not final. Within this regulation there is a purpose of purity. The line central and vital is not to be changed in its direction. God is not now making eternal statutes and judgments as to the separation of the nations one from another. His purpose is to have but one nation upon the face of the whole earth—a royal generation, a peculiar people, a new humanity, headed by a new and eternal Adam. Meantime, something must be done of a remedial and mitigatory kind. God's providence must begin where it can. The world was not prepared for the full blaze of the divine thought and meaning, so even God had to condescend to work in literal commandment, in striking limitation of human liberty, and in such details as of necessity occurred in the outworking of individual and social life. Even God is limited by human conditions, specially by human ignorance, more specially by human sin. He himself under some circumstances can only "stand at the door and knock." Meanwhile, the principle is a perpetual guide in Christian conduct. It is still true that things cannot be combined which are of different qualities, which have no essential and vital relation to one another. Nor is the inculcation or enforcement of this principle operative on one side only. Both the united people would be miserable. God is not only caring for those who are his own : he is also caring for those who are opposed to him—for by all. false alliances and unholy unions both lives are spoiled. The judgment does not fall upon one only : it falls upon both with tremendous force. Change the terms, soften them as much as you will, put them into modern form, and tone them down into modern softness and mellowness,—still there remains the vital principle that two things not being related to one another vitally and essentially, not in their innermost and best nature yearning for one another, can never come together in any form of marriage without involving both sides of the union in unutterable disappointment and distress.

Then the instruction was to deal severely with heathenish institutions and customs. This is proved by the fifth verse :— "Thus shall ye deal with them ; ye shall destroy their altars, and break down their images, and cut down their groves, and burn their graven images with fire." That is not the law of this day. It was the only possible law in the early time. Men must grow into right conceptions of force. There have always been men who have been impatient with Jesus Christ himself because he did not go quickly enough to the kingdom. In his own day the people sought to make him a King "by force," but Jesus Christ would have no kingship thus violently and prematurely instituted. The kingship of Christ is a necessity of the universe. The very first courses

of the foundations of creation, rightly interpreted, bear upon
their masonry this promise :—Jesus Christ shall reign over
the whole creation.   But the fulfilment of that promise belongs
to the providence of time.   There we enter into an evolution
transcending the imagination and mocking the patience of the
most devoted Simeon.   The only way in which Israel could deal
with the heathen nations was by the way of destruction, break-
age, downcutting, and burning.   The period was given up to
that species of force and urgency.   We have come to learn
that persuasion is mightier than arms, reasoning is more
potent than violence, and prayer will accomplish victories
which are impossible to sword and spear.   It would seem
to be an easy way to get rid of idolatry to burn the idol and
reduce their altars to ashes.   All this species of inroad might
be made upon the idolatry, but idolatry itself would remain
untouched, secure in the citadel of the heart's trust, and hardly
less secure in the castle of debased imagination.   Only truth
can destroy error; only love can burn all evil ; only heaven
can get rid of hell.   So the innermost thought remains.   The
principle of destruction abides for ever.   Everything that is
done by the most peaceful and patient servant of God has in
it the quality of destruction, only it is spiritual violence, moral
conquest, the victory of the soul.   " Put up thy sword into
the sheath : " " for all they that take the sword shall perish
with the sword."   Nay, Jesus will not have even embattled
angels crowding to his side to smite with lightning those
who assail him.   Jesus Christ says,—Let the truth be spoken
in a fair field, and in the long run light will conquer darkness.

The harshness was not arbitrary, but logical.   God is represented in the tenth verse in these terms :—he " repayeth them
that hate him to their face, to destroy them : he will not be
slack to him that hateth him, he will repay him to his face."
How such words could be read with spitefulness of tone !—as
if God were some petulant deity, vain and careful to assiduity
about all the decoration of his throne ; as if no hand must
touch it ; as if intruders would be thrust into the sea or burned
in the furnace.   There is no such meaning in the words.
The same law applies in nature.   It is the law of agriculture
as certainly as it is the law of theology and morals.   It is not

given to man—poor man—to overturn the divine decree in
any realm of life or action. Whoso would try to invert the
seasons shall find himself without bread in the day when
his garners should have been full; and if some imaginative
Moses, gifted with the power of vivid pictorial description,
should say, looking upon the empty barns,—"He repayeth
them that hate him to their face, to destroy them," he would
but vindicate a law which is not arbitrary but gracious—a
providential law; and providence is the dawn of grace.

But was the election itself arbitrary, fixed, and wholly
independent of the spirit and conduct of those who were
elected? The answer is given in the twelfth verse :—"Wherefore it shall come to pass, if ye hearken to these judgments,
and keep, and do them, that the Lord thy God shall keep
unto thee the covenant and the mercy which he sware unto
thy fathers." So election has been misunderstood. Men have
not been slow to say,—Once in grace always in grace; being
born again we may do what we please; we are not now under
the law; we are Jews no more; we are free to sin. Nowhere
is that doctrine taught in the Old Testament or in the New.
The contrary doctrine is put in every possible variety of
words, and is vindicated by every possible variety of event
and circumstance in human history. We are committed to
the law which demands righteousness. Over all controversies
and all endeavours to escape restraint and prohibition there
rises this great inquiry,—"What doth the Lord require of
thee, but to do justly, and to love mercy, and to walk humbly
with thy God?" That is Christian life,—not some metaphysical mystery which has no practical exemplification, but a
profound spiritual mystery which proves itself by conduct
as mysterious in its nobleness as its origin is mysterious in
its divinity. There are two mysteries in the Christian life :
the mystery of its beginning and the mystery of its maintenance,—the mystery of spirit and the mystery of conduct.
Whenever a man, smitten on the one cheek, turns the other
also, he sustains and completes the mystery of regeneration.
The man who is living on metaphysical conceptions, and
dreaming away his life in theological contemplation, without
unfolding the mysteries of grace in the mysteries of conduct,

has abused the covenant, and has committed high treason
against the throne of God.

Showing, as he always shows, a most penetrating mind,
Moses points to a very subtle temptation which would arise
in connection with the progress of Israel. The graven images
of the heathen nations were to be burned with fire. Moses
says in the twenty-fifth verse, — " Thou shalt not desire
the silver or gold that is on them, nor take it unto thee, lest
thou be snared therein." How subtle is the temptation in
that direction ! Might not this ointment have been sold for
hundreds of pence ? and might not the produce have been
given to the poor ? Shall we cast in the hideous gods and
the valuable gold and consume them both in the unsparing
fire ? How much better first to strip the god of his golden
coat and then burn the wood or clay or grind the stone to
powder ! Moses, foreseeing this temptation, and by the very
inspiration of God, knowing the mysteries of human nature,
said,—" Touch not ; taste not; handle not." In such abstention
is the only possible safety of the Church. The temptation
operates to-day. Men will sustain a questionable mode of
earning a livelihood on the pretence that they can gather
from the forbidden trade gold and silver which they can melt
down and mint with the image and superscription of God ;
they can allow the devastating traffic to proceed, reeking like
the pit of hell, destroying countless thousands of lives, and
yet justify the continuance of the iniquity by taking off the
gold and the silver and throwing part of it into the coffers of
the Church. Missions so sustained are dishonoured. The
gold torn from any evil way of getting a livelihood and given
to the Church is an abomination to the Lord thy God. He
does not want even good gold stolen for his purposes, or
gold won by unholy means thrown into his exchequer. His
Son could live without a place whereon to lay his head, but
he could not live in any house that had in it the Dagon of
the Philistines—unholy gains, patronage with a smiling face
but with a heart all but too bad to be damned. God's independence, Christ's independence, asserts itself in many ways
in the Old Testament and in the New ; and the Church must
be as independent as the God who created it. There is a

strong temptation to continue the mischief, and tax it for the good of the heathen or the benefit of the poor. God accepts no such money. It never can be changed; it has no real and permanent value in the sanctuary; it makes the treasury full, but it is the fulness which is the truest and veriest emptiness. Let us give honest money. Let us eat bread unleavened by wrong-doing; there may be little of it, but Christ will break it with his own hands, and it shall be more than our hunger needs.

Marvellous, too, is the prevision of Moses when he lays down the only law or principle by which all these abstentions and all these actions can be sustained. Do not let us ascribe these regulations to the prevision of Moses unless we understand by that term the inspiration of God. What is the principle which guarantees safety and protects the soul from the unclean things of heathen nations? That principle is laid down in the twenty-sixth verse. Speaking of heathen abomination Moses says,—"thou shalt utterly detest it, and thou shalt utterly abhor it." There is no middle feeling; there is no intermediate way of dealing with bad things. "If thy right hand offend thee, cut it off;" "if thy right eye offend thee, pluck it out." "Abhor that which is evil; cleave to that which is good." Thus the Testaments are one: the moral tone is the same; the stern law never yields to time,— its phrase changes, its words may come and go, its forms may take upon them the colour of the transient times, but the inner spirit of righteousness is the spirit of God, without beginning, without measure, without end. We are thus called to revulsion. How can this be made plain to every understanding? Perhaps it can scarcely be adequately explained by merely spiritual terms and suggestions, but it admits of some indication from a physical point of view. Imagine any preparation given for food from which the whole nature recoils with unutterable horror. That may be considered the beginning of the meaning of this verse in its spiritual application. Having had such an offer made, the soul loathes it; hunger itself will not look at the offensive bribe given to the agony of its pain; all nature shudders and turns away—if silent, only because the strongest speech would be but a mockery of the intensity

of its pain. Thus the body may help the mind to right construc-
tions of divine purposes and spiritual laws.   You do not dispute
about that which is offered which awakens the sensations of
horror, nor do you ask questions about it, nor do you look
on with partial approval if, haply, in some way, the inconvenience may be got rid of; but having seen that which is offered,
nature, asserting an eternal law, rises, flies insulted and
dishonoured. Abstain from the appearance of evil. Touch
not, taste not, handle not the unclean thing. Do not allow
the mind merely to disapprove of evil, merely to condemn
certain social customs and arrangements,—to keep in a kind
of hovering relation towards things upon which God has put
his veto; but seeing one of them, "thou shalt utterly detest
it, and thou shalt utterly abhor it,"—the soul shall rise against
it as if God himself had been pained by some sudden and
tremendous offence. How is this spirit to be created within
us? It is the miracle of Christ; it is the miracle of the Holy
Ghost. This spirit is not born with man, or by the will of
man : it is born in us by the incorruptible seed of God.
This is the wonder of the Almighty, who looking upon the
accomplishment of this miracle says,—"It is very good."

Deut. viii.

THE PLAN OF LIFE.

THIS chapter may be considered as laying down the sacred and stimulating doctrine that our life is planned and ordered for us as to its divine side and moral obligation. We are not called upon to consider the great questions of moral duty or righteousness or good conduct in any of its vital springs, with a view to conceiving some plan of our own as to the realisation of perfect character. The idea of this chapter is that all moral duties have been defined and all moral limits have been divinely described and imposed, so that all we have to do is to concede the homage of rational and thankful obedience. This is a difficult lesson for the unrenewed human heart to learn ; it is, however, the one lesson which runs through the entire scope of revelation from end to end. It would seem to be a tribute to human sagacity, and even a recognition of human responsibility, to have left every man to define right and wrong for himself and to discover on his own account the shortest and safest way to heaven. A conception of this kind represents a profound and fatal mistake ; that mistake being that we are in any sense upon equal terms with the Creator and Preserver of our spirits. To begin truly we must begin with the assumption that we are of yesterday and know nothing, and that appearances alone reveal themselves to our imperfect vision, the spiritual and eternal reality of things being of necessity hidden from faculties which could not comprehend it. Thus the Biblical doctrine is one of human dependence upon divine revelation. All our quests after first principles and final issues are in reality expressions of the heart's desire to find and understand the will of the eternal God. We may shrink from that form of expression as being perhaps almost superstitious to our present incomplete reason, but viewed in its largest issues it comes to this—that man is everywhere seeking for the complete word, the divine term, the sure and everlasting rock. Having the spirit of little children, and coming to the Bible tenderly reverent to know definitely what God would have us do, we shall receive from the sacred page light for every day, comfort for every sorrow, and inspiration for every duty. If we appeal to the law and the testimony for the sake of finding materials for argument or abstract philosophy we shall kick against the pricks and involve ourselves in endless vexations. The Bible has nothing to say to such a spirit. It will only speak to the meek and lowly in heart, and to men who ask with reverent earnestness what God would have them do.

The plan of life is happily vindicated by the experience of life. Moses calls upon Israel to " remember all the way which the Lord thy God led thee these forty years." This is the happy issue of faith. Faith began without evidence of an external and positive kind, but as life advanced one day after another shaped itself into indisputable testimony, and so fortified the faith with a sacred and unimpeachable experience. We must begin with the faith and end with its verification. God will not allow us to begin at the other end: his plan is to train by trust, and to vindicate himself by the illumination which he vouchsafes to every day, so that the night shall corroborate the morning, and at eventide men shall praise God for the trust with which they began the day. Israel was not called upon so much to remember the literal road, but " the way," that is the manner or method, or, as we might say, the genius of the whole journey. In the Acts of the Apostles the Christian life is more than once called " the way." The journey of life is not made up of mere details and separate incidents ; all these are strung upon what we may describe as the thread of a divine purpose, and it is to that thread we must constantly look if we would see the unity and the direction of the divine intent. It comes to this then, that every Christian believer must fall back upon his personal experience of " the way." To personal knowledge the Christian may add the history of the whole Church. Individual experience and universal history concurring in an indivisible testimony, the result is a conviction which no mere argument or intellectual scepticism can either obscure or disturb. When Christian life is thus verified, Christian testimony will assume a lofty and definite tone. No longer will

Christianity be found in the attitude of a mere apologist; it will rise to the dignity of a living witness conscious of perfect and even divine veracity. Without such consciousness what is preaching? what is public profession? what are Christian institutions? Everything depends upon the reality of the personal life, the true, deep joy of the renewed heart; to these experiences there is no answer, the attempted reply of mere words being without point and without effect.

In the third verse Moses lays down by inspiration the sublime doctrine that the sustenance of life is not confined to one method. His words are most remarkable :—" And he humbled thee, and suffered thee to hunger, and fed thee with manna, which thou knewest not, neither did thy fathers know; that he might make thee know that man doth not live by bread alone, but by every word that proceedeth out of the mouth of the Lord doth man live." These words were used by Jesus Christ in reply to the temptation of Satan. The sustenance of human life has ever been a divine mystery on which God has never condescended to cast any light. God will sustain life in his own way. He gives it " manna," a term which itself requires definition, and which has baffled all the attempts of investigators adequately and finally to solve. It is an utter mistake to suppose that God could not sustain human life or any other life without what is known as bread. We call bread the staff of life, and, as a general expression, the term is sufficiently accurate : but God is not dependent upon the processes of nature; he could support human life as he supports the angels in heaven : if he has made the eating of bread apparently necessary to the sustenance of the bodily frame, it is that he might make the cultivation of bread a practical means of human training and a bond of social union. It is not God who is dependent upon the bread as an instrument; it is man who is dependent upon it as a condition of commerce and the unit of the commonwealths of the world. By allowing the mind to assume that by bread only man can live, we direct our thoughts into a narrow and unworthy channel. We make man a debtor to the earth and a debtor to his own invention. The sublime doctrine of inspiration is that we live and move and have our being in God,—and are in no sense, other than is involved in the divine sovereignty, either children of the dust, or debtors to anything

which the ground can supply.   He who is most conscious of his
highest nature is least conscious of his bodily requirements.
Now and again we have had happy experiences which at least
remotely indicate that a time may come when life will be an
expression of thought and feeling and worship, rather than a
result of gratified appetite, or the cultivation of meaner things.
All this cannot be expressed in words. We are thankful to have
now and again a hint of that larger being, that holy consciousness
which is best described by the thrilling word Immortality.
Wonderful are the words of Christ upon this matter of the
sustenance of life :—" He that doeth the will of God abideth for
ever."

The seventh verse reminds us that obedience is always
associated with reward :—" For the Lord thy God bringeth thee
into a good land, a land of brooks of water, of fountains and
depths that spring out of valleys and hills," and so the promise
rolls on in noble eloquence,—" A land of wheat, and barley, and
vines, and fig trees, and pomegranates ; a land of oil, olive, and
honey." This has been the divine method of cultivating and
ennobling the human race from the beginning. Men can understand reward, or the coming in to great and abundant possession of
such things as can be immediately used in the promotion of
human comfort and human security. God has always availed
himself of the principle of rewards and punishments in the training of mankind. His delight has been in pointing to an infinite
and glorious heaven as the crown and glory of human obedience.
It is not to be supposed that any appeal is thus made to the
meaner nature, or the baser motives by which conduct is moved.
Man needs kindly stimulus, a gracious impulsion on the way
towards the city of light.   It is possible that Christians may have
outgrown the whole idea expressed by terms which ancient Israel
could understand, but the very outgrowth is itself a testimony to
the reality of the principle which is found in this chapter.   A
purely spiritual heaven would have had no meaning in the days
of the Israelites.   Moses and his people could only understand
such words as brooks, fountains, wheat, barley, vines, fig trees,
and pomegranates ; God meant all these words to be the beginning of spiritual terms, and the spirituality of the terms never
could be realised until human experience had passed through

all the consciousness excited and sustained by these practical promises.

Moses does not shrink from propounding the apparent contradiction that even a life of obedience must also be a life of chastening :—"Thou shalt also consider in thine heart, that, as a man chasteneth his son, so the Lord thy God chasteneth thee. Therefore thou shalt keep the commandments of the Lord thy God, to walk in his ways, and to fear him" (vv. 5, 6). It might be thought that obedience would escape chastening, and no doubt it would if the obedience were perfect; but obedience itself being, under present conditions, partial or imperfect, chastening is needed for the purification of motive and the subjugation of will. The wise man says that a wise parent seeketh chastening for his son. "Whom the Lord loveth he chasteneth"—is a doctrine which the greatest teachers of Christianity have not shrunk from declaring. Chastening does not always mean what is generally understood as punishment. Chastening may mean a trial of patience, so that the will may be taught the habit of waiting, and expectation may become the beginning of prayer. God has always recognised the value of the element of *time* in the schooling of the human race. He did not give all his revelation at once, he did not send his Son into the world at the beginning : he does not immediately answer all prayers : the mystery of the operation of time has never yet been fully understood ; day is to be added to day, and one event is to be linked on to another, periods of rest are to intervene between periods of activity, and the judgment which man may pronounce upon God is to be deferred until the divine way has been perfectly accomplished. The purpose of chastening is to reveal a man unto himself: "To humble thee, and to prove thee, to know what was in thine heart;" we do not know ourselves until after the test of many days. We are surprises unto ourselves. By the utterance of language, the adoption of policies, the accumulation of companionships and responsibilities we amaze ourselves by the variety, the subtlety, and the persistency of life. We learn in hunger what we could never understand in fulness. To be kept standing throughout the night dews and knocking at inhospitable doors may give us definitions of home and security which the enjoyment of such blessings might never originate. The humble and obedient soul rejoices

that life has not one burden too many to carry, or one tear too
hot to shed, or one difficulty too severe to encounter; it says,—
All these things are appointed as gracious necessities in the perfecting of my education; I know that my Redeemer liveth; I know
that all things work together for good to them whose love is set
upon the living God. This spirit drives away the demon of
impatience and blesses and tranquillises the soul with the angel
of heavenly confidence. If the children of God suffered nothing
but punishment, those who look on from the outside might well
wonder as to the rewards and issues of virtue even in this world:
but chastening is not punishment, it is training, it is education, it
is experience, it is part of an inscrutable but beneficent method.
Blessed are they who wait until the end, and who speak not
of the judgments of God until they have seen all the glory of
heaven.

It would seem that in this direction the thought of Moses
steadfastly moved. What was God's object in bringing out Israel
from the land of Egypt, from the house of bondage, and leading
the people through that great and terrible wilderness, wherein
were fiery serpents and scorpions and drought, where there was no
water ? Why did God bring forth water out of the rock of flint ?
Moses gives the tender and noble reply :—"That he might
humble thee, and that he might prove thee, to do thee good at thy
latter end." That is the sublime purpose ! If we exclude the
"latter end" from our view of divine methods we shall certainly
be entangled in the thicket of details. The latter end is not in
our keeping ; but it is set before us in order to restrain our
passion and attemper our imagination and cultivate our patience.
It is something to know that at the end God means to do us good.
That should be a steadfast fact in the mind, and may be used in
many different relations, but all for the same purpose. What of
the difficulties of the way if the end is to be bright and beautiful
heaven ? What of the battle and storm here and now if according to our steadfastness and loyalty to divine principles is to be
the splendour of the divine recognition in the land of glory ?
Thus we draw ourselves on by the latter end. Again and again
we tenderly exclaim : "Let me die the death of the righteous, and
let my last end be like his." The latter end will explain everything. On the last day of life we may see more than we have

ever beheld during the whole course of our pilgrimage. Sudden glory may drive away every cloud and shadow, and bring in eternal day. One whisper from the upper spheres spoken to the dying may dissolve every doubt, break down every bound and barrier separating the soul from God, and admit the spirit into celestial liberty. We will not be deterred by to-day's difficulties. We shall not be tempted by sneering opponent or bitter sceptic or godless life to regard the providence of heaven as bounded by any one day. Give God whatever time he requires, and when he has accomplished the hours claimed by his purpose and has declared the consummation of his design in our life, we may be permitted to give some opinion as to "the way" by which we have been led and the method by which our best life has been sustained.

But Moses will not stop at this point. He becomes eloquent in lofty religious warning. Towards the close of the chapter he says:—"And it shall be, if thou do at all forget the Lord thy God, and walk after other gods, and serve them, and worship them, I testify against you this day that ye shall surely perish. As the nations which the Lord destroyeth before your face, so shall ye perish; because ye would not be obedient unto the voice of the Lord your God" (vv. 19, 20). Thus the way of the Lord is equal. Disobedience means penalty as certainly as obedience means reward. The two courses are openly set before us. It is undoubtedly within our liberty to oppose God, to set up an altar of our own, to invent commandments out of our own imagination, and to serve whom we will and as we will; in these matters we have no right, but according to our moral constitution we have the liberty: but God has not hidden from us the consequences of such perverseness and idolatry: nor are those consequences partial in their operation or alterable in their pressure; they are tremendous consequences, too awful to be expressed in words, too appalling to be encompassed by the imagination. This is where I rest in the matter of everlasting punishment. What that term may mean it is impossible for any human mind to conceive. It would seem as if God himself felt the inadequateness of language to express the infinite idea. The prayer of every man should be,—My soul, come not thou into this secret. Men should never trifle with the idea of the punishment of sin; it is everlasting punishment; it is eternal penalty; it is an expression of the horror of God as his infinite holiness looks upon the abomination of sin. " Be not deceived ; God is not mocked : for whatsoever a man soweth, that shall he also reap." This is not a one-sided law; it is the impartial law which holds within its ample scope all that is terrible in the idea of perdition and all that is sublime in the promise of heaven.

PRAYER.

ALMIGHTY GOD, we seek the truth. Jesus Christ said : " I am the Way, the Truth, and the Life." We would see Jesus ; we would fix the attention of our love and expectation upon thy Son, and receive from him what he alone can give—life, pardon, peace. Without him we can do nothing. We are powerless when cut away from the Vine and the upper life, the divine and eternal ; then we fall back into the dust : we are without spirit or force or goodness of will. We can do all things through Christ which strengtheneth us,—yea, we can bear much fruit and make the Father glad. May we abide in Christ ; may we look to the Son of God ; may we fix our whole love upon Jesus, and, studying his law with a complete attention, may we obey it with a consenting will. We thank thee for all the words spoken by the Son of God ; they are spirit, they are life, they are full of tenderest love ; they lift the cloud from the outlook of the mind and shed eternal glory on things beyond. Never man spake like this Man. We wonder at the gracious words which proceed out of his mouth,—how full of wisdom ! how tender with heavenly unction ! how adapted to our necessity and pain ! When he concludes his speech the heart, grateful and enraptured, says,— My Lord and my God ! May Christ ever speak to us, ever abide with us, walk with us on the evening road, and begin at Moses and all the Prophets and the Psalms, and show unto us the things concerning himself; and as the wondrous speech proceeds our heart shall burn within us, and we shall know that we are near the bush out of which the Lord spake unto Moses. We bless thee for thine house, its security, its quietness, its spirit of holy peace. Be near us, every one. Touch the sad heart, and give it one hour's release from burdensomeness. Look upon the struggling life, and the glance of thine eye shall be as a guarantee of hope and conquest. Bring back the prodigal ; he has many a weary mile to return, but if it shall come into his heart that thou art expecting him and longing for him with all the yearning of love his steps may be hastened, and the miles will soon be passed. Comfort us in our sorrow ; carry our burdens a while for us. Seal our eyelids in peaceful sleep, and on the morning we shall rise invested with new energy and inspired with new hope.

This prayer we say, every word of it, in the name of him who, once crowned with thorns, is now crowned with all the crowns of heaven Amen.

Deut. viii. 16.

"That he might humble thee, and that he might prove thee, to ao thee good at thy latter end."

THE DESIGN OF AFFLICTION.

IT can never be inappropriate to address men upon the subject of affliction. In that one solemn fact there is a whole philosophy. How comes it that in this green world, with its blue skies, it can never be inappropriate to address a large assembly of human creatures on the subject of human sorrow ? Laughter would often be out of place, and merriment would be a sin ; but tenderness, sympathy, recognition of tears and heartache and weariness—why, almost at the wedding feast such allusions would evoke an assenting sigh. There must be some reason under all this. There is not a man living but knows what is meant by grief and pain, trouble and fear, suffering and sorrow. These are the well-known words that need no explanation—their utterance is their exposition. The heart knoweth his own bitterness. Every man's sorrow has an accent of its own, as every man's joy has a smile that he could find nowhere else. It is a notable fact that everywhere the Bible recognises the existence of affliction. In no other book is affliction so minutely and pathetically delineated. It seems to have been written on purpose to talk about affliction, sorrow, pain, death. It would seem as if the Book could have had no existence but for darkness and trouble, sorrow and anxiety. No feature of affliction escapes the attention of the Bible. The black image throws its fretted shadow over the whole area of the Book. You find affliction in Genesis. The Bible cannot begin except in the night-time, in the hour of darkness and under the gloom of sin. You cannot find a single historical book without finding the black line of affliction running through all the moving narrative. And the Psalms—why, affliction is the mournful inspiration

of the Psalter. The Psalter would not be a book were there
no affliction in the world. All that is noblest in its pathos,
sublimest in its solace, and grandest in its outlook, it owes to the
fact that at the root of human life is the worm of human sorrow.
Why is not the Bible all joyful ? Why is it not a series of
military marches ? Why does it not sound the timbrel and beat
the cymbal and cause the trumpet's blare of triumph and joy to be
heard on every page and through every scene ? Do let us get at
the reason of the mournful tone which pervades the holy revelation. That reason we give in one word. It may admit of controversy in terms ; but it admits of no dispute in facts. The
brief, grim, tremendous answer is—SIN. But my immediate
purpose does not lead me in that direction. The one inquiry
which challenges my mind, and to which I would venture to
call attention, is this : Granted that sin is the parent of sorrow,
and of affliction and death, what are God's uses of affliction ?
What does God mean when he afflicts the children of men ? Has
he condescended to explain his intention ? Does he thunder and
lighten upon the world without cause ? Do the arrows of his
wrath fly without moral intent, or gracious control ? What is
the meaning of chastening, loss, grief, disappointment, affliction,
in any, in all its dark and trying phases ? Happily we are not
left to conjecture. We go to the Book that speaks about affliction, to receive an answer to our urgent inquiry. What is God's
design in troubling and chastening human life ? Here is one
reason which I will quote directly from the Book itself. Let us
be silent, let us cause our nimble, but often faulty, fancy to sit
down whilst we listen with the attention of the heart to the
inspired explanation of human discipline : "Remember all the
way which the Lord thy God led thee, these forty years in the
wilderness, to humble thee and to prove thee to know what was
in thine heart, whether thou wouldest keep his commandments
or no." There is a twofold design of chastening. The first is
self-revelation, "to know what was in thine heart." Some things
can only be got at by fire. There are depths in our consciousness that nothing can sound but pain, anguish, bitterness, sorrow.
And these are not all bad ; sometimes pain works its way down
to our better nature, touches into gracious activity our noblest
impulses, and evokes from our heretofore dumb lips the noblest

prayer. Sometimes we see farther through our tears than through our laughter. It is better to go to the house of mourning than to the house of feasting. Many a man owes all that he knows about himself, in its reality and in its best suggestiveness —not to prosperity, but to adversity. Not to light, but to darkness. The angel of trouble has spoken to him, in whispers that have found their way into the inmost hearing of the heart.

The next design of affliction given in this quotation is "whether thou wouldest keep his commandments or no." Obedience is the purpose which God has in view. There can be no grand life until we have learned to obey. It is good for a man to have to obey. It is a continual lesson, a daily discipline. He gathers from it a true consciousness of his own capacity and his own strength, and he begins to ask questions of the most serious intent. From the beginning God's purpose was that we should obey. You cannot obey in any good and useful sense the spirit of evil. You only get good from the exercise of obedience when that exercise goes against your own will and chastens it into gracious submission. I say this the more clearly, lest some should imagine that there is no good in obedience in the abstract. A young person might say, "Then I will obey the spirit that bids me indulge myself, evade my lessons, my duties ; trifle with my engagements. That will be obedience." So it may. But it is an obedience that brings no good along with it. It goes with the current of your own evil nature. It is an acquiescence that pleases you, not a discipline that tests your noblest and most useful qualities. It is good for a man to obey —it shows him that he is not God. It brings him down to his proper level. It enables him to say, "I do not wish to do this. I would rather not do it ; the thing in itself is right, but I wish to evade it or do something that may be supposed to be equivalent to it, but in a pleasanter way." Now a man has that battle to fight ; every battle must begin in a man's heart. You cannot fight your battles with your hand, you must have thrown the devil in a secret encounter and crushed his head in the concealment of nightly agony of prayer and thought, and then in the open light and the broad highway your victories will come easily to you. Obedience is not abstinence of the hand ; it is acquiescence of the heart. The Lord therefore says, "I sent this trouble upon thee to know what was in thine heart, whether thou wouldest keep my commandments or no." Self-revelation and filial obedience—these are part of God's design in sending afflictions upon us.

Take another explanation : " I will forsake them, and I will hide my face from them, and they shall be devoured, and many evils and troubles shall befall them, so that they will say in that day, Are not these evils come upon us, because our God is not among us ? " Sometimes God's withdrawments evoke from the heart conscious of his absence the most poignant and eager prayers. He says, " I will go away that they may miss me." He says, " I will withdraw and cause the walls of their security to tremble and the roof of their defence to let the storm pour down through it in order that they may begin to ask great questions." He will not have us fretting the mind with little inquiries and petty interrogations. He will force us to vital questionings : " Are not these things come upon us, because our God is not among us ? " Why deal with symptoms and not with real diseases ? Why try merely to clean the window when you have shut out the sun ? Why paint the cheek when you know the disease is in the heart ? It is thus that men awake oftentimes to a great interest in spiritual things. They build up walls so far, and in the morning they find them thrown down. They say, " It is the wind." They build them again, and again they are thrown down, and they say, " It was the vibration caused by passing vehicles." They build them up again, and again they are thrown down. And now they say, " How is this ? Are the spiritual presences against us ? Are the secrets of the universe turned into our enemies ? Are we working along forbidden lines ? Why this overturning ? Why this daily mockery ? " And then, with faces upturned, they catch the secret in the light, not in the dust, and find that it was God himself who prevented their bricks cohering and who melted their cement—God who caused his geometry to fight against their bad masonry. That may be the reason why you sustained the tremendous disaster last week. That may be the reason why the postman brings you no deliverance, why every letter brings fire with it, why every envelope is full of stings, and why every communication becomes a threat and a fear. O man, *that* may be the reason, and you, poor fool, have been thinking all the time that it was some little accident or matter of detail ; not thinking that God's round heaven was fighting against you and from its every inch sending out stings and rebukes of fire.   Here is an exact explanation of the law.   God says : " I will withdraw, I will forsake them, I will go away that they may ask, ' Are not these evils come upon us, because our God is not among us ? ' "   That may be the reason you have no joy at home ; it is a God-forsaken house.   You may have your altar there, you may utter your morning and evening prayer there, you may turn over the sacred leaves as if seeking for something in the dust there.   But you have no God—great, fatherly, ever-shining presence, gentle benediction, brooding heart, and tender pity.   That may be the reason why your table is not steady, why the bread turns sour in your mouth, why the water is all fire-drinking, why the fire goes out suddenly and you know not why.   That may be the cause.   Search for God in the house, ask him to come back again, say you have found the reason now and you mourn it, and ask him to return.

Take another answer : " They shall bear the punishment of their iniquity . . . that the house of Israel may no more go astray from me."   Punishment—meant to bring men home again.   That is God's weapon, and you cannot steal it.   You do wrong, and the scorpion stings you.   You cannot bribe the scorpion, or tame it, or please it.   Do what you will, it is a scorpion still.   You say you will eat and drink abundantly, and grow your joys in your body, and the blood saith : " No ! " And every bone says : " No ! "   And the head and the heart say : " No ! we are God's, and not in us shall you grow any joy that is not of the nature of his own purpose and will." The bones, the joints, the sinews, the nerves, the whole scheme of the physical constitution of man, all fight for God. You have your enmities in the intellect and your oppositions in the imagination, and your troubles of a technical kind, and you try to wriggle your way out of the morality of Christianity. By some theological jugglery, by posing as an " honest doubter," you want to drink the wine of the dishonest glutton and wine-bibber.   But God will cause his laws to speak for him and defend him ; so you shall be beaten and punctured and troubled. You shall have no sleep, or in sleep a hell in sleep !   And what a hell there can be in a bad dream! What is God's purpose in this? To bring you home again, and nothing else.

Take another statement of the cause and purpose of God in this matter of afflicting men: "I will cause you to pass under the rod, and I will bring you into the bond of the covenant . . . there shall ye remember your ways, and all your doings, wherein ye have been defiled; and ye shall loathe yourselves in your own sight for all your evils that ye have committed." There again is the internal mystery. It is not the heart that needs must be revealed. You cannot argue with a man who is running down to hell with the consent of all his powers. Argue with him! Your argument and eloquence would be thrown away upon him. You must so show the evil of his doings as to work in the man self-loathing. You may show him pictures of evil, and he will gaze upon them—nay, he will buy them and hang them up in his rooms at home and point them out to his friends as works of vigour and power and wondrous artistic skill. He will not regard them as mirrors reflecting his own image. The work must be done in his soul. He must so see evil as to hate himself—self-disgust is the beginning of penitence and amendment. When the Prodigal came to himself—saw himself as he really was—he said: "I have sinned against Heaven." Every branch that beareth fruit, he purgeth it, that it may bring forth more fruit. That is another purpose of God in affliction. God sent his servant Paul a thorn in the flesh that he should not be exalted above measure. And to the text, "that he might humble thee and that he might prove thee," there is the sweet answer—After thou hast tried me thou wilt bring me forth as gold. How much education some of us need! I envy some men, because they so soon, to all seeming, get through their lesson and are good, and others of us require time after time affliction upon affliction, and still the furnace fire is heaped up, and still we remain in the burning, and we seem to become no better. One man had a death in his family, and from that moment he became a new creature. Others have carried out child after child, and still the home is without God and the life without hope in the world. Some men, after one debauch, have hated themselves so that hatred turned into prayer and penitence and trust in

God; and they stood straight up, renewed, redeemed, emancipated. And others have been for years in the mire and in the filth, and wallowed there and enjoyed it. Debauch after debauch, and become the worse for every experience. Some men have seen the error of their ways quite early, and yet seem to still go on repeating evil thought and deed without learning anything. The object of God is to do us good at our latter end. If the end of digging grave after grave is that we see our sin as God sees it, and hate it as Christ hated it, then all the loss has been for our good. God means us to be men, he means to purify us and sanctify us, to make us holy, to restore his image and likeness in us—in Christ, through Christ, by the power of Christ, by the ministry of his sacrificial blood, and the ministry of God the Holy Ghost. This is the will of God, even your sanctification, and to get that will accomplished he has to take away the first-born and the last-born, the dear old father or mother, the dearest friend, the kindliest presence, health, fortune, position. He has to get us down to the root, branch and stem and all, right down; but he says: "The root shall remain and become good and strong and young again, and out of this root shall come beauty and fruitfulness such as shall please the heavenly Husbandman."

We all have affliction. Yours seems to be greater than mine—mine may seem to be greater than yours. But let us know that there cannot be affliction in our life without its being under God's control, and he will not suffer us to be tried above that we are able to bear it, and with every trial he will make a way of escape. He does not willingly grieve the children of men. He is pruning us, cutting us, nursing us, purifying us by divers processes to the end that he may set us in his heavens—princes that shall go out no more for ever.

Let us now look at some portions of Biblical testimony, and see how far they cover what we ourselves know of the afflictions and distresses of life. Let us begin at the lowest point, and step by step move onward to the higher altitudes. Take as a starting testimony this pitiful speech of an ancient offender, "We are verily guilty concerning our brother, in that we saw the anguish of his soul, when he besought us, and we would not hear; there-

fore is this distress come upon us." Afflictions do not spring
out of the ground. Behind the meanest action there is a
whole philosophy. We could almost write a Bible ourselves,
so much have we seen of life, of guilt, of consequential pain,
and of possible hell. The brethren of Joseph were self-convicted. They did not refer their distress to some high theory
of the universe, with which they had little or nothing to do.
Placing their finger on the black line which that finger itself
had written, they said in candour (which is one element of
penitence), "This is our doing." What a world it would be
if distress did not follow crime! Life would be insupportable.
Society would be impossible. It is the biting serpent that
keeps us right. We make broad ways, along which the penal
hosts of God come armed with weapons of righteous vengeance
to inflict upon us the punishment appropriate to our guilt.
You are in distress ; ask the reason why. We have seen that
distress is not always a sign of divine indignation, because
distress is not always a consequence of personal guilt. But,
looking at the matter from the standpoint of the text which
is before us, let us ask ourselves this plain question, "How
did this distress come upon me ? " It is a pain of the body.
You can easily account for it. It is a pain in the conscience—
the witnesses are at the door. It is a dread fear of to-morrow.
The reason is in the way you lived yesterday. There is no
mystery about many a case of distress. If you have not a
home, a place of security and of defence and sacred retreat,
you know how you came to be in that position. You broke
the law. You were unkind to your brother. You neglected
your natural dependants. You sinned away your opportunities.
You know the reason why ; so do not make a mystery of it
and add to the distress consequent upon actual guilt the intellectual pain of making mysteries out of plain and indisputable
facts.

Take another instance of the result of affliction, which will
show a very pitiful aspect of human nature. "Pharaoh sent
and called for Moses and Aaron, and said unto them, I have
sinned this time : the Lord is righteous, and I and my people
are wicked." That was the right result. Wherein, then, is
the pitifulness of the aspect of human nature which is herein

disclosed ? It is in the fact that Pharaoh's speech was the expression of an insincere spirit. He did not mean what he said. He was ready to repent in words, but not in deeds. If confession of the lip would placate the angry heavens he would utter any number of confessions. But far down in his heart was the untamed spirit of rebellion and alienation and self-idolatry. Is it not so with you ? " If God will take away this pain that troubles my life and makes existence intolerable, I will confess my sin." " If God will be gracious this time, I will never offend against his law and sanctuary any more." " If the Lord will enable me to tear this lion in pieces, and rend this bear, then surely I will go up to his house, and mine shall be the loudest and sweetest voice in the holy psalm." You do not mean it. You want to get rid of a burden. This is not genuine repentance. You want to escape consequences, not to hate sin. And thus to the original criminality you add the petty offence of cowardice. Men do not like to walk in the hell which they enkindle. It is no love of heaven that makes them pray for a speedy and complete escape. But the criminal in every case is not a hero, but a coward. Sin is never valorous. Boastful it may be for a time ; but valour, nobility, courage, and chivalry are inconsistent with its nature. It lights its hell, and then would flee away from the flames. That is the reason why you are so far back in your moral progress. When you were last afflicted you said, " If God will raise me up this time, I will devote to him so much of my income, so much of my strength, and so much of my time." God did raise you up, and from that day to this your vow has lain upon his altar a dead letter. Do not escape the impeach-ment ; it is meant to be heavy, terrific, emphatic with the thunder of God's own anger. You will be laid down again, and prayer shall mock your pain, and the leaden heavens shall send back your piteous cry. Awake, thou that sleepest ! Remember your obligations, and now say, I will no longer withhold performance of a vow plighted under circumstances that can never be forgotten.

Take another instance of the effect of affliction, also an instance of the lower kind. "The people came to Moses and said, We have sinned, for we have spoken against the Lord, and against

thee; pray unto the Lord that he take away the serpents from
us." What a mean request! You breed serpents, and are then
afraid of them. You are responsible for their existence, and
then you cry to God to kill your own progeny. I cannot find
one instance of valour and nobleness in all the ranks of sin.
God teaches us by fear. It is impossible to look upon life in
all its scheme and outline without seeing that fear has an important part to play in the education of mankind. The child
is often ruled by fear. Imagination is called upon to magnify
penalties in the case of the child. Many a threat, inspired by
love, is directed to the child that the attention of the little
offender may be more completely and usefully awakened. And
no preaching can be complete that does not, now and again,
remind the people of the terrors of the law. It is no light
thing to sin; and, come to what conclusion you may about
the future of the wicked soul, there can be no doubt that that
future is one of tremendous agony. Who will dare it? Who
will willingly go forward to it? I know of no theory of the
Future of the soul which by some point or other does not
bring in the righteous punishment of offending man. You can
only affect some persons through fear. Without imagination
of the better kind, without high sentiment, without noble education, without generous impulses — they can only be touched
along the line of fear. So I do not visit with criticism of an
embarrassing kind the efforts of men who preach hell rather
than heaven to certain classes of hearers. High discourse
about the nobler spaces, the infinite liberties, the glorious
sanctuaries yet to be revealed and enjoyed, would be lost on
an audience so debased. God, therefore, has again and again
in his process of educating the human race, availed himself
of fear for the purpose of awakening the attention of the lost.

Take another instance. "After all that is come upon us for
our evil deeds, and for our great trespass, seeing that thou
our God hast punished us less than our iniquities deserve."
Man can only be taught that lesson by suffering. Without
suffering he would be as a worker in cold iron. He must be
made to see that at the root of all suffering is sin. Hence
the grandeur of the mission of Christ; hence its royal sublimity
and its divine beneficence. He came not to deal with symptoms,

but with realities—interior essences and facts; so he taketh away the sin of the world. It is an inclusive act. To take away the root is to take away the branches. To remove the sin is to destroy the disease. To heal the heart is to bring the flush of health to the cheek that was blanched through suffering. Do not look at secondary causes, and so play the practical fool. Look at beginnings, at springs, at fountain-heads, and find in sin the one secret of all suffering.

Now let us go to the higher ground, and let us hear this good confession: "Thou art just in all that is brought upon us; for thou hast done right, but we have done wickedly." That word "just" is a word which cannot be dropped out of the history of divine Providence without destroying the idea of Providence itself. "Thou art just." Hell opens its lips and says, "Thou art just." All sufferers who have come to the root and foundation of their suffering have said, "Thou art just." The pain is intolerable, but it is just. The night is dark, but not so black as the sin which gathered the appalling cloud. Confession must be kept in its right place in every review of Providence. It is not enough that we confess that Providence is royal, divine, wonderful, mysterious, perplexing; we must come to a moral word somewhere in our criticism and discourse, and that one moral word which is needful to give dignity to our survey and estimate is the eternal word, "*just.*" So says the suffering world; not a pain too many, not an agony too keen, not a night too dark, not a wind too cold, not a stream too deep or swift, not a sting too burning—thou, O Lord, King of angels, only Potentate, thou art just. When a man can truly say that, with the emphasis of his intelligence and affection, he is not far from the kingdom of God.

Take a still loftier instance. "Thou, O God, hast proved us: thou hast tried us, as silver is tried. Thou broughtest us into the net; thou laidst affliction upon our loins . . . but thou broughtest us out into a wealthy place." The road was difficult, but the end was grand. We came through thickets and thorns and stony places and rocky heights and over wildernesses, but the end is paradise —the end is heaven. A wealthy place here means a large place. God would enlarge our inheritance and add to our liberty, and no roof that we can build over our heads is grand enough for us, so he builds the roof of the sky, and sows it with the beauty of stars. He means to bring you into a large place; into new ideas, new relations, new opportunities, new hopes. " In my Father's house are many mansions." " Beloved, now are we the sons of God, and it doth not yet appear what we shall be." We are now learning the alphabet—hard work; it is difficult to bring together into picture and music and harmony; but presently a great light will shine upon us, and a new inspiration will seize our intelligence and our whole moral nature and lift it up to a sublimer plane, which shall read the revelation of God with new capacities and new sensations. Your affliction ought to have made you richer—richer in experience, richer in every department of life and thought; and if it has failed to do so God's design has not been successful.

Now let us hear an individual testimony. So far the testimony has been uttered in the plural number. Here is a man who will speak for himself, and in speaking for himself shall speak for the whole world. " Before I was afflicted I went astray : but now have I kept thy word. . . It is good for me that I have been afflicted ; that I might learn thy statutes." You cannot read the Bible in health with any true edification, or with any deep perception of its inner meaning. It is not in fatness and prosperity to deliver the music of revelation with effect upon the attention of those who are listening. The Bible can be best read when the throat is choked with some sob of penitence, or when the reading is made incoherent because the print is punctuated with falling tears. The Bible cannot be rhetorically read, so as to bring out its spiritual purpose and intent and force. It is best read when the voice shakes, when the eyes are dim, and when the whole heart is alive with conflicting joy and sorrow. Do not go to men of shallow and narrow experience to know what the Bible is. Religious questions cannot be discussed in cold blood. Religion, in the Christian acceptation of the term, is blood, is sacrifice, is agony, is life at its highest point. To refer to the figure just used —to come to the Bible in a merely cold and critical mood is attempting to unite pieces of cold iron by beating them. Without fire progress is impossible. So the flippant man can never be a great critic or a great preacher. The man destitute of veneration can never make his influence deeply and lastingly felt in the review or the recitation of the divine word.

Then comes the crowning result: "Remembering mine affliction and my misery, the wormwood and the gall. My soul hath them still in remembrance, and is humbled in me." Here we have mellowness of character. Your dignity, your energy, have fallen into their proper places, and the supreme characteristic of your life and spirit now is mellowness. Affliction has been sanctified to us, and so the character is enriched, the tone is subdued, our judgment of other people is larger and nobler, our capacity of sympathy is enhanced and ennobled, and now we can speak out of the heart, rich with the manifold treasures of God. Once there was uppermost in our thinking and our speech a feeling of cleverness, sagacity, intellectual force, or even some gleams of genius; but since we have had the grave dug and filled, and another dug by its side—since the favourite flower has been blighted and the heart has been taken away; since the delight of the eyes has been removed; since the roof has been battered in by the fierce and destructive storm; since the sky has been blackened with one fatal night, our voice has become mellow, tender, sympathetic, and the touch of our hand has been as the touch of a redeeming, saving power. Are we the better for our affliction? Are we the richer in all the higher elements of character? Let each ask the question for himself. Or has the wine of God become sour through neglect or misuse? What then? What is the preacher's last cry? This: "Come, and let us return unto the Lord; for he hath torn, and he will heal us; he hath smitten, and he will bind us up." Could a broader gospel be preached? Could a tenderer tone be uttered? "All we like sheep have gone astray; we have turned every one to his own way." Is there any voice to address us in faraway places in tones that can be well heard down in the soul? Yes. What does it say? "Come, and let us return unto the Lord." What then? "Let the wicked forsake his way, and the unrighteous man his thoughts: and let him return unto the Lord, and he will have mercy upon him; and to our God, for he will abundantly pardon." These are great words, these are grand offers. All other words and offers become mean and commonplace and contemptible in the presence of a word which means

Love, an offer which means Pardon, and a return which means
Heaven.

Let us next consider in what *spirit* affliction may be accepted.
We have studied God's design in afflicting men, and we have seen
some instances of the success of that method. Let us now see
how variously as to spirit and interpretation affliction may be
received at the hands of God. By " affliction " do not narrowly
understand mere bodily suffering, but trial of every kind ; yea, the
whole burden and discipline of life. Understand that affliction in
this large sense must be endured. The question is not whether
we will have affliction or not. Affliction we must have. No door
can be made to shut so closely as to keep affliction out of the
house. Seeing, therefore, that in some form or other we must
receive discipline ; or undergo trial ; or endure pain, the question
is, In what spirit shall we receive the inevitable discipline of life ?
Here we have choice of methods. At this point what is called
" free-will " operates most fully. We can be wise—we can be
foolish. It is for us—grasping, so far as we may be able to
include it, the whole purpose of God, in the constitution and
education of our life—to say in what spirit we shall regard our
subordination and the discipline which it inevitably implies.
The question is a great one, and as it must come before every
mind in some form, let us endeavour to give it adequate
consideration and becoming reply.

We must go to history for our illustrations ; and, turning to
history for my first illustration, I find that the discipline of life
may be received *impenitently.* Hear these words in solemn and
decisive proof : " If ye will not be reformed by me by these
things, but will walk contrary unto me ; then will I also walk
contrary unto you, and will punish you yet seven times for your
sins." That warning was addressed to impenitent hearts. The
rain fell upon the rocks and melted them not. The sunshine
poured its horn of light upon the sand, and it answered with no
tiny flower. But the case is put with tremendous force. God
will not yield. Who can last the longer, God or man ? The
Infinite or the finite ? Whose arrows will give out soonest—his
who has but a handful, or his whose quiver is the universe ?
Clearly understand that God will not yield, and understand that

his "will not" is not an instance of stubbornness or mere obstinacy. God cannot yield. Righteousness cannot give way. The
standard of the sanctuary cannot alter its height. The balances
of the sanctuary cannot accommodate themselves to conditions
and circumstances. Right is right, and no tittle or jot of it can
be abated. Not only so, God will increase punishment where
affliction is misunderstood or impenitently received. "I will punish
you yet seven times for your sins." That is, " I will give you
sevenfold more punishment." He begins with the little penalty.
He lays his finger-tip upon you to give you to know that you are
on the wrong road. If you flee further from him, he increases
the weight of his hand. If you repeat your sin, he smites you
with cords. If you renew it, he chastises you with scorpions.
It is a fearful thing to fall into the hands of the living God. Now
heed; say frankly with penitence and contrition, "Father, I have
sinned; the blame is all mine ; God be merciful unto me a sinner.
I thought to make my way in the universe in spite of thee. I
cannot do it. I do not yield because I am foiled, but because
I feel my folly and I sink under my sin. God pity me and save
me." Will you say that ? Then your affliction shall become
your strength. The night shall break into light and beauty, and
the wilderness shall blossom as the rose ; and the place where
your pain was keenest shall be the centre of your surest and
noblest joys. But I warn you, God will not give way—God
cannot give way. The one thing God can do is to multiply your
affliction seven times, and to cover up the arch of the sky with a
night denser than has yet blackened the firmament.

Turning to history again, I find that affliction may be received
self-approvingly, or self-excusingly, and so may fail of its benign
purpose. The proof is in these words : " In vain have I smitten
your children; they received no correction. . . . Thou sayest,
Because I am innocent, surely his anger shall turn from me."
The correction has been administered, but has not been received.
It has been misunderstood. It has been taken in hardness. It
has been resented as an injustice. It has been treated as if it
came from an enemy, and not from a friend. The deadly
sophism of your innocence must be rooted out before you can be
cured. The Pharisee must be destroyed before the man can be
saved. Will you understand that ? So long as you have one

little petty virtue that you indulge, and patronise, and exhibit, and trust to, God's back must be turned upon you. The difficulty of our life is our self-righteousness. The idea that we are good, and therefore do not deserve pain, sorrow, misfortune, loss, is the damning fallacy of life. We must die before we can live. We must feel ourselves to be empty-handed before we can be truly rich. Thou hast said, " I am rich, and increased with goods, and have need of nothing ; and knowest not that thou art wretched, and miserable, and poor, and blind, and naked." God will not share the house of your trust with any rival deity. He is not one who will sit down upon equal terms with your respectability, and virtue, and excellence. Until we understand that we can make no religious progress. Here the superficial reasoner has the advantage over the Christian thinker, because he says to you, " It is impossible you can be so very bad; you are kind, you have good thoughts about people, you are neighbourly, you are hospitable, you are socially honourable, you are in good repute amongst your fellows, you are not ill-natured, but kindly disposed." The man is telling you lies. You are none of these things, except in a relative and superficial sense. In the sanctuary we deal with realities, not incidental relations. We go to the core and root of things, and not to surfaces and to passing incidents. Judging ourselves by ourselves, we are all that the non-christian thinker has described us to be. But we are not now instituting a comparison between one man and another, but between the best man and God. Let that idea get well into your mind and heart, and you will say, " I have heard of thee by the hearing of the ear : but now mine eye seeth thee. Wherefore I abhor myself, and repent in dust and ashes." The great difficulty is for us to get rid of our respectability. Two men went up into the temple to pray ; the one a Pharisee, the other a publican. The Pharisee lauded himself; the publican hated himself, and asked for mercy. The Pharisee was a Pharisee after his prayer ; the publican was a justified man. Renounce excuses ; drop the hollow plea of self-justification, and throw yourselves wholly into the arms, yea, into the heart, of the Saviour of the world. Then your afflictions will be like angels that have taken you home. Your discipline will be a minister of God. Your loss will be the beginning of your gain, and you will spring up into a new youth and a fresh immortal strength, saying, "I can do all things through Christ which strengtheneth me." Other men have done it; why not **we**?

Turning again to history for illustration and argument, I find that affliction may be received *self-deceivingly*. The proof is in these words: "They have not cried unto me with their heart, when they howled upon their beds." Heart-crying is one thing, and mere howling is another. To howl is not to repent necessarily. We have howled enough, but our howling has not been of the right kind. There is a selfish howling. When some people are in pain they never think that they are paining their friends. They limit the suffering to themselves. Their thoughts never go out to those who watch and wait. They do not know that their pain inflicts distress upon the whole household. They confine themselves to themselves. There is no charity in their lamentations. There is no breadth in their sorrow, and therefore it is a selfish and a lost distress. Then there is a cowardly howling. Do not imagine that you are repentant merely because you are crying out. Perhaps you are only crying out because you have lost your property, lost your health, lost your standing —not because you have offended God and grieved the Spirit of Righteousness. The Lord takes notice of the howling, but he says, "They have not cried unto me with their heart, when they howled upon their beds." It was a selfish, cowardly, resentful howling, and not the sigh of penitence, or the storm of contrition. Here we have great difficulty. Men come to us with sad stories of distress, and they make long moans about pain and fear, about poverty and uselessness. They use the words which penitents might use, but not in a contrite spirit. Analyse their howling, and it is all selfish. Take their crying to pieces, so to say, and it is all because the place smarts on which God's whip fell. It is the flesh that complains; it is not the spirit that repents. When a bad man complains of his head, is he complaining of his sin? Is he not only waiting till he can gather himself together again that he may renew the contest against Heaven, and endeavour to find on earth a root that was never planted there?

One more point there is which I dare scarcely touch. How few know that the passage is in the Bible. It is a passage that proves that affliction may be received, in the fourth place, *despairingly*. Are there in any poems made by men such words as these? Tell me if any poet dare write such words: "They gnawed their tongues for pain, and blasphemed the God of heaven because of their pains and their sores, and repented not of their deeds." "My soul, come not thou into their secret." Some man wrote these words who had seen hell. We lightly utter the word. We try to modify its force and its meaning. We do what we can to mitigate the pressure of that tremendous punishment, which is implied in the use of such a term ; but when we have done our utmost at modification and mitigation, there remains this terrible fact, "They gnawed their tongues for pain," and with their gnawed tongues they "blasphemed the God of heaven." They felt their "pains and their sores," but they "repented not of their deeds," and God cannot give way. "As I live, saith the Lord God, I have no pleasure in the death of the wicked ; " but "the soul that sinneth, it shall die." Do not endeavour by any means to make God's hell a pleasure. Do not trifle with the idea of future punishment. Whatever it be, it is the last answer of Omnipotence to rebellious man. "It is a fearful thing to fall into the hands of the living God." This is not a question to be argued. It is not a theme for speculation. When logician and speculatist have accomplished their task, there remains the unexplained word—hell !

How are we receiving our afflictions ? "Come now, let us reason together." Ephraim of old was described as a "bullock unaccustomed to the yoke." In some countries the bullock is used for ploughing and for drawing vehicles. The poor ox is yoked, and, being unaccustomed to the yoke, it chafes under it. Its great shoulders protest against the violation of liberty. By-and-by the bullock becomes accustomed to the treatment, and submits itself to the service of man. Ephraim receiving the discipline of God was "as a bullock unaccustomed to the yoke." We do not take kindly to our troubles, afflictions, distresses, and losses. It is not natural that we should do so ; but, seeing that we have incurred them, we must receive them at God's hand, and become accustomed to the discipline ; and eventually submit ourselves to the service of God, which is the true liberty. How did Jesus Christ conduct himself under the afflictions which fell, in a plentiful rain, to his lot ? He was "a Man of sorrows, and acquainted with grief." His face was marred more than any

man's. He gave his back to the smiters, and his cheeks to them
that plucked off the hair. He bore the Cross. How did he
deport himself under the daily affliction of his life ? An affliction
not self-incurred, an affliction borne for others, an affliction
endured from before the foundation of the world ? Answer that
question. The reply is given : "Who for the joy that was set
before him endured the cross, despising the shame." Have we
that long look ? Is ours a narrow vision that sees the nearest
wall, or a keen, far telescopic eye that sees the horizon and the
land beyond ? Take in more field, make the worlds balance one
another and complete one another : life is not all earth. There is
a future state, and the future must interpret and ennoble the
present. How did Paul bear his afflictions ? By looking at the
things that are not seen. Keeping his heart's eyes fixed upon the
invisible, he said, " Our light affliction, which is but for a moment."
"We glory in tribulations also." What an " also " was that!
What an inclusive term ! How it dipped in and absorbed and
glorified all the processes and all the trials of this weary earthly
life ! "We glory in tribulations also." Only Christ can win that
conquest ! That field was never fought and won but by one
Captain, and his name is Christ. Receive your afflictions as of
the Lord's sending. Say, "The Lord gave, and the Lord hath
taken away ; blessed be the name of the Lord." I would kiss
his bereaving hand. "When he hath tried me, I shall come
forth as gold." " Thou hast been with me in six troubles, and in
the seventh thou wilt not forsake me." All tribulations can be
overcome in the grace and strength of Christ. "One of the elders
answered, saying unto me, What are these which are arrayed in
white robes ? and whence came they? And I said unto him, Sir,
thou knowest. And he said to me, These are they which came
out of great tribulation, and have washed their robes, and made
them white in the blood of the Lamb. Therefore are they before
the throne of God, and serve him day and night in his temple. . .
They shall hunger no more, neither thirst any more; neither shall
the sun light on them, nor any heat. For the Lamb which is in
the midst of the throne shall feed them, and shall lead them unto
living fountains of waters : and God shall wipe away all tears
from their eyes." It is enough ʟ It is heaven !

PRAYER.

ALMIGHTY GOD, do thou put thy Spirit within us; then shall we do the thing that is right, and walk steadfastly in the way of thy commandments. We would find the house of wisdom; her ways are ways of pleasantness and all her paths are peace. We would enter at her bidding, and partake of the feast which she has prepared. Yea, we would accept the hospitality which thou thyself hast offered: we would eat and drink abundantly at the table of the Lord, that we may renew our strength and be enabled to pursue our journey with fresh vigour, with burning zeal, with all-sustaining hope. They that wait upon the Lord shall renew their strength; yea, they shall become young again: the burden of the years shall fall away from them, and they shall stand up in all the freshness and power and buoyancy of early life. Such is the blessing which follows true and loving waiting upon God. We have not because we ask not, or because we ask amiss; the fault is in the prayer, not in the Giver. We have mistaken thy purpose, or thou wouldst surely have answered our petitions with great replies. We have sought to renew our youth vainly at other sources,—yea, we have hastened as if with frenzy to forbidden altars, that we might light the lamp of life with false fire; and, behold, the wind has blown out the flame, and we have been left in oppressive darkness. We will return unto the Lord; we will arise and go to our Father, and speak the language of penitence, and shed the tears of contrition, and make mention of the Cross, and avail ourselves of all the love of God. Thou hast guided us all our life long; not one day hast thou been absent from our life. Thou hast led thy people by a way that they knew not, and by paths they had not known. When we could not open the gate, thou hast thrown down the barrier; when the mountain was too high for our weariness to climb, thou didst touch the hill, and it vanished in smoke. Thou hast dried up for us rivers and seas; thou hast made solid the softest ground,—yea, thou hast wrought great wonders in our life; many a miracle hast thou set up in it as a witness of thy presence and thy power, and we are here to bless thee with unanimous praise, with a psalm of gratitude, uttered with all the fervour which memory can throw into our service, remembering how great has been thy goodness and how tender thy mercy. We will not be ashamed of thy providence: we will own to it; though there be many who mock us, we will say,—This is the Lord's doing, and it is marvellous in our eyes: this is our Father's will, and it is our desire to accept and obey it; this is the disposal of the Lord of the lot which we cast into the lap: we will accept his appointment and follow out his purpose. Enable us with heavenly strength so to say and so to do; then our life shall be no longer shattered and frayed out in weakness, but shall be gathered up in great strength, and in holy power shall proceed to the execution of the divine behest. Guide us, O thou great Jehovah! Jesus, still lead on! Be thou our light by night, our Captain in the daytime, a high power to which we may continually resort, a sanctuary in the wilderness. Afflict our afflictors, and save us from taking vengeance into our own hands. We fall into thine hands, thou Loving One; we rest in the Lord and wait patiently for him. The coming of Christ Jesus our Saviour shall be with the quietness of the dawn, and we shall not know it until a great light is round about us; we shall come with the silence of the growing corn, and we shall hardly be aware of the plentifulness of the divine bounty until we find ourselves standing in the midst of fields laden with golden wheat. Such blessings and honours fall to the lot of thy people—O may we be numbered in the host! Amen

Deut. viii. 18.

"But thou shalt remember the Lord thy God: for it is he that giveth thee power to get wealth."

THE THEOLOGY OF MONEY.

A DEEP conviction of this fact would turn human history into a sacrament. Receive into the mind the full impression of this doctrine, and you will find yourself working side by side with God, in the field, the warehouse, the bank, the shop, the office, the pulpit. What a blow this text strikes at one of the most popular and mischievous fallacies in common life—namely, that man is the maker of his own money! Men who can see God in the creation of worlds cannot see him suggesting an idea in business, smiling on the plough, guiding the merchant's pen, and bringing summer into a brain long winter-bound and barren. In the realm of commerce the Most High has been practically dethroned, and in his place have been set all manner of contemptible idols: we have put into the holy place trick and cunning, and to these we have sacrificed as if they had made our fortune and enriched our destiny with sunshine. We have locked up God in the church; or we have crushed him into the Bible like a faded rose-leaf; we have shut upon him the iron gate of the market-place; we have forced commerce into a kind of religious widowhood and compelled trade to adopt the creed of Atheism.

There is always danger in endeavouring to adjust the influence of second causes. The element of mediation enters very largely into God's government, one world being lighted by another, one man depending on another, and one influence diffusing itself in a thousand directions, and entering into the most subtle and complicated combinations; all this intercepts our vision of that which is original and absolute in energy. We have a difficulty in understanding anything but straight lines. If money fell from the sky like rain, or snow, or sunshine, we could perhaps more readily admit that it came from God; but because it comes through circuitous and sometimes obscure channels we do not feel upon it the warmth of the divine touch, and often we see upon it only the image of Cæsar. We are guilty, like an ancient harlot, on whose wicked head God poured out his wrath: "She said, I will go after my lovers, that give me my bread and my water, my wool and my flax, mine oil and my drink." But God hedged up her way with thorns, he caused her to lose her paths, and said in a tone which combined complaint and anger, "For she did not know that I gave her corn, and wine, and oil, and multiplied her silver and gold, which they prepared for Baal." He who gives the light of the sun gives also the oil which man enkindles into a flame, and supposes that result to be an invention of his own. Lebanon and Bashan are not more certainly divine creations than are the wool and flax which cover the nakedness of man. To the religious contemplation, the sanctified and adoring mind, the whole world is one sky-domed church, and there is nothing common or unclean.

God wishes this fact to be kept in mind by his people. In this instance, as in many others, God makes his appeal to recollection: "Thou shalt *remember.*" The fact is to be ever present to the memory; it is to be as a star by which our course upon troubled waters is to be regulated; it is to be a mystic cloud in the daytime, a guiding fire in the night season. The rich memory should create a rich life. An empty memory is a continual temptation. Mark the happy consequences of this grateful recollection. First of all, God and wealth are ever to be thought of together. "The silver and the gold are *mine.*" There is but one absolute Proprietor.

We hold our treasures on loan; we occupy a stewardship. Consequent upon this is a natural and most beautiful humility. "What hast thou that thou hast not received?" When the trader sits down in the evening to count his day's gains, he is to remember that the Lord his God gave him power to get wealth. When the workman throws down the instrument of his labour that he may receive the reward of his toil, he is to remember that the Lord his God gave him power to get wealth. When the young man receives the first payment of his industry, he is to remember that the Lord his God gave him power to get wealth. Thus the getting of money becomes a sacred act. Money is a mighty power; wealth occupies a proud position in all the parliament of civilisation. Trade thus becomes a means of grace and commerce an ally of religion. In one word, the true appreciation of this doctrine would restore every act of life to its direct and vital relation to the living God. There are men who say that the voice of the pulpit should never be heard in the market-place. They forget that they could not move a muscle but for the grace of God : nor could they originate or apply an idea but for the mercy of Heaven. Let us hold, in opposition to this atheistic commerce, that every ledger should be a Bible, true as if written by the finger of God ; that every place of business should be made sacred by the presence of righteousness, verity, honour, and justice. The man who can be atheistic in business could be atheistic in heaven itself. The man who never turns his warehouse into a church can hardly fail to turn the church into a warehouse. Even nominally Christian men are often unduly anxious that too much of what they call religion should not be introduced into places of trade. They speak about God with a regulated whisper, as if they were speaking about a ghost whose unfriendly eye was fixed upon them. When they refer to God it is with the motion of a trembling finger or an inflection of the voice which indicates anything but moral repose. Filial joy is wanting : the leaping heart is not known in the experience of such fear-ridden professors of Christianity. Men who make money with both hands, who run greedily after gain, and serve mammon with fervent zeal, are not likely to remember that the Lord their God gave them power to get wealth. Memory is occupied with other subjects. The heart is foreclosed. The whole nature acts as if it had entered into a bond to entertain no religious recollections. In enumerating the happy consequences arising from a grateful recognition of God's relation to wealth, the check upon all wastefulness and extravagance might be mentioned. Christianity enjoins frugality upon its disciples; its command is, "Gather up the fragments." The man who wastes money would also waste his moral dowry. An extravagant Christian—that is, a man who outruns his resources, his business, and his life—is likely to become a subtle felony. Money is one of the limitations of power, and to overstep that limitation is a practical blasphemy, an unpronounced but most terrible reproach upon divine arrangements. The temptation is for men to put forth their hand and appropriate forbidden wealth. The point of interdict may be in the sum, and not in the quality of the thing which is forbidden. It may be sometimes easier to abstain altogether from the fruit of a tree than to stop at a particular point in gathering that fruit, and to say to desire and appetite,—This is enough, and to take more is to commit theft in the sanctuary of God.

This, then, is the fundamental principle upon which Christians are to proceed—namely, that God giveth man power to get wealth, and consequently that God sustains an immediate relation to the property of the world. Take the case of a young man just entering business. If his heart is uneducated and unwatched, he will regard business as a species of gambling; if his heart be set upon right principles, he will esteem business as a moral service, as the practical side of his prayers, a public representation of his best desires and convictions. In course of time the young man realises money on his own account. Looking at his gold and silver, he says, "I made that." There is a glow of honest pride on his cheek. He looks upon the reward of his industry, and his eyes kindle with joy. Whilst he looks upon his first-earned gold the Bible says to him, gently and persuasively, "Thou shalt remember the Lord thy God: for it is he that giveth thee power to get wealth." Instantly his view of property is elevated, enlarged, sanctified. He was just about to say that his own arm had gotten him the victory, and to forget

that, though the image is Cæsar's, yet the gold is God's. What,
then, is the natural line of thought through which the successful
man would run under such circumstances? It would lie in some
such direction as this: What can be the meaning of this word
"remember"? Does it not call me to gratitude? Is it not
intended to turn my heart and my eye heavenward? As God
has given me "power to get wealth," am I not bound to return
some recognition of his goodness and mercy? A process of self-
examination like this must drive away from the mind many
thoughts and temptations which would subtract from its power
and degrade its influence. For want of asking questions, the
mind often goes without instruction and enrichment. The conscience should be required to put questions to the understanding
and the reason, and should gently constrain these noble powers
to make definite reply. Conscience is the great question-asking
centre of our constitution. All its questions are of a moral kind,
and a characteristic of them is that, however much they may be
silenced at the time, they recur with intenser energy as life nears
its solemn close. Better ask those questions at the outset, and
come to a clear understanding respecting them, than stifle their
purpose and condemn them to long speechlessness.

We speak of the "exceeding great and precious promises" of
God, but often overlook those which apply to our so-called
secular life. Is it to be imagined that Almighty God is an
unconcerned spectator of our commercial life? Does he leave
us without observation and sympathy in the field which is most
thickly occupied with all manner of well-adapted and urgent
temptations? The probability is that we need less protection in
the public sanctuary than we need in the public market-place.
Probably there is no point in all the mysterious line of life where
a man is so persistently and seductively attacked as at the point
of business. He sees how much he could do if he were not
limited by moral considerations; he thinks that even moral
breaches might be repaired by momentary compensations;
he detects with too keen an eye to what religious uses money
might be applied, whatever may have been the price of its
acquisition. It is altogether improbable, therefore, that God
would leave the tradesman without moral criticism and defence,
and lavish all his divine attention upon those who intermeddle

with theologies and philosophies. Very distinct, and even wonderful, are the references which are made in the Bible to the matter of trade, commerce, and business of every kind. "Honour the Lord with thy substance, and with the firstfruits of all thine increase." Supposing this to be done, what is the result which is promised to accrue? That result is stated in terms that are severely logical : "So shall thy barns be filled with plenty, and thy presses shall burst out with new wine." We have already seen that God has laid his claim upon the whole property of man in many an instance. "Thou shalt not delay to offer the first of thy ripe fruits, and of thy liquors" (Exod. xxii. 29). "The first of the firstfruits of thy land thou shalt bring into the house of the Lord thy God" (Exod. xxiii. 19). The very fact of Christians having been redeemed at an infinite cost is turned into an argument why all things, material and physical, to which they can lay claim, are to be sanctified and turned to religious uses : "Ye are bought with a price : therefore glorify God in your body." God has made the outpouring of spiritual blessing dependent upon man's faithfulness in observing the law of tithes, and firstfruits, and religious tributes of all kinds : "Bring ye all the tithes into the storehouse, that there may be meat in mine house, and prove me now herewith, saith the Lord of hosts, if I will not open you the windows of heaven, and pour you out a blessing, that there shall not be room enough to receive it." We may keep back part of the consecrated price, but the loss will be ours rather than God's. We may account ourselves even clever in making calculations as to how much we can save from the cost of piety and charity, but the great law of compensation will proceed disastrously in our case because of this calculated and irreligious penury : "He which soweth sparingly shall reap also sparingly." This law of compensation operates also in the other direction with noble impartiality : "He which soweth bountifully shall reap also bountifully." We imagine that all God's benefactions are spiritual ; we have shut him out from the field and the vineyard ; but hear his word : "The Lord shall command the blessing upon thee in thy storehouses, and in all that thou settest thine hand unto ; and he shall bless thee in the land which the Lord thy God giveth thee." But we must not attempt to make an investment of our charity: "Take heed that ye do not your alms before men, to be seen of them: otherwise ye have no reward of your Father which is in heaven." God cannot be outwitted in this matter. Not only must we sow the right seed at the right time, we must sow it in the right soil; in other words, all the conditions must be right, or the harvest will end in disappointment and sorrow. What is the true motive of all such action? —"The love of Christ constraineth us;" "For ye know the grace of our Lord Jesus Christ;" "Let this mind be in you, which was also in Christ Jesus." We must operate from an intensely spiritual and religious point of view: "I beseech you, therefore, brethren, by the mercies of God, that ye present your bodies a living sacrifice, holy, acceptable unto God, which is your reasonable service."

The text has called us to an act of remembrance, and in doing so has suggested the inquiry whether there is any such act of remembrance on the part of God himself? The Scripture is abundant in its replies to this inquiry: "For God is not unrighteous to forget your work and labour of love, which ye have shewed toward his name, in that ye have ministered to the saints, and do minister." Jesus Christ himself has laid down the same encouragement with even minuter allusion: "Whosoever shall give to drink unto one of these little ones a cup of cold water only in the name of a disciple, verily I say unto you, he shall in no wise lose his reward." The Apostle Peter preached to Cornelius the same doctrine: "Thy prayers and thine alms are come up for a memorial before God." Thus, on the divine side and on the human side there is an act of remembrance. God is always writing "a book of remembrance." We cannot work for God without reward, yet the reward must form no part of the motive under which we work. The sacred and awful ordinance of Heaven is: "Them that honour me I will honour, and they that despise me shall be lightly esteemed." Let us not suppose that we can ever owe anything to the oversight or forgetfulness of God. Everything is written down in the books which fire cannot consume, and we shall one day be called upon to face the minute and indisputable account.

PRAYER.

ALMIGHTY GOD, we, too, are in trouble, and in our hearts there is pain. Is there no balm in Gilead? Is there no physician there? We have been looking in the wrong direction: we have been turning towards ourselves for health, forgetting that we are all weakness, without any answer to the accuser, without any justification of our conduct. God be merciful unto us sinners! We will not speak to thee of our righteousness, or of our claim, for we have none; we will speak of our unrighteousness and of our forfeiture of thy regard, and will not spare ourselves in the day of examination and account. The heart is deceitful above all things and desperately wicked. The whole life has gone astray; the life has become a lie. But thy mercy still beams above the sun; thy tender love is more gracious than the showers of summer; thy tears outnumber the dew of the morning. We come not to thy judgment but to thy compassion; we are sure of thy love; we understand it in some degree. Towards thy righteousness we dare not look; it has no voice for us other than the voice of rebuke: but our eyes are towards the Cross—the living, dying, rising immortal mercy of the Cross; there we cannot die; there heaven's door stands wide open. We look unto the Bleeding Lamb; we feel the ministry of his blood; we cannot explain or understand, but in our soul there is a mystery of peace, a sense of newness of life, a beginning brighter than the dawning day; and this we accept as a seal and pledge of a covenant eternal as thine own duration and sure as the pillars of thine own throne. Amen.

Deut. ix.

CRITICISMS AND CAUTIONS.

THE expression of the first verse brings to our mind the truth that in life there are many days which are so special that they stand out by themselves, points of history, glittering aspects of time. Moses says,—"Hear, O Israel: thou art to pass over Jordan this day." Life focalises itself in a mere point. The preparation may be long and tedious, so much so as to tax our patience and sometimes throw our faith into sore vexation and trouble; but when God's providences do culminate they seem all to occur instantaneously, with a quite startling suddenness; and coming so we speedily forget all the waiting time and are ourselves suddenly startled into new praise. God does specialise the time of life. Thank God for every day that has a distinct individuality and that shoots an influence into all the other days immediately behind and immediately before. Thus the Sabbath day treats the week : it makes us forget the dulness of the day that is gone, and it throws an influence of a consecrating kind upon the day that is about to come. In the family we have such days :—the birth-day, the wedding-day, the day when the belfry shook with the resounding metal—a great burst of music and gladness; the day when we saw heaven opened, and had all that great liberty of prayer by which we seemed to enter therein in all the fulness of its breadth and all the glory of its splendour : it was a day of victory, quite a day of the soul, when the spirit was more than the body—not in some vain metaphysical theory of its constitution, but in sweet consciousness, in noble dominance over all life's vexation, and trouble, and sin, and shame. His is a mind not to be envied who does not mark the speciality of time—the day that had so much light in it ; the bright morning that raised our hopes from the dead ; the time of the coming of the angel who rolled the stone away and sat upon it, and filled the immediate space with heaven's glory. We should see more of God if we looked for more of him. The day would be more distinct if we opened its gate with the right key and if we approached its duties in the right spirit. We need preparation for such special days. It is well that there should be men amongst us who have foresight and who know that to-morrow will be a fighting day, and the day after a time of trial by fire and by water, and who with this genius of prevision have also the courage of a prophet to announce the coming time to prepare those of duller sight for the immediate providence. There are such men, but they are always in the family of the old kings of the Church. Nothing ever transpires that is not to be found in hint, or analogy, or distinct announcement in the Bible. No Jordan flows that is not related to the Bible Jordan by some very distinct arm or outlet ; and Moses may be taken as the type of those old men who, having understanding of the time, know what Israel ought to do, and speak their knowledge as Moses delivered his often severe Gospel. Men need to be girded up : they require the tonic word.

All sighing for comfort is an evaporating sentiment unless the meaning of it be that having received God's solace it shall all be turned into fighting material,—a determined and invincible strength levelled against the energetic weakness of hell.

Moses could not help preaching. It was not enough for him to make a bald announcement. Having stated all that was of the nature of law and commandment with sharpest clearness of expression, he went out into colour and exhortation, sentiment and impulse, towards heaven. He told the people in crossing Jordan and undertaking a severe task that "God is he which goeth over before thee." Having told Israel that the encountering people were "great and tall, the children of the Anakims, whom thou knowest, and of whom thou hast heard say, Who can stand before the children of Anak?" he said,—remember, or "understand"—grasp the theology of the case—God is at the head of the army, and the Anakim are before him as the grasshoppers of the earth. Moses insists upon Israel having a right theology—not a science, not merely formulated opinion, but a distinct, living grasp of the thought that God is, and is a rewarder of them that diligently seek him. He will not have an arm lifted but in God's almightiness; he will have no atheistic generalship; he will not speak of himself as the leader of Israel: God first; God midst; God last. Nothing stirs a man like a grand theology,—that is a living, perpetual grip of the eternal. Be right with God, and then you are within the range and flow of the music of creation; moving with the stars and yet grander than all the host of heaven, the soul falls into all the mystery and benediction of perfect peace. It is well to understand the difficulty that through its magnitude we may see somewhat of the greatness of God. Moses will not run down the Anakim as if any child could beat them back with a straw; he indicates their stature: he revives the memory of their prowess: he speaks of them as men who are in no wise to be contemned in the matter of strength and soldiership; within human limits they are tremendous foes, worthy of any foeman's steel; then, having so pictured them, without one touch of exaggeration, he says, Now understand that the Lord thy God is he who commands this army, and when he smites the nations reel and stagger like drunken men; have faith in God; have confidence in the covenant of Heaven; abide under the shadow of the Almighty; and when the Anakim fall—when they are brought down before thy face, when thou dost drive them out and destroy them quickly, remember a time of danger sets in. Give right interpretations to success; do not become atheists through prosperity; nor encourage the spirit of Pharisaism because all your little world seems ruled in obedience to your will.

Now the preacher takes his place. The legislator having given the law, the prophet begins; hence we hear Moses saying, in the fourth verse, "Speak not thou in thine heart, after that the Lord thy God hath cast them out from before thee, saying, For my righteousness the Lord hath brought me in to possess this land." No Pharisaism is allowed, no sacrificing to your own net or drag. God will not allow his soldiers to fall asleep after the day's battle upon the pillow of their own righteousness; nor will he allow them to say, See what virtue can do; see what good character will accomplish! behold, are not we men of clean hands? and in cleanliness of hands is there not strength of battle? Moses teaches that there is no righteousness on our side that can account for our success in life. God will not have boastfulness in his army or in his family. When we have succeeded we interpret the success aright if we regard it as having brought us one step nearer heaven. Are not men accustomed in the eventide, counting their gains and their successes, to say, This comes of sobriety, punctuality, attention to business; these are the natural and logical sequences of forethought and industry; how few there are who follow our path! were they as good as we they would be as rich? God will not allow such reasoning, if reasoning it may be termed. It is vanity; it is a misunderstanding of the real conditions of the case. Within limits we might assign all such talk has in it a measure of truth. No wise man will bring good conduct, forethought, punctuality, and all the elementary virtues of business into discredit: he will rather magnify them; but God does not pay us at night for the righteousness with which we have patronised him during the day. If we thus magnify our righteousness we would share the glory with Omnipotence, and God cannot permit us to divide the glory of his throne. Moses gives the true cause: "For the wickedness of these nations the Lord doth drive them out from before

thee ; " the nations are in error : they are inspired by the wrong
spirit : they are animated by the wrong motives : their ambitions
are perverted ; God could fight them with swords, God could
blind them with the hot dust of the wilderness, God could touch
their minds and make them reel so that they could not put
thought to thought or utter one desire in words ; that, however,
is not the divine plan, but in choosing other instruments those
instruments must not imagine that God could not have done
without them, and so imagining fall out of the humility of prayer
and the reverence of trust.

Now the preacher will be severer still. He knows his congregation and he speaks to them of their immediate character and
their assured and indisputable history. Moses says in the
seventh verse, "Remember, and forget not, how thou provokedst the Lord thy God to wrath in the wilderness : from the
day that thou didst depart out of the land of Egypt, until ye came
unto this place, ye have been rebellious against the Lord." Then
comes the history of Israel's wickedness. Moses will have the
people remember what their own character really is. He goes to
the root of the matter. He will not allow them to be fascinated
by a day's good conduct here and there, by some transient appearance of sound and honest religiousness : he says, You are a stiff-
necked and rebellious people. There is a substance of character.
There is a central quantity in man. For want of penetrating to
that central quantity we misunderstand man and we misunderstand one another. The central quantity may be bad when all
the fringework is of fine twined scarlet, lit up with spangles of
gold ; and blessed be God, the central quantity may be right,
though many of the changing circumstances and phases of life
may be such as to bewilder observers and to occasion sore distress
and trouble to the soul itself. Israel was stiff-necked and rebellious : Israel represented the hardness of the human heart in all
time. Showers of gracious rain were lost upon that sandy people ;
all heaven's sunshine produced no happy effect upon the rocky
heart of Israel. Let there be no self-deception ; let there be no
loss of history ; let the word be, " Remember, and forget not,
how thou provokedst the Lord thy God to wrath in the wilderness." Keep such hold of your bad old self as will frighten you
from repeating it. Do not carry it like a spectre to excite your

fear and drain your courage and your strength; but have such healthy apprehension of it, such a seizure of all its spirit and scope, as will help you to pray broader prayers and plead with humbler audacity all the promises tending in the direction of assured forgiveness. Men may carry their dead selves about with them so as to corrupt the present life and to take out of it all joy, and spring, and hope. In no such way are we to detain the past; we are to detain it in the sense of gathering its richest lessons, its best instructions; it is to be to us as a warning or as a finger pointing to dangerous places and to forbidden occupations and delights.

Now Moses will turn comforter. A wonderful man was Moses! A legislator with a hard mouth that could speak nothing but law; then a preacher whose tone softened into expostulation, here and there delicately hardened into rebuke,—a marvellous mixture of human tones. In this instance he will quote one of his own prayers, and through the quotation show the gentleness of the spirit which made him at once the severest and meekest man in history. Moses remembered his own prayers. There are those who would not have prayers published; nor need we wonder at their want of desire or approbation in this matter: they abuse what poor prayers they do offer; they turn them out and never inquire concerning their destiny or their reply; they are spoken and forgotten;—what wonder that they have no prayers to quote! Moses remembered every prayer he ever addressed to the ear of Heaven, and gathering Israel, as it were, closely around him, he says,—I prayed for you; and when God was quite near I availed myself of his condescension to say—"O Lord God, destroy not thy people and thine inheritance, which thou hast redeemed through thy greatness, which thou hast brought forth out of Egypt with a mighty hand. Remember—" Thus he would call God to recollection. The man's prayer was remembered by the memory of the heart; if he did not quote the exact words he quoted the precise substance. The petition went in this direction: for the people, for the covenant, for God's own sake; and if even new words were set to the music of the spiritual expression they in no wise altered the meaning of the suppliant's plea. This is the true consistency—not that a man shall remember his words, but that he shall be

faithful to his meaning. They who live in the consistency of
words are pedants, harsh judges, companions who ought to be
delighted with their own society and to be relieved of the association of other hearts. Consistency is in purpose, meaning, the fire
of the soul ; and where there is such integrity towards God the
words will often seem to contradict one another : eye-witnesses
can be called to make oath that such and such words were spoken
on such and such days ; it is false in the view of its want of
the larger truth ; it is exact without being true ; it is precise
without being philosophical and complete. A wonderful insight
into prayer is given in this quotation. Moses pleads for present
Israel on account of ancient Israel :—" Remember thy servants."
What was their name ? " Abraham, Isaac, and Jacob." Here is
a prayer with some leverage ; here is a breathing that comes up
from eternity. The plea is not to be argued within the present
five minutes. We belong to the ancient time, and to-day reap
the harvest which vanished men did sow. Answers are coming
from eternity because of God's love of Abraham, and Isaac, and
Jacob. The light that struck the little earth but last night left
the star whose gospel it brings some ten thousand years ago,—
and it only arrived yesternight ! Replies may be on their way
from the Old Testament saints for aught we know to the contrary.
The prayers we find in the Old Testament are so large it may
well have taken all this time to receive adequate replies. The
great prayers were offered in the Hebrew tongue—prayers that
stormed the heavens, that seemed to hold in their entreaty the
necessities of every possible age of time. Do not let us cut ourselves off by an unholy act of deletion from the ages of the
furthest past. God's ministry is wondrous ; God's providence is
spread all over the line of life. The joy we had yesterday was
the result of a reply that came from heaven in answer to a
mother's tender intercession. Moses went upon the plea that
Israel were still the people of God :—they are rebellious, they are
stiff-necked, they have broken all the commandments, they made
a calf and worshipped it ; but they are still thine ; they must not
be damned on the detail : they are still thine : they are in the
covenant, they are within thy gracious purpose. Were God to
judge us by the incident and trouble of to-day, the lapse of
yesterday and the trespass of to-morrow, his universe could not

cohere for twenty-four hours. He is a God of covenant, decree, sovereignty, meaning; and he is conducting the whole Church— old, new, present, to come—and whatever may be the inter- mediate steps, and difficulties, and provocations to himself, at last. the Lamb and the bride shall be wedded, and all heaven shall be the festal chamber.

SELECTED NOTE.

"*Hear, O Israel : Thou art to pass over Jordan this day, to go in to possess nations greater and mightier than thyself, cities great and fenced up to heaven, a people great and tall, the children of the Anakims, whom thou knowest, and of whom thou hast heard say, Who can stand before the children of Anak !*" (vv. 1, 2).—We seem to be looking on the remains of some Cyclopean city. These are scanty enough, but still sufficient to be remarkable. It is not merely, however, their size that strikes us, but their curiously mingled order and confusion, as they lie down in the ravine at our right, or rise above each other on the hill-slope at our left. We see no pillars, no ornaments, no inscriptions. Whatever city was here it belonged to a far antiquity, a time of rude, unadorned, but massive architecture, when men, few in number, and unable to apply any great amount of power, took advantage of natural peculiarities, such as the withdrawing cave, or the outstanding boulder, and instead of shaping their materials to their plan, shaped their plan to their materials. Yet the scene is not a bare one; far from it. There is no stream below, no rill trickling down the clefts, no moss vivifying the dead stone; but there is quite a wilderness of rich brushwood over- spreading the whole. Not shrubs merely, but trees, have taken possession of every free inch of soil; the ballut, the privet, and the fir rooting them- selves in each crevice, and forming an exquisite fringe, or rather network of green, through whose interminable meshes the grey patches of the old rock came up like the tombstones of some primeval cemetery.

It appears that this region was occupied at a very early period by the *Anakim*, who were of the *Rephaim* nations. Their chief city, Hebron, which we are just approaching, was one of the oldest cities of history, having been built seven years before Zoan, in Egypt (Numb. xiii. 22), the chief city of the Delta. The identity of the Anakim and Rephaim is of no consequence to our present statement; still, it is worth while noticing that Moses explicitly mentions this:—"The Emims dwelt therein in times past, a people great, and many, and tall as the *Anakims ;* which also were accounted *Rephaim*" (in our translation, *giants*), "as the Anakims" (Deut. ii. 10, 11). Thus the Anakim branch of the Rephaim were the original occupiers of Southern Judea. They were the first that took possession of its mountains, building cities, and swaying no feeble sceptre over a large region around. They were evidently not only an ancient, but a warlike and formidable tribe. It was not of hordes of savage wanderers or herds- men that Moses made mention (Deut. ix. 1, 2). And even though we may admit that the report of the spies was greatly coloured by their fears, still their language indicates the character of the Rephaim tribe (Numb. xiii. 33).

PRAYER.

ALMIGHTY GOD, how can we live so long as Satan is in our heart? It is not life: it is death twice dead. The pain is more than we can bear. All music is choked; all light is put out; all hope is killed. We are in fear of the enemy; yea, though we boast sometimes in his hearing we know that our boasting is vain. He is stronger than we are—older, wiser, more subtle than any beast of the field. He comes into Eden: he allures us by seductions which are fatal. This is our life's complaint; this is our heart's bitter testimony. When we would do good evil is present with us; the good that we would we do not: the evil that we would not that we do. We know this to be so, and who would tell us otherwise is but a messenger of falsehood, having come up from the depths of darkness to befool and curse us. If we say that we have no sin, we deceive ourselves, and the truth is not in us. We bless thee that we have not to fight the foe in our own strength. God is with us: God is our refuge and strength, a very present help in trouble; therefore will we not fear: no breaking up of earth or time shall cause us to quake, for hidden in the almightiness of God we are at rest, and blessed by heavenly love we live in everlasting summer. We are always denying Christ: thrice a day we say we do not know him; whenever the knowledge would involve difficulty, persecution, loss, pain, then we do not know the Man; and when we can use him as a passport, a key wherewith to open difficult gates, then we know him, and are proud of him, and speak his name quite loudly. God be merciful unto us, sinners! We have learned the art of hypocrisy: we are skilled in that evil way. Oh that we might be courageous, burningly in earnest, invincible, resolute in all holy purpose; then surely the world would hear of us, and listen to us, and in some degree obey the word which thou dost inspire us to speak. How many/blessings have we for which we ought to be thankful!—the home, standing on secure foundations; the table that is in the midst of it more than a table for bodily sustenance, a table of sacrament and memorial; and the lamps which shine upon it are let down from heaven; and the chair of peace, and the fire or comfort, and the bed of rest, and the word of love, and the bond of Christian fellowship—how can we speak of these things? We cannot speak of them: we must sing of them, call for an instrument of ten strings to help us to express inexpressible love. Thou hast given us a measure of strength and health and force; thou hast kept reason upon her throne, and the will is still under control; we are not altogether lost, even the worst of us. Say so to the bad man; tell him that even he may return, though so disfigured that none can tell who he is, and so utterly lost that it is impossible to miss him —even he may come back again: wide is mercy's door, loud is mercy's call,

tender are the tears of Heaven, yet red with blood. We bless thee for all
Christian hope, for all Christian security and spiritual prospect. We are no
longer prisoners : we hover upon the horizon as if ready to take flight over
broader space, where the light is clearer and the day without an eventide.
Inspired to do thy will, may we turn comfort into stimulus, may our
consolations be the beginning and the seal of strength ; and wherein our
tears have been dried and our hands have ceased to shake, may our watchfulness be the keener and our industry the completer. Take the bad man
out of our way when he would hinder us; let him go out into the night that
we may have a word together about better things, and speak that word as it
ought to be spoken.

Lord, hear us! Christ upon the Cross, save us! Blood of the eternal
covenant, take out the last stain of sin ! Spirit of the living God, Holy Ghost,
baptise us as with fire ! Amen.

Deut. x.-xi.

EDUCATED TOWARDS SPIRITUALITY.

HOW to introduce the spiritual element into all this instruction of an external and formal kind was the difficulty
even of inspiration. We have felt all along that the speeches
and instructions delivered to Israel meant, as to their purpose
and issue, something that was not expressed. We now come
to find an indication of that which is intensely spiritual. The
method of its introduction is—so it may be said, with reverence
—infinitely skilled. Great prizes of land were offered, wonderful
donations of milk and honey and harvest, and as for springs
and fountains of water, they were to rise in perennial fulness
and beauty. What wonder if considerable eagerness should
mark the spirit of the men to whom such promises were
delivered ? Who would not be eager for land flowing with
milk and honey, green all the year round because of the abounding waters, smiling with fruitfulness because of the blessing of
God ? But this could never be enough : the promises cannot
end in themselves ; when they have been uttered they quiver
with an unexpressed meaning. To bring that meaning under
the attention so as to secure the confidence of the people God
will set aside a tribe that is to have no land. That was a
subtle revelation of ulterior design. Out of that arrangement
was to come the inspiration that foretold the passing away of
the heavens and the dissolution of the earth and the destruction

of all things material as no longer worth holding. All things
have beginnings. The greatest literature traces itself back to
its alphabet. Levi is set forth as a spiritual symbol. "Levi
hath no part nor inheritance with his brethren." Is he then
poor ? Read the answer in chapter x. 9 :—" The Lord is his
inheritance, according as the Lord thy God promised him."
That was the lot of Levi. Is not that an anticipation of the
words which make all other instruction mean—" Seek ye first
the kingdom of God, and his righteousness; and all these
things shall be added unto you " ? It was well to have some
men who had no land, no golden harvest, no storehouses
rich with grain. They were the schoolmasters of the time
—the great spiritual philosophers and teachers, not knowing
themselves what they typified, still being there, the mystery
of life, a symbol of the sublime doctrine that men shall not
live by bread alone. Out of these incidental lines of history
gathers a great apocalypse of progress. The one tribe will
presently absorb the other tribe, and at the last we shall all
be kings and priests unto God ; and if globes were offered to
us, constellations and whole firmaments of glory, instead of
nearness to the divine presence, we should scorn the mean
donation. To that height we have to grow ; to that issue all
things will come that yield themselves to the movement of
the divine purpose.

We have read all the arrangements made for the ceremonial
worship of Israel: what was the meaning of it ? Here we
come again upon the same thought of ultimate spirituality.
Moses now, in the latter time, begins to reveal secrets. He
gave Israel long space in which to kill animals and offer them
by fire : he utterly wearied out the people by such impotent
ritual, and when they themselves began to turn their very
weariness into a kind of religious hope that surely something
orighter would presently be revealed, Moses spake these words :
—" And now, Israel, what doth the Lord thy God require of
thee ? " That is the question. What does it all mean ? Thou
hast slain thousands of bullocks and rams and sheep and goats,
" what doth the Lord thy God require of thee "—what has he
been meaning all this time,—" but to fear the Lord thy God,
to walk in all his ways, and to love him, and to serve the

Lord thy God with all thy heart and with all thy soul, to
keep the commandments of the Lord, and his statutes, which
I command thee this day for thy good?" (x. 12–13). That
was the divine intention from the very beginning. God does
not disclose his purpose all at once, but out of consideration
for our capacities and our opportunities and our necessities
he leads us one step at a time, as the wise teacher leads the
young scholar. What wise teacher thrusts a whole library
upon the dawning mind of childhood? A picture, a toy, a
tempting prize, a handful to be going on with, and all the rest
covered by a genial smile : so the young scholar passes from
page to page until the genius of the revelation seizes him, and
life becomes a sacred Pentecost. Such words spoken to Israel
at first would have been lost. There is a time for revelation ;
as certainly as for man, so certainly for God, there is a time
to speak, there is a time to be silent. It is a sublime addition
to our knowledge to realise the divine purpose, that all letters,
words, buildings, books, mean life, union with God, absorption
into God. Preachers and books and pulpits and altars and buildings are of use at the time, for the time most useful, in many
cases indispensable; but the issue of it all is perfect union
with the Father of our spirits, knowing him from within, a
perfect correspondence of our nature with his nature and his
purpose ; not a word spoken, a look exchanged, nor an attitude
but becomes a sacrifice. This thought supplies a standard by
which to measure progress. Where are we? To what have we
attained? What is our stature to-day? Are we still among
the beggarly elements? Do we still cry out for a kind of
teaching that is infantile and that ought to be from our age
altogether profitless? Or do we sigh to see the finer lines
and hear the lower tones and enter into the mystery of silent
worship—so highly strung in all holy sensibilities that even
a word jars upon us and is out of place under circumstances
so charged with the divine presence?

Still keeping by this same line of thought, notice how the
promises were adapted to the mental condition of Israel. What
promises could Israel understand? Only promises of the most
substantial kind. Moses addresses himself to this necessity
with infinite skill :—"Thy fathers went down into Egypt with

threescore and ten persons; and now the Lord thy God hath made thee as the stars of heaven for multitude " (x. 22). Israel cared nothing for thoughts: Israel cared for children: Israel knew not the poetry and the divinity of things: Israel understood acres, land upon land far-stretching, and harvests larger than any garners ever built. This being the mental condition of Israel, give Israel troops of children, thousands upon thousands outnumbering the stars,—a tumultuous throng, too vast for the space of the wilderness; as for harvests, let them grow upon the rocks, let the very stones burst into golden grain, for Israel is a great child and can understand only things that can be handled: let him have such things, more and more; God means them to be altar-steps leading upward, onward, into the place where there is no need of the sun or of the moon, no death, no night; Israel has a long journey to go, and he must be well housed and harvested on the road, or he will give way and fail before the time set for the fulness of the divine revelation. The same thought is expressed in many ways. It is given in chapter xi. 11, 12 :—" But the land, whither ye go to possess it, is a land of hills and valleys, and drinketh water of the rain of heaven: a land which the Lord thy God careth for: the eyes of the Lord thy God are always upon it, from the beginning of the year even unto the end of the year." What a child was Israel; what an infant of days; keep speaking to him much about prosperity and wealth and harvests and the rain of heaven, and you can lead Israel as you please, like a hungry beast following an offered bait which is withdrawn that he may be led and be caused to submit to a higher will. This also supplies a standard of progress. Do we care for the sanctuary because of its God or because of its conventional respectability? To what end besiege we the altar of Heaven, to pray or to profit?

Still preserving the marvellous consistency of the whole economy, we cannot fail to notice how beautifully the sacrifices were adapted to the religious condition of the people. This explains the sacrifices indeed. What was the religious condition of the people? Hardly religious at all. It was an infantile condition; it was a condition in which appeal could only lie with effect along the line of vision. So God will institute a worship accordingly: he will say to Israel, Bring beasts in great numbers, and kill them upon the altar; take censers, put fire thereon; spare nothing of your herds and flocks and corn and wine; have a continual burnt offering, and add to the continual burnt offering other offerings great in number and in value. Israel must be kept busy; leisure will be destruction. There must be seven Sabbaths in the week, and seven of those seven must be specialised by fast or festival or sacred observance. Give Israel no time to rest. When he has brought one bullock, send him for another; when he has killed a ram, call for a thousand more; this will be instructive to him. We must weary him to a higher aspiration; to begin this aspiration would be to beat the air, or to speak an unknown language, or to propound a series of spiritual impossibilities. Men must be trained according to their capacity and their quality. The whole ceremonial system of Moses constitutes in itself—in its wisdom so rich, its marvellous adaptation to the character and temper of the times,—an unanswerable argument for the inspiration of the Bible. It was the economy for the times. It could not be replaced, even imaginatively, to advantage, by the keenest wit of the brightest reader. It might be a profitable engagement now and then to try to amend the masonry of the Bible. Take out whole blocks of institutions, observances, and ceremonies, and put into the vacancies something better; let it be confessedly better in quality, but taken out of a further time and brought back to the early age. At once there is a sense of incoherence, unfitness, dissonance; the right thing is not in the right place; history is outraged; the genius of progress is misinterpreted. So with the Christian Scriptures. Take out, for example, the sermon upon the mount, and put into its place instructions regarding the building of the tabernacle. Men could not tolerate the alteration. The soul cannot thus go back. We have seen how wonderful a thing it was to write a New Testament: when the resources of language had been exhausted, when the sublimest poetry had been uttered, when the grandest altar had been built, it required a Son of God at once to begin the New Testament: begun by a feebler hand, the ages would have cast out the violence and the insult. The distributions of matter in the Bible are made by a divine hand;

the very placing of the materials is itself an argument—not, indeed, to the man who comes upon the Bible with effrontery and self-idolatry, beginning where he pleases, and moving up and down the sacred record with erratic will and taste, but to the man who makes the law his study, night and day, seeing how it looks in star-light, then how it bears the blaze of noonday, how it takes upon itself the fevers of the summer, and how amid the chills of winter it still thrills with forecasts of mercy. Only they ought to pronounce upon the Bible who have read it, and only they have read the Bible who have read it all, until it has swallowed up all manner of books and has become transformed into the very life of the soul.

So far the line has been consistent from its beginning, what wonder, then, if it culminate in one splendid word? That word is introduced here and there. For example, in chapter x. 12, the word occurs; in chapter xi. 1, it is repeated. What is that culminating word? How long it has been kept back! Now that it is set down we see it and acknowledge it; it comes at the right time, and is put in the right place :—" To love him." Then again in chapter xi. 1,—" Therefore thou shalt love the Lord thy God." Moses is almost a Christian, even in the historical sense of the term, and it is well that his name should be linked for ever with the name of the Lamb. Jesus uses no higher word than "love." Paul thought he would pronounce it aright by repeating it often,—and repetition is sometimes the only proper pronunciation : the word must be spoken so frequently as to fall into a refrain and attach itself to all the noblest speech of life. " Master, which is the great commandment ? " And Jesus answered,—" Thou shalt love." Here we have Moses and the Lamb. It ought to be easy to love God : we are akin to him; damn ourselves as we may, we are still his workmanship, his lost ones. We wrong our own souls in turning away from God : we commit suicide in renouncing worship; we are not surrendering something outside of us, we are putting the knife of destruction into our own soul. We have once more a standard of progress. We are in relation to this word love! Love means passion, fire, sacrifice, self-oblivion, daily, eternal worship. Who then can be saved? The word love does not destroy other elements which enter into the mystery of true worship. Moses says,—" What doth the Lord thy God require of thee, but to fear the Lord thy God, to walk in all his ways . . . and to serve the Lord thy God with all thy heart and with all thy soul, to keep the commandments of the Lord ? " The word love is found in this company. Recite the names that you may the more clearly understand the society of love. " Fear," " walk," " serve," " keep," —it is in that society that love shines like the queenliest of the stars. Love is not a mere sentiment, a quality that evaporates in sighing or that fades into invisibleness by mystic contemplation ; love calls fear, walking, serving, keeping, to its side, and they all together, in happy harmonic co-operation, constitute the divine life and the divine sonship of the soul. We, too, have mystery ; we have miracles ; we have ceremonies ; we have tabernacles and temples ;—what is the meaning of them all ? They cannot end in themselves ; read the riddle ; tell us in some short word which may be kept in a child's memory—the meaning of all the cumbrous machinery—the gorgeous ritual of the olden time, and even the simpler worship of the passing day. What is the meaning of prayer, and faith, and gift, and service, and outward profession? Would we learn the word ? We find it in the Old Testament and in the New: Moses speaks it, Christ speaks it, Paul speaks it, John speaks it,—they are all trying to say it— "Love." Love keeps nothing back ; love is cruel as fire in the testing of qualities ; love is genial as Heaven in the blessing of goodness. Though we have all knowledge, all prophecy, and are marvels in gifts of eloquence, and though we give our goods to feed the poor and our body to be burned, and outrun ancient Israel in costly and continuous ceremony, if we have not love— pure, simple, childlike, beautiful love—our music is noise, and our sacrifice is vanity.

PRAYER.

THOU wilt not show us thy glory now. Thou hast promised to show us thy goodness, and to make it pass before us: this thou art doing day by day; all things show the mercy of God. As for ourselves, goodness and mercy have followed us all the days of our life. We know this: our life speaks to this truth strongly and lovingly; therefore, we fear no evil: we smile upon the threatened darkness: the valley of the shadow of death is part of the way home. We have no real fear, no intense terror of heart; we are subject to passing dreads and alarms and foolish excitements, but all these do not touch the soul seated in the solemnity of an eternal covenant. Thou wilt accomplish all things; thou wilt not fail to bring on the topstone; having spent the ages in building the temple, the pinnacle shall not be wanting. Thou didst see the end from the beginning, and almightiness cannot fail. We stand in this security as within the munition of rocks; the wind cannot overturn our retreat; the tempest wastes its fury upon that stone; we are shut in by the hand of God. Help us to see the great beyond,—not to be too curious about it, but to use it as an allurement, a silent persuasion, a mighty compulsion towards stronger work, nobler purpose, larger prayer; thus the heavens shall help the earth; the sun shall be our light all day, and above it shall there be a brightness which the soul can understand. We bless thee for a sense of sin forgiven. Continue thy daily pardon. We feel as if we must be pardoned every moment, for since we have been pardoned and our eyes have been enlightened, we see more clearly, and we discern more critically: the things which once wore no face of offence now burn before us as if filled with all horribleness and as if carrying all shame. We would be pure as God is pure, perfect with the perfectness of God; but this end who can attain except through long ages, by the way of the Cross, by the ministry of blood, by the mighty power of the Holy Ghost? But our hope is in God: we shall yet be perfected; we shall stand before him without spot or wrinkle or any such thing, without a tear of shame in the eyes, without a flutter of misgiving or fear in the uplifted hands. The Lord have us in his holy keeping; the Lord build for us a pavilion in which our souls may daily trust; and when the end comes may we find it but a beginning; when the shadow falls may it be the background of many an unsuspected star; and when we stand before thee may we have on the robe of Christ—be clothed with him, not having on our own righteousness, which is of the law, but the righteousness of Christ, the purity of the Cross.

If this prayer may be answered now we shall not know but that we are already in heaven. Amen.

Deut. xi. 26-32.

26. Behold, I set before you this day a blessing and a curse;

27. A blessing, if ye obey the commandments of the Lord your God, which I command you this day:

28. And a curse, if ye will not obey the commandments of the Lord your God, but turn aside out of the way which I command you this day, to go after other gods, which ye have not known.

29. And it shall come to pass, when the Lord thy God hath brought thee in unto the land whither thou goest to possess it, that thou shalt put the blessing upon mount Gerizim, and the curse upon mount Ebal.

30. Are they not on the other side Jordan, by the way where the sun goeth down, in the land of the Canaanites, which dwell in the champaign over against Gilgal, beside the plains of Moreh?

31. For ye shall pass over Jordan to go in to possess the land which the Lord your God giveth you, and ye shall possess it, and dwell therein.

32. And ye shall observe to do all the statutes and judgments which I set before you this day.

PRACTICAL ALTERNATIVES.

THIS is the closing portion of a very long discourse delivered by Moses. The discourse begins in the twenty-second verse of the fifth chapter and extends to the end of the eleventh chapter. Within these points Moses rehearses the Decalogue and its leading principles; beyond the range of principles he has hardly yet gone. The next chapter opens with details, and insists upon special and clear applications of the morals which Moses had heretofore inculcated. The preacher winds up this portion of his discourse with a solemn appeal; he brings the great question to a point. He has not conducted himself merely as a lecturer upon moral philosophy, stating various theories with great learning and skill, and leaving his listeners to come to their own conclusions. There are no such lectures in an inspired book; they are in their right place in strictly human literature— an ample field within which men may indulge their genius and exhibit the results of their investigations. Moses comes with a law. Rightly or wrongly, that is the position which he assumes. He is not an intellectual reasoner merely—an inventor of systems, a critic of extinct ages; he says he has brought two tables written with the finger of God, measurable and intelligible as to letters and applications, but underneath them, and above them, and round about them is the mystery of Eternity. How does this noble preacher conclude his expositions and rehearsals ? He does not divide the people into two classes : he sets before them alternative courses :—proceed upon the line of obedience, and you come to blessing ; proceed along the line of disobedience, and a curse is the inevitable necessity,—not a threatening, not an exhibition of fretful vengeance, but a spiritual necessity : a curse follows evil-doing, not as an arbitrary punishment, but as the effect, which can never be changed, of a certain, positive, operating cause. This, therefore, takes out the personal element. We are not divided as on the right hand and on the left. Instead of classifying the hearers, Moses classifies the alternatives ; and thus grace follows law,—a species of mercy asserts itself in the midst of the severest and most critical of all moral legislation. The dart is not aimed at any particular man, nor is the favour dispensed in any spirit of selection and partiality ; but two great courses are indicated, two distinct issues are classified, and it is for us, reasoning upon history and observation, to say whether the prophet of the Lord touched the vital line— whether he trifled with the occasion, or whether he spake that which is to-day confirmed by experience and observation or human development and progress. What if everything round about us be confirming the testimony of Moses ? What if the Decalogue be written every day of the week ? What if in the operation of moral influence it can be distinctly proved that the Bible is one, that the word of the Lord abideth for ever, and that, whatever changes may have occurred, obedience still leads to blessing, disobedience still leads to cursing, and it is not within the wit or the strength of man to change that outgoing of law and consequence ?

A very precious thing it is that we have only to obey. At first it looks as if we were humbled by this course of service, but further inquest into the spiritual meaning of the matter shows us that in the definition of right and wrong, law and righteousness, God has been most tenderly-pitiful towards us, and law is but the practical and more visible and measurable aspect of love. Again and again we have seen that we are not moral inventors. God has not propounded a writing to us, to find out which is right and which is wrong; nor has he left to us the wild liberty, which would have been so full of disappointment and pain, of discovering for ourselves which way we would take, not knowing the definite issue of either course. There is nothing arbitrary in the revelation of eternal law : by its very nature it is a quantity which lies beyond our vision, and which does not submit itself to the rearrangements of our invention. Things relating to mere convenience, momentary rights, boundaries which are being continually enlarged and contracted as civilisation may require,— with regard to these we are legislators, makers of law, having in our right the gift of reward and the infliction of penalty ; but even these things are wrong if they are not built upon rocks we never laid, if they do not express the eternal harmoniousness, the infinite righteousness of God. In so far as they approach the divine thought, they will abide, they will daily vindicate their own justice ; and in so far as they do not express the decree of Heaven, all time is against them ; not a star in the wide heavens is on their side ; they must go down by a pressure as irresistible as it is immeasurable and invisible. Happy is the man who has discovered that he is not meant to be a moral inventor—a maker of morals,—that he has to accept a revealed morality and an offered righteousness : that God has been so kind to him as to arrange the whole way of life, so that the wayfaring man need not lose the path. This down-letting of a moral revelation is an aspect of the grace of God. When we come into fuller grace, clearer apprehension of the divine mind, we call the law an assistant guiding us to school—not so much a schoolmaster, as the English has it, as one who takes us by the hand and guides us to the schoolmaster ; but, even then we begin to see that the law, if written on stone, was written by a hand of love ; if set forth in letters that seem to burn in the intensity of their purity, yet did those very letters light us into inner meanings, into the very hidden sanctuary of God. When will men learn this ? When will they at once and for ever confess it, and so save themselves from endless and profitless trouble ? The Christian position is that the whole scheme of righteousness is revealed : whatever is right, true, pure, good, lovely, honest, and of heavenly savour has been given by God, so that the disappointing exercise of invention is superseded or is rendered of non-effect. One who knows the universe, because he made it, and all eternity, because he inhabits it, has condescended to tell us what is good, what is true, what is pure, what is right. If we were inspired by the right spirit, we would instantly stand up in thankfulness and bless the Giver's name, and ask but one other favour—that we might have eyes to see the innermost meaning of the law, and hearts trained, disciplined, and sanctified to accept and obey it, and express it in noble behaviour.

Is it true, within limits that we know, that obedience leads to blessing and disobedience to cursing? Sometimes we have to interrupt the divine reasoning that we may assist ourselves in its comprehension by the study of analogy upon lower ground. Is it true that there is a seed-time, which, if neglected, will be followed by desolation and death? Disprove that, and you will largely enable yourselves to disprove higher and more spiritual propositions. Is there a Bible of agriculture—a distinct revelation of the mysterious way of astronomic and agricultural and chemical forces? Is there a Moses of science—a man who comes to the ages with two tables of stone, telling us what nature has told him after waiting upon her day and night for many a year? The man abides by facts: he says, I have studied nature, I have been a patient student in her temple, and I have seen that this and that are essential to a harmonic association with her principles and requirements. He must leave the law; if he is wrong, he will soon be disproved; if he is right, then the critics cannot put him down. The appeal must always be to experience, to fact, to known circumstances, and provable assertions. A pity, indeed,—some might say,— that men cannot form their own opinions as to whether they will avail themselves of the day assigned to seed-sowing. Why should not men make a calendar of their own about these things? The calendars are copies: the writing of man is only what man has heard in the solemnity and silence of some Sinai. The appeal, after he has spoken, lies to earth, time, season, and by the issue—not by his pretence or claim—let him stand or fall. But may there not be many varieties of methods? Certainly; but the earth abideth for ever. We must study the effect of the central and eternal quantity within which we have no liberty, and then the changeable and adaptable circumstances and forces within which we may for the moment imagine ourselves to be masters and governors. A marvellous, mysterious combination is our life of necessity and freedom,—an eternal quantity and a continually-changing atmosphere; within that system we live. Is it true that there are laws of health —ten commandments, more or less, about the body? Then there is a Bible of physiology; there is a Moses who speaks with the authority of nature about the human system and its relations to all its environment. Is it true that want of exercise, accompanied by plentifulness of food, leads to the degeneration of muscle? Why were we not left to settle that ourselves? Is there a law upon this? Is it true that children born in the spring-time and in the winter are marked by greater vitality than children born at any other period of the year? Why were we not left to say in the family circle itself when children shall be healthy, when vitality shall rise and when it shall fall? Is there a law of sleep and of labour? If so, then, the Bible is a larger book than we supposed. If all these little outside Bibles are true and can challenge facts to prove their truth, it is not difficult to rise to the higher level, and to say, There may be a Bible meant for the soul; there may be a revelation addressed to the reason, and to the higher reason called faith, and to the higher self called the spirit. This higher revelation has not the immediate advantage of the lower Bibles, because they deal with earth, body, space, time, measurable quantities : but the higher Bible deals with soul, spirit, thought, will, eternity; by the very grandeur of its claim it dispossesses itself of that immediateness of proof which lies within the handling of the lower revelations and testimonies. But this must not be considered a disadvantage : this belongs to the glory and the necessity of the case. He who operates within a radius of a few inches can be, apparently, quicker in his movements, more precise and determined in his decisions, than the man who claims the globe as the theatre of his actions. So the Bible, having the disadvantage of dealing with spiritual quantities, must be judged, so far as we can approach it, by the spirit of the lower laws, or the laws applying to the lower economy. Is there any curse upon indolence? Does indolence rise for a moment from its pillow to smile satirically at industry, saying, I shall be to-night as rich as you are:

mean to slumber and sleep and doze in many a happy dream, and when you come back at eventide from the field where you have been wearying yourself my hands will be as full as yours ; go your unprofitable and vexatious way ? When did indolence say so ? Or, saying so, when did indolence prove the truthfulness and reality of its doctrine ? When was not indolence stabbed by its own satire, and made to tremble under the infliction of its own scorn ? Then there is a Bible relating to industry, service, stewardship, faithfulness,—who does not uphold that Bible ? Is there an employer of labour in the world who would not say, Such a Bible proves its own inspiration ? And is there an honest labourer in the world who would hesitate to accept that Bible, being compelled to its acceptance by the very constraint of necessity ? So then, we cannot do away with this law of blessing and cursing : we cannot set up a rival system of nature ; we are bound to accept the very earth ; we are driven—account for it as we may—to accept the light of the sun ; we are so pressed and humbled that we must wait for the former and the latter rain. Yet what liberty man has ! What pranks he plays in chemistry ! How he amuses himself in the invention of lights ! How, having once invented a candle, he cannot rest until he has invented a larger light, and when he has invented his largest light he takes care to put it out before the sun rises, or the sun will put it out for him ! God will not allow two creators : he himself reigns. He is still creating, and man is left but to invent, and arrange, and adapt, and borrow : find him where you will you find man a debtor; and the universe asks its brightest genius, "How much owest thou unto my Lord ?"

The argument is this : seeing that in the field, in the body, in the social economy, there is a law of blessing and a law of cursing, who shall say that this same reasoning does not culminate in a great revelation of heaven, hell ; "the right-hand," "the left-hand ;" eternal life, everlasting penalty ? If the analogies had been dead against that construction, we might by so much have stood in doubt and excused ourselves from completeness of service ; but every analogy becomes a preacher : all nature takes up her parable and speaks the revelations of her God: all life beats with a pulse below a pulse, the physical throb being but an indication of a growing immortality. We stand in a solemn sanctuary. We cannot get rid of law. The spiritual is a present blessing or a present curse. We cannot be happy with a bad conscience: it hardens the pillow when we need sleep most, it upsets all our arrangements, or makes our hand so tremble that we cannot clutch our own property; and we cannot be unhappy with a good conscience: without bread we are still in fulness, without employment we are still inspired by hope, without much earthly charity or largeness of construction of our motive and force we still retire within the sanctuary of an approved judgment and conscience. Blessing is not a question of posthumous realisation, nor is cursing. Heaven is here, and hell in germ, in outline, in hint, in quick, burning suggestion. Even now sometimes men know not whether they are in the body or out of the body by reason of religious entrancement and ecstasy; and there are men who, if they dare put their feeling into words, would say, "The pains of hell gat hold upon me." "There is no peace, saith my God, to the wicked;" "Though hand join in hand, the wicked shall not be unpunished;" "Be sure your sin will find you out." Who can fight God and win the battle?

The last words of Moses in this paragraph show us that new situations do not necessitate new morals. This is proved by verses 31, 32: "For ye shall pass over Jordan to go in to possess the land which the Lord your God giveth you, and ye shall possess it, and dwell therein. And ye shall observe to do all the statutes and judgments which I set before you this day." Morals do not change. Methods change, systems vary, theology readjusts its statements and retranslates itself into the growing language of a growing civilisation,—all that is true; but the abiding quantity is the law, the revelation of God in Christ, the living Son of the eternal God—Jesus Christ the same yesterday, and to-day, and for ever. We have no right that changes its claims according to the side of the river which it is upon: right is right on this side Jordan and on that side Jordan: there is no cis-Jordan righteousness and trans-Jordan morality. Right is right the universe through, because God

is one; evil is evil everywhere, because divine holiness is
unchangeable. Look not to time, place, change of circumstance
or situation, for the acceptance of a vicious morality: the universe is against it; eternity condemns it. Right is possible
here, and only in one way: the blood of Jesus Christ cleanseth
from all sin; there is a fountain opened in the house of David
for sin and uncleanness. Availing ourselves of that one way
we lose nothing; taking the very lowest view of the whole
mystery, we gain much because of an expansion of our own
view of human nature and human possibility, and, at the last,
when the great leap must be taken, if we leap into nothingness,
we have had a wonderful joy all the way we have taken—
wonderful communion, marvellous blessing in good-doing, intellectual and spiritual enlargement, in growing power of prayer;
but, if the leap be into life, judgment, an eternal state of
consciousness and apprehension, who wins: the fool who has
no God, or the Christian who has been trusting in the living
God and his Saviour Jesus Christ? To that inquiry who
will reply in words? To attempt an answer in syllables
would be to lower the occasion. That is an inquiry which
brings its own ineffable reply.

PRAYER.

ALMIGHTY GOD, thy Son Jesus Christ is our Saviour. He is mighty to save. The Son of man is come to seek and to save that which was lost. We were lost: we were as sheep going astray, turning every one to his own way; but we have returned to the Shepherd and Bishop of our souls. This is the Lord's doing, and it is marvellous in our eyes. We have been brought by a way we knew not and by paths we could not understand. This is the miracle of grace; this is the surprise of Heaven. Once we were blind: now we see; once we had no future: now life and immortality are brought to light. We long for the future; we live in heaven; we are the sons of God. We bless thee for a word of love and hope and joy: it fills the heart; it makes the spirit glad; it is the inspiration of heavenly grace. Meet with us when we gather together around thy Book, and help us to understand its best meaning, to feel its holy influence, and to respond to its gracious appeals. Thou knowest who are carrying heavy burdens, whose eyes are full of tears, whose hands are feeble and can no longer do life's pressing work; thou knowest also the prodigal children, thankless offspring, difficult to manage in business, in the home, and on the highway; our whole life is spread out before thee in clearest vision, and there is an answer in heaven to all the necessity of earth. Lord, answer thy servants; be gracious unto them who are clothed with the white linen of the saints. Thou wilt not see them put to shame; thou wilt try them with many a chastening sorrow, but in the deliverance of thy people thou wilt magnify thy grace. Wash us in the sacrificial blood; cleanse us from the condemnation of sin; make us pure with thine own purity; and in thine own due time gather us to the hills of heaven. Amen.

Deut. xii.

LIFE IN A NEW LAND.

THIS chapter opens a new section of the Mosaic legislation. Up to this time we have had copious and urgent discourses by Moses upon the law, its principles, and its purposes—more or less abstract and philosophical discourses; now we come into practical instruction and exhortation. The people are about to move into new circumstances and to sustain new relations, and Moses condescends to particularise, and seeks by almost tedious detail to impress upon the mind of Israel what is right, what is good, and what is expected of the people of God. The children of Israel could understand no other language. They were amongst the youngest nations of time. In studying their history we study beginnings, first lessons, and the proper methods of preaching to infantile minds—namely, methods of command, authority, illustration, and sparkling narrative. The people of Israel were called upon to illustrate in their own conduct the laws which God had pronounced from Sinai. The noticeable thing is that, although the circumstances were new and the land a strange land, no change takes place in the moral substance of the law. The law is one, the same in heaven as upon earth, the same in the dawn of earthly time as in the eventide of the terrestrial dispensation. Till heaven and earth pass not one jot or tittle of the law can be destroyed. It is in the very substance of the divine nature ; it is the mystery of the personality whose name is God ; it is the secret of eternal righteousness. But there are adaptations, accommodations, methods of addressing the life to unexpected or unusual or temporary conditions ; in all these matters Moses is specially detailed, critical, and exact in his statements, sometimes dwelling upon what to us may appear trifles. But there are no trifles in moral education : every monition has a purpose, every hint is the beginning of a revelation. Let us follow Israel into new lands and circumstances, and mark the operation of law.

The first thing Israel had to do appears to be a work of violence. All idols were to be destroyed :—"Ye shall utterly destroy all the places, wherein the nations which ye shall possess served their gods, upon the high mountains, and upon the hills, and under every green tree : and ye shall overthrow their altars, and break their pillars, and burn their groves with fire ; and ye shall hew down the graven images of their gods, and destroy the names of them out of that place " (vv. 2-3). Israel could understand no other language. This is not the language of to-day ; but the thing inculcated upon Israel is the lesson for the present time : words change, but duties remain. Violence was the only method that could commend itself to infantile Israel. The hand was the reasoner ; the breaking hammer was the instrument of logic in days so remote and so unfavoured. Forgetting this, how many people misunderstand instructions given to the ancient Church ; they speak of the violence of those instructions, the bloodthirstiness even of him who gave the instructions to Israel. Hostile critics select such expressions and hold them up as if in mid-air, that the sun-light may get well round about them ; and attention is called to the barbarity, the brutality, the revolting violence of so-called divine commandments. It is false reasoning on the part of the hostile critic. We must think ourselves back to the exact period of time and the particular circumstances at which and under which the instructions were delivered. But all the words of violence have dropped away. " Destroy," " overthrow," " burn," " hew down," are words which are not found in the instructions given to Christian evangelists. Has the law then passed away ? Not a jot or tittle of it. Is there still to be a work of this kind accomplished in heathen nations ? That is the very work that must first be done. This is the work that is aimed at by the humblest and meekest teacher who shoulders the Gospel yoke and proceeds to Christianise the nations. Now we destroy by reasoning, and that is a far more terrible destruction than the supposed annihilation that can be wrought by manual violence. You cannot conquer an enemy by the arm, the rod, or the weapon of war ; you subdue him, overpower him, or impose some momentary restraint upon him ; fear of you takes possession of his heart, and he sues for peace because he is afraid. That is not conquest; there is nothing eternal in such an issue. How, then, to destroy an enemy ? By converting him—by changing his motive, by penetrating into his most secret life, and accomplishing the mystery of regeneration in his affections. That mystery accomplished, the conquest is complete and everlasting ; the work of destruction has been accomplished ; burning and hewing down, and all actions indicative of mere violence have disappeared. Enemies are killed, false altars are burned, and graven images are hewn down, not manually but morally, not by some overpowering force of assault, but by the very men themselves who, having seen the hollowness of their gods, have deposed them from their sovereignty. So with all the other instructions with which the Bible is charged. Attention must not be fixed upon the letter, often apparently so hot, angry, and even vindictive ; we must get to the inner man, and there we shall find that God has all the while intended but one thing, namely, to establish the throne of righteousness, and to purge the firmament of every cloud that could obscure the brightness and beauty of his presence. It is but a perfunctory and unprofitable criticism that fastens upon outward circumstances, framings and settings of divine intentions; the true criticism is to penetrate to those intentions themselves, and history, observation, and experience concur in the solemn and grateful testimony that in every instance the intention of God has been a purpose of salvation.

But it was not enough to destroy. The negative word was to be succeeded by a positive service :—" But unto the place which the Lord your God shall choose out of all your tribes to put his name there, even unto his habitation shall ye seek, and thither thou shalt come : and thither ye shall bring your burnt offerings, and your sacrifices, and your tithes, and heave offerings of your hand, and your vows, and your freewill offerings, and the firstlings of your herds and of your flocks : and there ye shall eat before the Lord your God, and ye shall rejoice in all that ye put your hand unto, ye and your households, wherein the Lord thy God hath blessed thee " (vv. 5–7). It would delight many reformers to confine themselves to a merely negative work, because they delight in criticism; their ability lies along that narrow line ; they can see faults, they can detect discrepancies and inconsistencies, and with great fluency they can expose sophism of the subtlest kind, and with indignation they can expose outrages of a moral sort ; but the great work of Christianising the lands is first negative, and then positive. Israel must be faithful to his own God if he would completely destroy the graven images of the heathen nations ; Israel must go to the right sanctuary if he would pull down the noblest refuge of heathenism ; Christians must keep up their personal Christianity if they are to become great ministers, missionaries, lecturers, and teachers. Men belonging to such high classes must never forget their own devotions, their own deep reading ; they must maintain long periods of silence. If they are always talking, what wonder if their talk should become suddenly and completely commonplace and tasteless, without savour, or accent, or unction? They must contrast their great thunder-bursts of appeal by prolonged silence in solitary places. They will preach as they have prayed: their public invectives, encouragements, criticisms, and expositions will take tone from their private and secret communings with Heaven. The reason that we sink into commonplace and outgrow our power is that we have been talking too much. Whole days of silence should punctuate the history of the week—long hours of solitude, until there comes upon the soul a desire to see a fellow-creature, a public assembly,—a kind of hunger in the soul for social contact, presence, and influence. The Bible is full of teaching regarding the uses of solitude. Israel must keep up his own religion; go to the place chosen by the Lord, bring his burnt offerings, and his sacrifices, his tithes, and heave offerings, and vows, and freewill offerings, and the firstlings of his herds and of his flocks, and eat before the Lord his God; and then go forth Heaven-nourished, Heaven-inspired, to burn false altars and grind into powder the graven images of heathen ignorance. Have faith in men who live in God.

Amidst all this assault, denunciation, and sacred fury there was to run a line of perfect self-control:—"Ye shall not do after all the things that we do here this day, every man whatsoever is right in his own eyes" (v. 8). Individuality has limits. Where are there any individualities? We know nothing about them in the great Christian society; individuality has undergone distinct modification: we belong to one another; we are parts of a complicated but sentient and indestructible body; we are branches in a living vine; the individual will is destroyed by the beneficent presence of a social responsibility. There was to be personal watchfulness: hence we read in the thirteenth verse,—"Take heed to thyself;" and in the nineteenth verse again,—"Take heed to thyself;" and in the thirtieth verse, —"Take heed to thyself." That is where individuality comes in, every man watching himself. The Apostle Paul could use no higher form of words in charging the young soldiers of the cross: said he to one and another,—Take heed unto thyself; and again, speaking to the Church, he said, Let every man examine himself. Where are there instructions binding upon us in the direction of social criticism—the examination of other people, and keeping guard over the consistency of our brethren ?   We are admonished to look after them along another line—to see that they want nothing that is for their good, to care for them, to put our strength at the disposal of their weakness ; but there is no responsibility thrown upon us in the matter of watching other people in any critical or suspecting sense.   Each man must look to himself : his head may be right whilst his heart is a thousand miles away from the path prescribed by God ; his head and his heart may be comparatively consistent, and yet appetite, passion, desire, may be set on fire of hell.   Every man must watch himself at his weakest point, and must suspect himself where other people least suspect him.   No attempt, therefore, is made to do away with individual responsibility ; that will grow in proportion as there is personal watchfulness, personal severity with our own judgment, heart, and conduct.   Let a man try himself as by fire.   He who beats himself, to use the apostolic expression, " in the eyes," that he may the less see the faults of other people, is in least danger of becoming a castaway.   If all public criticism and all social contempt could be turned in towards individual uses, there would be an outgoing from the self-suspected and self-disciplined heart of a stream of beneficence and charity and Christian hope towards all the prodigals of the world.

Now there will be an act of marvellous condescension : there will be a tone of mercy amid all this outflow of legislation ; the burden will not be made heavier than Israel can bear.   Read verse 21 :—" If the place which the Lord thy God hath chosen to put his name there be too far from thee, then—"   And here comes the divine condescension, the concession of Heaven to the limitations of earth.   Calvary is in the Old Testament. The condescending, saving Cross is in the books of the law. Love was never absent from the inspired record.   If the place be too far ; if there be local difficulty ; if there be a weight to carry too heavy for thy poor strength, God will meet thee : he will make thy weakness the basis of a new negotiation ; instead of standing away upon the hills of eternity and frightening little earth by all the thunder of infinity, he will come down and see what can be done,—measuring, adjusting, and arranging, so as to suit human weakness. When there was no eye to pity; when there was no arm to save, his own eye pitied and his own arm brought salvation. Grace and truth go together; pity follows law; the iron statute is bedewed with tears : God is love. Nor is God concerned only about the living: he is concerned about those who have yet to appear in life. So we read in the twenty-eighth verse, —" Observe and hear all these words which I command thee, that it may go well with thee, and with thy children after thee for ever, when thou doest that which is good and right in the sight of the Lord thy God." God is concerned for posterity. We may mock the suggestion, and put foolish questions concerning the generations yet to come, but the Book of God is as careful about the child unborn as about the old pilgrim born into the higher spaces. God does not insulate himself by the little present; he contemplates the end from the beginning. All souls are his. He also puts it into our care to regard the welfare of our successors. There is a sense in which we all have a posterity—some in a narrower, some in a larger sense; but we all have a succession : we are influencing to-morrow by our spirit and action to-day. How mad are they and how guilty of the cruellest murder who go on indulging every desire, sating every appetite, satisfying every wish, forgetting that they are involving the yet unborn in pain, weakness, incapacity, and dooming them to life-long suffering and distress. Here is the greatness of the Bible, the noble condescension of God, the infinite solicitude of the eternal Father. His speech runs to this effect: take care: not only are you involved, but your child and child's child, for generation upon generation : your drunkenness will re-appear in the disease of ages yet to come; your bad conduct will repeat itself in a long succession of evil-minded men; your behaviour appears at present to be agreeable, to have some aspects that might be called delightful, but things are not what they seem : actions do not end in themselves : every bad thought you think takes out some spark of vitality from your brain—robs you, depletes you, leaves you nearer lunacy; be careful : have some regard for those who have to succeed you;

learn from those who went before you how evil a thing it is to have sown bad seed, and by what you have learned from them conduct yourself aright; if you are true, wise, pure, generous, well-conducted altogether, generations will arise to bless you; if you take care of the poor, if any of your succession should be doomed to poverty, with what measure ye mete it shall be measured to you and them again; blessed are the merciful: for they shall obtain mercy; with what judgment ye judge ye shall be judged. Life is one: touch it where we may, we send a thrill, a vibration, along all the vital lines. The law is two-fold: sow evil, and reap evil; sow good, and reap good. This is no partial law, dealing with penalty and shame only: it is an impartial righteousness, dealing with reward and glory, and promising delight vast and tender as the heaven of God.

SELECTED NOTE.

The consequences of parental wrong-doing fall on the offspring, as we plainly see in the case of the drunkard; the laws of heredity have been carefully studied during late years with many remarkable results.

The belief in the transmission of penalty to offspring was in ancient times very widely extended, as may be illustrated by the following extract from the laws of Menu, the most ancient lawgiver of the Hindoos:—

"Even here below an unjust man attains no felicity:
  Nor he whose wealth proceeds from giving false evidence:
  Nor he who constantly delights in mischief.

"Though oppressed by penury, in consequence of his righteous dealings,
  Let him (the good man) never give his mind to unrighteousness;
  For he may observe the speedy overthrow of iniquitous and sinful men.

" Iniquity committed in this world produces not fruit immediately;
  But like the earth, in due season, and advancing little by little,
  It eradicates the man who committed it.

"Yes, iniquity once committed fails not of producing fruit to him who
    wrought it;
  If not in his own person, yet in his sons,
  Or if not his sons, yet in his grandsons.

" He grows rich for awhile through unrighteousness;
  Then he beholds good things; then it is that he vanquishes his fear;
  But he perisheth at length from his root upwards."

PRAYER.

ALMIGHTY GOD, our eyes are fixed upon the Cross of Christ. God forbid that we should glory, save in the Cross of our Lord Jesus Christ. We crucified him; we mocked him; we cast all taunting condemnation into his teeth. We do not discharge ourselves of the tremendous responsibility: we hang down our heads in mourning and shame and self-reproach which burns to agony, knowing that we murdered the Son of God. We crucify the Son of God afresh, and every day we put him to an open shame. The white robe of his holiness is not safe in our keeping; the purity of heaven we stain even by our highest thoughts. Do thou have mercy upon us day by day, ever being more merciful than before, because our sin is aggravated by time, and we sin to-day more deeply than we could sin yesterday. God be merciful unto us sinners! Only thy mercy can reach our estate: the best of us is a lost, dead man. But we have read thy word, and we have heard it uttered by lips of sympathy, and it is a word which comes into our life like an angel from heaven,—the very angel of the divine presence, the angel of the covenant, the all-present and all-directing spirit that has ruled the destinies of the race. We bless thee for words we can understand— simple words, notes of music, speeches of love. When our pain burns most acutely, then thy Gospel is most to us; in our fatness and prosperity and abounding strength we forget God, and look upon ourselves with approbation and delight; but when we see one glimpse of our real self—the evil one within us, charged with the poison of malice, disfigured by the passions of hell, helpless because of self-destruction—then rises the Cross upon our vision, the very beauty and glory of God. We bless thee for thy day, sanctifying all the week; for thy Book, giving life to all books that are good, and drawing them back to itself to have all their beauty renewed; for all friendships that lift us higher in the scale of thought and being; for all hopes that drive the darkness away and plant flowers upon the tomb; for all the lights which outshine the stars and give us hope of a day yet to come;—these are thy mercies; these are thy benefits; these are thy appeals to our souls; and our souls would answer them in rising gladness, because they are gifts ineffable and everlasting. Give us the quietness of the sanctuary in our own soul; breathe the peace of heaven upon us, every-one; give release from anxiety, from tormenting memory, from foreboding fear; and in one moment of vision of better things and heavenly gladness we shall bury a lifetime of sorrow, and recover ourselves, and claim the future with all the conscious ease of strength divinely sustained. Let thy mercy be our inner day; let thy love in Christ Jesus be our secret thought;

let the whole priesthood of the Saviour be to us as bread on which the soul may feed, and wine sacramental, the drinking of which shall be as the utterance of an oath. Amen.

Deut. xiii.

DANGER AND SECURITY.

THIS passage, by the inspiration of God, touches upon all the possible points of danger in a religious course. Suppose, for the moment, we do not admit the inspiration, still there remains the fact that in a book so old as Deuteronomy some master hand has touched the three great points of vital danger in religious progress. We bow to genius : we acknowledge power : we say it is but decent to uncover the head in the presence of superiority ;—bound by this law, we cannot read this chapter without feeling that, be the writer who he may, he was a man who knew human nature : he saw clearly every point of danger, and with delicate, but resolute, courage pointed out the only course which such dangers involved and required.

What are the points of danger ?   The first may be described as being somewhat after a philosophical sort. There is nothing rude in the assault, nothing violent, or startling, or shocking, from a merely animal or physical point of view; it is a very delicate encroachment upon religious thought : it is shadowy as a vision : it is impalpable as a dream, and the speaker of his dream assumes, with amazing appearance of innocence, a total want of responsibility in the matter, forasmuch as he is simply relating, with a child's ingenuousness, what he saw in the dark and what he heard in the silence. What creature could be less objectionable ?   Here is no blatant vulgarity of denunciation, no audacious assault upon conservative piety.   Who would not allow a man to relate a dream ?   Who does not like to have his imagination touched as by fire, and invited to the hospitality of spaces boundless and lights that outshine the sun ?   What harm can come of a trip to the upper air ?   What possible injury can come from a survey of clouds which break now and again to let the glory through ?   Surely this is harmless : it is more than harmless : it is instructive : it may be a lesson in the deeper philosophy; it may be the beginning of a widening revelation. Besides, an approach of this kind is marvellously graded so as to suit human nature: you do no harm to your cause by assuming that the man to whom you are speaking is a fellow-dreamer, a brother-poet, gifted with the same imagination, and by gently insinuating that he may have had still higher experiences of the night-scenes, the star-fields, the glory-lands that burn above. A man likes to be accosted as if he were an intellectual gentleman. To tell him a dream is to beget his confidence; to ask him to listen to the minor tones of the soul is to confer the highest of favours upon his manhood. The mischief is this, that a man who would listen to such a dreamer, or seer of visions, and allow his religion to be affected by the nightmare, would turn the man out of his presence if he attempted to offer him a single idea upon any practical subject under heaven. We are easily beguiled from the religious point. "O foolish Galatians, who hath bewitched you?" Surely this is a mystery of a profound and solemn kind, that we are always ready to listen to dreamers and visionaries concerning the faith of Christ, and give them credit for penetration amounting almost to inspiration, and yet upon all other subjects we withdraw the confidence of our judgment and heart from such men. We allow any thief to steal our religion,—mayhap, because we want to get rid of it; we lay it where the thief can purloin it without trouble: he knows where to find it. In politics we laugh at him; in business we deny his right to speak, and call it impertinence if he cough in the presence of commercial men; and were he to offer a judgment upon literature, propriety would shudder, intellectual dignity would recoil lest the man should stain its purity; but let him tell a dream or a vision that will imperil the faith of the rising life of the country, and he may be listened to. It would seem as if it were easier to murder the soul than to kill the body. The first point of danger, therefore, is thus clouded in a golden veil; and the man who may be said to be preparing for that danger is dreamy, hazy-minded, speculative, always looking into a mist if, haply, he may find a star: such a gentle, dozing creature, so harmless, and really so very attractive in many qualities of his character.

What is the second point of danger? It is not at all philosophical; it may be ranked among the social forces that are constantly operating upon life:—" If thy brother, the son of thy
mother, or thy son, or thy daughter, or the wife of thy bosom,
or thy friend, which is as thine own soul, entice thee" (v. 6).
All kindred would seem to be written under this designation, and
the friend who is akin to the soul,—your very other self,—he of
whom you ask no questions even when you least understand him,
because he is golden gold, true as the geometry of the universe,
—upright, square, thoroughly well-related in all the parts and
qualities of his nature,—a building of God. Social influences are
constantly operating upon our faith. The youngest member of
the family has been reading a book, and has invited the head of
the house to go and listen to some new speaker of theories, speculations, and dreams: the service is so beautiful: the idea is so
novel : a great deal of the rush and tumult common to elementary
religious life is totally escaped ; the intellectual brother—the man
supposed to have all the brains of the family—has got a new
idea,—an idea which in no wise associates itself with historical
churches and traditional creeds, but a bran-new idea, altogether
sparkling and daring, and whosoever professes it will at once
take his place in the synagogue of genius ; or the darling friend
has caught a voice down some by-way, and he will have his other
self go with him in the evening to hear this speaker of anti-
Christian ideas,—a man who has undertaken to reconstruct so
much of the universe as will allow him to touch it : a person of
exquisite mind, of dainty taste, and of quite latent power. The
subtle purpose is to draw men away from the old altar, the old
Book, the God of deliverance and beneficence, of mercy and redemption, to another god who will condescend to be measured for
a creed, and who is not above sitting for his portrait. So we
blame the family for alluring us from old centres: the older
members of the family would not have gone, but under pressure
from the brother, the son, the daughter, the wife, or the family
friend. Why betake yourself to such cowardly language? Why
add insult to injury when you leave the old altar, saying you
would not have gone but that some other man enticed you?
The fact is you have gone : better stand straight up and claim
your going to be the expression of a conviction, the out-working

of what you believe to be a true inspiration. Do not follow a multitude to do evil. Do not always be at the string end, led about by those who are of more forceful and energetic will than yourselves. Be sure as to what they are taking you to; have a clear understanding before you begin. You would not allow those persons to interfere with anything practical : when the discussion of commercial questions arises, you stand at the front and say,— There I can bear testimony, and there I ought to be heard. Why claim such a solemn responsibility in the settlement of nothing, and allow anybody to settle for you the great questions of religious truth and personal destiny ? There is no need to violate courtesy, or to suspend friendly relations; but it ought to be needful to every man to know exactly what is proposed to be done with his soul by the prophet who has dreamed a dream, or the member of a family who has been seized with a desire to entice other members of that family from the historical altar.

What is the third point of danger ? It is not philosophical; it is not, in the narrow sense of the term, social; it is a point of danger which may be characterised as public sentiment, public opinion,—a general turning round, and a wholesale abandonment of old theologies and old forms of worship :—" If thou shalt hear say in one of thy cities, which the Lord thy God hath given thee to dwell there," that the cities have turned round, as it were, *en masse*, and have gone after "other gods, which ye have not known " (vv. 12–13). Some men may have courage to laugh at the dreamer : others may have virtue enough to resist the blandishments of the nearest friend; but who can resist the current or tendency of public opinion ? Say to some men,— Public opinion is against you; you are talking a forgotten language ; you have not associated yourself with the tendency of the times ; all your speech is not without benevolence and the attraction of quaintness : there is an archaic flavour in your speech that is very touching and that might for a moment bring with it a species of rest to the soul, but new thought has arisen, new language has been coined, new music is expressing a new worship : the whole city has turned round—obey that public opinion ; to be in a minority is to invoke mockery and contempt; and they will instantly yield.

Thus the writer of the chapter has given the three points of danger,—philosophical, social, and public. The great advantage of all seducers from the true faith lies in the marvellous mystery that some people like to be in danger. A species of capital is made out of the religious vote. Various candidates for the throne of confidence ask you what you will take for your vote. It places men in an interesting condition to be regarded as intellectual invalids, spiritual convalescents, and in some degree of danger from the fever of heterodoxy; it pleases them to lay their empty heads upon their indolent hands, and to be regarded as persons whose condition excites the solicitude of Christendom. A marvellous human nature this! And the persons who so pose—not knowing whether they will vote for Barabbas or Christ, the living God or the god of wood and stone,—such persons are utterly wanting in moral robustness, intellectual health, spiritual vigour that begets confidence and assures security.

What is the course to be taken under circumstances of danger? Moses had no difficulty about his reply: let us see what it was, and consider whether we can adopt it. " And that prophet, or that dreamer of dreams, shall be put to death " (v. 5). The seducer in the family brings upon himself this penalty. " Neither shall thine eye pity him, neither shalt thou spare, neither shalt thou conceal him : but thou shalt surely kill him "—(vv. 8–9)— " thou shalt stone him with stones, that he die " (v. 10). And as for the city—representative of public opinion,—" Thou shalt surely smite the inhabitants of that city with the edge of the sword, destroying it utterly, and all that is therein, and the cattle thereof, with the edge of the sword. And thou shalt gather all the spoil of it into the midst of the street thereof, and shalt burn with fire the city, and all the spoil thereof every whit, for the Lord thy God : and it shall be an heap for ever ; it shall not be built again. And there shall cleave nought of the cursed thing to thine hand " (vv. 15–17). That was a drastic course : there is no touch of compromise in that stern provision ; there is no line of toleration in that tremendous answer. The same course is to be taken to-day, as to its spiritual meaning. Physical violence there must be none : the day of physical pains and penalties for spiritual offences has closed ; but the great lesson of destruction remains for ever. We have just seen that the truest destruction is moral ; we have admitted to ourselves that no conquest is worth achieving that is not based upon the consent of the conquered man or nation; we must destroy by spiritual influence, by moral dignity, by such assuredness of conviction and simplicity of faith on our own part as will be as a burning fire to every suggestion bearing upon apostasy or treason.

Why are such temptations permitted? The answer is given in the third verse:—" The Lord your God proveth you, to know whether ye love the Lord your God with all your heart and with all your soul." Every man's faith must be tried. Every man is tried in business, so that the honest man is known from the dishonest, and the power of temptation upon the integrity of the trader is estimated with appalling accuracy. We are tried by success; we are proved by prosperity; the thief may actually be sent to us that we may know whether every door and window has been fastened. We close the house night by night with simple confidence: the round has become so monotonous a course that we take it for granted that all things are secure. The thief will find out the one point of weakness; and the night after we shall be much more careful than we were the night before. It is a notable feature of human nature that after the property has been stolen it is quite excited with new solicitude. Such is the noblest creature that traverses the little mean space called earth! After he has lost all he had, he puts in every bolt he can lay his hands upon, and turns every lock with expressive violence. O that men were wise! In such an hour as ye think not the thief cometh. If the good man of the house had known at what hour the thief would come, he would have been sitting up waiting for him armed. We live in circumstances of uncertainty, in periods full of excitement; the voice of Christ is—" Watch."

But are we not living in the days of toleration? Is there not, in some countries at least, an Act of Toleration? There is: toleration has still its place; but toleration must not be misunderstood. Who are the men who claim the exercise of toleration? Are they consistent men? From point to point in all the line of social intercourse and confidence do they carry out this idea of toleration? Let us test. They are very large in their toleration of aberrations and eccentricities in theology; along that line there is no end to their sublimity. Are they consistent? Let us try them by the standard of life. Here is a man who says,—Morality is quite a parochial term : morality is a question of circumstance ; as to right and wrong, they vary with latitude and longitude ; morality must be considered a variable quantity. Do you tolerate that man ? Would you leave him in charge of your business for one calendar month ? Would you allow him to have full control over your family circumstances for the same limited period of time ? Would you trust such a man with signed cheques, the money lines of which were blank ? You are lovers of toleration ; you preach toleration ; you would die (if you could not help it) for toleration. Are you consistent ? Where does your toleration begin ? Where does it end ? Here is a man who comes with a new creed, untouched by ministerial fingers, unpolluted by pulpit senility and ignorance ; he says,—Weak people have no rights : strength is right : he who can get has a right to get, and the weak must go to the wall ; the weak are an offence to nature : they are out of harmony with the constitution of things ; they must be got rid of ; strength, health, force,—these are the masters of the world. Do you tolerate him ? Would you like him to sit up for the nights of one whole week with your little sick child ? Would you like him to take out, in its little perambulator, the pale-cheeked one of the family— the little creature whose life trembles in the balance ? You love toleration ; you are fond of toleration ; you clap your sweltering hands in applause of infinite nothings mouthed by irresponsible speakers about toleration. Where does the toleration begin ? Where does it end ? We make people welcome—a thousand welcomes—to all the theology ; but when they touch our money, or our family, or our little ones, we say we must have the very highest references about them. Why refer ? Why submit to such pointless routine ? Refer !—be tolerant, be magnanimous, be trustful. You, who can afford to let a man do what he pleases with theology, ought not to be so scrupulous as to what he may do with your bank-book. Here is a man who lays down the doctrine that property is robbery. His creed is,—Share and share alike. He says he is a "democrat" ; he says he will have no boundary walls, and no entails and primogenitures and rights and deeds and Chancery injunctions and decrees ; he would have all equal.

What a splendid man! What an original thinker about all things created! What an administrator! What a Daniel come to judgment! Shall we tolerate him? Shall we be very gentle to him?—and shall we begin by handing him over whatever we have about us? We are tolerationists! As for theology, you may turn into that field all the beasts you own, and let the quadrupeds trample the fair gardens under their hoofs; but you will not tolerate the man who says,— What is yours is mine, and I have a right to it, and I claim it now. We admire toleration: we think it is an excellent abstract idea: we believe there is a whole heaven of beauty in it, if anybody could discover it; but, in the meantime, we will have no toleration of liars, thieves, evil persons, who seek to disturb the foundations of society and property. We are " fearfully and wonderfully made."

What penalty, then, shall we inflict upon men who seek to destroy our faith? I hesitate not in my reply : Avoid them ; pass by them; they would injure your soul. Wherever there is matter of mere opinion there should be the largest measure of toleration—not upon one side, but on both sides. It is a marvellous thing that the men who cry out for toleration are often the most reluctant to exercise it. There is much mockery addressed to the Christ of to-day ; there is not a little penalty inflicted upon the Christian thinkers of the time ; there are disallowances and disabilities and disqualifications of many kinds attached to deep religious conviction. Do not suppose that toleration is a one-sided quantity; when it is established it will operate from two opposite centres. Meanwhile, what are our religious convictions? If they are large, vital, well-reasoned; if they have borne the burden of the day; if they have sustained the heat of noontide ; if they have survived the thick rains of night ;—if our convictions have been potent in life, comforting in affliction, inspiring in death, he does not violate the genius of conviction who says,—Beware of any man who would tamper with those convictions, who would kill your spiritual enthusiasm, who would tempt you from the service of passion into the passivity of indolence or the uncertainty of insincere confession. We are not intolerant.

We believe, and therefore speak. Our convictions are our life. If they were mere opinions, we should compare them, compromise with others, make arrangements for the settlement of controversies; but where convictions are positive, either on the one side or the other ; where they are real convictions men must abide by them, and beware of the thievish hand. This is our position ; we have tested it by manifold experience.

SELECTED NOTE.

"*Thou shalt stone him with stones, that he die*" (v. 10).—The mode of capital punishment which constitutes a material element in the character of any law, was probably as humane as the circumstances of Moses admitted. It was probably restricted to lapidation or stoning, which, by skilful management, might produce instantaneous death. It was an Egyptian custom (Exod. viii. 26). The public effusion of blood by decapitation cannot be proved to have been a Mosaic punishment, nor even an Egyptian ; for in the instance of Pharaoh's chief baker (Gen. xl. 19), " Pharaoh shall lift up thine head from off thee," the marginal rendering seems preferable—" shall reckon thee and take thine office from thee." He is said to have been "hanged" (xli. 13) ; which may possibly mean posthumous exposure, though no independent evidence appears of this custom in ancient Egypt. The appearance of decapitation, " slaying by the sword," in later times (2 Sam. iv. 8 ; xx. 21, 22 ; 2 Kings x. 6-8) has no more relation to the Mosaic law than the decapitation of John the Baptist by Herod (Matt. xiv. 8–12) ; or than the hewing to pieces of Agag before the Lord by Samuel, as a punishment *in kind* (1 Sam. xv. 33) ; or than the office of the Cherethites, כרתי (2 Sam. viii. 18; xv. 18; xx. 7-23), or headsmen, as Gesenius understands by the word, from כרת, " to chop off " or hew down (executioners belonging to the body-guard of the king) ; whereas execution was ordered by Moses, probably adopting an ancient custom, to be begun first by the witnesses, a regulation which constituted a tremendous appeal to their moral feelings, and after-wards to be completed by the people (Deut. xiii. 10 ; xvii. 7 ; Josh. vii. 25 ; John viii. 7). It was a later innovation that immediate execution should be done by some personal attendant, by whom the office was probably considered as an honour (2 Sam. i. 15 ; iv. 12). Stoning, therefore, was probably the only capital punishment ordered by Moses. It is observable that neither this nor any other punishment was, according to his law, attended with insult or torture. Nor did his laws admit of those horrible mutilations practised by other nations. For instance, he prescribed stoning for adulterers (comp. Lev. xx. 10; Ezek. xxiii. 25 ; xvi. 38-40 ; John viii. 5) ; but the Chaldeans cut off the noses of such offenders. Mutilation of such a nature amounts to a perpetual condemnation to infamy and crime. Moses seems to have understood the true end of punishment, which is not to gratify the antipathy of society against crime, nor moral vengeance, which belongs to God alone, but prevention. " All the people shall hear and fear, and do no more so presumptuously."

PRAYER.

ALMIGHTY GOD, help us to understand thy law and to do it obediently and lovingly, that we may enjoy the happy issue of such action, and find in experience a light upon many a mystery. If we do the will, we shall know the doctrine. How hard it is to do the will thou knowest. Thou understandest us altogether—in the mystery of the mind, in the peculiarity of the whole constitution; thou knowest how sensitive we are to evil suggestion, how profoundly we love the darkness, and how we love to be liberated from the restraints of law. Yet herein is our greatness as well as our infirmity. Thou hast made us in thine own image and likeness; but we have lost our uprightness and sought out many inventions, and now we are following after wind and vanity, and grasping energetically at the nothings of time. So we come before thee to mourn our fall, our personal apostasy, and to utter our personal prayer for pardon, liberty, and hope. We rejoice that there is a door standing wide open, and that within the opened home is our Father waiting to be gracious, his great love tarrying for us, his infinite compassion ready to welcome us. This is the Gospel we have heard; this is the good news which has filled our life from the very first. We have heard that God is love, God is light, God hath no pleasure in the death of the wicked, God says—Turn ye, turn ye, why will ye die?—and he stands at the door of the heart and knocks, and asks to be admitted to the guest-chamber of the soul. Behold, we delight in this Gospel: it is music to our ears—a sovereign balm for every wound. We need such speech, for the darkness is often very burdensome, and the wind so cold, and the pit-falls so many, and our readiness to go astray so eager. So we require to hear, now and again, of thy love and tenderness as revealed in the sacrifice of Christ, the oblation of the Son of God, the atonement wrought for sin. We reply to such Gospel by new vows and oaths and utterances of thankfulness; may we live this utterance in all obedient and noble life. Amen.

Deut. xv. 1-11.

"At the end of every seven years thou shalt make a release. And this is the manner of the release: every creditor that lendeth ought unto his neighbour shall release it; he shall not exact it of his neighbour, or of his brother; because it is called the Lord's release" (vv. 1-2).

THE PLACE OF BENEFICENCE.

GOD is putting lines of mercy amid all the black print of the law. It would seem as if wherever God could find a place at which he might utter some word of pity or compassion he filled up that place with an utterance of his solicitude for the welfare of man. Loving words always look beautiful; perhaps they look most beautiful when surrounded by contrastive words of stern righteousness, of unyielding law, of severe prohibition. Flowers look lovely everywhere, but what must be the loveliness of a flower to the wanderer in a desert? So these Gospel words are full of charm wherever we find them, but they have double charmfulness being found in connection with institutions, instructions, precepts, and commandments marked by the severest righteousness. In the midst of time God graciously puts a year of release. Time needs to be jewelled; time is an appalling monotony. What can be so dull as the days that have no business, no pleasure, no special engagement for faculties which have been prepared for specific work? How dull the time is then, without a sparkle of dew, without a glint of superior light, without a note of supernal music! But God will mark off special periods; the very boundaries shall be gold; the very limits shall glitter with diamonds. How many beautiful days (as we have already seen) has God set in the commonplace of life:—the restful Sabbath, the hilarious festival, the time of family joy. Memory will supply many such dates and engagements which fill the heart with highest gladness. The poor man must have his year of release—the debtor, the slave, the servant, the disappointed heart. The rich have many friends—they can turn the whole week into a gala-day; but the poorest and weakest of mankind must have a year set amid the succession of the days to which they can look with religious expectation. It is something to know the limit of one's endurance. When no date of liberation is fixed, the heart aches because of the burdensome monotony; but when a time is appointed—a specified line laid down—courage rises: the spirit says,—Now I must be brave; every day brings the year of release nearer; I must fire my courage and heroically try again. We know what this is in various departments of life. How often have men sighed, expressing the thought, which they could scarcely put into words sufficiently delicate, that if but a limit could be assigned—say a year hence, or seven years, or ten—they could grapple with a given quantity: they could face a specific and measurable

difficulty; but to look upon the everlasting when that everlasting is one of darkness and trial cows the spirit, subdues and
humiliates the soul.

We must have the element of hopefulness in life: without
hope we die. To-morrow will be a day of ransom and
liberty—if not to-morrow by the clock, yet to-morrow in
feeling: already the dawn is upon our hearts, already we
hear noises of a distant approach: presently a great gladness
will descend upon the soul. The child will be better in a day
or two; when the weather warms (the doctor assures us), the
life will be stronger. When arrangements now in progress are
consummated—and they will be consummated presently—the
whole house will be lighted up with real joy and thankfulness.
So the spirit speaks to itself; so the heart sings songs in the
night-time; so we live by hope and faith—the higher Self, the
grander Reason. Nor is this pitiful dreaming on our part.
There is something in man that will hope. Blessed be God
for the singing angel; when we quench his song, we quench
ourselves. There is a pressure, as of prophecy within us, so
that in our degree we are all foretellers: we have each a
gleaming vision on which the soul's bright answering eyes
are fixed; we know that right will conquer, that light will
chase away the shadows, that truth will be enthroned, and
that earth shall yet be beautiful with her Maker's blessing. This
is the larger hope, the Christian expectation, the evangelical
prophecy. We have but to multiply what is in ourselves,
instinctively and educationally, to find in the expansion of that
great power all that is brightest in prophecy, all that is gladdest
in Christian forecast. What applies to the individual life applies
to the associated life which is denominated the Church.

We find in this year of release what we all need—namely,
the principle of new chances, new opportunities, fresh beginnings. To-morrow—said the debtor or the slave—is the day of
release, and the next day I shall begin again: I shall have
another chance in life; the burden will be taken away, the
darkness will be dispersed, and life shall be young again.
Every man ought to have more chances than one, even in our
own life. God has filled the sphere of life with opportunities.
The expired week is dead and gone, and Christ's own resurrection

day comes with the Gospel of hope, the Gospel of a new
beginning, the Gospel of a larger opportunity ; and the year dies
and buries itself, and the new year comes with silver trumpets,
with proclamations from heaven, and Life says, when it is not
utterly lost,—I will begin again : I will no longer blot the book
of life : I will write with a steady and careful hand. But where
moral questions are concerned a process must be indicated
which is indispensable. Institutional arrangements can be
changed at given dates, but moral releases can only be accomplished by moral processes. The man who is in prison must
take the right steps to get out of it. What are those right
steps ?—repentance, contrition, confession—open, frank, straightforward, self-renouncing confession ; then the man must be
allowed to begin again ; God will, in his providence, work out
for such a man another opportunity ; concealment there must be
none, prevarication none, self-defence none. Where the case
lies between the soul and God—the higher morality still—there
must be an interview at the Cross—a mysterious communion
under the blood that flows from the wounded Christ. "If we
confess our sins, God is faithful and just to forgive us our sins,
and to cleanse us from all unrighteousness." With regard to
this higher order of release we may say,—" Now is the accepted
time ; now is the day of salvation;" the year of jubilee has
come ; the year of release is shining upon us ; whosoever will
let him rise—a man. It is well, notwithstanding, to accustom
the mind to all the lower revelations of release, forgiveness, new
opportunity, that so, step by step, we may ascend the ladder
the head of which is in heaven.

All this being done on the part of the creditor and the
owner, what happens on the side of God ? The answer to that
inquiry is :—

" The Lord shall greatly bless thee in the land which the Lord thy God
giveth thee for an inheritance to possess it " (v. 4).

God never allows us to obey the law without immediate and
large compensation. We cannot obey the laws of health without
instantly being the healthier ; we cannot obey the laws of
cleanliness without the flesh instantly thanking us, in stronger
pulsations and wider liberties, for what we have done to it.

A blessing is attached to all obedience, when the obedience is rendered to law divine and gracious. The reward is in the man's own heart : he has a reward which no thief can take away from the sanctuary in which it is preserved : heaven is within. None can forestall God, or outrun God, or confer upon God an obligation which he cannot repay; he takes the moisture from the earth only that he may return it in copious showers. No man can serve God for nought. The devil has found this out, as in the case of Job; the enemy sees that round about the true life there is a hedge and protection, not planted by man, and by man not to be uprooted. But the commandment is most critical and exacting. The commandment is marvellously adapted to certain infirmities of the human mind. For example, as the seventh year was nearing, men might abstain from doing things that would terminate in the year of release : they could postpone arrangements which would be to their advantage the day after to-morrow; but the spirit of the law foresaw this, arranged for this, and specifically cautioned the heart against this obvious temptation. In the ninth verse we read :—

"Beware that there be not a thought in thy wicked heart, saying, The seventh year, the year of release, is at hand; and thine eye be evil against thy poor brother, and thou givest him nought."

The book which contains this caution by so much vindicates its own inspiration. A book which so knows human nature, understands its every pulse and thought, is a book which was written by more than human wisdom. In incidental instances of this kind we see into the real quality of the book. It is comparatively easy to make broad laws and to give general directions without following them into their issues and all their involutions of consequence and relation; but here is a book which searches the heart, tries the reins,—sharper than any two-edged sword, piercing to the dividing asunder of the joints and marrow : an awful book of judgment. "Beware that there be not a thought in thy wicked heart, saying, The seventh year, the year of release, is at hand"—so I will slacken my endeavours; I will begin the next period of seven years lavishly; then I will show my true nature ; but seeing this obligation is just running off and will exhaust itself in a week or two, I will withhold, and stand still, and wait for the new time. God denounces such reasoning as selfish, vicious, hostile to the spirit of the law. We are to work up to the last moment: to-morrow is the time of release, yet this very eventide is to be marked by the richest generosity, the tenderest regard for human rights, and the seventh year is to end with a benediction. Beware that there is not a thought in thy wicked heart, not a speech upon thy tongue, not a broad, open confession of indifference and carelessness; but a thought in thy wicked heart—speechless, formless, a little spectre on the man's horizon,—beware! God searches the heart: "all things are naked and opened unto the eyes of him with whom we have to do:" "As a man thinketh in his heart, so is he;" though both his hands be full, if the spirit of grudging is in his heart, his oblation is a worthless gift.

A marvellous expression occurs in the eleventh verse: —"The poor shall never cease out of the land." That is a remark which is not understood. Poverty is not an accident; there is a moral mystery connected with poverty which has never yet been found out. The sick-chamber makes the house; the infirm member of the family rules its tenderest thinking. Poverty has a great function to work out in the social scheme; but whilst we admit this we must not take the permanence of poverty as an argument for neglect : it is an argument for solicitude, it is an appeal to benevolence, it is an opportunity to soften the heart and cultivate the highest graces of the soul. It is perfectly true that the bulk of poor people may have brought their poverty upon themselves; but who are we that we should make rough speeches about them ? What have we brought upon ourselves ? If we are more respectable than others, it is still the respectability of thieves and liars and selfish plotters. We, who are apparently more industrious and virtuous and regardful, are not made of different clay, and are not animated by a different blood. It is perfectly true that a thousand people may have brought to-day's poverty upon themselves, and they will have to suffer for it; but beyond all these accidents or incidents there is the solemn fact, that poverty is a permanent quantity, for moral reasons which appeal to the higher instincts of the social commonwealth. We have that we may give ; we are strong that we may support the weak; we are wise that we may teach the ignorant. " Let this mind be in you, which was also in Christ Jesus." No man has the slightest occasion or reason for reproaching any other man, except in relation to the immediate circumstance. If the assize were on a larger scale and we were all involved in the scrutiny, the issue would be this : " There is none righteous, no, not one." It seems ruthless to dash the painted cup of personal respectability out of the hand of any Pharisee; but the Pharisee, with all his praying and fasting and criticism, is a bad and all but unpardonable man; his prayers aggravate his perfidy; because he is a Pharisee it will be difficult for him to be saved.

Very handsomely had the poor man to leave on the day of liberation. The Hebrew man and the Hebrew woman were to leave under happy circumstances : —

"Thou shalt not let him go away empty : thou shalt furnish him liberally out of thy flock, and out of thy floor, and out of thy winepress : of that wherewith the Lord thy God hath blessed thee thou shalt give unto him" (vv. 13, 14).

It was God's before it was yours; it is only yours in the sense of stewardship. When the poor slave leaves, he is to leave with both hands full, and with a gracious burden upon his bended back, and with a blessing in his thankful heart. Law may be obeyed perfunctorily, arbitrarily, grudgingly; or law can be carried out with all the beauty of blossoming fruitfulness, and all the joy of music. Whatever we do we must do handsomely, graciously, not with ungratefulness and begrudging, for work so done is not done, and the blessing is neither with him that stays, nor with him that goes. After this inquiry we may well ask, Where, then, is the superiority of Christianity over Judaism ? Perhaps there is no institutional superiority. I know of no finer laws than are to be found in the Mosaic economy : they are laws of righteousness, and laws of mercy—a wonderful line of grace running through all the severest legislation. Judaism was, as to all these blessings, local and limited : the stranger was not always involved in the spirit of grace : certain blessings or benefactions were limited to the Israelites ; Christianity asserts its superiority by viewing the world as one, the human family as one,—God having made of one blood all nations of men ; Christianity recognises neither Jew nor Greek, neither Barbarian nor Scythian, neither circumcision nor uncircumcision, neither bond nor free ; its spirit is universal ; its love seeks out that which was lost that it might be saved: "This is a faithful

saying, and worthy of all acceptation, that Christ Jesus came into
the world to save sinners;" "The Son of man is come to seek
and to save that which was lost." There is nothing local, nothing
limited : wherever there is a sinner there is an offered Saviour ;
wherever there is abounding sin there is superabounding grace.

SELECTED NOTE.

*" There shall be no poor among you ; for the Lord shall greatly bless thee in
the land which the Lord thy God giveth thee for an inheritance to possess it"*
(v. 4).—The design of the jubilee is that those of the people of God who,
through poverty or other adverse circumstances, had forfeited their personal
liberty or property to their fellow-brethren, should have their debts forgiven
by their co-religionists every half-century, on the great day of atonement,
and be restored to their families and inheritance as freely and fully as God
on that very day forgave the debts of his people and restored them to perfect
fellowship with himself, so that the whole community, having forgiven each
other and being forgiven by God, might return to the original order which
had been disturbed in the lapse of time, and being freed from the bondage
of one another might unreservedly be the servants of him who is their
Redeemer. The aim of the jubilee, therefore, is to preserve unimpaired the
essential character of the theocracy, to the end that there be no poor among
the people of God (Deut. xv. 4). Hence God, who redeemed Israel from the
bondage of Egypt to be his peculiar people, and allotted to them the
promised land, will not suffer any one to usurp his title as Lord over those
whom he owns as his own. It is the idea of grace for all the suffering
children of man, bringing freedom to the captive and rest to the weary
as well as to the earth, which made the year of jubilee the symbol of
the Messianic year of grace (Isa. lxi. 2), when all the conflicts in the
universe shall be restored to their original harmony, and when not only we,
who have the firstfruits of the Spirit, but the whole creation, which groaneth
and travaileth in pain together until now, shall be restored into the glorious
liberty of the sons of God (comp. Isa. lxi. 1-3 ; Luke iv. 21 ; Rom. viii.
18-23 ; Heb. iv. 9).

The importance of this institution will be apparent if it is considered what
moral and social advantages would accrue to the community from the sacred
observance of it. (1) It would prevent the accumulation of land on the part
of a few to the detriment of the community at large. (2) It would render it
impossible for any one to be born to absolute poverty, since every one had
his hereditary land. (3) It would preclude those inequalities which are
produced by extremes of riches and poverty, and which make one man
domineer over another. (4) It would utterly do away with slavery. (5)
It would afford a fresh opportunity to those who were reduced by adverse
circumstances to begin again their career of industry, in the patrimony which
they had temporarily forfeited. (6) It would periodically rectify the dis-
orders which crept into the state in the course of time, preclude the division
of the people into nobles and plebeians, and preserve the theocracy inviolate

PRAYER.

ALMIGHTY GOD, we need great words to cheer us. Our life is dark and dreary. Where can those great words be found but in thine own book ? They were made for our sin ; they are shaped by our sorrow ; they are attuned to our grief. We know that this is thy word because it meets our sad necessity. This is no light of man's enkindling, for such light can struggle but feebly with the heavy darkness. This is the light of the Lord, for it fills the whole sky, and all night flees away, in terror and in shame, from its infinite brightness. We know thy word by the inward witness. A stranger will not we follow, we know his voice to be strange. It has not in it the love-tone which lifts it up to the level of thy speech. We turn away from it, for it would lead us into solitude and danger and death. Let thy voice fill the heart. Let thy music sing in all the chambers of our life and make the life-house glad. We rejoice that the heavens do stoop to the earth, and that God holds converse with man. This is the work of Christ and none other. This is the incoming of the Son of man unto our life bringing with him morning and liberty, pardon and growth in grace. Even so, Lord Jesus, come quickly! Take up thine abode in our heart ; turn our tears into precious jewels. Make music of our sighing! When our heart is ill at ease quiet us with thine own peace. Undertake for us altogether, cleansing away our sin, redeeming us from all captivity, sanctifying us by the continual ministry of grace, and ennobling us by daily inspiration. We are very frail : let our feebleness become a cry unto the clement heavens. We are poor—let our poverty be its own prayer. We are sinful exceedingly—not wholly with the hand, but oftentimes wholly with the heart. Let our sense of sin be a cry for mercy and for pardon. Let this hour be a memorable one in our history. May men see angels to-night. May the worldly spirit be liberated from its bondage and have entrance into the upper places, where the light is cloudless and where the music is clear. Let backsliders return with heavy hearts but eager feet, and let the door of thy grace be found already open to every prodigal who would come home again. Strengthen every heart that has made a good vow. Thou knowest how difficult it is to live up to the sacred hope. How prone we are to the earth, how beset we are by temptation, how old associations gather around us and form themselves into a body of attack. Thou knowest us altogether. Sustain us, therefore, in the great fight, and, at the last, through the blood of the everlasting covenant, may we be able to speak of a well-fought field, and of a crown of glory laid up for us. Give us great thoughts, noble aspirations, pure and heroic impulses ; and, in all things, make us like thy Son Jesus Christ, brightness of thy glory, and express image of thy person. Amen.

Deut. xv. 12-18.

"And if thy brother, an Hebrew man, or an Hebrew woman, be sold unto thee, and serve thee six years; then in the seventh year thou shalt let him go free from thee" (v. 12).

GREAT PRINCIPLES APPLIED.

IT appears, then, that even bondage does not destroy brotherhood. Observe how the permanent and the temporary are joined in this verse. The brother continues for ever. It is not brotherhood but slavery that ceases. When the man goes out he goes out a brother: his old yesterday of bondage is a cloud blown away; but the fraternal instinct and the fraternal responsibility can only end with life. Yet how wonderfully accidents or temporary circumstances modify all things and create somewhat curious and often difficult relations between man and man! Why should one brother be master and another brother be bondman? The question cannot be answered abstractly or argumentatively. We must recognise facts as they are. Of all the most obvious facts which appeal to our attention there is none more obvious than that one man is set over another, that one man is destined, for a period at least, to be the servant of another. Were we creating a society upon a philosophical basis we might try to create some other kind of structure; but we are not called to the creation of society but to its interpretation. We are servants one of another. The Queen is the subject of her kingdom. No man can be a true king who is not first a subject. There is a greater king than any merely nominal monarch who represents an individuality: a kinghood of humanity, the royalty of right, the princeliness of strength helping weakness and being the guarantee of weakness against unjust and overwhelming oppression. Let the situation be accepted. To chafe under the yoke is to destroy some of our best faculties and to render progress simply impossible. Good is to be obtained from servitude. We learn to rule by learning to serve; we learn to be good men by being good little children. There is a period of bondage in every life. Even those who are apparently born to great masterliness and even royalty have to stoop and serve and accept discipline and find their way to any throne worth occupying through a process of labour and self-denial.

" And when thou sendest him out free from thee, thou shalt not let him go away empty " (v. 13).

Duty on the one side does not end with service on the other. We ought to be careful how we apply this word duty to our life. Duty is in some respects a cold word, and quite measurable : it begins at a certain chime of the clock, and ends with a certain other and nameable chime; it lives within the day; it does not carry its work home with it, or dream about it, or discover the poetry and religiousness of service; it is in some respects duty— mere duty, very severe duty, performed to the last jot and tittle ; but still it is only a hireling's service. The Lord would add love to duty; he would add beauty to strength. The value of the gift is at the point where it begins to run over. What we give is to be given after the fashion of a vessel filled, filled to the brim, pressed down, running over ; with somewhat of the poetry of wastefulness about it—wastefulness, that is, as interpreted by dull and worldly eyes, but quite celestial poetry and music after the fashion of the Cross of Christ, when viewed by him who is the Giver of every good and every perfect gift. We cannot do our duty to a good servant ; there must be more than duty ; there must be remembrance, thoughtfulness, gratitude,—downright, frank affection : for the work has been well done : no hireling fingers have touched it, but a devoted heart has thought about it, dreamed about it, planned it in a hundred different ways, and loving attention has been given to every detail. Let no man leave your life empty-handed. You may give him at least a flower, a smile, a grip with meaning in it, a look charged with the radiance of gratitude. Do not regard life as a temporary arrangement, and all social relations but so many mechanical puttings together for transient and vanishing ends ; life should be a religious solidity, a complete unity, so that whether one member suffer all the members shall suffer with it, or whether one member rejoice all the members shall share its gladness. Towards this happy consolidation of social relations and rights all things under Christian inspiration are tending; whilst they are tending in this direction there will be misunderstanding, jarring, somewhat of bitterness of criticism, it may be, and a good deal of exasperation and reproach : yet all the while the central line is moving towards understanding, sympathy, confidence, liberality.

All good work should be well rewarded, and all human connections should be so conducted that it costs the heart grief to give them up. Men have been so brought into unity of mind and feeling in a short Atlantic trip that the good-bye spoken the last day on the ship has quite made strong men quiver with tender emotion. The breaking-up of the ship's company seemed to have in it the breaking-up of all things ; men go on their different ways : they see one another no more; they remember the days and the nights, and the talks upon the dreary waste of water, and one touch of the hand dissolves the company. How sad to part in ill-feeling, with misunderstanding and bitterness of heart !—and how sadder still—only with a solemn and noble pathos—to part in real friendship, genuine love, mutual, unquestioning trust and confidence ! The parting *will* come ; we can so arrange our relations now that when the parting comes its sorrow shall be sweet, its sadness shall be but a cloud for a moment veiling a celestial light.

The same idea is continued in the fourteenth verse :—

"Thou shalt furnish him liberally out of thy flock, and out of thy floor, and out of thy winepress."

He who has served well should be treated well. That must be the law in all our life. We must have done with all merely mechanical and hireling relations if ever we are to realise Christ's idea of society. There should be no orphan children; there should be no unattended sick ; there should be no outcast city. It is worse than vain—it reaches the highest point of profanity ; it aggravates itself, indeed, into an appalling blasphemy—that we should first cast out the city and then make a charity of attending to the city we have outcast. Something has to be done within all operating social arrangements that will prevent the catastrophe. Service has no right to end in poverty. After a man's day's work is done he should carry with him liberally out of the flock, and out of the floor, and out of the winepress ; this he should do by right : the issue should not be a happy accident but a logical and just conclusion. The idea is of universal application. If any man be mean enough to serve as a man-pleaser and with a view to the ultimate bounty, he ought to be disappointed—and disappointed he certainly will be. All such men will exist to the end of time ;

but we cannot arrange society upon a basis of suspicion and distrust. Whoever has served well should have a quiet eventide, no wolf of hunger pursuing him, no dark cloud lying over the roof like a burden which the house can but ill bear. Preacher, merchant, thinker, writer, tradesman of every kind, master, servant—the time of labour completed—should go into green pastures, and walk by still waters, and have a quiet watching and waiting time, bread being given and water being made sure, and a "Well done, good and faithful servant," floating upon the whole life like a blessing from heaven. Many men render this impossible by their own misconduct. Misconduct would ruin creation ; a selfish and rebellious spirit would render heaven impossible, on earth or otherwhere. Why fix attention upon the exceptions— unless it be with a view to reduce their number ? Our love-duty remains the same. If we would be well served we must rule well. It seems as if we escaped with all our bounty : we allowed the good servant, of whatever name or degree, to go, and we gave nothing ; the arrangement that had existed for years—two, four, six, seven years—was dissolved without a single gift out of the flock, or the floor, or the winepress ; and we have reasoned that therefore we have saved so much. It is a fallacy. That is a selfishness that lives upon its own life-blood. Only generosity can be happy ; only liberality puts the top-stone on justice. In forgetting the liberal donation we have laid up wrath against the day of wrath even for our own souls : we have shut out light from the south : we have wronged our own spirits.

"And thou shalt remember that thou wast a bondman in the land of Egypt, and the Lord thy God redeemed thee : therefore I command thee this thing to-day" (v. 15).

Memory should be called in to the aid of duty. We must not forget the great general principles in looking at the momentary details. One man is master, we say ; but only in a very narrow sense. The master now was himself once a slave. We were all slaves. If any man now is good, he must remember the mire out of which he was lifted, and the hole out of which he was digged. No man amongst us has come down from the untainted clouds, and is conferring a favour upon human society by mingling with it. The whitest robe is blackness compared with the snow of celestial righteousness. We are respectable as

amongst ourselves and between ourselves, and in contrast with
other nameable people ; but boasting ourselves amongst ourselves
we become foolish : the standard is not with us :—" Be ye therefore perfect, even as your Father which is in heaven is perfect."
The great principle of this direction involves all life. Memory is
to play a wonderful part in the education of the soul. When we
see a prodigal, are we to gather our skirts about us and assume
a relation of severe respectability to the poor sore-footed
wanderer ? Remember we are all prodigals. One man is seen
more upon the road than another, and is more obviously departing from the Father's house ; but movement is a very subtle
action. Some men move in the night-time,—ay, they move at
flying pace ! In the day they are at church : in the light they
are demure : in society they are irreproachable ; but no sooner
does the cloud curtain out the sun—no sooner does night come
than they fly : their feet are swift in the way of destruction.
Remember ! When we hear of men getting wronged in this way
or in that way—in the city, at home, in all the various relations
of life—it suits our illicit and calculated piety to sigh over the
ruin which we have perceived. It may be a hypocritical sigh.
Remember ! We need not go into words ; reproach is useless.
Let the soul look backward—steadily, closely, fully, critically—
and in that retrospect there will be fire enough to light a hell.
We are cursed through not looking back far enough. We now
have "respectable" people in the Church—the Church that ought
to be the gathering-ground of prodigals, broken hearts, shattered
lives,—a place of tears ! It has become a boasting-ground—the
paradise of a Pharisee. We have forgotten the Egypt of our own
bondage and humiliation.

"It shall not seem hard unto thee, when thou sendest him away free
from thee ; for he hath been worth a double hired servant to thee, in serving
thee six years " (v. 18).

Religious inspiration should be mightier than selfish instincts.
Man must be conquered by God. That which is natural must be
chastened out of the soul : " Ye must be born again." Does it
not seem a hard thing for a servant to be taking away liberally
out of the flock, and out of the floor, and out of the winepress ?
Does it not seem a hard thing that the servant should have both
hands filled and should be blessed with a sense of fulness and

prosperity? It all might have been saved. Such is the reasoning of the hard heart. Whatever you save as against righteousness, justice, and love has no lasting in it: there is a ghost among the money. God's judgment or blessing rests upon the whole flock, floor, and winepress. The money saved from the man who had a right to it shall be lost. Do not imagine that God has abandoned all the commercial relations of life and handed over marts and exchanges to the dominion of the devil. The Lord still reigneth, and all history, interpreted by a Christian spirit, ends in this: that whoever endeavours selfishly to upset the divine regulation is never really the richer for the money he has stolen. We dare not spend stolen money: we are quite sure if we lay it down on the counter that the man who looks at it will see written upon it—" This money was stolen." We dare not unroll the sheaf of stolen notes: in the very crinkle of the paper there is an accusation. Honest money goes far, and brings sweetness with it and light and hope, and a blessing full of unction may be asked upon the little loaf bought by the honestly-earned penny. Whatever we have let it be honest money, and then the more we have the more everybody else will have, for we shall be but trustees and stewards, sowing with both hands and reaping with both hands night and day. This is God's law; this doctrine lies at the very root of divine legislation and social economy.

All this would be interesting in itself, and would be full of holy and happy impulse as mere matter of history—Hebrew, or Greek, or Roman; but the matter does not end there. The legislator is seen in the legislation. You find the mind of God in the law of God. What does God ask? He only asks what he has first given. The fourteenth verse proves this:—

" . . . of that wherewith the Lord thy God hath blessed thee thou shalt give unto him."

We do not create property; we do not create gold. It pleases us to think ourselves creators and proprietors, and it delights our misguided spirits to constitute ourselves into boards of directors and managers and comptrollers: whereas we have nothing that we have not received; a Voice sounds from heaven, saying,—The gold and the silver are mine, and the cattle upon a thousand hills; all souls are mine. God opens his hand and satisfies the desire of every living thing. God only asks what he has first given; the Giver condescends to become the Suppliant. Reading such legislation, how easy it is for us to believe that "God is love"! It required a highly spiritual Christian to put that revelation into words: "God is love"—but all such sayings go back over the whole field of history, and express in their conciseness what all the best men have been long thinking. One of the greatest of our departed statesmen defined a proverb as "the wisdom of many, and the wit of one." So with this sentence, "God is love"; it is the instinct of many; it is the experience of many; it is the utterance of one. The Old Testament is as full of love as the New Testament. The legislation of Moses culminates in the redemption of Christ.

SELECTED NOTE.

"*And thou shalt remember that thou wast a bondman in the land of Egypt, and the Lord thy God redeemed thee : therefore I command thee this thing to-day*" (v. 15).—The Israelites were frequently reminded, after their exode from Egypt, of the oppressions they endured in that "house of bondage" from which they had been delivered by the direct interposition of God. The design of these admonitions was to teach them justice and kindness towards their servants when they should become settled in Canaan (Deut. v. 15; viii. 14; x. 19; xv. 15; xxiii. 7, etc.), as well as to impress them with gratitude towards their great Deliverer. The Egyptians had domestic servants, who may have been slaves (Exod. ix. 14, 20, 21; xi. 5). But the Israelites were not dispersed among the families of Egypt—they formed a special community. They had exclusive possession of the land of Goshen, "the best part of the land of Egypt." They lived in permanent dwellings, their own houses, and not in tents (Exod. xii. 22). Each family seems to have had its own house (Exod. xii. 4; comp. Acts vii. 20); and judging from the regulations about eating the passover, they could scarcely have been small ones (Exod. xii., etc.). They appear to have been well clothed (Exod. xii. 11). They owned "flocks and herds, and very much cattle" (Exod. xii. 4, 6, 32, 37, 38). They had their own form of government; and although occupying a province of Egypt, and *tributary* to it, they preserved their tribes and family divisions, and their internal organisation throughout. The service required from the Israelites by their taskmasters seems to have been exacted from males only, and probably a portion only of the people were compelled to labour at any one time. As tributaries, they probably supplied levies of men, from which the wealthy appear to have been exempted (Exod. iii. 16; iv. 29; v. 20). The poor were the oppressed; "and all the service, wherewith they made them serve, was with rigour" (Exod. i. 11-14). But Jehovah saw their "afflictions and heard their groanings," and delivered them, after having inflicted the most terrible plagues on their oppressors.

PRAYER.

ALMIGHTY GOD, thou hast set apart a time for worship, and a place for the sacrifice of praise. This is the day the Lord hath made: we will rejoice and be glad in it; this is the place where the Lord's name is recorded: here he will be and show himself unto those who lift up towards him eyes of expectation. We bless thee for the holy time, for the holy place, and for the holy book,—a time that is separate, a place that is made a sanctuary, a book that stands above all other books, alone in its completeness and authority. May we understand these appointments, and respond to all their meaning: may the time be as a jewel among the days; may the place sanctify our habitations; may the book inspire and direct our thought and feeling and action. Thus, may we be the better—not the worse—for our meeting together in thy name: may we feel the mystery of sympathy; may we enter into the joy of fellowship; may we have communion one with another and with our Lord Jesus Christ by the power of the Holy Ghost. Thus, united in thy love and worshipping at thine altar, we shall be prepared to endure the burden and the suffering of life, and to wait with expectancy and hope the day of thine appearing. We bless thee for the flowers in the wilderness, for water among the rocks, for a cooling breeze at noonday; for all the mercy and lovingkindness, so tender and abundant, which have followed us all the days of our life, and made it a time of sunshine and liberty. That we have not lived up to all this call of thine, enforced by providences so tender, and ennobled by a pathos so wondrous as the sacrifice of thy Son, is our bitterest complaint: we accuse ourselves; we know that we have come short in all things, and that we have offended against thee. But thy mercy is great to forgive as well as to provide; thy lovingkindness is a redemption as well as a providence; so we come to the Cross, owning our sickness of heart, our rebellion of will, our whole evil-mindedness, asking for the pardon of God. Comfort us according to our necessities; how many they are thou knowest, how bitter and sharp thou alone canst tell. Withhold not thy consolations: let thy solaces be more in number than our sufferings; then shall we magnify God in the house of our affliction. Regard our loved ones for whom it is our delight to pray. Some are not here: they are far away upon the sea, or beyond the sea, in strange lands, in difficult places; or they are in the chamber of sickness, or in the shadow of a great sorrow, counting their loss, and not able to find the gain which thou hast hidden amid its tears; the Lord look upon them, be tender and gracious unto them, comfort them with stimulus, that they may be stirred up to nobler service and not be allowed to sink under the burden of their grief. Make the old young; make the young glad with a double joy ; and may business teach us that we are children of heaven and not of earth, of eternity and not of time, and that there are no good things to be found below which can satisfy the capacity of the soul.

The Lord hear us in these things : his attention shall be a blessing; his condescending to listen shall be a help ; and as for the reply—the holy answer, the gracious response of Heaven—will it be less than the Cross ? Will it be more than the earth and time can receive ? Will it be a surprise of benefaction ? We know it will be worthy of the name in which our prayer is prayed, and there we rest. Amen.

Deut. xvi.

" Observe the month of Abib, and keep the passover unto the Lord thy God : for in the month of Abib the Lord thy God brought thee forth out of Egypt by night " (v. 1).

CONDITIONS OF WORSHIP.

THE time is specified, and the reason is given. This is the law, rather than a mere accident. The law is : that every month has a memory, every day has a story, every night has a star all its own. Selected instances help us to ascertain general principles. Acting upon those instances, we become familiar with their spirit and moral genius, so much so that we begin to ask, Are there not other memorable events ? Are there not other times of deliverance ? Have we been brought out of Egypt only ? Are not all the days storied with providential love ? Thus, from the particular we pass into the general, and from the general to the universal ; and thus all time is lighted up by the divine and comforting Presence. The time is only dull when we make it such. If the events of our life had been brighter, then our moments of temporal rejoicing would have been more numerous : every day might have been a birthday ; every hour might have been labelled with some deed of love ; the whole week long we should have had festival as well as fast, the sound of trumpet and mirthfulness as well as the voice of groaning and confession of sin. The Lord knows what he has done for every month of the year. It would seem as if the calendar were kept in heaven. We may not consult the diary, but God looks at it, and according to the time of day and the time of year he expects the psalm and hymn of earth. Why do we blur the pages of the daily journal so that we cannot tell what happened this day twelvemonth, so that the day shall be but a moral vacancy in the life? Who died this day year? Whose death does this day for ever commemorate—what martyr, what apostle, what great leading thinker, what sweet life at home? Were these questions asked at every dawn, what time in the whole year would there be that might not be an "Abib"— a "time of putting in the sickle," a reaping time, having even in the winter a touch of harvest gladness? We should try to make the time more memorable. This is impossible to some, if heroic and chivalrous deed be required, but it is possible to all who can love and serve and think and patiently endure.

If God is so careful about time, has he any regard for place?

"Thou mayest not sacrifice the passover within any of thy gates, which the Lord thy God giveth thee :

"But at the place which the Lord thy God shall choose to place his name in, there thou shalt sacrifice the passover at even, at the going down of the sun, at the season that thou camest forth out of Egypt " (vv. 5, 6).

This is morally consistent with God's claim for gracious recollection of definite times. May we not slay the passover where we please? The answer is, Certainly not. May we not insulate ourselves, and upon little church appointments of our own creation carry out the ceremony of our worship? The answer is, Certainly not. We should strive to move in the direction at least of unity, commonwealth, fellowship, solidarity. The sacrifice is the same, the man who offers it is the same; but because it is not offered at the place which God has chosen the sacrifice and the sacrificer go for nothing. That is in harmony with all the social arrangements which experience has approved. There are fit places for all things, as well as fit times. Has God chosen a place? There can be no hesitation as to an affirmative reply. God has always been solicitous about a house for himself: he would have a building put up from foundation to pinnacle for his own service—a house that should be called by his own name, and that should owe all its dignity and worth to his presence and sanction. But, whilst all questions of locality have their importance within given limits, the great doctrine of the text is that there is an appointed place, where God and man shall, so to say, face one another in solemn and joyous interview. There is only one place, and all related places are only of importance and value in proportion as they are vitally related. What is that one place ? It is called Golgotha—Calvary,—the place of the Cross, the shadow of the altar on which the Saviour died. We can only meet God at the Cross, if we have to meet in the name of mercy, compassion, hope. If we would meet on Sinai, we have no answer; if we would meet on Golgotha, the answer is with God—an infinite reply of love and pardon and release. It is wonderful how God has fixed certain great centres and allowed us liberty only within the radius. Dwelling upon that radius, we call it liberty ; but, fixing the mind upon the centre, we call it law, divine sovereignty, heavenly supremacy. The centre is not fixed by us, but by the Lord ; and our liberty is also determined by his wisdom. There are, then, holy places, and there are holy times. There are holy places without referring to the Church, distinctively so called ; and there are holy times without referring to the Sabbath day. The grave is a holy place. Blessed be God, there are yet men who cannot play a fool's game within the boundaries of the churchyard filled with the sleeping dead. There are places marked by moral strife, which happily ended in conquest wrought by righteousness and truth. There are altars where we prayed victorious prayers ; there are times of light—well-remembered light : we know just when the light came, how full it was, how it struck us to the earth for one moment, and how amidst its lustre we heard appeals and directions, out of obedience to which came our noblest life. Want of veneration is want of dignity. To be able to treat all places and all times alike is simply to be able to say that we have destroyed the very faculty which may become the beginning of the noblest life and service.

The time having been fixed and the place having been determined, what remains ?

"And thou shalt keep the feast of weeks unto the Lord thy God with a tribute of a freewill offering of thine hand, which thou shalt give unto the Lord thy God, according as the Lord thy God hath blessed thee " (v. 10).

Here is the beginning of another kind of liberty. A wonderful word occurs in this verse ; there is no larger word in all the language of devotion and service. That word is "a freewill offering." Reading the Scriptures carefully up to this point,

we would suppose that everything had been claimed, taxed, and
insisted upon that could possibly be given to God's altar ; yet we
are reminded that such is not the case : the very opportunity of
giving unto the Lord a "freewill" offering shows that still something has been left. How wonderfully God educates the human
race : he will insist upon definite claims and obligations being
answered, and yet he will also give opportunity for freewill
action, as if he had said,—Now we shall see what you will do
when left to yourselves ; the law no longer presses you : the great
hand is lifted, and for the time being you shall do in this matter
as it may please your own mind and heart. That is an element
in the divine education of the human race. God gives us opportunities of showing ourselves to ourselves. He only would count
the gift : no one should know what had been done : the sweet
transaction should lie between the one soul and the living Lord.
The Church could not live upon that to-day. Here and there
instances would occur of almost superhuman liberality—instances
amounting to complete devotion and sacrifice : blessed be God for
these ; but remove public opinion, public criticism, and all the
other considerations which operate upon human action, and then
stand in amazement at the result which would accrue. The soul
must be revealed to itself ; the man must be compelled to drag up
the coward that lies asleep within his own nature, and he must
look that coward in the face, and call that coward by his own
name. We are not to be permitted to live in rush and tumult
and such tempestuous excitement as shall lead to false estimates
of ourselves. At given periods of time we have to see what we
are in God's sight ; and whether we be saint or sinner, coward,
liar, or hero and truthful man, we must know the reality of the
ase. What is given under pressure is not given : what is given
to a subscription list in order to keep up the harmony of the
numbers is wasted money ; only that is given which cannot be
kept back ; only that is accepted which carries with it the blood
of the heart.

Another singular word occurs in this tenth verse :—"a tribute."
The literal meaning is that the gift is to be proportional. It is
a word with a strong arithmetical or numerical aspect : not only is
there a gift, but the gift is the result of thought, calculation, and
expresses the serious and responsible judgment of the giver.

That consideration alters the whole case.   It would have been easy to throw a dole to the Lord that had no reference whatever to what was left behind : that would be a broad, easily-opened gate to heaven ; but such is not the condition stated in the bond. Even the freewill offering is to be tributary : it is to be based upon the original substance, the actual property, whatever is in the hand as momentary possession.   Thus, sacrifice is to be calculated ; worship is to be the result of forethought ; nothing is to be done of mere constraint or as consultative of ease and indulgence. A word of taxation touches the very poetry and pathos of oblation.

"And thou shalt rejoice before the Lord thy God, thou, and thy son, and thy daughter, and thy manservant, and thy maidservant, and the Levite that is within thy gates, and the stranger, and the fatherless, and the widow, that are among you, in the place which the Lord thy God hath chosen to place his name there " (v. 11).

This gives us the joyous aspect of religion.   An ancient Jewish annotator has made a beautiful remark upon this verse, to the effect that "thy four, O Israel, and my four shall rejoice together." Observe how the numbers are divided into fours, and how the one four may be said to be man's and the second four may be said to be God's.   This is the distinction drawn by Rashi, the Jewish commentator : "Thy son, and thy daughter, and thy manservant, and thy maidservant"—let them rejoice, let them be glad in response to music, and let them call for more music to express their ever-increasing joy ; but my four must be there also : the Levite, the stranger, the fatherless, and the widow ; they represent the divine name as authority for admission to the feast.   The religious servant, the poor stranger, the orphan, and the widow,—they sit down, in seats divinely claimed for them, at the festive board.   So the company shall be representative : —son, daughter, manservant, maidservant ; priest, stranger, orphan, widow ;—this is the typical company sitting down at the symbolical feast.   God will not have our small houseparties, made up of people of one class, equally well-dressed and accosting one another in the language of equality ; he will have a large feast.   We can have no true feast that some orphan child does not partake of.   If the desolate and the stranger eat nothing of our feast, the feast will be but an evil memory to the

very appetite which it has sated. Every man should have
connected with his house, however small the house may be,
some child, or poor creature, or outcast dog, that looks to him
for crumbs, or cup of water, or caressing hand, or stimulating
word. Your house is not a little structure of four walls: it is
only four little walls that it may typify, as by an arithmetical
symbol, an inexpressible quantity. There should be no waste
meat in the house; there should be no vacant seat at the
table; and if there are some who cannot come to the table the
table must be sent to them. Wherever there is hunger, however brought about, it claims to be a guest at the best man's
table.

The Lord will have joy, as well as law and tribute and
appointed time and defined and circumscribed space: "Thou
shalt rejoice before the Lord thy God." A wonderful turn of
events is indicated by this permission. Instead of the word
being one expressive of fear, hopeless solemnity, and utter
dejection of mind, it is a word which could be used upon
birth-day, wedding-day, midsummer-day, when the flowers are
richest and greatest in number. "Thou shalt rejoice"—
rejoice and be glad; rejoice and give thanks; rejoice and dance
and sing, the very ecstasy of love and worship. Where there is
such joy the stranger and the fatherless and the widow must
be included. It is not in the nature of joy to exclude. We wait
for each other to be in some happy temper that we may ask
permission to introduce the exiled child or friend; we say we
must watch our opportunity; when the master of the house is
glad, when his heart is overflowing with love, when he must
sing because of the fire that is burning within him—a holy fire
of joy—then, at the critical moment, we will ask if he will not see
the face he has not beheld for many a day; in his joy he will say
Yes; in the festival of his heart he will forgive. Joy does not
shut doors and close windows and silence birds that sing and
children that laugh; joy says, Let the strangers hover at the
door, and look in: they will do no harm; and if they come
forward a pace or two, so be it; this is a night of gladness, a
day of banqueting; turn none away; if you can spread the
table far enough to take in some outsiders, spread it; the day is
bright, the day is a day of heaven. Joy must be inclusive; joy

must have large things. The critical thought is often severe. In calculating moods we number our friends and our guests; but when the great wave of gladness rolls through the heart—rises, swells, breaks, and rises again, who could be critically exclusive or meanly particular? Who would not say,—Yes, that other child may come in: by sitting closer together we can make room for two poor friends still? Who does not lift up the goblet and say, There remains enough in it to satisfy the thirst of yet another wanderer; go into the highways and the hedges, and compel the people to come in with the sweet compulsion of love? That is the meaning of the Church. It is not meant for " thy son, and thy daughter," seated in one respectable place, and " thy manservant, and thy maidservant," seated in a secondary and inferior place; but it is meant for thy son, and thy daughter, and thy manservant, and thy maidservant, and the stranger, and the fatherless, and the widow, and the man who has no inheritance—a glorious Church! Each Church should ask what it is doing for the stranger, and the fatherless, and the widow, and the man who has no definite position or inheritance in society. It is no Church that does not spread a table every week for the very poorest people in the district; it may be a congregation—a set of persons who luxuriate in what they believe to be excellent provisions; but it is not a Christian Church. The Christian Church should have tables spread for the fatherless, and the stranger, and the widow, and the lost, and the weary. The measure of the hospitality should be the measure of the hunger of those who come. But if we should be taken in? Thank God for it! to be taken in sometimes is educative, and is not without some moral advantage. The counterfeit proves that there is a good deal of reality; the counterfeit is a tribute to Christian generosity. We may never have been taken in, and therefore may laugh the pharisaic laugh over our own shrewdness; but in proportion as we laugh that pharisaic laugh are we ourselves trying to take in omniscience. In the Old Testament, therefore, there were times of joy. It has been pointed out as remarkable that the Feast of Tabernacles was proverbially a time of rejoicing: the dedication of Solomon's temple, the commencement of the second temple, and the dedication of the wall of Jerusalem, all took place in or about the time of the Feast of Tabernacles.

"Thou shalt not plant thee a grove of any trees near unto the altar of the Lord thy God, which thou shalt make thee. Neither shalt thou set thee up any image; which the Lord thy God hateth" (vv. 21, 22).

Thus, imagery is forbidden—even religious imitation and attempted reproduction of things divine and inexpressible. We are prone to do something to show our handiwork in God's sanctuary; it pleases us to try to add something to the circle; it delights us to run one rim of gilt around the refined gold which burns with the image and superscription of God. We are told not to interfere; we must keep our hands off everything. We must learn to stand still; sometimes to do everything by doing nothing; and we must learn to rebuke our inventive faculty and become learned in the utterance of simple prayer. God will have his altar untouched.: he will have human attention undistracted by any human devices. The altar is to stand alone in its simple dignity—most adorned when unadorned. There must be no attempt to link true religion and false religion, inspired worship and idolatrous worship, groves humanly planted and altars divinely built. The Lord will have a time for himself, and place for himself, a gift for himself, an altar for himself. Why for himself? Because he is the Lord, and because he means to train the human mind and heart without distraction towards the highest sublimity of law. Who will not set up his reason against the altar, and delight because his religion is rational?—as well hold up a candle to the sun, because all fire is of the same quality; because there is but one fire in the universe, and that is GOD. The sun says,—Thou shalt not light a candle in my presence. We do it, but the candle is literally of no service in the presence of the mid-day sun. Jesus Christ is the Light of the world—the Sun of the great firmament of the soul—and he alone can light the space that is to be illumined. Who will not throw the little flower of self-approval upon the altar, saying,—I am not as other men: I fast, I pay tithes, I do not practise extortion: I am not as the publicans are? The Lord has forbidden all groves and all images and all distractions. Only one man is permitted near the altar; only one soul is heard in heaven. His name?— *the broken-hearted sinner!*

PRAYER.

ALMIGHTY GOD, thy word is a living word, coming into our hearts from heaven, full of promise, full of consolation, and full of stimulus. We cannot read it without answering it; our souls know it to be a divine word, so tender, so full of music, calling us upward to broader and nobler life. The word of the Lord abideth for ever: amid all changes it is the same: it changes not; its great word is a word of love, and hope, and forgiveness, for the erring sons of men. Thy word is a gospel; if there is in it the severity of judgment, it is that sinners may be affrighted out of evil, and brought under the blessing of condescending and redeeming Heaven. The terrors of the Lord are meant to persuade men. May we—by terror or by love—all be brought to thyself, thy house, the Cross of Christ the way, and Christ himself the Truth. We bless thee that we have hope in this direction. We thank thee that when we are most overcast, brightness arises from the Cross; we rejoice that when the burden is heaviest, it is Christ's almighty hand that lifts it from our weakness. In thy house we have security; in the temple of God we have the beginning of heaven; in the light of the Sabbath we have the dawn of eternal rest. For all these mercies we bless thee with united heart, with fervent love, with undistracted attention and will. Our heart is fixed, O God, our heart is fixed. For these suggestions we bless thee. Once we were as children, tossed to and fro, driven about; but now, being men in Christ Jesus, we stand in the security of thy love, we are blessed by the tenderness of thy grace, and we are made strong by all the promises which thou hast addressed to us. We give one another to God. We ask for one another blessings suited to the need of each life. Thou knowest us altogether: thou knowest the weakest and the poorest, the man who has no words with which to utter his desire, and the soul which bends itself down in burning shame before thee because of remembered sin. We pray thee to look upon us according to our need, and out of the unsearchable riches of Christ do thou supply all our wants; how many they are we do not ourselves know: thou knowest every necessity; thou hast numbered the hairs of our head, how much more hast thou considered the necessities of our soul! We leave ourselves in thy hands; they are mighty, they are gentle, they are full to abounding with all heavenly riches and grace. Send none unblessed away: may our homes be the happier for our having been to church; may our business life be the nobler for our having bent at the altar; and may our whole course upon the earth be upright and straightforward because we have been with Jesus and learned of him, and are inspired by his spirit and illumined by his mind.

The Lord hear us; the Lord come closely to us that we may whisper our prayers; and may we know that our prayers have been heard through the blood of the everlasting covenant, because of deep peace, and sacred joy, and radiant hope, which only are the gifts of God.   Amen.

Deut. xvii.

" If there be found among you, within any of thy gates which the Lord thy God giveth thee, man or woman, that hath wrought wickedness in the sight of the Lord thy God, in transgressing his covenant, and hath gone and served other gods, and worshipped them, either the sun, or moon, or any of the host of heaven, which I have not commanded " (vv. 2, 3).

TRUE WORSHIP.

THIS makes our relation to God very definite.   There is to be no intermediate worship.   Closeness—almost visible closeness—is to be the rule and standard of our communion with God.   Nothing must stand between.   We are permitted to come boldly to the throne of grace, that we may obtain mercy and find grace to help in time of need.   There must be no intervening system of priests, or officers of any kind, or angels of any degree : every soul must have right of way to God, and must not stop on the road, but go straight up as it were to the presence-chamber of the king.   This honour have all the saints ; this delight is the portion of all broken hearts and contrite spirits. The publican may stand with eyes down-cast and breast smitten as if in reproach, and say, " God be merciful to me a sinner !" Only two parties are named in the covenant—God and the sinner himself.   Observe the definiteness of God's command.   There is to be no counterfeit ; there is to be no pretence.   Even the sun is not to be worshipped, nor the fair moon, nor any of the stars that make night rich.   The temptation is very strong.   If anything visible might be worshipped, surely it would be the sun, at any point of what we call his career—in the whitening east, in the dazzling noontide, in the solemn westering of that day-making glory.   God foresaw this.   It was dangerous to make a sun : it looks so like a God.   Other spirits might find in the soft moon somewhat of motherliness and gentleness, and condescending interest in the affairs of men—a sweet, sweet light that has come out in the darkness, that is never seen in the mid-day glory ; a seeking mother, a solicitous sister, a gentle

friend that may and dare come out in the night ;—who could fail
to fall down and say,—Bless thee, thou spirit of light, thou art
at least a symbol of the living God ?   And some of the stars
seem to speak : they glitter so ; their sparkling is so vivid; their
appeal so direct, as if we must answer such voices.   God has
said,—Sun, moon, and the host of heaven are not to be worshipped.   So much for nature-homage ; so much for the altar
of the universe, as represented by things bright and beautiful
and most alluring in their tenderness.   All altars, but one, are
thrown down.   Those who believe the Bible have, therefore, no
alternative.   They hear poems about nature, about sun-light and
moon-light, and babbling brooks, and sparkling dew, and bending
corn, and birds trilling out their very throats in song ; and they
say,—If the Bible had not spoken so definitely, we might have
been persuaded to halt and build a tabernacle and worship the
host of heaven and the singing tenants of the air and all the
beauty of the bespangled carpet under our feet ; but the Bible
is emphatic and definite : we are not to stop at the creature,
but to go up to the Creator ; we are not to uncover our heads in
the presence of the lamps at his gate, but are to pass on that
we may find himself, and in prostration of heart worship only
his living Majesty.   It comes to this, then : Is the Bible our
guide ?   Are we intelligent and resolute believers in a divine
revelation, which is now given to us in our own tongue, and the
substance of which we can all understand ?   We must take care
how we defraud God of his rights.   God will make up to us for
any loss we may sustain in obeying his commandments.   The
green field is alluring : where the sunshine plays surely there
must be a ladder the head of which reaches unto heaven ; but
if we have honestly said,—We leave all these things and betake
ourselves to the appointed place, and worship in the appointed
way,—God will make up to us for all the green fields we have
forfeited, and as for the light of the sun, a light above its noontide
brightness shall delight the vision of the soul.

"Then shalt thou bring forth that man or that woman, which have
committed that wicked thing, unto thy gates, even that man or that woman,
and shalt stone them with stones, till they die " (v. 5).

The letter has passed.   He who lives in the letter lives in the
shell or in the bark, as the old Roman law has said.   We must

live in the spirit, and not in the letter, so though all physical
pain and penalty have disappeared, death is still and ever must
be the result of false worship. He who worships the wrong
deity does not worship. That is a suggestion which has risen
into a fact by reason of multiplied and even immeasurable
observation and experience. It is not the body that dies : it
is the soul that pines, withers, decays, and gradually sinks away,
—a notable truth, a profound thought indeed, most solemn, and
one which can be tested. The meaning simply is this : Lose
touch of God, and you cannot live. " As the branch cannot bear
fruit of itself, except it abide in the vine ; no more can ye, except
ye abide in me. . . Without me ye can do nothing." The
thought, therefore, is not extraordinary as to its claim upon our
attention or arbitrary in its authority : it simply means : Leave
hold of God, and you must wither ; abandon the centre of life,
and though you may go forward for a moment or two by reason
of the impulse derived from the original contact, you must halt
and die. It is so intellectually, it is so morally, it is so socially ;
in all these departments there are living centres, recognised
authorities, and if we neglect or despise them, the result is seen
in intellectual, moral, and social feebleness, pollution, and death.
We are not made to invent our own gods, and be as healthy and
robust of intellect as if we were worshipping at the true altar.
We are seeking by foolish worship to establish a lie : we are
endeavouring to show that being mortal we can become immortal ;
that being fallible we can find out and worship infallibility without
going to the living God ; that being ignorant we can write for
ourselves a law and constitute for ourselves a light and guide.
The man who has no Bible may talk so, and he forfeits nothing
of consistency ; but the man who holds to the Bible must hold to
the true God, the one altar, the only Priest, the fountain opened
for sin and for uncleanness. We cannot have a Bible, and yet
live as if we had it not ; to have seen it is to have incurred a
responsibility ; to have read one of its living chapters is to
separate by an infinite distance our souls from all the ignorance
and bondage of the past. Although, therefore, physical death
is no longer to be inflicted and outward stoning is happily
unknown, there remains the eternal truth that false worship is
death, misconceived worship is loss of soul, and right worship

is daily sustenance and the continual enhancement of highest strength.

In the fourteenth verse we have an instance of God's deep reading of the human heart. It is a verse full of forecast; it is, indeed, charged with surprise, and must have come upon the people startlingly :—

" When thou art come unto the land which the Lord thy God giveth thee, and shalt possess it, and shalt dwell therein, and shalt say, I will set a king over me, like as all the nations that are about me."

This opens up a marvellous sphere of divine operation in the affairs of men. It would seem as if God himself had almost suggested the evil that has been committed. Take the instance of our first parents in the days of their innocence. God said unto them, " Of every tree of the garden thou mayest freely eat : but of the tree of the knowledge of good and evil, thou shalt not eat of it : for in the day that thou eatest thereof thou shalt surely die." And here God indicates a rising in the mind of his people of a rebellious spirit against himself, expressing its purpose in a desire for a king. The thought had not occurred to the people at this moment ; no such idea had ever touched the minds of the people to whom these words were addressed. Here, then, we are called upon to distinguish between fore-knowledge and predestination. That there is foreknowledge in God is a necessity of his being God : without foreknowledge he is without Godhead ; but when he predestinates he predes-tinates to caution, to vigilance: he calls men to be upon their guard, and to pray with increasing energy and precision of meaning, that they may be saved from false issues and from criminal acts. To fore-know is not to fore-determine. The eating of the fruit of the tree was not an act of predestination, nor was the call for a king in Israel to be traced to the decree of God ; in both instances there was warning and there was a call to vigilance, and to certain lines of policy and conduct in the case of the choosing of a king.

Very beautiful is the portrait of a king that is given by God himself. God will have a king of his own creation :—

" Thou shalt in any wise set him king over thee, whom the Lord thy God shal choose " (v. 15).

Royalty must be created by divinity. This is the same
principle that we have laid down in regard to worship. We
must have God at the head, the Creator upon the throne ; there
must be no settlement with intermediate causes and influences :
in all things we must have direct communication with the living
Creator, the eternal Sovereign of the universe. Have a king,
says God, but have one of my choosing. In other words : If you
will insist upon having a monarch, call upon me to name him.
A marvellous condescension in the one case and a complete
submission in the other. There cannot be two Gods, equal in
authority and power, ruling over the human mind. The Lord
reigneth ; all kings are his subjects : he is Lord of lords ; the
crown is God's creation, if a crown of righteousness, justice,
purity, and charity.

The Lord is pleased to go into detail about this possibly coming
king that should reign over his people. He was to be fraternal :

"One from among thy brethren shalt thou set king over thee" (v. 15).

The basis was a basis of equality : there was to be no idea of
a heavenly descent or a coming from some other and invisible
world with superhuman and impossible claims. There are such
kings, and there always must be such kings, in every republic,
in all time and in all space. Republics do not destroy kings ;
only they indicate and worship with loyalty the right kind of king.
There will always be larger men, elder men, wiser men ; men
in whom there is a greater quantity of manhood than in others ;
far-seeing men ; men whose hands combine the grasp of strength
with the caress of gentleness. God will, therefore, have the
fraternal principle asserted. We live in brotherhood : otherwise
we live in bondage and in fear and in distressing humiliation.

But the king must be guarded : he will have his temptations.
Against two of those temptations God guards his people. The
king shall not be a vain man :

"He shall not multiply horses to himself" (v. 16).

Horses were the symbols of power. To have many horses
was to be a right royal king, according to conventional construction of the situation. The horse was supposed to be the image
of power, the seal of great might and glory. God cautions the
king that is to reign over his people against trusting in horses—

against the whole strength and genius of worldly vanity : being
a king, he must not be foolish ; being royal, he must not be
unwise ; his very greatness should make him ambitious to be
greater still in moral qualities—in fraternal solicitude and in
beneficent action.

Not only was he cautioned against vanity, but against self-
indulgence :

"Neither shall he multiply wives to himself, that his heart turn not
away : neither shall he greatly multiply to himself silver and gold " (v. 17).

These are the temptations of the great ones of the earth—to
have many horses, to gratify every appetite, and to have all that
money can buy, and to boast themselves that they can purchase
what they wish to possess. All these impulses must be kept
down ; the whole desire of the man must be chastened. The
king must know himself to be the vicegerent of God, the
messenger of Heaven, the errand-bearer of the eternal covenant.
How is this to be brought about ? Only by the inculcation of
great principles, by the spread of spiritual knowledge, by a truer
estimate of the scope and function of law.

But all this is cautionary, and may be described as largely
negative. What more must take place in the history and
government of the true king ? He must be a student :

"And it shall be, when he sitteth upon the throne of his kingdom, that he
shall write him a copy of this law in a book out of that which is before the
priests the Levites : and it shall be with him, and he shall read therein all
the days of his life : that he may learn to fear the Lord his God, to keep
all the words of this law and these statutes, to do them : that his heart be
not lifted up above his brethren, and that he turn not aside from the
commandment, to the right hand, or to the left : to the end that he may
prolong his days in his kingdom, he, and his children, in the midst of
Israel " (vv. 18-20).

The law is divinely given. Any laws we may make, if they
are to be righteous and beneficent, must be of the quality of
law which has been already revealed from heaven. Whatever
is not of that quality must go down. False worship leads to
death ; false legislation leads to social dissolution. The Book
has been written ; everything that human life can need is in
the Bible : there is no law touching human life, property, interest
—past, present, future—which is not to be found in the Book of
God. This is not a claim set up on behalf of the Book : it is the

record of the world's profoundest reading; it is the testimony of the world's amplest and purest experience. We must make laws for momentary purposes that we may direct into proper channels certain actions and relationships; but all the law which we make must be of the nature of the law which is revealed. That being so, we must study the revealed law : we must read it by the dazzling noontide light, and read it by the lamps which men have made to dispel the darkness. The law must be read in all lights, day and night, from beginning to end, in all its varieties, relationships, and issues ; and he who reads the law so will instantly discern the spirit of all human law, and be able to say with authority,—This is right; this is just; this is true. Or,—This is unrighteous, unjust, untrue, and must, as such, be done away. Great Bible readers are great reformers. We cannot have any profoundly beneficent change in social life, custom, and usage, except we have it through the inspired revelation. Spread the Bible ; make all men read the Bible so that they may understand it ; spare no expense in circulating the Book ; those who can explain it, devote yourselves to it day and night: turn the Book of God into the language of the people, and thus create in them, under the blessing of Heaven, a true spirit, a keen discernment, a sure touch that knows in the darkness as in the light what it is that claims attention and confidence.

We are called to true worship. "God is a Spirit: and they that worship him must worship him in spirit and in truth." "For the Father seeketh such to worship him." True worship inspires and ennobles character. No man can pray well and live badly. He may pray well in a literary sense : the structure of his sentences may be perfect : the flow of his poetry may be as the running of a river ; but to pray well, with sense of divine nearness, with all the trembling pathos of self-accusation and self-conviction, is to live well. We must never own it to be possible that a man can worship truly and live iniquitously. He may direct his eyes to the right heavens, he may name the name of the right God, he may be found in recognised and honoured sanctuaries ; but his worship—the inner action of the soul—is wrong : otherwise it would be possible to construct a perfect hypocrisy, by pleasing God at one end of life and outwitting him at the other.   Where the true worship is the true life must be—not the perfect life, not the ideal life; but the life that would be right—the life inspired by noble purpose directed to the highest ends, the life that longs to be like the God it adores.   To such worship we are called.   We lose when we do not worship; we go down in the volume and quality of our being when we cease to pray.   To pray is to multiply life; to pray to the right God, to bend before the appointed throne, to cling to the one Cross in which alone there is virtue, is to increase the volume of life, intellectual capacity, moral emotion, and every attribute that gives purity and dignity to man.   For this reason we uphold the sanctuary, we open the book of revelation; and we must not be allured from the altar where we renew our youth, and where we daily read the record that can alone make wise.

SELECTED NOTE.

"*He shall not multiply horses to himself*" (v. 16).   It appears to be substantiated that the horse was derived from High Asia, and was not indigenous in Arabia, Syria, or Egypt.   They are not mentioned among the presents which Pharaoh bestowed upon Abraham, and occur in Scripture for the first time when the patriarch Joseph receives them from the Egyptians in exchange for bread (Gen. xlvii. 17)—evidently as valuable animals, disposed of singly, and not in droves or flocks like cattle and asses.   They were still sufficiently important to be expressly mentioned in the funeral procession which accompanied the body of Jacob to his sepulchre in Canaan (Gen. l. 9); and, for centuries after, it does not appear that, under the domestic management of the Egyptians, unless the murrain had greatly reduced them, horses had multiplied as they would have done in a land more congenial to their habits, since only six hundred chariots appear to have pursued Israel (Exod. xiv. 7)—even admitting that there were other chariots and horsemen not included in that number.   In the sculptured battle-scenes which are believed to represent victories of Sesostris, or Thothmes II. and III., over nations of Central Asia, it is evident that the enemy's armies, as well as the foreign allies of Egypt, are abundantly supplied with horses, both for chariots and for riders; and in triumphal processions they are shown as presents or tribute—proving that they were portions of the national wealth of conquered states sufficiently valuable to be prized in Egypt.   At a later period, the books of Deuteronomy (xvii. 16, for the future kings of Israel are forbidden to possess many) and Joshua (xi. 4) furnish similar evidence of abundance of horses in the plains of Syria; and in Job occurs a description of a perfect war-horse, couched in the bold, figurative language of inspiration, such as remains unequalled by any other poe·, ancient or modern.

PRAYER.

OH that we might do thy will, thou loving Father of us all! Not our will but thine be done; thy will be done on earth as it is done in heaven. It is not the will of our Father in heaven that one of these little ones should perish. Thou hast no pleasure in death; thou art the God of life and immortality: thou dost live for ever, and thou hast offered us life eternal in Jesus Christ thy Son. This is life eternal: to know thee, the only true God, and Jesus Christ whom thou hast sent. Give us such knowledge of thyself as we are able to receive. May we know thee by thy love, thy tenderness, thy daily compassion; may we feel thy nearness and answer thy touch, and return thy whispered love in many a vow of consecration. Thou hast been very kind to us, and merciful even unto tenderness; thy kindness has been lovingkindness; thy mercy has been tender mercy. Thou hast caused us to invent new words to meet the beauty of thy revelations; so we speak of thy lovingkindness and thy tender mercy, and say that thy mercy endureth for ever. May we realise this; may we answer this; may our whole life show that this is no mere assent to what we do not understand, but the utterance of a soul that has tested its own faith. We bless thee for all thy care: thine arms are round about us. The old man's journey is not yet concluded, because thou hast more light on earth for him to see; the little child is nursed and caressed and comforted that he may become strong in moral quality and noble in moral temper; the man of business is still taught that life is not in the ground but in the sky, and thou art offering to descend from above and make him live. Our houses are precious to thee: thou dost send the sunshine upon them; thou dost surround them by protection; and we are here to-day in thy house in a common language and with a common feeling blessing the one Father of the race. Thou hast raised up a Prophet for us: thou hast sent a Teacher from thyself to teach us. We know that Jesus has come from God, for no man could do the miracles which he did except God were with him; and we say to him every time we draw near to his feet,—Rabbi, we know that thou art a Teacher sent from God. May the hearer meet the Teacher in a right spirit, in a sweet temper, in an expectant mood of soul; and between the Teacher and the taught may there be a bond of vital sympathy; and may we all sit togeth r at thy table, and eat and drink abundantly according to the terms of thy welcome. Amen.

Deut. xviii. 15-22.

15. The Lord thy God will raise up unto thee a Prophet from the midst of thee, of thy brethren, like unto me; unto him ye shall hearken;

16. According to all that thou desiredst of the Lord thy God in Horeb in the day of the assembly, saying, Let me not hear again the voice of the Lord my God, neither let me see this great fire any more, that I die not.

17. And the Lord said unto me, They have well spoken that which they have spoken.

18. I will raise them up a Prophet from among their brethren, like unto thee, and will put my words in his mouth ; and he shall speak unto them all that I shall command him.

19. And it shall come to pass, that whosoever will not hearken unto my words which he shall speak in my name, I will require it of him.

20. But the prophet, which shall presume to speak a word in my name, which I have not commanded him to speak, or that shall speak in the name of other gods, even that prophet shall die.

21. And if thou say in thine heart, How shall we know the word which the Lord hath not spoken ?

22. When a prophet speaketh in the name of the Lord, if the thing follow not, nor come to pass, that is the thing which the Lord hath not spoken, but the prophet hath spoken it presumptuously : thou shalt not be afraid of him.

THE PREDICTED PROPHET.

A WONDERFUL desire is this—no marvel that it elicited divine commendation :—

" Let me not hear again the voice of the Lord my God, neither let me see this great fire any more, that I die not " (v. 16).

On hearing these words the Lord himself said,—

" They have well spoken that which they have spoken " (v. 17).

The divinity that is in a man seems to lie a long way down. Great circumstances are required really to rouse a man that he may see for a moment *himself*. It needed Sinai to make the people of Israel know that God could not be known. When God thundered upon them and spoke to them as it were face to face they begged that the interview might close. The very thing we desire is the very thing we could not endure. Why do we not learn from history, and draw wise conclusions from events within our own knowledge ? But for the clouds, and the atmosphere, we could not bear the very sun without whose light and warmth we die. We seem to owe the sun · to the very atmosphere that attempers his shining. It would occur to us that if God would speak directly from his throne all mankind with one consent would say, " The Lord he is God." That experiment has been tried ; and the very people who might be presumed to have

required it were the people who prayed that it might be concluded; they prayed that there might be no repetition; to have
come so near to God was to have come too near in their then
condition of mind and heart. All our plans have been tried, and
they have failed. Some of the most obvious plans have been
pronounced unwise, unnecessary, or fruitless. Once a man
prayed a prayer to which many might have said Amen; but he
was told from heaven that he was wrong. His idea was that
if one rose from the dead his brethren, five in number, would
repent; but he only saw part of the case. We see points, not
lines; roofs of our own building and decorating, not skies arched
and lighted by Deity. The Voice replied in effect,—Your plan
seems to be natural and good; in reality it is worthless for all
practical purposes: "If they hear not Moses and the prophets,
neither will they be persuaded though one rose from the dead."
We cannot amend God's way of coming to us; he made us, and
not we ourselves: he knows what we can bear; his revelation in
all its method and scope is not the least proof of his lovingkindness and tender mercy. Our own plans we should be the first to
wish to have forgotten. We are called to acceptance, obedience,
acquiescence with the divine will,—to say all prayers in one
prayer: "Not my will, but thine, be done." How God seems to
be pleased when we say anything that is really in the soul of it
along the lines of his own thought and purpose! We speak so
many foolish words in his hearing, and do so many unwise
deeds under his observation, that when we do touch the right
chord the vibration is answered in heaven: when we do happen
to speak the wise word in the right tone God himself descends
upon us and leaves a new benediction. "They have well spoken
that which they have spoken;"—they do not know how wise
they have been. This is inspiration in its practical expression—
to come to right conclusions regarding divine disclosure, divine
approach to the soul, to have a right distance set between man
and God. In such a temper God can deal with us, and enrich us
largely with noble and unimagined riches.

The prophet who can do us good must be akin to us:

"I will raise them up a Prophet from among their brethren, like unto
thee" (v. 18).

A beautiful word is the "like unto." It is a word frequently

used in the New Testament by the predicted Prophet himself.
We have been educated by analogies, examples, and pictorial
representations of things. "Like unto"—then Moses was the
analogy. Solomon likened his loved one to a company of horses
in Pharaoh's chariot. Jesus Christ likened the kingdom of heaven
unto a thousand things beautiful, vital, poetical, apocalyptic,—
things whose history was known and yet whose issues were
immeasurable. So it must be in every degree. The teacher
must be akin to the scholar or no good will be done—evidently
not, if only on the ground that the language which is spoken by
the teacher is not known to the wonder-struck scholar who
listens to him with amazement and partial stupefaction. There
are many languages within the bounds of the same language.
All words are not the same words, even though they belong
to a common tongue ; moreover, the meaning is often in the
emphasis, not in the word, the word being a mere convenience
or starting-point—something on which the soul strikes its thought
into accent and expression, which must be done in a moment or
the whole idea is lost. Words are tormentors. Words are the
occasion, as also the cause, of endless controversy. No two
men pronounce the same word exactly alike in the ear of God.
Tone holds meaning ; the revelation is in the emphasis ; and
except we speak a common language, in the spiritual sense, there
will be no increase of intellectual light or moral understanding,
how eloquent soever may be the exposition of the unknown
prophet. The scholars must exclaim, "How hear we every man
in his own tongue, wherein we were born . . . the wonderful
works of God ?" This is the secret of the masonry between the
teacher and the scholar : the one understands the other. The
teacher can afford to be elliptical, because he knows the acuteness
and the sympathy of the scholars to whom he is speaking : they
can fill in all the vacant spaces : they know exactly the words
which the speaker himself would have chosen but for pressure of
time ; so the lesson, though short is long, though brief as to words
is endless as to suggestion. The teacher of the highest truths
must speak in the language of sympathy. It is probably of no
consequence in what tone a man expounds the physical sciences :
they are not resentful in this matter of vocal expression : they
will permit rudeness and violence of tone : the teacher need not

study the music of expression in endeavouring to make clear some geometrical problem; but Christ must be preached in Christ's own tone. The wise teacher will spend, if need be, days in trying to find out how to say: "Our Father, which art in heaven;" or "God is love;" or "Come unto me, all ye that labour and are heavy laden, and I will give you rest." Words like these might be spoiled by the speaker; such heavens might be robbed of all their stars by a felonious interpreter of the higher things. We read: "The Lord God hath given me the tongue of the learned, that I should know how to speak a word in season to him that is weary." But the word surely would be there whether the tongue was learned or unlearned? In a narrow sense that is true: the word is there, composed of so many syllables and so many letters; but there must be a soul of its own quality to repeat the syllables, to give the letters force, to turn the printing into music, and by subtle persuasion tempt the soul to receive the celestial solace. God must, therefore, give not only the word but the tongue; and the true learning is in sympathy, kinship, unity of mind, and that peculiar knowledge of human nature which if it be not born in a man never can be put into him;—this is the gift of God.

Israel prayed that some other method of communication might be established between heaven ..d earth, saying,—Do not repeat this awful process, "that I die not:" let the life be spared. I can hear nothing—says the soul—because the thunder is so loud, and there is nothing in thunder to hear. At the great torrent of Niagara the one thing you cannot get is a draught of water. The traveller could quench his fiery thirst at a cool spring or a gentle stream, and lift up his head and be glad with religious thankfulness; but who dare, in the very agony of thirst, approach that infinite cascade? So God must not come to us in great thunder-bursts and torrents: he must not plead with us with his great power; he must conceal himself, dwarf himself, unmake himself in a sense known to the soul but difficult to explain in words; he must humble himself and take upon himself the form of a servant, and become obedient unto death;—in this quiet way, in this gracious approach, we make vital acquaintance with God. We do not know what we owe to quiet influences and to almost silent ministries. When the prodigal son—not the vulgar criminal, but the prodigal son who has been wasting his life in any way you please—goes back to his mother—not his father, but his mother Nature—the *alma mater*, the loving mother, —all she wants him to do is to lie upon some sunny height, and think nothing, plan nothing, and release himself from the torment of his own genius and inventiveness, not to say anxiety and memory : she says—Poor prodigal, all you have to do is to do nothing : I will do it all ; lay your weary head down on some grassy knoll and have no mind : dismiss your great intellectual self and be a little child in your mother's house. Then with soft breezes and summer light and the ministry of birds far away yet near at hand, she will seem to be doing nothing, yet all the while she is pouring life-blood into the wasted one. Presently he will look around and feel himself a giant refreshed ; and he who thought he was spent feels the old spirit stirring within him, saying,—I must be back to the city, to the scene of legitimate strife, the places where the prizes are won ; my old mother has had me in her lap and has nursed me into thankfulness. They never recover who cannot do everything by doing nothing : they are diseased with the spirit of superfluous energy ; they are over-weighted with the demon of fussiness ; they cannot lie down absolutely and say,—Mother Nature, I have sinned against Heaven and in thy sight, by sitting up too long, by wearing out my poor energies ; I have almost committed suicide, and I have struggled home : now I am going to say nothing and do nothing but lie down here, and I know you will not let me die. What profit we might attain in the house of God if we could leave our genius outside—our cleverness, our theological prejudices, our mental sharpness, and say to the living God,—" A guilty, weak, and helpless worm, on thy kind arms I fall ! " Then the sweet music, and the nobler music of the read word, and the tender prayer, and the exposition, alight with so many glories, would all combine to renew our youth, and after the service we should mount up with wings as eagles, and ask the runner to compete with us, and walk down the young man in the pride of strength. Thus God teaches us by gentle prophecies, by apparently undemonstrative ministries—above all by One whose voice was not heard in the street, who did not lift up nor cry, nor cause his voice to be heard more than was really necessary, who adapted the thunder of his infinity to the weakness of our mortality. We should do more if we did less. We do not come to hear the prophet for the purpose of entering into disputation with him, but for the purpose of receiving streams of vitality, without name, without measure, too subtle for analysis, too delicate and divine for controversy. Thus, we must come to God's Book. If we come to it merely as literalists and critics it can be as silent as speechlessness itself; if we come with the broken heart it will heal our diseases.

If the prophet is not hearkened to, penalty will follow :—

"And it shall come to pass, that whosoever will not hearken unto my words which he shall speak in my name, I will require it of him" (v. 19).

An opportunity of reading the Bible is an opportunity of increasing manhood. The hearing of any vital exposition of God's Book creates a responsibility in the life of the hearer which is absolutely immeasurable. If the people will not hearken unto the divine word spoken in the divine Name their not hearing shall be accounted an aggravation, an offence, and a sin. This must be so philosophically as well as morally. To have been near a great teacher is to have been close to an open gate, the entrance of which would have brought one into a kind of paradise ; but to have been near a great teacher sent from God, and not to have observed him or profited by him or blessed him in the name of the Lord, is to have gone down in the volume and in the quality of manhood. Do not imagine that men can despise the Bible and be as good as ever. To scorn the divine is to lose the human. Not to pray nobly is to live narrowly. We do not only offend God by our impiety, we wrong our own soul.

The false prophet was to be known by the thing not coming to pass which he spake (v. 22). That is a right test ; that is a proper standard. If the proof is not in the result there is no proof. If the wicked man be really and truly happy in his soul the Bible is a falsehood. If vice can create heaven—the heaven of purity, innocence, and the rest which comes of harmony—then the Gospel is an exaggeration and a pretence. Let everything be judged by the result. Christ himself said so : judge the tree by its fruit. He would have no praise of the tree ; he will not have himself spoken of merely from a horticultural point of view, nor will he have his people described as trees only—large trees, noble in height, umbrageous, the refuge of singing birds, beautiful in leafage : such compliments are hateful to him : "Herein is my Father glorified, that ye bear much fruit." The Bible is thus the most rational of all books as to its judgments. The issue is plain and clear. If the thing the prophet says—meaning by prophet a teacher sent from God—does not come true, then he has not spoken the words God told him to speak. Christianity must lay claim to this same standard : she must consent to be judged, not by her metaphysics but by her beneficence ; not because she has a theory of the Godhead, but because she can redeem humanity.

SELECTED NOTE.

Deut. xix. 1-13.—Moses set apart out of the sacerdotal cities six as "cities of refuge." There were, on the eastern side of the Jordan, three, namely, "Bezer in the wilderness, in the plain country of the Reubenites, and Ramoth in Gilead of the Gadites, and Golan in Bashan of the Manassites" (Deut. iv. 43) ; on the western side three, namely, "Kedesh in Galilee in Mount Naphtali, and Shechem in Mount Ephraim, and Kirjath-arba, which is Hebron, in the mountain of Judah" (Josh. xx. 7). If found desirable then other cities might be added. To *any* of these cities a person who had unawares and unintentionally slain *any one* might flee, and if he reached it before he was overtaken by the avenger of blood, he was safe within its shelter, provided he did not remove more than a thousand yards (Numb. xxxv. 5) from its circuit, nor quit the refuge till the decease of the high-priest under whom the homicide had taken place. If, however, he transgressed these provisions, the avenger might lawfully put him to death. The roads leading to the cities of refuge were to be kept in good repair. Before, however, the fugitive could avail himself of the shelter conceded by the laws, he was to undergo a solemn trial, and make it appear to the satisfaction of the magistrates of the place where the homicide was committed that it was purely accidental. Should he, however, be found to have been guilty of murder, he was delivered "into the hand of the avenger of blood, that he might die."

And the Israelites were strictly forbidden to spare him either from considerations of pity or in consequence of any pecuniary ransom. This disallowal of a compensation by money in the case of murder shows a just regard for human life, and appears much to the advantage of the Hebrew legislation when compared with the practice of other countries (Athens, for instance, and Islam), in which pecuniary atonements were allowed, if not encouraged, and where, in consequence, the life of the poor must have been in as great jeopardy as the character of the wealthy.

PRAYER.

ALMIGHTY GOD, who can find out the meaning of thy word? It is exceeding broad. Thy word is quick and powerful, sharper than any two-edged sword; it hurts us whilst we read it, but it kills that it may make alive again. Thy word is full of gentleness, though so severe. If thou hast torn us, thou wilt heal us; if thou hast rent us, thou wilt bind us up again: in a day or two all will be well: the wound will be healed and the pain will be forgotten. Thou dost give life: thou art the God of immortality; thou healest disease; thou hast written thy condemnation upon death; thou lovest health and life and growth and all beauty and fruitfulness;— towards the creation of these all thy ministries tend: we would be found within the sphere of their operation; we would obediently submit ourselves unto their requirements and laws, that, being brought into the harmony of thy movement, we might respond to thy word with delight and turn thy statutes into songs. But who can do this for us? Is not Jesus Christ thy Son able to work even this miracle? We now pray that the miracle may be accomplished. Lord, that we might see! Lord, if thou wilt, thou canst make us clean! Jesus Christ, Son of David, have mercy on us! Other men have passed by and paid no heed to us: they could not touch our inmost complaint; but thou art almighty: the key of the house of David is upon thy shoulder: thou hast all power and all grace, and thy love will accomplish our redemption. We bless thee that there is no case beyond thy reach. Thou knowest altogether what we are and what we need, and fulness of provision has been made in the Gospel: the Cross of Christ healeth the diseases of the soul. We return to the Saviour. We have gone after other leaders, and they have led us into the ditch, for we were both blind; but now we come to Jesus Christ again and again, and he is gracious enough to forgive our wanderings and receive us home. We would that thy word might be made plain to us, that we might see somewhat at least of its meaning and feel its unction and acknowledge its power. Thy word is truth. Truth will touch our life at every point, granting unto our necessity an answer of fulness, to our pain an answer of ease, to our desire an answer of contentment. Lead us into all truth—the infinite palace of God, the inner universe towards which all other things point in wonder and with delight. Pity us in our weaknesses, and count them not against us in the judgment. Thou wilt not pity our sin, but thou wilt pity the sinner; and as for our sin, what is it compared with thy grace? Where sin aboundeth grace much more aboundeth, pouring itself in ocean fulness over all the marks of the wrong-doer. Help us to live our few remaining days well: we will be gone to-morrow, and the day after is the judgment; we walk along the brink over which we must presently slip: we are seen a moment, yet in a little while we are not seen—but with the eyes of recollection.

May we work while it is called day, for the night cometh wherein no man can work. We are not needful to thee. Thou dost take us away, and behold the world is not aware that we have been removed. Thou dost so teach us not to rely upon one another, but to live and move and have our being in thyself. Thou art the same, and thy years fail not: amid all rising, flourishing, and dying thou lookest on in eternal youth. Regard our loved ones; if they will not make prayers for themselves, Jesus, our Intercessor, will surely pray for them, and they will receive replies without having offered requests. Thou doest exceeding abundantly above not only what we ask but what we think: our thought is left below, and the fountains of thy grace are opened in the skies, and great rains of blessing are poured out upon the thirst of life. Hear us in these things. Hear us for the land we love, for the throne to which we are bound, for all the institutions that represent the highest thought and best ambition of life; and overrule all things to the inbringing of the kingdom which is all purity and sunshine and music. Amen.

Deut. xix.

"When the Lord thy God hath cut off the nations, whose land the Lord thy God giveth thee, and thou succeedest them, and dwellest in their cities, and in their houses; thou shalt separate three cities for thee in the midst of thy land, which the Lord thy God giveth thee to possess it " (vv. 1, 2).

DIVINELY-PROVIDED REFUGE.

WHEN a blessing has been conferred a duty is to follow. This would seem to be the method of the divine kingdom. That kingdom does not consist wholly of blessing, sentiment, ease, and honour; the kingdom of God is a kingdom of duty and discipline, calling upon its possessors to be faithful and gracious, to obey certain commandments, and to hold the kingdom feudally, —not as of right, but as from the Lord, to whom an account must be rendered. Whenever the Lord gives us cities we have a work of separation to do. The cities are not given to us wholly: they are only given to us partially. The Lord still maintains his position upon earth, though he is throned in heaven; he has cities upon the earth that are peculiarly his own. Whatever city is given to us must have part of it set aside as God's, for God's use, and concerning which an account must be rendered to God. Had the message been all upon one side, how subtle and tre-mendous would have been the temptation addressed to human vanity and ambition !—the Lord will give you cities ; he will cast out the heathen and the stranger before you; you shall enter into the palaces of their kings and enjoy the riches of all their generations. Had the message run in that line it would have been an evil. There is nothing really in the very soul of it good that does not involve the element of discipline. Regard it as a fact established by all history and approved by all the philosophy that is founded upon experience, that at some point man must bow the knee, and acknowledge lordship and divine right and claim ; and wherever he thus bows the knee man sets up an altar. Human will must be broken. This is a doctrine which benevolent but foolish parents endeavour to evade : they bring up their children with an unbroken will, and call it graciousness and good-nature ;—it is baseness, selfishness, cruelty : it is leaving that to be done by a stranger which ought to have been done by the spirit of home and the genius of love. We are called upon to acknowledge God in all our possessions, to have our will broken in the sense of rejecting the idea of sole proprietorship or absolute claim, and in the sense of saying concerning many a fair city,—This is God's, not mine ;—concerning many a wedge of gold,—This is the Lord's, not mine. When the human spirit has been brought to that concession, and can make the surrender graciously, lovingly, and thankfully, the miracle of grace has been accomplished in the reluctant or obdurate heart. Israel could keep the cities, and include the three that ought to have been separated in the bill of ownership; but the Lord could have withheld the rain, and no city could live without the clouds : the Lord could have shifted the wind into the quarter whence cometh blight, cold, and desolation ; no city can live without the southwest wind. We may claim all, but we cannot keep all. To put the three cities into our bag and lodge them with the usurer is not to outwit God : the Sovereign will take out his claim in health, or wealth, or peace : but his claim must be recognised and satisfied. Listen not to the sophism which says that all cities are God's : there is a morality which is too grandiloquent ; reject the suggestion that all days are God's : there is a liberality that gives nothing. God has always secured three of the cities or more, part of every harvest-field, a few grapes at least out of every vineyard, one day in the week ; the claim has not been great in extent in relation to the territory which has been covered, but the making of it is the assertion of sovereign right, and the satisfaction of it is an expression of human obedience.

"Thou shalt prepare thee a way, and divide the coasts of thy land, which the Lord thy God giveth thee to inherit, into three parts, that every slayer may flee thither" (v. 3).

There was to be public proclamation of the existence of the cities of refuge. The picture is a very striking one. There were signs put up along the road leading to the cities of refuge, and on the signs was written the word "miklot"—refuge. What a sign to come upon in the hour of despair and oppressed weakness! The man who was fleeing, having shed innocent blood, looked anxiously around that he might observe the standard bearing the magic word *miklot;* seeing that word, he fled along the road which was indicated by the gracious term. Fix the mind upon the picture until the picture itself glows into a beauteous gospel. A man has done wrong: he knows the consequences of his wrong-doing, even though the wrong was a misadventure: instantly he flees for refuge ; he did not make the city of refuge: he may not know in what direction the city of refuge lies; but here and there and again the standard is lifted up and on it written—*refuge.* The man does not run the other way, or ask who wrote the *miklot,* or enter into discussion as to the form of the letters and the right of those letters to be where they are ; nor does he ask the age of the standard, or why it is not on the other side of the road : the man is in earnest : the avenger is behind him : he has no time for questions or controversy about the refuge ;—Where lies the city ?—and seeing an indication of its position he "flees for refuge" to the city that is set before him. Our public roads should have no lack of standards of a higher and nobler kind : the wrong-doer should have no doubt left upon his mind as to what direction to take in the time of self-accusation and self-despair. Every Christian should be a stranger, having written upon him "miklot"— refuge ; every church should be an open door, opened towards heaven, pardon, and peace. We must not be afraid to say that all our Christianity exists in the first instance for the purpose of saving the wrong-doer who wishes to be saved. That is the primary purpose of the Church ; other purposes are no doubt included, but the one initial, all-commanding object of the Church is to be a city of refuge, a place where the lamp of hope burns brightly, a sanctuary where the gospel words are spoken with gospel fervour and unction. The Church of the living God should resound with the cry :—Flee for refuge to the hope set before you in the Gospel. The enormous—the incalculable—difficulty is that men do not recognise themselves as in need of refuge. We must have destroyed within us the sophism that we are fit to be at large. So long as we walk up and down the city complacently approving ourselves and quoting instances of our own wisdom and virtue, any standard bearing the word *miklot* —refuge—is an offence to us. The Gospel was never meant for any man who can take care of himself : it is a city of refuge ; and men only ask for refuge when they hear the pursuit of the avenger, or know themselves to be objects deserving punishment. Where do we find the refugees in the church ? Men are not there as refugees : they are there as upon equal terms with the Lord of the sanctuary ; they patronise that Lord : they subscribe to his reputation upon the earth : they light his lamps for him, and they expect to be rewarded for their loyalty ;—whereas men ought to be in the church in a state of breathlessness, then in a state of thankfulness for security ; then, sometimes, as if hearing just outside the stroke of the avenger, they should pray more mightily and sing their praises more fervently, knowing that the avenger may smite the wall and hurt himself, but can never reach those who are hidden in the place of refuge—" Jesus, Refuge of my soul, let me to thy bosom fly." We should realise this conception of the Church, and doing so we shall not be slow to put up in the city the sign-post and the index-finger ; nor shall we scruple to use the word " refuge," or the word " salvation," for we shall speak the word with the emphasis and the unction of personal gratitude.

"And this is the case of the slayer, which shall flee thither, that he may live: Whoso killeth his neighbour ignorantly, whom he hated not in time past : as when a man goeth into the wood with his neighbour to hew wood, and his hand fetcheth a stroke with the axe to cut down the tree, and the head slippeth from the helve, and lighteth upon his neighbour, that he die ; he shall flee unto one of those cities, and live : lest the avenger of the blood pursue the slayer, while his heart is hot, and overtake him, because the way is long, and slay him ; whereas he was not worthy of death, inasmuch as he hated him not in time past " (vv. 4-6).

Here is the principle that actions as between man and man are to be discriminated. Everything depends upon motive. The action is not complete in itself, and remains a mystery or an enigma until the motive has been penetrated and understood. This discrimination of actions would destroy many a sacred phantasm. The law applies in both directions. Supposedly good actions are to be examined in the light of this law as well as actions that are supposedly vicious. If everything depends upon the motive, what becomes of the fabric of a life-time? How much easier it would be to live from the outside than to live from an interior centre! The hand can do so many things easily as an expression of skill and mechanical cleverness, whilst the heart may be away committing murder and theft, and breaking all the commandments at one tremendous stroke. The word of God is sharper than any two-edged sword, piercing to the dividing asunder of the joints and marrow. What temples of charity are thrown down because the action of an evil motive was in the midst of them!—the action itself was beautiful, reputable, and was accepted by society with applause; but the spirit of the Book asks for the motive which originated the charity or the action, and finding that to be of base quality the action itself goes for less than nothing, and in the great book of account is set down against the doer. If our good actions are set down against us, who can pay the sum-total of the debt? Thus, we are thrown back upon spiritual thoughts and spiritual considerations. All our mechanical and outside arrangements and institutions go for nothing : the Lord asks but one question, —What is your motive? What do you really mean? What is your purpose?—and the answer to that inquiry being in the right tone, all the rest will be accounted to us : even our dreams shall be temples, and our cup of cold water shall be as a goblet of wine.

But there was another kind of man-slayer—what was to become of him?—

" But if any man hate his neighbour, and lie in wait for him, and rise up against him, and smite him mortally that he die, and fleeth into one of these cities : then the elders of his city shall send and fetch him thence, and deliver him into the hand of the avenger of blood, that he may die. Thine eye shall not pity him, but thou shalt put away the guilt of innocent blood from Israel, that it may go well with thee " (vv. 11-13).

The universe was not constituted to give security to murderers : there is no shelter for a man-hater. He may get into a city of refuge, but he is to be dragged out of it: the evil-doer may make a profession of religion, but his cloak, though of velvet and gold-braided, must be torn from his shoulders. The universe has no lodgment for the man of malicious heart and murderous spirit; the city of refuge in Israel was not built for him: he has no right in it; to pity him is to despise the law: to pity the murderer is to forget the murdered. The eyes of justice are fixed upon both points in the case. When justice weeps, it weeps over the murdered life, not over the hand that killed it. It is an evil sentiment that spares the wrong-doer and forgets the wrong-endurer, the sufferer of wrong. There is one place appointed for the murderer. Who is the murderer? Not the shedder of blood :—whoso hateth his brother without a cause is a murderer. We must have frank speech in the sanctuary. The terms themselves are awful, but they are disinfected by the very spirit of the sanctuary in which they are uttered; and it ought to be possible in God's house to speak any word that can be spoken by human tongue, so that it may be approved or condemned—acquitted or sentenced to unquenchable fire. The only place for the malicious man is hell,—and hell cannot burn out the spirit of malice. The spirit of malice is the spirit of evil, or the evil spirit,—the stranger from God, the further from the spirit of love. This is the great law not of Israel only, but of the Church of Christ in all ages. Beware of malice! It does not always begin in its broadest form, or leap at once in all its intensity into human action : it begins in little frets and spites and jealousies; it starts out of a root of criticism, of fault-finding, and investigations into consistency; it may begin as a clever action, showing the spirit of judgment, and proving itself to be equal to the analysis of the most hidden motive; but it grows; disappointed, it begins to justify itself; foiled in its attempts to succeed, it retires that it may increase the supposed evidence that is at command; then it returns to the onslaught; it grows by what it feeds on; at last, philanthropy—love of man—dies, and misanthropy—hatred of man—takes its place. Then is the soul a murderer; and, thank God, there is no city of refuge for the murderer of life, of hope, of love, of trust!—open the door and thrust ye the unprofitable servant into outer darkness!—the sun will not spare a beam to bless the murderer. Again and again ask the question,—Who are the murderers? There are murderers who never shed blood—men who are killing their household circle every day, mothers who are killing their children every hour, supposed friends who are living upon the agony of those whom they oppress with their kindness. Let the word of God have free course in the soul—not only as a blessing, but as a criticism and as a judgment; and let us, hearing the sentence, obey the command.

Then is it even so? May accidental sins be provided for, but is there no provision made for those who cry out in the bitterness of their souls, each for himself,—I am a murderer: I have slain the good; I have entertained malice where I ought to have entertained nothing but gratitude; I have been unjust and cruel;—is there no refuge for me?—the *miklot* is a mockery to me if the city be meant only for those who are chargeable with misadventure? Now comes the great gospel speech: Christ is the city of refuge—but understand in what sense, lest the very goodness of God be profaned and prostituted. Christ is not a refuge in the sense of a criminal being able to outrun justice. The picture in Israel was the picture of a man fleeing for refuge and an avenger fleeing after him, and if the avenger were swifter of foot the man-slayer might be killed outside the city. There is no such picture in Christianity. In Christ we do not outrun justice: justice itself, by a mystery we can neither understand nor explain, has been satisfied by Christ. This is not to be made a matter of words: the controversialist is not here to offer his impertinent opinion; the question lies entirely between men who are in agony and Christ who offers refuge. There is no place for controversy or criticism, or coming to an understanding with all the factors in the case; this is an instance of self-convicted men, conscious of having done wrong and only wrong, asking if there is no *miklot* in all the universe for them, when they hate the wrong and repent it with bitterness of soul. Christianity is not a clever contrivance for outwitting justice. The mystery of the Cross lies within that thought. What that mystery is we cannot say. Now and then we seem to see somewhat of its meaning. God is just, and yet the justifier of the ungodly; Christ bore our sins in his own body on the tree; he suffered the just for the unjust; he was wounded for our transgressions; he was bruised for our iniquities; the chastisement of our peace was upon him. We do not know what it means; but there are times when we need just these words and no other: they are full of rest, hope, music; to analyse them is to slay the life that you may find its secret. The soul can but hear them now and then, but when they are heard, suddenly there is with the soul a multitude of the heavenly host singing,—"Glory to God in the highest, and on earth peace, good-will toward men." Do not ask to have that great light brought within the sphere that is visual and comprehensible: let it stand in its own place, fixed by the hand of God; and when we are weariest, saddest, and most severe with ourselves we shall see that light and call it heaven. The refuge in Christ is based upon confession, repentance, and restitution. Let us flee for refuge to the hope set before us in the Gospel. The action is one of intensity. We are not loitering upon the road, talking upon indifferent subjects as we ramble along: we are fleeing—running at our utmost speed: if we attract attention at all, it is by the swiftness of our motion and the eagerness of our action. How does a man run when the wolf is pursuing him over the snow?—how the horses plunge and urge forward then! How do men flee when fire is following them?—when the whole prairie is ablaze and the wind is a weapon of fire? How do men flee from a building that is tottering and might at any moment fall? From all such images gather some hint of the meaning of the words:—flee for refuge: make haste: heed nothing but the attainment of the sanctuary which has been built by God: its open door is a welcome: it was meant for sinners, it was built for sinners: it was not set up for righteous men, but for men unrighteous and lost. This is the Gospel which Christianity has to preach. It has no other Gospel; and it can only preach it with effect to men who are conscious of having done wrong. If any man say,—I have no sin,—the Gospel has no speech of welcome to make to him, but a speech of condemnation, saying,—He is a liar; "if we confess our sins, God is faithful and just to forgive us our sins, and to cleanse us from all unrighteousness." But we cannot understand the mystery: the evil deed was done, and God in his omnipotence says to us—Leave me to expunge the evil; as for you—flee for refuge!

PRAYER.

ALMIGHTY GOD, though we dwell in tabernacles of clay, yet dost thou not withhold thy light from our window, but dost surround us with the morning glory, and call us, in the midst of all the joy of light, to the joy and sacrifice of labour. Though we are consumed before the moth, to teach us how little we are, yet are we also conscious of being immortal in God : so shall we outlive all stars and suns and worlds, and be for ever with the Lord. We thank thee for this lifting up of the heart in sacred rapture : it makes us feel thy nearness when we yield to thy power, and it gives strength to our confidence when we hear the voice of thy grace. Surely thou art nigh unto them that call upon thee, and thine hand is outstretched in almightiness to those who put their trust in thee in the time of fear and danger and great distress. It is our joy to believe in thy nearness, in the tenderness of thy love, in the long-suffering of thy patience, in the all-helpfulness of thy power. We have heard of thy Son—that this Man receiveth sinners and eateth with them. He came to seek and to save that which was lost : he did not come to call the righteous but sinners to repentance. We confess our sin : we mourn it with bitterness; yet we cannot but rejoice that Jesus Christ came in answer to it. Our sin brought thy Son into the world that he might save us from its guilt and consequence. A wondrous mystery this in thy rule ! We see the stars in the darkness, not in the light : we see all thy mercy, compassion, love, and tears in the darkness of our sin. Oh, how the stars glitter ! How great their number ! Blessed be God, all these are witnesses of thy care for us. Thou wilt not willingly see the sinner die : thou hast no pleasure in the death of the wicked. Turn ye, turn ye, why will ye die ?—is a word which has been traced to thine own lips. We accept it now ; it is addressed to ourselves; it is an inquiry of love. Lord, by thy grace we will not die : we will arise and go to our Father, and speak words of penitence and self-loathing. We know that whilst we are yet a great way off thou wilt see us, and run and have compassion and fall upon our neck and kiss us, and adopt us into the family again;—this is the exceeding love of God ; this is the mystery of infinite pity. God be merciful unto us sinners ! The Lord magnify his grace over our guilt that we may see how great is the compassion of God, and how infinite the resources of love. We pray that thine house may be as a door opening upon heaven. We desire that this elevation may enable us to see beyond the boundary of time and behold somewhat of the gleaming and beauty of the city that lies beyond. O fair city ! beauteous home of beauteous souls ! We yearn for its purity, we weary to enter its rest, we long to know the mystery of its service. We bless thee that thou hast set a city of allurement before us—a fascination in the skies, a Jerusalem above, a mother city, waiting for us and bidding us come up higher. We need such exhortation and comfort, such stimulus and solace, all our days; and this great privilege we attain and secure through Jesus Christ our Saviour, who died for us and rose again, and is able to make intercession for us at the right hand of God; he is our Surety, our Saviour, our Propitiation; we flee unto him as pursued men flee into a city of refuge. Jesus, Refuge of my soul, let me hide myself in thee. This is the cry of the heart;—to such a cry thou wilt send a great answer. Amen.

Deut. xx. 8.

" And the officers shall speak further unto the people, and they shall say, What man is there that is fearful and fainthearted ? let him go and return unto his house, lest his brethren's heart faint as well as his heart."

FAINTHEARTEDNESS.

IN order to see the full beauty and meaning of this charge we must read the words which lead up to it. Arrangements are being made in view of possible battle. It is well in life always to be prepared for war even whilst we are praying for peace. The question might arise in the minds of the children of Israel,— What shall we do in the day of battle ? Instructions having distinct reference to that inquiry are given in this chapter.

" When thou goest out to battle against thine enemies, and seest horses, and chariots, and a people more than thou, be not afraid of them : for the Lord thy God is with thee, which brought thee up out of the land of Egypt " (v. 1).

There is an exhortation :—"Be not afraid of them." Following the exhortation is the reason upon which it is founded : " For the Lord thy God is with thee." No matter what the number of the enemy ; it is of no consequence how many horses he has, and how their necks are clothed with thunder : there is One who maketh the mountains smoke before him ; thy God is the Almighty and Eternal God, and he will see that the battle ends on the side of right. This verse calls us to take the religious view of every engagement in life. We must be sure that we start aright,—that is to say, that our cause is good at the core— just, wise, reasonable, and generous. The cause being right, everything in the universe that is right is of necessity on its side : the stars of heaven fight for righteousness. Whatever may be the nature of accidental or temporary circumstances, the issue is perfectly certain :—he shall come and reign, whose right it is. Ever the right comes uppermost. Acting upon this conviction, how calm is the man whose conscience approves him! He knows that the waves can only come to a certain line; he says, "Why do the heathen rage, and the people imagine a vain thing?" "The Lord reigneth;" the God of heaven is the God who battles on the side of right. This exhortation does not apply only to national wars, but to all the controversies which constitute the action and the tragedy of life. Every man is called to battle in some way, at some place, at some time. Life itself is a battle : we wrestle not against flesh and blood, it may be, but against principalities, against powers, against the rulers of the darkness of this world—the invisible host banded in a common oath to destroy the kingdom of truth. "Take unto you the whole armour of God, that ye may be able to withstand in the evil day, and having done all, to stand." This is the foundation upon which all further instruction given in this chapter is based. The battle puts our religion to the test : we do not know whether we are religious or not, in the profound sense of the term, until we come to battle. It is easy to sing at midsummer, when all visible nature challenges us in gracious tones to lift up our voice in solemn praise. There is no strain upon a man to thank God when he sits under his own blossoming trees and hears the birds trilling their incoherent hymn. That is not piety : it is selfishness of the vilest kind—the selfishness which electroplates itself with piety : the mean, personal consideration which cloaks itself with a sentiment thin as a morning cloud. See what men are when they are under stress— when the storm pours upon the roof, when the enemy thunders at the door, when death takes away the delight of the eyes, when every room in the house is a sick-chamber, when business is unprosperous, and all things seem to conspire in a desperate confederacy against the progress of life ;—it is then we know whether our religion is solid, healthy, rational, and built upon eternal foundations.

The officers were commanded to order off certain people :—

"What man is there that hath built a new house, and hath not dedicated it? let him go and return ɔ his house, lest he die in the battle, and another man dedicate it " (v. 5).

He might be thinking about his new house and its appointments, its luxuries and manifold enjoyments, and thus he would cease to be a soldier. A soldier must have no home, or find a home wherever he finds a field.

" And what man is he that hath planted a vineyard, and hath not yet eaten of it ? let him also go and return unto his house, lest he die in the battle, and another man eat of it " (v. 6).

He will be thinking about his grapes, and wine, and luscious delights, and by so much he will lose the quality of a soldier. A soldier must have no vineyards, no wine-goblets, no table at which to satisfy the desires of the epicure : he must drink the living air, he must eat the food he finds at his foot; he must always be ready for the sound of the trumpet calling to battle.

" And what man is there that hath betrothed a wife, and hath not taken her ? let him go and return unto his house, lest he die in the battle, and another man take her " (v. 7).

We must have no softness, no sentiment, no yielding stuff in this army,—nothing but steel, iron, adamant, determination, incorruptible and invincible.

Having ordered off all these people, the officers proceeded still further to weed the army :—

" What man is there that is fearful and fainthearted ? let him go and return unto his house, lest his brethren's heart faint as well as his heart " (v. 8).

The army might thus be greatly reduced ; we must remember, however, that reduction may mean increase. We do not conquer by number but by quality. One hero is worth ten thousand cowards. Cæsar is in himself more than all his legions. Quality counts for everything in the greatest battles and the most strenuous moments of life. Given the right quality, and the issue is certain. Quality never gives in : quality is never beaten ; quality flutters a challenge in its dying moments, and seems to say, I will rise again and continue the fight from the other side. So the army was reduced, and yet the army was increased in the very process of reduction. To-day the great speech is made over again :—" What man is there that is fearful and fainthearted ? let him go and return unto his house, lest his brethren's heart faint as well as his heart."

We cannot deny the fact that most Christian professors
are fainthearted ; they are not heroic souls. The great proportion of Christian professors are people who are "not well."
The number of invalids in the Church would surprise the imagination of the most audacious dreamer. This is not a world
for the fainthearted . it is a world of strife, wear and tear,
conflict, tumult, trial by fire, and temptation by the chief intellect
of hell ; it is a rough world ; it has well been described as being
out of joint. Those who would take hold of the world aright
must be inured to hardship : they must " endure hardship as
good soldiers of Christ." We are not speaking of the weak, but
of the fainthearted ; not of men inflicted with an infirmity, but
of hearts that have lost—if ever they had—the heroic nerve.
The Church is now the most timid of all influences in the world.
Granting that there are sections of the great Christian Church
marked by marvellous energy—for which we thank God—yet,
speaking of the Church as a whole, it is suffering from faintheartedness, timidity, fear : that spirit which cannot live in the
society of love, that gruesome, dark-faced thing that dare not look
at love : for love would slay it with light. What is the explanation of faintheartedness ? Want of conviction. Given a convinced Church, and a heroic Church is the consequence ; given
a Church uncertain, unconvinced, and you have a Church that
any atmosphere can affect and any charlatan can impose upon.
We must, therefore, return to foundations, to central principles,
to primary realities ; and having made sure of these the rest will
arrange itself. Where is conviction ? There may be a good
deal of concession : there may be a strong indisposition to object
to, or to deny, or to bring into discredit, theological problems and
religious usages, but what is needed is something more : clear,
well-reasoned, strongly-grounded conviction ; and where this
rules the mind every faculty is called into service, and the
battle of life is conducted with heroic decision and chivalrous
self-forgetfulness.

It was well understood in Israel that the fainthearted man
does more harm than he supposes he does. It is the same all
the world over and all time through. The timid man says,—I
will sit behind. Does his retirement behind mean simply one
man has gone from the front ? It means infinitely more : it is a

loss of influence, a loss of sympathy, a loss of leadership. A Christian professor is not at liberty to say he will abide in the shade : he will allow the claims of others : any place, how obscure soever, will do for him. Have no patience with men who tell such lies ! They have no right to be behind : their mission should be to find the best place, and to wake up every energy—to stir up the gift that is in them ; and every man should feel that the battle depends upon him. The discouraging influence of faintheartedness it is impossible to describe in words. Better have a congregation of six souls of light, and fire, and love, than have a great crowd without conviction, easy-going, flaccid in sentiment and thought,—without central realities and foundations that can be relied upon. " What man is there that is fearful and fainthearted ? Let him go "—he is not a loss : his going is the gain of all who are left behind : he made other people cold, he discouraged the young, he threw a gloom and a frown upon all that was proceeding in the Church : he disliked passion and music and beauty and brightness ; no genial word ever came out of his lips ; his hands never grasped the hand of soldier with heroic firmness ;—he must go, and we will send no blessing after him, for he would have no capacity to receive it. The great work of weeding the Church army must be carried out. It must be carried out in the ministry. There are men, unquestionably, in every ministry who have no right to be there—respectable, pedantic, literal, self-considering, afraid of giving offence, so prudent as to be imprudent, so wise as to become foolish. The ministry must be rid of them : they are not created in heaven, and they have no right to be in this position upon earth. So with all ranks, classes, and stations in the Church. The one man we must get rid of is the fainthearted man—the timid, cowering, self-considering professor, who is thankful when all is over without any accident having occurred,—a fear-ridden soul, a fear-darkened mind ; he must be exhorted—unhappily for his destina-tion—to return to his own house, probably because no other house would receive him. Let him go : the pulpit will be the better for his absence, the Church will be the warmer for his retirement, the young will then lift up their voices and be glad. Who has not seen the saddest of all pictures—a child beginning to dance and sing the moment the father has left the house ? That is a scene to make the soul sad. The child should never dance and sing so much as when his father comes back : and the father should dance and sing with the child, and *be* the child, and thus gladness should sound in every room of the house.

How marvellously faintheartedness shows itself! In one case it is fear of heresy. We hear of certain young people throwing off old habits and ways, and thereupon we become fainthearted, forgetting that there is a time in life when cleverness is the little imp that tempts men to their own destruction,—forgetting that there is a very critical period in life when the boy is *too* tall for a jacket and too young for a coat! We should bring into our view all the intermediate periods of life, and all transitional processes, assured that outside the Church there is nothing but a mighty famine, swine-feeding, and the bitterness of soul will send the young wanderer back again. In another case it is fear of criticism. What will the people next door say ? What will the adjoining Church think ? What will other men declare their judgment ? The false and cowardly speech runs thus :— I have no wish myself about the matter : personally I should say nothing to obstruct the suggestion ; but I am afraid it will be misunderstood, and that others will form an improper or inaccurate opinion about it. A man talking so representing other people! A man assuming a penetration like that ought to have had a courage equal to his genius. In another case it is fear of sensation. Our ministry has been wrecked in many instances by cold-hearted and mean-spirited men who ought never to have had the influence associated with official promotion. We must not advertise, because some people might misunderstand it ; we must not have too much music, because there are persons unable to follow the mystery of praise ; we must not have anything unusual. To have such fainthearted men in the Church is the bitterest trial that Christ has now to undergo. As for his enemies, he will rule them with a rod of iron, and dash them in pieces like a potter's vessel ; but the fainthearted and the timid—those who have no conviction or daring or chivalry—they wear out the life of the true minister, and they curse the home where they live. There is another faintness which is rather to the credit of the man who experiences it—a faintness arising from great service, long-continued effort, and noble sacrificial consecration. When a man pours out his life for the cause he may well be faint now and then. A beautiful sentiment in Scripture describes his condition :—" faint, yet pursuing "—putting out the arm in the right direction, looking along the right road, and saying in mute eloquence,—Give me breathing time, and I will join you again ; let me rest awhile ; do not take my sword away : in a day or two at most I will be at the front of the fight. That is a faintness which may be the beginning of great strength. So God is gracious to us : having no sympathy with timidity and fear and coward-liness, he has infinite compassion upon those who, having worn themselves out in service, need space and time for breathing. This exhortation comes back in a great trumpet-blast :—" What man is there that is fearful and fainthearted ? let him go and return into his house, lest his brethren's heart faint as well as his heart." It is difficult to stand against discouragement : it is awfully, awfully hard to keep warm in the presence of an iceberg. Not only is the man himself a coward : he is making cowards of others. So with regard to the pulpit and to every department of Christian service, this word must sound out more and more clearly : if any man wants money, let him go and return unto his house ;—if any man wants ease ; if any man would be exempt from criticism and hardship ; if any man is seeking to abound with the decaying and withering tributes of life ; if any man is ambitious for mere applause, let him go and return unto his own house. Christ can do without him : he is hindered by him.

PRAYER.

ALMIGHTY GOD, thou spreadest our table in the sight of our enemies; our cup runneth over; goodness and mercy have followed us all the days of our life. When we went into a far country and there felt the pains of hunger, we were moved to return again, saying,—In our Father's house there is bread enough and to spare. Lord, evermore give us this bread! This is the true bread that cometh down from heaven, of which, if a man eat, he shall hunger no more. Lord, evermore give us this bread! We have thought to satisfy ourselves with the stones of the field, and, behold, we have become more and more an hungered. Give us the true bread which cometh down from heaven. May we eat the flesh and drink the blood of Jesus Christ thy Son, and thus have life abiding in us, even eternal life. We have followed the way of evil, and have been stung by disappointments beyond all number; but now we return to our Father's house, where the feast is spread, where hospitality is offered to the poorest and the meanest; and we would sit down here at thy bidding, King of the feast, Master of assemblies, and eat and drink abundantly of the wisdom and grace and love of the Triune God. We have longed for this mystery: we have become weary with things we can handle and understand and measure and set back in our contempt: we have longed for the tabernacle in the wilderness, for the shekinah-cloud, for the trumpet of convocation, for the descending Deity. Having come into thine house, may we enter into the mystery of its grandeur and the deeper mystery of its peace; here may we enjoy conscious pardon through the blood of our Lord Jesus Christ: may we arise from this attitude of prostration into a pasture of triumph, release, joy, through the Holy Ghost, and go out to do life's duty with new strength, new hope, immortal courage. We are in the Lord's banqueting-house; we are not in the wilderness, we are not in stony places, we are not exiles; but, through the Lord Jesus Christ, Son of man, Son of God, we are children at home. Let our hearts be glad and let our eyes lift themselves up to the heavens, and see how much there is yet to begin, and what spaces have to be covered, and what possible services may have to be rendered. Thus may we bring the power of an endless life to bear upon the concerns, the burdens, the pains of the passing hour. Speak comfortably to those whose hearts are sore with a bitterness they cannot explain, and come thou, as thou only canst come, to hearts that are bowed down in self-distrust, in utter penitence and contrition, and are crying for the rest that can only come through pardon. Send messages, sweet singing gospels, to our loved ones at home, whether well or ill, but with special tenderness to those who are shutup in the chamber where they must soon die. The Lord comfort those who are weak, and when heart and flesh do fail be thou more than ever to the faith that has hung upon thee in simple love. Double the joy of those who are drinking deep of gladness to-day, but chasten their delight lest they become presumptuous and forget God. Lead, kindly Light—go before us, Spirit of Peace, make us quiet with thine own security, make us strong with thine own power. Amen.

Deut. xx. 19.

'When thou shalt besiege a city a long time, in making war against it to take it, thou shalt not destroy the trees thereof by forcing an axe against them: for thou mayest eat of them, and thou shalt not cut them down (for the tree of the field is man's life) to employ them in the siege."

CUTTING DOWN FRUIT-TREES

IT will be observed that this instruction is given to the Jews in the event of their going to war against any city. No question of mere horticulture arises in connection with this injunction. It is wantonness that is forbidden; it is not art that is decried. Trees that did not bear fruit were of course available for war, but trees that could be used for purposes of sustaining human life were to be regarded as in a sense sacred and inviolable.

A prohibition of this kind is charged with lofty moral significance. When men go to war they are in hot blood; everything seems to go down before the determination to repulse the enemy and establish a great victory. But here men in their keenest excitement are to discriminate between one thing and another, and are not to permit themselves to turn the exigencies of war into an excuse for wantonness or for the destruction of property that bears an intimate relation to human sustenance. It would be easy in times of calmness to admire and preserve beautiful fruit-trees, but imagine an army of soldiers rushing up to an orchard, and standing still before it as if they had suddenly come upon an altar—a god! surely that were a severe trial of human patience. If one of the trees could have been cut down the victory might have been won, or certainly the enemy might have been baffled; but even under such circumstances law was to be religiously respected. Dropping all that is merely incidental in the instruction, the moral appeal to ourselves is perfect in completeness and dignity. Civilisation has turned human life into a daily war. We live in the midst of contentions, rivalries, oppositions, and fierce conflicts of every kind, and God puts down his law in the very midst of our life and calls upon us to regulate everything by its sacredness. God has not left human life in a state of chaos ; his boundaries are round about it ; his written and unwritten laws constitute its restraints, its rewards and its penalties ; and even war in its most violent form is not to blind our eyes to the claims of God. Men say that all is fair in love and war, but this proverbial morality has no sanction in holy scripture. We are too apt to plead the exigency of circumstances in extenuation of acts that would not have otherwise been committed. It is evident that there are points in life at which circumstances must triumph or law must be maintained. Thus an appeal is made to reason and conscience in nearly every day. When the human or the divine must go down, the Christian ought to have no hesitation as to his choice.

Victories may be bought at too high a price. He who gives fruit-bearing trees in exchange for his triumphs may be said to have paid his soul for the prizes of this world. " What is a man profited, if he shall gain the whole world, and lose his own soul ? " What is a warrior profited if he gain the province, and cut down every fruit-tree, and burn up every harvest-field, and dry all the wells and fountains of the land ? Thus again and again comes upon us the certainty of the law that a man may purchase even his victories at too high a price. This applies to all kinds of victories,—victories, for example, which relate to property, influence, social position, and all the vanities of life. This is the danger which Christ was constantly pointing out. " What shall a man give in exchange for his soul ? " " Fear him who hath power to destroy both body and soul in hell." " A man's life consisteth not in the abundance of the things which he possesseth." A wonderful foresight is discovered in the injunction of the text. The speaker is endeavouring to show that the present victory may be overborne by future suffering. We shall require the fruit-trees after the victory has been established : but if we have cut down the fruit-trees to achieve the victory, where then is our reward and what is its value ? We may get our own way in life, but we may have burnt down all life's fruitful orchards in gaining the worthless prize. A whole philosophy of life is involved in this text. The fruit-tree is symbolical and not literal. God sometimes gives men the desire of their hearts, and sends leanness into their souls. What if a man shall come back from the field of learning, having won his honours, if, in doing so, he has lost his health ? What if a tradesman, at the end of a long period of service, should retire with a whole bankful of money, but have lost his power of enjoying the beauties of nature or the comforts of social life ? "A little that a righteous man hath is better than the riches of many wicked." Were it possible for a man to adorn his house with all the riches of sculpture and painting, what would he be profited if, in the process of bringing all these treasures together, he should have lost his sight ? Which is the more valuable possession, a picture which cannot be seen, or eyes which may for ever satisfy themselves upon the beauties and glories of nature ? Many men override this law, and insist upon having the pleasure whatever may be the price that is paid for it. An account is steadfastly kept against them, and one day they must discharge it, or be thrust into prison until they have paid the uttermost farthing. The young life, boastful of its energy, insists upon having its pleasures, cost what they may, and the old man is left to ruminate that in his youth he won his victories by cutting down his fruit-trees.

Two views may be taken of the circumstances and objects by which we are surrounded ; the one is the highest view of their possible uses, and the other the low view which contents itself with immediate advantages. The wood of the fruit-tree might be as useful as any other wood for keeping back an enemy or serving as a defence ; but the fruit-tree was never meant for that purpose, and to apply it in that direction is to oppose the intention of God. We are to look at the highest uses of all things—a fruit-tree for fruit ; a flower for beauty ; a bird for music ; a rock for building. It is not enough that things be put to some use, we must endeavour to discover the particular use which God intended them to serve, and the adoption of that use alone will bring us into harmony with the divine will. Music was never intended to celebrate evil or give notoriety to things that are unholy, or purposes that are morally mischievous. Music can be used for these purposes, but the use of it in this direction is

a profanation. Eloquence was never intended to advocate unrighteous claims or dishonourable causes; eloquence can bring
together all its words and sentences and thunders even for this
base purpose, and in the choicest language may defend the foulest
criminal : but this was not the original purpose of eloquence ;
man's tongue was not made that the interests of falsehood might
be subserved, or that vice might outwit virtue in some display
of wordy skill. Eloquence was meant to expound truth, equity,
law ; it was intended to be a tongue for the dumb, and to speak
boldly for those who could not speak for themselves in all
righteous causes and claims. So, as a fruit-tree might have been
used for military purposes, but was yet forbidden to be so used,
many human faculties, if not all, might be turned to inferior or
even forbidden uses, but the mere fact that they could be so
perverted is no justification of the perversion. In all things
respect the highest purpose, the chief intent, the manifest destiny,
and, working along that high line of appointment and ordination,
the issue must be one of contentment and harmony. A man may
be able to clean a boot, but if he be also able to paint a picture the
time which is spent upon the inferior service may be time wasted.
He may be able to carve a face upon a cherry-stone, but if he
can also teach a child, all his carving, however exquisite, is but
a proof of his perverseness. The question we ought to put
to ourselves constantly is, What is the highest purpose of
my being ? What is the real intent of my creation ? Can I do
some larger and nobler thing than that which now absorbs my
energies ? Unless we study such questions as these, and answer
them righteously, we shall certainly be cutting down fruit-trees
to help us to gain temporary triumphs. A man has a brook
to cross and is unable to cross it without assistance ; he can cut
down a fruit-tree which will form a bridge, or he can pull up a
gate-post which would serve exactly the same purpose ; is he at
liberty to desecrate a fruit-tree when he might have crossed the
stream by other means, involving no act of wantonness, and
inflicting upon society no sense of loss ? No man is at liberty
to beg for bread so long as he can work for it. He must turn
himself to the highest advantage,—that is to say, realise the very
purpose of God in his creation and fulfil all its obligations. A
man has the power to hide his talent, but not the right. This

is a distinction which is not always made with sufficient clearness. Power and right are not coequal terms. We have the power to cut down fruit-trees, but not the right ; we have the power to mislead the blind, but not the right ; we have the power to prostitute our talents, but not the right. The right is often the more difficult course as to its process, but the difficulty of the process is forgotten in the heaven of its issue. To have the power of cutting down fruit-trees is to have the power of inflicting great mischief upon society. A man may show great power in cutting down a fruit-tree, but he may show still greater power in refusing to do so. The first power is merely physical, the second power is of the nature of God's omnipotence. Forbearance is often the last point of power. We may have power to starve an enemy, or injure an opponent, or lead away business from a rival, or turn aside the current which would fertilise the garden of an antagonist ; all these things we might do at great cost, and show great expertness and ability in bringing about our purposes : we forget that we should show a more distinguished power in abstaining from every one of these wicked things. To love an enemy is to show greater strength than could possibly be shown by burning up himself and his house, and leaving nothing behind but the smoking ashes. This is a great spiritual mystery, and seems indeed to have in it all the elements of a palpable contradiction, and is not to be understood or realised in all its gracious possibilities but by long-continued practice in obedience to the divine will. Such issues as these often come upon the mind with the surprise of a revelation.

There are times when even fruit-trees are to be cut down. Perhaps this is hardly clear on the first putting of it. The meaning is that a fruit-tree may cease to be a fruit-tree. When Jesus came to the fig-tree and found on it nothing but leaves, he doomed it to perpetual barrenness, and it withered away. Even the husbandman pleaded that if the fruit-tree did not bear fruit after one more trial it should be cut down as a cumberer of the ground. Fruit-trees are not to be kept in the ground simply because in years long past they did bear fruit. Trees are only available according to the fruit which they bear to-day. " Herein is my Father glorified, that ye bear much fruit." Christians themselves are only to be tolerated as such in proportion to the fruit which

they bear. Profession often aggravates disappointment. Orna-
mental churches, ministries, and institutions generally, how
bold and loud soever their professions, must perish under the
condemnation of the society they have mocked by their false
appearances. A tremendous possibility must not be overlooked
here : it is possible to bring forth evil fruit. The question,
therefore, is not, Are we bearing fruit ? but, Are we bearing
good fruit ? The Christian can have no difficulty as to the kind
of fruit which he is expected to bring forth. He is to be as
a branch in the Living Vine. "From me is thy fruit found."
"Every tree which bringeth not forth good fruit is hewn down,
and cast into the fire." "Little children, abide in him ; that, when
he shall appear, we may have confidence, and not be ashamed
before him at his coming." There is to be a judgment of trees.
"Now also the axe is laid unto the root of the trees." Here
again we are brought into close proximity with our own text, for
in Deut. xx. 20, we read : "Only the trees which thou knowest
that they be not trees for meat, thou shalt destroy and cut them
down." There must be no mistake about the fruit. Leaves are
not enough. Shapeliness is not enough. Abundance of wood is
not enough : "That which beareth thorns and briers is rejected,
and is nigh unto cursing ; whose end is to be burned."

PRAYER

ALMIGHTY GOD, our hands are withered; bid us now stretch them forth. Thou art the Healer, O Christ of God ! Thou dost live to heal; thou hast no pleasure in disease, or death, or the grave: thy joy is in health and life and heaven. May we rise into the spirit of thy joy, and respond to all the ministries thou hast set in motion for the preservation of the soul's health and the opening out of great views concerning the soul's destiny. We bless thee for thine house, its comfort, its security, its peace ; it is a place of calm: the storm is outside : the high wind blows over the roof but does not come within. Thou hast hidden thy people as in the cleft of a rock until the calamity be overpast, and thou hast spoken comfortably unto them and assured them of deliverance and liberty. We bless thee for thy Book; it is in our native tongue : we understand most of it ; when we most need it, it is most to us—so comforting in sorrow, so inspiring in dejection, and so enriching when the mind realises its true capacity. May we read thy Book with attentive eyes, with hearts eager to learn the meaning of the message; and may we retire from our perusal of holy pages stronger, purer, wiser, more resolute in the cause of good, and more resigned to all the mysteries of thy rule. Thou hast a word for every one : the old man trembling on his staff and looking into his grave ; the little child to whom life is a cloud full of stars, or a night full of voices, or a day bright with hope ;—send a message to each of us : let each feel that this is the Father's house, and as for bread, there is enough and to spare. Dry our tears ; lift our burdens awhile that we may recover breath and strength ; attemper the wind to the shorn lamb; speak to those who have little, and who live in backward places and positions, in the shadow and in the cold, and so reveal thyself to them that the spirit may triumph over the flesh, and that even in unexpected places there may be a sense of thy presence. The Lord grant unto us light, peace, pardon, comfort,—all we need, to do the remainder of this day's work with both hands, and to enter on to-morrow's labour with Christian hope.

We pray at the Cross : we name the Name that is above every name ; we cannot understand the mystery which it represents, but we feel its redeeming love. Amen.

Deut. xxii. 1-4.

1. Thou shalt not see thy brother's ox or his sheep go astray, and hide thyself from them: thou shalt in any case bring them again unto thy brother.

2. And if thy brother be not nigh unto thee, or if thou know him not, then

thou shalt bring it unto thine own house, and it shall be with thee until thy brother seek after it, and thou shalt restore it to him again.

3. In like manner shalt thou do with his ass; and so shalt thou do with his raiment; and with all lost thing of thy brother's, which he hath lost, and thou hast found, shalt thou do likewise: thou mayest not hide thyself.

4. Thou shalt not see thy brother's ass or his ox fall down by the way, and hide thyself from them: thou shalt surely help him to lift them up again.

FRATERNAL RESPONSIBILITIES.

THE word "brother" is not to be read in a limited sense, as if referring to a relation by blood. That is evident from the expression in the second verse:—"if thou know him not." The reference is general—to a brother-man. In Exodus, as we have seen, the term used is not brother, but "enemy":—"If thine enemy's ox, or ass, or sheep——." It is needful to understand this clearly, lest we suppose that the directions given in the Bible are merely of a domestic and limited kind. "Thou shalt not see thy brother's ox or his sheep go astray." That is not the literal rendering of the term; the literal rendering would be,—"Thou shalt not see thy brother's ox or his sheep *driven away*"—another man behind them, and driving them on as if he were taking them to his own field. The term, therefore, is much stronger than the term which is thus rendered in English. Not only is the animal going astray, as if by misadventure, but it is being driven away— carried off, feloniously claimed by some other man. We are not to see actions of this kind and be quiet: there is a time to speak; and of all times calling for indignant eloquence and protest there are none like those which are marked by acts of oppression and wrong-doing: "Thou shalt not hide thyself"—thou shalt stand up, go to the front, play the man, accost the wrong-doer in a tone he cannot misunderstand, and insist upon right being done to brother, friend, or enemy. This is the tone of the Bible; this is the moral inspiration of the Holy Book: it speaks up for right, it never countenances wrong-doing, it never crowns a felon: it hangs its Iscariot, it drowns its blasphemers.

We are now upon familiar ground, these sentiments having come under our observation in earlier readings. As the sentiments are the same, their applications must not be substantially varied. What are those applications? The argument must proceed from the lower to the higher. We must reason thus: If a certain line of action is to be adopted under such and such temporary circumstances and within such and such limited scope, what action will be appropriate to higher occasions and within larger boundaries ?   This is the divine method of revelation ; this is the only method which God himself could adopt in coming near to us. He tabernacled in the idea o fatherhood ; he said in effect, The people understand the word FATHER : amid all their wrong they still cling to the fatherly idea with some measure of fondness and loyalty : I, therefore, will be as a father to them, and will instruct my servants to say, " like as a father ; " and I will instruct my Son to say, "how much more shall your Father ! " and when the disciples gather around him that they may ask concerning the mystery of prayer and request him to hand them the key of heaven, I will teach them to say, " Our Father." This is a principle of Biblical interpretation—namely, movement from the lower to the higher, from the contracted to the boundless, from human tears to the infinite compassion of God.

Adopting this principle, how does the passage open itself to our inquiry ? Thus : If we must not see our brother's ox being driven away, can we stand back and behold his *mind* being forced into wrong or evil directions ? It were an immoral morality to contend that we must be anxious about the man's ox but care nothing about the man's *understanding.* We do not live in Deuteronomy : we revert to it as men revert to ancient history, inquiring into the roots and origins of things : we live within the circle of the Cross : we are followers of the Lord Jesus Christ ; our morality or our philanthropy, therefore, does not end in solicitude regarding ox, or sheep, or ass : we are called to the broader concern, the tenderer interest, which relates to the human mind and the human soul.   Are not *minds* driven away ? Some minds are stronger than others : and is not dominance sometimes used to compel inferior judgments to accept sophistical or even immoral conclusions ? Is there no man to whom the truth has been given as a sacred trust and in whom it burns so that he cannot run away when he sees other minds being driven into darkness, or attempts made to debase and prostitute the intelligence of the soul ? There need not be any dogmatism in the man's manner or tone ; but, in proportion as he has a sense of right, will he speak emphatically, clearly, in round and penetrating tones, so that his exercises of a philanthropic description may not be taken as efforts that cost nothing—interpositions which express officiousness rather than the earnestness of the Cross of Christ. It would be singular indeed, amounting to an irony intolerable, were we taught to be solicitous about oxen and sheep and cattle of every name, but to care nothing about the man himself. How contradictory! How painfully ironical could we read such words as these :—If thou seest thy brother's ox driven away, stand up, insist upon the ox being taken back, speak a word for honesty; but if thou shalt see thy brother *himself* being driven into slavery, pass by on the other side, take no heed of an action of that sort, confine solicitude to the ox, remit concerns in relation to the individual man! Evidently the argument must run in the other direction : If careful about the ox, how much more about the mind! If careful about the sheep, how much more careful about the owner! Reasoning in this direction, we soon find ourselves approaching the mystery of the Cross : all this neighbourliness, philanthropy, tender, anxious solicitude about cattle and property leads by a straight and open road to the mystery of the divine concern for the soul of man, as revealed in the Cross of him who died the just for the unjust.

Take it from another point of view. If careful about the sheep, is there to be no care concerning the man's *good name?* Are we permitted to stand by and see the man's fame and reputation driven away without protest upon our part ? We could not see one sheep taken from his flock without instantly being excited and hastening to the owner to tell him that some petty felony had been committed ; we might even be more courageous, and, assured that others were looking on and were near at hand to help us, we might venture to protest to the felon himself and insist upon the property being returned. We are courageous when we are in considerable numbers. The individual and solitary observer might not have courage to protest, but the most timid of hearts acquires boldness in the assured presence and society of others. Can we, then, see the good name driven away without jealousy for our brother's fame, without concern for that quality of reputation without which life is not worth living? We are told that to steal the purse is to steal trash—it is something—nothing; 'twas mine, 'tis his—a mere rearrangement of property; "but he that filches from me my good name, robs me of that which not enriches him, and makes me poor indeed." Do we leave the poets to express this high sentiment in golden terms, whilst we engage ourselves with the small solicitude which is satisfied with the fate of oxen and sheep? We are the keepers of our brother: his good name is ours. When the reputation of a Christian man goes down or is being driven away, the sum-total of Christian influence is diminished; —in this sense we are not to live unto ourselves or for ourselves: every soul is part of the common stock of humanity, and when one member is exalted the whole body is raised in a worthy ascension, and when one member is debased or wronged or robbed a felony has been committed upon the consolidated property of the Church. Thus we are led into philanthropic relations, social trusteeships, and are bound for one another; and if we see a man's reputation driven away by some cruel hand—even though the reputation be that of an enemy—we are to say, "Be just and fear not"—let us know both sides of the case; there must be no immoral partiality; surely in the worst of cases there must be some redeeming points. When the Church cares for itself in this way the hireling will be afraid to approach the fold: even the wolf will know that the flock is well sheltered.

Take it from another point. "In like manner shalt thou do with . . . his raiment." And are we to be careful about the man's raiment, and care nothing about his *aspirations?* Is it nothing to us that the man never lifts his head towards the wider spaces and wonders what the lights are that glitter in the distant arch? Is it nothing to us that the man never sighs after some larger sphere, or ponders concerning some nobler possibility of life? Finding a man driving *himself* away, we are bound to arouse him in the Creator's name and to accuse him of the worst species of suicide. Aspirations are the beginning of great character: they express discontentment: being turned into our mother tongue they might be thus read: This world is not enough: I beat my hands against its narrow boundaries: my soul longs for something broader, brighter, grander: I know

these glittering points are not nails driven into a door to prevent
its being opened—these glittering points are invitations, calls,
allurements; I would respond, Is there no God in all the void?
Hear a man talking so, and instantly leap upon his chariot, join
him, and ask him if he understands what he says, and when
he tells you that he has no understanding but is sighing after
solutions of mysteries, read to him the great words of Christ—
the solemn Gospel of the Son of God—and as you speak, in
Christ's name and in Christ's tone, his heart will burn within
him, and at eventide he will say, Abide with me. Man knows
the truth when he hears it : there is an answering voice in
the constitution of man. There are some words which cannot
be palmed off upon man as true ; when he himself is really
in the agony of earnestness there are other words which come
into his darkness like great lights. The light proves itself.
Light instantly chases away the creatures of darkness ; one little
flame sends a vibration of light into every corner of the building.
How light troubles darkness ! how the darkness writhes under
the gleam of light !—it is in sore distress. So the soul knows
the light as the flowers know the sun.

Can we see our brother's ass being driven away and care nothing
what becomes of his *child ?* Save the children, and begin your work
as soon as possible. The traveller who wants to get home does
not wait until the sun is high up in the sky : the moment he sees a
little whitening line in the east he grasps his staff and stands up
ready to go onward to his home and the sanctuary of his love.
Were we more anxious about the children we should do a greater
work of a Christian kind. The old man seems to be beyond our
reach, but the little child seems to be made for Christ. It would
seem—do not let us shrink from the term—*natural* for every
little child to put out his arms to cling to the Child of Bethlehem.
Save the children, and you will purify society ; expend your
solicitude upon young, opening, tender life, and you shall see
the result of your concern after many days. Services should be
constituted for children ; the old people have had the sanctuary
too long : their ears are sated with eloquence : their minds are
stored with names which never turn into inspirations ; churches
might be built for children, and preachers trained to speak
to them alone. We have reversed all things, and thus have

gone astray. Baptism is for the little speechless child—a great mystery of life : a throb that has in it immortality; and that other sacrament of blood, that mystery of pain, that apocalypse of love might be given to little children ; when we touch it with our reason, we profane it : when we claim it because we under-stand it, we become idolaters : " Except ye be converted, and become as little children, ye shall not enter into the kingdom of heaven." See a little child without knowledge, and do not " hide " yourself, but say, That little child is mine. We hold our knowledge for the benefit of the ignorant; we are trustees of our strength that we may save the weak from oppression. It is sad to see the little children left to themselves; and there-fore ineffably beautiful to mark the concern which interests itself in the education and redemption of the young. A poet says he was nearer heaven in his childhood than he ever was in after-days, and he sweetly prayed that he might return through his yesterdays and through his childhood back to God. That is chronologically impossible—locally and physically not to be done; and yet that is the very miracle which is to be performed in the soul—in the spirit; we must be "born again."

It is a coward's trick to close the eyes whilst wrong is being done in order that we may not see it. It is easy to escape distress, perplexity, and to flee away from the burdens of other men; but the whole word is, "Thou shalt not hide thyself" but "Thou shalt surely help him." Who can under-value a Bible which speaks in such a tone ? The proverb, " Every man must take care of himself," has no place in the Book of God. We must take care of one another : "Whoso hath this world's goods, and seeth his brother have need, and shutteth up his bowels of compassion from him, how dwelleth the love of God in him ?" If thou sayest,—Behold, I knew it not,—will not he who makes inquisition for blood bring the matter to a positive and inevitable test ? Christians are not called upon to close their eyes, to run away from danger, and to lay down some narrow doctrine of *mine* and *thine.* Christianity means nothing if it does not mean the unity of the human race, the common rights of humanity : and he who fails to interpose in all cases of injustice and wrong-doing, or suffering which he can relieve, may be a great theologian, but he is not a Christian.

PRAYER.

ALMIGHTY GOD, we cry unto thee, each for himself, "Create in me a clean heart, O God; and renew a right spirit within me." The leprosy is in the heart; the flesh is good and sound and right, but our hearts are full of sin and evil and bitterness. "Lord, if thou wilt, thou canst make me clean." But thou dost ask us to be willing in this case: Lord, we are willing; we would be clean; we would know the mystery of holiness, the rest of purity, the music of unity with God. We do not know what cleanness is; we cannot wash our own hearts. Thou alone canst cleanse the spirit and sanctify the whole will, making every passion a pure flame, and the out-going of the soul a sacred yearning after larger knowledge. We cannot do the miracles of God. Work in us mightily, and show thy great power in the cleansing of hearts that are deceitful above all things and desperately wicked. This is the purpose of thy Cross, O Christ, this is the meaning of the blood that was shed,—to take away all sin, to cleanse the sinner, to make the evil-doer a right-doer, so that not only shall the works be changed, but the worker shall be transformed. We bless thee for this revelation of thy purpose; it enables us to seize the Book in which it is written, and to lay hold upon it with our judgment and affection, and to expect from it further light, more ardent warmth, and larger hospitality. Thou wouldst have all hearts clean; from the great heaven thou hast written this word, addressed to all the sons of men: "Be ye holy, as your Father in heaven is holy." Thou dost call us to no minor character; thou hast not set before us that which is uncertain, incomplete, fickle, and changeable; thou art thyself the standard of holiness, the character to whose grandeur we must aspire. To God all things are possible. In that consolation we rest, and from that point we begin our poor endeavour, knowing that our weakness shall be perfected by the divine power, and what we cannot do, God will abundantly accomplish. We have been a long time at school; we are poor scholars; we misspell the simplest words, and misapply the deepest, and in the midst of our reading we burn with unholy passion. When we are at church, we bring with us forbidden guests. When we read thy Book, we think of other music and fascination. Life is difficult, the discipline is hard; every day smites with its own fist, and we spend our time in vainly trying to get up again. But it is thy life, not ours; thy way of doing things, and therefore it is right: we accept it; even when the burden is heaviest, we do not pray that it may be destroyed, but that our strength may be equal to it. Thou hast carried thy servants through many a mile of the life-journey; some of them are willing to turn right back again, and begin all the road once more, thinking they would avoid the mistakes, and never repeat the errors which have filled the life-way with difficulty and judgment. Some are in a strait betwixt two : wanting to stay, willing to go; wanting to go, willing to stay ; having no will in the matter, but waiting thy revelation. Others are impatient to go, for they have seen the end of things; they have heard all the roaring wind, and have tasted its emptiness, and now they long to be in the better land, where every day is harvest, and where there is no black night. We pray for one another : for the little child and the old man, for the sick heart, for the wounded spirit, for those whose hopes are dead, and whose best trusts are blighted. We remember those whose sin cannot be spoken, whose suffering lies beyond the reach of words, who die in secret, and waste away whilst they are deceiving their friends with smiles. Thou knowest us altogether : in our robustness and force and great strength, in our weakness and delicateness, in our pining and fear, in our richness, in our wealth and poverty,—in all our relations thou knowest us wholly; there is not a word upon our tongue, there is not a thought in our heart, but, lo, O Lord, thou knowest it altogether. Thy knowledge is mercy : to know is to pity, to know is to look with inward kindness on the objects of suffering and despair. The Lord send messages to us, every one ; make the reading of his Word like the dawning of a birthday ; and may there be festival in the house, eating and drinking abundantly at God's great table, and may all the guests rise from the feast, saying,—Blessed be the Master, and to the King be the loyalty of every heart. Amen.

Deut. xxii. 6, 7.

" If a bird's nest chance to be before thee in the way in any tree, or on the ground, whether they be young ones, or eggs, and the dam sitting upon the young, or upon the eggs, thou shalt not take the dam with the young : but thou shalt in any wise let the dam go, and take the young to thee; that it may be well with thee, and that thou mayest prolong thy days."

BIRDS' NESTS.

A SINGULAR word to be in a Book which we might have expected to be wholly occupied with spiritual revelation. Men are anxious to know something about the unseen worlds, and the mystery which lies at the heart of things and palpitates throughout the whole circle of observable nature, and yet they are called upon to pay attention to the treatment of birds' nests. Is this any departure from the benevolent and redeeming spirit of the Book ? On the contrary, this is a vivid illustration of the minuteness of divine government, and as such it affords the beginning of an argument which must for ever accumulate in volume and force, on the ground that if God is so careful of a

bird's nest he must be proportionately careful of all things of
higher quality. Jesus Christ so used nature. "If then God so
clothe the grass," said he, "how much more will he clothe you,
O ye of little faith?" So we may add, If God is so careful of
birds' nests, what must he be of human hearts, and human homes,
and the destinies of the human family? It is not enough to keep
the law in great aspects, such as appeal to the public eye, and by
keeping which reputation is sometimes unjustly gained. We are
called upon to pay attention to minute and hardly discernible
features of character, for these often indicate the real quality of
the man. God's beneficence is wonderfully displayed in the care
of the birds' nests. God is kind in little things as well as in
great. The quality of his love is one, whether it be shown in
the redemption of the race, in numbering the hairs of our head,
in ordering our steps, or giving his beloved sleep. Did we but
know it we should find that all law is beneficent—the law of
restriction as well as the law of liberty. The law which would
keep a man from doing injury to himself, though it may appear
to impair the prerogative of human will, is profoundly beneficent. Was not man to have dominion over the fowls of the
air? Truly so; but dominion is to be exercised in mercy.
Power that is uncontrolled by kindness soon becomes despotism.
The psalmist heard that power belonged unto God; at that point
he might have trembled with awe or bowed himself down in
servile fear, for little and frail is the strength of man; but the
psalmist seems to have heard at the same time the other and
comforting truth—namely, "Also unto thee, O Lord, belongeth
mercy." This is completeness of sovereignty : this is not only a
hand that can rule but a heart that can love. We are apt to think
that right and wrong are terms which only apply to great
concerns, and so we lose the element of morality in things that
are comparatively insignificant in volume and temporary in
duration. The Bible insists that right and wrong are terms
which belong to everything in life. There is a right way of
appropriating the contents of a bird's nest, and there is a way
that is equally wrong. We may do the right thing in the wrong
way. All men know what it is to speak the right word in the
wrong tone, and so deprive the word of all its natural music and
proper value as a moral instrument. There is a right way of

chiding, and there is a chastisement which becomes mere malice, or the wanton expression of superior physical force. The morality of the Bible goes down to every root and fibre of life. In offering a salutation, in opening a door, in uttering a wish, in writing a letter, in using titles of deference, in every possible exercise of human thought and power the moral element is present. Phebe was to be received by the Christians at Rome "as becometh saints." A New Testament injunction is " Be courteous." Charity itself is courteous, graceful, savoured with the highest degree of refinement, and expressive of the completest reach of dignity. So the Bible will not allow our life to fray itself out in loose ends, content if the middle portion of the web be comparatively well-connected and serviceable; every thread-end is to be attended to, every fibre is to be considered of value, and conscience is not satisfied until every question which righteousness can ask has been answered in a satisfactory manner. The treatment of birds' nests is a sure indication of the man's whole character. The act does not begin and end in itself. He who can wantonly destroy a bird's nest can wantonly do a hundred other things of the same kind. It is here that we see the value of all such moral restriction and injunction. To be cruel at all is to be cruel all through and through the substance and quality of the character. Men cannot be cruel to birds' nests and gentle to children's cradles. The man who can take care of a bird's nest because it is right to do so—not because of any pleasure which he has in a bird's nest—is a man who cannot be indifferent to the homes of children and the circumstances of his fellow-creatures generally. It is a mistake to suppose that we can be wanton up to a given point, and then begin to be considerate and benevolent. We are all apt scholars in a bad school, and learn more in one lesson there than we can learn through much discipline in the school of God. The little tyrannies of childhood often explain the great despotism of mature life. Is not kindness an influence that penetrates the whole life, having manifold expression, alike upward, downward, and laterally, touching all human things, all inferiors and dependants, and every harmless and defenceless life? On the other hand, we are to be most careful not to encourage any merely pedantic feeling. Hence the caution I have before given respecting the purpose for which a man considerately handles even a bird's nest. Every day we see how possible it is for a man to be very careful of his horse, and yet to hold the comfort of his servant very lightly. We have all seen, too, how possible it is for a man to be more careful of his dogs than of his children. But the care which is thus lavished upon horse or dog is not the care dictated by moral considerations, or inspired by benevolence; it is what I have termed a pedantic feeling, it is a mere expression of vanity, it is not an obedience to conscience or moral law. There are men who would not on any account break up a bird's nest in the garden who yet would allow a human creature to die of hunger. The bird's nest may be regarded as an ornament of the garden, or an object of interest, or a centre around which various influences may gather; so whatever care may be bestowed upon it, it is not to be regarded as concerning the conscience or the higher nature. We must beware of decorative morality; hand-painted feeling: calculated consideration for inferior things; for selfishness is very subtle in its operation, and sometimes it assumes with perfect hypocrisy the airs of benevolence and religion. What if in all our carefulness for dumb animals we think little of breaking a human heart by sternness or neglect? According to an ancient authority it was better to be Herod's pig than to be Herod's child; an anomaly which in literature is impossible, but in actual experience is an indisputable and tragical fact.

Kindness to the lower should become still tenderer kindness to the higher. This is Christ's own argument when he bids us behold the fowls of the air that in their life we may see our Father's kindness, he adds, "Are ye not much better than they?" When he points out how carefully a man would look after the life of his cattle, he adds, "How much then is a man better than a sheep?" It ought to be considered a presumptive argument in favour of any man's spirit that he is kind to the inferior creatures that are around him; if this presumption be not realised in his case, then is his kindness bitterest wrong.

It is true that all such injunctions are not literally repeated in the Christian economy. We have not in the Christian Church to guard ourselves by sections and sub-sections of technical precepts. How then does the case stand with us who have come into a complete inheritance of so-called liberty? We have passed from the letter to the spirit; God has put within us a clean heart, so that we are no longer true, or kind, or noble, merely because of a literal direction which is guarded by solemn anction, but because the Holy Ghost has sanctified us, made our hearts his dwelling-place. It is utterly in vain for us to attempt to satisfy even our own sense of right by attending merely to what is known as duty or propriety. If we have not within us the Holy Spirit as our Teacher and Ruler, the efforts of our hand will but disappoint and mock our expectation. We cannot build a great character with the hand. At first the hand was called into active requisition, and was made to do a great deal in the way of moral industry, but he who called the hand into such service intended through it to find a way into the heart. Again and again we must repeat, "As a man thinketh in his heart, so is he." If we pass by a bird's nest and forbear to destroy it simply because a law has forbidden its destruction, we are in our souls as if we had torn the little home to pieces and slain its helpless occupant. We do the things which we would do, even though they be not accomplished by the action of the hand. We pass through the wheat-field and do not touch a single ear of corn, yet if in our heart we covet the produce, or begrudge the farmer the result of his labour, we are in the sight of God spiritually guilty of having burned the wheat-field and thus destroyed the bread of man. The morality of Christianity is intensely spiritual. To hate is to murder. To covet is to steal. To desire is to appropriate. We are prone to measure things by vulgar aspects and broad appeals to human attention; consequently we have come to think that thieving can only be accomplished by the hand, whereas Christ teaches us that without laying our hands upon a single article of property belonging to another man we may in reality be guilty of the most wicked appropriation. Our prayer should continually be, "Create in me a clean heart, O God." The hand may commit mistakes, it is the heart that commits sin. No matter how pedantically we may fulfil the literal law, if the spirit of righteousness is not in us we are not credited with obedience: the light that is within us is darkness, and when that is the case, who can estimate the gloom of so terrible a night?

PRAYER.

ALMIGHT. GOD, thou knowest what is good for us; we will not choose: to choose is to spoil the life when thou hast undertaken to choose for us. Do with us what thou wilt; thou canst not do wrong: God is Light; God is Love. We rest in God; we wait patiently for him. Let him come when he may: at the cock-crowing, or in the hot mid-day, or in the depth of the darkness. Come when thou wilt, as thou wilt; delay not thy coming—is the one prayer upon which our faith and hope would venture; and thou hast permitted us to go thus far in our pleading with thee: thou hast not forbidden it to be written in thy Book,—Even so, Lord Jesus, come quickly. We know not what quickly means: it is a word that expresses our present failing, but we know not all that it contains. A thousand years are in thy sight as yesterday when it is past: one day is as a thousand years. Thou dost not reckon as we do. So we stand speaking our little language, uttering words which express only part of our thought, knowing that thy love will interpret our meaning and send an answer to itself rather than to our pleading. Thou dost permit us to pray. It relieves the heart to talk upward; the life is the better for the vision directed on high;—there we see majesty, vastness, grandeur, points of light as tender as they are dazzling, and behold gates open upward into heaven, and we hope to enter the gleaming portals. We bless thee for the thought that is upward, for the aspiration that is like fire, for every wish of the heart that purifies the lips that utter it. These are thy creations; these are the testimonies of God to man; these are the proofs that thou hast not forsaken thy creatures. Pardon us wherein we have done wrong; grant unto us a sense of forgiveness; give us to feel as men feel who, staggering under great burdens, lose the way, and are permitted to spring forth into liberty. That will be early heaven; that will be a pledge of immortality; that will be the crown of Christ. O Christ! we bless thee. Our hearts know none other; they love thee: thou hast redeemed them. Our whole life is a tribute to thy power and thy grace. We come to thee, we rest upon thee; touching thy wounds, we say, These shall save us; opening thine hand to see the print of the nails, we say, This hand is mightier than all other; it will protect and deliver us; and to Christ shall be the praise of every age. Amen.

Deut. xxii. 8.

"When thou buildest a new house, then thou shalt make a battlement for thy roof, that thou bring not blood upon thine house, if any man fall from thence."

BATTLEMENTS.

NOT only is this an extraordinary instruction, it is the more
extraordinary that it appears in a Book which is supposed
to be devoted to spiritual revelations. But in calling it extraordinary, do we not mistake the meaning which ought to be
attached to the term "spiritual revelations"? Are not more
things spiritual than we have hitherto imagined? It is due to
the spirit of the Bible, and indeed to the whole genius of the
providence of life, to enlarge the term spiritual rather than to
enlarge the word material. What if in the long run it should
prove that things are in reality not material at all but
intensely and eternally spiritual? It will be observed that
according to this instruction man is not at liberty altogether to
please himself even in the construction of a dwelling-place.
What is there indeed in which a man is permitted altogether to
consult himself or gratify his own desires? Self ought to have
no place in human thinking. At first this may appear to be an
impossibility, and indeed it is a natural impossibility, and is one
of the miracles which can be wrought in human thought and life
only by the spirit of the Son of God. This instruction recognises
the social side of human life, and that side may be taken as in
some sense representative of a divine claim; it is not the claim
of one individual only, but of society; it may be taken as representing the sum-total of individuals; the larger individual—the
concrete humanity. Socialism has its beneficent as well as its
dangerous side. Socialism indeed, when rightly interpreted, is
never to be feared; it is only when perverted and prostituted to
base uses, in which self becomes the supreme idol, that socialism
is to be denounced and avoided. The social influences continually
operating in life limit self-will, develop the most gracious side
of human nature, and purify and establish all that is noblest and
truest in friendship.

There are certain conditions under which an instruction such
as is given in the text may excite obvious objections. Suppose,
for example, that a man should plead that his neighbour calls
upon him only occasionally, and should upon that circumstance
raise the inquiry whether he should put up a permanent building
to meet an exceptional circumstance. The inquiry would seem to

be pertinent and reasonable. On the other hand, when closely looked into, it will be found that the whole scheme of human life is laid out with a view to circumstances which are called exceptional. The average temperature of the year may be mild, for most of the twelve months the wind may be low and the rain gentle ; why then build a house with strong walls and heavy roofs ? Could we be sure that there would be only one tempestuous day in the whole year—if we did not know when that day might occur, the element of uncertainty being of great consequence in this argument—we should build the house strongly in order to prepare for the advent of the stormy visitation. Thus in reality we do build our houses for exceptional circumstances. The ship-builder builds his vessels not for smooth waters and quiet days only, but for the roughest billows and the fiercest winds. He does not know when the tempest may come upon his vessel, and therefore he has prepared for it under all possible emergencies. The vessel would be absurdly too strong were it always to sail in unrippled water ; but even if the navigator knew that for nine days out of ten the water would be without a ripple, and knew not on what particular day a great wind would arise to try the timbers of his ship, he would not stir an inch from port until he was sure the ship was so built as to be able in all probability to weather the most trying storm. Our neighbour may call to-morrow—see then that the battlement be ready ! Though his visits be uncertain, yet that very uncertainty constitutes a demand for a permanent arrangement on our part ; as the uncertainty is permanent so also must be our means of meeting it. We are continually exhorted to be prepared for crises, to expect the unexpected, and be sure of the uncertain ; he who is so defended for his neighbour's sake will be found to be equal to the most sudden emergencies of life.

A man who is anxious to save himself the expense of erecting a battlement for his roof may easily suggest reasons for evading the law which is laid down in the text. He might plead that it would be time enough to build the battlement when anything like danger is in prospect. Or he might suggest that it would be time enough to consider the desirableness of building the battlement after someone had proved the inadequacy of the roof to prevent accident or injury. But all these excuses are selfish and pointless. Life is to be regulated by the doctrine that prevention is better than cure. We are not at liberty to make experiments with the lives of people, for example, seeing whether they will in reality fall off the roof which we have built. Life is too short, too valuable, to justify such experiments. He who prevents a life being lost, actually saves a life. The preventive ministries of life are not indeed so heroic and impressive in their aspects as ministries of a more affirmative kind, yet are they set down in the Book of God as most acceptable services, often requiring his own eye to discern them, and requiring his own judgment to fix their proper estimate and value. To prevent a boy becoming a drunkard is better than to save him from extreme dissipation, though it will not carry with it so imposing an appearance before the eyes of society. All workers engaged in the holy service of prevention should be sustained and encouraged in their noble work. It lacks the ostentation which elicits applause, and may indeed bring upon itself the sneer of the unreflecting, but God himself continually operates in what may be called a preventive direction, and prevention in his case is equal to an act of creation.

But ought not men to be able to take care of themselves when they are walking on the roof without our guarding them as though they were little children? This question, too, is not without a reasonable aspect. It might even be urged into the dignity of an argument, on the pretence that if we do too much for people we may beget in them a spirit of carelessness or a spirit of dependence, leading ultimately to absolute disregard and thoughtlessness in all the relations of life. We are, however, if students of the Bible earnestly desirous to carry out its meaning, bound to study the interests even of the weakest men. This is the very principle of Christianity. If eating flesh or drinking wine make my brother to offend, I will eat no more while the world standeth. "Him that is weak in the faith receive ye." "Destroy not him with thy meat, for whom Christ died." Thus we are continually exhorted to consideration for other people. The whole house is controlled by the weakness that is within it. The sick-chamber shuts up the banqueting hall. The dying child puts an end to the intended feast. It will be found in examining all the conditions of social life that it is around the centre of weakness that solicitude, and affection, and beneficence continually revolve. The house itself may be strong, but if the battlement as a sign of grace be not above it, it is wanting in that beauty which is pleasant to the divine eye. You yourself may be able to walk upon your roof without danger; but another man may not have the same steadiness of head or firmness of foot; and it is for that other man that you are to regulate your domestic arrangements. "Thou shalt love thy neighbour as thyself." By thinking of one another we lay claim upon the affection and trust of neighbour and friend. We are not to reason as if this action were all upon our own side. Whilst we build our battlement for the sake of another man we must remember that that other man in building his house builds a battlement for our sake. All services of this kind are reciprocal; no man, therefore, is at liberty to stand back and decline social responsibilities : in every sense, whether accepted or rejected, no man liveth unto himself.

The Christian application of this doctrine is clear. That Christian application we have seen in many other instances in the course of these readings. If we are so to build a house as not to endanger the men who visit us, are we at liberty to build a life which may be to others the very snare of destruction ? Is there not to be a battlement around our conduct ? Are our habits to be formed without reference to the social influence which they may exert ? It would be a poor defence to say that we had put up our houses with excellent battlements, but had forgotten to put a battlement upon the house of our life and conduct. The house of stone is admirably built; but the house of life is practically a ruin! This would seem to be an impossibility, and in our poor thought it is such; but facts are continually showing us the bitter and disastrous ironies which men can perpetrate. Remember that children are looking at us, and that strangers are taking account of our ways, and that we may be lured from righteousness by a licentiousness which we call liberty. Is the Christian, then, to abstain from amusements and delights which he could enjoy without personal injury lest a weaker man should be tempted to do that which would injure him ? Precisely so. That is the very essence of Christian self-denial. Perhaps a man may say in self-excuse, "I am so little known or of so little account that my example can do no harm to any one."

This reasoning is not to be credited with humility, but is to be charged with direct iniquity. It is to no man's credit that as a Christian his example is of so little moment. When men make out that they have lived a long life in the world, and at the end of it must be considered as of small account, they forget that they are making out a bitter self-impeachment. If we had been more faithful to our Master in the circle in which we moved we should have been more known. Consistency always acquires a very high and wide reputation. The consistent man is remarked, and is applauded or avoided according to the moral quality of the observer. The very fact of our not being widely known as Christian men, men of living conscience, and self-sacrificing spirit, may constitute a very heavy charge against our personal fidelity.

A question kindred to inquiries which we have often raised recurs at this point : has God given directions for the building of a house and forgotten to give directions for the building of a life ? Is it like him to do the little and forget the great ? Is he not more careful about the tenant than about the house ? He has given the most elaborate and urgent exhortations upon the matter of life-building. "With all thy getting get understanding." "The fear of the Lord is the beginning of wisdom." "Wisdom is the principal thing ; therefore . . . with all thy getting get understanding." To know how carefully God has given instructions for the formation and development of a strong life, we may profitably peruse the book of Proverbs ; added to this study will come a careful investigation of all the sayings and counsels of Jesus Christ. "Whosoever heareth these sayings of mine, and doeth them, I will liken him unto a wise man, which built his house upon a rock." The specification for a well-founded, commodious, and beautiful life-house is to be found only in the Book of God. Not one detail is omitted by the divine architect. To body, soul, and spirit counsel is immediately directed. Whoever goes to the Book of God with an earnest desire to discover the way of salvation and the secret of vital growth will assuredly receive the mystery of God as a gift never withheld from the heart of the devout and diligent man. It is indeed utterly impossible to plead with truth and reason that we should be better men if we knew exactly how to live. Whatever force such a plea may have had many centuries ago, it has been utterly divested of all value since the revelation of Jesus Christ. The Son of God himself never allowed that the plan of a true life was a modern invention even of his own day. When the lawyer asked him what was to be done in order that eternal life might be inherited, Jesus Christ referred him to a life thousands of years old. God has at no time left human nature without illumination and guidance. Even in the earliest ages the way upward and heavenly was disclosed to the eyes of attentive men. Balaam exclaimed—and his exclamation cannot be improved either in eloquence or in doctrine—" What doth the Lord require of thee, but to do justly, and to love mercy, and to walk humbly with God ? " Let us be careful not to leave the house unfinished. It is not enough to have many good rooms, and some beautiful views ; we must regard the house as a whole, and consider that no house is stronger than its weakest part. It is impossible to deny that many men who make no profession of Christianity have life-houses not without strength and beauty. But they cannot be complete houses. The law of God is immediately opposed to the idea that completeness can be secured without divinity. However great the house of the wicked man, however commodious the space, however splendid the decoration, however costly the furniture, there is in it a vital defect, a weakness which the enemy will discover, and that house is doomed to fall because it is not founded upon a rock. How many life-houses there are which apparently want but some two or three comparatively little things to make them wholly perfect ! In one case perhaps only the battlement is wanting, in another case it may be but some sign of spiritual beauty, in another case there may be simply want of grace, courtesy, noble civility, and generous care for the interests of others. Whatever it may be, examination should be instituted, and every man should consider himself bound not only to be faithful in much, but faithful also in that which is least ; and being so he will not only see that there is strength in his character but also beauty, and upon the top of the pillars which represent integrity and permanence will be the lilywork of grace, patience, humbleness, and love.

PRAYER.

ALMIGHTY GOD, thou hast laid a great charge upon us, and in the very greatness of the charge we see thine own wisdom and grace. Behold, this sacrifice is of the Lord's appointing: we see his hand in the arrangement and none other. The Lord who gave is the Lord who commands. We are not our own: we have nothing that we have not received; we are bought men; bought not with silver and gold, but with the precious blood of Jesus Christ,—a price beyond all words, all thought, yet touching the feeling with marvellous power and stirring the noblest emotions of the soul. May we answer the great demand; may we be no longer our own, even in name, or in thought, but hold ourselves at God's bidding, ready to do all his will: to accept the law from heaven and to make thy statutes our songs in the house of our pilgrimage. We bless thee for the greatness of the claim. Thou art a great God and a great King above all gods, and thou dost ask what they never ask, and by the very fact of thy doing so thou dost show thy greatness. We would respond to thy claim: not our will, but thine, be done. Whatever we have that we most prize, we lay it down, we place it upon the altar; we say, It is not ours first, but God's, and ours to use, enjoy, and turn to highest purpose. Thus shall we live a sweet life, full of grace and tenderness and great joy, saying, All things work together for good to them that love God. We will have no fear; no spirit of dejection shall rule us; but the joy of the Lord shall be our strength, and all our cry shall be, Thy kingdom come; thy will be done in earth, as it is in heaven. The Lord work in us this miracle of grace by the mighty power of the Holy Ghost; subdue every rebellious thought, and bring our whole will into loving obedience and resignation. So shall our heaven begin even upon earth, and whilst yet in the house of death we shall feel the joy and the nobleness of immortality. Amen.

Deut. xxix. 29.

" The secret things belong unto the Lord our God: but those things which are revealed belong unto us and to our children for ever, that we may do all the words of this law."

SECRET THINGS.

WE have here two words of permanent significance, the confusion of which would lead to all kinds of spiritual disaster. These words are " secret " and " revealed." It is

something to know that this distinction was so early made in
human thinking. The distinction, in fact, can be found in the
communications which passed between God and man in the
garden of Eden itself. The simple law is that some "things"
belong unto the Lord our God; we have nothing to do with
them ; we are not concerned in their investigation or adjustment;
other things belong to us and to our children, and our definite
duty and relation to these is to see that they are realised in all
their meaning and purpose.

Things that are secret and revealed occupy, from one point
of view, distinctly different spheres, yet from another point of
view it is obvious that the secret and the revealed are at some
points vitally related. One would say that nature is a full
revelation; that the heavens and the earth are books wide open;
and that there can be no law of trespass in the outer creation.
But this is not the case. We find that even nature has her
mysterious or secret things, and that many a door is marked
" private," and that phenomena only, and not essences, are open
to the investigation of human science : there is a law of secrecy
even in the apparently open and unwatched fields of nature. In
other words, there is a point of unknowableness in the construction of a grass-blade as certainly as in the creation of a human
mind. Inquiry is circumscribed. There is a limit to the "ask,
seek, knock" of all investigation. Emphatic importance attaches
to this fact. We imagine that prayer and spiritual benefits,
exclusively so designated, are alone comprehended under the
statement—"ask, and it shall be given you;" whereas experience shows that that simple law is at the very root and core
of every kind of progress. "Ask, and it shall be given you"—
is as truly a canon in science as it is a law in religion. It is
written alike in the Bible of nature and the Bible of the Gospel.
It is inscribed as distinctly on the heaven and the earth as on
the solemn temple and the Mosaic altar. And so indeed with
many other of the laws of the Holy Book. When the ages
shall give birth to the seer who shall have in all its fulness and
vigour the faculty of interpretation, he will teach men that
science and gospel stand on the same basis, and that the one
serveth the other as the younger the firstborn.

Here is a man who is learned in the writing of the stars. The heavens are the broad pages, and the worlds are the words, and systems are the sentences which he attempts to make out. Many a brilliant paragraph he succeeds in interpreting, at least to some extent. But how did he attain his wisdom? Simply by the old Gospel plan—" ask, seek, knock ; " by patience often severely tried ; by labour that brought sore weariness ; by perseverance often toilsome,—this is the way by which men acquire wisdom of all kinds. What is called cant in religion is called philosophy in science. Every time the astronomer turns an inquiring eye to the stars he actually stands in the attitude of mute prayer. Every turn of the telescope really represents the action of asking, seeking, knocking. Every conclusion arrived at as the result of investigation seriously conducted may in some sort be described as an answered prayer. The difficulty which the Christian teacher has to contend with is that men willingly acknowledge that they are studying, botanising, anatomising, and the like; but they will not carry up their action to the term which comprehensively expresses the whole method and purpose of the inquiry : that term is Prayer, the highest asking, the most reverent solicitude, the most persistent, and the most rational application of human powers. We could not read a line upon the face of nature if an unseen hand did not hold the light for us. We could not read the book of the stars if that unseen hand did not turn over the pages.

The practical point to be kept in view is that although God encourages man to ask, seek, and knock ; though he has made man an inquisitive and a progressive being ; though he has endowed man with faculties, instincts, capacities that yearn to transcend the limits which humiliate him, yet human ambition is to be regulated by divine law, and man is to keep within prescribed boundaries and avoid the iniquity of trespass. This is so in nature, and it is so in what we have come to understand by the term Providence. No man can find out the work that God doeth from the beginning to the end. We cannot see how God interposes in every combination and adjusts the place of every detail in life. We see something of God in the vastness of the heavens, but are baffled by the minuteness which makes the dewdrop as perfect a sphere as the greatest planet that burns in unknown heights. The Bible teaches that in the every-day affairs of life God is constantly interposing. He hath compassed us behind and before, and laid his hand upon us. There is not a word on our tongue, there is not a thought in our heart, that is not known altogether to God. This is the Bible theory of human life ; our inquiry is into the reality of that theory,— a question which cannot be determined by words, but which can only be concluded by a careful study of individual and general human experience. Wonderful are the hidings of the divine purpose ! We lay our plan, we boldly predict a bright future, we see everything exactly as we would wish it to be, and our imagination is that all we have to do is to advance and enjoy the gracious result ; yet we know that in the midst of our dreams an invisible hand has overturned our glittering temple and ploughed up its deep foundation. In walking down the highway we have unwittingly changed sides ; we knocked at the wrong door when in quest of a friend ; in sorting our correspondence for the post we have mismatched some of the letters and envelopes ; or we had set our heart on a certain journey and had made much preparation for it, but on the appointed morning we were arrested by severe affliction, personal or relative. We could not understand these things at the time. Some of them appeared to be of no consequence. But time disclosed a wonderful purpose, even in things which were so small as to be made no account of. We were amazed that events so trivial could have concealed purposes so great, and that afflictions so unexpected and so cruel should have lain at the very threshold of the kingdom of God. But the divine Worker disdains nothing. He holds everything in high value. He will have the fragments gathered up that nothing may be lost. An atom may be necessary to the completion of a temple. As out of so common a thing as the dust of the earth God fashioned man, so out of the ordinary trifles of life he builds the greatest realities of the future. That we cannot understand these things is no argument against the certainty of their existence and action. We have to understand God as much as God intended us to understand, and leave the rest. What do you do when in reading the great books of ancient religious authors you meet with passages written in an unknown tongue ? Paragraph after paragraph you read with all possible fluency, instantly appre-

hending the author's purpose ; but suddenly the writer throws
before you a paragraph written in Greek or in Latin, or in some
language you have not learned ; what then ? If you are
absorbed by the book you will eagerly look out for the next
paragraph in English, and continue your pursuit of the leading
thought. Do likewise with God's book of providence. Much of
it is written, as it were, in our own tongue ; read that, master its
deep meaning, and leave the passages written in an unknown
language until you are farther advanced in the literature of
life—until you are older and better scholars in God's first school.
The day of interpretation will assuredly come. A beam of
light will pierce the mystery. Meanwhile, there should be
sweet rest in the reflection that " secret things belong unto the
Lord our God."

The Christian admitting all this, and even contending for it
as a necessity of Christian philosophy and life, turns with still
higher wonder and reverence towards a scene which compels him
to exclaim, " Great is the mystery of godliness ! " All the
mysteries of nature and providence are but as the riddles of
childhood compared with the problem of the Atonement. The
Cross is the meeting-place of the highest intelligences. " Which
things the angels desire to look into." Pilate's superscription in
Hebrew, and Greek, and Latin we can decipher ; but the writing of
that other hand—the hand that wrote on Belshazzar's proud walls
—that hand, so awfully distinct, yet so rapid, so delicate, as to
be " something between a thought and a thing "—the writing of
that other hand we cannot read in all the depth and scope of its
meaning. The oldest wisdom looks on and wonders, wrinkled
sages can but sigh in amazement ; and angels make no progress in
that infinite study. Yet we are not to turn away from the Cross as
from a mystery that has no aspect of a practical kind. There are
revealed things even in the Cross of Christ. We have not so much
to do with the top of the ladder which is lost in the brightness of
heaven as with the foot of it which resteth on the earth ; nor have
we so much to do with the bright angels who throng that ladder as
with the messages of mercy and hymns of hope which they bring to
our attention. Fool is he who in running from a town in flames
will not cross the river until he speculates concerning the architect
of the bridge and makes inquiry into the origin and date of its

building. The illustration may be applied to the sinner who wishes to escape from his sin. His first business is to reduce to practice what little he does understand, to manifest a disposition to accept all the arrangements of divine wisdom, and in child-like trust to give himself up to God. The Cross has a side that is " secret," and a side that is " revealed "—a side that shines towards God and a side that shines towards a sinning world. The Cross may be so treated as to be an overwhelming and discouraging mystery; or it may be so treated as to show the infinite love, and mercy, and righteousness of God in the great endeavour to rescue men from wickedness and restore them to the image and favour of God.

We have come to associate secrecy with selfishness, yet all nature proves that in divine administration secrecy and benevolence may co-exist. As rapidly as we are pointed to the mystery we should direct our eyes to the fatherhood. Do men say that God keeps to himself the mystery of the sun? Our answer should be that he turns upon us the full revelation of the light. Does God keep to himself the secret of germination? On the other hand, he gives us the revelation of golden harvests; the spring kept the secret in her heart, but autumn has filled our barns with plenty. Thus, enough is kept back to prove the power, and enough is given to establish the mercy. It is not only right, it is necessary that the father should know more than the child. Is the father less a father because of his superior knowledge? Is not his very superiority of knowledge one of his highest qualifications for discharging his duty as a father? Mystery is the seal of the infinite, yet benevolence is perpetually present in the providence which guides human life. You have seen a blind man led along the highway by a little child, to whose young bright eyes he commits himself in faith and hope. Man is that poor blind wanderer through the way of God's mysteries, and that little guide represents the benevolence, the mercy, the tenderness, with which God leads us from day to day and will lead us until the time of the larger revelation. The commonest mercy of the daytime flames up into a fire column that lights men through the gloom and trouble of the night. We must not look at the mystery and forget the benevolence. The very wealth of God makes us covetous Does poverty provoke envy ? We look not so much at what God has given as at what he might have given. We read the love through the mystery, rather than the mystery through the love. Men like to penetrate into the hidden. They flatter it, they exalt it, they say it is given for good, and pleasant to the eyes, and a tree to be desired to make one wise ; and having wrought themselves up into this delusive appreciation of its value, they put forth the thievish hand, and the fancied blessing turns to a scorpion's sting. We are not to anticipate our course of study : the volumes will be handed to us one by one. Let us understand what we now can, and in doing so let us increase in knowledge ; understand that in all the wastes of folly there could be no greater fool than he who will not believe his father's telegram because he cannot understand the mystery of the telegraph.

The sense in which things revealed belong unto us is distinctly specified in the text—"that we may do all the words of this law." We know revelation by a power which is within ourselves. There is a spirit in man, and the inspiration of the Almighty giveth us understanding. Whether that power has been correctly designated by the expression " verifying faculty " or not, there it is, constantly operating within us, and constantly confirming or disputing our conclusions. That power does not affect to deal with the incident, the colour, and the local or transient detail to be found in a book : it deals with great moral disclosures, and supreme moral appeals, and profound moral obligations. Looking in this direction, the inward light is an unfailing guide, the verifying faculty never fails to cry out, This is the very truth of God : this is the very beginning of heaven. Observe the expression—" all the words of this law." We are not called upon to consider the words of a speculation, or a theory, or a new suggestion regarding the constitution and destiny of things. God puts himself before us distinctly as Lawgiver. All the moral institutes issue from God's wisdom. All that man lays down as law is, so far as it is right, but a modification or interpretation of God's own word of government. The heavens and the earth are full of proofs as to the omnipotence of the Creator, but in such a word as " Thou shalt love thy neighbour as thyself " we may find a profounder testimony to Christ's Godhead than in all the wonders of creation. Here is a moral mystery only to be interpreted by moral obedience. This doctrine is only attainable through doing the will; blessed be God, through doing the will we do come into the full appreciation of this religious mystery, and are enabled from that point of progress to advance to immeasurably greater distances in the upward way. To have lost our identity in the interests of others, and for their real good, is to have begun to realise the mystery of divine love.

The law is to be translated into action: "That we may do all the words." A very beautiful picture thus appeals to the attention. A word is to become a deed: a thought is to be embodied in expressive action; and between the word and the deed, the thought and the action, there is to be obvious and undeniable consistency. Religion has, indeed, its contemplative side, but it has also its practical side of action. The architect draws his plans not that they may be exhibited as pictures but that they may be built up into visible and useful edifices. If the builder has taken the architect's plans, framed them in gold, and hung them up in the best room of his house, he has not honoured the plans but dishonoured them: the architect will presently come and ask for the mansion, and he will not be satisfied to be told that instead of the mansion having been built the plans have been carefully framed and exhibited only to admiring eyes. But have we not framed the law of God and made a picture of it and worshipped the letter with a species of idolatry? What have we done with the Bible? We have published it in letters of gold; we have bound it in richest morocco; genius, art, taste, have conspired to beautify and adorn and decorate the sacred book; but where is the mansion of a noble, holy, and useful life? We received the law that we might "do" it; if we have failed in the doing our admiration is hypocrisy and our loudest applause is but our loudest lie.

We are not only called to obedience, we are called to hope. We shall make some conquest yet even in spheres which at present are absolutely mysterious. At present we know in part, and prophesy in part, because we see through a glass darkly. What thou knowest not now thou shalt know hereafter. We have a hope which is as an anchor of the soul both sure and steadfast, a hope which entereth into that within the veil, and we are confident that one day we shall know even as also we are known. They will know most of the mystery who have done most of the law. If we are waiting for the solution of the mystery before we begin obedience to the law, the mystery will never be revealed to us other than in clouds and storms of judgment. We walk by faith, not by sight. Jesus said unto one of his disciples, "Thomas, because thou hast seen me, thou hast believed: blessed are they that have not seen, and yet have believed." This is the Christian's law of action. He acknowledges the mystery; he has no reply whatever to many an enigma; but he is sure that in doing justice, loving mercy, and walking humbly with God, he is preparing himself for those great revelations which are promised to faith, obedience, and love.

SELECTED NOTE.

One of the most sad and saddening aspects of modern life is the lack of a humble acknowledgment of the limitation of human powers. There has been engendered a pride and even arrogance of thought which knows not how to veil its face in the presence of the infinite God, and of Truth which is as infinite as he. There is an audacity of speculation which will acknowledge no mystery, and which rejects all that transcends the limits of reason.

And especially is this the case in those departments of truth which relate to the moral and spiritual government of God. Concerning the material world there is no such presumptuous daring. Men feel that as yet of this they know but in part—and in small part. No man of science will step forth and profess a universal acquaintance with the universe. He would be regarded as a laughing-stock. He might as soon pretend that he can hold the waters in the hollow of his hand, or that he can mete out heaven with a span, or comprehend the dust of the earth in a measure, or weigh the mountains in scales and the hills in a balance. Slowly and patiently do men of science work, winning now the knowledge of one fact, and then another, but feeling as Newton felt when he had achieved even his noblest discoveries, that they have but picked up a shell or a pebble on the great shore of truth, while the vast ocean lies yet undiscovered before them. The map of science is filled in here and there, but over the greatest portion of it is written the words "unknown land." Year by year a little more is filled in, and yet a little more, but when shall the whole be defined, and when shall the map itself be large enough to include the whole material creation which stretches illimitably around us on every hand? There is no discovery that has yet been made, which has not immediately suggested new mysteries, and the wisest men are those who feel that the disproportion seems ever growing between the limits of the human mind, and the boundlessness of the creation which it seeks to explore.—ENOCH MELLOR, D.D.

PRAYER.

ALMIGHTY GOD, thou abidest for ever though thy servants are cut off in the midst of their days. We are as a shadow, and there is none continuing ; but thou remainest the same, and thy years fail not. One generation goeth, and another generation cometh ; but the Lord abideth evermore. Thou art the living Sovereign, thou art the living Redeemer, and thy mercy, like thyself, endureth for ever. We have heard of thy mercy all the ages through, since thou didst put skins of beasts upon the shoulders of those who fell in the garden. Thy promise has always been singing in mid-air, cheering the heart and touching the imagination of the world ; and, behold, we have seen thy promise fulfilled : it is no longer a promise, it is a reality, for Jesus Christ hath come into the world to save sinners. May we believe in him that we may rejoice in him, and rejoicing in him may serve him with both hands earnestly, knowing no joy but in his approbation, and expecting no heaven that is not involved in his blessing. Few and evil are our days upon the earth : our days are as a post or as a weaver's shuttle flying to and fro ; we are driven before the wind ; we are consumed by the moth ;— all things press against us destructively. Yet have we hope that cannot be extinguished—confidence in immortality : if our earthly house of this tabernacle were dissolved, we have a building of God, a house not made with hands, eternal in the heavens ; now we see beyond the night-line : now the cloud is but a door which will presently open, and through the opening gloom we shall see the ineffable glory of heaven. We have learned all this in Jesus Christ thy Son ; he is our Teacher and our proof ; we witness to him : we have sat beside him and heard the gracious words which proceed out of his mouth, and our souls are glad ; we have entered into a great inheritance : we are rich in faith : we can be poor no more ; we shall see our Redeemer face to face, and bless him even for the trials of the road. Keep us steadfast in the love of the truth : may we abide in the Vine and bring forth much fruit ; may our love be in Christ and for Christ and towards Christ—a bloom for ever seeking the sun. For all thy care we bless thee ; for the guiding of thine eye we magnify thee. We owe all we are and have to thee : by the grace of God we are what we are. Hear our hallelujah ; receive the hosanna of our grateful hearts ; and help us to live all our prayers. Amen.

Deut. xxxi. 14.

"And the Lord said unto Moses, Behold, thy days approach that thou must die."

NEARING THE END.

THERE is no day fixed : it is an " approach " that is spoken of. The word may, therefore, be addressed to every man well-advanced in life. There is a period at which the road becomes a slope downwards, and at the foot of the hill is the last earthly resting-place. This is the way of God. He tells them that the end is " approaching." Now and again he seems to cut them off suddenly as with an unexpected stroke; yet perhaps the suddenness is in appearance rather than in reality. To be born is to have notice to quit ; to live is to die. If men speak of " suddenness," it is because they have not interpreted the circumstances which have constituted their surroundings :—" We all do fade as a leaf." Every sin takes out of us some portion of life ; we cannot have an evil thought without the quantity of life within us being diminished. We cannot think a noble thought, or find a free way in our hearts for a sublime impulse, without increasing the sum-total of our life—without beginning our immortality. Thus is a man stronger after prayer than before ; thus does every sweet and holy hymn send a thrill of gladness through the soul that sings. Let every man take notice that he must die. From a literary point of view that is a pitiful commonplace ; but from the point of view of actual experience and all the issues of death it is a sublime and an appalling announcement. But Moses must die. We have never associated the idea of death with Moses. He has always been so strong : the camp never halted because of his ill-health; he was always at the head ; his voice was clear and mellow ; his eye was bright and darting, and yet so genial—as if it could not conceal the smile that was in his heart. His has been the strong arm and the uplifted hand and the commanding tone, and to associate death with such strength was to be guilty of irony and to perpetrate an almost palpable contradiction. Yet the strongest trees yield to silent time ; the mightiest strength bows down itself in weakness and trouble : Samson dies, Hercules becomes but a figure in ancient history ; there is no man who abideth for ever. It is becoming, therefore, under an announcement of this kind, that we should revert to the beginning with which we have become so familiar. The woman of the Hebrews hides her little thr ee months' child in a basket of bulrushes, and

trusts him to the river. How weak the child! "The babe wept."
Did he ever weep again? Were those his first and final tears?
He never looked like a weeping man; but men who do not look
so often weep more than those whose lives are given up to
chronic sentimentalism:—"Jesus wept." Compare the child
upon the river with the hundred-and-twenty-year-old man, going
up the hill never to come down again. He walks up steadily.
If he was a weak man, how seldom he showed his weakness! he
had a gift of concealing infirmity, so much so that only now and
again, in some flashing outbreak of temper, do we find that he
was a man of like passions with ourselves. The end is not like
the beginning: those who studied the beginning could not have
forecast the end. Suppose any ardent imagination had attempted
whilst looking at the weeping babe to cast the horoscope of the
man, to say what he would be—as history has proved him—how
he would die on the top of Nebo—no absurdity could be more
glaring. Out of such weakness none could have predicted the
issue of such virile might. Is not God always teaching us by
these great changes that he is secretly working out a still grander
mutation? It doth not yet appear what we shall be : weeping
babes have become mighty legislators ; poor little outcast lives
have towered up into the majesty of leadership and sovereignty ;
and God by these palpable analogies is for ever suggesting the
possibility of our own development and final coronation. Oh that
men were wise, that they would read the Bible which God is
writing every day, and put together, until they accumulate into
massiveness and overwhelming moral authority, the incidents
which characterise our varied life. What greater distance is
there than between the weeping Moses on the Nile and the culminating Moses as he gathers himself together to obey in sweet
patience and uncomplaining resignation the last demand? Regard
the whole process : note its variety, swiftness, tumult; and then
observe the deep tranquillity, the sabbatic calm, the ineffable
dignity, and say whether after such a perusal of historical facts
it does not become easier to believe that we ourselves—weak,
lonely, misunderstood, harshly treated, ill-behaved, unruly,—shall
one day, by the ministry of the Holy Ghost and through the
blood of atonement, become, as it were, princes, priests, kings,
in the upper spaces—the holy sanctuary of the heavens. Let

analogy teach ; let history become theological ; let the palpable incidents of life connect themselves into an argument and vindicate the page of Holy Scripture.

Now that Moses is walking up the mountain, we cannot but think of the life-long hardship he has endured. Read the history of his association with Israel, and say if there is one "Thank you" in all the tumultuous story. Does one man speak out of the host and say, In the name of Israel I give thee thanks ? We do not know some men until we see them wandering away from us. The back of Moses is now turned : we shall see his face no more ; he will be a great man in Israel now that he is gone : the people may make an idol of him—of him whom they have so much abused ; they may quote his words, repaint his lineaments, and tell their descendants of his heroic days. When had he any times of peace ? When does Moses ever say, Now I am in a green country full of verdure, and flowers, and birds, and this is ample compensation for all the horrors of the way ? Marvellous is the providence which calls some men to continual labour and other men to almost continual contemplation, or such monasticism of life as protects them from the roughness of the storm ! We owe much to our labourers : we reap harvests which were sown by heroic swords. It is easy to gather the harvest, for we go out in the autumn time when the sky is richest in all brightness and beauty, when the wind is cool and vitalising, and when the fields are white or golden, according to the crops they bear ; but these harvests were sown in tears : the seed now fructified was dropped into furrows moistened with blood. Let not the harvester rejoice as if he were the sower : we reap what nobler men have cast into the ground. Some men cannot do without encouragement, but Moses was left to pursue his way in its absence. Who ever cheered him ? He was always called upon to cheer others, to stimulate them, to cry,—Higher ! forward !—as if he were bidding them to mountains rich with harvests and to prospects bright as heaven.

What a strain there was also upon the religious side of his nature ! He had no recreation : the bow was never unbent ; he was always being called up to hear the Lord communicate some new law, some new charge or address. To his veneration a continual appeal was addressed. What wonder if his face wore the aspect of solemnity ? What wonder if his eye was alight with the very splendours he had beheld ? For the face of Moses not to shine would be a contradiction and a defiance of fact. We are ourselves like what we most like or what we most admire. Moses dwelt in the presence of God, entered into the very spirit of the divine purpose, accustomed himself to the throb and music of the divine utterance, and when he came down from the mountain he wist not that his face did shine. We do not know all that we gain by divine communion ; we seize only part of the treasure : we do not comprehend or appreciate the unsearchable riches. It is customary to speak of the sternness of Moses, his rigour and his definiteness of command and tone ; but we cannot deeply peruse his story without observing the womanly instincts which gave the tenderness of dignity to the man. He was father and mother of that great house of Israel ; he did all kinds of work ; if there was sickness, he was the man to speak about it in healing tones ; if there was bitterness in the pool, he was the man to find the purifying and sweetening plant ;—in a sense he gathered the lambs in his bosom and carried them with shepherdly solicitude ; he was the mother, the nurse, the sister, the woman, in that great and rebellious house of Israel. Such always is the complete man : his tenderness is always equal to his dignity, or by so much he is a defective character. The greatest men in history have, in spirit, temper, and patience, been the greatest women. What was the motive of such a life ? Who can explain the inward and all-moving force ? We must wait for the keyword until we come to the most eloquent epistle in the New Testament. How is Moses accounted for by the writer of the Epistle to the Hebrews ? " By faith Moses——." Now we begin to get light upon that mysterious word " faith." It is ascribed to Moses as a motive—an animating and sustaining force ; it must, therefore, mean insight into the purpose and tendency of things—penetration into the very philosophy of right, religion, and duty ; it must mean self-surrender, self-abandonment, complete trust of God. Such is the meaning as read in the light of history, and such is the meaning vindicated by the richest learning of philosophy. Faith could find a way through the wilderness ; faith could build a sanctuary in the desert ; faith could carry a great household of rebellious

children through dangerous places ; faith could see Canaan with
closed eyes, and awaken imagination to sing to adequate music
the delights of that promised country. We perish for want of
faith. Knowledge we have, and tongues many, and sense of the
value of things : nor are we without veneration or prayerfulness
of attitude and tone ; but we have not the all-firing faith, the all-
ennobling trust, the sight that sees the invisible, the hands that
clutch the very omnipotence of God ;—our life is a calculation, an
excited prudence, a boastful cowardice. Do we say, "Lord, I
will follow thee whithersoever thou goest " ? He replies : No,
" The foxes have holes, and the birds of the air have nests : but
the Son of man hath not where to lay his head." "Who follows
in his train ? " Few men go along that line ; if they ever join
it, it is because they have come upon it along some incidental
path. Christianity is the religion of faith : it is not a new
variety of philosophy ; it is not a specimen of intellectual
legerdemain : its watchword is faith, its keyword is love, its
purpose is the pardon of the world.

Then is Moses not to see Canaan ? Moses would not care now
to see any land flowing with milk and honey. He shall see the
upper Canaan,—the happy land where the flowers never wither,
where the summer is guaranteed to last eternally. Thus God
educates men. He promises them something for the end, and
under the animation of that promise they pursue their duty, and
they so pursue it that at the last they ask for something for the
heart ; the hand could not hold what they want : it is not equal
to the answer of their bolder prayer. The Lord promises a land
flowing with milk and honey, the only promise that could then
be understood. Men arose to search for the land, and by daily
education, gracious discipline, gentle admonition, continual and
regulated instruction, they came to say what God at first meant
them to say,—We seek a country out of sight : we seek a city on
high—a city whose Builder and Maker is God. We have seen
that a time comes when by right spiritual education and true
spiritual sympathy with Christ the world shrivels into mean
proportions, and is hurried into contempt by the very religion
which we supposed would enable us to enjoy it. After a certain
period of well-received lessons we say, We will not have the
earth : we do not feel that it is worth carrying ; it is but a handful

of dust, it is but a flutter in the air,—let it return to the nothing-ness out of which it came ; we yearn for God, we sigh for the infinite, we cannot rest without the eternal Father.

Moses goes upon the mountain to die. It is well : such a man ought to die upon a mountain. The scene is full of symbolism ; it is quick with moral and spiritual suggestiveness. Men may die upon mountains if they will ; or men may perish in dark valleys if they like. To die upon the mountain is to die into heaven. The place of our death, as to its significance and honour, will be determined by the life we lead. We die just as we live, and, so to say, where we live. Moses lived a mountain life : he was a highlander ; he lived on the hills, and on the hills he died. May it not be so with us ? By well-done duty, by well-endured affliction, by well-tested patience, by complete self-surrender, by continual imitation and following of Christ, we may die on some lofty hill, cool with dew or bright with sunshine, the point nearest to the skies. To die at such an elevation is to begin to live. Men can die in the valleys if they please ; by meanness of life, by self-consideration, by baptised prudence, by bastard piety, by feigned prayer, they can hasten swiftly down into deep places and die in the shadows and gloom of despair. We can so live that none will care where or how we die : the only gospel they ever hear of us will be that we are dead. But who will live this life ? Who can think of it ? Who that knows the value of influence, who that regards the love of children and the love of posterity, could live a life so ignoble, so devoid of practical sentiment, so wasteful in all that is most sacred in energy ?

Moses died with a song upon his lips. What that song was we shall in our next reading see. The image, however, may now, for the moment, be detained before the mind as full of the best suggestion. Moses died singing : a song was part of the last utterance of the heroic man. What a song it was we may be eager to .know. How strong; how tender; how valiant ; how nearly a law ; how next to a judgment ; how close to a cross ! The song of Moses marks a period in the progress of the soul. The song tells what the life has been, and the song touches with infinite delicateness the future of the spirit. We may die with a song upon our lips, or we may die in cruel

silence—in the dumbness of despair. By a song do not understand the term literally : he dies singing who dies contentedly,
hopefully, at peace with the world, at rest in Christ, confident
that the Cross he has served will light him through the valley ;
it may be no sound of a vocal kind, no triumph, no rapture, as
commonly understood ; but tranquillity may be music, resignation
may have about it the triumph and gladness of a song.

Die we must : there is no discharge in that war. How we
shall die may be determined by ourselves, as to its moral
characteristics and benedictions ; where we shall die, as to
elevation of thought and mind, is left to ourselves very largely
to decide ; but know this, that if any man believe in Christ Jesus
with his whole soul, he cannot die : he that liveth and believeth
in him, though he were dead, yet shall he live. "I am come
that they might have life, and that they might have it more
abundantly." "Believest thou this ?" Let the question be
the most solemn appeal ever addressed to the attention
of the soul.

PRAYER.

ALMIGHTY GOD, thou hast been eyes unto us : thou hast seen the way when it was hidden from our vision; the darkness and the light are both alike unto thee. We delight to worship thee as the God ruling among the armies of heaven and among the children of men, for we are all thy creatures: we represent thy breath: thy life is in us, and thy touch is even upon our ruin. We are still thy children, fashioned by thee, redeemed with blood by thy Son, and to us are revealed the unsearchable riches of Christ. We desire, therefore, to claim every privilege, and to rejoice in every honour, and to say, This is the Lord's doing, and it is marvellous in our eyes; this is the gift of God, this is the light of heaven, this is the miracle of the Holy Ghost. So there is no boastfulness: we are humbled in the dust; when thou dost show us how thou hast loved us we are the more cast down in our own esteem : but thou dost recover us and re-establish us,—yea, thou dost set our feet upon a rock, and thou dost put a song into our mouth: we will sing of thy goodness and mercy; we will bless thee for thy judgments too, often strange and heavy, yet every one needed to chasten and subdue the soul on which it falls. We bless thee for thine house: we love every stone of it; its light is sanctified; its very air is charged with a ministry of light. Thy Book is wide open before us, and we can understand somewhat of it, and can respond to its great appeals; and above all that it unfolds and reveals we see the Cross of our Lord Jesus Christ—the Priest of the universe, our Advocate with the Father, the Daysman between God and our souls—laying his hand upon both and making reconciliation. We love the Cross because of its representation of God's love, God's pity, God's omnipotence;—may we cling to it, and glory in it, and magnify it, and die under the inspiration of its holy mystery. Amen.

Deut. xxxi.-xxxii.

19. Now therefore write ye this song for you, and teach it the children of Israel : put it in their mouths, that this song may be a witness for me against the children of Israel.

22. Moses therefore wrote this song the same day, and taught it the children of Israel.

THE LAST SONG.

THE old man whom we have known so long dies singing. All men should die so ; all men may so die : God is not sparing in his gift of song or privilege of music : music was in

his purpose long before speech : all things are to end in a great
song. What speeches may be delivered on high we cannot tell :
few if any have been reported even by dreamers and seers ; but
they have all told us of the singing that characterises life in the
upper spaces : they quote the very words of the noble song; they
give some idea of the innumerableness of the numbers who sing
the triumphant hymn. God means, therefore, that every life
should end in a song—not necessarily in the mechanical definition
of that term, but as to its spiritual scope and meaning : there is
triumph in serenity—yea, serenity may be the last expression
of triumph. There are songs without words : there is singing
without articulate and audible voice : we may sing with the
spirit and with the understanding. Blessed are they who, before
going up to Nebo to die, sing in the valley, and, so to say, pass
out of sight with their singing robes around them ;—to this end
we are invited in Christ, and in Christ this is the only possible
end—namely, triumph, song; the rapture of expectancy, and
the inspiration of hope.

The song was to be a "witness" for God "against" the
children of Israel,—say, rather, as between himself and the
children of Israel. Witness does not always imply accusation :
it quite as frequently implies confirmation, endorsement, approval ; it embodies in itself a sure testimony, strong because
of its indisputableness. God is said to be "Judge," and we too
frequently attach somewhat of harshness to that word ; in many
of its relations it is noble in its tenderness : it is a refuge to
which the soul may continually flee. God is the "Judge" of the
widow and the fatherless. Does the Scripture mean that God
will hold them to standards that are severe and bind upon them
penalties which are intolerable ? On the contrary : instead of
Judge, say "Vindicator." God is the Judge of the widow and
fatherless : he will hear their cause and determine it ; he will
attemper judgment with mercy : in wrath he will remember
mercy ; to the Judge of all the earth all good causes may appeal,
and all weakness, and all inculpable infirmity, and all broken-
heartedness. God is the Judge of the little, the mean, the
helpless,—the widow, the orphan. The word "witness" is to
be interpreted after some such fashion. The song is not to be
put up to accuse the children of Israel only : it is not an im-

peachment merely; it is a witness, a record, a testimony,—a distinct writing that can be appealed to in all critical or ambiguous circumstances.

Moses wrote the song "the same day." We speak of our efforts of genius, and the time required for the elaboration of this or that attempt to serve the sanctuary; but if you can write a song at all you can write it at once. Herein the great French poet's dictum is true : said one to Victor Hugo, "Is it not difficult to write epic poetry?" "No," said the great genius of his day, "No : easy or impossible." "Difficult" implies that the poetry can be written with due time, and after due effort; but the French judge would have no such construction put upon the term. Poetry is breathing, looking,—the last expression of inspired genius. Moses wrote the song "the same day :" he could not stop the rush of the musical storm : the moment he got the first note he had all the rest in him. How many men would be burning lives, in all the best sense of ardour, if they could but get the first spark!—they have fuel enough in them : they have great latent power ; but they have not the starting spark, the first ignition, which would set on a blaze whole volumes of noble matter.

Moses has been trained to this effort : he has sung before ; but he always sings after great disclosures of the divine face— after the most vivid consciousness of the divine presence and touch. His songs are all in the same key : they roll along the same lofty level ; they never beat into weakness, they are never impaired by meanness ; from end to end they are God's own songs, and Moses seems to have been but a hand in the grasp of Omnipotence when he traces the immortal words. Such is to be our ministry ; such is to be our life : "We have this treasure in earthen vessels, that the excellency of the power may be of God, and not of us."

What are the characteristics of a great song ? The first most noticeable characteristic of this song is that it is intensely theological. The keyword is GOD—in his majesty, in his compassion, in his righteousness, in his tears—God in a species of incarnation thousands of years before the event of Bethlehem. Without God there is no song that fills the whole arch ; there are snatches of song that want unity, cohesion, and massiveness,

—stray notes, wandering chords, confused vibratio.is ; but in
God you have the upgathering of every chord, bar, suggestion,
and tone of music : he is the centralising, uniting, all-cohering
force. Have nothing to do with songs that do not lead up to
God. This will not exclude many songs that are supposed to be
of a secular kind. Who made the earth ? Who cut off the little
slice from eternity which we call time ? God is the God of
the whole world, and his is the fulness of the sea. Many a
song that dips down towards recreation, amusement, entertain-
ment, may have in it the true music of heaven ;—let such be the
beginning, and let the end be grand as thunder, solemn as
lightning, appalling as the height of heaven.

Another characteristic of the song is its broad human history.
Read the thirty-second chapter from end to end, and you will
find it a record of historical events. Facts are the pedestals
on which we set sculptured music. We must know our own
history if we would know the highest religious arguments, and
apply with unquestionable and beneficent skill great Christian
appeals. The witness must be in ourselves : we must know, and
taste, and feel, and handle of the word of life, and live upon it,
returning to it as hunger returns to bread and thirst flies swiftly
to sparkling fountains. We do not live upon the history of other
people : we only read the history of Israel to show how true it
is that God is one and that his government is an indissoluble
whole. To the Christian student there is no ancient history in
the sense of history that is antiquated, obsolete, and no longer
applicable to human circumstances. What we call ancient history was done yesterday from a divine point of view ; from
that point of view, indeed, there is but one day, quick with the
tumultuous pulses of a thousand years. As we have often
seen, we impoverish ourselves and lower the temperature of all
noblest history by causing great spaces to intervene between our
personal consciousness and the actual transaction of the events.
Everything has occurred to-day. Early on the summer morning
God said, " Let there be light," and the east whitened, and the
dawn blushed, and over all the hills and vales and streams there
came a tender glory. This very morning God shaped us in
his own image and likeness. He was with us in the darkness,

bearing our aching and weary heads, remaking us, reconstructing us, putting a distance between ourselves and our last sin and our most recent failure, and setting us up in the strength of recruited power to attempt the labour of another day. Speak not of ancient history in any sense that severs present consciousness from the eternal providence of God. When you are doubtful as to religious mysteries, read your own personal record; when metaphysics are too high or too deep, peruse facts,—put the pieces of your lives together : see how they become a shape —a house not made with hands, a temple fashioned in heaven. The days are not to be detached from one another : they are to be linked on and held in all the symbolism and reality of their unity.

Hence, another characteristic of the song is its record of providence. God found Jacob—

"In a desert land, and in the waste howling wilderness; he led him about, he instructed him, he kept him as the apple of his eye. As an eagle stirreth up her nest, fluttereth over her young, spreadeth abroad her wings, taketh them, beareth them on her wings : so the Lord alone did lead him, and there was no strange god with him " (xxxii. vv. 10-12),

—and then comes all the detail of providential care and love and tears, and all the sublime appeal arising out of the undisputed goodness of God. We do not need providence to be proved by wordy argument, for we ourselves are living illustrations of God's nearness, and greatness, and love. We must never give up this arm of our panoply : this weapon is a weapon strong and keen ; we must in the use of it testify what we have seen and known, what has been in our own experience ; and we must magnify God by facts that have occurred within the limits of our own observation and experience. Every Christian man is a miracle ; every Christian life is a Bible ; every devout experience is a proof of the possibility of inspiration.

The song is also accusatory :—

"Jeshurun waxed fat, and kicked : thou art waxen fat, thou art grown thick, thou art covered with fatness ; then he forsook God which made him, and lightly esteemed the Rock of his salvation " (v. 15).

When a song accuses, how terrific is the indictment ! Who expects a song to double back upon the singer and accuse him of ingratitude, presumption, or forgetfulness ? Our hymns are witnesses for us and against us ; our very music has some plain things to

tell us; even in song we do not escape justice. The songs of the
Bible are not mere sentiments melodised and turned into a species
of æsthetic luxury : Bible songs are Bible theology, Bible statutes,
Bible precepts, divine interventions, and providences. They
misinterpret the Bible who suppose that it is a piling up of one
sentiment upon another, until the sentiments bulge upon the
clouds and are lost in the obscure distance; in the songs of the
Bible there is law : the very songs of our pilgrimage are statutes
that are turned into music.

Moses able to say all this after such experience as he knew!
This is a noble testimony; this, indeed, is a complete and happy
vindication of the ways of God to man. It is Moses who writes
this; no poet was created for the purpose : no hidden genius
or flower born to blush unseen and waste its sweetness on the
desert air was developed for the purpose of writing these noble
stanzas, these rolling, thunderous bursts of song. The old legislator, the holy leader, the man who had to bear so much, who
knew all the providence of God in human history even from
the beginning to the end—he was elected to be poet. That is
God's way. Serve on faithfully; bend the back, use your arms,
toil in the dust; but whatever you do carry it out with both
hands, with reality and simplicity of purpose; and, by-and-by,
when the poet is wanted, you, toiler, may be told to stand up and
sing. This is the loving way of God : those who pass his
scrutiny go in through the gate of pearl to sing on the inner side :
after hearing God's " Well done, good and faithful servant,"
everything but a song becomes impossible; from that poetry
there can be no apostasy into prosaic moods and contracted
spaces.

In this song we have the commandments all repeated,—that is
to say, you find nothing in the Ten Commandments, as to the
formation of human character and the shaping of human destiny,
that is not to be found in this great song. Commandments must
be the severe side of true music; duty is only the outer aspect of
song. Without the commandments of God there could be no songs
of men with reality in them and with the fire pentecostal and the
touch that gives immortality God will have his commandments

honoured : first he will state them in plain, stern terms :—
" Thou shalt," " Thou shalt not:" there shall be no mistake
about the literal meaning of the commands of God ; but after long
years every commandment will come back again upon us in song,
in appeal, in persuasion, in tears, in the Cross of Christ, and in
all the love spoken by the Gospel. Thus the Bible is one : the
spirit of the Bible is a spirit of righteousness, truth, compassion,
redemption. Everything in human history is in the Pentateuch ;
every romance that can be read aloud and every true work of
fiction repeats the commandments of Sinai. Men do more than
perhaps they mean to do. We cannot escape the circle of God in
any lawful industry, in any conscientious effort. A man shall set
himself to depict in parable or fiction the life of his day ; he may
describe himself as an artist, he may even go so far as to describe
himself as a *mere* artist—a devotee of art, a student of proportion,
perspective, and colour ;—he little knows that in proportion as
he succeeds in rightly interpreting life he is a preacher. Great is
the company of preachers ! They would not be called by that
name : they are suspicious of that limited term, because it has
been limited by the very men who should have glorified it. You
find all the fiction in the world that is true to human life in the
parable of the Prodigal Son : the pen of fiction has never touched
a point that is not involved within the sweep of that nobler
delineation. The parables of Christ contain everything—every
spark of genius, every throb of poetry, every moral of sound
teaching. So we return to find all the commandments of God in
the last song of Moses ; as God first gives the commandments, and
then gives the history, and then gives the song, so all life is under
his control, and he is revealing his purposes and providences in
many a book never meant to call attention to his sovereignty.
Many are called they know not why, or how, or to what end :
the first may be last, the last may be first. As for those who
are nominally Christians and preachers—baptised men, anointed
with a sacred unction—what if they fall short of their calling and
other men should come from the east and from the west, from
the north and from the south, and they—the supposed lineage of
God—should be shut out ! The Christian reader of all history
should make it his business to include, wherever he can, every
effort and attempt made to lighten human burdens, to soothe

human misery, and disentangle human perplexity; we cannot have such service described as worldly, secular, atheistic. He who dries a child's innocent tears is by so much serving God; he who but closes his eyes silently before partaking of his food recognises a Hand unseen—a Giver quite near; he who writes a poem for the purpose of brightening family life and cheering solitary wanderers—he who leaves behind him some sign which may be seen after many days, that a forlorn and shipwrecked brother seeing may take heart again, is a minister—not ordained by human touch or recognition of an ecclesiastical kind, but a helper in the human strife, a friend of the friendless. Do not reject commandments because they come in the form of song, and do not regard song as being destitute of the inspiration and virility of righteousness. The Bible combines strength and beauty, law and gospel—Moses and the Lamb. Our life is meant to fall into music. Music is an abused term. The musicians have been as unkind to music as the theologians have been unkind to theology. Definitions need enlargement; terms need ampler reference and application. Many a man is musical who cannot sing; the spirit of music is in the man: he knows the true tone when he hears it—not from the critical point of view—but it touches his soul, comes into his being like an inspiration, and soothes him like a benediction, or stirs him like a war-trumpet. Music is the inheritance of little children—the angel that sits upstairs watching the weak and the dying when hired eyes tire and fall into needed slumber. So with the Gospel of Jesus Christ: it has its stern theology, its profound metaphysics, its awful morality—the very snow of heaven, the spotless whiteness of the ineffable purity; but it has its song, its musical strain, and it calls us all to walk in step—to go processionally: our feet are to fall harmoniously: the whole motion of the Church is to be a motion united, massive, coherent, resonant,—providences turned into psalms, afflictions elevated into music, and righteousness itself—the stern commandment—is to be made to take up the harp and re-express itself in tender strains. Do be musical, do be harmonious in life; as for the mere vocal exercise, that may be poor or uncultivated, but there is another kind of music—a spiritual, intellectual, moral music, and to that we are all called—a blessed, a sacred destiny.

PRAYER.

We would see Jesus. He is the fairest among ten thousand, and altogether lovely. Our eyes ever desire to look upon him, and now we have come to the place of his appointment. Where two or three are gathered together, there Jesus is in the midst; he is always the centre. We know him to be the way, the truth, and the life, and none may dispute his place. We will have this Man to reign over us, for it is his right to reign. We call him King of kings; we hail him Lord of lords; we bow down before him, and worship the Son of God, God the Son, Immanuel—God with us. We have praises to sing, and we would sing them with a loud, clear voice. We are not ashamed of the providence of God. Thou art our Father : thou dost guide us with thine eye; thine arms are round about us; thy smile is our soul's day, thy frown the night in which our soul trembles. Thou hast spread our table bountifully, so that our hunger has been more than satisfied; thou hast kept our house, so that there is peace at home; thou hast given us music in every room and light on every point of the dwelling; —verily, thou art the God of the families of the earth, and our households trust in thee. As for our afflictions, it was good for us that we were afflicted : we were chastened, sobered, refined; there came into our voice a tenderer tone, and there settled in our hearts a nobler trust : thou hast sanctified thy chastening, and turned our smarting to our spiritual account. We bless the rod, we kiss the hand that lifted it, and at the grave-side we desire to say, It is well. For all thy mercies we bless thee—for every flower that blooms, for every bird that sings, for every stream that moistens the green grass, for all the promise of the year,—for a good seed-time and hay harvest, and prospect of plentifulness of bread; the Lord has been in the field, and the orchard, and the garden, and has filled the river with riches. Blessing, and honour, and glory, and power be unto the name of the God of Providence! We will not ask thee for the earth : it is too small a gift for a King; we want thyself, we desire thy Spirit, we yearn for clearer sight of thy love and for further hold of thy purpose, that when we are tossed upon the deep, the tumult may be but local, for in our souls immortal there is rest—a deep and eternal tranquillity. We desire to read thy word with new vision, to enter into the spirit of its history and its prophecy, its minstrelsy and gospel, that the word of Christ may dwell in us richly, abounding in gracious fulness, so as to make the enemy afraid because of the holiness of our souls. We desire to see thee in all the way of life, to say every day, This is the Lord : lo, God was here, and I knew it not; and even among these rocks he has set up his ladder. We pray for one another : for the young, and the bright, and the tuneful, that they may rise up into nobleness and usefulness of life; for the sad and the weary; for the man who has just seen life's emptiness, and turned away with discontent from the place where he meant to find his pleasure. Thou dost send that revelation upon us all; we say, Surely on the mountain-top we shall find our home, and, lo, we cannot stay there, because of the darkness, and the cold, and the dreariness of stony places. We said, Surely now we shall find what we needed of wealth, and beauty, and comfort, and enjoyment; now will begin the dance of pleasure, now will break out the music of lasting gladness;—and, behold, we fell among serpents and into dangerous places, and every tree shook as with alarm, and the wind was full of fear. We now see that light is in heaven only, and rest in truth, and peace in faith, and joy in purity; thou hast scourged out of us our old vanities and misleading sophisms and false expectations, and now we see where the garden of the Lord is, and that it opens but at one place, and with one key—Jesus, Son of Mary, Son of man, Son of God. We pray for the friends we love, and without whom we could not live—the hearts we look for, the travellers we expect with joy, the souls that light every room of the house with tender glory; for our friends who are far away, across the great sea, in the colonies—wanderers in places they have not yet known. We pray for those in trouble on the sea—that great and terrible waste. We pray for all who are visiting us from distant places: may they feel at home; may there be some touch in thy house that they shall recognise with ardent love and thankfulness. We pray for our sick ones: some nigh unto death; some are sick of body—weary, utterly exhausted: the grasshopper is a burden; others are ailing in mind: they are disappointed, they are mortified, they have not found what they expected: they dug in earth that they might find heaven, and, lo, heaven was not there. We pray for those whose graves are quite new, for the grass has not yet had time to grow upon them, there is not a flower upon the mould that hides the dead; be thou the resurrection and the life in the hearts of such, and make them glad even in the churchyard: turn that last resting-place into a garden of flowers, and make it a place where they will keep appointments with those who from death would learn how to live. The Lord be with us now; and we need no other presence. Amen.

Deut. xxxii.

THE SONG OF MOSES.

WHAT interest can we have in the study of events which occurred thousands of years ago? If that is the question which we put to ourselves, no wonder the answer is sometimes disappointing. We do not study the events which happened thousands of years ago. That would be too narrow a way of putting the case; we might then be mere antiquarians, deeply interested in something that transpired innumerable centuries since. We are not studying the events. We are studying the

God that overruled them. Persons are apt to imagine that there
is nothing in the Old Testament but old history; they forget that
God is in the Old Testament, as in a bush that burns but is not
consumed. How often we hear the question, Seeing that all
these events occurred so long ago, what have we to do with them
at this distance of time? The events certainly did occur long
ago, but the God who originated them, or sanctified them, or
overruled them, is the God who lighted the lamp of this morning.
We study God in studying the Old Testament; and in looking
into the events which constitute the narrative line and substance
of the Old Testament, we look into them as men look into
caskets where they expect to find choice treasure. The events
are dead, but God lives. The profoundest and most exciting of
all questions is,—Does the God of the Old Testament reappear
in the New? Is he the God of to-day? He has proclaimed
himself the God of the living—in what large sense are we to
interpret that term " living " ?—does it include all beating pulses,
all throbbing hearts, all eyes uplifted that they may find
satisfaction in the heavens? We must get rid of all narrow
definitions. We must purge the mind of the folly that in reading
the Old Testament we are digging in a grave; we are keeping
company with Jehovah, we are walking with God, we are being
charged by the subtle yet broad consistency which unites all
human history, and shows the eternal in the very midst of the
mutable. Moreover, true songs are never old; music is the
youngest of all angels, with a glorious and incalculable ancestry,
yet here to-day to take up all oldest words, and make them thrill
and quiver and vibrate with new energy and new passion.

The preface of the song is in the first four verses. The song
opens with a noble appeal :—

" Give ear, O ye heavens, and I will speak ; and hear, O earth, the words
of my mouth " (v. 1).

Who is the speaker that he must have the heavens for auditors ?
Who is this claimant of human attention that he must hush the
earth and have a silent universe to listen to his harmony ? This
verse is not a human creation : something a good deal smaller in
the way of theatre would suit any human speaker. The voice
of man is limited ; his vocal strength is but a dying strength.
Who is this man who says, " O heavens, incline your ear ; O

earth, listen to me"? The subject determines the theatre; the doctrine regulates the space. Let those who handle mean subjects content themselves with corners, and obscurities, and favoured spots, and elected listeners; the Gospel will have all the world to roam in :—"Go ye into all the world, and preach the Gospel to every creature." This Bible, whether in Hebrew or in Greek, speaks for large spaces; it will not have any spot excluded from its appeals; it will cause its pearly music drops to fall into all the realms tenanted by man; and not a single human hearer shall go without some message of tenderest love and hope. Moses asks that the earth may hear and that the heavens may listen;—why? Because his subject is the Creator of them all : he will sing of God; his topic shall be Deity; he will lift up his song high as heaven's throne. There is nothing narrow or exclusive in the tone of the Bible; it would have every man hear, it would find a place for every man, and if the man will not come to the place, it would go after him, and never rest until the man is found. So we must not speak timidly. If we are uttering words of our own making and propounding theories of our own invention, then the fewer the hearers the better, and the easier will go our fortune in the mean attempt to satisfy human learning; but he who speaks God's truth must stand in God's zone, and ask all the stars to wait to catch some tone of his inspired tongue. Thus we find nobleness everywhere in the Bible—great massiveness, incalculable solidity, ineffable dignity; as to mere flash, or foam, or sparkle, they have no place in God's great Book : it is a Book built as it were on rocks and lighted with suns. The Bible pays little or no attention to mere nature; the inspired books never go into rhapsody about flowers, and birds, and colour; in that sense of the word the Bible is not æsthetic. The great Pagan writers hardly pay any attention to nature; in all their poems they never dream of the beauties of merely natural scenery; they philosophise, they moralise, they idealise, but it has been left to modern seers to note how closely God identifies himself with every leaf in the whole forest, and every star in all the hosts of night. But the Bible always worships the God of nature : it is a theological Book, it is charged with theological inspiration and theological purpose; all things it holds in contempt in comparison with the revealed God. If he can be found, everything less than he falls away into cloud, perspective, and is not reckoned in the presence of the glory of his smile. God himself will call the heavens and the earth to witness :—" Hear, O heavens, and give ear, O earth : . . . I have nourished and brought up children, and they have rebelled against me." "O stars of night, I have had no trouble with you, great blazing glories : you have come and gone hither and thither, obeying my voice with precision ; but my children have left me, they have set their teeth in me, and their words have been stout against me ; yet how can I give them up? I have laid up in store thunderbolts for their destruction, and I have dissolved those thunderbolts in dew ; how can I give them up ? " Still the great Bible songs and the great Bible appeals roll through the firmament, sound through all space, and justify their avarice of room by the splendour of their subject.

" My doctrine shall drop as the rain, my speech shall distil as the dew, as the small rain upon the tender herb, and as the showers upon the grass " (v. 2).

What an easy condescension from the sublime to the minute and the comparatively insignificant ! "My doctrine "—that is, my learning, the truth which I hold, the spiritual philosophy which I grasp and value—"shall drop as the rain "—that is, shall be handed on and down, shall be regarded as the right and inheritance of the ages. No man is to be the perpetual custodian of God's truth ; doctrine is not to be locked up within any four corners, and to be closeted as a private possession. Whoever has a truth must speak it ; he will get two truths back for the one which he delivers. Every man must sow his ideas, and reap great harvests of thought. We spoil doctrine by keeping it within confined air ; doctrine must go forth, and challenge attention, and ask for audience, and persuade men to adopt it ;— why ? Because doctrine is not a mere sentiment, or idea, or high and audacious thought : it is inspiration ; it cannot co-exist with indolence, or selfishness, or disregard of human sin and need ; wherever the doctrine is benevolence follows it : both hands are put out to help, and the eyes are made quite quick to detect the necessities and errors of all men. Doctrine, therefore, is not a set of words, an elaboration of phrases : it is an inspiration ; a movement, an energy in the soul. All inspired thought

says, Speak : correct the mistake, run after the wanderer, help
the helpless, make the poor rich. A doctrine of that kind was
never meant to be shut up within private quarters, or to be
claimed as an individual possession ; it is the wealth of the race,
it is the treasure of God. He who takes natural objects as his
symbols and guides will often act very beautifully as well as
very exactly or correctly :—" My doctrine shall drop as the rain."
The earth without rain cannot grow one tiny grass-blade ; when
the clouds keep away the flowers hang down their heads, and
shrivel and burn, and represent the very spirit of necessity and
pain. We must have the black clouds ; how welcome they are
after a time of drought and scorching, when the earth is opening
its mouth and asking for a draught of water ! So God's doctrine
is to be poured out upon thirsty souls, burnt and scorched lives,
ruined and unproductive natures. The rain-plash is a sweet
music, a minor music, a tender appeal, a liquid persuasion. The
rain will accommodate itself to all forms and shapes, and it will
impartially visit the poor man's little handful of garden and the
great man's countless acres. Such is the Gospel of Christ : it is
impartial, gentle, necessary ; it finds the heart when the heart is
scorched, and asks to heal its burning, and to make the barren
land of the inner life beautiful with summer flowers. " My
speech shall distil as the dew,"—it shall come in the twilight, not
in the great burning noontide. The sun no sooner goes than
the dew says, I must make the best of my time, and give the
scorched landscape its nightly bath, and in the morning all the
face of the land sparkles and glitters as if a king had poured out
upon it all jewellery and precious stones. When does the dew
come ? How does the dew come ? " The wind bloweth where
it listeth, and thou hearest the sound thereof, but canst not tell
whence it cometh, and whither it goeth : so "—and thus it is
with the dew. When do the vapours become dew ? Who can
gather the dew without spoiling it ? Who can take one dewdrop into his hands and place it back on the rose-leaf? Some
beautiful analogies of nature must exert a fascination over us by
suggestion rather than submit to be handled by rude and heavy
touch. We cannot tell how the word gets into the heart—how
softly, how silently : it is there, and we knew it not ; we expected
it, and at the very time we were looking out for it, it was already

there ; it is the secret of the Lord, and it moves by a noble mystery of action, so that no line can be laid upon it, and no man may arbitrarily handle the wealth of gold. "As the small rain upon the tender herb, and as the showers upon the grass." There shall be adaptation between the one and the other : if the herb is "tender" the rain must be "small." Do not thunder upon us with thy great power ; do not plead against us with all the winds of thine eloquence, for who could stand against the storm ? On the other hand, the tenderer the grass the better it can bear even the scudding shower and the heavy downpour. Your big things are broken ; your little ones bend themselves until the calamity is overpast, and then they lift up their heads and bless God. Great trees are torn, or are wrenched from their roots, or are thrust down in contempt, but all the grass of the meadow is but the greener for the winds which have galloped over it, or the great rivers that have poured themselves upon the emerald bed. Thus may it be with man : in his pride and vanity, and strength, and fatness the winds scorn him, and all nature says he must be pulled down, and thrown into the dust and trampled upon until he learn to pray. Jesus will bless the meek, the merciful, the pure in heart, the peace-loving; but as for those who in heathen vanity set themselves up against him, he will dash them in pieces like a potter's vessel. The word does not always produce an instantaneous effect : the word has sometimes to filter well down into the thought and into the heart and the life ; and the word does not report itself in the mere quantity of the doctrine, but in the greenness of the young grass, in the beauty and fruitfulness of the tender herb : no statistical return shall be made of the number of discourses heard, or the number of chapters read, but the life shall be the more verdant in spring-like beauty, and the more splendid in all the colouring of summer.

Why are the heavens called and the earth silenced ? Why is the doctrine to drop as the rain, and the speech to distil as the dew, as the small rain upon the tender herb, and as the showers upon the grass ? What is the occasion ? The answer is given in the third verse :—

"Because I will publish the name of the Lord : ascribe ye greatness unto our God.

Now the noble tone is resumed. The second verse brought us down into a new level—into the places of channels : we left the mountains and walked by the silver streams made by the dropping rain and the distilling dew ; now we are lifted up to the level of the first verse :—"I will publish the name of the Lord." I will not be ashamed of it, I will make it known; I will associate God's name with human life and human providence ; I will make all things theological. Begin by ascribing "greatness unto our God." Greatness even of bulk may be used for religious purposes. What is the mountain ? No ten feet of it are worth looking at ; but when hundreds of feet are added to hundreds more, and when the hundreds become thousands, and the great hill bulges against the cloud, that is a dull eye which cannot see the beginning of majesty. "Ascribe ye greatness unto our God." Gather up what he has done, put his acts together, add providence to providence, day to day, mystery to mystery, until reason says, I am tired, and imagination takes up the mighty task of calculation. God is great ; his greatness is unsearchable and past finding out. There is something in the divine greatness which appeals to the best faculties of the human mind. At first we are amazed by it, perhaps afraid of it; gradually, by much chastening and all the mystery of daily education, we approach it, and at last we seem to ascend it as men climb mountains ; and we rest upon God's greatness : we find a hiding-place in the very majesty we dreaded ; the greatness of God becomes the base on which stands in beauty God's love. We must beware of low ideas of God. Herein reason needs to be cautioned and warned very sternly. A God that can be measured by reason is no God ; a God that can be understood is no God ; we must have a God we can worship, and to worship we must be moved by impulses of fear rising and sobering into veneration, and must have some sense of kinship with the God which we adore. We cannot worship a "strange god ; " we may bow down before it and make an idol of it, but we cannot worship it in the sense of heart-trust, heart-love, intelligent confidence. What is a "strange god " ? It is a god to which we are not akin : there is no blood-relationship between us ; the god is hand-made, hand-painted. The true God is a spirit—as man is a spirit—and must be worshipped in spirit and in truth, away from language and possible representation of thought, in ineffable quietness, in the speechlessness of sympathy.

"He is the Rock, his work is perfect : for all his ways are judgment : a God of truth and without iniquity, just and right is he " (v. 4).

That is doctrine. In that verse there is substance to be grasped, appreciated, and appropriated. "He is the Rock." God only is called "the Rock" in all Holy Scripture. The Hebrew word which is translated "rock" is here and there wrought into other names and may be found in the middle of a name or at the end, but is qualified by its human accretions or attachments ; but here we have "the Rock"—otherwhere translated feebly "everlasting strength"—a multitude of syllables instead of this one, solid, quiet word. "He is the Rock" without which the earth would be impossible—the symbol of strength. "His work is perfect." An imperfect God is not a God. The work may not be measurable within two given points : within those two visible points it may seem to be imperfect work, as in the momentary flourishing of the wicked and the temporary distress of the righteous ; but when God's work is spoken of, it must be measured by God's own space. Then comes the grand assurance without which religion would be a fiction :—"God is a God of truth and without iniquity, just and right is he." The moral basis is strong ; the moral claim is complete. The purity of God is the guarantee of providence and is the pledge of redemption. "Just and right is he"—then no good cause need fear ; no misunderstood life may evade the divine judgment, as if misunderstanding would be added to mis-understanding. We must have a God of whom we can say, He is "right." We must not be ashamed of the geometrical term "he is right ; " we must magnify it into moral senses, and still say, "He is right." If any suspicion could be fixed upon his rightness, his majesty would be a dissolving cloud, a glittering nothing. It is because God is right, true, just, that the universe stands ; and, at the last, Providence will be vindicated, and human history disclose itself as one of the tabernacles of the Most High.

In the fifth verse the whole tone changes :—

"They have corrupted themselves, their spot is not the spot of his children : they are a perverse and crooked generation."

Is this true to human history ?　The contrast itself is so violent
as to excite the spirit of incredulity.　As a poetical conception it
would seem to be out of proportion and out of colour ;—what is
it as a solemn fact ?　Can we, as human creatures, accomplish a
miracle so stupendous ?　Are we, as intelligent men, capable of
corrupting ourselves,—sowing in our own hearts the seeds of
decay, cultivating a cancer, taking delight in our withering powers,
and viewing with a kind of mad satisfaction our decrepit faculties ?
The answer must be in ourselves.　There is no reply in poetry ;
poetry is offended by the juxtaposition of majesty so sublime and
corruption so putrid.　The answer must be in ourselves : let the
heart reply ; let human life lay down its testimony.　Who does
not know that the testimony of human life would be a ghastly
confirmation of that which appears to be a violent and incredible
irony ?　Moses says, before singing the song, "I know that after
my death ye will utterly corrupt yourselves."　The word
"utterly" is to be read "surely," with moral if not literary
emphasis.　The people had corrupted themselves, but there
would seem to be a difference between "corrupting," and "utterly
corrupting"—between wounding and suicide, between a momentary offence and premeditated treason.　The word "utterly"
expresses their fate when great influences are removed.　Some
of us are only kept apparently right by a very subtle and
sympathetic hand : if such and such a ministry were removed,
we know not to what depths we would fall ; were a certain
praying voice, at home or otherwhere, to cease its intercession,
our life would fall down in absolute humiliation and wastefulness.
The word is "corrupt," "corrupting," "utterly corrupt"—
signifying rottenness, putridity,—absolute decay that has not
in it one element of hope.　"Their spot is not the spot of his
children"—they are not his children ; the spots that are upon
them are disguises : they are not signs of adoption, not proofs of
election to which the soul has consented ; these people are aliens,
strangers : their garments are not known at God's wedding-feast ;
they have accomplished the miracle of sinking their identity.
"They are a perverse and crooked generation" where they are
not positively sinful, they are difficult, unmanageable ; where
they are not utterly rotten, they are "crooked :" it is impossible
to straighten them ; everything they say is upside-down as to its

meaning : there is no straightforwardness, sweet candour, beautiful frankness about them ; they are knotty, they are difficult of understanding, never saying exactly and straight on what they mean,—doubling back upon their friends, twisting language into a false meaning, making promises and not sealing them with their hearts. Again we have to ask, not so much—Is this true ? as, Is this possible ? Can a man corrupt himself ? Can a soul depart so far from its innocence as to become learned in all evil and iniquity, and wickedness of every name and degree of intensity ? Can trees of the Lord's right-hand planting twist themselves, as it were, into knots that never can be disentangled ? Does it lie within finite strength to accomplish miracles so astounding ? The song is based upon history, this music comes out of fact ; this noble strain of praise and complaint interprets in the language of music the horrors of an actual human tragedy.

Now a question arises :—

"Do ye thus requite the Lord, O foolish people and unwise ? is not he thy father that hath bought thee ? hath he not made thee, and established thee ? " (v. 6).

So human actions are not dissociated from divine economies and heavenly thoughts. Human actions are replies to divine providence ; human conduct is a commentary upon the providential method of God. We cannot take our actions and set them up solitarily, and say, We began the action, continued it, and completed it without any reference to heavenly ministries and providential interpositions and judgments. We cannot cut off our actions from the great currents of the universe. The lifting of a hand may be a prayer, or it may be a token of rebellion ; the uplifted eye may be a speechless supplication ; a cup of water given to a disciple in the name of Christ is given to the Master himself. Every act of condescension and benevolence ought to be considered an echo of a divine appeal. Thus the reference is once more to conscience and to reason :—"Do ye thus requite the Lord, O foolish people and unwise ? "—people of a withered heart, people who have put out the lamp of understanding, people who have forgotten the first principles of human responsibility. What is it that has been omitted from the policy and worship of the unwise and foolish people ? It is the fatherhood of God :—"Is not he thy father that hath bought thee?" Having

got rid of the Father, all the rest is an easy run into the devil's
arms; having accomplished the moral excision—having cut off
ourselves from consenting to God's sovereignty—we become the
guest of the enemy, and are easily led into ever-deepening depths
of humiliation and disgrace. Is this possible? We will not ask
—Is it true? But does not possibility itself shudder at the suggestion, and say, Do not prostitute fancy; break your little moral
commandments, trample your ethics in the dust: they are but
vain theories of vain minds; but let imagination alone, do not
defile the sanctuary of high fancy, the thing which you suggest
is impossible? The plea has reason in it, the protest is not
without force from a philosophical point of view. It ought not to
be possible to forget father, God, law, love, providence; it ought
to be impossible for a man to be ungrateful. Are men ungrateful? Can any father testify even to the possibility of an ungrateful child? Unthankfulness ought to be impossible. We
find it in this song; we are, therefore, driven back upon our own
consciousness once more for confirmation or rebuttal. Have *we*
been ungrateful? Have *we* forgotten the Father who made us
and the God who established us? Have *we* taken our lives into
our own hands, and treated ourselves as if we were almighty and
all-wise objects of self-idolatry? Better leave these inquiries;
do not ask for replies in terms: the inquiry must be left as its
own pregnant and appalling answer.

Now the Psalmist will reason with the people. He will change
for a moment the tone of the great Psalm; he will call a council
and examine minutely the sacred past :—

" Remember the days of old, consider the years of many generations: ask
thy father, and he will show thee; thy elders, and they will tell thee " (v. 7).

God's providence is no novelty. In searching out its root and
origin, so to say, we have to pass by every ancient book: we
have to pass by the very written letter of the Bible itself. We
always revert to the former generations—the ages that are gone.
When God made us he began to be kind to us: not a day were
we left alone; he has watched our downsitting and our uprising
from the very beginning of human history. Search far back as
we may, there is still a yesterday to that past; examine as profoundly as we can, there is still a sacred depth to which we have

not penetrated. What is the consistent testimony? How does history mass itself up into argument and accumulate itself into the shapeliness of a sanctuary? The whole tendency of history is to prove the existence of an unseen hand, the watchfulness of an unseen eye, the government—critical and beneficent—of an unseen Sovereign. We are not left to the testimony of some mean ten years, or some mean ten centuries: still the years double upon themselves in æons, ages, millenniums. Thus the fact of God's care, love, presence, and providence, is based upon the simple induction of facts large as time and solid as the foundations of the earth. It is something to be able to make so wide and penetrating an appeal. We might have been afraid of the yesterdays of history; we might have said, Draw a line, and do not go beyond that: begin at a certain defined period in human history, and from that period draw all your induction and argument. But the Bible knows nothing of mythological periods—periods anterior to formulated and certified history; the Bible insists upon the retrospect being absolutely complete, so that every grass-blade may say, God nourished me—and every man may exclaim, Without God I can do nothing. This is the appeal to time; this is the determination to abide by the arbitrament of history.

"When the Most High divided to the nations their inheritance, when he separated the sons of Adam, he set the bounds of the people according to the number of the children of Israel" (v. 8).

The nations, then, are God's creation. We have drawn lines upon our paper-world, and called them by significant and convenient names; but in doing so we were endeavouring to follow the broad line of fact and reality. He who made the map did not make the world which it represents. We are so prone to think that if we can make a map we can fashion the earth. Our map is but a plan of what is already done. We have gone forth to scan the shape of the continents, and to number the islands, and to estimate the varieties which distinguish the geography which is accessible to us; but the facts were all there to be examined and tested and reasoned about. God has been building all the time. The Almighty has not been bringing together an infinite amount of human material, and leaving it without shape or purpose: he has been building nations, setting

up empires and communities of every name ; and he has so
watched them that surge as they may into what foaming tumult
may be possible to rebellion, they are still brought back like
leashed hounds within range and hold of the divine grip.   God's
globe is God's garden : he is growing in it all manner of trees,
and flowers, and things beautiful and useful ;—let the shapeliness
thereof be an argument ; let the daily continuance thereof suggest
some religious thought ; let the whole build itself up into an altar,
and invite us to humble prayer and holy psalm.

"For the Lord's portion is his people ; Jacob is the lot of his inheritance "
(v. 9).

As if we were of consequence to him, as if he could not do
without us, as if even our disfigured countenance, made ghastly
by skilled iniquity, had still a fascination for the Maker's eye.   It
is long before God can give up the sons of men : mothers yield
before he surrenders ; he cares for man, and values the sons of
men, and has made man a little lower than himself—as it were
in jealousy, a little lower, but still quite near ;—this is a mystery :
instead of overwhelming our understanding it should touch our
faith, and set an unconsuming fire to our imagination, and make
us glad with premillennial joy.   Nowhere is man made so much
of as in the Bible.   It is true that many a Bible doctrine humbles
man, drives him into the dust, makes him ashamed of himself,
causes burning to scorch his countenance ; but even such humiliation is but a pledge of the divine solicitude and a proof of the
culprit's greatness.

"He found him in a desert land, and in the waste howling wilderness; he
led him about, he instructed him, he kept him as the apple of his eye"
(v. 10).

A wonderful word is this " found." It occurs often in Holy
Scripture.   Let it mean here—God *disclosed* himself to man in a
desert land—manifested himself to man in the wilderness.   Thus
God found Jacob at Bethel.   Thus the word is used by Jesus
Christ with significant repetition in the three great parables in
the fifteenth chapter of Luke :—" Rejoice with me; for I have
found my sheep which was lost . . . Rejoice with me ; for I have
found the piece which I had lost . . . Let us eat, and be merry :
for this my son was dead, and is alive again ; he was lost, and is
found,"—a word we dismiss lightly.   We have forgotten the

deep significance of many a familiar word. We know not in
what words God may be specially discovered. When God
" finds " a man, the meaning often is that he *discloses* himself to
the man, so that a dreaming Jacob sees what he did not expect
to see, and when he speaks it is to say, " Surely the Lord is in
this place ; and I knew it not." It was not Jacob who found
God, but God who found Jacob : " We love him, because he first
loved us." Having discovered himself to Jacob, what course did
he pursue ? " He led him about, he instructed him." He did not
pursue a straight course with the wanderer, for that would have
been too brief, and would certainly have been misunderstood ;
but Jacob was " led about," now a little forward, now a little
backward ; now a little aside, now through a city ; now across a
mountain, now in rocky places where human hands could find no
sustenance. That is life ; that is our own life, if we rightly
understood it. We cannot go forward galloping, running, fleeing,
in a straight line, and making what we call progress : it would
be but lineal advancement : all we should leave behind us would
be a mere thread of a way. Education consists in being brought
back, in being called upon to advance—retire—halt ; to rise at
unexpected times, to meet surprising perils, and to be cast back
upon our own resources to learn that resources we have none.
" No chastening for the present seemeth to be joyous, but
grievous : nevertheless afterward it yieldeth the peaceable fruit
of righteousness." Education is not a leap, a bound, an easy
course ; it means a great deal of returning, redoubling, gathering
up the fragments,—going over our life again day by day, perusing
old diaries, acquainting ourselves with ancient journals, and out
of the past bringing an inspiration for the future. Thus was
Jacob treated ; and in that sense Jacob is a symbolical term,
standing for the sum-total of the human race : for God's education of Jacob is God's education of the world.

A beautiful figure represents a portion of the divine way with
man :—

"As an eagle stirreth up her nest, fluttereth over her young, spreadeth
abroad her wings, taketh them, beareth them on her wings " (v. 11).

Imagination must fancy the picture. The eagle has taken out
the little eaglets upon her wings : suddenly she has dropped

from under them, and left them to try their own pinions : they
are weak, they will fall,—see how the great eagle darts down
and receives the tired eaglets upon her wings, and mounts again
into still higher levels ; then she will try again, and the little one
is cast off into the immeasurable air, and its destiny is partially
realised : it flutters as if in its native clime ; presently the little
pinions become tired, and the eaglet will fall, but the eagle
descends again and receives it on mighty pinions of iron, and
rises again to the gate of heaven ; and thus the eaglet is trained
to fly, and there comes a period when the little ones become
strong, when the eaglet drops its diminutiveness and becomes
complete as the eagle itself, and has thus been trained to swim
in God's air, to fly in God's firmament, and beat its strengthened
pinions against the gate of the sun.   This is God's way with us.
We fly sometimes but poorly : we fall, and suddenly the great
pinion of the Almighty, the wing of the Most High, is under us,
and we rest upon it ; and then we fly a little more and discover
our weakness, and just at the moment of peril the pinion returns
and we rest in high-up places amidst what appears to us to be
infinite dangers.   We do not always fly as we should like to do :
our fear overcomes what little strength we have ; we must not
be scoffed at or mocked ; we are only learning to fly ; by-and-by
we shall fly well and fear nothing, and in all our flying we shall
return at eventide to hover over the nest of heaven and find
peace in the shelter of the skies.   Give us time : " They that
wait upon the Lord shall renew their strength ; they shall mount
up with wings as eagles ; they shall run, and not be weary : and
they shall walk, and not faint."   It is easy to stand below and
laugh at the young eaglets in their early flying ; but God's wing
is under them : God will not forsake them ; not one of his birds
shall perish ; not a sparrow falleth to the ground without your
Father ; and if he treats us as his larger creatures, his nobler
creations, he will guide us with his eye ; under the shadow of
his wing we shall find protection, and at last it will be infinitely
pleasant to us to be able to mount above the earth—to tower
away and mingle with the blaze of day.

PRAYER.

ALMIGHTY GOD, it is a fearful thing to fall into thine hands. Thine arrows are of great number, and when they strike they pierce fatally. Who can set themselves against God and live? Whose arm is strong enough to repel thy stroke? We are consumed before thee; thou hidest thy face, and we are lost in darkness. It is a fearful thing to fall into the hands of the living God. Our God is a consuming fire. Them that honour thee thou wilt honour, and they that despise thee shall be lightly esteemed. Now we turn and behold thy mercy, and are amazed at the tearful compassion of God. Our hearts exclaim thankfully, God is love; God is light; he has no pleasure in death: he would that the wicked might turn and live. Thou criest after the lost one that he would return ; thou hast the best robe ready for him; yea, thou art waiting to be gracious, to receive us, one and all, wanderers, into thine house, and thou wilt call upon thine angels to be glad. We thank thee for all thy tender mercy, thy loving care, thy pity, thy tears. We live in God's love; we are upheld by God's omnipotence ; the light of his countenance is our day, and his love in Christ is our hope for eternity. We come to the Cross—the wondrous Cross—the mystery of God, the mystery of eternity; into these things the angels desire to look. Behold the Lamb of God, which taketh away the sin of the world. We look, and live in the looking; it is thy way: thou hast called us to look unto Christ and be saved ; Lord, help us to look, to fasten our eyes upon the dying Sacrifice. We commend one another to thy loving care : hold us, guide us, make us stronger day by day; and then, when the day's work is well done, call us into rest, and joy, and glory. Amen

Deut. xxxii.

"But Jeshurun waxed fat, and kicked : thou art waxen fat, thou art grown thick, thou art covered with fatness ; then he forsook God which made him, and lightly esteemed the Rock of his salvation " (v. 15).

THE SONG OF MOSES.—(*Continued.*)

IS this true ? Do not trifle with the inquiry. First of all, is it possible? As we have already inquired, is it not too astounding to be credible ? Does it not shock the imagination ? Do strong men cease to pray ? Do men who are covered with the fatness of prosperity cease to sing God's praise ? Is there some

thing in the world, in time and in sense, that crowds out the
divine, the supernatural, and the future? We are able to
answer these questions : they are not metaphysical, subtle, out of
reach ; they come strictly and literally within the lines of our
own consciousness and experience ; so we can affirm or deny
these great historical portraitures of mankind. The history of
poverty is more likely to be a history of religion than is the
history of wealth. We, perhaps, never see human meanness
so conspicuously as when we see foiled, defeated, disappointed
men crawling back to the altars which they had abandoned in
the time of sunshine and abundance. We easily dismiss our
ministers ; they soon become a nuisance to our prosperous life ;
we will call for them in the day of sickness, and ask them to
whine out their prayers in our hearing when we cannot pray for
ourselves, or when we think Heaven is so offended with us that
any prayer of ours would be answered only with contempt.
The world does not sit comfortably with true spirituality of mind ;
they speak different languages, they belong to opposing spheres,
they cannot occupy an equal position. To speak of making the
best of both worlds is to speak about that which has no relation
the one part to the other. One world is to be kept under our
foot : it is never to sustain any relation to our head ; it is never to
come within the operation of our highest and strongest thought ;
the other world is lined outside with bright blue, flecked here
and there with silver and woolly clouds, and at night punctured
and enriched with the embroidery of stars,—a high world, out of
reach, yet still pouring upon us its light and warmth and eternal
comfort. We must keep the varying worlds in their places.
We, too, have a kind of astronomic sovereignty to maintain.
We cannot disturb the relations of the worlds : each star must
throb in its own place, each planet burn within its own sphere,
and everything must be kept in regular system and exact relation,
or we shall be troubled in our thinking and foiled and mortified
in our prayers. "Jeshurun" is a diminutive ; it is a term of
endearment ; it is, so to say, that loving cunning twist in the
proper name which indicates the playfulness of affection ; it is
a fancy name ; it was meant to please the man-child to whom it
was applied. Even the endeared one "waxed fat, and kicked"
—that is to say, grew too prosperous to be truly godly, grew too

rich in matter for the hand, to have any real and lasting property in the heart. Who, then, is the rich man?—The man who has laid up treasures where moth and rust cannot corrupt, and where thieves cannot break through and steal ; the man of great thought, energetic mind, copious understanding, spiritual insight, love of the invisible and the divine; the soul mighty to triumph in the great art of prayer-war—the violence that storms heaven's gate and forces omnipotence to terms. God is willing to be thus conquered ; he waits to be gracious; he wants to have us press down his almightiness, as the strong man loves the little child to draw him nearer to its own stature. We speak of forcing omnipotence to terms, meaning thereby to pay a tribute to the omnipotence that is willing to be forced. Even the endeared soul may become too prosperous to find in spiritual endearment its richest heritage and noblest blessing. How easily we are led away from the altar! "How hardly"—that is, with what infinite difficulty—"shall they that have riches enter into the kingdom of God!" Nor is the term "riches" to be taken in its merely monetary or arithmetical sense : whoever is contented with earth cannot pray—in other words, whoever can find satisfaction within the bounds of time and space cannot need a revelation, and cannot understand one. The Bible is a blank book to blank eyes. Thus there is a place for poverty in the discipline of life; thus there is a sphere in which the black minister called affliction can preach his sombre discourse, and touch with feelings akin to religion hearts that are otherwise likely to be led astray.

"They provoked him to jealousy with strange gods, with abominations provoked they him to anger" (v. 16).

Is this little on the part of God? If we say so, we do not understand what we say. This is true of all love, of all spirituality, of all honesty and decency. The purer the object, the more easily is it excited to jealousy—not the jealousy which expresses itself in censoriousness, in petulance, in mean revenge ; but the jealousy which expresses a wounded heart, a disappointed love, a mortified trust. That which is but partially honest is not moved to jealousy by felonious action : by its very nature it connives at it ; it has a mind skilful in the formation of excuses for outrages so detestable : it attributes them to custom, to the manner of the times, to the atmosphere of the place; it does not judge them in the eternal light and at the infinite bar. The whiter the snow, the more easily it shows every black spot there is upon it; the more vital the love, the more easily does it respond either to the homage which is due or to the humiliation which is undeserved. God thus expresses precisely what we should wish him to express; even here he is not transcending our reason : he is magnifying himself so as to lay a broader claim upon our veneration and trust. It is right that it should be a fearful thing to fall into the hands of the living God; and it is right because God is love. Outraged love is the severest, the most terrific, of enemies; offended honesty has no pity upon the thief. It is right that it should be so. We must in some quarter of the universe find a throne that cannot be bought, a sceptre that cannot be bribed, an authority that cannot be deterred. All these ideas are gathered up in a final expression and in a sublime representation in the Bible term—GOD.

A very marvellous expression occurs in the seventeenth verse, full of the subtlest sarcasm. There is one set of words in this verse that has upon it the keenness of a sword. Speaking of what apostate Israel did, the song says :—

"They sacrificed unto devils, not to God."

That we can perfectly understand : the matter is put in the broadest and most impressive form, so much so as to be little better than a commonplace; but the sentence grows and sharpens as it advances—thus :—

"to gods whom they knew not."

There is a hidden excuse for them there—meaning, perhaps, if they had known their gods they never would have worshipped them : if they had known their gods, they would have known their emptiness, their vanity, their weakness, their self-helplessness ; they would have poured contempt where they were invited to offer prayer ; but the expression that is so sharp and keen, biting like satire and mocking like irony, is this :—

"to new gods that came newly up."

There is no finer wit in all literature, having regard to the keenness of the satire and to the infinite suggestiveness of the

weak-mindedness of Israel. " To new gods "—to new toys, new
objects of fascination, new theological theories, new speculations
—"that came newly up "—as if they were twice new, double-
dyed novelties, new things " newly up "—just to hand—toy
gods brought by the last ship ; fall down and worship these
fancy deities ! They have everything you want—except wisdom,
righteousness, love, and omnipotence ; they have everything
as gods you can desire—except elements that are divine and
energies that are supernatural ; come, worship them ! they are
so new, they are brand-new, the paint is hardly dry ; they have
come " newly up," they are just to hand ; first come, first
served ; gods in plenty—new—newly come. We need not therefore invent any present-day satire to inflict upon theological
novelty ; a better phrase than is found in the seventeenth verse
can never be invented. Think of a " new " god ! The expression is a contradiction in terms. To be God is not to be new ;
to be new is not to be God. As we have said, there can be no
" mere " preaching ; if it is preaching, it is not *mere* preaching,
and if it is *mere* preaching, it is not preaching. If the god is
new, it is not God ; if the god is real, he is not *new*. So with
theological theories, doctrines, speculations, and confidences.
Let us allow for new letters, new settings, new framings ; but
the things uttered, and set, and framed must be venerable as
eternity. He who can adopt a new god can give a new god up.
A new god that has come newly up can be easily abandoned.
Have no faith in lovers of novelty ; your confidences will become
old to them, and they will seek a new confidence ; they will
become accustomed to your love, and cast it off as a burden.
Men cannot love novelty in theology, and yet love antiquity and
thoroughly-solid establishments in friendship, in household love,
or in commercial confidences. We are doing injustice to the
spirit of truth in supposing that a man can be here and there
and elsewhere in religion, and yet keep firm in love, honest in
social confidence, and the standard-bearer in business and in the
family. The man is what he is religiously : if he can accept a
new god, he can accept a new love ; if he can be pleased with
a new religious toy, he can be pleased with new conversation,
new faces, and new relationships ; the novelty which is most
conspicuous at the religious end runs through and through, like

a stain, the whole substance and quality of the character. We
have to-day an abundance of "new gods that came newly up,"
whom our "fathers feared not." They must be left to play off
their little novelty, wear out their paint; they must be permitted
to expose their complexion until the sun has devoured it; gods
that can be new grow old very soon, and are cast out by the
love that never really trusted them.

"Of the Rock that begat thee thou art unmindful, and hast forgotten God
that formed thee" (v. 18).

How is it that men soon forget the solid, the real, the
substantial? What is it that delights men in spluttering rockets,
in coloured fountains, in lamps swinging upon trees that are
offended by their presence? See the great seething crowd
waiting for the coloured fountains to spring up, and for all the
little electric lamps confined in tinted globes to shine among the
swaying branches! What exclamations of idiotic delight! How
stunned is modern intelligence at the marvellous display of
colour! Who heeds the quiet moon that looks on with unutterable amazement, and that in her motherly heart is saying,—O
that they were wise, that they were less given to toy-worship
and to playfulness of that kind! Here I have been shining ages
upon ages—who heeds me? Which of all the sweltering, over-
fed throng turns a bleared eye to my course to watch me in my
gently sovereignty? And the stars, too, look down upon the
coloured fountains without being moved to envy by their
momentary blush and by their unheard splash! We forget the
Rock so soon; we prefer the toy; we want something light,
something that can be spoken trippingly on the tongue—an easy
fluent nothing. We do not care to bow down the head to study,
to criticism, to the examination and estimation of evidence, and
commit ourselves to the acceptance of sound conclusions. Can
we go anywhere to see a coloured fountain? Men who do not
travel half-a-mile to the greatest pulpit in the world, or the
greatest altar ever built to the God of heaven, would put
themselves and their families to any amount of inconvenience
and expense to gaze with the admiration of idiocy upon a coloured
fountain! Blessed are they who love the permanent stars, the
lamps of heaven, and who set their feet broadly and squarely

on God's everlasting Rock. Let us turn to the real, to the substantial, to the very revelation of God's truth, and abide there ; the coloured fountain can only come now and again, but the eternal heavens are always full of light or rich with beauty.

How could the Lord meet this case ? He says :—

"I will hide my face from them " (v. 20).

Withdrawment is the only defence of outraged holiness. Men do not know what they are enjoying until their enjoyments are withdrawn. Hence the ordinary quotation—" Blessings brighten in their flight." Who knows what he owes to the Church of the living God until he is put down in a strange land where the opportunity does not occur, where the altar is not to be seen ? Who knows even how comparatively good a Christian community is until he is thrown amongst aliens and strangers, who never heard the Christian name, and never uncovered in reverence to the Christian God ? Few men there are who have been driven into such circumstances who would not have been thankful for an opportunity to return to the most imperfect Christian community in their native land.

But withdrawment is not understood by the fattened prosperity of Jeshurun ; so God will proceed further. He lays down his policy in the twenty-first verse:—

" They have moved me to jealousy with that which is not God ; they have provoked me to anger with their vanities: and I—"

—for a rod has two ends—

" —and I will move them to jealousy with those which are not a people; I will provoke them to anger with a foolish nation."

Men must be met upon their own ground. We cannot address high arguments to men who have blinded their intelligence and dismissed their conscience : we reduce ourselves to a lower level than that upon which we began ; and God must bring himself down to that level if he is to inflict upon sinners appropriate chastisement. Jeshurun shall feel the jealousy he himself has provoked. What will God do then ? He will put honour upon nations that have hitherto been without name or status : their men shall become kings, their nameless ones shall become famous; they shall arise to dispute the primacy of Jeshurun. Then Israel will begin to think. He will say, Who are these that come up from the north ? what men are these, of whom I have never heard before ?—and then he will return in memory to old covenants, and promises, and vows, and will ask Heaven's explanation. There is always an explanation in heaven. Afflictions do not spring out of the dust. Your tower of strength was not thrown down because a feather blew against it. There are no accidents in the great issue and outcome of human life. When competitors arise, and you feel that the standing of your favouritism is imperilled, you will begin to wonder, and he who wisely wonders often timidly prays. The man will talk to himself in plain terms : he will say,—How is this ? I have been king; I have had none to dispute my sceptre or my authority; and now the dog barks at me on the streets, and men whom I would not have numbered with the dogs of my father's flock mock me, and ask for my name, and look upon me as they would look upon some intrusive curiosity. How is this ? The elders used to rise at my approach, and strong men owned me first amongst equals : now wherever I put my foot I have a sense of insecurity, and wherever I look I see no beaming face. How is this ? The answer is religious : I have forgotten my appointments with God ; I have hurried through a Book amid the fruitful pages of which I ought to have lingered with delight and desire and love ; I have abandoned the God of my fathers : I have taken interest in new gods that came newly up; this is the reason : I am speaking truly to myself; all this I would not care at first to speak in the hearing of other people, but I will tell the truth to myself, and the truth is that my love of God has cooled, my loyalty to truth has become impaired, my communion with the heavens has become less intimate ; I am not the man I was ; and now God is permitting chatterers to arise around me who mock me and insult me ; I have retained everything but the rod of my strength, the eloquence of my prayer, the almightiness of my faith. When men speak to themselves thus—ruthlessly, sternly, with religious frankness—they will end the monologue by saying, " I will arise, and go to my Father, and will say unto him, Father, I have sinned." Never did erring child say that to the Father in heaven without the Father calling for festival and music and infinite joy.

God blamed Israel because they were

"children in whom is no faith" (v. 20).

Do not misunderstand that word "faith." It is a Christian word ; here it does not occur in its spiritual or Christian sense. "Faith" is a word which belongs to Christ, not to Moses. The word "faith" here means covenant-keeping, reality, honesty to vows. They have signed a paper, but they will break the bond : they are children in whom is no faith, no reliance, no trust. This is not the "sixth sense," this is not reason on wings ; this is simple truthfulness and covenant-keeping honour. Faith is not born yet in the Bible, as to name and definite influence—though many a man in the old book was moved by faith who could not account for his own motive and impulse. We are called to faith in its highest sense ; and in being called to faith in its highest sense, we are not called upon to renounce reason. Should I say to a child, Dear little one, your two hands are not strong enough to take up that weight, even of gold, but I could find you a third one, and with that you could lift it easily, and with that it would be no weight ; you could carry it always without weariness and without fatigue—do I dishonour the other hands ? Do I put the child to some humiliation ? Do I ignore what little power it has ? Certainly not : I increase it, I magnify it, I honour it ; so does the great and loving One, who wishes us to pray without ceasing, magnify reason by saying,—It wants faith ; faith magnifies the senses by saying,—They are five in number, and I can make them six ; do not dispense with any one of them, keep them all in their integrity, but you want the sixth sense that lays hold upon the invisible and the eternal. We cannot, therefore, keep covenants and honour vows in the sense in which the word "faith" is used here, with any completeness, until we are inspired by the higher faith—that all-encompassing trust in God, that marvellous sixth sense which sees God. Lord, increase our faith ! May our prosperity never interfere with our prayer ! Give us what thou wilt—poverty, riches, health, disease, strength, or weakness, but take not thy Holy Spirit from us.

PRAYER.

ALMIGHTY GOD, guide us with thine eye in all the way of life. We need some sense of thy nearness, for the wind is cold, and the way is hard, and the end is not clearly seen. We are hardly born until we die; there is no time for anything upon the earth. Surely this is not all! The days become shorter rather than longer; we thought they would lengthen out and give us light to do some work in, but, behold, they close quickly, and the years are all gone, and there is no time to repair the past or make much of the present. There is no present: it flies whilst we describe it. We are driven on as by a mighty wind; we are withdrawn as by a hand unseen; we are spoken to by voices that have no figure; and, behold, we cannot tell what it is we see, or hear, or do. But thou hast sent word to us of thy nearness and presence and purpose; we are told that thou art a God nigh at hand and not afar off—nearer to us than we can ever be to ourselves,—a mystery of nearness, as if we were part of thee, as if thou wert part of us, as if we were one. This is a great mystery, full of solemnity and full of pathos. That we have done wrong we very well know. It is easy to do wrong: it is easy to eat honey, because it is sweet. Behold, we have indeed done wrong, and so far spoiled thy purpose and stained the handiwork of God. But we are sure that we are not so great as thou art. If we have done wrong, the remedy is in thee and not in ourselves. Thou canst not be at peace so long as wickedness remains. Thou hast endeavoured to reclaim us by punishment, and thy penalties have left us harder than ever; thou hast burned us with hunger, thou hast cut us with the sword, thou hast filled the soul with terrors; and we have shed tears of fearfulness and uttered cowardly prayers and promised to be better for fear that we should be crushed; but Pharaoh-like we have turned again in the morning and defied thee to thy face; then thou hast whispered to us and persuaded us with all gentleness, and led us out to a place called Calvary to see thine agony, to behold thy love, to look upon the sacrifice for sins. This is the Lord's doing: herein is mercy combined with righteousness holding counsel with law, herein is grace abounding over sin. The devil is not Lord, the enemy is not on the throne; he sets up his purposes, and they are foiled and thrown down and buried in the grave of contempt. The Lord reigneth; the Cross is the symbol of triumph; thy Son shall have the heathen for his inheritance and the uttermost parts of the earth for his possession. As I live, saith the Lord, the whole earth shall be full of the glory of the Lord. This thou wilt work out in thine own way and in thine own time, but it shall be done, because the mouth of the Lord hath spoken it. Surely thou wilt remember us in our low estate; our weakness shall be our plea, our sin shall be the mighty reason of our prayer; because we cannot save ourselves thy power to save shall be magnified. As for our afflictions, difficulties, disappointments, all the black things that make up life, all the miseries that chasten the heart, they are under thy control every one of them : no spark has in it more heat than thou hast entrusted to it, and no chain is longer than the links thyself hast forged. We still believe in God and have no confidence in ourselves, and have perfect distrust of the enemy when we muse upon thine almightiness and see somewhat of thy love. Reconcile us to our lot wherein we cannot amend it. Life is an infinite difficulty to some : the morning brings no light of hope, the evening no shade of rest, and the noontide is a fierce enemy ; they cannot fight the battle ; the bread they earn is too little, and it is embittered by many a reflection which cannot be controlled or explained ; the house is lonely and dark, the children are sickly and unequal to the task of life, the whole day is full of shadows, and the night is a darkness unrelieved ;—come to such ; explain a little of the mystery to them ; if they could but sing one note in the night-time, they would take heart again. Have pity upon those who are too successful ; thou art causing them to see what prosperity means, and, behold, we regard them with compassion as they open the glittering parcel to find it full of nothingness. The world grows bitter herbs : all time and sense are like a garden-land bringing forth nothing but bitter aloes ; behold, the garden is on high, where the sweet fruit grows, where the pure flowers bloom, where the birds sing God's gospels. May we set our affections upon things above, and by a mightier gravitation than that of earth be drawn towards the throne that is established for ever. Break the bad man's purpose ; turn his counsel to confusion ; set him upside down on the wayside that men may laugh at him who mocked their God. Prosper every good cause : give it energy and hope and secretly-multiplying resources, and may it win the whole battle, and set up God's standard— pledge of victory, pledge of peace. Amen.

Deut. xxxii.

THE SONG OF MOSES.—(*Continued.*)

WE find a record of what may be called the penal resources of God in the paragraph beginning with verse 20 and ending with verse 25. That paragraph is a kind of armoury ; it is a special chamber set apart in the great creation into which we may reverently look if we would know some resources which are available in reference to the punishment of sin. The paragraph should be read alone,—that is to say, it should be taken out of its literary setting and perused as a solitary writing. In the New Testament we find an armoury available to Christian soldiers ; in that armoury we find sword and shield and breast-plate, and all the other parts of an invincible panoply. In these verses we find an armoury which is not to be used by men, but which is to be solely employed by Almighty God himself. Quite a new aspect of the divine character is here

revealed. How after perusing such words can we read the
sweet message given in sweet syllables—"God is love"? He
is a God full of terribleness according to the description given in
verses 20-25 of this chapter. What is God's penal reply to sin
according to this record? It is a reply in the first instance of
withdrawment :—"I will hide my face from them"—(v. 20)—
let them see what they can do with life; grant unto them their
own hearts' desire, and "I will see what their end shall be"
—they claim to be wise, let them light the lamp of their wisdom
and see how long it will burn without my presence and blessing.
This withdrawment of the divine face is the most terrific punishment that can befall the life of the human soul. It is not a
stroke, or a sharp pain, or an open wound out of which the
blood flows in a hot flood : all such pains can be borne with some
degree of fortitude ; possibly some man may have found a balm
for such wounds : send for him, pay him well, ask him to
make haste, to leave all other patients and clients, to flee to your
side because you can reward him handsomely ; but here is a
punishment man cannot touch : it may be described in a sense
as abstract, as purely spiritual. What are we waiting for?
We are waiting for light. Who can bring it? It is not carried
in the waggons of men ; it cannot be fetched by the horses of
kings ; it lies beyond the line of our arm. For what are we
pining ?—for a smile. Who can buy it? None can buy it : it
is not sold in the market-place for gold. We want a touch, a
glance, a feeling of divine nearness ; we cannot tell in words
what it is we need, but such a necessity never before strained the
soul and pained it with agony. So long as we can describe our
suffering, our very description becomes a species of mitigation.
When words fail, when our attempted utterance returns upon
ourselves, the hearer being unable to make out one word we say,
then the mind staggers and eloquent lips babble an idiot's tale.

God will thus punish his people homœopathically,—an ancient
plan, full of philosophy, but failing sometimes even in the hands
of God. He will address like to like ; he will encounter the
sinner in his own mood. Says God,—"They have moved me to
jealousy . . . I will move them to jealousy"—and jealousy
falling into collision with jealousy, there shall be destruction of
the unholy feeling and return to peace and concord. It is not so

in reality. As a piece of abstract philosophy it sounds well ; but jealousy does not cure jealousy in this sense. For a time a happy effect seems to accrue, but in the end the wickedness is deeper than before. Says God, They have set up in my place a not-god ;—that is the charge he brings against them, namely, that Israel worshipped a not-god. I will vex them with a people that are not a people : I will raise up compeers out of the dust, and rivals shall spring out of the dung-hill, and men who had no name shall stand up as children of renown. That homœo-pathic principle also failed. For a time it operated well : Israel began to look around, and to wonder at the mockery and humiliation ; but we may become accustomed to miracles, we may become so familiar with providences as to fail to observe them. Now God will be more energetic :—

" For a fire is kindled in mine anger, and shall burn unto the lowest hell [*sheol*, pit], and shall consume the earth with her increase, and set on fire the foundations of the mountains " (v. 22).

That will have no effect on sin. The terms do not co-ordinate. " Sin and hell " may be associated as crime and punishment, but never as crime and salvation. Punishment does not save, hell does not cure ; there is nothing in perdition, whatever that term may involve and imply, to bring the soul to penitence and for-giveness. A man comes out of a gaol a greater criminal than when he entered it, so far as the gaol is concerned. There is no light in darkness ; there is no pardon in law. Our God is a consuming fire ; not a soul in all the universe takes up its psalm to sing that God's wrath saved him or the fire of his judgment redeemed him. When gospel songs are sung they will be associated with grace rather than fire, burning, anger, hell, con-suming ; in these there is no gospel, in these there is no hope. The harvest is a heap, and a day of desperate sorrow is sent upon the earth, and men think they pray ; but lift off the pressure and they curse with a double energy.

" They shall be burnt with hunger, and devoured with burning heat, and with bitter destruction : I will also send the teeth of beasts upon them with the poison of serpents of the dust " (v. 24).

That is God's translation of the term sin. When he puts the term sin in equivalent terms of punishment, we begin to see what sin really is in the divine eyes. No man can interpret the

word sin. God himself fails to make it clear to human perception. The sinner cannot judge sin: he says it was a mistake, he
did not mean it; if more time had been given to him the error
never would have been committed; he meant to turn it to good
uses; he was tempted suddenly, his soul was not in it; now
that he sees its issue, he is sorry he began the process. So long
as we can talk of sin we cannot feel it. If we make of it a
matter of words, we shall make of it evaporation. He made the
most of sin who simply said whilst his eyes were piercing the
dust,—" God be merciful to me a sinner." He did not know
what he said as to all the fulness of its meaning; but our noblest
eloquence is forced out of us.

God will now send another punishment—namely, the " terror
within" (v. 25). That is worst of all. We can deal with any
force that is visible, measurable, and otherwise estimable as to
quality and energy; but who can fight a shadow? Who can
put down an army of fears? Who has weapons fine enough to
fight impalpable ghosts and shed blood where there is none?
We cannot account for the fear: the man lies there on his couch
visibly and talks with some degree of coherence; his eye has
in it no unsettledness, and his voice is as firm and resonant as
ever; but he has a fear in his heart: presently he will speak of
it; a great terror sits upon the throne of his reason; it is in
vain to laugh at the man, or mock him, or challenge him to high
and sober reasoning; on all subjects but one perhaps he is sane,
clear of mind, but at a certain point he breaks down and is no
more a man. We are fearfully and wonderfully made. Half
of the journey we gallop on steeds that cannot tire; and in one
moment we are thrown upon the ground and cannot move a
limb. The division between life and death is very frail; the
partition between genius and insanity can almost be seen through:
it is so thin that at any moment the mightiest man in society
may be unable to find his own door, to recognise his own
children, to return the common salutations of life. So God's
armoury is very large, made up of jealousies and provocations,
fires kindled in anger, fires that burn downwards as well as
upwards, fires that leap upon the foundations of the mountains
as hunger might leap upon food; and as for mischiefs, God piles
them up in heaps; and as for his arrows, he spends them upon

the wicked as a thunderstorm drenches the earth. Punishment has been exhausted. Where God has failed, let not man attempt to succeed.

Why did God withhold his hand and not carry punishment to extremity? The answer is here:—

"Were it not that I feared the wrath of the enemy, lest their adversaries should behave themselves strangely, and lest they should say, Our hand is high, and the Lord hath not done all this" (v. 27).

What is the meaning?—clearly, that God will not allow the enemy to suppose that evil providences are not under the control of God,—in other words, the enemy would arise and say, Do not quote the name of Jehovah in connection with the overthrow of this people: this is our doing; we have brought them to nought, we have humbled their pride, we have stained their vanity: they are under our control. This is a very delicate aspect of divine providence. God would punish his own sinning children more but for fear the enemy should put a false construction upon the penalty. The enemy is always ready to sacrifice unto his own net and drag, and to say how able he is, and altogether potent and good. Vice says,—I have put all these things where they are: I have thrown down the altar, I have burned the holy books, I have silenced the saintly men, all praying hosts I have driven into corners and scattered into stony places. God restrains himself lest the enemy should unduly boast. When we have seen judgments come upon people who have excited our dislike, we have been too prone to say, This comes of their having acted so towards us: we are really the occasion of all this humiliation and distress; these people ought to have behaved themselves better, then this disaster had not lightened upon them. God will have the case between himself and the sinner: he will not have external criticism, nor will he have men imagine that they are the fountain and origin of affliction. Men may be secondary causes: they may be instruments of the occasion; but affliction following crime of the heart is the direct angel and minister of God.

What charge does God bring against the people?

"For they are a nation void of counsel, neither is there any understanding in them" (v. 28).

The most difficult of all people to deal with. When people go beyond the line of remonstrance, counsel, entreaty, they become their own idolaters, and worshipping at their own altar they get no answers to their prayers. " Void of counsel "—too proud to receive advice, too self-contented to heed social criticism, too self-complacent to accept a hint from older and wiser men. You cannot deal with such people with any happy effect : there is nothing to work upon ; you have excellent seed, but they have no soil into which to receive it; nothing attaches itself to their mind : the mind has become a vacuity, it has lost its apprehensive power,—that is to say, its power of taking hold and profiting by that which is offered to it graciously and liberally; self-conceit has deposed the spirit of prayer, and self-contentment has rendered heaven unnecessary. " Neither is there any understanding in them "—they thought to be reasonable; and the very worship of reason always ends in its extinction. Reason must be fed by faith ; reason must eat out of the hand of God ; our understanding is not a self-perpetuating power, it also must wait among the servants of God.

Now comes a strain—a minor tone; almightiness whispers, the God of thunders lowers his voice, and says :—

"O that they were wise, that they understood this, that they would consider their latter end !" (v. 29).

O that there were something in them to take hold of—any living reason, any sensitive conscience, any religious aspiration, any one element that even kind and omniscient Heaven could find to begin with! How does God wish them to regard the present and the past ?—by considering their latter end. What is the literal meaning of these words ? That meaning may be taken as calling upon the people to consider their future, their destiny, the summing up and real meaning of things. Here and there in the Old Testament we get some dim hint of what in the New Testament is described as immortality. The blood of Abel cried from the ground. If we could have heard that cry in its articulateness, we should have heard in it some hint of another world—a place and time of settlement, justice, compensation, heaven, hell. "That they would consider their latter end !" look at things in their largeness, in their final meanings, in their bearing upon other spheres and aspects of life yet to be revealed. Thus we come back to spiritual thought, spiritual consideration, and spiritual life and fire. No man can treat any single day wisely who does not treat it in the spirit of eternity,—then he makes an isolated stone of the day : he does not regard it as a piece of an infinite temple. No man can use earth aright who is not religiously minded. The uses of prayer herein are subtle and far-reaching. No man can make a right bargain until he can pray once; he may be clever, momentarily profitable—so clever as to justify a secret laugh at the greenness of the man upon whom the felony has been perpetrated, but there is no fine gold in the issue : children will come up and search the bank for the gold, and find in the bank ashes where they expected to find golden treasure. When men " consider their latter end " wisely and healthily, the recollection has a happy effect upon the immediate business of the day; then the man says, I must meet this action further on, or my children must meet it. Time goes round; a great wheel is in perpetual circulation; harvest comes after seed-time. " Be not deceived ; God is not mocked : for whatsoever a man soweth that shall he also reap." He would be disappointed in the field if this were not so ; he shall not be disappointed in the larger field of life.

So the Bible is full of . solemn calls, noble and pathetic reflections, calling men to understanding, to the acceptance of counsel, to obedience and wisdom, and the consideration of the end of all things. Pagans exclaimed, Let us eat and drink, for to-morrow we die ! If so, it were a pity to put off death until to-morrow, for a man might " his own quietus make with a bare bodkin " to-day. Better die before meals than after them, if that be all. The Bible is conceived in another spirit ; the Bible utters another tone: the Bible asks us to eat and drink abundantly of spiritual provision ; and in asking us to think about eternity it does not relax our industry in any affair of time. The Bible says, in effect, He who studies most the subject of eternity best discharges the duty of the passing day ; he who prays best works best ; he who loves God most loves his neighbour as himself. The Bible will have no hand-painting or decoration of exteriors ; it will have the heart made right, the fountain of life cleansed, the tree itself made good at the very root and core; and then it says, the rest will follow in beauty of foliage, in ampleness and sweetness of fruit.

PRAYER.

Almighty God, thy way is not open to us that we may understand it. We know not what thou art doing day by day, but we know that when the days are all ended we shall say with thankfulness, He hath done all things well. Thou dost make disappointments help the soul's life; thus thou dost turn disappointed eyes to heaven. There is no land upon the earth we want when we have been trained to see thy purpose and to behold the things unseen; thou dost fill us with contempt for all time so short, for all space so small, for all earthly joy that plays its frivolous tune for one brief moment. We seek a country out of sight; we are strangers and pilgrims; our eyes are already beginning to look for a city which hath foundations, whose Builder and Maker is God. Thus thou dost train us. We have laid down all our childish entertainments and pleasures and mockeries, and we have laid down much beside, saying, Lo, heaven is not in these, nor is the sky of God in these small blessings. We know that what we want is beyond—beyond the smiling and the weeping, beyond the sowing and the reaping; it is not here. There lies a river between us and what we really need; thou wilt divide the water for us, and we shall pass through the channel as upon dry ground, and not know until we are upon the other side mingling our voices with heavenly music. Now and again thou dost show us somewhat of that land—in dream, in new and daring thought, in rapturous praise, in ecstatic prayer, in some unexpected power of contemplation, when all the heavens show themselves in symbol; then we begin to think somewhat of the upper place and the great reserve. We would use this to our encouragement and inspiration; we would not accept it as a reward for indolence, or a guarantee of self-indulgence, but as an impulse to make haste, and to be true and faithful and wise, waiting in all the dignity of patience for the Lord's coming, that the waiting and the coming may be of one quality—calm with the tranquillity of thine own throne. We are here for a day or two: we shall be dead and forgotten to-morrow; yet may we live in remembered deeds, in holy charities, in sacrifices acceptable unto God;—for this immortality we would now live. God's blessing be upon us, a plentiful light filling all the heavens and the earth, yet with no sense of burdensomeness. The Lord's great love be our defence and our hope, our present inspiration and our lasting reward.

This we say in the sweet name of Jesus—name to sinners dear—Son of man, Son of God, who loved us, and died for us, and gave himself the just for the unjust. His name is our prayer; his sacrifice is thy Amen.

Deut. xxxii.

"How should one chase a thousand, and two put ten thousand to flight, except their Rock had sold them, and the Lord had shut them up ?" (v. 30).

THE SONG OF MOSES.—*(Continued.)*

THIS is an appeal to reason, based upon obvious and indisputable facts. There is a law in warfare; there is a probability in battle, as in every other occupation and event of life. It is unreasonable and incredible that one man should chase a thousand and two men put ten thousand to flight. This must be accounted for. All the probabilities of the case are against the statement; the presumption is a violent one, and we must begin our argument by throwing it out : we must not have the imagination shocked by such a startling contrast of numbers. It is simply impossible that any one man should chase a thousand men, though they be the veriest cowards; their very numbers should give them courage; in a throng there should be some measure of audacity. How, then, is this chasing to be accounted for? The answer is :—"Except their Rock had sold them, and the Lord had shut them up "—in other words, except their Rock had given them over to the enemy, had taken out of them whatever courage might naturally belong to them, and had thus shown that, when the religious passion goes down and the religious intelligence is insulted, even natural bravery turns to helpless cowardice. With the ancient history we have next to nothing to do, but with the moral which inspires it every man ought to feel himself concerned. Why are we driven before the wind ? Why do apparently little oppositions cast us down, or fill us with great dismay, or drive us from our standing-ground? Physically we are numerous, and physically we are not without strength, and some little time ago we were not destitute of courage; how comes our present state, and what is the explanation of it ? We have lost faith ; we have gone down in spiritual quality ; we have inverted our prayers, so that they no longer ascend to a welcoming heaven but descend to an unanswering or mocking earth. Failure is to be attributed often to loss of religious faith, loss of communion with God, loss of spiritual inspiration. How to account for the failures that are upon the right hand and upon the left—not failures from the beginning, which may

be attributed to some freak of nature in the constitution of the
individuals who are defeated, but failures coming after victory,
the course of a lifetime turned upside down, the once-victors now
suppliants for their fate ;—these are the mysteries. Some men
are from the beginning without hands or eyes or faculties : whatever they touch they touch at the wrong end, and whatever they
look upon withers under their glance ; we are not speaking of
such now : they are mysteries in providence which we cannot
explain, riddles to which we have no answer ; but here are
men who have fought and conquered, who have spoken with
their enemies in the gate, and sent them reeling back in
dismay and pitiful weakness,—now, the same men are fleeing a
thousand before one and ten thousand before two ! Watching
the incredible anomaly, we ask, How can these things be? The
answer comes from heaven : They are faithless men, they have
taken to the worship of themselves ; they must be allowed to test
their own vanity, and try the new gods with new conditions.
God does give men up ; God does sell men to the enemy, and
shut them up in a corner and turn the key upon them as if they
were left in prison. Strange things does God do among the
children of men ! He will not be mocked ; we cannot do so well
without him as we do with him. If we think we can demon-
strate our independence of him, he may let go his hold and leave
us to run swiftly into destruction. Do not mock God. Have
your solemn questionings, and now and then it may be your
dark doubts ; but let there be no self-conceit, no offering to
personal vanity, no self-confidence, no mockery of God ; when
the mind is dazzled, rest awhile : after three days some capable
Ananias may call upon you with answers from heaven.

The mystery is increased by another consideration :—

"For their rock is not as our Rock, even our enemies themselves being
judges" (v. 31).

This verse admits of a new setting as to its meaning. It is
taken thus by one of the most eminent Jewish commentators,
namely : "Their rock is not as our Rock, and yet they have become
our judges"—they are following the wrong course, and yet they
are exalted above us, and they judge our life, and they condemn
us, and they drive us away from their judgment-seat in contempt

and scorn ; this is a miracle in philosophy, this is an impossibility in morals ; their rock is not as our Rock, and yet somehow they have ascended the judgment-seat, and we turn pale before their tribunal and humbly receive the sentence of their scorn.   These inversions of natural courses have to be acounted for.   We are not at liberty to allow history to perpetrate infinite jests, and to taunt us with incredible ironies.   There must be harmony in history ; there must be in it a tendency—a central line, always moving onward with nobleness and majesty of revelation and purpose ; much that is incidental and. temporary may associate itself with that line but must fall into the harmony of the central movement. But here is an instance which cannot be accounted for on any ordinary principles.   Here are people with the wrong god and the wrong law and the wrong policy, and somehow they are on the judgment-seat, and men who have the right theology in sentiment and the right law in the letter stand before them like doomed culprits.

Or take it in the other or more common way :—"For their rock is not as our Rock, even our enemies themselves being judges."   We have the larger providence, we are under a more benevolent dispensation than themselves, our God is abler than their god ; they acknowledge this, and though this acknowledgment is made to us in theory, yet in practice they seem to have the best of it : they are at home, they are in prosperity, they stand in the midst of their vineyards, they make their bread of the kidneys of wheat, whilst we are strangers and exiles and wanderers.   We have the right God, but we are suffering under an afflictive providence.   Let it be so anyhow, if only men will think.   There is hope of any man who feels an arresting hand upon his shoulder and hears in his ear an accusatory voice, and who asks questions upon the arrest and the accusation : he is dead, but not " twice dead ; " he is withered, but not " plucked up by the roots ; " he is as a felled tree, but still here and there are signs of sprouting : he yet may fully live.   Let every man ask himself how it is that he can have a right theology, and a right Church, and the very book of God, and yet be mocked of the enemy, chased by straws that are driven by the wind, and made afraid by withered leaves that crinkle on the ground.   The reason is religious.   There is something wrong at the centre ; every accident seems to be right, but the central life is wrong.

"For their vine is of the vine of Sodom, and of the fields cf Gomorrah: their grapes are grapes of gall, their clusters are bitter : their wine is the poison of dragons, and the cruel venom of asps " (vv. 32-33).

This is perversion; this is the embittering of God's sweetness ; this is what is meant by the light that is in a man becoming darkness. Israel has spoiled the vine, Israel has turned wine of heaven into poison, Israel has made productive fields barren as the ashes of Gomorrah. This always lies within our power. We can dwarf the Church, we can prostitute the altar, we can make the sweetest things the bitterest. This corrupting, pestilential power seems to belong to the man who was made in the image and likeness of God. We can so treat the Church as to hate it ; we can so worship ourselves, our vanity, our ability, our love of so-called progress, that we can only go back to the altar to spit upon it, and to the ministers of God to call them liars. This possibility is quite within the compass of our faculty ; the heart can perform this astounding and iniquitous miracle. Israel performed it in the wilderness, and men are performing it with awful repetition to-day.

So the song rolls on, speaking of vengeance, speaking of the enemies of God, and promising them an awful reward. When the song was ended :—

"Moses came and spake all the words of this song in the ears of the people, he, and Hoshea the son of Nun" (v. 44).

He will die like old Jacob with a blessing upon his lips; but practically he ceases here. The legislator has become the poet, and in song he seems to die. He must bless the young and bless the future : he must assume the prophetic mantle and become an Elijah before the time ; but the history would seem to end here at the forty-third verse, and to be continued by the hand of Joshua, or by the hand of some scribe unknown. Now Moses is told to go up into the Mount Abarim and Mount Nebo :—"And die in the mount whither thou goest up." And a reason is given :—

"Because ye trespassed against me among the children of Israel at the waters of Meribah-Kadesh, in the wilderness of Zin; because ye sanctified me not in the midst of the children of Israel" (v. 51).

Do not misunderstand these words. These words represent the

conception of ignorance. This is an after-thought by which the so-called premature death of Moses is to be accounted for; but the event as it stands here is out of analogy with the whole current and flow of the story, as if it could be accepted just as it here appears, it would throw infinite discredit upon all that had gone before. We want to be clever above that which is written, and so we will account for the decease of Moses before he enters the promised land. We are fond of attributing evil motives to men : it suits us to trace their death to their particular sin. Does the case stand thus—that all the people are to go into the promised land, but Moses is not, because Moses once ascended a hill and struck a rock, or was once or twice impatient? It is impossible. The whole people behaved so respectably, so virtuously, and so decorously, that they were permitted to go into the promised land, but their veteran leader was cut off—a sinner buried in the mountains, because he struck a rock or uttered an impatient word ! Does God thus acknowledge "respectability"? Israel ancient and modern has been doing little but wrong all the way through. Moses has lived a life of suffering and of prayer, of communion with God, and has displayed meekness beyond the meekness of any other man that ever lived ; on no shoulders up to his time have such burdens been laid ; never was human temper or patience so tried : and is all the multitude of evil-doers, mockers, scorners, worshippers of false gods, to go into the promised land and leave Moses a culprit buried without consecration, interred without acknowledgment of service, left to rot in a place unknown ? This cannot be : God cannot deny himself. Moses was the only man who would have been dis satisfied with the promised land. He had been so trained, chastened, enriched in mind, sanctified in heart, that to have led him into Canaan would be to lead him into an unutterable disappointment. What was Canaan ? even if a fruitful field, it was but a field that was fruitful. If the eyes of Moses had seen Canaan, and his feet had trod the soil, surely his heart would have died within him for very vexation. No Moses ever gets to Canaan on earth. He is trained by its promise : he is so trained that the promise drops out of his vision whilst a larger scene glows upon it and a nobler issue challenges the imagination. We are promised great wealth; and when we are young we

count the gold, and hear the music of its chink, and say what we
will do with it when it falls into our hands; the days pass on,
life reveals itself, we see what a tragedy is operating at the
heart of things—what intolerable agony is burning at the core
like an unnamed hell; we then enlarge in mind, we become
elevated in thought, we hear voices and see sights, and have our
attention struck by revelations hitherto unapprehended, and as
we grow in the upward and spiritual direction all our young
dreams vanish, and we see what may be : the stars are what
we want, the heavens conceal our estate,—the only inheritance
worth living for, worth dying for, is an inheritance of holiness,
capability for higher service, communion face to face with God.
As for others, let them have the gold : they are mean enough to
seize it, poor enough to need it; they never read the grander
books, they never peruse the deeper revelation, they never hear
the ineffable music; lead them forth, let them devour the pasture,
and die of grossness.   Offer Canaan to Moses !   Our training has
done nothing for us if it has not made us so rich in thought as
to cause the earth to dwindle into a handful of soil not worth
taking up.   This is the end of Christian training; this is the
meaning of all Christian chastening.   But when we are called
upon to account for Moses not seeing Canaan, we begin to say,
What did he do ?—True, he once struck a rock ; true, he once
gave some signs of impatience; but really now we think of it
we can count his sins upon our fingers, but they must have been
greater sins than we thought of at the time : he was not allowed
to go into Canaan, therefore the sins must have been very great
indeed.   This is very much like us : it is marked by our lean
charity, it is characterised by our shallow judgment.   Though
the speech is attributed to God, and put as it were into his very
lips, it is the conception of the man who wrote it—the after-
thought of the historian.   We are emboldened to say this
because of all the previous history.   If sin could disqualify a
man for entrance into Canaan, then not a man in all the host
ought ever to have seen the promised land.   But Moses was
trained for the true Canaan—the Jerusalem that is above.   He
repeats the experience of Abraham : when Abraham came to a
land flowing with milk and honey he said he would not have
it ; he did not want it ; it was a paltry reward and no dis-

appointment worth speaking of; said the old traveller, I seek a country out of sight ; give me all the earth, and I will throw it away, all the rivers, and pastures, and vineyards, and wheat-fields, and I will present them to a child—a toy to play with, a confection to suck ; I want heaven—all heaven ; I want the eternal God.   So the righteous are taken away from the evil to come : the righteous are taken away from disappointment. They want to see their families all " comfortably settled,"—that is to say, all so beautifully settled as to have nothing to do. They want to see their sons come to manhood, and all the education of their children completed, and their houses set forth without a purpose and without a faculty ; they will work and slave night and day that the eldest sons may have ten thousand more, and that some daughter may be saved from " stooping " to work.   An evil purpose !   A vicious cruelty !   If you leave every child you have a million sterling, but with no taste for work, with a sense of indignity attaching to all labour, you cannot put him into a hotter hell on earth.   You meant it well :   it was pleasing to think that the boys would have nothing to do and that the girls would be enclosed in a garden of flowers ; there is no such garden under the blue heavens, and there is no difficulty greater than to get over an evil training.   And sometimes our purpose is good, it is a healthy purpose : we will see certain works completed, certain columns built right up to the last shaping point ; we will see certain institutions thoroughly founded and brought into noble and beneficent working order : then having seen all this accomplished, we shall be satisfied.   God does not allow us to see even these sacred issues : he says, I can do without you ; you have been faithful, now you must enter heaven and look upon some things from above.   We wonder why the good man was not permitted to live ten years longer to have seen all the reward of his labour upon earth ; it is a mean wonder, an unworthy surprise.   We wonder that the good man was not kept ten years longer in prison, ten years longer in banishment, ten years longer in weakness ; but let us magnify the mercy of God that sent an angel down in the night-time, shook the foundations of the prison, and led out his servant into liberty and rest.

PRAYER.

ALMIGHTY GOD, thou art our Father, though Abraham be ignorant of us; thou didst not in saving man take on thee the nature of angels, thou didst take upon thee the seed of Abraham; thou didst come in the image and likeness of man, which is in very deed the image and likeness of God. When thou didst so come unto us we knew thee not, for thou wert as one of ourselves, kindred in quality, the same in speech, neighbourly, friendly, social, so that we spoke of thy brethren and thy sisters, thy father and thy mother. We did not know the meaning of our own speech; we could not tell what we said, but we felt that our speech and thy vision were in contradiction; we felt thy greatness. When we did but touch the hem of thy garment we knew that thou wert more than man—than any man known to us—and we ourselves called thee Immanuel: God with us; near us, part of us, one with us; a great mystery of life, an eternal problem, not the less an eternal blessing. We thank thee for all religious thought; we bless thee that the altar elevates whomsoever touches it; we thank thee that we cannot look downward whilst we are thinking of God and the future, truth and immortality, development, and heaven; then the mind kindles; then our nature puts forth its wings and flies up to the gate of the morning and the dwelling-place of the sun, and we love the light and sing in it as birds do. May we always be faithful to the altar, may our inquiry go deeper and deeper every day, and may our love burn until perfectly disinfected of all selfishness and earthliness and limitation, until it become a great flame, aspiring in continual hope and sacrifice to the very throne of God. We bless thee for all Christian fellowship, for communion in Christ Jesus, that we can speak through him and with him, that he is our Advocate and Intercessor: our Priest, eloquent through his own blood, mighty through the weakness of the Cross, the greater for us because so pained in Gethsemane and unable to save himself on Calvary. The Lord send the mysteries of the Cross into our hearts as songs without words, great inspirations, deep and holy comfortings. Amen.

Deut. xxxiii.

THE DISTRIBUTION OF BLESSINGS.

MOSES cannot die. We have been told about his approaching death again and again; but he cannot yet be released. He has just been singing his great song, and now he is about to

utter a blessing worthy of its doctrine and music ; and whether
he will yet die, who can tell ? He does not die hard, in any
severe and arbitrary sense of that term ; instead of dying, he
seems to live more, to double his vitality, and to cause his
energy to express itself in song and benediction. To become a
poet is not to die. To rise up into the stature and majesty of a
priest is not to lie down and expire as an incident on the way to
oblivion. We must follow this man further. If men can die as
dogs die, why these songs, these blessings, these earnest solici-
tudes about the future ? No dog sings ; no dog utters benedictions. What dog cares for the future of the world ? There
cannot be a hand so cruel as to crush Moses after such a song
and such a series of beatitudes. There are some lives we
cannot kill : they are so great, so capable, so full of sacred
mystery, so near being something higher, that to touch them,
except with reverence, is itself an act of profanity. We cannot
reason about this, or be cross-examined as to mere process of
argument : we feel it, we know it ; we should contradict our own
instincts and every quality that constitutes manhood were we to
deny it. We thought Moses was about to die like an unforgiven
criminal. Against this doctrine we have just protested with
vehemence. It would be impossible. If there be two things in
which it is impossible for God to lie, it is impossible for the God
of justice to speak to Moses as a criminal. Whatever may have
been written on the margin by some unskilled or malicious hand,
and whatever may have been transferred from the margin into
the body of the text, all nature, all justice, all truth says : Moses
must not die on the ground of being a criminal. Such an assumption would prove too much or too little. Surely we cannot be
allowed to part with Moses under some charge and impeachment
of sin ? We recover our composure. Justice herself, with grave
face, smiles a sweet contentment as we read the words—"Moses
the man of God " (v. 1). We were in great sorrow when we
read about his sin and his being ordered to Abarim because he
had sinned at the waters of Meribah-Kadesh, in the wilderness
of Zin. Our heart said " *No !* " We may not be prepared with
a critical or grammatical answer, but we have an answer older
than all criticism and all grammar—the answer of a just instinct.
Now we read of Moses as " the man of God." That term was

never applied to any man before. It will be applied to another
prophet as we advance in the perusal of the sacred records; but
to Moses alone, at this moment, is the term applied—and it fits
him well; it is a grace he seems to have earned, a crown he
seems to have won. "The man of God"—the man loving God,
trusting God, knowing God, communing much and tenderly in
solitary wastes and heights with God—the one man to whom God
has spoken, as it were, face to face, and almost looked him into
a kind of inferior deity, so grandly did his face burn and shine
after long interviews in solitude with God. This is right; this is
in harmony with all the story; the great rhythmic movement
concludes itself in this solemn and majestic tone.

"—The man of God blessed the children of Israel." Rights
come with character. The man of God has a right to bless; and
men recognise in him an undisputed dignity, and look to him as
a lower fountain and origin of blessing. Who has not longed for
certain men to touch them? Who has not desired to pluck the
good man's gown and share his smile? Who would not have
had one look from men whose names are immortal in all purest
honour and goodness? To have spent a day with them would
have been an education; to have heard their utterance of the
mother-tongue would have been an epoch never to be forgotten.
Great character carries with it great rights. There is a primacy
of character; there is a throne which is never begrudged to goodness. The blessing does not read like the utterance of a man
who is about to die from sheer weakness and exhaustion. There
is no sign of intellectual decay here; the moral flavour is as
delicate as ever, the penetration as keen, the tone as firm. This
is not dying; it is passing on to greater spheres and nobler
service. For death, in any inclusive and final sense, to come
after this blessing would be an irony which imagination could
not tolerate and which justice never could permit.

Let us look at the blessing as a whole. We need blessing.
We have been so long in want of rain, it will do us good to go
out and stand with uncovered head in the plentiful shower—so
soft, so gentle, so impartial as to blessing, yet so discriminating
as to its apportionment. All men could not receive the *same*
blessing. A general "God bless thee!" would have amounted
to nothing; or even some studied and pompous form of benedic-

tion, given with uplifted hands and priestly attitude and voice, would have been a gift unappreciated. It is a singular fact in human constitution that all men could not receive the same blessing—that is to say, what is a blessing to one man is not a blessing to another. Let us thank God that such is the case. It is in this way that variety becomes not only permissible but infinitely desirable, and even inevitable. The discourse which blesses one man has no music in it to another; neither is the discourse to be blamed, nor is the man to be blamed : there was no relation between the two things brought for one unhappy moment into connection. Give a landscape to a blind man! Would you blame the landscape? Would you blame the blind man because of want of appreciation? It is not a blessing to the blind man : he could not receive it. What does the blind man want? Believing that none could ask that question but God, he says, "Lord, that I might receive my sight!" Give him vision, and even partial darkness will be an opening heaven to his rejoicing and grateful heart. The earth is not equally appreciated in all its parts and distributions of clime and production. Some could hasten through a garden. There are men so made that they could walk faster through a garden than through a market-place. They could not receive the blessing which another quality of soul could receive. Some ears hear nothing in the bird-song and the bird-language but noise ; they would slay the winged singers! Some men never lift their heads up to see how big the sky is. If they turn to the sky it is to forecast the weather, not to read the writing of God upon the blue beauty. So all men could not receive the same blessing or an inclusive blessing ; there must be discrimination, allotment, individualisation; that we find in this great utterance of the dying Moses.

All men can receive *some* blessing. Let us thank God for that, otherwise some things in nature and life would go without appreciation. There are men so constituted that they want nothing but innumerable insects to gather, to classify, to name, and to study. They must have their portion in Israel ; and God has plentifully endowed them with resources, blessed be his gracious name! He sends none away empty. If men would possess themselves, intellectually and scientifically, of stars,

worlds, planets, God feeds them at a plentiful table ! when they
have satisfied themselves for the moment, they are filled with
a knowledge that they have not begun to know the building of
God.   We must provide for the constitution and capacity of every
man.   Every man must find something in the Church for himself,
set down, as it were, by the hand of God directly and immediately
for his appropriation.   This is the sublime possibility of the
sanctuary.   The weary man here finds rest, or hears of it, and
in hearing of it dying hopes are rekindled and failing strength
begins to take heart again.   The man of sorrow wants healing.
Alas ! all men are more or less men of sorrow : every heart has
its own wound, every life its own pain, every spirit its own tears.
Such men must be blessed ; and they can be plentifully blessed
only in the house of God : every stone of it was put up for such
men ; the whole sanctuary was roofed in for their security, and
the whole book of revelation and all the noble psalms, written,
by inspired men, are so many contributions made to the healing
and the comforting of men of sorrow—now a great light for the
intellect, now a tender tone for the hearing sated with the noises
of the world, now a royal, soldierly exhortation to duty, service,
sacrifice—a trumpet-blast which soldiers answer with a life of
fire.   Every man has a blessing in Israel—a special blessing,
addressed, as it were, individually and exclusively to his very
soul.   Blessed are they who seize the benediction and live upon it !

The distinct appropriateness of some blessings is a proof of the
possible appropriateness of others.   Here and there we can join
the line and say,—This we know to be appropriate ; and therefore the benedictions which we cannot follow in the letter may be
equally appropriate could we as fully comprehend them.   Levi
has been a mystery to us all the way through.   He has had no
land ; he has been unlike his brethren ; he has been, so to say,
the praying man of the ever-changing company, busying himself
about sacrifices and law, and all manner of religious ceremony
and instruction.   What can he have ?   Can Moses fit him with a
blessing ?   Read verses 8-11 :—

"And of Levi he said, Let thy Thummim and thy Urim be with thy holy
one, whom thou didst prove at Massah, and with whom thou didst strive at
the waters of Meribah ; who said unto his father and to his mother, I have
not seen him ; neither did he acknowledge his brethren, nor knew his own

children : for they have observed thy word, and kept thy covenant. They shall teach Jacob thy judgments, and Israel thy law : they shall put incense before thee, and whole burnt sacrifice upon thine altar. Bless, Lord, his substance, and accept the work of his hands: smite through the loins of them that rise against him, and of them that hate him, that they rise not again."

Could any blessing be more exquisitely adapted to Levi as we know him from history than this peculiar benediction ? Levi is commended to God because he had not known his father, or his mother, or acknowledged his brethren, or known his own children, because he was so absorbed in his work. This is the Christian call before the time. This is the dawn, white and tender, trembling and quivering in the far-away east of time ; the fulness of this light we shall find in Christ's own day, and in Christ's own speech—" Follow me ; and let the dead bury their dead ; " " If any man come to me, and hate not his father, and mother, and wife, and children, and brethren, and sisters, yea, and his own life also, he cannot be my disciple." Levi in a sense had done this, and Levi is to have the great blessing ; the Urim and the Thummim are to be with the holy one for ever—Light and Perfection, glory and peace, radiance and security. As for what substance he has—Lord, bless it, and he shall have enough and to spare ; his loaves are but five in number, break them with thine own hands, and he will call " Halt ! for my hunger is satisfied." When we do come upon a divine explanation of a divine mystery, it is so clear, so complete, so profound and satisfying that we can with ineffable comfort pass on to the next mystery of which no explanation has been given, knowing that God could explain that enigma were it right that the riddle should be read.

Look for a moment at the unenvied blessings of some men. When Jacob came to Joseph the speech rolled from him like a river ; the old man did not know how eloquent he was until the name of Joseph came to his lips. We have perused that great speech of old Israel, and found it to be like a garden of delights, a fountain in the wilderness,—a surprise to the man who uttered it as well as to the man who received it. Moses almost quotes the blessing, yet he varies it ; for when was love ever short or the inventive faculty of adding new colour and new tone to the utterance of her homage ? " And of Joseph he said "—then flows the river :—

"And of Joseph he said, Blessed of the Lord be his land, for the precious things of heaven, for the dew, and for the deep that coucheth beneath, and for the precious fruits brought forth by the sun, and for the precious things put forth by the moon, and for the chief things of the ancient mountains, and for the precious things of the lasting hills, and for the precious things of the earth and fulness thereof, and for the good will of him that dwelt in the bush : let the blessing come upon the head of Joseph, and upon the top of the head of him that was separated from his brethren. His glory is like the firstling of his bullock, and his horns are like the horns of unicorns : with them he shall push the people together to the ends of the earth : and they are the ten thousands of Ephraim, and they are the thousands of Manasseh" (vv. 13-17).

Who can read the blessing with music expressive and tender enough ? It must be looked at ; we should profane it by vocally repeating it. A man should graduate for a lifetime in the utterance of words, in the balancing of emphasis, before he attempts to read this speech addressed to the name of Joseph. The man himself is not here, but his name stands for progeny, a posterity, a whole family of men, the world over and time through. Nothing is to be kept from this man :—

"Blessed of the Lord be his land, for the precious things of heaven, for the dew, and for the deep that coucheth beneath, and for the precious fruits brought forth by the sun, and for the precious things put forth by the moon" (vv. 13-14).

He dreamed of the sun and the moon and the stars long, long ago, and saw them in a spirit of homage. Let the sun shine for him, and let the moon pour her gentle beams upon sea and land for him, and let all things that grow gather themselves into sheaves that he may carry them in his bosom ; let his glory be like the firstling of the bullock, and his horns be like the horns of the unicorn (v. 17). Only God has such blessings to give. To no earthly treasure-house does this man come for Joseph, but to heaven ; and does heaven contain anything too good for him ? And none envied his blessings. Men felt it to be right. When the portions were given out, men felt that this man had that which was right. Not one cried out saying : "That is too much for any one man ; make the distribution more equal ; do not create favouritism in Israel." There are times when men feel that compensation must be paid, when old wrongs come into the memory as so many prompters, saying, "You remember me ; you cannot have forgotten my ghastliness ; your recollection must

vividly recall the night of revenge and cruelty, and the day of
sale and expatriation." And when all these black memories
crowd upon the soul, and we hear some great, royal, priestly
voice outside pronouncing blessing upon blessing, piling mountain
upon mountain, we say, " It is right : let it be done ; God save
the king !" There is a spirit in man, and the inspiration of the
Almighty giveth him understanding. Blessed are they whose
trust is in the living God, for they shall in due time see the result
of all their labour, and be comforted with tenderest and divinest
solaces.

So every man in Israel had his blessing. Reuben was to have
innumerable men ; the voice of Judah was to be blessed as God
might bless an instrument of music ; Levi was to have the
continual presence of the Thummim and the Urim ; Gad was to
be liberated from the mountains of Gilead, and to have great
liberty ; and all the children of Israel were to have a blessing
adapted to the circumstances of each.

In blessing men we take nothing from God. When all the
blessings were given, the poet-prophet said :—

"There is none like unto the God of Jeshurun, who rideth upon the heaven
in thy help, and in his excellency on the sky. The eternal God is thy refuge,
and underneath are the everlasting arms ; and he shall thrust out the enemy
from before thee; and shall say, Destroy them " (vv. 26-27).

More blessing is left than is given. Giving doth not impoverish
God. His sun, running his daily course, is as bright after he has
kissed all the lands with light, as he was when he first came to
begin the glowing task of the day. The sun is not wasted ; when
he dips in the western water, he dips with a promise that he will
be back again soon. We may nod a moment and get ourselves
ready to behold the vision, because before we can well close our
eyes he will be up again, making the east white and glistening.
There is no end to the divine blessing. " Ho, every one that
thirsteth, come ye to the waters !" and when you have slaked
your thirst, the fountain will seem to abound the more for the
water which you have withdrawn : there will be more at the end
than at the beginning. " Prove me now herewith, saith the Lord
of hosts, if I will not open you the windows of heaven, and pour
you out a blessing, that there shall not be room enough to receive
it." As the ancient beneficiary cried out, " I have no more

vessels, let the oil be stayed," so now it is man who gives in, it is never God who is exhausted.

But there are always interstices—crevices that may have been left without a blessing ; provision must be made for that possibility, so we conclude with a general blessing. Now, here is a shower that will fill everything up, leaving no cavity without its benefaction :—

" Happy art thou, O Israel : who is like unto thee, O people saved by the Lord, the shield of thy help, and who is the sword of thy excellency! and thine enemies shall be found liars unto thee ; and thou shalt tread upon their high places " (v. 29).

This is the general benediction, the great comforting word that rolls like a river over the whole life of Israel.

Are we blessed ? Have we each some blessing, great or small, all our own—a blessing of hope, of contentment, of aspiration, of reverent inquiry, of sure confidence in God ? Do we read the Bible as if it had been written expressly, and this very moment, for us, for our guidance, stimulus, comfort and reward ? If so, we are blessed with blessings. What is the Christian blessing ? It may be mentioned in one word—a word which is often misunderstood, because too narrowly defined. The Christian blessing is Peace : " Peace I leave with you, my peace I give unto you : not as the world giveth, give I unto you " —the peace of God, which passeth all understanding, the peaceful peace, the tranquil calm, the sabbatic rest, the peace of God. Do not neglect the true meaning of that word peace ; it is an inclusive term, it involves reconciliation—the harmonisation of the nature of man with the nature of God, the cessation of rebellion, the acceptance, upon divine terms, of pardon ; it means the Cross, in all the typical eloquence of its blood, in all the unbeclouded splendour of its eternal glory. " Acquaint now thyself with him, and be at peace." O that we had hearkened unto his law, then had our peace flowed like a river !

PRAYER.

ALMIGHTY GOD, thou hast given a voice unto the morning and a voice unto the evening. May we have understanding thereof, and know what thou art speaking to us by the rising light and by the departing sun; may all things round about us teach somewhat of thy providence and thy sovereignty, and may we receive the simple and tender lesson into an opening and responding heart. We all do fade as a leaf. We are cut down like the grass and are mown down like the flowers of the field. Thou dost give unto thy beloved sleep; thou sayest unto thy servants who have faithfully served thee, Well done! To dying eyes thou dost show the crown of righteousness gleaming through the deepening cloud. We bless thee for all thy care—so minute, so continual, so grand in patience, so ineffably careful and loving. We bless thee that thy hand is upon us, and behind us, and before us, and round about us, that we live and move and have our being in God. Let thy merciful presence come near us—a shining light, a glowing warmth in the heart, a speech of benediction, a token of heavenly deliverance and glory. We have come to praise thee for all the mercies of the passing time. The hours have been full of thy love, the ages have been alight with symbols of thy presence; our whole life lifts itself up in fearless testimony, and each Christian believer becomes a witness to the mighty power, the redeeming efficacy, of the blood of Jesus Christ. May we grow in the knowledge of our Saviour. We have not begun to know him; his riches are unsearchable; he cannot be found out unto perfection; he allures us onward, upward, heavenward; and by many a token he shows how near he is, and then he rises above our touch, and asks us to follow on. May we not be disobedient unto the heavenly vision, but rather arise and do God's bidding with all love, with the energy of both hands, with the consent of the whole man. We own our sin, but when we bring to bear upon it the omnipotence of thy Cross, behold, where sin abounds grace doth much more abound, and is not to be heard of, because of the wonderful ministry of Christ. Blessed Saviour of the world, thou hast destroyed sin; thou hast beheld Satan fall like lightning out of heaven, and all his power is under thy foot, and the world is thine, and the whole earth, and thine the fulness of the sea; and all is hastening towards reconcilement and unity, completeness of homage and unbrokenness of service: the mouth of the Lord hath spoken it, and none may set aside his oath or destroy the divine covenant. As surely as thou dost live, the whole earth shall be covered with the glory of heaven. This is our hope, and this our confidence, and this our joy. We think of it until our heart burns within us, and we know that surely thou wilt hasten it in thy time, and we shall then see the meaning of light, the very glory of day. What we want, or what we need most, thou knowest. Thou understandest us altogether; our whole heart is laid bare before thee, like an open page, and thine eye can see the secret springs of our thought. Grant unto us some assurance that our emptiness shall be filled up, that our desire shall be construed into a sacred prayer and answered with largest blessing; may our aspirations be regarded as uttering the necessities of the soul, at least in hint, how feeble soever, and may they return upon us with great benedictions. Thou art shortening our days, thou art limiting our opportunities of doing good, thou art pointing us to the descending sun, and telling us that the day is swiftly speeding to its close; may we work in the light, for the night cometh when no man can work; may we walk as children of the day and not of the night— children of light, who are ashamed of darkness rather than afraid of it, and who glory in being sons of God, in purpose, in uppermost desire, how far short soever we fall in actual execution and realisation. We bless thee for this hope, for this inspiration, for this resolve; these are the miracles of God, these are the triumphs of grace; we praise thee for them as for good and perfect gifts of God. We pray for all whom we ought never to forget: for those who do not pray for themselves; for self-idolaters; for those who are their own confidence and strength, and who know not that their strength is in heaven and not upon earth; for the spiritually blind and deaf and dumb; for prodigals, wandering in the darkness and reaping nothing but its blackness; for all loved ones in trouble, perplexity, or sore straits; for all who travel by sea and land; for all who are in great crises of life, full of pain, or full of hope that becomes almost agony, because of its uncertainty; the Lord grant unto such all needful succour, tender blessing, ministry of grace; and lead them on still day by day, until the end nears and the meaning seems clearer to the mind. We give thee all we are and have— ourselves, our families, our houses, our businesses, our whole life. Lord, come thou, whose right it is, and reign over us all, that we may, in obedient love, do homage before thee night and day, and express the homage of our minds by the industry and sacrifice of our hands.

This prayer we pray, as we pray all our prayers and sing all our hymns, in the sweet name of the Son of Mary, Son of man, Son of God, God the Son—the Word made flesh. Amen.

Deut. xxxiv.

NILE AND NEBO.

IT is a long way from the Nile to Nebo—a long way, not in mere distance geographical, but in experience, in trial, in work, in suffering—in all that goes to make up the sum total of the mystery of human life. It is well for us to have opposite points, that we may sometimes look at the one and at the other, at the beginning and at the intermediate end: and so measure off life in great sections, and consider it well, as if it were an entirety between the two points. Thus we set up judgment-seats, and form exact moral estimates of what we are and what we have done; and thus we hasten on to the day of audit and final and irrevocable settlement. If Moses could have seen the whole at one view, could he have lived? No man can see God and live: can any man see his own life, in all the minuteness of its detail, in every throb of pain, in every streak of blood, in every strife of battle, and go through it? Would not the sight kill him? Would it not become a burden which he could not sustain, from which he would shrink in utmost terror and despair, saying, I cannot undertake it; let me die, and not live? Thus God is the supreme mystery. But there are mysteries under his being which help to illustrate its profoundness and its majesty. We ourselves are mysteries, and life is an invisible wonder, and is dealt out to us a moment at a time, for who of us could be entrusted with a whole week together? Our breath is in our nostrils; the little light that is in our eye is but a flash upon the surface, and may pass in a moment. Our life is but a vapour which cometh for a little time, and then passeth away. The vision is shown little by little—just one circumstance at a time; and we cannot take up the next loop along with the present loop: we must knit patiently, tediously, a loop at a time, taking up all the allotted thread until our portion of work is completed. Let us study our own life in the light of this suggestion. Let any man who has lived—not merely existed—any man who has had to struggle for life, to fight for bread, to scheme with all cunningness of thought that he might maintain his foothold upon the land,—compare the first point of his recollection with his present position, and then say whether he would like to do all the battling over again, and endure all the suffering once more; or say whether it would be possible to live the whole life in one day's agony. This is God's way of educating us. This is the way against which we chafe and kick, as men might kick against pricks: so we bruise ourselves, and let our life ooze out in blood, instead of accepting the method, saying, We brought nothing into this world, nor did we ask to come into it: but loyally, with fulness of homage, we submit to thy way in the world, reading all its books one by one, gathering up what little store of wisdom it may hold; and at the end, not now, we can pronounce our opinion upon it. Every man who has lived a varied, eventful, struggling life is himself a miracle. Let him soberly think over the case—where he began, where he has for the moment ended; let him compare the Nile with the Nebo, and say whose handiwork is displayed in all the figure of life—who drew that geometry, who coloured that picture, who brought all those innumerable lines into focus and final meaning. The individual lines appear to be simple enough, little and short enough to have sometimes next to nothing in them; then they become related, mutually attached and reciprocal in influence and in colour. Behold how the miracle expands and brightens, until standing before it we say,—Surely this is God's handiwork; all this looks like what we behold in wondrous nature; there is unity here, shape, meaning; presently we shall hear voices in this temple, and own our life-sanctuary to be the house of God.

Could we see life as a whole, would it be worth living? No man can answer that question, because having lived it we answer it with our experience, not with our imagination. Still, the question is not without keenest interest. Could we see the whole, is life worth living? It is often a weary experience, a keen disappointment, a reaping with blunt sickles in fields that grow nothing but darkness; the morning brings its hope, and night never fails to come with its disappointment; in the morning good resolutions nerve the little strength, and at night the good resolutions are brought home—dead angels, white and cold. We must not answer from our imagination, from our momentary passions and affections, from individual instances, saying, Yes: to have seen that one face was worth living a life of agony; to have felt that one little gentle touch was worth all the sorrow that could be crushed into seventy years. That is an emotional or imaginative, not a philosophical answer. The question is, Could we see life as a whole, all its days and nights of joy and sorrow, life and death, anguish and gladness, mountain and vale, light and gloom—is it worth living? What does it all come to? To die on the softest bed, what is it but to have a luxury in which there is no enjoyment? To die amid all pomp and circumstance, what is it but to see the perfection of irony? Thus we talk outside the Bible. To open the Bible

for our answer is not our immediate purpose. We are speaking
now of life in itself, by itself, and without any of those religious
influences and ministries which constitute what is known as
supernatural action. Begin your life upon the earth, study
it within the lines of the earth, and finish it at the grave, so
that the last dig of your spurs into the steed of your life shall
make that steed leap into the tomb—the goal! the winning
post! Is it worth doing? Occasional joys say, Yes; great
disappointments say, No. A noisy controversy goes on within
the mind and heart: now we say it is worth living, and now
we declare in another tone that life is not worth living; and
thus we are of no certain opinion for two days together, so
quickly do tears follow laughter.

Read the fourth verse :—

" And the Lord said unto him, This is the land which I sware unto
Abraham, unto Isaac, and unto Jacob, saying, I will give it unto thy seed :
I have caused thee to see it with thine eyes, but thou shalt not go over
thither."

Is this mocking the man ? Is this God's providence, to show
a man what he might have had, and then assure him that he
shall not have it—to dangle food before the eyes of hunger,
and then throw it away, so that the hand of need cannot follow
it ? Is it God's way to lift a man up to some Pisgah whence
he can see heaven, and then cast him down into hell ? Is it
not cruel refinement ? Is this not unworthy of a God of care
and compassion and love ? Everything depends upon the tone
of the reading. The verse might be so read as to involve a
charge of mockery against God. The man whose heart is
wrong could so read this verse as to turn it into an impeachment
against God's considerateness of human feeling. There is a
barbarous as well as a civilised mode of reading ; there is a
reading that misses the whole emphasis, that by a cold monotony
levels the hills rather than raises the valleys. Some words are
not to be read aloud, because the meaning is not in the letters
but in the tone. By looking long at the words and allowing the
heart to utter them, we may get some hint of their spiritual
music; but to hear our words read by those who do not understand us is to suffer the worst of pain. The iron voice, or the
hireling voice, the heartless voice, the grinding, crushing voice—

how it slays all things! How it will not allow anything to live
that has in it one touch of beauty or one hint of immortality!
Who can utter the words of the Lord? Reading the words,
"Thus saith the Lord," we might well pause there for ever, and
say, What he said he must repeat, for it does not lie within the
compass of the human voice to reproduce the music of God.
Moses was to see that the promise had been fulfilled. He was
to be ranked with Abraham, and Isaac, and Jacob, in that it was
unworthy of him to go into so little a land, so mean a home;
enough for the scholars who were behind him, enough for those
who were still reading and half-blind, who could scarcely discriminate between the right hand and the left—schoolhouse enough
for them; but as for Moses—after Sinai, after forty days'
communion upon the mountain, after the shining face, after all
the experience that made him what he was—his next movement
must be to the eternal Canaan, the better land, the Jerusalem
which is above. Moses understood the speech; Moses did not
reproach the providence of God. His very acceptance of it was
the noblest human confirmation of its beneficence that could
possibly be supplied. Where Moses was content we need not
chafe.

"And Moses was an hundred and twenty years old when he died: his
eye was not dim, nor his natural force abated" (v. 7).

Then why did he die? He might have been of use still. If
his faculties had all exhausted themselves, it was time for him to
lie down, and he was not called upon to work his jaded powers
when they complained of weariness and sighed for the rest of
the grave; but his eye was as bright as ever, and his natural
physical force as complete as ever. From a physical point
of view he needed not to die. Nor did he die. The word
"die" in relation to Moses is used conveniently, momentarily, as the best word that could indicate a passing incident.
Men in the condition of Moses do not die: they are raised,
they are translated, or transferred, they ascend; they do not
die in the common and general sense in which that term is
accepted. Moses was not killed by work. It is said by some
that work never kills any man. What authority they have for
speaking so we cannot tell. It is certain, however, that the

greatest workers have been amongst the longest livers. Those who have done most have lived most, and sometimes even in natural terms they lived longest. Not always. Herein we must not meddle; there is no calendar by which these things can be fixed, or upon which certainties can be built or speculation affirmed. Moses was not dismissed for inefficiency; he was still the greatest prophet in Israel. It was the king who died when Moses died. Joshua was a child to him, and Joshua would have been the first to say so. Not a man in all Israel dare stand before him, saying, "I could wear thy mantle." When it came to real issue and test of strength, to penetration of insight and reach of judgment, and solidity of character, all men stood in the plain to admire this mountainous man. He was not, therefore, unable to work; he was not inefficient in the service he rendered; he was abler on the day of his death than he had ever been on any day of his life. Then why did he die? He did not die, he ascended. Searchers upon the mountains, diggers in the valleys, said to one another, as they searched and dug in vain, "He is not here: for he is risen." God knows when men ought to die. Do not intermeddle with God. Sometimes the work is completed in our early years. A short day have some lives, but a crowded one; within very limited hours they speak words which can never be forgotten, or sing songs the world will never willingly let die. Thus God keeps us in patient uncertainty, whether we shall perish upon the Nile, or pass away upon mount Nebo, or be found with death set upon the face as a period put to a process of sleep. All this God keeps in uncertainty. We cannot open these doors of mystery. In the midst of life we are in death. No world is so near to us as the world eternal. We speak of making the most of the present: what is the present and the near?—It is the eternal, it is the heavenly, it is the divine. It is our mistake to suppose that earth is nearer than heaven. Eternity crowds out time, and presses into interstices which time could never fill. All our days are in God's hands. There is an appointed time to man upon the earth. "One dieth in his full strength, being wholly at ease and quiet. . . . Another dieth in the bitterness of his soul, and never eateth with pleasure." Forecast we do, and add up the whole multitude of figures, and publish arithmetical results with prodigal hands, but we cannot tell when the dart will strike. We have surrounded the mystery with calculated probabilities, but the mystery itself is a door that cannot be opened.

Were there no mitigations in the close of the life of Moses? Was all wrought out according to some process of iron necessity? Was it merely a walk up the mountain and a falling down dead, and a being covered with an anonymous sod? There were mitigations in the case, which are open to the eye of ordinary attention. Moses died in God's company :—

> "—the Lord shewed him all the land " (v. 1).
> "—the Lord said unto him " (v. 4).

They were together at the last. Is there no meaning in this? We are told that the Lord spake unto Moses; and the literal translation of that expression is that Moses died *on the mouth of God.*

> "So Moses the servant of the Lord died there in the land of Moab, according to the word of the Lord " (v. 5).

Read :—

> "So Moses the servant of the Lord died there in the land of Moab, on the mouth of the Lord."

What wonder that the Jewish commentator should have said that the Lord kissed his servant Moses? It would have been a fitting farewell within such a sphere as Moses had so long and arduously occupied. What if, after all his service, he had been kissed into rest—kissed into heaven? God can come nearer to us than the physician. What he does to the soul in the hour and article of physical expiring, who can tell? "Let him kiss me with the kisses of his mouth." Who shall say what sweet communion passes between the servant and the Lord when not a word is spoken? Not a word is heard from Moses. His was an expressive silence. There was but one Speaker and one auditor. The auditor who had talked so much, with so noble a voice, with so positive and royal an eloquence, spoke nothing, but died on the mouth of God—died in the embrace of his Lord. Who can say what the measure of that reward was? We cannot enter into these mysteries; we can be drawn upward by them, impelled in noble directions by their influence. To have

God's kiss, God's well-done, God's smile is not to die; it is but
to "languish into life."

"And he buried him in the valley in the land of Moab, over against
Beth-peor " (v. 6).

These are figurative expressions. We do not know the meaning of them—and yet we know it well. The text could be so
degraded as to present great difficulties to the untutored and
unsubdued imagination ; but to the fancy that has been chastened
by suffering, the picture is full of tenderness. God has buried
much in his time; he has been the great grave-digger, he has
filled up the tombs of the ages and written the epitaphs of æons.
How he buried Moses we can never know ; but having buried
him, God knew where he was. The grave was as a footprint to
the Almighty : the tomb was as a chosen garden of God. It
warms the poor heart, and cheers the dreariness of the spirit to
think that God knows where every grave is—away out on the
sea, down in the green waters, hidden among the marine rocks
that human eye may never look upon ; in ground blessed by
the priest, in land unblessed by any human voice ; the great
grave loaded with marble and almost resonant with pompous
eloquence and eulogium : and the nameless grave, where the
beggar who might have been a prince is laid, where the silent
poet rots, according to the flesh. God knows every grave—
the little child's few inches of sod, and the old man's last resting-
place, and the sweet mother's, without whom the world would
have been a waste. It is enough. These regions are not in our
keeping, except in some cases as to their surfaces. The key is in
heaven, and as to the time when the door will open, we know
not ; enough to know where the key is, and to know that it
cannot be lost.

"... no man knoweth of his sepulchre unto this day " (v. 6).

There are unknown graves ; there are places that are sacred
only to God, because God only knows them. We cannot tell
upon what ground we are treading ; we do not know who is
buried just under our feet. The earth has been a long time
in building, bold men—and wise men—say thousands upon
thousands of ages and incalculable periods. What little singing
birds were buried just under our feet we cannot tell ; or what

majestic beasts, or what hints of nobler life, or what men, women, and children, what prophets, sages, martyrs—we cannot tell. The house of the living is built upon the house of the dead. The whole world is sacred. We ought to hush our voices in the presence of its historic majesty, and call it the House of God.

Were we to finish here our perusal of the life of Moses, we should feel the incompleteness of the story. It has been full of event : it has kindled into heroic interest here and there, and again and oftentimes ; but this cannot be the end. If we had courage enough to turn over the page, we should find that there is more to be read. What we lack in positive instruction, we find realised in positive instinct, in real and indisputable intuition. We do not possess all our riches in the letter. Writing can only go to a certain point ; at its best it is but a make-believe, a help by the way, a hint to be going on with. We still have our instincts, intuitions ; our mental impulses, convictions, inspirations. We cannot tell anything about them ; we feel it is with them as it is with the wind : we hear the sound thereof, but we know not whence it cometh or whither it goeth : so is every one that is born of the Spirit—that has the spirit-eye, the spirit-genius, the prophetic faculty, the seer's agonising gaze. We are not to be bound by letters, and chapters, and verses ; we cannot end here. As Moses went up, so must we, and on a later day we must hear more about this man. We are bound to do so by the very covenant of God, for he cannot have made man in his own image and likeness merely for the purpose of burying him in an unknown grave.

Great was Moses !

" And there arose not a prophet since in Israel like unto Moses, whom the Lord knew face to face " (v. 10).

He was unique ; he stands alone ; no man can go near him. And yet he that is least in the kingdom of heaven is greater than Moses !